BANKRUPTCY AND INSOLVENCY LAW

SECOND EDITION

Other Books in the *Essentials of Canadian Law* Series

International Trade Law

Family Law

Copyright Law

The Law of Sentencing

Administrative Law

Securities Law

Computer Law 2/e

Maritime Law

International Human Rights Law

Franchise Law

Legal Ethics and Professional Responsibility 2/e

Refugee Law

Statutory Interpretation 2/e

National Security Law: Canadian Practice in International Perspective

Public International Law 2/e

Individual Employment Law 2/e

The Law of Partnerships and Corporations 3/e

Civil Litigation

Conflict of Laws

Legal Research and Writing 3/e

Religious Institutions and the Law in Canada 3/e

Detention and Arrest

Canadian Telecommunications Law

Intellectual Property Law 2/e

Animals and the Law

Income Tax Law 2/e

Fundamental Justice

Mergers, Acquisitions, and Other Changes of Corporate Control 2/e

Criminal Procedure 2/e

Personal Property Security Law 2/e

The Law of Contracts 2/e

Youth Criminal Justice Law 3/e

Constitutional Law 4/e

Bank and Customer Law in Canada 2/e

The Law of Equitable Remedies 2/e

The Charter of Rights and Freedoms 5/e

Environmental Law 4/e

Pension Law 2/e

International and Transnational Criminal Law 2/e

Remedies: The Law of Damages 3/e

Freedom of Conscience and Religion

The Law of Trusts 3/e

The Law of Evidence 7/e

Ethics and Criminal Law 2/e

Insurance Law 2/e

Immigration Law 2/e

Criminal Law 6/e

The Law of Torts 5/e

ESSENTIALS OF CANADIAN LAW

BANKRUPTCY AND INSOLVENCY LAW

SECOND EDITION

RODERICK J. WOOD
Faculty of Law
University of Alberta

IRWIN LAW

Bankruptcy and Insolvency Law, second edition

Published in 2015 by

Irwin Law Inc.
14 Duncan Street
Suite 206
Toronto, ON
M5H 3G8

www.irwinlaw.com

ISBN: 978-1-55221-402-2
e-book ISBN: 978-1-55221-403-9

Library and Archives Canada Cataloguing in Publication

Wood, Roderick J., author
Bankruptcy and insolvency law / Roderick J. Wood, Faculty of Law, University of Alberta. — Second edition.

(Essentials of Canadian law)
Includes bibliographical references and index.
Issued in print and electronic formats.
ISBN 978-1-55221-402-2 (paperback)—ISBN 978-1-55221-403-9 (pdf)

1. Bankruptcy—Canada. I. Title. II. Series: Essentials of Canadian law.

KE1485.W66 2015 346.7107'8 C2015-906544-5
KF1536.ZA2W66 2015 C2015-906545-3

Canada
Ontario
Ontario Media Development Corporation
Société de développement de l'industrie des médias de l'Ontario

Printed and bound by CPI Group (UK) Ltd, Croydon, CR0 4YY

1 2 3 4 5 19 18 17 16 15

For Susan, Mary, and Kat

SUMMARY TABLE OF CONTENTS

DETAILED TABLE OF CONTENTS

CHAPTER 7:
ENHANCING THE BANKRUPT ESTATE *188*

CHAPTER 9:

THE PROOF, VALUATION, AND PAYMENT OF CLAIMS 260

CHAPTER 10:
DISCHARGE OF THE BANKRUPT 295

PREFACE
to the Second Edition

Canadian bankruptcy and insolvency law continues to evolve at a rapid pace. However, there has been a significant shift in the type of legal change that has predominated. When the first edition of this book was published in 2009, a sweeping set of amendments had been enacted in 2005 and 2007 but had not yet come into force. The first edition incorporated these statutory changes in the anticipation that they would soon be proclaimed into force, and this was indeed how events unfolded. Although Industry Canada completed a statutory review in 2014, the next step in the process will involve a parliamentary committee review and report. As a consequence, no legislative amendments are on the immediate horizon. The recent developments in the law have therefore had their source primarily in the decisions of the courts. Over the past six years since the publication of the first edition, numerous judicial decisions have interpreted the new legislative provisions and have greatly enhanced our understanding of how these provisions will operate in actual legal context.

In addition to the work of interpreting new and untested legislative provisions, there has been significant judicial development of principle and doctrine. The Supreme Court of Canada has been at the forefront of this process. In 2010, the Court rendered its important decision in *Century Services Inc v Canada (AG)*[1] that explored the exercise of judicial authority under the *Companies' Creditors Arrangement Act* (*CCAA*).

1 2010 SCC 60.

In 2011, it dealt with the intersection of matrimonial property law and bankruptcy law in *Schreyer v Schreyer*.[2] In 2012, the Court rendered its decision on the vexing issue of environmental remediation claims in *Newfoundland and Labrador v AbitibiBowater Inc*.[3] In 2013, it issued a long awaited decision in *Sun Indalex Finance, LLC v United Steelworkers*[4] that considered the duties of the insolvent corporation as pension administrator while in restructuring proceedings.

The organization of the book has not changed substantially, although a number of new topics have been introduced into the framework. These are summarized below:

- In Chapter 4, new sections have been added on the anti-deprivation rule of bankruptcy law as well as on veto rights.
- In Chapter 7, a new section has been included on recovery by secured creditors through use of the preference and transfer at undervalue provisions.
- In Chapter 8, a new section examines appeals from the decision of a trustee in light *of Re Galaxy Sports Inc*[5] and its progeny.
- In Chapter 9, a new section has been added on environment remediation claims and another has been written on contracting out of the bankruptcy scheme of distribution.
- In Chapter 10, a new section examines multiple bankruptcies and discharge of the bankrupt.
- In Chapter 11, a section has been added that discusses the appropriateness of using restructuring proceedings for liquidation.
- In Chapter 12, a new section considers balance of convenience in connection with the stay of proceedings in restructuring law.
- In Chapter 13, there are three new sections covering roll-ups, stalking horse bids and other sale processes, and credit bids.
- In Chapter 14, three new sections have been added on conflicting duties as pension plan administrator, on breach of the monitor's duties, and on appointment of representative counsel.
- In Chapter 15, three new sections have been added on post-filing interest and expenses, on the priority of court ordered charges, and on the allocation of restructuring costs.
- In Chapter 16, a new section on third-party releases has been included.

---

2 2011 SCC 35.

3 2012 SCC 67.

4 2013 SCC 6.

5 2004 BCCA 284.

- In Chapter 17, two new sections on national receivers and on the dwindling use of privately appointed receivers have been added.
- In Chapter 18, a new section has been included on the definition of a receiver.
- In Chapter 21, a new part on *Canada Business Corporations Act* arrangements has been written to take into account the increased use of this process by insolvent corporations.

Abbreviations have been used for the *Bankruptcy and Insolvency Act* [*BIA*] and the *Companies' Creditors Arrangement Act* [*CCAA*] due to the sheer volume of references to these two statutes within this book. The citation for these two statutes are:

BIA *Bankruptcy and Insolvency Act*, RSC 1985, c B-3
CCAA *Companies' Creditors Arrangement Act*, RSC 1985, c C-36

I am grateful for the support that I received as the FR (Dick) Matthews QC Professor of Business Law at the Faculty of Law, University of Alberta, and as the Estey Chair in Business Law at the College of Law, University of Saskatchewan during my visit to Saskatoon during the 2014–15 academic year. I would like to thank Jeffrey Miller and Alisa Posesorski for their help and support in bringing this book to publication. I also owe a debt of gratitude to the lawyers, judges, and insolvency professionals who in many discussions over the years have helped me gain a deeper insight to this vast area of law.

Roderick J. Wood

PREFACE
to the First Edition

There are some who think that insolvency law is a narrow and technical topic. They are wrong. The breadth of its domain is quite astounding. A salient characteristic of insolvency law is that it cuts across almost every field of private law. The rights that are created in these other fields of private law can no longer be vindicated in the usual forum through the ordinary civil process once insolvency proceedings are commenced. Instead, the rights are enforced through the insolvency proceedings, and in some cases the nature and characteristics of the rights are significantly transformed. The impact of insolvency law on social and economic conditions both within Canada and worldwide is equally breathtaking. The fate of the Canadian blood supply system, the future of our national airlines, the recovery afforded to victims of institutional abuse, and the survival of entire communities have all hung in the balance. If by "technical" what is meant is that insolvency law is sometimes difficult, well then that will be conceded. But who would reasonably think that it could be otherwise?

One method of organizing a book on insolvency law is to include chapters that discuss the effects of insolvency law on particular kinds of legal relationships. This would entail separate chapters dealing with bankruptcy and family law, bankruptcy and landlord-tenant law, and the like. The weakness of this mode of organization is that the animating principles of insolvency law tend to fade into the background. I have chosen to organize this book in a way that will illuminate the structure of insolvency law, its aims and objectives, and its foundational principles. This means that if you want to learn about the effect of insolvency on a landlord-tenant relationship you must go to Chapter 5 to find out about the effect of bankruptcy on a landlord's right to distrain, Chapter 9 to know about the proof and ranking of the landlord's claim, and Chapters 6 and 13 to study the disclaimer of leases. This inconvenience is more than justified. A focus on the underlying principles of insolvency law permits us to see how these principles work in a variety of different situations and contexts. This, in turn, gives us a deeper understanding of their nature and operation.

One limitation of this book is that it assumes that the private law rules and principles that interact with insolvency law are derived from a common law system. With regret, I came to the conclusion that I did not possess a sufficient knowledge of Quebec's civil law system that would permit me to produce a truly bijural book. A second limitation is that it does not discuss the various reform proposals that have been considered but have not found their way into the recent amendments to Canadian insolvency statutes. Although many of these topics are dear to my heart, I have restricted my inquiry to the law as we presently find it in order to produce the greatest possible degree of clarity in this work. I have, for the most part, referred to the two recent amending statutes to the Canadian insolvency statutes as the 2005/2007 amendments. This is simply recognition that the two amending statutes are so interconnected that there was little to be gained from attempting to separately attribute the amendments to one or the other source.

I wish to acknowledge the University of Alberta for awarding me with a McCalla Research Professorship. This provided me teaching relief for the 2006/2007 academic year, and made it possible to produce this book sooner than otherwise would have been the case. I wish to thank Jeffrey Miller and Alisa Posesorski of Irwin Law for their work in bringing this book into publication. I also wish to thank Rick Reeson for our many discussions over the years on a variety of commercial law and insolvency law topics.

In writing this book, I have analyzed the law on the basis that the 2005 and 2007 amendments to the *Bankruptcy and Insolvency Act* and the *Companies' Creditors Arrangement Act* are fully in force. At the time this book went to press, this had not yet occurred. Some of the more politically sensitive provisions—such as those involving the *Wage Earner's Protection Program Act*, RRSPs, and student loans—were proclaimed into force on 7 July 2008. However, the bulk of the amendments were not in force at the time of writing, although the expectation was that this would occur sometime in the fall or winter of 2008. I would therefore caution the reader not to rely upon this book as a statement of the current law unless and until the reader has confirmed that these amendments have been fully proclaimed into force. And even in this case, the reader should be aware of the transition rules. These generally provide that the new provisions do not apply unless the amendments had come into force before the commencement of the insolvency proceedings.

CHAPTER 1

AN INTRODUCTION TO INSOLVENCY LAW

A. THE NATURE, PURPOSE, AND BOUNDARIES OF INSOLVENCY LAW

1) The Relationship between Bankruptcy Law and Insolvency Law

In Canada, it is common to see the terms bankruptcy and insolvency law used in tandem. The *Constitution Act, 1867* confers exclusive authority on the Parliament of Canada to make laws in relation to bankruptcy and insolvency,[1] and the primary federal statute in the field is named the *Bankruptcy and Insolvency Act* (*BIA*). The only danger with this usage is that it might suggest to some that bankruptcy law and insolvency law are two distinct though related legal fields. In fact, insolvency law is the wider concept, encompassing bankruptcy law but also including other non-bankruptcy insolvency systems. The usage has probably come about because bankruptcy is the oldest and most established of the insolvency regimes and therefore takes pride of place at the beginning of the phrase, with all of the other insolvency regimes lumped together at the end. This terminology should not obscure the fact that bankruptcy is merely one of several different legal regimes that respond to the insolvency of a debtor.

---

1 30 & 31 Vict, c 3 (UK), reprinted in RSC 1985, App II, No 5, s 91(21).

2) The Single Proceeding Model of Insolvency Law

At its core, insolvency law is concerned with the inability of a person to pay claims owing to others. A person who is in this state of affairs is considered to be insolvent, and insolvency law provides a set of legal responses to address this problem. Insolvency law is premised upon a debtor's inability to pay, rather than upon a debtor's unwillingness to pay. If the debtor has the means to pay but simply refuses to do so, a claimant can commence and prosecute a civil action against the debtor. If the claimant is successful, the claimant will obtain a judgment from the court. This permits the claimant to invoke judgment enforcement law in order to obtain satisfaction of the claim. The judgment enforcement system is established by provincial law and gives the claimant a set of enforcement remedies against the assets of the debtor.

Insolvency law is not primarily concerned with coercing payment from reluctant debtors. Rather, it comes into play when the debtor does not have sufficient assets to satisfy the claims of all of the claimants. In most cases, the debtor's insolvency results from an inability to pay contractual claims voluntarily incurred by the debtor. Some of these claims may arise from the extension of credit by a person who has provided goods or services to the debtor and who has agreed to accept payment for them at some future date. Others may arise from contracts of loan under which the debtor borrows a specific sum of money from a lender and agrees to repay it according to a fixed schedule (term loans) or under which amounts that are advanced are repayable on demand (demand loans). However, insolvencies may also occur because the debtor does not have sufficient assets to satisfy claims that are not associated with an extension of credit. These may involve claims against the debtor for breach of contract, as in the case of a construction firm that is liable in contract for the shoddy construction of a building. They may also involve claims against the debtor in tort for injuries caused by wrongful acts or omissions, as in the case of a manufacturer whose use of asbestos in a product has rendered it liable in negligence to victims suffering from asbestosis and mesothelioma.

The various insolvency regimes have different objectives. Some are primarily concerned with the liquidation of the debtor's assets. Others provide a means by which a debtor can attempt to rescue a business by seeking an arrangement or compromise in which creditors agree to accept less than they are entitled to. Some are concerned with the economic rehabilitation of the debtor. Others are not. In spite of these differences, there is one feature that is common to all insolvency regimes. They all provide a collective proceeding that supersedes the usual civil process available to creditors to enforce their claims. The creditors' remedies are collectivized in order to prevent the free-for-all that would otherwise prevail if creditors were permitted to exercise their remedies. In the absence of a collective process, each creditor is armed with the knowledge that if they do not strike hard and swift to seize the debtor's assets, they will be beaten out by other creditors. The fundamental importance of "single control" in a collective insolvency proceeding has long been recognized in Canadian law.[2] The single control policy furthers the "public interest in the expeditious, efficient and economical clean-up of the aftermath of a financial collapse."[3]

The race to grab assets in the absence of a collective insolvency regime does not provide an environment within which an efficient and orderly liquidation can occur. The process is inefficient because each creditor must separately attempt to enforce their claims against the debtor's assets, and this produces duplication in enforcement costs. The piecemeal selling off of assets also results in a much smaller recovery than if a single person were in control of the liquidation. Similarly, the race to seize assets does not produce an environment within which negotiations with creditors can easily occur. A reasonable creditor who is inclined to negotiate with the debtor will be unlikely to do so if other creditors are actively taking steps to make away with the debtor's realizable assets; instead, the creditor will feel compelled to join the wild dash to seize assets. Although some of the creditors (those who are able to strike first) are better off in such a scenario, the creditors as a group receive less than if a more orderly liquidation or negotiated arrangement had taken place.

There is one insolvency regime that only partially conforms to the single proceeding model. The privately appointed receiver is sometimes viewed as an insolvency regime but at other times is characterized as being primarily a secured creditor remedy. Although the commencement of a private receivership does not give rise to a stay of proceedings on the other claimants, the priority afforded to the secured creditor is such that the other creditors have little to gain in attempting to seize assets. The lack of a stay of proceedings, therefore, is not a particular impediment to the sale of a going concern. Because the statutes have imposed obligations on receivers that are owed to persons other than the secured creditor and because the statutory priority rules that apply to bankruptcy are increasingly being extended to cover receiverships

---

2 *Century Services Inc v Canada (AG)*, 2010 SCC 60 at para 22; *Re J McCarthy & Sons Co* (1916), 38 OLR 3 (SCAD); *Stewart v LePage* (1916), 53 SCR 337.

3 *Re Eagle River International Ltd*, [2001] 3 SCR 978 at para 27.

as well, it is now sensible to treat the privately appointed receiver as a type of insolvency regime.

3) The Objectives of Insolvency Law

The various insolvency regimes impose a single, collective proceeding within which the creditors must participate in order to vindicate their claims against an insolvent person. However, the fundamental objective of the process is not always the same across the various insolvency regimes. In respect of the commercial insolvency regimes, there are two fundamentally different objectives — liquidation and rescue. Liquidation regimes, such as bankruptcy, seek to liquidate the debtor's assets and distribute the proceeds to the creditors. Restructuring regimes (which are also referred to as reorganization regimes) seek to preserve the business as an operating entity by reducing or adjusting the claims of the creditors so as to provide the debtor with a new viable capital structure.

Consumer insolvency regimes similarly involve either the liquidation of the debtor's assets or an alternative to liquidation in which the consumer debtor retains his or her assets and satisfies all or part of the claims out of future earnings. Despite this difference, the fundamental objective that underlies all consumer insolvency regimes is that of economic rehabilitation of the debtor. Although consumer bankruptcy is formally a liquidation regime, the reality is that in many instances the consumer has very little property of value and therefore the liquidation process is not engaged.

In addition to these fundamental objectives, there are several other objectives that are pursued in the design of insolvency regimes. The UNCITRAL *Legislative Guide on Insolvency Law* states that, in order to establish and develop an effective insolvency law, the following key goals should be considered:

- Provide certainty in the market to promote economic stability and growth.
- Maximize value of assets.
- Strike a balance between liquidation and reorganization.
- Ensure equitable treatment of similarly situated creditors.
- Provide for timely, efficient and impartial resolution of insolvency.
- Preserve the insolvency estate to allow equitable distribution to creditors.
- Ensure a transparent and predictable insolvency law that contains incentives for gathering and dispensing information.

- Recognize existing creditors' rights and establish clear rules for ranking of priority claims.[4]

Many of these objectives are directed towards increasing the efficiency, predictability, and transparency of the insolvency process. This ensures that there will be more assets available to satisfy the claims of creditors and reduces the costs of credit by making it easier for creditors to predict future outcomes.

4) The Relationship between Private Law and Insolvency Law

Private law is the part of our legal system that involves relations between legal persons as opposed to relations between a person and the state. Private law is made up of three components: (1) the law of persons; (2) the law of rights; and (3) the law of procedure.[5] The law of persons defines the entities that are afforded legal personality — those who are considered to be persons in law and who are thereby capable of holding and enforcing rights. The law of rights is concerned with the nature and scope of rights. It deals with three fundamental questions. The first is about the reach of the right and whether the right can be demanded against the world in general (a proprietary right) or whether it can be demanded against only a particular person (a personal right). The second question deals with the content of the right — what the right gives to the holder. The third question looks to the events that create the right — whether the right arises out of a consensual agreement, a wrong, through unjust enrichment, or out of some other event. The law of procedure describes the legal processes that must be invoked when seeking to enforce a right.

Insolvency law, in large measure, is procedural in nature.[6] The commencement of insolvency proceedings will typically prevent a claimant from pursuing a claim through an ordinary civil action before a court or enforcing it through the judgment enforcement system. Instead, the person holding the right must assert the right through the collective procedure provided for by insolvency law. The mechanism provided by insolvency law for asserting, proving, and enforcing a claim is radically

4 (New York: United Nations, 2005) at 14.

5 See P Birks, ed, *English Private Law*, vol 1 (Oxford: Oxford University Press, 2000) at xxv–li.

6 See J Duns, *Insolvency: Law and Policy* (Oxford: Oxford University Press, 2002) at 12.

different from the ordinary civil process that is used when the debtor is not insolvent.

Insolvency law does not generally affect the law of persons, but it may restrict access to certain of the insolvency regimes on the basis of the kind of person involved. For example, the *Companies' Creditors Arrangement Act* (*CCAA*) applies only to corporations, while the consumer proposal provisions apply only to individuals. However, insolvency law does not involve itself with the creation of legal personality, instead leaving this to be determined by other branches of private law.

Insolvency law does not generally involve itself with the content or creation of rights. For the most part, pre-insolvency rights remain unaltered in insolvency. A claim for damages for breach of contract is validated and enforced through a different legal process under an insolvency regime, but the basic legal entitlement is not otherwise affected. There are, however, several important exceptions to this principle. For example, insolvency law gives a supplier of goods a special right of repossession that can be exercised against a receiver or a trustee in bankruptcy. This right carries with it a priority over secured creditors and has no counterpart in ordinary private law principles. Insolvency law proceeds from the premise that private law rights are not affected by insolvency unless an insolvency law rule specifically alters the private law right.

5) The Relevance of Proprietary Rights and Personal Rights in Insolvency Law

There are two fundamentally different kinds of rights that are recognized in private law: proprietary rights (also referred to as real rights or rights *in rem*) and personal rights (also referred to as rights *in personam*). This forms the division between property and obligation, between what I own and what I am owed. The difference between these kinds of rights is the extent to which the right can be demanded against other persons. A proprietary right is a right in relation to a thing. The right can be demanded against any other person who takes possession or control of or who asserts an interest in the thing. By way of contrast, a personal right can be asserted only against the person who owes the obligation.

Insolvency law, for the most part, preserves the distinction between proprietary rights and personal rights. The distinction is most critical when analysing the position of persons who have claims against the insolvent debtor. Those who have personal rights against the debtor can recover only out of the assets of the debtor. These claimants cannot look to property that belongs to third parties to satisfy their claims;

the purpose of insolvency law is not to confiscate property of others or to redistribute wealth in society. Those who have proprietary claims are generally free to assert those rights unaffected by the claims of those who have personal claims against the debtor. This explains why secured creditors are entitled to look to their collateral to satisfy their claims free from the claims of ordinary unsecured creditors.

This is not to say that those with proprietary rights are unaffected by the insolvency regime. In some cases, the insolvency regime treats proprietary claims as largely falling outside the scope and ambit of the insolvency regime. For example, in bankruptcy a secured creditor is permitted to withdraw its collateral from the bankrupt estate and to realize on it outside the bankruptcy proceedings.[7] In other cases, persons with proprietary rights are participants in the insolvency proceedings. For example, in restructuring proceedings a secured creditor cannot enforce its remedies, is entitled to vote on the plan, and is bound by a compromise or arrangement that is approved by a majority of the creditors and the court. However, the priority afforded to secured creditors over unsecured creditors is recognized and preserved in the restructuring proceedings.[8]

6) The Relationship between Insolvency Law and Provincial Law

Private law comprises common law principles as modified by statutory enactments. As the provinces have the legislative authority to enact laws pertaining to property and civil rights, statutory modification of common law principles is predominantly provincial in origin. For example, provincial statutes have extensively modified the common law position respecting secured transaction law through the enactment of personal property security legislation. Insolvency law is primarily procedural and does not generally redefine the substantive rights held by claimants. As a result, provincial statutes that alter common law rights are usually fully effective in insolvency.[9] Occasionally, there is a conflict between the federal and provincial statutes. In these instances, the federal insolvency

---

7 See Chapter 5, Section B(2).

8 See Chapter 16, Section D.

9 This idea is codified in s 72 of the *BIA*, which provides that the Act does not abrogate or supersede the substantive provisions of any other law or statute relating to property and civil rights that are not in conflict, and gives a trustee all rights and remedies provided by that law or statute as supplementary to and in addition to the rights and remedies provided by the *BIA*.

provision is given pre-eminence through the constitutional principle of federal paramountcy.

Provincial legislation also plays a supplementary role by creating additional rights that can be exercised by an insolvency administrator. For example, a trustee in bankruptcy can invoke provincial fraudulent preference legislation to avoid a pre-bankruptcy transfer, and can invoke personal property security legislation to subordinate an unperfected security interest.[10] A trustee can also resort to provincial legislation in order to occupy temporarily the leased premises following the bankruptcy.[11] In other instances, the federal insolvency statute expressly incorporates a rule or concept created by a provincial statute. For example, the bankruptcy statute provides that property that is exempt under provincial law is not divisible among the creditors.[12]

B. THE CONSTITUTIONAL DIMENSIONS OF INSOLVENCY LAW

The Parliament of Canada has the exclusive legislative authority to enact law in relation to bankruptcy and insolvency. Until the Great Depression of the 1930s, Canadian insolvency legislation was primarily concerned with proceedings under which an insolvency administrator liquidated the insolvent debtor's assets and distributed the proceeds to creditors. Two statutes passed by Parliament in the wake of the Depression, the *Companies' Creditors Arrangement Act*[13] and the *Farm Creditors Arrangement Act*,[14] adopted a fundamentally different approach in that they created insolvency proceedings where the objective was the negotiation of an arrangement under which the creditors compromised their claims and the debtor was permitted to carry on the business or farming operations. Both of these statutes were challenged, and in both cases the constitutional validity of the legislation was upheld.[15] The Privy Council held that the power to enact laws in relation to bankruptcy and insolvency was not intended to be "stereotyped" so as to confine Parliament to the types of insolvency regimes then in existence.

---

10 See Chapter 5, Section B(3) and Chapter 7, Section A(1).

11 See Chapter 6, Section B(3).

12 See Chapter 4, Section C(2).

13 SC 1933, c 36.

14 SC 1934, c 53.

15 *In re Companies' Creditors Arrangement Act*, [1934] SCR 659; *Attorney General for British Columbia v Attorney General for Canada* (1937), 18 CBR 217 (PC).

The element essential to constitutional validity is that the legislation must be directed towards debtors who are unable to meet their liabilities.

The attitude towards provincial attempts to establish insolvency regimes has evolved significantly over time. Following the wholesale repeal of Canadian insolvency legislation in 1880, provinces enacted voluntary assignment legislation to partially fill the gap. The legislation permitted a debtor to make an assignment of his or her property to a trustee who would liquidate it and distribute it among the creditors. The Privy Council held that this legislation was *intra vires*.[16] It noted that the proceedings were not compulsory and that the legislation did not require that the debtor be insolvent. This led to the belief that provincial insolvency legislation might be valid in the absence of a similar federal insolvency regime. Subsequent cases have rendered this view doubtful.

In 1937 Alberta enacted the *Debt Adjustment Act*.[17] This legislation prevented creditors from enforcing their remedies against a debtor without first obtaining a permit from the Debt Adjustment Board. The board also had the power to compel a creditor to accept a compromise or arrangement. Both the Supreme Court of Canada[18] and the Privy Council[19] held that the statute was *ultra vires* of the Alberta legislature. In 1959 the Alberta *Orderly Payment of Debts Act*[20] was struck down as beyond the powers of the provincial legislature for essentially similar reasons.[21] The majority opinion of the Supreme Court of Canada expressly cast doubt upon the decision of the Privy Council in the *Voluntary Assignments* case.

Although it is beyond the powers of the provincial legislatures to create insolvency regimes, provincial laws that create or adjust rights within the context of a bankruptcy or insolvency have been upheld. Provincial fraudulent preference legislation gives a creditor the right to set aside preferential transfers made by an insolvent debtor to a creditor. The Supreme Court of Canada in *Robinson v Countrywide Factors Ltd*[22] upheld the legislation. The majority opinion accepted the proposition that many of the institutions concerning credit and security are explicitly or implicitly predicated on the risk of insolvency, and that the

16 *Attorney General of Ontario v Attorney General for Canada (Voluntary Assignments)*, [1894] AC 189.

17 SA 1937, c 9.

18 *Reference Re: Debt Adjustment Act, 1937 (Alberta)*, [1942] SCR 31.

19 (1943), 24 CBR 129 (PC).

20 SA 1959, c 61.

21 *Reference re: Orderly Payment of Debts Act, 1959 (Alta)*, [1960] SCR 571.

22 [1978] 1 SCR 753.

federal power to enact legislation in relation to bankruptcy and insolvency should not deprive provinces from regulating property and civil rights. This recognizes that there may be some degree of overlap between federal and provincial legislation as long as the provincial legislation is concerned with rights in insolvency and does not purport to create an insolvency regime. The Supreme Court of Canada has also upheld provincial personal property security legislation that permits a trustee in bankruptcy to subordinate an unperfected security interest.[23]

Questions of constitutional law also come into play when valid provincial legislation comes into conflict with federal insolvency legislation. This issue has arisen most often in relation to priorities in insolvency. Provincial legislation confers a special proprietary right on certain classes of claimants, such as employees, a right that usually takes the form of a non-consensual security interest or deemed trust. The Supreme Court of Canada has held in a series of decisions that, to the extent that federal bankruptcy legislation mandates the affording of some other priority status to such claims, provisions conferring a special proprietary right on certain claimants are inoperative.[24] There has been an expanded federal legislative presence in relation to receivership law with the enactment of provisions that permit the appointment of a national receiver in 2009, and there is now a greater likelihood that provincial legislation that restricts the enforcement of creditor's remedies will be held to be inoperative in receivership proceedings due to the principle of federal paramountcy.[25]

C. THE SOURCES OF INSOLVENCY LAW

The framework for Canadian insolvency law is found in several statutes enacted by the Parliament of Canada. However, these statutes are not the only sources of insolvency law, and for a full picture it is necessary to understand the interplay between the federal insolvency statutes and the other sources of insolvency law.

---

23 *Re Giffen*, [1998] 1 SCR 91.

24 *Quebec (Deputy Minister of Revenue) v Rainville*, [1980] 1 SCR 35; *Deloitte Haskins & Sells Ltd v Alberta (Workers' Compensation Board)*, [1985] 1 SCR 785; *Husky Oil Operations Ltd v Canada (Minister of National Revenue)*, [1995] 3 SCR 453.

25 *Lemare Lake Logging Ltd v 3L Cattle Company Limited*, 2014 SKCA 35, appeal to the SCC heard 21 May 2015.

1) The Common Law

Although most of the insolvency regimes are overwhelmingly legislative in character, there is one that has its origins primarily in the common law. Receivership law began as a mixture of contract law and equitable principle. Although there has been a significant overlay of provincial and federal legislation, the common law core of receivership law remains in place and defines many of the operative concepts and principles. It is impossible to understand the current state of the receivership law without having a detailed knowledge of these common law principles.

Even in insolvency regimes that are predominantly statutory in nature, such as the bankruptcy regime, there is a residue of common law principle that continues to operate. Courts have developed a "fraud on the bankruptcy law principle" that renders it unlawful for parties to use contractual provisions that result in a forfeiture of property upon the occurrence of bankruptcy.[26] As well, a common law rule, referred to as the rule in *Ex parte James; Re Condon*,[27] confers upon a bankruptcy court the power to prevent the trustee from acting in a high-handed or unreasonable manner. Courts have also used their inherent jurisdiction in order to fill gaps in the statutory rules.[28]

2) Statute Law

The following federal insolvency statutes create or regulate the various insolvency regimes:

- *Bankruptcy and Insolvency Act (BIA)*;
- *Companies' Creditors Arrangement Act (CCAA)*;
- *Winding-up and Restructuring Act* (*WURA*);
- *Farm Debt Mediation Act (FDMA)*;
- *Canada Business Corporations Act* (Part IX, ss 94–101; and s 192) (*CBCA*); and
- *Canada Transportation Act* (sections 106–10).

---

26 *Canadian Imperial Bank of Commerce v Bramalea Inc* (1995), 33 OR (3d) 692 (Gen Div). And see R Wood, "Direct Payment Clauses and the Fraud upon the Bankruptcy Law Principle: *Re Horizon Earthworks Ltd (Bankrupt)*" (2014) 52 *Alberta Law Review* 171.

27 (1874), LR 9 Ch App 609. And see Chapter 4, Section E.

28 *Re Residential Warranty Co of Canada Inc* (2006), 25 CBR (5th) 38 (Alta CA). And see Chapter 11, Section D(1).

By far, the largest and most encompassing of the federal insolvency statutes is the *BIA*. This statute governs the bankruptcy regime but also creates or governs several of the other non-bankruptcy insolvency regimes. The last three statutes in the list are more specialized. Part IX of the *CBCA* contains provisions governing receiverships in relation to corporations that are incorporated under the federal Act. The *FDMA* applies only in respect of farmers. The provisions of the *Canada Transportation Act* apply only to insolvent railway companies.

Provincial statutes play a less central role. These statutes also set out rules governing receiverships in business corporation legislation and personal property security legislation. There are as well a number of provincial statutes that have an auxiliary or supplementary function in that they confer additional powers on an insolvency administrator.

3) Subordinate Legislation

The *BIA* gives the Governor in Council the power to make General Rules.[29] The *Bankruptcy and Insolvency General Rules*[30] cover a broad range of procedural matters concerning applications before a bankruptcy court, as well as rules governing consumer proposals, rules governing mediations in bankruptcy proceedings, and an extensive code of ethics for trustees. Regulations promulgated under the *FMDA* provide procedural rules respecting mediations,[31] while regulations promulgated under the *CCAA* provide the details of the information that must be filed with the Superintendent of Bankruptcy.[32]

4) Superintendent's Directives and Forms

The *BIA* provides that the Superintendent of Bankruptcy may issue directives to facilitate the carrying out of the purposes and provisions of the Act.[33] Several important directives have been issued, such as the Surplus Income Directive, which is an essential component of the rules governing the distribution of post-bankruptcy income earned by the debtor. The Act also gives the Superintendent of Bankruptcy the power to prescribe forms of documents,[34] and a large number of forms have been prescribed pursuant to this power.

---

29 *BIA*, s 209.

30 CRC, c 368.

31 *Farm Debt Mediation Regulations*, SOR/98-168.

32 *Companies' Creditors Arrangement Regulations*, SOR/2009-219.

33 *BIA*, s 5(4)(c).

34 *Ibid*, s 5(4)(e).

D. THE VARIOUS INSOLVENCY REGIMES

The various insolvency regimes will be discussed in depth in later chapters of this book. It is useful at the outset to outline the salient characteristics of the different regimes in order to identify their objectives and to highlight the means through which they attempt to achieve these objectives. There are ten[35] different insolvency regimes in Canada, namely:

- bankruptcy;
- restructuring under the *CCAA*;
- restructuring under the *BIA*;
- restructuring under the *CBCA*;
- receivership;
- consumer proposals;
- orderly payment of debts (OPD);
- mediation under the *FDMA*;
- liquidation or restructuring under the *WURA*; and
- railway insolvency.

This book is primarily concerned with insolvency regimes of general application rather than those that pertain to particular regions or special types of debtors. For this reason, its focus will be primarily upon the first five of these insolvency regimes.

1) Bankruptcy

Bankruptcy law is the oldest insolvency regime. In Canada, it applies to both natural persons and artificial entities such as corporations. Bankruptcy proceedings may be initiated either by the debtor (voluntary bankruptcy) or by the creditors (involuntary bankruptcy). Bankruptcy utilizes a liquidation approach to the debtor's insolvency. Upon the occurrence of bankruptcy, the assets of the debtor vest in a trustee in bankruptcy. The trustee then sells or otherwise disposes of the assets and distributes their proceeds among the creditors who prove their claims in the bankruptcy. This distribution is made according to a specified scheme of distribution. In the case of a natural person, bankruptcy law also pursues a policy of debtor rehabilitation by the

35 This treats court-appointed receivers and privately appointed receivers as a single insolvency regime. Although there are important differences between the two types of receiverships, many of the statutory provisions that govern receiverships apply to both kinds. Therefore, it is preferable to regard them as two variants within the same insolvency regime.

discharge of most pre-bankruptcy claims in order to give the debtor a fresh start. The statutory framework governing bankruptcy is set out in the *BIA*.

2) Restructuring under the *CCAA*

The *Companies' Creditors Arrangement Act* is one of two commercial restructuring regimes that are of general application. In the past, a reorganization or restructuring regime (the terms are used interchangeably) usually did not involve a liquidation of the debtor's assets. It was premised on the idea that the business may be more valuable as a going concern and that all parties may benefit if a forced liquidation can be avoided. The proceedings are initiated (usually by an insolvent debtor) by bringing an application before a court for a stay of proceedings. The debtor then attempts to negotiate a compromise or arrangement with its creditors, and the plan is placed before the creditors and voted on. If a specified majority accepts the plan and a court approves it, the plan will bind all the affected creditors. The *CCAA* is the restructuring regime under which most of the largest financially distressed Canadian corporations have restructured. The *CCAA* applies only if the debtor is a corporation and if the total claims against the debtor exceed $5 million. It is characterized by a high degree of court involvement. More recently, it has become common to use this regime as a means of liquidating the business assets through a sale of the business as a going concern. In a liquidating *CCAA*, a plan of arrangement is not developed and there is no voting by the creditors.

3) Restructuring under the *BIA*

Division 1 of Part III of the *BIA* was enacted in 1992. It establishes a second commercial restructuring regime of general application. Unlike the *CCAA*, it is not restricted to corporations but also applies to natural persons and to artificial entities other than corporations. Nor does its application depend upon the size of the indebtedness owed by the debtor. The debtor is given a specified period of time within which to devise a commercial proposal to place before the creditors for consideration. The commercial proposal provisions use a more rule-based approach than the *CCAA* in order to reduce the costs associated with multiple court applications. In spite of this basic difference in approach, the commercial proposal regime and the *CCAA* share many key features and elements, and caselaw decided in respect of one of the regimes is often applicable to the other. The debtor usually remains in control of the assets while the reorganization is being attempted. As in the case of the *CCAA*, the proceedings can now be used to carry out a going-concern sale of the business.

4) Restructuring under the *CBCA*

Restructurings that affect only the interests of bondholders or other holders of debt securities are also undertaken pursuant to the arrangement provisions in section 192 of the *Canada Business Corporations Act*. Although the statute provides that this provision applies only to a corporation that is not insolvent, courts have interpreted this requirement in such a way that it will rarely constitute an obstacle.

5) Receiverships

A receivership involves the appointment of a receiver-manager who takes possession and control of the debtor's business. The receiver-manager may operate the business, but in most cases the ultimate goal is to liquidate the assets either as a going concern or through their break-up and sale. Unlike a bankruptcy, the debtor's assets do not vest in the receiver-manager. A receiver-manager may be appointed by a secured creditor pursuant to a contractual power in a security agreement or may be appointed by a court. Although the legal distinctions between these two types of appointments have been diminished by legislation, there remain many important differences. A complex mixture of common law and equitable principle and federal and provincial legislation governs receiverships. The *BIA* now permits the appointment of a national receiver who will be afforded recognition across Canada.

6) Consumer Proposals

The consumer proposal provisions were added to the *BIA* in 1992 as Division II of Part III of the Act. They provide individuals with an alternative to consumer bankruptcy. A consumer proposal may be made only by a natural person whose debts, excluding any debts secured by the person's principal residence, do not exceed $250,000. In order to make a consumer proposal, the debtor must obtain the assistance of an administrator who assists the debtor in preparing the proposal, investigates the consumer debtor's property and financial affairs, and provides counselling to the debtor. A meeting of creditors is not ordinarily required. The creditors may simply indicate their assent or dissent regarding the consumer proposal when they file their proof of claim.

7) Orderly Payment of Debts

Part X of the *BIA* sets out the orderly payment of debts procedure. These provisions were added in 1965 after the Supreme Court of Canada struck down similar provincial legislation as *ultra vires*. The OPD provides an inexpensive procedure under which a debtor can apply to a clerk of a court for a consolidation order. The consolidation order fixes the amounts to be paid into court by the debtor and the times of payment until the amounts owing to all creditors are paid in full. The OPD provisions are in force only in those provinces that accept it. Alberta, Saskatchewan, Nova Scotia, and Prince Edward Island have all elected to do so.

8) *Farm Debt Mediation Act*

The *Farm Debt Mediation Act* was enacted in 1998. It attempted to improve the efficiency of earlier federal legislation enacted in 1986, which it replaces. The proceedings are initiated when an insolvent farmer applies to an administrator for a review of his financial affairs and mediation for the purpose of facilitating an arrangement with creditors. The administrator assists the farmer in preparing a financial recovery plan. The administrator then appoints a professional mediator who will attempt to arrive at a mutually acceptable arrangement between the farmer and the creditors. No party is bound to the arrangement unless they consent to it.

9) *Winding-up and Restructuring Act*

Federal winding-up legislation was originally the means through which insolvent corporations were liquidated. Its role was substantially undercut in 1919 upon the enactment of bankruptcy legislation that applied to both natural persons and to artificial entities such as corporations. The *Winding-up and Restructuring Act* (*WURA*) is the only insolvency regime that can be used in connection with the insolvency of banks, insurance companies, trust companies, and loan companies. Proceedings under the *WURA* are characterized by a higher degree of court involvement; the court appoints a liquidator and supervises the liquidation of the debtor's assets. The *WURA* contains some brief and skeletal provisions for restructuring, as well as special provisions governing insolvencies of authorized foreign banks and the restructuring of insurance companies.

10) Railway Insolvency

Sections 106 to 110 of the *Canada Transportation Act* provide an insolvency regime in respect of insolvent railway companies. This is the only insolvency regime that can be invoked, since railway companies are excluded from the scope of the *BIA*, the *CCAA*, and the *WURA*. The provisions are very brief and do not contemplate liquidation of the debtor. The Act provides skeletal rules for the filing of a scheme of arrangement in the federal court. These provisions are wholly inadequate, and courts have eroded their application by interpreting "railway company" to mean only those that are incorporated under special legislation.[36]

E. THE CONCEPT OF INSOLVENCY

1) The Legal Significance of Insolvency

It is important from the outset to distinguish between the insolvency of a debtor and the initiation of an insolvency regime. Insolvency is a fact. It occurs when a debtor is unable to pay his or her creditors. The insolvency regimes provide a legal definition of insolvency in order to determine precisely when this state of affairs is considered to exist. The various insolvency regimes provide different legal responses to the fact of the debtor's insolvency. These insolvency regimes do not come into operation simply by the occurrence of insolvency. They must be initiated by some action or proceeding taken by the creditors or the debtor. Often the initiating party must make a choice between two or more insolvency regimes in order to pick the one that provides the most appropriate solution to the problem.

The concept of insolvency serves a number of different purposes. First, it has a gatekeeping role. The various insolvency regimes typically require that the debtor be insolvent before insolvency proceedings can be initiated.[37] The federal insolvency regimes that use insolvency as a precondition are enumerated below:

---

36 *Montréal, Maine & Atlantique Canada Co (Arrangement relatif à)*, 2015 QCCS 3236.

37 The initiation of involuntary bankruptcy proceedings by creditors does not conform to this pattern. The creditors do not need to prove that the debtor is insolvent. It is sufficient if they prove an act of bankruptcy. However, the application must be dismissed on proof that the debtor is able to pay creditors.

- voluntary assignments in bankruptcy;[38]
- restructuring proceedings under the *CCAA*;[39]
- commercial proposals;[40]
- receiverships;[41]
- consumer proposals;[42]
- orderly payment of debts;[43]
- liquidation or restructuring under the *WURA*;[44]
- farm debt mediation;[45] and
- railway insolvencies.[46]

Second, the concept of insolvency is used in a number of provisions that give the trustee the right to impugn pre-bankruptcy transactions. In order to attack a pre-bankruptcy transaction as a fraudulent preference, the trustee must prove that the debtor was insolvent at the time of the transaction.[47] An insolvency requirement is also imposed where the trustee seeks to recover against the directors or shareholder of a corporation in respect of a dividend, redemption, or share purchase.[48]

Third, provincial law uses the concept of insolvency in fraudulent preference statutes as well as statutes that impose liability on directors for distributions to shareholders that were made at a time when the corporation was insolvent. These provincial statutes do not create insolvency regimes. However, a trustee in bankruptcy is able to use these provisions and therefore their operation is of great significance. Although the federal and provincial insolvency tests are roughly comparable, they are not identical.

Fourth, a court cannot grant an absolute discharge in bankruptcy if the debtor has continued to trade after becoming aware of being insolvent.[49]

---

38 *BIA*, s 49.
39 *CCAA*, s 2(1) "debtor company."
40 *BIA*, s 50.
41 *Ibid*, ss 243(1) & (2).
42 *Ibid*, s 66.1 "consumer debtor."
43 *Ibid*, s 217 "debtor."
44 *Winding-up and Restructuring Act*, RSC 1985, c W-11, s 6(1)(a) [*WURA*].
45 *Farm Debt Mediation Act*, SC 1997, c 21, s 6 [*FDMA*].
46 *Canada Transportation Act*, SC 1996, c 10, s 106(1).
47 *BIA*, s 95(1).
48 *Ibid*, s 101.
49 *Ibid*, s 173(1)(c).

2) The Definition of Insolvent Person

The legal definition of insolvency in the *BIA* is contained in the definition of "insolvent person."[50] The definition contains the following tests of insolvency:

> (*a*) [The debtor] is for any reason unable to meet obligations as they generally become due.
> (*b*) [The debtor] has ceased paying his current obligations in the ordinary course of business as they generally become due.
> (*c*) The aggregate of [the debtor's] property is not, at a fair valuation, sufficient, or, if disposed of at a fairly conducted sale under legal process, would not be sufficient to enable payment of all obligations, due and accruing due.

The three tests set out in the definition are alternatives. It is sufficient to show that any one of them is satisfied.[51]

The Canadian approach[52] differs slightly from that in two other common law countries, the United States and the United Kingdom, which provide two tests for insolvency rather than three. The first test, known as the cash flow test, examines if the debtor is able to pay debts as they fall due. The second test, known as the balance sheet test, determines if the debtor's liabilities exceed the debtor's assets. The first two tests in the Canadian formulation are essentially cash flow tests, while the third is a balance sheet test. However, there is an important difference between the two cash flow tests in that the first is forward-looking while the second is backward-looking.

3) The Cash Flow Tests

The first insolvency test requires proof of the debtor's inability to meet current obligations as they generally become due. This is a cash flow test that contains an element of futurity. It is not directly concerned with whether the debtor has not paid his or her current obligations in the past. The question is whether the debtor is able to pay. A debtor who is able but unwilling to pay does not satisfy this test of insolvency.[53] A debtor is insolvent under this test even though there are no payments currently due if it is shown that the payments will become

50 *Ibid*, s 2(1).

51 *Re Selmas-Cromie Ltd* (1975), 21 CBR (NS) 10 (BCSC).

52 The insolvency tests contained in the definition have remained substantially unchanged since the enactment of the first Canadian bankruptcy statute in 1919.

53 *Thorne Riddell v Fleishman* (1983), 47 CBR (NS) 233 (Ont HCJ) [*Thorne Riddell*].

due in the immediate future and the debtor does not have the means to satisfy these obligations.[54] In order to determine the debtor's ability to pay, it is necessary to assess the assets available to the debtor to meet these obligations. A lack of liquid funds is not determinative. A debtor who has a line of credit or other credit facility that can be drawn on to satisfy the obligations is not insolvent under this test.[55] However, the assets that are to be considered do not include assets that are not normally liquidated in the ordinary course of business.[56]

The second cash flow test requires proof that the debtor has ceased paying current obligations in the ordinary course of business as they generally become due. This test looks to the past. It is not concerned with the debtor's inability to pay obligations in the immediate future. The question is whether the debtor has ceased to pay them. The second test is more limited than the first in that it applies only to a debtor who carries on a business.

Under either of these cash flow tests, it may be necessary to determine if a particular obligation qualifies as a current obligation. Long-term liabilities that are payable at some future date should not be considered.[57] Unliquidated claims or debts that are subject to a *bona fide* dispute should also be excluded. A debt may be presently due and payable, but the creditors may have agreed to defer payment to a later date. If this is the case, the debtor will not be insolvent under the cash flow tests.[58] The mere failure by a creditor to seek recovery by commencing a legal action or taking some other step is not enough to qualify as an agreement to defer payment.[59] In principle, the date specified in the contract should be used to determine the date that the debt is due and payable unless there is some express or implied agreement between the parties, or a course of conduct sufficient to ground an estoppel.[60]

---

54 *King Petroleum Ltd, Re* (1978), 29 CBR (NS) 76 (Ont HCJ) [*King Petroleum*]; *Re Viteway Natural Foods Ltd* (1986), 63 CBR (NS) 157 (BCSC) [*Viteway*].

55 *Re Bel Air Electric Inc* (1962), 3 CBR (NS) 252 (Que Sup Ct).

56 *Re Pacific Mobile Corp* (1979), 32 CBR (NS) 209 (Que Sup Ct).

57 This is subject to what has been said concerning obligations that are payable in the immediate future in relation to the first insolvency test.

58 *Thorne Riddell*, above note 53.

59 *Viteway*, above note 54.

60 See *Southern Cross Interiors Pty Ltd v Deputy Commissioner of Taxation*, [2001] NSWSC 621.

4) The Balance Sheet Test

Under the balance sheet test, a debtor is insolvent if the assets of the debtor are insufficient to satisfy all liabilities of the debtor. In applying this insolvency test, it is necessary to decide what things constitute assets and then appraise their value. It is also necessary to decide what things constitute liabilities and then assess their amount. The assets that can be considered are those that belong to the debtor at the time that the insolvency test is conducted. They do not encompass assets that may be acquired in the future or an anticipated profit or increase in value of the assets that may occur sometime in the future.[61] Exempt assets must be included, even though these assets will not be available to satisfy the claims of creditors in insolvency or other enforcement proceedings.[62]

The balance sheet test contemplates two methods for the valuation of assets — the fair valuation of the assets and the disposal of the assets at a fairly conducted sale under legal process. The valuation of assets set out on the debtor's balance sheet is the starting point, but the liquidation value of the assets must also be considered.[63] The values set out on the balance sheet reflect the historic cost of assets, rather than their current value. The valuation of assets on the balance sheet can be departed from if it is shown that some of the accounts receivable are unlikely to be collected or that certain of the assets have depreciated in value.[64]

There is some disagreement over which liabilities must be taken into account under the balance sheet test. The statutory language refers to "all obligations, due and accruing due." Some cases have held that this does not encompass all future liabilities but only "obligations currently payable or properly chargeable to the accounting period during which the test is being applied."[65] Other cases have held that all future obligations, including contingent liabilities, must be included.[66] In principle, the balance sheet test should include all future liabilities. A failure to include these into the calculation unfairly prejudices long-term creditors.

---

61 *Re Consolidated Seed Exports Ltd* (1986), 62 CBR (NS) 156 (BCSC).

62 *Re Schroeder* (2000), 17 CBR (4th) 135 (Man QB); *Re Derksen* (1995), 34 CBR (3d) 252 (Man QB).

63 *King Petroleum*, above note 54.

64 *Touche Ross Ltd v Weldwood of Canada Sales Ltd* (1983), 48 CBR (NS) 83 (Ont HCJ); *633746 Ontario Inc (Trustee of) v Salvati* (1990), 79 CBR (NS) 72 (Ont HCJ).

65 *Enterprise Capital Management Inc v Semi-Tech Corp* (1999), 10 CBR (4th) 133 (Ont SCJ) [*Enterprise*]; *Re Oblats de Marie Immaculée du Manitoba* (2004), 1 CBR (5th) 279 (Man QB); *Industries Cover inc (Syndic des)*, 2015 QCCS 136.

66 *Re Stelco Inc* (2004), 48 CBR (4th) 299 (Ont SCJ) [*Stelco*]; *Viteway*, above note 54; *Optical Recording Laboratories Inc v Digital Recording Corp* (1990), 2 CBR (3d) 64 (Ont CA).

The insolvency test must be met before a payment or transfer of property can be impugned as a preference. A failure to include all liabilities would permit short-term creditors to be paid despite the fact that this will result in insufficient assets to satisfy the claims of long-term creditors. Courts that have refused to include all obligations have expressed a concern that this may result in too many businesses falling within the definition.[67] This concern is misplaced. The excess of liabilities over assets is not an act of bankruptcy, and therefore involuntary bankruptcy proceedings cannot be forced upon a debtor even if the debtor is insolvent under the balance sheet test.

The statutory language associated with the balance sheet test refers to obligations rather than debts. Contingent claims and unliquidated claims are therefore included.[68] The valuation of contingent claims poses a particular difficulty. The contingency may or may not arise, and the probability that it will can range from an almost complete certainty to a very remote possibility. Where the probability is at one of these extremes, the courts will simply include the full value of the high probability claim[69] and reduce to zero the value of the low-probability claim. Matters become less certain when the likelihood of occurrence is somewhere in between these two extremes.

Professor Goode identifies two approaches to valuation of contingent liabilities.[70] One approach is to determine if there is a probability that the claim will occur (i.e., a greater than 50 percent chance). If so, the full value of the claim is included; if not, the obligation is valued at zero. The alternative approach would be to value the claim at the percentage likelihood of its occurrence. Under this approach, a claim for $100 that has a 60 percent chance of occurring would be valued at $60. Courts have adopted the second valuation approach to deal with problems of valuation that arise in connection with the proof of contingent claims by claimants who wish to participate in the proceeds of bankruptcy liquidation. There is no reason why this approach should not also be applied in connection with the balance sheet test.[71]

---

67 *Enterprise*, above note 65.

68 *Re Challmie* (1976), 22 CBR (NS) 78 (BCSC).

69 *Ibid.* The contingent liability was a personal guarantee in respect of a company that was in financial difficulties. The court simply added the full value of this claim to the liabilities of the debtor.

70 R Goode, *Principles of Corporate Insolvency Law*, 4th ed (London: Sweet and Maxwell, 2011) at 145–47.

71 *Re Wiebe* (1995), 30 CBR (3d) 109 (Ont Ct Gen Div). And see Chapter 9, Section A(8).

5) The Insolvency Tests in Restructuring Proceedings

In order for a company to attempt a restructuring under the *CCAA*, the company must be insolvent. The *CCAA* does not define the term and does not expressly incorporate the insolvency tests of the *BIA*. The *BIA* restructuring provisions apply to an "insolvent person," and this brings into play the insolvency tests embedded in that definition. This raises a number of important questions. Is the test of insolvency contained in the *CCAA* the same as that used in the *BIA*? If it is not, what formulation is to be used? And, in respect of restructurings under the *BIA*, are the insolvency tests applied in precisely the same manner to both liquidations and restructurings?

Justice Farley considered these questions in *Re Stelco*.[72] The case involved a looming insolvency crisis. The company had not failed to meet any of its current obligations, but it was anticipated that it would run out of funding in ten months. Justice Farley held that the insolvency test in the *CCAA* is distinct from that contained in the *BIA*. Although there is an element of futurity in the first of the cash flow tests in the *BIA*, this encompasses only debts that become payable in the immediate future. Justice Farley was of the opinion that this insolvency test was inappropriate when the issue involved restructuring proceedings. He observed that often debtors wait too long before initiating restructuring proceedings, and that to be successful the proceedings must be commenced before the death spiral of the company. For this reason, he held that a company is insolvent under the *CCAA* "if it is reasonably expected to run out of liquidity within reasonable proximity of time as compared with the time reasonably required to implement a restructuring."[73] As virtually all *CCAA* proceedings will take at least six months and complex ones will frequently exceed a year, the ten-month period fell within the normal range and the company was held to be insolvent.

Justice Farley also considered the matter on the basis that the *BIA* insolvency tests applied to the proceedings. He held that the first cash flow test in the *BIA* operates differently depending on the nature of the proceedings. In bankruptcy proceedings or proceedings to set aside a transfer of property as a preference, the conventional test with a short horizon is employed. But in restructuring proceedings, a much longer time horizon is used. This interpretation would equally apply to restructuring proceedings under the commercial proposal provisions of

72 *Stelco*, above note 66.

73 *Ibid* at para 26.

the *BIA*, although the time frame would be limited to six months since that is the maximum length of those proceedings.

The decision has been followed in other *CCAA* cases.[74] It is less clear whether courts will be as receptive to the idea that the meaning of the *BIA* insolvency test changes depending on whether bankruptcy or commercial proposal proceedings are involved.

FURTHER READINGS

AUSTRALIAN LAW REFORM COMMISSION. *General Insolvency Inquiry*, Australian Law Reform Commission Report 45 (Sydney: Australian Law Reform Commission, 1988) (*Harmer Report*)

GOODE, R. *Principles of Corporate Insolvency Law*, 4th ed (London: Sweet and Maxwell, 2011) ch 4

HOGG, P. *Constitutional Law of Canada*, 5th ed (Toronto: Thomson Carswell, 2007) ch 25

JACKSON, T. *The Logic and Limits of Bankruptcy Law* (Cambridge, MA: Harvard University Press, 1986) ch 1

KEAY, A. "The Insolvency Factor in the Avoidance of Antecedent Transactions in Corporate Liquidations" (1995) 21 *Monash University Law Review* 305

REVIEW COMMITTEE OF INSOLVENCY LAW AND PRACTICE. *Report of the Review Committee of Insolvency Law and Practice*, Cmnd 8558 (London: HMSO, 1982) ch 4 (*Cork Report*)

SENATE STANDING COMMITTEE ON BANKING, TRADE AND COMMERCE. *Debtors and Creditors: Sharing the Burden: A Review of the Bankruptcy and Insolvency Act and the Companies' Creditors Arrangement Act* by Richard H Kroft & David Tkachuk (Ottawa: Standing Senate Committee on Banking, Trade and Commerce, 2003)

STUDY COMMITTEE ON BANKRUPTCY AND INSOLVENCY LEGISLATION. *Report of the Study Committee on Bankruptcy and Insolvency Legislation* (Ottawa: Study Committee on Bankruptcy and Insolvency Legislation, 1970) ch 2 and 4 (*Tassé Report*)

UNCITRAL. *Legislative Guide on Insolvency Law* (New York: United Nations, 2005) Part One

74 See *Lemare Holdings Ltd (Re)*, 2014 BCSC 893; *Redstone Investment Corporation (Re)*, 2014 ONSC 2004.

Ziegel, J. "Should Proof of the Debtor's Insolvency Be Dispensed with in Voluntary Insolvency Proceedings" in Janis P Sarra, ed, *Annual Review of Insolvency Law, 2007* (Toronto: Carswell, 2008) 21

PART ONE

BANKRUPTCY LAW

CHAPTER 2

THE FOUNDATIONS OF BANKRUPTCY LAW

A. SHORT HISTORY OF BANKRUPTCY LAW

Blackstone claimed that the term bankruptcy was derived from the Italian and signified that a trader's bench had been broken.[1] Coke believed that it came from the French and denoted a merchant who, along with his trading bench, had disappeared without a trace.[2] Whatever its origins, it is undeniable that bankruptcy law has a very long history. Roman law contained procedures that were similar in function and operation to bankruptcy proceedings.[3] These were incorporated into the law merchant — a body of law that drew upon the customs and practices of merchants.[4] Although much of the law merchant was absorbed into English commercial law, its influence on insolvency law was more limited. Anglo-Canadian bankruptcy is overwhelmingly statutory in character. Its origins, growth, and development can be traced through a series of bankruptcy statutes beginning in the sixteenth century.

---

1 *Blackstone's Commentaries on the Laws of England*, vol 2 (Oxford: Clarendon Press, 1765–69) at 472.

2 Edward Coke, *The Fourth Part of the Institutes of the Laws of England* (London: W Clarke, 1817) at 266.

3 I Fletcher, *The Law of Insolvency* (London: Sweet & Maxwell, 1990) at 5–6.

4 See LE Levinthal, "The Early History of English Bankruptcy" (1919) 67 *University of Pennsylvania Law Review* 1.

1) The Development of English Bankruptcy Law

The first English bankruptcy statute was enacted in 1542 during the reign of Henry VIII. It was directed against debtors who attempted to escape their obligations by either leaving the country or by staying within their homes, which effectively prevented the service of legal process.[5] The Act permitted a creditor to lodge a complaint before a bankruptcy commissioner, who would summon the debtor. If the debtor did not appear, the debtor could be found to be outside the king's protection. The commissioner could then break down the debtor's door and seize and sell the debtor's assets. This early statute displayed two central features of bankruptcy law that have persisted to the present day. First, it created a summary and collective procedure that operated for the benefit of all the creditors, and not simply for the creditor who initiated the process. Second, it adopted a *pro rata* sharing principle in respect of the distribution of the debtor's assets among the creditors.

A more detailed bankruptcy statute was enacted in 1571 during the reign of Elizabeth I.[6] This statute created additional acts of bankruptcy that were required to be proven by the creditors before the debtor could be adjudged bankrupt. The present Canadian bankruptcy statute still requires proof of an act of bankruptcy in respect of involuntary bankruptcy proceedings, although some of the other common law countries have dispensed with the concept and instead require proof that the debtor is insolvent. The Act was also notable for its restriction of bankruptcy to debtors who were merchants or traders.[7] This limitation on the scope of the Act remained in place for almost three hundred years, until it was done away with in 1861.

The bankruptcy statutes provided creditors with enhanced powers of enforcement against merchant debtors. However, it came to be recognized that bankruptcy law could produce extraordinary hardship for debtors whose ships were lost at sea or whose losses were otherwise caused by no fault of their own. Daniel Defoe, a merchant, journalist, and pamphleteer who is most well known for his novel *Robinson Crusoe*, went bankrupt in 1691. His *Essay upon Projects*, written in 1697,

5 34 & 35 Hen VIII, c 4.

6 13 Eliz I, c 7. The *Fraudulent Conveyances Act*, 13 Eliz I, c 5 was enacted in the same year. This statute, which permits creditors to set aside fraudulent conveyances of property, remains in force as a received imperial statute in many of the Canadian common law jurisdictions.

7 A sizeable portion of bankruptcy law during this period was devoted to determining which activities qualified a person as a trader and which did not. See I Duffy, "English Bankrupts, 1571–1861" (1980) 24 *American Journal of Legal History* 283.

captures this sentiment. Defoe argues that bankruptcy law failed to differentiate between the "Honest Debtor, who fails by visible Necessity, Losses, Sickness, Decay of Trade, or the like" and the "Knavish, Designing, or Idle, Extravagant Debtor, who fails because he has run out his Estate in Excesses, or on purpose to cheat and abuse his Creditors."[8]

In 1705 bankruptcy legislation was passed to respond to this concern by introducing the concept of the discharge of a bankrupt.[9] Prior to this, a bankrupt remained liable for all amounts remaining unpaid to the creditors following the bankruptcy. The Act marks a key moment in the history of bankruptcy law. Although the original purpose behind the discharge may have been to offer an incentive for cooperation on the part of the bankrupt, the concept would ultimately expand and transform bankruptcy law. Bankruptcy would no longer be viewed solely as a powerful collection tool for creditors, but would be recognized as having an additional objective. Bankruptcy provides an honest bankrupt with a means of escaping the crushing burden of debt.

The bankruptcy discharge was afforded only to bankrupts who cooperated and assisted in the proceedings. The Act dealt harshly with uncooperative and fraudulent bankrupts through the imposition of capital punishment by hanging.[10] The death penalty for this offence was abolished in 1820, once it became widely apparent that the penalty was seldom exacted and therefore did not provide an effective deterrent.[11] The task of distinguishing between the honest but unfortunate debtor and the undeserving debtor who is responsible for the financial crisis is not always easy to do. Modern bankruptcy law continues to struggle to find proper techniques to achieve this purpose.

The nineteenth century is regarded as an era of sweeping law reform, and it is during this period that the law respecting remedies of creditors was fundamentally recast. By then, the restriction of bankruptcy to traders had produced two very different regimes. Merchants

---

8 (London: np, 1697) at 206–7.

9 4 & 5 Anne, c 17.

10 Prior to this the penalty had been to stand in a pillory or to have an ear cut off if the debtor failed to show that bankruptcy was solely due to misfortune. See 21 Jac I, c 19 (1623). See also E Kadens, "The Last Bankrupt Hanged: Balancing Incentives in the Development of Bankruptcy Law" (2010) 59 *Duke Law Journal* 1229.

11 1 Geo IV, c 115. Basil Montagu commented that: "There had been at least 40,000 bankrupts; that there had not been ten prosecutions, and only three executions; and yet that fraudulent bankruptcies and concealment of property were of daily occurrence, were so common as almost to have lost the nature of crime." B Montagu, *Thoughts upon the Abolition of the Punishment of Death, in Cases of Bankruptcy* (London: Butterworth, 1821) at 3.

and traders were subject to bankruptcy proceedings. Against non-traders, unpaid creditors had to elect between one of two modes of collection. The creditor could seek to execute against the property of the debtor through seizure and sale of the debtor's assets or against the debtor's person through imprisonment of the debtor. Because of a number of technical difficulties in pursuing execution against property, creditors frequently elected to execute against the person. The Victorian reforms significantly improved the creditor's remedies against the debtor's property. During this period, imprisonment of the debtor was curtailed and finally largely abolished.[12] As a consequence, execution against property became the primary remedy of the creditor. The division between insolvencies of traders and non-traders was abolished in 1861, thereby extending the availability of bankruptcy to non-traders.[13]

Bankruptcy law also underwent a series of significant reforms during this period. Many of the reforms were concerned with curtailing abuse of the bankruptcy system. At the beginning of the nineteenth century, the administration of the bankrupt's assets was carried out by an assignee selected by the creditors. This produced a "continual danger of negligence or fraud or both."[14] The administration by the 700 commissioners who oversaw the bankruptcy system was chaotic, and they were unable to exert any effective control to counter these abuses. In 1831 a policy of official administration was adopted under which official assignees appointed by the lord chancellor had control over the management of the bankrupt estate.[15]

The reforms failed to produce a suitable bankruptcy system, and they were criticized by various segments of the business community. The dissatisfaction stemmed chiefly from the high administrative costs that substantially eroded the assets available for distribution to the creditors. In 1869 the official assignee model was scrapped in favour of the reinstitution of creditor control.[16] This was soon regarded to be a disastrous failure. In some cases, a minority of creditors would take control of the bankruptcy administration and improperly sacrifice the

---

12 See J Cohen, "The History of Imprisonment for Debt and Its Relation to the Development of Discharge in Bankruptcy" (1982) 3 *Journal of Legal History* 153. The *Debtors Act 1869*, 32 & 33 Vict, c 62 provided a general abolition of imprisonment for debt.

13 24 & 25 Vict, c 134, s 69.

14 V Lester, *Victorian Insolvency* (Oxford: Clarendon Press, 1995) at 45, quoting from a newspaper report of 1830. Debtors were also able to abuse and manipulate the system through a number of devices. See E Welbourne, "Bankruptcy before the Era of Victorian Reform" (1932) 4 *Cambridge Historical Journal* 51.

15 1 & 2 Will IV, c 56.

16 32 & 33 Vict, c 71.

interests of the other creditors for their own benefit. Sometimes the debtor would obtain control of the process through the use of confederates and fictitious creditors, and then drain the assets through exorbitant trustee and solicitor fees.[17] Bankruptcy was in danger of "degenerating into a scramble" between debtors and creditors.[18]

The English *Bankruptcy Act, 1883*[19] discarded the pure creditor-control model and in its place instituted a new model of joint official and creditor control that continues to be the foundation of modern English and Canadian bankruptcy legislation.[20] The legislation created the office of official receiver and put in place a number of measures designed to ensure accountability on the part of the trustees in bankruptcy and to prevent abuses on the part of creditors and debtors. The overarching philosophy behind the reforms was contained in the idea that bankruptcy was not simply a private dispute between creditors and debtors. The community also had a strong interest in measures "to improve the general tone of commercial morality, to promote honest trading, and to lessen the number of failures."[21] Although English bankruptcy law continued to evolve in the years that followed, the influence of English bankruptcy reforms on Canadian bankruptcy law diminished significantly after the 1883 statute.

2) The Development of Canadian Bankruptcy Law

Post-Confederation Canadian insolvency statutes were passed in 1869 and 1875.[22] The *Insolvent Act of 1869*[23] provided for both voluntary and involuntary insolvency proceedings, but applied only to traders. The *Insolvent Act of 1875*[24] sought to give creditors greater control over the proceedings. It restricted the ability of debtors to obtain a discharge and dropped the provisions that permitted a debtor to make a voluntary assignment. Apparently these changes were not enough to quell

---

17 Lester, above note 14 at 178–79.

18 Review Committee of Insolvency Law and Practice, *Report of the Review Committee of Insolvency Law and Practice*, Cmnd 8558 (London: HMSO, 1982) at 19 [*Cork Report*].

19 46 & 47 Vict, c 52.

20 The features of this joint model are described in Chapter 8.

21 Joseph Chamberlain, Resident of the Board of Trade, speaking on the second reading of the bill. *Hansard* (19 March 1883) at col 817.

22 For a history of pre-Confederation Canadian insolvency legislation, see L Duncan, *The Law and Practice of Bankruptcy in Canada* (Toronto: Carswell, 1922) at 4–15.

23 SC 1869, c 16.

24 SC 1875, c 16.

criticisms directed against the insolvency statutes. The opponents of these laws argued that the current laws allowed dishonest administration of estates, and that the availability of a discharge produced fraud and recklessness in trading. There was also a feeling that it was unfair that persons classed as traders could obtain a benefit denied to others. However, instead of implementing measures that would check these abuses and expand the coverage of bankruptcy law to include all individuals, the statutes were repealed in 1880.[25] As a result, Canada had no bankruptcy law at all during the period from 1880 to 1919.

During this thirty-nine-year period, the provinces enacted legislation that provided *pro rata* sharing among judgment enforcement creditors, as well as legislation that permitted creditors to impugn fraudulent preferences.[26] The provinces also enacted legislation that provided a form of insolvency process. Under this legislation, an insolvent debtor could make a voluntary assignment of his or her property to a trustee who would liquidate the estate under the supervision of inspectors appointed by the creditors. The legislation did not provide for any involuntary insolvency proceedings initiated by creditors. Nor did it provide for a discharge of the debtor.

The deficiencies in the provincial legislation together with a downturn in the economy in 1913 produced a renewed interest in bankruptcy law in Canada. Credit-granting institutions wanted to be able to institute involuntary proceedings against insolvent debtors.[27] The absence of any provision for discharge of the debtor meant that some debtors fled the country while others evaded their creditors by trading under the name of others.[28]

Although a consensus was emerging that bankruptcy legislation was needed,[29] there was debate over the model that should be used. The Canadian Bar Association struck a committee to draft a bankruptcy statute. This generated a concern among credit grantors and licensed insolvency trustees that a bankruptcy statute drafted by lawyers would

---

25 See T Telfer, *Ruin and Redemption: The Struggle for a Canadian Bankruptcy Law 1867-1919* (Toronto: University of Toronto Press, 2014) for a detailed examination of the history both before and after the repeal of the insolvency statutes.

26 See Duncan, above note 22 at 20–22.

27 See T Telfer, "The Canadian *Bankruptcy Act* of 1919: Public Legislation or Private Interest?" (1995) 24 *Canadian Business Law Journal* 357 at 383.

28 See T Telfer, "Access to the Discharge in Canadian Bankruptcy Law and the New Role of Surplus Income: A Historical Perspective" in R Rickett & T Telfer, eds, *International Perspectives on Consumers' Access to Justice* (Cambridge: Cambridge University Press, 2003) 231 at 254–59.

29 See SW Jacobs, "A Canadian Bankruptcy Act: Is it a Necessity?" (1917) 37 *Canadian Law Times* 604.

adopt a court-controlled administration that would produce heavy expenses and delays. For this reason, the Canadian Credit Men's Trust Association, a national organization of authorized trustees, retained HP Grundy, KC, of Winnipeg to draft a statute that displayed a greater element of creditor control. This draft formed the basis for the *Bankruptcy Act*,[30] which was enacted by the Parliament of Canada in 1919.

The English *Bankruptcy Act, 1883* heavily influenced the drafting and conceptual structure of the Canadian *Bankruptcy Act* of 1919.[31] However, the Canadian Act departed from the English model in a number of important respects. For one thing, it was deliberately structured so as to reduce the occasions where an application to court was needed. An individual who wished to make a voluntary assignment into bankruptcy was not required to bring a bankruptcy petition before a court. As well, the Canadian model did not embrace official administration to the same degree as the English Act, and official receivers in Canada were not given investigative responsibilities comparable to those in England.

The *Winding-Up Act*[32] had been enacted in 1882 in order to deal with insolvent companies. In England, Australia, and New Zealand, there is a basic division between insolvency of individuals and insolvency of corporations. Bankruptcy law governs the former, while corporate insolvency legislation governs the latter. The Canadian bankruptcy statute, in common with United States bankruptcy law, covers both individual and corporate insolvency.[33] The benefits of a single insolvency regime for both individuals and corporations were appreciated at an early date. A noted bankruptcy expert observed that the existence of two codes that "contain different provisions on such important matters as priorities, fraudulent preferences and fraudulent conveyances, tend to obscure the law."[34]

Despite the passage of the legislation, there continued to be incompetence and collusive conduct on the part of some trustees. In 1932 the Office of the Superintendent in Bankruptcy (OSB) was created in order to

30 SC 1919, c 36.

31 Although there was a 1914 English *Bankruptcy Act*, the *Cork Report*, above note 18 at 20, describes it as a "tidying up operation" that "did not alter in any material respect the system devised in 1883."

32 SC 1882, c 23.

33 The *Winding-Up Act* was not repealed upon the enactment of the 1919 Act. The use of the winding-up regime remained mandatory in the case of insolvencies of certain types of debtors, such as banks and insurance companies, and could still be employed as an alternative insolvency regime for other kinds of corporations. It was not until 1966 that precedence was given to bankruptcy proceedings.

34 Duncan, above note 22 at vii.

supervise and establish qualifications for bankruptcy trustees. In 1949 a new, streamlined procedure was created for the administration of small estates. In 1966 the powers of the superintendent were widened through the creation of additional investigatory powers. The courts, too, were given additional powers to review pre-bankruptcy transactions at undervalue between parties who were not bargaining with one another at arm's length. Surplus income provisions were also added to ensure that a sufficient portion of the bankrupt's post-bankruptcy income would be available to meet the bankrupt's necessary living expenses.

3) Modern Reform Efforts in Canada

During the 1970s and early 1980s, a major effort was made to revise the whole bankruptcy system. In 1970 the *Tassé Report*, which called for a major overhaul of the system, was released.[35] Several bills were later introduced to achieve this objective, but none of them was enacted. Following this, an incremental approach to bankruptcy law reform was proposed.[36] Instead of replacing the old bankruptcy statute with a new one, the existing structure of the statute was maintained and reforms in discrete areas of bankruptcy law were introduced by amendment. Amending statutes were passed in 1992 and 1997.

The 1992 amendments made significant changes to the treatment of Crown claims in bankruptcy, created a new right of suppliers to repossess unpaid goods, provided for the automatic discharge of first-time bankrupts and mandatory credit counselling, and protected trustees against liability for claims for environmental damage.[37] The 1997 amendments provided new surplus income rules respecting post-bankruptcy earnings, as well as new provisions on international insolvencies.[38]

The 1997 amendments provided for a review of the bankruptcy legislation after five years. Industry Canada issued its *Report on the Operation and Administration of the Bankruptcy and Insolvency Act and*

---

35 Study Committee on Bankruptcy and Insolvency Legislation, *Report of the Study Committee on Bankruptcy and Insolvency Legislation* (Ottawa: Study Committee on Bankruptcy and Insolvency Legislation, 1970) [*Tassé Report*].

36 See J Ziegel, "Canada's Phased-In Bankruptcy Law Reform" (1996) 70 *American Bankruptcy Law Journal* 383. And see also Canada, Advisory Committee on Bankruptcy and Insolvency, *Report of the Advisory Committee on Bankruptcy and Insolvency* by GF Colter (Ottawa: Supply and Services, 1986) [*Colter Report*].

37 SC 1992, c 27.

38 SC 1997, c 12.

the Companies' Creditors Arrangement Act[39] in 2002. A separate task force on personal insolvencies, established by the superintendent in bankruptcy, issued its report in 2002.[40] The Insolvency Institute of Canada and the Canadian Association of Insolvency and Restructuring Professionals created a joint task force on business insolvency reform, and it also released its report in 2002.[41] The Senate Committee on Banking Trade and Commerce considered these reports and issued its own in 2003.[42]

Bankruptcy reform suddenly became a hot political topic just before the dissolution of Parliament and the calling of the 2006 federal election. The controversy centred on the low status of wage-earner claims in insolvency. A bankruptcy reform bill was introduced, the centrepiece of which was the *Wage Earner Protection Program Act*. The bill was quickly passed[43] with support from all the political parties.[44] Unfortunately, in the rush to enact, a number of problems went undetected, requiring a further amending bill. The first attempt died when Parliament was prorogued,[45] but the amending legislation was subsequently reintroduced and passed on 14 December 2007.[46]

These bankruptcy reforms were far-reaching in scope and included the following elements:

- an insurance program (the Wage Earner Protection Program) that gives workers the right to make claims for unpaid wages when their employer goes into bankruptcy or receivership;
- new provisions concerning disclaimer, affirmation, and assignment of executory contracts;

---

39 (Ottawa: Industry Canada, 2002).

40 Canada, Office of the Superintendent of Bankruptcy, *Final Report of the Personal Insolvency Task Force* (Ottawa: Office of the Superintendent of Bankruptcy, 2002).

41 Insolvency Institute of Canada and the Canadian Association of Insolvency and Restructuring Professionals Joint Task Force on Business Insolvency Law Reform, *Report to Industry Canada* (Toronto: Insolvency Institute of Canada and the Canadian Association of Insolvency and Restructuring Professionals Joint Task Force on Business Insolvency Law Reform, 2002).

42 Senate Standing Committee on Banking, Trade and Commerce, *Debtors and Creditors: Sharing the Burden: A Review of the Bankruptcy and Insolvency Act and the Companies' Creditors Arrangement Act* by Richard H. Kroft & David Tkachuk (Ottawa: Standing Senate Committee on Banking, Trade and Commerce, 2003).

43 SC 2005, c 47.

44 See JS Ziegel, "The Travails of Bill C-55" (2006) 42 *Canadian Business Law Journal* 440.

45 39th Parliament, 1st Session, Bill C-62.

46 SC 2007, c 36.

- a federal exemption that shelters registered retirement savings plans (RRSPs) from the claims of creditors;
- reformulated provisions governing preferences and transactions at undervalue that allow a trustee to impugn pre-bankruptcy transactions;
- changes to the rules that govern discharge of a bankrupt; and
- a new set of cross-border insolvency provisions based on the UNCITRAL Model Law on Cross-Border Insolvency.

This incremental approach to the reform of bankruptcy law has its drawbacks. Although some aspects of the bankruptcy statute are modernized, other features have become progressively obsolete and outdated. At some point a thorough revision of the entire statute will be required.[47]

B. THE OBJECTIVES OF BANKRUPTCY LAW

The Supreme Court of Canada has stated that the purpose and object of bankruptcy law is to (1) distribute equitably the assets of the debtor and (2) permit the rehabilitation of the debtor as a citizen.[48] This provides a very useful starting point for examining the objectives of bankruptcy law. The first objective is to create a collective process through which the assets of the debtor are liquidated, the claims of the creditors are assessed, and the proceeds of the liquidated assets are distributed to the creditors. The second objective is to afford the debtor a fresh start when it is appropriate to do so. The entire history of bankruptcy law reform reveals a third objective: the prevention of fraud and abuse of the bankruptcy system, the promotion of commercial morality, and the protection of the credit system.[49]

---

47 R Wood & D Bryan, "Creeping Statutory Obsolescence in Bankruptcy Law" (2014) 3 *Journal of the Insolvency Institute of Canada* 1.

48 *Industrial Acceptance Corp v Lalonde*, [1952] 2 SCR 109; *Vachon v Canada (Employment & Immigration Commission)*, [1985] 2 SCR 417.

49 The three foundational objectives of bankruptcy law have been recognized for over two hundred years. Basil Montagu commented in 1805 that the "laws of bankruptcy are a system of laws constructed by statute for the benefit of trade (a), to secure an equal and speedy distribution of an insolvent or improvident trader's property amongst all his creditors (b), to discharge the unfortunate trader from his debts (c), and to suppress fraud." See B Montagu, *A Digest of the Bankrupt Laws*, vol 1 (London: Butterworth, 1805–7) at 1.

1) Liquidation and Distribution of the Debtor's Assets

The insolvency of a debtor typically means that there will not be sufficient assets to satisfy the claims of all the creditors. Bankruptcy is a legal process that seeks to maximize the recovery of the creditors as a group. In a world of no bankruptcy, some of the creditors — those who are able to grab assets before the other creditors are able to do so — are better off. But the creditors as a whole are worse off. There are two reasons why this is the case. First, in the absence of bankruptcy, each creditor must incur the cost of obtaining judgment and of enforcing it. This produces duplication in adjudication and enforcement costs that might be reduced if there was a collective liquidation proceeding carried out on behalf of all the creditors. Second, under a regime where the ranking among creditors is determined by a principle of first come, first served, each creditor will have a strong incentive to rush in and grab the assets even though a more orderly liquidation of assets would produce a higher return for all the creditors as a group. Bankruptcy law protects the integrity of a collective liquidation proceeding by imposing an automatic stay of proceedings that pre-empts the enforcement remedies of the creditors. In doing so, it provides "a way to override the creditors' pursuit of their own remedies and to make them work together."[50]

A collective liquidation proceeding requires a process for the assessment of creditors' claims and the distribution of assets to creditors. Creditors do not invoke the usual civil process for the adjudication of their claims. Instead, an administrative rather than a judicial process is created under which a trustee in bankruptcy assesses and values their claims. This ensures that the claims can be processed more quickly and cheaply than would otherwise be the case. Bankruptcy law also provides rules for the ranking of the claims of creditors. Historically, bankruptcy law has adopted a *pro rata* sharing principle among creditors. This has sometimes been said to form one of the foundational principles of bankruptcy law. The pre-eminence of this principle, however, is undercut by the recognition of a number of exceptions under which certain creditors, such as preferred creditors, are given a higher ranking. Rather than a fundamental principle, *pro rata* sharing might better be regarded as a sensible rule for ranking among claims of the same

---

50 T Jackson, *The Logic and Limits of Bankruptcy Law* (Cambridge, MA: Harvard University Press, 1986) at 17.

type where there is no convincing reason for preferring one claim over another.[51]

2) Rehabilitation of the Individual Debtor

The second objective of bankruptcy law looks to the economic rehabilitation of the debtor. This objective is not engaged if the debtor is an artificial entity, such as a corporation. Bankruptcy proceedings in respect of corporations and other artificial entities are mostly concerned with issues of liquidation and distribution. It is in respect of individuals that the second objective of bankruptcy law comes into play. Indeed, in many cases of consumer bankruptcy, the debtor owns very few assets. In these "no asset" cases, debtor rehabilitation is the primary objective that is being pursued.

The rehabilitation of the debtor is accomplished through a number of means, the most important of which is the ability of a debtor to obtain a bankruptcy discharge. Because of illness, loss of employment, or other cause, a debtor may be left in a position where there is no reasonable prospect of repayment of all debts. The bankruptcy discharge gives the honest but unfortunate debtor the ability to be freed from the crushing burden of debt that cannot be met. This gives the debtor a fresh start that will permit his or her reintegration into society. Discharge releases the debtor from the claims of creditors that were in existence at the time of the bankruptcy. The creditors may resort to the debtor's assets, including after-acquired assets, up until the date of the discharge. Assets acquired after that date are not available to the creditors.

The bankruptcy discharge is not the only means through which bankruptcy law seeks to foster the economic rehabilitation of the debtor. Bankruptcy law also pursues this objective by ensuring that the debtor is not stripped of all assets during the course of the bankruptcy but is permitted to retain sufficient assets to provide the debtor and his or her family with food, accommodation, and other necessaries of life. Bankruptcy law does so through its treatment of exempt property and through the surplus income regime that covers the post-bankruptcy, pre-discharge earnings of the debtor. Bankruptcy law also pursues the objective of debtor rehabilitation through mandatory credit counselling that attempts to reduce the occurrence of repeat bankruptcies.

---

51 See R Mokal, "Priority as Pathology: The *Pari Passu* Myth" (2001) 60 *Cambridge Law Journal* 581.

3) Enhancing Commercial Morality and Protecting the Credit System

The third objective of bankruptcy law is premised on the idea that bankruptcy is not simply a private matter between creditors and debtors but a subject where there are legitimate matters of public interest at stake.[52] Bankruptcy law seeks to protect commercial morality by preventing fraudulent debtors from abusing the credit system. Equally, creditors and trustees in bankruptcy are prevented from engaging in practices that abuse the bankruptcy system or undermine public trust in the credit economy. The Supreme Court of Canada, in an early decision, stated although one of the objects of bankruptcy law is to secure a speedy and equitable distribution of the bankrupt's assets, it is not confined to this purpose and also has as its goals the prevention of fraud and bad faith.[53] It therefore "acts as a preventative to fraud and collusion on the one hand, and as an encouragement to honest and cautious trading on the other."[54]

Bankruptcy law imposes a set of bankruptcy offences that can be used to discipline persons who transgress the norms of commercial morality. It also provides for a system for the licensing of trustees to force out those who are fraudulent or incompetent. Additionally, bankruptcy law possesses an investigatory apparatus that permits public officials to investigate complaints, and it recognizes the importance of an information-gathering function concerning the causes of insolvencies and the operation of the various insolvency regimes. The ability to compile insolvency statistics is now regarded as a crucial element in effective bankruptcy law reform.

The integrity of the bankruptcy process can be seriously weakened if the debtor's assets are dissipated before the bankruptcy is invoked. This can occur if a debtor transfers assets to a third party and does not receive their fair value in exchange. Such payments and transfers have the effect of undermining the ranking of claims established by the insolvency regime. This is the problem of the fraudulent preference, which is not unique to bankruptcy law and is liable to arise whenever creditors seek recovery from the debtor's assets. Bankruptcy law provides rules that allow the creditors to recover value that has been transferred to third parties to address this problem. In essence, these

---

52 See *Tassé Report*, above note 35 at 87–88; *Cork Report*, above note 18 at 62–63. See also *Re Posner* (1960), 3 CBR (NS) 49 (Man QB).

53 *Shields v Peak* (1883), 8 SCR 579.

54 *Ibid* at 588, Ritchie CJ.

rules prevent creditors from jumping the queue when bankruptcy is imminent.

C. THE FUNDAMENTAL PRINCIPLES OF BANKRUPTCY LAW

One might embark upon the study of bankruptcy law by reading the *Bankruptcy and Insolvency Act* from beginning to end. Although this is a sensible strategy for reading most things, it is not recommended as a path to enlightenment when learning about bankruptcy law. The unfortunate reader would quickly become discouraged by a disorderly mass of rules and would discern little of the overarching structure of the law. In order to comprehend bankruptcy law, it is necessary to understand the fundamental principles that form its backbone. Only then will the detailed rules begin to make sense.

1) Bankruptcy Proceedings Are Collective

Bankruptcy is a collective proceeding that can be initiated by the creditors or by the debtor. Creditors who initiate bankruptcy proceedings against the debtor do so on behalf of all the creditors who are entitled to participate in the distribution of the debtor's assets. This has several different implications. First, non-initiating creditors can replace initiating creditors who do not diligently prosecute the action.[55] As well, courts will closely examine bilateral agreements between a debtor and an initiating creditor for the discontinuance of bankruptcy proceedings to ensure that the interests of other creditors are not prejudiced.[56] The collective nature of the proceedings is also seen in the rule that the legal costs of the initiating creditor and the administration costs of the bankruptcy are paid out of the bankrupt estate,[57] a provision that ensures that all participating creditors share in the costs of the bankruptcy. It is manifested, too, in the stay of proceedings that prevents creditors from opting out of the bankruptcy proceedings by exercising their ordinary civil remedies for the recovery of their claims.

---

55 *BIA*, s 43(13).

56 *Re Abu-Hatoum* (1987), 63 CBR (NS) 60 (Ont HCJ).

57 *BIA*, ss 45(1) and 136(1)(b).

2) The Debtor's Assets Vest in the Trustee

Upon the occurrence of bankruptcy, all of the debtor's assets vest in the trustee in bankruptcy. The vesting of assets is automatic through operation of law and does not require a transfer or conveyance by the debtor. The assets that vest in the trustee form the bankrupt estate and include contractual rights and other rights of action that the debtor has against third parties. The trustee takes the assets subject to the same rights, equities, and defences as the bankrupt. This is what is meant when it is said that the trustee steps into the shoes of the bankrupt.[58] The trustee does not occupy the position of a *bona fide* purchaser for value and therefore cannot claim priority over a person who holds an earlier equitable interest in the debtor's assets. Bankruptcy does not generally cause contractual rights held by the debtor to come to an end. A right of set-off that could be asserted against the debtor can similarly be asserted against a trustee.

Although the general rule is that pre-bankruptcy rights remain unaltered, there are exceptions to this principle. In some cases, the trustee will be in a superior position than that occupied by the debtor in relation to a third party. Although a pre-bankruptcy transfer of an asset by the debtor to a third party may be binding as between the parties, the trustee may be able to exercise a power to set aside the transaction as a fraudulent conveyance or fraudulent preference. A security interest in personal property that is not properly perfected under provincial law is binding as between the debtor and the secured creditor. However, the trustee may invoke provincial legislation that gives the trustee priority over the secured creditor.

3) Proprietary Rights of Third Parties Are Unaffected

It is only the debtor's assets that vest in the trustee. The trustee cannot look to assets belonging to third parties to satisfy claims against the debtor. If the debtor is in possession of property belonging to another, the trustee is obliged to return it to the owner. Sometimes both the third party and the debtor have an interest in an asset. The basic principle remains the same: it is only the debtor's interest in the asset that vests in the trustee. For this reason, a secured creditor's right to realize against the collateral in the event of a default is not generally affected by the bankruptcy. So long as the secured party has properly complied with any registration requirement that is needed to ensure priority over

58 See *Re Giffen*, [1998] 1 SCR 91 at para 52; *Saulnier v Royal Bank of Canada*, 2008 SCC 50 at para 50.

a trustee, the secured party can exercise its secured remedies against the collateral outside the bankruptcy process.

4) Personal Rights of Creditors Are Converted into Rights of Proof

A fundamental distinction is drawn between persons who hold a proprietary right in an asset and persons who hold a personal right against the debtor. This represents the difference between what I own and what I am owed.[59] As discussed above, a person who has a proprietary right in a thing is not generally affected by the bankruptcy of another. But, if the party has a personal claim against the debtor, that party loses the right to enforce the claim through ordinary legal process and must instead pursue the claim within the bankruptcy proceeding. Bankruptcy law provides a procedure by which persons who hold personal claims against the debtor can establish their claims and participate in the liquidation of the debtor's assets. The claimant must file a proof of claim with the trustee. This gives the claimant the right to share in the liquidation through payment of a bankruptcy dividend. Contingent and unliquidated claims can also be proven in bankruptcy, but a valuation procedure is required in order to establish their monetary value. Bankruptcy has the effect of accelerating a creditor's right to payment. The claimant can file a proof of claim and obtain a bankruptcy dividend even though the amount would not have been payable until some future time.

5) A Statutory Scheme of Distribution Governs Payments to Creditors

It is often claimed that the rule of *pari passu* sharing among creditors who prove their claims in bankruptcy is one of the fundamental principles of bankruptcy law. The rule of *pari passu* sharing among the ordinary creditors was established in the very first English bankruptcy statute and remains to this day. There is, however, a difficulty with regarding it as a fundamental principle. The reality is that in most bankruptcies there is unequal sharing among the participating creditors. Therefore, a wider formulation of the principle is needed. A more accurate statement of the principle is that the proceeds of the liquidation of the debtor's assets are distributed to the proving creditors ac-

59 RM Goode, "Ownership and Obligation in Commercial Transactions" (1987) 103 *Law Quarterly Review* 433.

cording to a statutory scheme of distribution. Although this scheme of distribution provides for *pari passu* sharing among ordinary creditors, certain kinds of claims are promoted and given more favourable treatment than the ordinary creditors (preferred creditors) while other kinds of claims are demoted and given less favourable treatment (postponed creditors).

Secured creditors are not governed by this scheme of distribution. They are entitled to exercise their secured remedies against the collateral, thereby withdrawing it from the bankrupt estate. A secured creditor who claims for a deficiency following a sale of the collateral is asserting a personal right against the debtor rather than a proprietary right against an asset, and is therefore treated the same as any other ordinary unsecured creditor.

6) Discharge Releases the Debtor from Pre-bankruptcy Claims

Only a natural person (i.e., a human being as opposed to an artificial entity such as a corporation) can obtain a discharge in bankruptcy in the absence of full satisfaction of the claims of creditors. A discharge releases the bankrupt from all claims provable in bankruptcy. There are certain special types of claims, such as family support orders and government student loan obligations, which are not released upon a discharge of the debtor. Claims that arise after the commencement of bankruptcy proceedings are not provable claims, and therefore they are also not released by the bankruptcy discharge. The bankruptcy discharge also affects the property that will be available to satisfy the claims of the creditors. Property that is acquired by the debtor before the bankruptcy discharge is divisible among the creditors. Property acquired after discharge is not.

D. THE CAST OF PLAYERS

In addition to the debtor and the creditors, there are a number of important players involved in the administration of bankruptcies. Their respective roles will be discussed in greater detail elsewhere in the book.[60] The purpose of this discussion is to provide a brief introduction of their titles and roles within the bankruptcy proceeding.

---

60 See Chapter 8.

1) The Trustee in Bankruptcy

The trustee in bankruptcy is the person who is responsible for assembling and liquidating the assets of the bankrupt estate, reviewing the proof of claims, and distributing the proceeds to creditors whose proofs of claims have been allowed. The trustee is required to complete certain steps, such as calling the first meeting of creditors and the submission of reports to the court and to the superintendent in bankruptcy. A trustee in bankruptcy is not a government official. The trustee is a private-sector actor who is licensed by the superintendent in bankruptcy. The trustee in bankruptcy is an officer of the court and owes a fiduciary obligation to the creditors and to the bankrupt.

2) The Superintendent of Bankruptcy

The Office of the Superintendent in Bankruptcy is responsible for supervising the administration of bankrupt estates. The OSB licenses trustees to administer estates. In order to obtain a licence, a trustee must complete a three-year qualification course administered by the OSB and the Canadian Association of Insolvency and Restructuring Professionals (CAIRP).[61] The OSB investigates complaints from debtors, creditors, or the public concerning fraud, incompetence, or wrongdoing within the insolvency system. The OSB can also set standards of conduct for trustees through the issuance of directives. Finally, the OSB maintains a registry system that provides a record of insolvency proceedings in Canada.

3) The Official Receiver

The official receiver is a federal civil servant employed by the OSB. A debtor who wishes to declare bankruptcy voluntarily must file an assignment in bankruptcy with the official receiver. The official receiver appoints the trustee on the assignment. In both voluntary and involuntary bankruptcies, the official receiver examines bankrupts under oath as to their conduct and the causes of the bankruptcy, and will chair the first meeting of creditors or nominate someone else to do so. Unlike their counterparts in the United Kingdom, the official receiver does not take interim control of the debtor's property prior to the appointment of a trustee.

---

61 CAIRP is a national professional association that represents trustees and other insolvency professionals.

4) The Inspectors

Creditors who attend the first meeting of creditors will be asked to affirm the appointment of the trustee or substitute another in his or her place, and to appoint inspectors. The board of inspectors that is appointed supervises the trustee's administration of the bankrupt estate. The trustee is required to obtain the approval of the board of inspectors on a wide number of matters. The inspectors are under a fiduciary obligation to act in the interests of the creditors as a group and are not permitted to act in their own self-interest.

5) The Bankruptcy Court

The bankruptcy statute does not create a separate bankruptcy court but instead vests the superior courts of the provinces and territories with "such jurisdiction at law and equity as will enable them to exercise original, auxiliary and ancillary jurisdiction in bankruptcy."[62] A court that is exercising this jurisdiction is commonly referred to as a bankruptcy court in Canada. The bankruptcy court has a number of different functions in respect of bankruptcy proceedings. In involuntary bankruptcy proceedings, the court makes a bankruptcy order against a debtor once the creditors prove that the debtor committed an act of bankruptcy. The bankruptcy court also hears applications for discharge of the debtor in cases where an automatic discharge is not granted. The trustee can seek directions from the court in matters of uncertainty, and other parties to the bankruptcy proceeding can apply to have the decision of the trustee reversed or modified. In appropriate cases, such as those involving fraud or conflict of interest, the court can replace the trustee. The bankruptcy court also will make determinations as to the rights of parties on a wide variety of matters. If the matter concerns the rights of a "stranger to the bankruptcy," the matter must be resolved by an action in the ordinary civil courts, and not by an action in the bankruptcy court.[63]

FURTHER READINGS

BAIRD, DG. "Loss Distribution, Forum Shopping, and Bankruptcy: A Reply to Warren" (1987) 54 *University of Chicago Law Review* 815

---

62 *BIA*, s 183(1).

63 *Clarkson Gordon Inc v Falconi* (1987), 61 OR (2d) 554 (HCJ).

CANADA, ADVISORY COMMITTEE ON BANKRUPTCY AND INSOLVENCY. *Report of the Advisory Committee on Bankruptcy and Insolvency* by GF Colter (Ottawa: Supply and Services, 1986) (*Colter Report*)

CANADA, OFFICE OF THE SUPERINTENDENT OF BANKRUPTCY. *Final Report of the Personal Insolvency Task Force* (Ottawa: Office of the Superintendent of Bankruptcy, 2002)

GOODE, R. *Principles of Corporate Insolvency Law*, 4th ed (London: Sweet & Maxwell, 2011) ch 2

INSOLVENCY INSTITUTE OF CANADA AND THE CANADIAN ASSOCIATION OF INSOLVENCY AND RESTRUCTURING PROFESSIONALS JOINT TASK FORCE ON BUSINESS INSOLVENCY LAW REFORM. *Report to Industry Canada* (Toronto: Insolvency Institute of Canada and the Canadian Association of Insolvency and Restructuring Professionals Joint Task Force on Business Insolvency Law Reform, 2002)

JONES, WJ. "The Foundations of English Bankruptcy: Statutes and Commissions in the Early Modern Period" (1979) 69 *Transactions of the American Philosophical Society* 1

LESTER, V. *Victorian Insolvency* (Oxford: Clarendon Press, 1995)

REVIEW COMMITTEE OF INSOLVENCY LAW AND PRACTICE. *Report of the Review Committee of Insolvency Law and Practice*, Cmnd 8558 (London: HMSO, 1982) ch 2 (*Cork Report*)

SENATE STANDING COMMITTEE ON BANKING, TRADE AND COMMERCE. *Debtors and Creditors: Sharing the Burden: A Review of the Bankruptcy and Insolvency Act and the Companies' Creditors Arrangement Act* by Richard H. Kroft & David Tkachuk (Ottawa: Standing Senate Committee on Banking, Trade and Commerce, 2003)

STUDY COMMITTEE ON BANKRUPTCY AND INSOLVENCY LEGISLATION. *Report of the Study Committee on Bankruptcy and Insolvency Legislation* (Ottawa: Study Committee on Bankruptcy and Insolvency Legislation, 1970) ch 2 (*Tassé Report*)

TELFER, T. *Ruin and Redemption: The Struggle for a Canadian Bankruptcy Law 1867–1919* (Toronto: University of Toronto Press, 2014)

WARREN, E. "Bankruptcy Policy" (1987) 54 *University of Chicago Law Review* 775

WOOD, R, & D BRYAN. "Creeping Statutory Obsolescence in Bankruptcy Law" (2014) 3 *Journal of the Insolvency Institute of Canada* 1

ZIEGEL, J. "Canada's Phased-In Bankruptcy Law Reform" (1996) 70 *American Bankruptcy. Law Journal* 383

CHAPTER 3

COMMENCEMENT OF BANKRUPTCY

There are three different means by which bankruptcy proceedings can be commenced. In the vast majority of cases, the debtor initiates the bankruptcy. This is known as a voluntary bankruptcy. In a voluntary bankruptcy, it is the debtor who takes the steps that are required to bring the bankruptcy regime into play. In most cases, the debtor will contact an insolvency professional who will then assist the debtor in completing and processing the necessary documents. The debtor is required to disclose the assets that are owned by the debtor and the creditors who have claims against the debtor. Voluntary bankruptcy involves a relatively simple process that does not require a court application. The insolvent person merely signs a document called an assignment in bankruptcy and files it with the official receiver.[1]

The creditors can also initiate a bankruptcy. This is known as an involuntary bankruptcy. Here, it is the creditors who take the active steps in commencing bankruptcy proceedings. The procedure used to initiate an involuntary bankruptcy is more complex and requires a court application. One or more of the creditors must apply to a bankruptcy court for a bankruptcy order against the debtor.[2] This terminology is relatively new. Until recently, the bankruptcy order was referred to as a receiving order and the application was called a petition for a receiving

1 *BIA*, s 49(1).

2 *Ibid*, s 43(1).

order.[3] The creditors must establish through evidence that the debtor has committed an act of bankruptcy, and a debtor may appear at the hearing and dispute the truth of the alleged facts. If the court is satisfied that there has been proper service and proof of the alleged facts, it may make a bankruptcy order.

Bankruptcy proceedings can arise automatically without the intervention of either the debtor or the creditor. This will occur when an attempt to negotiate a commercial proposal fails for one of a number of different reasons. The *BIA* provides that the debtor is deemed to have made an assignment in bankruptcy when this happens.

A. ELIGIBLE PERSONS

In many countries, including the United Kingdom and Australia, bankruptcy proceedings are available only in relation to individuals. A separate insolvency regime operates in relation to corporations and other artificial entities. Canada and the United States do not take this approach. Both natural persons and artificial entities are subject to bankruptcy proceedings.

Several key definitions in the *BIA* are used to delineate the kinds of persons who are subject to bankruptcy proceedings. In the case of an involuntary bankruptcy, the Act provides that one or more creditors may bring bankruptcy proceedings against a debtor. The definition of "debtor" imposes certain eligibility requirements on the types of persons who can be forced into bankruptcy.[4] In the case of voluntary bankruptcy, the Act provides that an insolvent person may make an assignment in bankruptcy. The definition of "insolvent person" is similarly used to impose certain eligibility requirements on the types of persons who can make an assignment.[5] The Act also makes it clear that bankruptcy proceedings are available in respect of an estate of a deceased person.[6]

Both the definition of "debtor" and that of "insolvent person" use the term "person," which is defined in the Act as including a partnership, an unincorporated association, a corporation, a cooperative society, or an organization.[7] Banks, insurance companies, trust companies, loan

---

3 The terminology was changed in 2004 as part of the federal harmonization project to ensure that both language versions of the statute take into account both the common law and civil law systems.

4 *BIA*, s 2 "debtor."

5 *Ibid*, "insolvent person."

6 *Ibid*, "person," ss 44 and 49(1).

7 *Ibid*, "person."

companies, and railway companies are not subject to bankruptcy. These entities are excluded from the Act because other special insolvency statutes govern their liquidation or restructuring.[8] Unfortunately, a clumsy drafting approach is used to achieve this result. The term "person" includes a corporation, while the term "corporation" excludes those entities just mentioned.[9] "Creditor" is also defined using the term "person."[10] A literal reading of the definitions would lead one to the conclusion that banks and other excluded corporations cannot prove a claim as a creditor in a bankruptcy, since they are not persons within the meaning of the Act and a creditor must be a person. Courts have overcome this problem by holding that this restricted meaning of "corporation" was not intended to be used in all of the provisions of the Act.[11]

A partnership is an aggregate of persons rather than a separate legal entity, and therefore bankruptcy proceedings must be initiated by or against the partners who make up the firm. Unless authorized, a partner does not have the power to make a bankruptcy assignment on behalf of the other partners.[12] All of the members of a firm should therefore execute an assignment if the firm wishes to initiate a voluntary bankruptcy.[13] Creditors who initiate involuntary bankruptcy proceedings against a firm are not required to present a bankruptcy application against all the partners.[14] However, a failure to do so will mean that the bankruptcy will encompass only the bankrupt partner's separate assets as well as his or her joint interest in the partnership assets. Because the *BIA* defines a person as including a partnership, the creditors of a firm can bring a bankruptcy application in the name of the partnership.[15] This does not transform the partnership into a separate legal entity. It simply has the same effect as if the bankruptcy application named each of the partners.[16]

The *BIA* provides that the Act applies to limited partnerships in the same manner as if they were ordinary partnerships.[17] A bankruptcy

8 See Chapter 21.

9 *BIA*, s 2 "corporation."

10 *Ibid*, "creditor."

11 *Re Selkirk Spruce Mills Ltd* (1958), 37 CBR 11 (BCSC); *Re Fischel* (1991), 10 CBR (3d) 282 (NBCA).

12 *Re Union Fish Co* (1923), 3 CBR 779 (Ont SC).

13 *Re Squires Brothers* (1922), CBR 191 (Sask KB) [*Squires Brothers*]. The bankruptcy estate includes the separate assets of the individual partners as well as the partnership assets. See *Taylor v Leveys* (1922), 2 CBR 390 (Ont SC).

14 *BIA*, s 43(15).

15 *Langille v Toronto-Dominion Bank*, [1982] 1 SCR 34 [*Langille*].

16 *Re Gottingen Street Food Market* (2002), 31 CBR (4th) 250 (NSSC).

17 *BIA*, s 85(1).

order that is obtained against the name of a limited partnership therefore operates as a bankruptcy of the general partner and vests in the trustee all the assets of the general partner, including the non-partnership assets of the general partner.[18] However, in respect of the limited partners, only the interests of the limited partners in the partnership assets vest in the trustee.[19]

Bankruptcy proceedings cannot generally be brought against a trust, since a trust does not fall within the Act's definition of a person. A trust has no legal personality. Contractual obligations are incurred by the trustee in the trustee's own name. Creditors therefore have a claim against the trustee for any breach of contract and will not typically have any claim against the beneficiaries of a trust. Although property held in trust is not available for distribution to the creditors of the trustee,[20] a trustee has a right to be indemnified out of the trust assets for liabilities incurred in respect of acts properly done in performance of the trustee's duties.[21] This right to indemnification is an asset that will vest in a trustee in bankruptcy upon a bankruptcy of the trustee.[22] The creditors may, however, encounter difficulties in reaching the trust assets if the trustee's right to indemnification is not available because of lack of capacity, lack of authorization, breach of an equitable duty, or the existence of an unconnected indebtedness owed by the trustee to pay funds into the trust.[23] As well, the right to indemnification may be excluded by agreement between the trustee and the beneficiary.[24]

The 2009 amendments to the *BIA* have altered this principle in one instance. The definition of a corporation[25] was changed so as to include an income trust. An income trust is defined as a trust that has assets in Canada if its units are listed on a prescribed stock exchange or the majority of its units are held by a trust whose units are held

---

18 *Re Kingsberry Properties Ltd Partnership* (1997), 3 CBR (4th) 124 (Ont Ct Gen Div), aff'd (1998), 3 CBR (4th) 135 (Ont CA) [*Kingsberry*]; *Ornge Global GP Inc (Re)*, 2013 ONSC 4518.

19 *Kingsberry*, above note 18. See also *BIA*, s. 85(1).

20 *BIA*, s 67(1)(a).

21 See D Steele & A Spence, "Enforcement against the Assets of a Business Trust by an Unsecured Creditor" (1998) 31 *Canadian Business Law Journal* 72 at 73–78.

22 *Jennings v Mather*, [1902] 1 KB 1 (CA).

23 See Trust Law Committee, *Rights of Creditors against Trustees and Trust Funds* (1999), online: www.kcl.ac.uk/law/research/centres/trustlawcommittee/otherpapersandreports/TLCCredRightsReport1404991.pdf.

24 *Graybriar Industries Ltd v South West Marine Estates Ltd* (1988), 21 BCLR (2d) 256 (SC).

25 *BIA*, s 2 "corporation."

on a prescribed stock exchange.[26] Although this provision makes it clear that an income trust is a person for the purposes of commencing bankruptcy proceedings, there is nothing in the *BIA* that provides that the creditors have a direct claim against the assets of an income trust. Without an ability to bring an action against the assets of the trust, the creditors will be unable to prove their claims in the bankruptcy of the income trust. It is possible that the courts will hold that the amendments impliedly give the creditors a direct right, but it is unfortunate that the legislation was not more careful in working out the implications of this change.

Bankruptcy proceedings are limited by a territorial requirement.[27] Prior to 1997, both voluntary and involuntary bankruptcy proceedings were available only if a person resided or carried on business in Canada.[28] The 1997 amendments widened the definition of an "insolvent person" by providing that it was also sufficient that the debtor own property in Canada. Voluntary bankruptcy is therefore available so long as that condition is met. In the case of an involuntary bankruptcy, the fact that there is property in Canada is not sufficient; the debtor must reside or carry on business in Canada.[29] This difference in treatment can be readily justified. A foreign debtor may be put to the expense of disputing the matter in Canada, and it is reasonable to impose a requirement that this person have some greater connection to the jurisdiction beyond mere ownership of property.

Individuals whose principal occupation and means of livelihood is fishing, farming, and wage earners who earn less than $2,500 cannot

---

26 *Ibid*, "income trust."

27 See Chapter 22 for a discussion of cross-border insolvencies.

28 A debtor who carries on business in Canada but later shuts down the business operations and departs from Canada without paying its creditors is nevertheless considered to carry on business in Canada so long as the creditors are unpaid. See *Solloway (Re)* (1939), 20 CBR 309 (Ont CA).

29 The term "debtor" is defined as "an insolvent person and any person who, at the time an act of bankruptcy was committed by him, resided or carried on business in Canada." It is unlikely that the widening of the term "insolvent person" was intended to permit involuntary bankruptcy proceedings where the debtor is not resident or did not carry on business in Canada. The term "debtor" is used in many other sections of the Act, and the definition was designed to ensure that it covered persons in both voluntary and involuntary bankruptcy proceedings. The first portion of the definition (the reference to an "insolvent person") was likely intended to cover voluntary bankruptcies, while the remainder of the definition (which makes specific reference to an act of bankruptcy and which imposes a requirement of residence or business activity) covers involuntary bankruptcies.

be forced into bankruptcy,[30] but they are able to place themselves voluntarily into bankruptcy by making an assignment. The restriction on involuntary bankruptcy proceedings against farmers applies only to individuals who carry on farming or fishing operations. It does not apply if the operations are carried out by a corporation or partnership,[31] nor does it apply to a hobby farmer or fisher whose principal occupation is not farming or fishing.[32]

B. CONSOLIDATION OF PROCEEDINGS

There is a significant difference between procedural consolidation and substantive consolidation of bankruptcy proceedings. In procedural consolidation, the court directs that bankruptcy proceedings against two or more related persons be consolidated in a single proceeding. This is merely an administrative convenience that reduces the time and expense involved in maintaining separate proceedings. Procedural consolidation does not alter the substantive right of claimants against their respective debtors.

Substantive consolidation involves a pooling of assets and a pooling of claims. All of the assets of the various debtors are liquidated. The funds generated from the disposition of these assets are then used to satisfy the claims of all the creditors. Substantive consolidation can significantly affect the substantive position of the creditors. Suppose that A has assets worth $100,000 and $200,000 in debts, while B has assets worth $200,000 and $800,000 in debts. In the absence of substantive consolidation, the creditors of A will receive 50 cents on the dollar and the creditors of B will receive 25 cents on the dollar by way of dividend. With substantive consolidation, all creditors will receive 30 cents on the dollar.

---

30 *BIA*, s 48.

31 *Langille*, above note 15; *Re Witchekan Lake Farms Ltd* (1974), 20 CBR (NS) 91 (Sask CA).

32 The provision originally stipulated that the debtor must be engaged solely in fishing, farming, or the tillage of the soil, and courts held that it therefore did not apply where the debtor earned off-farm income. See *Newell v McIvor* (1996), 38 CBR (3d) 173 (Sask CA). The provision was amended in 1997 by substituting "individuals whose principal occupation and means of livelihood" in place of "individuals engaged solely in fishing, farming or the tillage of the soil." A debtor who has discontinued the non-farming activity will nevertheless continue to be considered to be engaged in that activity if the debts associated with it have not been paid. See *In re Gartrell* (1923), 3 CBR 874 (Sask QB), aff'd (1923), 4 CBR 103 (Sask CA).

The *BIA* contains several statutory provisions governing procedural consolidation of bankruptcy proceedings. Where more than one application for a bankruptcy order is against the same debtor or against joint debtors, a court may consolidate the proceedings.[33] A court is also permitted to consolidate bankruptcy proceedings against members of a partnership where a bankruptcy order is obtained against one of the members.[34] The court's power to make consolidation orders is not limited to these specific situations. A bankruptcy court has the inherent jurisdiction to control its own processes, and this permits it to make such orders in appropriate cases.[35]

The *BIA* provides for substantive consolidation in respect of the summary administration of the estates of individuals who, because of their relationship, could reasonably be dealt with as one estate.[36] A joint assignment may be made where the debts of the individuals making the joint assignment are substantially the same and the trustee is of the opinion that it is in the best interest of the debtors and creditors. While the court's power to make substantive consolidation orders extends to other situations as well, it will not exercise that power if substantial consolidation would operate at the expense or possible prejudice of any particular creditor.[37] Courts will usually exercise the power only when the financial affairs of the debtors are so intertwined that it is difficult or impossible to separate them.[38] In such a case, an order for substantive consolidation does not operate to prejudice a creditor, since the making of the order benefits all creditors.[39] The issue of substantive consolidation also arises in restructuring proceedings, and Canadian courts have displayed a willingness to consider the more extensive United States caselaw on the topic.[40]

33 *BIA*, s 43(4).

34 *Ibid*, s 43(16).

35 *Ibid*, s 183(1). See also *Re JP Capital Corp* (1995), 31 CBR (3d) 102 (Ont Ct Gen Div).

36 *BIA*, s 155(f) and Directive No 2R.

37 *Ashley v Marlow Group Private Portfolio Management Inc* (2006), 22 CBR (5th) 126 (Ont SCJ).

38 *Envision Engineering & Contracting Inc (Re)*, 2014 ABQB 474.

39 *Re Associated Freezers of Canada Inc* (1995), 36 CBR (3d) 227 (Ont Ct Gen Div); *Re A & F Baillargeon Express Inc* (1993), 27 CBR (3d) 36 (Que Sup Ct).

40 See Chapter 12, Section B.

C. INVOLUNTARY BANKRUPTCY

1) The Application for a Bankruptcy Order

One or more of the creditors may bring an application for a bankruptcy order. To succeed, it must be proven that a debt of at least $1,000 is owing to the applicant or applicants, and that the debtor committed an act of bankruptcy within a six-month period immediately before the filing of the application.[41] The application must be filed in the court having jurisdiction in the judicial district of the locality of the debtor.[42] This is defined as the principal place of business or the residence of the debtor.[43]

The application must be accompanied by an affidavit of the applicant or an authorized person who has personal knowledge of the facts. Because of the very serious consequences to the debtor of a bankruptcy order, courts have required the strict proof of the facts alleged in the bankruptcy application.[44] Bankruptcy law does not afford the applicant creditor any process for discovery or examination of the debtor in aid of the bankruptcy application.[45] A debtor who wishes to dispute the application must file a notice setting out the contested allegations.[46] The bankruptcy court may stay proceedings on the application and direct a trial of the issue on the disputed facts.[47] In a disputed application, the debtor may cross-examine on the affidavit of truth.[48]

The Act provides that an application cannot be withdrawn without leave of the court.[49] An application for a bankruptcy order is a collective proceeding that is for the benefit of all the creditors of a debtor. For this reason, it is inappropriate for the application to be withdrawn by virtue of a bilateral agreement for settlement of a debt between one creditor and the debtors until the court is satisfied that it will not prejudice other creditors.[50]

An application for a bankruptcy order has a wider legal significance beyond its function of bringing the matter before the bankruptcy

---

41 *BIA*, s 43(1).

42 *Ibid*, s 43(5).

43 *Ibid*, s 2 "locality of a debtor."

44 *Re Selkirk* (1961), 2 CBR (NS) 113 (Ont CA) [*Selkirk*].

45 *Re Tunnell Ltd* (1923), 4 CBR 261 (Ont SC) [*Tunnell*].

46 *Bankruptcy and Insolvency General Rules*, CRC 1978, c 368, s 74 [*BIGR*].

47 *BIA*, s 43(10).

48 *BIGR*, above note 46, s 14(2).

49 *BIA*, s 43(14). And see *Re Nurmohamed* (2006), 21 CBR (5th) 42 (Ont SCJ).

50 *Re Abu-Hatoum* (1987), 63 CBR (NS) 60 (Ont HCJ); *Guarino v Loewen* (1988), 72 CBR (NS) 167 (Man QB).

court. The filing date of the application is one of the events described in the definition of "date of the initial bankruptcy event."[51] The *BIA* gives a trustee the power to impeach certain types of pre-bankruptcy transactions. These provisions are limited by a time period that runs backwards from the date of the initial bankruptcy event.[52] As well, non-consensual security interests in favour of the Crown enjoy secured creditor status only if they are registered at the date of the initial bankruptcy event.[53] Finally, transactions that are entered into after the date of the initial bankruptcy event are invalid unless they are made for adequate valuable consideration.[54]

2) The Requirement of a Debt

The Act defines a creditor as a person who has a claim provable in bankruptcy.[55] This covers both liquidated and unliquidated claims.[56] Although a person who has an unliquidated claim can prove this claim and participate in the bankruptcy, that person does not have sufficient standing to bring an application for a bankruptcy order. The application can be brought only by one or more creditors who are owed debts amounting to $1,000.

The monetary threshold of $1,000 has not been altered since 1949, and it is increasingly unlikely to pose much of a hurdle. The requirement that the claim be in the nature of a debt is more likely to create difficulties for an applicant. A debt is a sum payable in respect of a liquidated money demand, recoverable by action.[57] The characterization of a claim as a debt depends upon the liquidated nature of the claim rather than upon the source of the obligation. A claim in the tort of negligence for damages is an unliquidated claim. If the plaintiff obtains a judgment for the loss, the claim will be converted into a liquidated claim. Although most debts arise by virtue of a contract between the parties, there are many contractual claims that do not qualify as debts. An action for damages for breach of contract merely gives rise to an

---

51 *BIA*, s 2.

52 See Chapter 7, Section A(8).

53 See Chapter 5, Section E.

54 See Chapter 7, Section E.

55 *BIA*, s 2 "creditor."

56 *Ibid*, s 121 provides that all debts and liabilities at the date of bankruptcy are provable claims.

57 *Diewold v Diewold*, [1941] SCR 35; *Re Central Capital Corp* (1996), 132 DLR (4th) 223 (Ont CA).

unliquidated claim,[58] but it can be converted into a liquidated claim if a judgment is obtained. The claim will be characterized as one for the recovery of a debt if it is subject to a liquidated damages clause that can be ascertained by calculation or fixed by positive data. But, if the contractual provisions merely set out the methodology and depend upon the underlying opinion of experts, it will be characterized as a claim for damages.[59]

A secured creditor can apply for a bankruptcy order but must either surrender the security for the benefit of the creditors or give an estimate of the value of the security.[60] A secured creditor is unlikely to surrender its security unless the collateral is valueless,[61] since one of the major reasons for taking security is to give the secured creditor priority over unsecured creditors. If the value of the collateral is less than the obligation it secures, the secured claim qualifies as a debt only for the balance in excess of the value of the collateral. A court will not review the secured creditor's estimation of the value of its security unless the estimate is a sham or absurdly low.[62]

Claims in unjust enrichment for the recovery of money are considered debt claims.[63] This characterization extends as well to claims for the recovery of the value of services rendered despite the fact that a court must assess the value of the services.[64] The idea that claims founded in unjust enrichment qualify as debts is based on the now discredited quasi-contractual theory that such claims are premised on an implied promise to pay. Canadian law departed from this position and now regards unjust enrichment as a third subdivision within the law of obligations (the other two being contract and tort).[65] Given this, courts may be willing to re-examine the reasoning in these cases and to conclude that they are unliquidated claims rather than debts.

---

58 *LG&E Natural Canada Inc v Alberta Resources Inc* (1997), 224 AR 201 (QB).

59 *Citibank Canada v Confederation Life Insurance Co* (1996), 42 CBR (3d) 288 (Ont Ct Gen Div), aff'd (1998), 1 CBR (4th) 206 (Ont CA).

60 *BIA*, s 43(2).

61 This might occur upon the loss or destruction of the collateral, or it might also occur when a failure to register or perfect a security interest in personal property results in its subordination to a trustee in bankruptcy.

62 *Columbia Properties Ltd v Commonwealth Mortgage Corp* (1963), 6 CBR (NS) 321 (BCSC); *Re Hugh M Grant Ltd* (1982), 41 CBR (NS) 28 (Ont HCJ).

63 *Re Down* (2000), 19 CBR (4th) 46 (BCSC); *Re 207053 Alberta Ltd* (1998), 7 CBR (4th) 32 (Alta QB).

64 *First Avenue Research Corp v Donar Chemicals Ltd* (1987), 11 BCLR (2d) 136 (SC); *Van Ripper v Bretall* (1913), 4 WWR 1289 (Alta SC).

65 *Deglman v Guaranty Trust Co of Canada*, [1954] SCR 725; *Sorochan v Sorochan*, [1986] 2 SCR 38.

A reference to a "debt" is sometimes intended to cover a debt that is immediately payable. At other times it is intended to include an existing debt that becomes payable at a certain future time (referred to as a *debitum in praesenti, solvendum in futuro*). Canadian cases are divided on whether the debt must be immediately payable, although the weight of authority is that it is sufficient that the debt be payable at a future time.[66] This latter view fits better with the aims and objectives of bankruptcy law. A failure to pay debts as they generally become due is an act of bankruptcy, but there are many other acts of bankruptcy that do not require any default in payment. The purpose of the debt requirement is simply to ensure that the claimant has a sufficiently certain claim to justify the invocation of bankruptcy proceedings. If the debtor has made a fraudulent conveyance or preference or an admission of insolvency, the fact that a debt is not yet payable is not of any relevance. However, if the payment obligation requires some future performance on the part of the person to whom it is owed or if the obligation is conditional on the occurrence of some future condition or event (other than the mere passage of time), the obligation will not constitute an existing debt.[67]

It is not enough to show that a debt was owed at the time of the hearing. It must be shown that the debt was in existence at the time the application for a bankruptcy order is filed.[68] Although there is English authority for the view that the debt must also exist on the date that the act of bankruptcy occurs,[69] this conclusion is difficult to justify. The Act does not stipulate this as a requirement and it runs counter to its underlying policy, which is simply to ensure that the person pursuing the bankruptcy order has a sufficiently certain claim.

The debtor may dispute that it owes a debt to the creditor. In such cases, the court will either stay the application or dismiss it so that the matter can be resolved in the civil courts.[70] The court is not compelled to dismiss the application whenever the debtor disputes liability. It can

---

66 See, for example, *Tunnell*, above note 45; *Re Lakin Builders Ltd* (1961), 2 CBR (NS) 15 (Ont HCJ); *Re It's Hear Co* (1991), 8 CBR (3d) 78 (Ont Ct Gen Div); *Re Columbia Properties Ltd* (1963), 5 CBR (NS) 258 (BCSC); *Re Dhillon* (1997), 49 CBR (3d) 24 (BCSC); *Re Inex Pharmaceuticals Corp* (2005), 17 CBR (5th) 135 (BCSC). See *contra Re Rasminsky* (1922), 3 CBR 160 (Ont SC); *Brown v St John Garage and Supply Co* (1925), 7 CBR 62 (NBKB).

67 This will include the making of a demand under a demand loan, since something other than the mere passage of time is required in order for the loan to become payable. See *Re George Coles Ltd* (1951), 31 CBR 209 (Ont HCJ).

68 *Re Fred Walls & Son Holdings Ltd* (1999), 13 CBR (4th) 60 (BCSC).

69 *Re Debtors*, [1927] 1 Ch 19; *Ex p Debtor v Scott*, [1954] 1 WLR 1190.

70 *In re Amalgamated Rare Earth Mines Ltd* (1958), 37 CBR 168 (Ont CA).

make a bankruptcy order if it concludes that the dispute is not *bona fide*[71] or that at least $1,000 is owing even though there is a dispute as to total amount owing.[72]

The debt requirement was likely intended to screen out claims that are either subject to a contingency or more likely to be disputed. It is questionable whether it succeeds in this function. Debt claims are often disputed, and bankruptcy courts frequently dismiss applications for bankruptcy orders on the ground that the existence of a debt was not clearly established. Furthermore, the requirement can produce hardship for claimants who are unable to quickly reduce their claims to judgment debts. Persons who merely have claims for damages are unable to invoke bankruptcy even if the debtor is insolvent and judgment enforcement creditors are taking active steps to satisfy their claims from the debtor's inadequate assets. An enterprising claimant might obtain an assignment of a creditor's claim in order to acquire standing to bring the application,[73] but this is not always a feasible option. American bankruptcy does not limit standing to claimants who are owed debts. Instead, it requires that the claims be non-contingent and not subject to a *bona fide* dispute,[74] and this seems better designed to achieve the aims of bankruptcy law.

3) Proceedings against Securities Firms

Although the general rule is that only creditors may bring an application for a bankruptcy order against a debtor, the *BIA* provides a special rule where the debtor is a securities firm.[75] Provincial securities commissions, securities exchanges, customer-compensation bodies, and receivers or liquidators of a securities firm are permitted to apply for a bankruptcy order against a securities firm. In such a case, the applicant need show only that there was an act of bankruptcy within the six months before the filing of the application.[76] The *BIA* also provides an additional act of bankruptcy if the debtor is a securities firm. A

---

71 *Cargill Ltd v Compton Agro Inc* (1993), 23 CBR (3d) 285 (Man QB); *Re Catear Resources Ltd* (1990), 2 CBR (3d) 173 (BCSC).

72 *Re Vermillion Placers Inc* (1982), 41 CBR (NS) 173 (Ont HCJ); *Re Central Coast Carriers Ltd* (2002), 32 CBR (4th) 200 (BCSC).

73 *Re Prototravel Ltd* (1993), 21 CBR (3d) 101 (Ont Ct Gen Div).

74 *United States Bankruptcy Code*, § 303(b)(1).

75 See *BIA*, s 253, where "securities firm" provides a definition of a securities firm. It covers a person who carries on the business of buying and selling securities from, to or for a customer.

76 *Ibid*, s 256(1).

suspension of the securities firm's registration to trade in securities or membership in an exchange constitutes an act of bankruptcy if it is due to a failure to meet capital adequacy requirements.[77]

4) Acts of Bankruptcy

Creditors who seek a bankruptcy order must also allege in their applications that the debtor committed an act of bankruptcy within a six-month period immediately before the filing of the application.[78] The Act sets out a list of ten acts of bankruptcy.[79] A creditor may allege more than one act of bankruptcy, and a failure to prove all acts of bankruptcy is not fatal so long as one of the alleged acts is proven.[80] These acts of bankruptcy involve two different types of conduct. One is conduct that demonstrates that the debtor has violated certain norms of commercial morality by attempting to frustrate the legitimate collection efforts of creditors. The other is conduct that shows that the debtor is insolvent. It is not uncommon for a creditor to assert more than one act of bankruptcy, and a single event may constitute more than one act of bankruptcy.

a) Conduct that Defeats or Delays Creditors

The Act lists four grounds involving conduct in which the debtor in some manner has attempted to defraud, defeat, or delay creditors. The debtor commits an act of bankruptcy if the debtor: (1) makes a fraudulent gift, delivery, or transfer of the debtor's property;[81] (2) transfers or charges property such that it would be void as a fraudulent preference under the Act;[82] (3) departs or remains outside Canada, departs from his or her dwelling house, or otherwise absents himself or herself with the intent of defeating or delaying creditors;[83] or (4) assigns, removes, secretes, or disposes of property with the intent to defraud, defeat, or delay creditors, or attempts or is about to do so.[84] There is considerable overlap between the first and fourth of these grounds as they both encompass a fraudulent conveyance. However, the fourth ground is

---

77 *Ibid*, s 256(2).

78 *Ibid*, s 43(1).

79 *Ibid*, s 42(1).

80 *Parax Development International Inc (Bankruptcy of)*, 2003 SKQB 27; *484030 Ontario Ltd (Re)* (1992), 12 CBR (3d) 302 (Ont Ct Gen Div) [*484030*].

81 *BIA*, s 42(1)(b).

82 *Ibid*, s 42(1)(c).

83 *Ibid*, s 42(1)(d).

84 *Ibid*, s 42(1)(g).

wider in that it covers events other than transfers, such as the hiding of assets, and also extends to attempted transfers and imminent future transfers. Because of the difficulty of establishing fraudulent intent, these grounds are less likely to be relied upon when other bankruptcy grounds are available.

There is an incomplete correspondence between the acts of bankruptcy that target fraudulent conveyances and fraudulent preferences and the avoidance powers available to a trustee. The fact that a trustee has the power to avoid a transaction as a fraudulent preference is not sufficient to constitute an act of bankruptcy. The conduct must specifically fall within one of the enumerated grounds. A transfer of property that can be impugned under provincial law as a fraudulent preference does not constitute an act of bankruptcy, since the relevant bankruptcy ground covers only those transactions that can be avoided under the *BIA*. Nor will every transaction impeachable as a fraudulent preference under the *BIA* constitute an act of bankruptcy. Under bankruptcy law, a payment of money as well as a conveyance or transfer of property can be set aside as a fraudulent preference.[85] However, the bankruptcy ground does not refer to a payment of money but is limited to a transfer of property. Courts have held that this more limited language was intended to exclude a payment of money even though it could be set aside as a fraudulent preference under the federal statute.[86]

b) The Insolvency Grounds

Six of the enumerated acts of bankruptcy are insolvency-related grounds. Three of these grounds involve either an admission of insolvency or a communication of an impending insolvency by the debtor. The debtor commits an act of bankruptcy by notifying the creditors that the debtor is suspending payment of debts[87] or by exhibiting at a meeting of creditors a statement of assets and liabilities that shows that the debtor is insolvent.[88] The remaining ground involves an indirect admission of insolvency. The debtor commits an act of bankruptcy by making an assignment of the debtor's property to a trustee for the benefit of

---

85 *Ibid*, s 95.

86 *Re King Petroleum Ltd* (1973), 19 CBR (NS) 16 (Ont HCJ); *Re Tysak Ltd* (1981), 38 CBR (NS) 142 (Ont HCJ).

87 *BIA*, s 42(1)(h). The notice of suspension may be oral. See *Re King Petroleum Ltd*, above note 86.

88 *BIA*, s 42(1)(f). The statement that is shown must be in writing. See *Brown v England Estate* (1923), 3 CBR 812 (BCCA). A compelled examination of a judgment debtor by a judgment creditor in aid of the enforcement of a court order does not constitute a meeting of creditors. See *Ivany (Re)*, 2012 ONSC 7058 [*Ivany*].

the creditors generally. This covers voluntary bankruptcy proceedings initiated by the debtor in other countries, but it does not encompass involuntary proceedings.[89]

One of the bankruptcy grounds applies only if the debtor has concluded a commercial or consumer proposal with her creditors. A default in the proposal constitutes an act of bankruptcy.[90] This has largely been rendered a dead letter by the inclusion in the Act of a specific procedure for automatic bankruptcy upon the annulment of proposals for default.[91]

The other two bankruptcy grounds, discussed in greater detail below, focus upon an event or conduct that is typically associated with persons in insolvent circumstances. One is established when a judgment enforcement remedy or other legal process against the debtor's property is taken to a certain point.[92] The other is established when the debtor ceases to meet liabilities generally as they become due.[93] The latter ground uses a cash flow test rather than a balance sheet test of insolvency. Creditors therefore cannot obtain a bankruptcy order on the ground that the debtor has an excess of liabilities over assets.

c) Exercise of Judgment Enforcement Remedies

The bankruptcy ground dealing with the exercise of judgment enforcement remedies is useful to creditors in two situations. First, a creditor who has not obtained judgment against a debtor may be concerned that the exercise of judgment enforcement remedies by other creditors will leave insufficient assets to satisfy his or her claim.[94] In this case, the creditor invokes a bankruptcy primarily to ensure a *pro rata* sharing of the debtor's property. Second, a judgment creditor may choose to invoke bankruptcy if provincial judgment enforcement remedies have failed to satisfy the creditor's claim.[95] In this case, the creditor invokes the bankruptcy in the hope that the wider powers conferred upon the

89 *Bayerische Hypotheken - Und Wechselbank Aktiengesellschaft v Kaussen Estate* (1988), 67 CBR (NS) 81 (Que CA) [*Kaussen Estate*].

90 *BIA*, s 42(1)(i).

91 *Ibid*, ss 63 and 66.3.

92 *Ibid*, s 42(1)(e).

93 *Ibid*, s 42(1)(j).

94 Although a *pro rata* sharing rule is provided under provincial judgment enforcement law, it extends only to creditors who have obtained a writ or judgment.

95 There is no requirement that the judgment enforcement creditor exhaust other enforcement remedies before invoking a bankruptcy. See *Re Mastronardi* (2000), 21 CBR (4th) 107 (Ont CA). However, the judgment enforcement creditor in most cases will attempt to recover under the provincial judgment enforcement system in order to avoid sharing the funds recovered with other claimants.

trustee in bankruptcy may result in a greater prospect of recovery.[96] This can be a double-edged sword since bankruptcy also engages a stronger *pro rata* sharing rule, with the result that the recovery will be shared among a wider class of claimants than would be the case under provincial judgment enforcement law.

The provision is highly complex in structure and covers several different events. The bankruptcy ground can be broken into the following four grounds:

1) the debtor permits any execution or other process issued against the debtor under which any of debtor's property is seized, levied, or taken in execution to remain unsatisfied five days before the time fixed by the executing officer for the sale of the property or for fifteen days[97] after a seizure, levy, or taking in execution;
2) the debtor's property is sold by the executing officer;
3) the execution or other process has been held by the executing officer for a period of fifteen days after written demand for payment without seizure, levy, or taking in execution or satisfaction by payment; and
4) the execution or other process is returned to the effect that the executing officer can find no property on which to levy, seize, or take.

The first ground is relatively easy to apply where the judgment enforcement measure involves a seizure of tangible personal property, but it is less clear on its application to other types of judgment enforcement remedies that do not involve a seizure. For example, enforcement against real property does not involve an actual seizure of the land. Instead, the executing officer initiates a legal process that eventually results in an enforcement sale of the land to a buyer. Despite this, the legislation in several provinces refers to a seizure in respect of enforcement against land, and courts have struggled to give effect to this by holding that some preliminary step in the sale process (such as the notice of sale) qualifies as a seizure.[98]

Some provinces, in reforming their judgment enforcement law, have discarded the idea of a seizure of land as a necessary element of

---

96 This will often occur when a judgment creditor attempts to enforce a writ but the writ is returned *nulla bona* indicating that there are no exigible goods available to satisfy the writ. See, for example, *Montreal Trust Co v Schultz* (1993), 22 CBR (3d) 287 (Sask CA) [*Schultz*].

97 If interpleader proceedings are brought, the fifteen-day period does not begin to run until the interpleader proceedings are finally disposed of.

98 See CRB Dunlop, *Creditor-Debtor Law in Canada*, 2d ed (Toronto: Carswell, 1995) at 358–62.

the sale process.[99] In these provinces, a sale of the land pursuant of writ proceedings undoubtedly constitutes an act of bankruptcy under the second ground, but it is less clear whether an act of bankruptcy occurs prior to that event. Although the first ground refers to the fixing of time for sale of the property by the executing officer, this applies only if the property is seized, levied, or taken in execution. Other judgment enforcement remedies such as garnishment and the appointment of a receiver (sometimes referred to as equitable execution) involve neither seizure nor a sale of property but typically operate by diverting money that would otherwise be paid to the debtor. The reference to a levy does not appear to be wide enough to cover such remedies, since a levy involves a receipt of money as a result of a seizure of property.[100]

The third ground provides that an act of bankruptcy is established if the execution or other process is held by the executing officer for a period of fifteen days after written demand for payment without a seizure, levy, or taking in execution. The difficulty with this language is that it does not seem to accord with the actual operation of the judgment enforcement remedies. Although provinces and territories have judgment enforcement remedies that do not involve a seizure or taking of the property, these do not involve a written demand for payment from the creditor or the executing officer that is communicated to the debtor.[101] The provision therefore does not appear to cover garnishment, equitable execution, or the enforcement against land prior to its actual sale. One case has held that this ground is satisfied if a requirement to pay (the statutory garnishment remedy in respect of income tax) is issued and remains unpaid for fifteen days.[102] This is a highly doubtful proposition, since the third party's failure to pay the demand is frequently due to the fact that the third-party claims that no money is owed to the debtor.

The provision also covers the situation where the writ or other process is returned endorsed to the effect that the executing officer cannot find any property against which to seize or take. This covers a return of *nulla bona* on a writ that indicates that there are no goods or chattels available to satisfy the writ. The return of *nulla bona* on a writ provides *prima facie* evidence that can be rebutted if the debtor can prove that the executing officer did not in fact engage in a genuine attempt

---

99 *Civil Enforcement Act*, RSA 2000, c 15, ss 67–76.

100 *Benjamin Moore & Co v Finney*, [1955] 1 DLR 557 (Ont Co Ct). The money may result from a sale of the property or it may result from payment by the debtor.

101 *Re Roy* (1982), 44 CBR (NS) 86 (Ont HCJ).

102 *Re Southernmost Point Enterprises Ltd* (2002), 33 CBR (4th) 312 (NSSC) [*Southernmost Point*].

to find exigible assets.[103] The return of *nulla bona* as an endorsement on the writ has been replaced in some jurisdictions by a report of the executing officer that sets out details of the seizure.[104] This report probably satisfies the requirements of the *BIA* since it constitutes a formal report required by law that records the outcome of the writ proceedings. Informal correspondence between the executing officer and the instructing creditor in respect of the enforcement proceedings will not suffice.[105]

This act of bankruptcy is not restricted to judgment enforcement measures but applies as well to other legal process. One decision held that it extends to the process issued by the federal revenue agency in respect of unpaid income tax.[106] The decision is likely correct to the extent that it holds that this bankruptcy ground covers legal process that is issued by an administrative authority rather than a court. A seizure or other enforcement remedy instituted by a secured creditor against the collateral or a right of distress exercised by a landlord likely does not qualify under this bankruptcy ground. These remedies to not arise by virtue of "an execution or other process issued against the debtor." Instead, they arise out of a security interest in the debtor's property that is granted to the secured creditor or by virtue of a landlord-tenant relationship between the creditor and debtor.[107]

d) Ceasing to Meet Liabilities Generally

The act of bankruptcy most often relied upon by creditors is the ceasing to meet liabilities as they generally become due. It is not necessary to show that the debtor is failing to pay all of the creditors. A creditor will usually seek to satisfy this ground by providing evidence of the existence of the claims of at least two other unpaid creditors.[108] It is not necessary that these other creditors join the bankruptcy application or to show that the other creditors were pressing for payment; the applicant need only prove that they have debts that are not being paid.[109] A

103 *Schultz*, above note 96.

104 See *Civil Enforcement Regulation*, Alta Reg 276/95, s 13; Alta Reg 203/2002, s 13; *Rules of Civil Procedure*, RRO 1990, Reg 194, r 60.14(1).

105 *Selkirk*, above note 44.

106 *Southernmost Point*, above note 102.

107 The more limited language used in s 42(1)(e) should be contrasted with the more open-ended language used in s 69(3), which creates the automatic bankruptcy stay of proceedings that encompasses judicial and extra-judicial proceedings. See *Vachon v Canada (Employment & Immigration Commission)*, [1985] 2 SCR 417.

108 *Re Joyce* (1984), 51 CBR (NS) 152 (Ont HCJ).

109 *Re Cappe* (1993), 18 CBR (3d) 229 (Ont Ct Gen Div); *Re Hayes* (1979), 34 CBR (NS) 280 (BCSC).

court will not draw an inference that the debtor is not paying liabilities generally simply on the basis that the claim of the applicant creditor has not been paid.[110]

Although non-payment of a single creditor will not usually satisfy this bankruptcy ground, there are a number of exceptional instances where this restriction is relaxed. Courts have identified three special circumstances in which a failure to pay a single creditor can constitute a general cessation of payment.[111] The first is where the applicant creditor is the only creditor of the debtor and the debtor has failed to pay despite repeated demands for payment by the creditor. There is an ambiguity in the manner in which this is expressed. Some courts have indicated that to fall within this exception, the creditor must prove that the debtor has not entered into a debtor-creditor relationship with any other person.[112] This will be difficult to satisfy, since most debtors will owe money to more than one creditor. However, most cases take a wider view and hold that it is sufficient if the applicant is the only unpaid creditor.[113] The second exception is where the creditor is a significant creditor and there is fraud or other circumstances that make access to bankruptcy proceedings imperative for the protection of the whole class of creditors. The third is where the debtor admits an inability to pay creditors generally even though the identity of the individual creditors is not disclosed.

Justice Henry in *Re Holmes*[114] provides a rationale for the single creditor restriction. Resort to the statutory machinery of bankruptcy law is for the benefit of the creditors as a class. Therefore, it is necessary to show a failure to pay other creditors as well.[115] If there are no other creditors, bankruptcy is not appropriate and the creditor is expected to enforce the debt through the provincial judgment enforcement system. Although this reasoning illuminates the policy in respect of the general cessation of payment ground, it does not fully explain the structure of the other legislative provisions. In particular, it does not explain why

---

110 *Re Paperback Printing Services Ltd* (1977), 24 CBR (NS) 41 (Ont HCJ).

111 The classic statement of these special circumstances was enumerated in *Re Holmes* (1975), 20 CBR (NS) 111 (Ont SC) [*Holmes*] and has been quoted in many decisions such as *Re Valente* (2004), 47 CBR (4th) 317 (Ont CA) [*Valente*] and *Re Kenco Developments Ltd* (1985), 58 CBR (NS) 92 (BCCA).

112 See *Holmes*, above note 111.

113 See *Valente*, above note 111; *Re Freedman* (1924), 4 CBR 499 (Ont HCJ), rev'd on other grounds (1924), 5 CBR 47 (Ont SCAD).

114 Above note 111.

115 The policy rationale supports a more narrow interpretation of the first exception, since there is no reason why the unpaid creditor should not simply resort to the provincial judgment enforcement system to satisfy the claim.

the single-creditor restriction applies only where the alleged bankruptcy ground is the general cessation of payments to creditors and not to other bankruptcy grounds.[116]

There is no doubt that the availability of bankruptcy proceedings as an efficient collective remedy of creditors is one of the fundamental purposes of bankruptcy law. However, it is not the only objective of bankruptcy law. One of the original justifications for bankruptcy law was to provide creditors with more powerful remedies where a debtor has breached certain standards of commercial morality. Bankruptcy law gives the trustee in bankruptcy the power to impeach transactions under which the debtor transfers property to others. Bankruptcy is available even though only a single creditor may have a claim against the debtor. As well, a judgment enforcement creditor can use bankruptcy in order to overcome delays or obstacles that prevent it from enforcing its claim under provincial judgment enforcement law.[117] Although some commentators argue that the only goal of bankruptcy law should be to provide a collective proceeding where there are insufficient assets to satisfy all claims,[118] this does not describe the position taken under Canadian bankruptcy law.

e) Stale Acts of Bankruptcy

A "stale" act of bankruptcy — one that occurred outside the six-month period prior to the filing of the application — cannot be used to obtain a bankruptcy order. For example, a sale under judgment enforcement proceedings that occurs outside this period does not satisfy the requirements of the *BIA*. The cases are divided on the question of timing where the alleged act of bankruptcy is the debtor's ceasing to meet liabilities as they generally become due. Debts may have become due more than six months before the filing of the application for a bankruptcy order, and the issue is whether these can be considered in making a determination that the debtor has ceased to meet liabilities. Some cases take the view that a failure to pay a debt when it is due is a continuing act

116 See *Stancroft Trust Ltd v Asiamerica Capital Ltd* (1992), 15 CBR (3d) 175 (BCCA) [*Stancroft Trust*].

117 See *Re Dixie Market (Nurseries) Ltd* (1971), 14 CBR (NS) 281 (Ont HCJ) in which bankruptcy proceedings were utilized to circumvent a limitation under provincial judgment enforcement law that required a judgment enforcement creditor to wait one year before proceeding against land.

118 See T Jackson, *The Logic and Limits of Bankruptcy Law* (Cambridge, MA: Harvard University Press, 1986).

and therefore no further step needs to be taken.[119] Others hold that the relevant date is when the debt first became due.[120] Cases that adopt this latter approach are divided on a further issue. Some take the view that a fresh demand for payment that falls within the six-month period is incapable of reviving a stale debt.[121] Others hold that a fresh demand for payment within the six-month period will revive a stale debt.[122] However, if the debtor has obtained a judgment, it is considered to be a continuing demand and therefore there is no need to make an additional demand for payment within the six-month period.[123]

In principle, the focus of the inquiry should not be on whether a demand for payment occurred within the six-month period. The issue is whether in the six-month period before the bankruptcy application the debtor has ceased to meet liabilities generally. If the application for a bankruptcy order is based upon a failure to pay a single creditor, the special requirements for this type of claim must be satisfied. If it is based upon a failure to pay more than one creditor, it must be shown that the creditors are generally not being paid. The court must make a determination on the evidence before it whether or not this has occurred, and a failure to make a current demand is only one element that must be considered. A court may very well conclude that a failure to make a current demand is of no relevance, such as in the case where it would be clearly futile for the creditor to do so.[124] For example, the institution of foreign bankruptcy proceedings against the debtor renders it pointless for the creditors to make further demands for payment.[125] Given the uncertain state of the law, a creditor would nevertheless be well advised to make a current demand before bringing the bankruptcy application when relying on this particular ground.

---

119 *Re Rayner* (1934), 16 CBR 411 (PEISC); *Re The Pas Foundation & Excavation Ltd* (1975), 21 CBR (NS) 154 (Man QB). In *Re Pan-Atlas Financial Group Ltd*, 2008 BCSC 1198, the continuing act theory was extended to cases where the act of bankruptcy is a fraudulent conveyance under the *BIA*, s 42(1)(g).

120 *Brown v Kelly Douglas Co*, [1923] 1 WWR 1340 (BCCA).

121 *Re Atlas Hardware Ltd* (1978), 20 Nfld & PEIR 67 (Nfld SCTD); *Re Cedarhurst Properties Ltd* (1979), 34 CBR (NS) 278 (BCSC).

122 *Re Raitbait*, [1925] 2 DLR 1219 (Ont SC), aff'd [1925] 3 DLR 446 (Ont SCAD); *Federal Business Development Bank v Poznekoff* (1982), 143 DLR (3d) 370 (BCCA).

123 *Malmstrom v Platt* (2001), 24 CBR (4th) 70 (Ont CA); *Valente*, above note 111. The latter decision holds that, although the judgment constitutes a continuing demand for payment, it does not by itself constitute a special circumstance making a single debt evidence of an act of bankruptcy.

124 See *Bombardier Credit Ltd v Find* (1998), 2 CBR (4th) 1 (Ont CA); *Ivany*, above note 88.

125 *Kaussen Estate*, above note 89.

5) Debtor's Ability to Pay Debts

Even though the creditors may have shown that the debtor committed an act of bankruptcy, a court must nevertheless dismiss the application if the debtor can demonstrate that the debtor has the ability to pay the debts.[126] A debtor who has the ability to pay but who is unwilling to do so may nevertheless take the benefit of this provision, and a court is compelled to dismiss the application upon proof of the ability to pay.[127] The onus is on the debtor to demonstrate an ability to pay,[128] and this may require the production of financial statements or other documents.[129]

It may seem surprising that a debtor who has committed an act of bankruptcy and who is not willing to pay debts that are due can avoid bankruptcy proceedings simply by showing an ability to pay. However, this approach makes sense when the overall goals of bankruptcy law are considered. The statutory provisions governing involuntary bankruptcy are designed to identify instances of debtor insolvency. One of the fundamental purposes of bankruptcy law is to provide a collective proceeding against a debtor when the debtor has insufficient assets from which to satisfy the claims of creditors. In theory, a balance sheet test of insolvency would be the best measure of suitability for bankruptcy proceedings, since it would directly assess whether the debtor has sufficient assets to meet the claims of the creditors. However, there are a number of practical difficulties with the use of a balance sheet test as the standard for commencement of involuntary bankruptcy proceedings. First, the test involves information that is in the control of the debtor, and therefore difficult for the creditors to prove, particularly given that the creditor cannot resort to any discovery or examination of the debtor in aid of the bankruptcy application.[130] Second, the test itself depends upon a valuation of assets, and this can produce controversies over the appropriate valuation methodology.

Canadian bankruptcy legislation deals with this problem by first identifying a number of acts of bankruptcy that are commonly associated

---

126 *BIA*, s 43(7).

127 *Ashton v Moody* (1997), 47 CBR (3d) 91 (Sask CA); *Re Redbrooke Estates Ltd* (1967), 13 CBR (NS) 117 (Que Sup Ct). The Saskatchewan Court of Appeal in *Ashton v Moody* preferred the reasoning in *Re Redbrooke Estates Ltd* and did not follow the Saskatchewan decision of *Re Freeholders Oil Co* (1953), 33 CBR 149 (Sask QB), which held the debtor must be able and willing to pay the debts within a reasonable time.

128 *Re Hayes* (1979), 34 CBR (NS) 280 (BCSC) [*Hayes*].

129 *Re Omni-Stone Corp* (1991), 4 OR (3d) 636 (Gen Div); *484030*, above note 80.

130 *Tunnell*, above note 45.

with insolvent debtors. These are not in themselves reasons for bankruptcy proceedings, but rather they are symptoms that are often associated with an inability to pay debts. These acts are ones that can be proven by creditors without access to the financial information or documents that are in the control of the debtor. If any of these acts are established, the onus will then fall on the debtor to show that the debtor has sufficient assets to meet the claims of the creditors.[131] This provides a mechanism through which the relevant financial information will be disclosed. It also addresses valuation difficulties by placing the burden on the debtor to show a sufficiency of assets in cases where there is uncertainty over the appropriate valuation of the assets.[132]

Although the balance sheet test of insolvency is not one of the enumerated acts of bankruptcy, it nevertheless constitutes the ultimate test in disputed applications. Correspondingly, cessation of payments to creditors, although an act of bankruptcy, will not justify bankruptcy proceedings if the debtor can demonstrate an ability to pay creditors. In such a case, the creditors can resort to provincial judgment enforcement law to satisfy all of their outstanding claims.

6) Judicial Discretion

A court has the power to dismiss a bankruptcy application despite the fact that all necessary prerequisites and grounds alleged in the bankruptcy application have been proven.[133] The Act provides little guidance on when this discretion is to be exercised since it merely permits the court to do so if there is "sufficient cause." The discretion must be exercised judicially based on credible evidence.[134] There are three types of situations where such discretion is exercised by the courts: (1) where bankruptcy proceedings would be futile; (2) where the proceedings were brought for an improper purpose or there has been improper conduct on the part of the applicant; and (3) where the matter is one that is better resolved through civil proceedings.

---

131 See *Stancroft Trust*, above note 116, in which the court characterized an act of bankruptcy as a *prima facie* indicia of insolvency following which the court will consider if there is a reason why the bankruptcy order should not be made. See also *Schultz*, above note 96.

132 The debtor must show that it has the ability to pay the debts in the sense that his assets exceed liabilities. It is not enough to show that the creditors are not presently pressing for payment. See *Hayes*, above note 128.

133 *BIA*, s 43(7).

134 *Re Churchill Forest Industries (Manitoba) Limited* (1971), 16 CBR (NS) 158 (Man QB).

Courts will sometimes dismiss bankruptcy applications if it is clear that the proceedings would be of no benefit to the creditors. This might be established if it can be shown that the debtor has no assets and has no prospect of acquiring any in the future.[135] This will not be the case if there are suspicious circumstances that suggest that there have been pre-bankruptcy transfers by the debtor that may be investigated and impugned by a trustee in bankruptcy.[136] The discretion can also be exercised if it is shown that bankruptcy proceedings produce additional costs without conferring any benefit to the creditors.[137]

Courts will also dismiss a bankruptcy application if it is shown that the applicants brought it for an improper purpose.[138] This occurs where the bankruptcy application is brought against the debtor out of spite or vengeance or as part of a vendetta.[139] It also occurs where the application is brought in order to obtain a business advantage such as the elimination of a competitor[140] or the termination of a contract.[141] However, it is not improper for creditors to invoke bankruptcy for the sole purpose of elevating their claim over that of some other competing claimant.[142] A creditor will also be prevented from using bankruptcy where it is the creditor's illegal activity that has caused the cessation of the business.[143]

Courts sometimes state that the bankruptcy courts ought not to be used as a collection agency.[144] This is a rather misleading way of casting the proposition, since most creditors will bring the bankruptcy application with the hope that at least a portion of their claim will be satisfied.[145] Courts will invoke this as a cause for dismissal of the

---

135 *Re Benson* (1936), 18 CBR 99 (Ont SC).

136 *Re Hutchens* (1983), 46 CBR (NS) 234 (Ont HCJ).

137 *In re Stone* (1925), 7 CBR 103 (Ont SC). In that case there was only one creditor who had a claim against the debtor, and provincial judgment enforcement proceedings were sufficient to provide recovery.

138 *Diena (Re)*, 2012 ONSC 5849.

139 *Re Westlake* (1984), 53 CBR (NS) 207 (Ont HCJ); *Vipond v Ewing* (1939), 21 BR 129 (Que KB).

140 *Re De La Hooke* (1934), 15 CBR 485 (Ont SC); *Re Hydrofoil Lake Jet Lines Inc* (2000), 18 CBR (4th) 212 (Ont SCJ).

141 *Re Pappy's Good Eats Ltd* (1985), 56 CBR (NS) 304 (Ont HCJ).

142 *Re Scott Road Enterprises Ltd* (1988), 68 CBR (NS) 54 (BCCA).

143 *Re Kadri Food Corp* (1996), 41 CBR (3d) 272 (NSSC).

144 *Re Wells* (1944), 25 CBR 291 (Ont SC).

145 *Re Four Twenty-Seven Investments Ltd* (1985), 55 CBR (NS) 183 (Ont HCJ) [*Four Twenty-Seven*].

bankruptcy application only where it was launched in order to pressure the debtor to abandon or settle a dispute under litigation.[146]

Finally, courts have dismissed a bankruptcy application if the matter would be better resolved through a conventional civil action.[147] In many cases, the bankruptcy court will dismiss or stay the application on the ground that the creditor has not proven a debt amounting to $1,000.[148] However, the entire debt might not be in dispute, and in these cases the use of judicial discretion to dismiss for sufficient cause remains important. The use of judicial discretion to dismiss the bankruptcy application is more likely to be used where there are only a few creditors and these are actively engaged in disputed litigation with the debtor. Bankruptcy is said to be for clear-cut cases where liability is not in dispute, while the ordinary civil courts have a superior ability to resolve controversies concerning liability between the parties.[149]

7) The Bankruptcy Order

If the court is satisfied that the facts alleged in the application have been proven and the application has been properly served on the debtor, it may make a bankruptcy order.[150] The court in making the order will appoint a licensed trustee.[151] Bankruptcy occurs on the date that the bankruptcy order is granted by the court.[152] The relation back doctrine, which deemed the bankruptcy to be effective from the date of the filing of the initial application, was abolished in 1992. If the debtor appeals the bankruptcy order, the bankruptcy proceedings are stayed until the appeal is disposed of,[153] but the debtor's property will remain vested in the trustee pending the appeal and the debtor does not have the capacity to deal with the property.[154]

---

146 *Re Aarvi Construction Co* (1978), 29 CBR (NS) 265 (Ont HCJ); *Canada (Attorney General) v MacDonald Estate* (2001), 27 CBR (4th) 16 (BCSC).

147 *Re La Scala Bakery Ltd* (1984), 54 CBR (NS) 194 (Ont HCJ).

148 *Re Bearcat Exploration Ltd (Bankrupt)*, 2003 ABCA 365.

149 *Re Abalone Holdings Ltd (No 2)* (1979), 29 CBR (NS) 174 (Ont HCJ).

150 *BIA*, s 43(6). This is subject to s 43(7), which provides that the court must dismiss the application if the debtor proves that it has the ability to pay the debts, and that the court may dismiss for sufficient cause. See Sections C(5) & C(6), above in this chapter.

151 *BIA*, *ibid*, s 43(9). The person appointed will most often be the one proposed by the applicant creditors.

152 *Ibid*, s 2 "time of the bankruptcy."

153 *Ibid*, s 195.

154 *Black & White Sales Consultants Ltd v CBS Records Canada Ltd* (1980), 36 CBR (NS) 125 (Ont HCJ).

8) Interim Receivers

A plaintiff who commences a civil action against a defendant is subject to the risk that the defendant might transfer or dissipate the assets so that there will be no assets remaining to satisfy a judgment if the litigation is successful. This risk is ameliorated by the availability of the *Mareva* injunction and statutory pre-judgment remedies. A similar risk exists in the bankruptcy context. Creditors who have brought an application for a bankruptcy order may have a legitimate fear that the debtor will dispose of the assets before a bankruptcy order is obtained. Bankruptcy law provides a remedy that is analogous to the pre-judgment remedy in civil actions. A court may appoint an interim receiver after the application is filed but before a bankruptcy order is made if it is shown to be necessary for the protection of the estate of the debtor.[155] The interim receiver's purpose is to conserve the property and ensure that it is not disposed of from the time the bankruptcy application is launched until the time it is heard on its merits.[156]

A mere unfounded concern on the part of the applicant is not enough. In deciding whether to appoint an interim receiver, the court will assess two elements: first, the strength of the applicant's claim to a bankruptcy order; and second, the likelihood that harm will be suffered by the creditors if an interim receiver is not appointed. In respect of the first element, the creditor must demonstrate a strong *prima facie* case.[157] In other words, the evidence must be such as to convince a court on a balance of probabilities that the applicant will succeed.[158] In respect of the second element, there must be grave danger that assets would not be recovered.[159] In order to succeed, there must be evidence of some imminent threat, and not merely speculation or conjecture that the asset may be in jeopardy.[160]

The appointment of an interim receiver does not result in a vesting of the debtor's property in the interim receiver.[161] The function of an interim receiver is only to act as a watchdog or monitor,[162] and the Act directs that the interim receiver shall not interfere with the debtor in the carrying out of the debtor's business except as may be necessary to

---

155 *BIA*, s 46(1).

156 *Re Independent Gypsum Supply Ltd* (1983), 47 CBR (NS) 290 (Alta QB).

157 *Re Strain* (1976), 23 CBR (NS) 206 (Man CA).

158 *La Hougue Financial Management Services Ltd v One Shaftsbury Community* (2005), 13 CBR (5th) 217 (Ont SCJ).

159 *Re Pure Harmonics* (1983), 50 CBR (NS) 170 (Ont HCJ).

160 *Re Austroquip Manufacturing Co* (1988), 68 CBR (NS) 161 (Ont HCJ).

161 *Re Soren Brothers (No 2)* (1926), 7 CBR 545 (Ont SC).

162 *Re Big Eddy Shops Ltd* (1977), 24 CBR (NS) 90 (Ont HCJ).

conserve the property or comply with the court order.[163] The interim receiver normally cannot sell the debtor's property, although a sale of perishable property is permitted if the court order confers this power.[164] The appointment of an interim receiver does not stay the right or remedies of other creditors and therefore the interim receiver cannot prevent the payment to judgment enforcement creditors of funds that were paid into court under garnishment proceedings.[165] If the application for a bankruptcy order is successful, it is common for the interim receiver to be appointed trustee, since the interim receiver will have become familiar with the affairs of the debtor.[166]

D. VOLUNTARY BANKRUPTCY

Bankruptcy law confers a benefit on debtors as well as on creditors. Indeed, the vast majority of bankruptcies are ones where the debtor has voluntarily entered into the proceedings. In the case of individual bankrupts, it provides relief from legal action of the creditors and the prospect of obtaining a fresh start upon obtaining a bankruptcy discharge. Even in the case of artificial entities that do not typically survive the bankruptcy, voluntary bankruptcy provides an efficient mechanism for liquidating the entity and distributing the proceeds to the creditors.

Bankruptcy law provides the exclusive avenue through which insolvent debtors can make voluntary assignments of all of their property for the general benefit of their creditors.[167] In order to make an assignment in bankruptcy, the debtor must fall within the definition of an "insolvent person."[168] This definition specifies four elements that must exist in order for a debtor to make an assignment in bankruptcy. First, the claims of the creditors must amount to $1,000.[169] Second, the person must not be an undischarged bankrupt. Third, the person must reside, carry on business, or have property in Canada. Fourth, the

163 *BIA*, s 46(2).

164 *Ibid.*

165 *Arthur C Weeks Ltd v BC Contract Sales Ltd* (1961), 3 CBR (NS) 47 (BCSC).

166 *Re Continental Record Co* (1965), 8 CBR (NS) 73 (Ont HCJ).

167 *BIA*, s 42(2).

168 *Ibid*, ss 49(1) and 2 "insolvent person."

169 The debtor may make an assignment in bankruptcy even though the debtor owes money to a single creditor. See *Canada (Attorney General) v Gordon* (1992), 15 CBR (3d) 100 (Sask QB).

debtor must be insolvent as measured by the cash flow tests or balance sheet test for insolvency as set out in the definition.[170]

The process is simple and does not involve a court application. A sworn statement that discloses the debtor's property, the names and addresses of the creditors, and the amounts of their claims must accompany the assignment.[171] The assignment and sworn statement are filed with the official receiver in the locality of the debtor.[172] The official receiver will appoint a licensed trustee and will complete the assignment by filling in the name of the trustee. The debtor becomes a bankrupt on the date and time of the filing.[173] The debtor usually selects the trustee in the first instance, and that trustee will typically assist the debtor in the preparation of the documents. However, if the creditors want some other person to act as trustee, their wishes are to govern.[174]

An individual partner may make a bankruptcy assignment, but the bankruptcy affects only the partner's individual assets along with that partner's interest in the assets of the firm. In order to create a bankruptcy of the entire interest in the firm's assets, all partners must be parties to the assignment.[175] In the case of an artificial entity, the assignment must be signed by the person or body authorized to bind the entity. A resolution of directors is the vehicle that is usually used to effect the assignment where the debtor is a corporation,[176] but the power to make an assignment in bankruptcy is one that can be delegated to an officer of the corporation through the bylaws.[177]

E. AUTOMATIC BANKRUPTCY THROUGH FAILURE OF A COMMERCIAL PROPOSAL

A bankruptcy can also come about automatically without the intervention of either the creditor or the debtor. This occurs when an attempt by the debtor to reach a commercial proposal with the creditors fails. This can happen if the cash flow statements and associated documents or the proposal are not filed within the time periods set out in the

---

170 See Chapter 1, Section E.

171 *BIA*, s 49(2).

172 *Ibid*, ss 49(3) and 2(1) "locality of a debtor."

173 *Ibid*, s 2 "time of bankruptcy."

174 *Ibid*, s 49(4). And see *Re Roussel* (2001), 28 CBR (4th) 102 (Que CA).

175 *Squires Brothers*, above note 13.

176 *Re Tru-Value Investments Ltd* (1970), 15 CBR (NS) 6 (Ont HCJ).

177 *Re Regional Steel Works (Ottawa - 1987) Inc* (1994), 25 CBR (3d) 135 (Ont Ct Gen Div).

statute,[178] if the creditors vote down the proposal[179] or are deemed to have done so,[180] if a court decides not to approve the proposal,[181] or if a court later annuls it.[182] Once one of these events occurs, the debtor is deemed by the statute to have made an assignment at the time of the occurrence of that event. There is no similar provision in the *Companies Creditors' Arrangement Act* providing for automatic bankruptcy in the event that a corporate restructuring fails under that statute.

F. ANNULMENT OF A CONSUMER PROPOSAL

A failure of a consumer proposal caused by its non-approval by the creditors does not result in an automatic bankruptcy. Instead, the stay of proceedings comes to an end and the creditors are free to exercise their remedies against the debtor and the debtor's property.[183] However, if a consumer proposal that was made by a bankrupt is annulled, the consumer debtor will be deemed to have made an assignment in bankruptcy as of the date of the annulment.[184]

G. TERMINATION OF BANKRUPTCY PROCEEDINGS

In most cases, bankruptcy proceedings come to an end when the trustee's duties have been completed and the debtor, if a natural person, has obtained a bankruptcy discharge. However, under certain circumstances, bankruptcy proceedings can be interrupted before they reach this normal state of completion. Annulment of bankruptcy is available for both voluntary and involuntary bankruptcy. A court may annul a bankruptcy if it is of the opinion that a bankruptcy order ought not to have been made or an application ought not to have been filed.[185] If the bankruptcy was involuntary, the bankruptcy order can also be

178 *BIA*, s 50.4(8).
179 *Ibid*, s 57.
180 *Ibid*, ss 50(12.1) and 57.
181 *Ibid*, s 61(2).
182 *Ibid*, s 63(4).
183 *Ibid*, s 69.2(1).
184 *Ibid*, ss 66.3(5)(a) and 66.31(4)(a).
185 *Ibid*, s 181(1).

contested through an appeal[186] or by a motion for rescission.[187] As well, a bankrupt can initiate a consumer or commercial proposal, and approval of it operates to annul the bankruptcy and revest the property in the debtor.[188]

1) Termination of Involuntary Bankruptcy

There are three different processes that might be invoked after a bankruptcy order has been granted by a court, namely (1) an appeal of the bankruptcy order; (2) annulment of the bankruptcy; and (3) rescission of a bankruptcy order. An appeal of the bankruptcy order is the appropriate response where the controversy concerns a question of law.[189] For example, the controversy may be over whether the accepted facts constitute an act of bankruptcy. An order annulling a bankruptcy is the appropriate response where there is new evidence of a substantial nature that shows that the order should not have been made.[190] An order for rescission of a bankruptcy order is the appropriate response where the bankruptcy order was properly made in the first instance, but there are fundamentally new circumstances that arose after the bankruptcy order was granted or facts that were not known at the time the order was made.[191] For example, the bankrupt may have acquired additional property following the bankruptcy such that the bankrupt is able to pay all the creditors in full.[192] Annulment of the bankruptcy is not the appropriate response in this instance, since the applicant must show that the bankruptcy order ought not to have been made on the facts in existence at the time of the order.

---

186 *Ibid*, s 183(2).

187 *Ibid*, s 187(5).

188 *Ibid*, ss 61(1) and 66.4(2).

189 If a bankruptcy order is appealed, the bankruptcy proceedings are stayed until the appeal is disposed of. See *BIA*, s 195. However, the proceedings are merely suspended and the property continues to be vested in the trustee. See *Four Twenty-Seven*, above note 145.

190 *Re Trenwith* (1933), 15 CBR 107 (Ont HCJ); *Re Knight* (2003), 44 CBR (4th) 227 (BCSC).

191 *Re Bryden* (1975), 21 CBR (NS) 166 (BCSC); *Vince v Cinezeta Internationale Filmproduktionsgesellschaft MHB & CO KG*, 2013 SKQB 423. The motion should be made before the judge who granted the order in the first instance. See *Re Garritty* (2006), 21 CBR (5th) 237 (Alta QB).

192 *Christiansen v Paramount Developments Corp* (1998), 8 CBR (4th) 220 (Alta QB).

2) Annulment of Voluntary Bankruptcy

Unlike an involuntary bankruptcy, a voluntary bankruptcy is commenced without a court order. An application to annul a voluntary bankruptcy therefore provides interested parties with the opportunity to contest the bankruptcy. There are two grounds that are most commonly used in seeking an annulment of a voluntary bankruptcy. The first is where the debtor was not within the definition of an insolvent person at the date of the filing of the assignment. For example, a debtor may have failed to disclose assets or may have entered into sham transactions,[193] with the result that the debtor may not be insolvent under the balance sheet test. However, in order to be successful, the creditor must also show that the debtor was not insolvent under either of the cash flow tests. This may prove to be an obstacle for the creditor, since a business debtor who ceases to pay current obligations in the ordinary course of business satisfies this definition even if the debtor had the ability to pay such obligations.[194] An assignment may also be annulled on the ground that the person who purported to make the assignment was not authorized to do so.[195]

Courts will also annul a voluntary bankruptcy if it is an abuse of process of the courts or a fraud on the creditors. It is not enough to show that the debtor was seeking to obtain some collateral benefit as a result of the bankruptcy. It is therefore not an abuse of process to invoke a bankruptcy in order to terminate a shareholder agreement.[196] Nor is it sufficient to demonstrate that the claims that the creditors have against the debtor arose as a result of the fraudulent conduct of the debtor or that the debtor engaged in deceitful conduct. In such cases, the court can take fraudulent or deceitful conduct into account when considering the discharge of the debtor.[197] In order for an application to annul a voluntary bankruptcy to succeed, it must be shown that the debtor attempted to use the bankruptcy process as part of a fraudulent or deceitful design. This may occur where the bankruptcy process is invoked as one part of a larger scheme to hide or destroy assets in order to defeat a matrimonial property claim.[198]

---

193 *Hannay v Hannay* (2005), 16 CBR (5th) 52 (Sask QB).

194 *Re Wale* (1996), 45 CBR (4th) 15 (Ont Ct Gen Div) [*Wale*]. The same would not hold true for a non-business debtor, since the applicable cash flow test provides that the debtor must be unable (rather than unwilling) to meet obligations as they generally become due.

195 *Re Tartan Gold Fish Farms Ltd* (1996), 41 CBR (3d) 245 (NSSC) [*Tartan Gold*].

196 *Kalau v Dahl* (1985), 57 CBR (NS) 296 (Alta QB).

197 See *Funston v Gelberman* (2004), 5 CBR (5th) 223 (Ont SCJ).

198 *Wale*, above note 194; *Blatherwick v Blatherwick*, 2014 ONSC 1433.

3) Effect of Annulment

Annulment of a bankruptcy causes the bankrupt to revert to his or her former position as if the bankruptcy had not occurred. The stay of proceedings comes to an end, and the debtor is liable for all pre-bankruptcy and post-bankruptcy debts even though the debtor may have obtained a discharge prior to the annulment. The debtor's property that vested in the trustee on the bankruptcy is revested in the debtor unless the court orders that the property vest in some other person. Annulment of a bankruptcy does not invalidate transactions or payments made by the trustee.[199] If the trustee has sold or otherwise disposed of property, the purchaser is unaffected by an annulment of the bankruptcy. If the trustee has made distributions to the creditors, these payments are valid and effectual.

Outside these clear-cut situations, the effect of annulment of a bankruptcy becomes more controversial. One decision has held that civil proceedings that are commenced after the bankruptcy but before an annulment are a nullity, and that the annulment does not breathe new life into them.[200] The difficulty with this position is that it seems to run contrary to another line of cases that holds that actions that are commenced when the stay is in force are not a nullity but are merely subject to an irregularity that can be cured if the court subsequently grants leave *nunc pro tunc*.[201] In another decision, the court held that a creditor is bound by a decision of the trustee to reject a proof of claim if the appeal period has expired.[202] The creditor is therefore unable to bring civil proceedings in respect of the claim following the annulment of the bankruptcy. How far this reasoning can be extended is unclear. The same kind of argument can also be made in respect of a valuation of a contingent or unliquidated claim by a trustee,[203] a proprietary interest in an asset that is disputed by a trustee,[204] or a disallowance of a security interest by a trustee,[205] where in each instance the appeal period has expired.

---

199 *BIA*, s 181(2).

200 *Tartan Gold*, above note 195.

201 *McGillivray v Everall Construction (Edmonton) Ltd* (1981), 38 CBR (NS) 313 (Alta QB); *Blais v Bankers' Trust Corp* (1913), 14 DLR 277 (Alta SC). See also *Trusts and Guarantee Co v Brenner*, [1933] SCR 656.

202 *Re Bouvier Co* (1933), 14 CBR 446 (Ont HCJ).

203 *BIA*, s 135(1.1).

204 *Ibid*, s 81(2).

205 *Ibid*, s 135(3).

FURTHER READINGS

BLOCK-LIEB, S. "Why Creditors File So Few Involuntary Petitions and Why the Number Is Not Too Small" (1991) 57 *Brooklyn Law Review* 803

FROST, C. "Organizational Form, Misappropriation Risk, and the Substantive Consolidation of Corporate Groups" (1993) 44 *Hastings Law Journal* 449

GUNDY, S, & L ROGERS. "When the Cash Doesn't Flow: Dealing with Income Trusts in Financial Difficulty" in Janis P Sarra, ed, *Annual Review of Insolvency Law, 2004* (Toronto: Carswell, 2005) 29

HONSBERGER, J. "Failure to Pay One's Debts Generally as They Become Due: The Experience of France and Canada" (1980) 54 *American Bankruptcy Law Journal* 153

———. "Reaching Canadian Assets of Foreign Debtors through Local or Foreign Bankruptcy Proceedings" (1993) 18 *Canadian Bankruptcy Reports* (3d) 301

TREIMAN, I. "Acts of Bankruptcy: A Medieval Concept in Modern Bankruptcy Law" (1938) 52 *Harvard Law Review* 189

CHAPTER 4

PROPERTY OF THE BANKRUPT

A. THE CONCEPT OF PROPERTY IN BANKRUPTCY LAW

The concept of property is central to bankruptcy law. In order to understand its use, one must know something about the meaning of this concept in the wider context of the general law. Most often, the concept is employed to distinguish between two fundamentally different kinds of rights — personal rights and proprietary tights. A personal right (also referred to a right *in personam*) is one that is enforceable against an identifiable person or a definite class of persons. When a creditor lends money to a debtor, the creditor obtains a personal right against the debtor to recover the debt. The right is enforceable only against the person who incurred the obligation. A proprietary right (also referred to as a right *in rem*) is a right in respect of a thing. The right is available against an indefinite class of persons.[1] However, the concept of property is also sometimes used in a wider, less technical sense to denote all valuable rights without regard to whether they are personal rights or proprietary rights.

---

1 It is sometimes said that it is a right enforceable against the entire world, but this is not a necessary condition for a property right. For example, a finder has a property right in the goods that is good against the world except for the true owner, and a subordinate secured creditor has a property interest in the collateral that is trumped by that of a senior secured creditor.

Bankruptcy law uses the wider meaning of property in one context and the narrower meaning in another. One must be careful when using the term in order to understand which sense is intended. The wider meaning is used in identifying which of the debtor's assets will be available to satisfy the claims of the creditors. The Act defines property in a very broad manner that sweeps both personal rights and property rights into the bankrupt estate. For example, a personal right held by the bankrupt to recover a debt from another vests in the trustee, who thereby obtains the right to commence an action to recover the debt. In this respect, the definition of property is not drawing a distinction between personal rights and property rights but rather is using the term in the broad sense as including all the assets of the bankrupt. This does not pick up absolutely every right held by the bankrupt. A right of action to recover damages in tort for pain and suffering does not vest in the trustee. Nevertheless, most economically significant rights will be caught by the definition.

The narrower concept of property is used to differentiate between claims against the bankrupt that are administered within the bankruptcy regime and claims against the bankrupt that remain enforceable outside it. It is here that the distinction between a personal right and a property right is of fundamental importance. A person who has a personal right against the bankrupt loses the right to enforce the claim upon the occurrence of the bankruptcy.[2] In its place, the claimant obtains the right to prove the claim in bankruptcy and obtain a dividend from the liquidation of the bankrupt's assets. The matter is entirely different if the claimant has a property right in the asset. Only those assets that belong to the bankrupt vest in the trustee.[3] If the asset is not owned by the bankrupt but is the property of the claimant, the claimant will have the right to recover the asset from the trustee.

In many instances, both the bankrupt and the claimant will have property rights in the same thing. Consider the case of a bankrupt who operated a jewelry store and repaired a watch owned by a customer. The bankrupt has a property right in the watch in the form of a possessory lien, while the customer remains the owner of the watch. The right to the lien is a property right that vests in the trustee, and it can be asserted by the trustee against the customer. However, the lien secures only the cost of the repairs and does not give the trustee the right

2 The right is not lost but is merely suspended in respect of certain kinds of claims that survive the discharge of an individual bankrupt. See Chapter 10, Section G.

3 *BIA*, s 71.

to the full value of the watch unless it happens to be less than the cost of the repairs.

The bankrupt and the claimant may have conflicting claims to a right. For example, a person to whom a debt is owed may have assigned the right to both the bankrupt and to another claimant. Property law provides priority rules for the resolution of conflicting claims to the thing.[4] In the example above, priority between the trustee in bankruptcy and the claimant is resolved according to the order of registration in the personal property registry if the assignments were within the scope of personal property security legislation.[5] If not, priority is given to the first person to notify the debtor of the assignment.[6]

B. THE BANKRUPT'S ESTATE

1) Property Vesting in the Trustee

Upon the occurrence of a bankruptcy, the debtor's property vests in the trustee in bankruptcy.[7] The definition of property is very wide and encompasses any type of property "whether real or personal, legal or equitable, as well as obligations, easements and every description of estate, interest and profit, present or future, vested or contingent, in, arising out of or incident to property."[8] The definition covers both personal rights and property rights that are held by the bankrupt at the time of the bankruptcy. The vesting of property in the trustee occurs through operation of law without the need for any document or act of conveyance to give effect to the transfer.

The assets that vest in the trustee are subject to all the limitations or defences that could be asserted against the bankrupt.[9] This is what

---

4 The subject matter of the property right can be a personal right, such as a debt. Property law defines who has the better claim to the debt. However, the subject matter against which the competing claimants assert their proprietary claims — the debt — remains a personal right. It is enforceable by legal action against the person who owes the obligation (the account debtor). If the account debtor also goes bankrupt, the party who has the better claim to the debt will nevertheless lose the right to sue on it and will instead obtain only the right to prove for a dividend in the bankruptcy of the account debtor.

5 See R Cuming, C Walsh, & R Wood, *Personal Property Security Law*, 2d ed (Toronto: Irwin Law, 2012) at 157 and 402–4.

6 *Dearle v Hall* (1828), 3 Russ 1.

7 *BIA*, s 71.

8 *Ibid*, s 2 "property."

9 *Yale v MacMaster* (1974), 18 CBR (NS) 225 (Ont HCJ).

is meant when it is said that the trustee "steps into the shoes" of the bankrupt.[10] Another way of putting it is that the trustee obtains the property "warts and all."[11] This principle does not operate where bankruptcy or other legislation gives the trustee a power to subordinate or avoid certain property rights of third parties. In such cases, the trustee may have a better right to the asset than that held by the bankrupt.

The principle that the trustee takes the property subject to any limitation affecting it is nicely illustrated in the case where the debtor obtains property from another through fraud or other circumstances that entitle the transferor to rescind. At the time of the bankruptcy, the debtor holds legal title to the property and the transferor has merely a right of rescission in respect of the property. A right to rescind is lost when the asset is transferred to a *bona fide* purchaser for value and without notice. However, the trustee does not occupy the position of a purchaser but is subject to the same limitations that could be asserted against the bankrupt. The right of rescission can therefore be exercised against the trustee, thus causing the property to fall out of the bankrupt's estate and revest in the transferor.[12]

The operation of this principle can also be observed in relation to shared property rights. A bankrupt may share ownership of property with another person through joint ownership or co-ownership. Only the bankrupt's interest in the property will vest in the trustee. In the case of a joint tenancy, the occurrence of bankruptcy changes the nature of the interest. The vesting of the interest in the trustee results in the loss of the unity of title. This severs the joint tenancy and converts it into a tenancy in common.[13] The trustee obtains an undivided one-half interest in the property, and a death of one of the co-owners that occurs after the bankruptcy is of no consequence because the right of survivorship is lost upon severance. The trustee does not have the right to sell the entire interest in the property to a buyer and pay out the other co-owner with a portion of the sale proceeds.[14] If the property is land, the trustee may commence proceedings for the partition and sale of the property, but the trustee has no better right than the bankrupt in respect of this application, and a court may refuse to grant the order

10 See *Re Giffen*, [1998] 1 SCR 91 at para 52.

11 See RM Goode, *Principles of Corporate Insolvency Law*, 4th ed (Sweet & Maxwell: London, 2011) at 97. See also *Saulnier v Royal Bank of Canada*, 2008 SCC 58 at para 50 [*Saulnier*].

12 *Re Lethbridge Equipment Exchange Ltd* (1967), 11 CBR (NS) 104 (Alta SCTD).

13 *Re White* (1928), 8 CBR 544 (Ont SC).

14 *Re Reeder* (1995), 37 CBR (3d) 228 (BCSC).

where it causes serious hardship.[15] Similar proceedings are not available in respect of personal property, which renders such interests less marketable since the purchaser of the bankrupt's interest will hold the interest in common with the other co-owner. A trustee in bankruptcy acquires property subject to a dower right or homestead right held by the non-owning spouse. The trustee is permitted to dispose of the interest but remains subject to the requirement that the non-owning spouse consent to the transfer or that the consent be dispensed with by a court.[16]

The trustee in bankruptcy may claim that a third party who has legal title to property holds that property in trust for the bankrupt. The bankrupt's interest in the trust property clearly falls within the definition of property. Some courts have been hesitant to give full effect to this principle. The British Columbia Court of Appeal in *Blackman v Davison*[17] indicated that actions for remedies based on a resulting or constructive trust are matters that are "strictly and exclusively between the spouses" and are not available to creditors. There is little justification for the view. Resulting trusts and constructive trusts arise in a number of different circumstances and encompass both commercial and non-commercial activity.[18] The trust principles apply to relations between spouses, cohabitants, parents and children, friends, and strangers. The same trust law principles are applied in all these different contexts, and there is no basis in law for the view that trust claims in a marital setting are subject to their own unique rules.[19] Other courts have recognized that a trustee in bankruptcy can assert trust claims to such assets.[20] The Ontario Supreme Court in *Elkaim v Markina*[21] declined to follow *Blackman* and instead resolved the matter by concluding that a claim in unjust enrichment is not established until there is a separation since it is only then that the retention of the benefit can be considered unjust.

The crucial date for the vesting of the property is the date of the bankruptcy — the date of the bankruptcy order in the case of an involuntary bankruptcy, and the date of the filing of the assignment in

15 *McKenzie (Trustee of) v McKenzie* (2005), 11 CBR (5th) 116 (Man CA).

16 *Re Gates* (1973), 18 CBR (NS) 289 (Alta SCTD).

17 (1987), 64 CBR (NS) 84 (BCCA). The court also found that the facts necessary to obtain a declaration of a trust had not been established, so that the trustee in bankruptcy's claim to the asset failed on this ground as well.

18 *Peter v Beblow*, [1993] 1 SCR 980.

19 *Syncrude Canada Ltd v Hunter Engineering Co*, [1989] 1 SCR 426 at para 175.

20 See *Kopr v Kopr* (2006), 24 CBR (5th) 205 (Alta QB) [*Kopr*].

21 2010 ONSC 874.

the case of a voluntary bankruptcy. If the debtor disposed of the asset prior to that date, then the asset will not vest in the trustee. The trustee under certain circumstances is given the power to avoid pre-bankruptcy transactions.[22] When this happens, the asset is clawed back into the bankrupt estate. Assets that are acquired by the bankrupt following the bankruptcy also vest in the trustee.[23]

2) The Anti-deprivation Rule

Canadian courts have recognized that a contractual provision that is designed to remove value from the reach of an insolvent person's creditors is void on the basis that it violates the public policy of equitable and fair distribution on bankruptcy.[24] This is referred to as the "fraud on the bankruptcy law principle." The principle can be usefully broken down into two distinct components: the anti-deprivation rule and the *pari passu* rule. The anti-deprivation rule operates by invalidating provisions that withdraw an asset that would otherwise be available to satisfy the claims of creditors upon the insolvency of the party or the commencement of insolvency proceedings.[25] The *pari passu* rule invalidates contractual provisions that circumvent the statutory provisions distribution and thereby gives one creditor more than its proper share, and is examined separately in Chapter 9.

One of the earliest limitations was the distinction drawn between provisions that provide for the defeasance of an absolute interest and those that create determinable or limited interests.[26] The former involve the outright transfer of an interest that is forfeited upon the occurrence of bankruptcy.[27] These violate the anti-deprivation rule. The lat-

---

22 See Chapter 7.

23 *BIA*, s 67(1)(c). And see Section D, below in this chapter.

24 See *Canadian Imperial Bank of Commerce v Bramalea Inc* (1995), 33 OR (3d) 692 (Gen Div) [*Bramalea*] in which an agreement that provided for the transfer of a partner's partnership interest to the other partners at less than market value solely in the event of an insolvency of the partner was held to be void on the ground that it was a "fraud on the bankruptcy law." See R Wood, "Direct Payment Clauses and the Fraud upon the Bankruptcy Law Principle: *Greenview (Municipal District No 16) v Bank of Nova Scotia*" (2014) 52 *Alberta Law Review* 171.

25 A classic statement of the anti-deprivation rule is found in *Whitmore v Mason* (1861), 2 J & H 204 at 212: "no person possessed of property can reserve that property to himself until he shall become bankrupt, and then provide that, in the event of his becoming bankrupt, it shall pass to another and not to his creditors."

26 *BIA*, s 84.2.

27 *Ex parte Jay* (1880), 14 Ch D 19.

ter involve a determinable interest in which the quantum of the interest is limited by the stipulated event so that the occurrence of the event marks the end of the duration of the interest.[28] These do not violate the anti-deprivation rule. The distinction has been criticized as "little short of disgraceful" when applied to "a rule professedly founded on considerations of public policy."[29] Nevertheless, the courts adhere to this distinction, and in the result leases and licences that terminate upon the occurrence of bankruptcy are unaffected, as are protective trusts that are granted by the settlor to a beneficiary until the beneficiary's bankruptcy. A second limitation on the efficacy of the anti-deprivation rule is that it only applies if the triggering event is either the insolvency of the party or the commencement of insolvency proceedings.[30]

The anti-deprivation has undergone a major transformation in England as a result of the 2011 decision of the United Kingdom Supreme Court in *Belmont Park Investments PTY Ltd v BNY Corporate Trustee Services Ltd*.[31] The court in *Belmont* held that a deliberate intention to evade the insolvency laws is required before the anti-deprivation rule is engaged. Where the parties are acting in good faith and the transaction serves a legitimate commercial purpose, the rule will not apply. In determining if the transaction was a commercial one entered into in good faith the court may consider the fact that the source of the bankrupt's asset is the person to whom it is to go on bankruptcy. The emphasis on good faith and a sensible commercial purpose appears to have weakened the hold of the earlier limitations. The court was unwilling to discard the distinction in respect of leases on the basis that it was far beyond the judicial function to do away with a 200-year-old principle. But beyond these traditional exceptions, the distinction between defeasible interests and determinable interests is no longer relevant.

It should not be assumed that Canadian courts will follow *Belmont* in adopting an intent-based test in respect of the anti-deprivation rule. The decision has been criticized in England,[32] and it is clearly contrary to existing Canadian decisions that do not require proof of actual

---

28 *Re Knechtel Furniture Ltd* (1985), 56 CBR (NS) 258 (Ont HCJ); *Money Markets International Stockbrokers Ltd v London Stock Exchange Ltd*, [2001] EWHC 1052 (Ch).

29 *Re King's Trust* (1892) 29 LR Ir 401 at 410.

30 *Whitmore v Mason*, above note 25.

31 [2011] UKSC 38.

32 See Sarah Worthington, "Good Faith, Flawed Assets and the Emasculation of the UK Anti-deprivation Rule" (2012) 75 *Modern Law Review* 112 at 121. H Beale, M Bridge, L Gullifer, & E Lomnicka, *The Law of Security and Title-Based Financing*, 2d ed (Oxford: Oxford University Press, 2012) 350 describe the rule as "unacceptably obscure."

fraud in cases involving insolvency triggered forfeiture.[33] It also moves against the tide of legislative reform in Canada. The 2009 amendments to the *BIA* has partially codified an anti-deprivation rule.[34] This legislative modification of the anti-deprivation rule does not apply to bankruptcy proceedings against corporations or other artificial entities. This means that the statutory anti-deprivation rule applies in respect of consumer bankruptcies, and the common law anti-deprivation rule applies in respect of commercial bankruptcies.[35]

The statutory anti-deprivation rule[36] prevents any person from terminating an agreement with an individual bankrupt by reason only of his or her bankruptcy or insolvency. This legislative approach goes well beyond the common law anti-deprivation rule in several respects. First, the traditional exclusion of determinable interests such as leases and intellectual property licences is rejected. Second, in the case of leases and services provided by public utilities, the anti-deprivation rule applies to a non-insolvency triggering event in the form of a non-payment of rent or past goods and services.[37] The common law anti-deprivation rule, in contrast, only applies where the deprivation is triggered by insolvency or the commencement of insolvency proceedings. Third, the elements of good faith and sensible commercial purpose that are part of the English common law anti-deprivation rule are not relevant in respect of the statutory anti-deprivation rule.

In some respect the statutory anti-deprivation rule is more limited than the common law rule. First, the statutory rule only covers termination provisions that are contained in an agreement. Although this covers most of the ground there may be instances where the transaction arises out of a grant rather than an agreement or involves a transfer of an asset to a third party so as to take it outside the ambit of the statutory provision.[38] The common law rule is wider in that it may apply to

---

33 *Bramalea*, above note 24; *1183882 Alberta Ltd (Sok's Contracting) v Valin Industrial Mill Installations Ltd*, 2011 ABQB 440.

34 *BIA*, s 84.2. And see Chapter 6, Section B(2).

35 *Aircell Communications Inc (Trustee of) v Bell Mobility Cellular Inc*, 2013 ONCA 95, suggests that both the statutory rule as well as the common law rule will be applicable where the transaction falls within the scope of the statutory anti-deprivation rule.

36 The provisions are based on legislation in the United States that is designed to regulate "ipso facto" clauses — contractual provisions that are triggered by the occurrence of insolvency or bankruptcy proceedings. See 11 USC §§ 365(b)(2) and 365(e)(1).

37 *BIA*, ss 84.2(2) & (3).

38 The US *Bankruptcy Code* is wider in that it contains a second provision that applies to a "provision in an agreement, transfer instrument, or applicable non-

transfers of assets that do not arise out of an agreement between the parties. Second, the statutory anti-deprivation rule does not apply to derivatives contracts[39] whereas the common law anti-deprivation rule had potential application to such contracts. Third, the statutory anti-deprivation rule can be declared by a court to be inapplicable if the applicant satisfies the court that its operation would likely cause the applicant significant financial hardship.[40]

3) Non-transferable Property

Many contracts provide that a party cannot assign or transfer his or her rights to another. Ordinarily, the trustee in bankruptcy is in no better position than the bankrupt in exercising contractual rights that have vested in the trustee, and therefore the trustee would be bound by this limitation on transfer. However, the *BIA* has modified this rule in order to give the trustee the power to transfer the right in circumstances where the debtor would have been unable to do so.

This power was originally restricted to the assignment of a lease of real property. The *BIA* did not directly confer this power on trustees. Instead, it incorporated provincial law by providing that the rights of lessors were to be determined according to the law of the province in which the leased premises are situated.[41] Provincial legislation gave courts the power to approve an assignment of a lease by a trustee in bankruptcy notwithstanding a non-assignment provision contained in the lease agreement.[42] The court could not make the order unless the arrears in rent were paid to the landlord and the assignee agreed to observe and perform its terms of the lease and not conduct a more objectionable or hazardous business than that conducted by the bankrupt.

The 2009 amendments to the *BIA* expand the court's power to assign the rights and obligations of the debtor to a specified person who agrees to the assignment.[43] The new provision applies to all contracts except for post-bankruptcy contracts, eligible financial contracts, collective agreements and rights that are not assignable by reason of their

---

bankruptcy law . . . that effects or gives an option to effect a forfeiture, modification, or termination of the debtor's interest in property." See 11 USC § 541(c).

39 *BIA*, ss 84.2(7)–(9).

40 *Ibid*, s 84.2(6).

41 *Ibid*, s 146.

42 See, for example, *Landlord's Rights on Bankruptcy Act*, RSA 2000, c L-5, s 8(2)(b).

43 *BIA*, s 84.1(1). Notice of the application must be given to every party to an agreement.

nature.[44] The power can be exercised in respect of an individual only if the individual is carrying on business and only to the extent that the rights and obligations that are assigned relate to the business.[45] In deciding whether to make the order, the court must consider whether the person to whom the rights and obligations are to be assigned is able to perform the obligations and whether it is appropriate to assign the rights and obligations to that person.[46] The court is not permitted to make the order unless it is satisfied that all monetary defaults will be remedied before the date specified in the order.[47]

The new provisions apply to commercial leases and replace the provincial law concerning the assignment of leases by a trustee that was formerly incorporated by the *BIA*.[48] Nevertheless, some of the caselaw decided under the provincial statutes remains useful. In deciding whether a person is able to perform the future obligations under the agreement, it is likely that a court will continue to require evidence of the proposed assignee's business reputation in the community or creditworthiness.[49]

Commercial shopping mall leases frequently contain restrictive covenants that limit the kinds of business that can be carried out on the leased premises by the tenant or which limit the power of the landlord to permit the premises to be used for certain purposes. These types of clauses are designed to ensure that the mix of stores and the layout of the mall produces an economically viable enterprise for the benefit of all the tenants. Prior to the 2009 amendments to the *BIA*, the trustee had the power to assign a lease without the consent of the landlord under provincial statute, but the assignee was subject to any restrictive user provisions that limited the business activities that could be under-

---

44 *Ibid*, s 84.1(3). In *Ford Motor Company of Canada Ltd v Welcome Ford Sales Ltd*, 2011 ABCA 158 at para 50 [*Welcome Ford*] the court stated that an automobile dealership agreement is not a personal contract, but "a rather standard commercial franchise which could be performed by virtually any business person and entity with some capital and experience in automotive retailing."

45 *BIA*, s 84.1(2).

46 *Ibid*, s 84.1(4). It is not necessary to first seek the consent of the other party, but an unreasonable withholding of consent is a factor that a court may consider under s 84.1(4). See *Welcome Ford*, above note 44.

47 *BIA*, s 84.1(5).

48 *Ibid*, s 146 makes it clear that s 84.1 of the *BIA* is intended to replace the provincial law that formerly governed the assignment of commercial leases.

49 *Griff v Sommerset Management Services Ltd* (1978), 26 CBR (NS) 205 (Ont CA); *Peat Marwick Ltd v Kingswood Holdings Ltd* (1983), 50 CBR (NS) 201 (BCSC).

taken on the leased premises.[50] The same approach will most likely be taken in respect of the new *BIA* provisions.

4) Copyrights and Patents

Although a trustee will ordinarily be bound by the same restrictions or limitations that pertain to the debtor's enjoyment of the right, the *BIA* gives a trustee the power to sell patented articles free and clear of any restrictions or limitations that were binding on the debtor.[51] A manufacturer or vendor who objects to the disposition is given the right to purchase them from the trustee at the invoice price subject to a reasonable deduction for deterioration or depreciation.[52]

In the case of a manuscript and any copyright that has been assigned to the debtor, the trustee obtains a more limited right than that enjoyed by the debtor.[53] If the work has not been published and put on the market at the time of the bankruptcy and no expense has been incurred in connection with it, the manuscript and copyright revert to the author.[54] If the work has been put into type and expenses incurred, the work reverts to the author on payment of the expenses. If after six months the trustee decides not to carry out the contract, the work reverts without expense to the author and any contract or agreement is terminated. If the work is published and put on the market, the trustee is entitled to deal with the published work. The author is entitled to receive the same royalties that he or she would have received from the bankrupt, and the trustee is not permitted to assign the copyright except on terms that would give the author at least the same rate of royalties.[55] Before disposing of copies of the manufactured work, the trustee

---

50 *Micro Cooking Centres (Canada) Inc (Trustee of) v Cambridge Leaseholds Ltd* (1988), 68 CBR (NS) 60 (Ont HCJ). A court could, however, approve an assignment of a lease of a bankrupt tenant despite the fact that the landlord gave a covenant to another tenant not to assign the lease. See *Re Robinson, Little & Co* (1987), 67 CBR (NS) 23 (Alta CA).

51 *BIA*, s 82(1). And see A Duggan & N Siebrasse, "Protection of Creators' Rights in Insolvency" (2014) 26 *Intellectual Property Journal* 271.

52 *Ibid*, s. 82(2). The provision only applies to patents and courts are not prepared to extend its application to other forms of intellectual property rights. See *Scanwood Canada Ltd (Re)*, 2011 NSSC 393.

53 The *BIA* provisions apply to musical works and sound recordings as well as to written works. See *Re Song Corp* (2002), 31 CBR (4th) 97 (Ont SCJ).

54 *BIA*, s 83(1).

55 *Ibid*, s 83(2).

must offer them to the author at such price and on such terms and conditions as the trustee may deem fair and proper.[56]

5) Licences and Quotas

Some rights, though valuable, do not fall within the definition of property and therefore do not vest in the trustee. A licence is a right to do something that would not otherwise be lawful to do. Some licences fall within the definition of property while others do not. A professional licence that recognizes the skill and competency of an individual cannot be transferred or used by any other person and is not considered property. A transferable licence is considered property, but any procedures or restrictions imposed by the person who issues the licence must be respected.[57]

The difficult cases are those where a statute provides that a licence or quota is the property of the issuing authority and provides that it cannot be transferred. Despite the apparent non-transferability of the licence, the authority that issues the licence frequently gives effect to a sale or other transfer of the licence by cancelling the old licence and issuing a new licence in the name of the purchaser. Although the authority will sometimes claim that there is no transfer of rights between the licence holder and the purchaser when a new licence is issued to replace a licence that has been relinquished, the reality is that there is an active trade in them and they are often sold for large sums of money.[58]

Courts have divided on whether the licence should be considered property for the purposes of bankruptcy law.[59] A similar controversy exists as to whether licences should be regarded as property under personal property security legislation. Some courts have held that a licence is not property if the issuer has an absolute and unfettered discretion to grant or withdraw licences.[60] Others have held that the existence of a commercial market for the licence is a significant factor in its characterization.[61]

---

56 *Ibid*, s 83(3).

57 *Re Rogers* (2001), 42 CBR (4th) 310 (Alta QB).

58 See *Green v Harnum* (2007), 263 Nfld & PEIR 241 (NLTD).

59 See *Re Bennett* (1988), 67 CBR (NS) 314 (BCSC) (fishing licence regarded as property); *Re Jenkins* (1997), 32 CBR (4th) 262 (NSSC) (fishing licence not regarded as property). See also T Telfer, "Statutory Licences and the Search for Property: The End of the Imbroglio?" (2007) 45 *Canadian Business Law Journal* 224.

60 *National Trust Co v Bouckhuyt* (1987), 43 DLR (4th) 543 (Ont CA).

61 *Saskatoon Auction Mart Ltd v Finesse Holsteins*, [1993] 1 WWR 265 (Sask QB).

In *Saulnier v Royal Bank of Canada*,[62] the Supreme Court of Canada dealt with the question of whether a fishing licence was property as defined in the *BIA*. The legislation provided that the licence was the property of the Crown, that it was not transferable, and that the minister enjoyed an absolute discretion in issuing licences. The reality was that there was a commercial market for fishing licences based on the assumption that they could be transferred with the consent of the existing licence holder. The Court held that because the licence gave the licence holder a right to acquire property in the fish that were caught, it bore a resemblance to a *profit à prendre* and therefore should be regarded as property for the purposes of the *BIA*. The decision therefore is very narrow in its scope. Although it provides an answer in respect of fishing licences, it is not helpful in respect of licences or quotas in which the licence holder already owns the resource but needs the licence or quota to be allowed to produce or market it. Subsequent cases have tended to ignore this aspect of the judgment and have interpreted the decision widely so as to bring a licence within the definition of property even when it does not result in the holder directly acquiring property in an asset in respect of which the holder would not otherwise be entitled.[63]

6) Veto Rights

In some cases, a statute may confer a right to veto or withhold consent. Upon a bankruptcy of the holder of this right, the question arises whether it is property that vests in the trustee in bankruptcy. Some statutes confer a veto right to a non-owning spouse to withhold consent to a disposition of a homestead.[64] Others provide that a lender is required to offer to lease the land back to a farmer who has defaulted on a loan.[65] The Saskatchewan Court of Appeal has held that the right is not property that vests in the trustee if the right is available exclusively to the debtor and cannot be assigned.[66] If the right is transferable it will be regarded as property that vests in the trustee even if the right to assign is limited by statute to a small class of persons.[67] The

62 Above note 11.

63 *Stout & Co LLP v Chez Outdoors Ltd*, 2009 ABQB 444.

64 See, for example, *Homesteads Act*, CCSM c H80, s 4.

65 See, for example, *The Saskatchewan Farm Security Act*, SS 1988-89, c S-17.1, s 27.2(1).

66 *Czerwonka v Paslawski* (1989), 77 Sask R 206 (QB), aff'd (1989), 8 RPR (2d) 73 (Sask CA).

67 *Mulatz v Toronto Dominion Bank* (1994), 111 DLR (4th) 601 (Sask CA).

Manitoba Court of Appeal departed from this approach and characterized the veto right as property if it is a power that relates to property and is capable of being surrendered or waived for valuable consideration even though it was not capable of being assigned.[68] The court was heavily influenced by the Supreme Court of Canada's treatment of licences in *Saulnier*.[69]

7) Rights of Action

Despite the wide definition of property employed by the *BIA*, courts have limited its ambit in respect of certain kinds of assets. Courts have drawn a distinction between a cause of action that relates to an injury to the bankrupt's property and one that relates to a personal injury of the bankrupt. Courts have justified this distinction on the principle that "it is not the policy of the law to convert into money for the creditors the mental or physical anguish of the debtor."[70] A claim in the tort of conversion for interference with the bankrupt's goods will therefore vest in the trustee, but a personal injury claim to recover damages for physical injury, loss of expectation of life, pain and suffering, loss of amenities of life, and mental suffering will not.[71] A claim for damages for loss or damage to exempt property, however, will not be available for distribution to the creditors.[72] Causes of action that relate to divorce or custody[73] and a right to claim solicitor-client privilege[74] are similarly viewed as purely personal rights that do not vest in a trustee in bankruptcy. The principle has been extended even further in England, where it has been held that the personal correspondence of the bankrupt, being of a nature peculiarly personal and private to the bankrupt, does not vest in the trustee.[75]

The victim of the wrongdoing may have received money from a settlement of the claim or from successful litigation. If the cause of action is characterized as personal to the bankrupt so as not to be considered property of the bankrupt, then the funds recovered in respect

68 *Chartier v MMP Ltd*, 2013 MBCA 41. Compare *Phan v Lee*, 2005 ABCA 142.
69 Above note 11.
70 *Re Holley* (1986), 59 CBR (NS) 17 at para 44 (Ont CA).
71 *Re Ritenburg* (1961), 3 CBR (NS) 294 (Alta SCTD).
72 *Re Brodie* (1968), 12 CBR (NS) 172 (Ont HCJ).
73 *Gano v Alberta Motor Assn Insurance Co* (1997), 46 CBR (3d) 144 (Alta QB) [*Gano*].
74 *Bre-X Minerals Ltd (Trustee of) v Verchere*, 2001 ABCA 255.
75 *Haig v Aitken*, [2001] Ch 110.

of the claim also share this status and do not vest in the trustee.[76] It is uncertain whether this status extends to traceable non-exempt property that the bankrupt acquires using these funds.

Claims for injury to reputation resulting from defamation or malicious prosecution are also considered to be injuries that are personal to the bankrupt.[77] Although claims for punitive damages are non-compensatory awards in the nature of a judicial fine, they respond to the wrongdoer's conduct towards the victim and not the victim's property and therefore also do not vest in the trustee.[78]

Upon the occurrence of a bankruptcy, the bankrupt ceases to have any capacity to dispose of or otherwise deal with his or her property.[79] This affects the bankrupt's ability to commence or continue legal action.[80] If the right of action is one that vests in the trustee, the bankrupt will have no right to bring or continue the action. If it does not vest in the trustee, the bankrupt will maintain the right and ability to pursue the action.[81] A bankrupt will therefore retain the right to pursue the claim where the injury is personal to the bankrupt (such as a claim for pain and suffering) or where the claim is for income or revenue that is governed by the surplus income provision.[82] A single cause of action may give rise to both types of claims. In such a case, the cause of action vests in the trustee. If the trustee pursues the action, the trustee must hold any damages recovered in respect of the personal injury claim on a constructive trust for the bankrupt.[83] Where the claim is clearly a personal one but a head of damage might turn out to be property vested in the trustee in bankruptcy, the bankrupt is permitted to pursue the action and the characterization of the head of damage may be left to be determined after a trial.[84]

A bankrupt who causes injury to another person may carry insurance against that loss. If the insurance policy provides that the money is payable to the insured, the right of action vests in the trustee and all creditors of the bankrupt can share in these funds.[85] Courts are

---

76 *Re Airey* (1989), 77 CBR (NS) 74 (Ont HCJ); *Re Brodie*, above note 72.

77 *Cherry v Ivey* (1982), 43 CBR (NS) 174 (Ont HCJ); *Eggen v Grayson* (1956), 36 CBR 72 (Alta SCTD).

78 *Gano*, above note 73.

79 *BIA*, s 71.

80 *McNamara v Pagecorp Inc* (1988), 68 CBR (NS) 303 (Ont HCJ).

81 *Gano*, above note 73.

82 See *Wallace v United Grain Growers Ltd*, [1997] 3 SCR. 701 [*Wallace*]; *Re Landry* (2000), 21 CBR (4th) 58 (Ont CA).

83 *Ord v Upton*, [2000] 1 All ER 193 (CA).

84 *Clement Estate v Canada (AG)*, 2012 ONSC 5823.

85 *Re Harrington Motor Co Ltd*, [1928] Ch 105.

reluctant to reach this conclusion, since it permits creditors to reach insurance monies at the expense of the injured party for whose benefit it was intended. Where possible they have interpreted insurance policies as providing for payment to the injured party rather than to the bankrupt.[86] Provincial insurance statutes give the injured party a direct right to proceed against the insurer in respect of liability for motor vehicle accidents despite the fact that the injured party is not a party to the contract.[87] If the bankrupt carries property insurance, the funds are payable to the trustee in the event of loss, notwithstanding any law or contractual provision that provides otherwise.[88]

In order to fall within the definition of property, the claim must be one that is capable of being pursued in a court. The ability to apply for a discretionary award for compensation from a criminal injuries compensation board is not considered property, even if the award compensates an injury to the victim's property.[89] The test is whether the bankrupt could have sustained an action to recover the amount. As the award is completely discretionary, the claim is not one that vests in the trustee. A right that is cognizable in a court of law, but that is subject to the exercise of discretion on the part of the judge, is nevertheless a right of action that falls within the definition of property of the bankrupt.[90]

Provincial matrimonial property legislation typically gives a spouse the right to apply for a division of assets upon the occurrence of specific triggering events such as the separation of the spouses.[91] The right to seek a division of assets is a right that vests in the trustee if a triggering event has occurred at the date of the bankruptcy.[92] If the triggering event occurs after bankruptcy but before discharge of the bankrupt, the right of action will vest in the trustee as after-acquired property.[93] If there has

---

86 *Re Major* (1984), 54 CBR (NS) 28 (BCSC); *Eurasia Auto Ltd v M & M Welding & Supply (1985) Inc* (1991), 5 CBR (3d) 227 (Alta QB); *Re Miller* (2001), 27 CBR (4th) 107 (Ont SCJ).

87 See, for example, *Insurance Act*, RSA 2000, c I-3, s 579(1). Section 145 of the *BIA* provides that nothing in the Act affects the right afforded by provincial statute to have the proceeds of a motor vehicle liability insurance policy applied in satisfaction of the claim of the injured party.

88 *BIA*, s 24(2).

89 *Re Campbell*, [1997] Ch 14.

90 *Tinant v Tinant* (2003), 46 CBR (4th) 150 (Alta CA) [*Tinant*].

91 Saskatchewan's *The Family Property Act*, SS 1997, c F-6.3, does not adopt the concept of a triggering event. This raises the possibility that a trustee in bankruptcy may attempt to pursue an action in cases where there has not been a breakdown in the family relationship.

92 *Tinant*, above note 90; *Blowes v Blowes* (1993), 21 CBR (3d) 276 (Ont CA) [*Blowes*].

93 *Re Gray* (1988), 67 CBR (NS) 161 (Ont HCJ).

been no triggering event, the right to seek a division of assets at some future time is merely an inchoate right that does fall within the definition of property.[94]

One commentator has argued that a right to seek a matrimonial property order should not vest in the trustee unless there has been a triggering event *and* the spouse has commenced an action for a division of the assets.[95] Cases in Alberta and Saskatchewan have rejected this additional requirement.[96] The position in Ontario is less clear. The leading Ontario case did not mention this as a requirement in the decision, but in fact the spouse had brought an action for a division of the assets.[97] In the opinion of the author, the argument for an added requirement of commencement is not convincing and should be rejected. The courts have drawn a distinction between causes of action that relate to an injury to a person and causes of action that relate to an individual's property. An action for a division of assets clearly falls within the latter. If all conditions necessary for a commencement of an action have been satisfied, it is an existing right that vests in the trustee.

8) Set-Off

If a cause of action vests in the trustee and the person who owes the monetary obligation fails to pay it when it is due, the trustee's recourse is to bring an action against the party and obtain a judgment. The value of this right of action can be diminished or eliminated altogether if the party has a right to set-off. If a right of set-off is successfully asserted, the amount owed by the party to the trustee is reduced by the amount that the bankrupt owes to that party.

The consequences of a right to set-off are illustrated in the following example. C owes $1,000 to B. B, in turn, owes $2,000 to C. B goes bankrupt, and the right of action in respect of the $1,000 vests in the trustee. If C is unable to assert a right of set-off, C will be liable to pay the full $1,000 to the trustee. C will be able to prove a claim for the $2,000 in B's bankruptcy. However, it is unlikely that C will get anything close to full recovery of the claim. Assume that the assets are sufficient to pay to general creditors a dividend of ten cents on the dollar. C will only recover 10 percent of its claim ($200). C is therefore subject to a net loss of $800. The situation is vastly improved for C if a right of set-off is available. C is

94 *Kopr*, above note 20.

95 R Klotz, *Bankruptcy, Insolvency and Family Law*, 2d ed (Scarborough, ON: Carswell, 2002) (loose-leaf) at 6.1(f).

96 *Tinant*, above note 90; *Etsell (Re)*, 2009 SKQB 226.

97 *Blowes*, above note 92.

able to set-off the two claims, with the result that B's claim against C is extinguished and C's claim against B is reduced from $2,000 to $1,000. C can prove for this amount in B's bankruptcy and obtain a *pro rata* share of the assets. C will therefore recover $100.[98]

The *BIA* expressly preserves the right to claim set-off in respect of all claims made against the estate of the bankrupt and also to all actions instituted by the trustee for the recovery of debts due in bankruptcy.[99] The provision does not define the conditions when a right to set-off is available but instead leaves this to the general law applicable in the province. The common law did not permit the mutual setting off of claims. The right of set-off was created by statute as well as by the intervention equity. The former is called legal set-off, and it was created by the English statutes of set-off.[100] The latter is referred to as equitable set-off. The right to set-off can also arise by virtue of an agreement between the parties. This is referred to as contractual set-off.

Legal set-off is available in respect of claims that are unconnected with or independent of one another. For this reason, it is also referred to as "independent set-off" in England. It is available only if both the claims are debts or ascertainable amounts at the date of the bankruptcy. A party who has a claim for unliquidated damages against a bankrupt, therefore, cannot claim this kind of set-off in relation to a money claim owing to the trustee. The fact that a debt is payable in the future does not prevent legal set-off.[101] But, if the debt does not arise until some act is performed or some condition is satisfied other than the simple passage of time, then it is not possible to claim a legal set-off in respect of this future debt.[102] There must also be a mutuality of parties in order to

---

98 This assumes the same 10 percent rate of recovery in the bankruptcy. In fact, this figure will usually not be exactly the same. The exercise of a right of set-off changes the total assets available for distribution as well as the total provable claims. However, if the total assets and total liabilities are significantly greater than the amount of the set-off, there will not be very much of a change.

99 *BIA*, s 97(3).

100 *Insolvent Debtors Relief Act, 1728*, 2 Geo II, c 22, s 13, and *Set-Off Act, 1734*, 8 Geo II, c 24, s 5.

101 *Coopers & Lybrand Ltd v Lumberland Building Materials Ltd* (1983), 50 CBR (NS) 150 (BCSC). The courts originally required that both debts be in existence and payable at the time the action was commenced. See *Richards v James* (1848), 2 Ex 471. However, the requirement was subsequently relaxed so that it was sufficient that the debt became payable before the judgment was rendered. See *Burman v Rosin* (1915), 26 DLR 790 (Ont SC).

102 In *Re Associated Investors of Canada Ltd* (1989), 76 CBR (NS) 185 (Alta QB), the court held that legal set-off was not available in respect of demand loans that did not have any set repayment terms since the debt was conditional upon a demand for payment.

exercise the right of legal set-off. In other words, the cross-claims must be between the same parties and in the same right.

Upon the occurrence of the bankruptcy, there is a change of mutuality. A debt that arises after the bankruptcy cannot be set-off against a debt that arises before the bankruptcy.[103] This is illustrated in the following example. Suppose that C owes $1,000 to B prior to B's bankruptcy. After the bankruptcy, B becomes indebted to C for $500. C cannot set-off the two claims, since they are not mutual debts. The debt for $1,000 is no longer owed to B but has vested in the trustee. The converse also holds true. Assume that it is now B who is indebted to C prior to the bankruptcy. C cannot exercise legal set-off in respect of a debt payable to B that arises after B's bankruptcy. The claim that C holds has been transformed on bankruptcy into a claim against the trustee for a dividend to be paid out of the bankrupt estate. The requirement of mutuality of debts is lacking.[104]

The bankruptcy of the debtor does not destroy a right of set-off that is available at the date of bankruptcy.[105] However, it will operate so as to prevent legal set-off in respect of a contingent claim that does not become a debt until after the bankruptcy. Assume that C has given a personal guarantee in respect of a debt owed by B, the bankrupt. C is also indebted to B. If C has not been called upon to pay on the guarantee at the date of the bankruptcy, the obligation remains a contingent liability and cannot be set-off against the indebtedness that C owes to B.[106]

The requirement of mutuality also prevents a claimant from exercising set-off in respect of claims that have been acquired from other creditors after the bankruptcy. In this scenario, C owes a debt to B. After B's bankruptcy, C obtains an assignment of a claim of another creditor against B. The claim acquired by C is a claim against the trustee for a dividend to be paid out of the bankrupt estate. There is no mutuality, and therefore legal set-off is unavailable.[107]

The most significant difference between legal set-off and equitable set-off is that the latter allows an unliquidated claim to be set-off against a debt or other liquidated claim.[108] For this reason, equitable set-off is also referred to as "transaction set-off" in England. In order

---

103 *Re Air Canada* (2003), 45 CBR (4th) 13 (Ont SCJ); *Coopers & Lybrand Ltd v Lumberland Building Materials Ltd* (1983), 50 CBR (NS) 150 (BCSC).

104 *Re Kryspin* (1981), 40 CBR (NS) 67 (Ont HCJ).

105 *Re Paquet* (1997), 46 CBR (3d) 249 (Alta QB).

106 *Mitchell, Houghton Ltd v Mitchell, Houghton (Que.) Ltd* (1970), 14 CBR (NS) 301 (Ont HCJ).

107 *Northern Electric Co v Auto Service Co* (1961), 2 CBR (NS) 218 (Nfld SC).

108 *Telford v Holt*, [1987] 2 SCR 193.

to assert equitable set-off, it is neither necessary nor sufficient that the two claims arise out of the same contract.[109] Equitable set-off is available if the transactions or dealings are so inseparably connected that it would be manifestly unjust to allow the plaintiff to enforce payment without taking into consideration the cross-claim.[110] Equitable set-off is illustrated in the following example. A enters a contract with B under which B agrees to construct a piece of heavy machinery and A agrees to pay for it. The construction is completed and payment is due, but A has a claim against B for defective work. A is able to set-off its unliquidated claim for damages against B's claim for the money that is due.[111] This right of equitable set-off is unaffected by the bankruptcy of B.

Contractual set-off is derived from an agreement between the party that expressly provides the extent to which obligations may be set-off against each other. For example, the contract may provide that a party has a right to set-off any unliquidated claims against debts owing in respect of claims that are not closely related and lack mutuality.[112] This would give the claimant a right of set-off in circumstances in which neither legal nor equitable set-off would be available. A contractual right of set-off may be vulnerable to invalidation as contravening the *pari passu* principle, but will be effective in respect of set-offs that are completed before bankruptcy proceedings are initiated.[113] Instead of expanding a right of set-off, the contract may narrow or eliminate it. In such a case, a trustee can enforce the provision and prevent the other party from asserting legal or equitable set-off in the bankruptcy.[114]

9) Non-realizable Property

A trustee may form the opinion that an asset of the debtor that has vested in the trustee is incapable of being realized. In such a case, the trustee must return the property to the debtor before the trustee ap-

---

109 *Coba Industries Ltd v Millie's Holdings (Canada) Ltd* (1985), 20 DLR (4th) 689 (BCCA).

110 *Canada (Attorney General) v Confederation Life Insurance Co* (2002), 39 CBR (4th) 182 (Ont SCJ). In Canada, there are several different formulations of the test that is to be employed to determine if a sufficiently close connection exists. See K Palmer, *The Law of Set-Off in Canada* (Aurora, ON: Canada Law Book, 1993) at 89–94.

111 *Newfoundland v Newfoundland Railway* (1888), 13 App Cas 199 (PC).

112 See *Re Brunswick Chrysler Plymouth Ltd* (2004), 11 CBR (5th) 10 (NBQB).

113 See Chapter 9, Section B(5).

114 *Columbia Trust Co (Liquidator of) v Nasby's Auctioneering (1985) Ltd* (1991), 10 CBR (3d) 298 (Alta QB); *National Foundation for Hepatitis C (Trustee of) v GWE Group Inc* (1999), 8 CBR (4th) 281 (Alta QB).

plies for a discharge.[115] If a trustee determines that it is inappropriate to bring a lawsuit after weighing its costs and benefits, the right of action is considered to be an asset incapable of realization and must be returned to the debtor.[116] If the trustee fails to act, the debtor may seek an order for the return of the property.[117] There is not an automatic revesting of unrealizable property in the debtor upon the discharge of the debtor.[118]

Sometimes a trustee obtains a discharge without either realizing on the property or returning it to the debtor. If the trustee has come to the conclusion that the property is unrealizable, the trustee is under an obligation to reconvey the property to the debtor. The trustee cannot thereafter seek to realize on the property if the trustee is mistaken and the property turns out to be more valuable than earlier thought to be the case.[119] A trustee may also be precluded from realizing on the property if the trustee has misled the debtor into thinking that the trustee would not seek to realize the property.[120] The trustee will not be prevented from realizing against the asset if the debtor has misled the trustee as to the existence of the property or its value.[121]

C. NON-DIVISIBLE PROPERTY

The *BIA* identifies two classes of property — trust property and exempt property — as property that is not divisible among the bankrupt's creditors.[122] At one time it was thought that this meant that these assets did not vest in the trustee in bankruptcy.[123] This view is no longer tenable following the decision of the Supreme Court of Canada in *Ramgotra*

115 *BIA*, s 40(1).

116 *MLA Northern Contracting Ltd v LeBrun* (2007), 39 CBR (5th) 95 (Ont SCJ).

117 *BIA*, s 40(2). The application cannot be brought by a third party, even if the party is the sole shareholder and director of a corporate debtor. See *Petro Canada Inc v 490300 Ontario Inc* (1989), 74 CBR (NS) 33 (Ont HCJ).

118 *Canadian Imperial Bank of Commerce v Woodgrove Hills Developments Ltd* (1982), 43 CBR (NS) 239 (Ont HCJ); *Alsask Farm & Ranch Supply Ltd v Texaco Canada Inc* (1989), 74 CBR (NS) 73 (Sask QB).

119 *Re Shelson* (2004), 4 CBR (5th) 76 (Ont CA); *Zemlak v Zemlak* (1987), 66 CBR (NS) 1 (Sask CA) [*Zemlak*].

120 *Marino (Trustee of) v Marino* (2004), 2 CBR. (5th) 290 (Ont CA).

121 *Rocher v H & M Diamond & Associates* (2003), 43 CBR (4th) 134 (Ont CA).

122 *BIA*, s 67(1).

123 See *Gano*, above note 73.

(Trustee of) v North American Life Assurance Co.[124] The Court held that property designated as non-divisible property vests in the trustee in bankruptcy, but that the property cannot be liquidated and distributed to the creditors who prove their claims in the bankruptcy. Because these assets are incapable of realization by the trustee, they must be returned to the bankrupt before the trustee applies for a discharge from his or her duties.[125]

This theory can produce difficulties for bankrupts and third parties in respect of dealings with the property. There is a period following the bankruptcy and before a transfer back to the bankrupt during which the trustee in bankruptcy holds legal title to the assets. During this period, the bankrupt does not possess any right to the asset and also has no power to transfer or otherwise deal with it. This creates a problem for a bankrupt who wishes to deal with exempt property following the bankruptcy. As the exempt property is vested in the trustee, the bankrupt has no right or power to transfer title to the asset to the transferee. To avoid this problem, the bankrupt should obtain a disclaimer or other document revesting property in the bankrupt before dealing with the property.[126] Problems can also arise where the bankrupt holds the property in trust for a beneficiary. Upon bankruptcy, legal title to the trust property vests in the trustee in bankruptcy. The bankrupt is therefore unable to administer the trust for the beneficiary until the trustee in bankruptcy transfers the property back to the bankrupt. In Ontario, the bankruptcy of a trustee is an event that permits the non-judicial replacement of the trustee.[127] In any event, the court has the inherent jurisdiction to appoint or replace a trustee and this has often been codified in legislation.[128] The trustee in bankruptcy should transfer the trust property to the new trustee if one has been appointed.

1) Trust Property

A trust is an equitable obligation that is imposed on a person (the trustee) to hold and administer the subject matter of the trust for the benefit of another (the beneficiary). The subject matter of the trust can be a property right or it can be a personal right. For example, a person who

---

124 (1996), 37 CBR (3d) 141, (*sub nom Royal Bank of Canada v North American Life Assurance Co*) [1996] 1 SCR 325.

125 *BIA*, s 40.

126 *Ibid*, s 20(1). And see *Re Firestone* (2003), 42 CBR (4th) 34 (Alta QB).

127 *Trustee Act*, RSO 1990, c T.23, s 3.

128 See, for example, *Trustee Act*, RSA 2000, c T-8, s 16. And see *Newbank Group Inc (Trustee of) v Handelman* (1991), 6 CBR (3d) 240 (Ont Ct Gen Div).

is owed money by another can create a trust of that right in favour of a beneficiary. If the person who is owed the money goes bankrupt, the personal right of action to recover the debt is not available to the creditors who prove their claims in the bankruptcy.

In order for a beneficiary to assert a trust on a bankruptcy of the trustee, the subject matter of the trust or its traceable value still must be in existence. A beneficiary will be unable to identify the trust *res* if the trustee has wrongfully disposed of the asset and the proceeds of disposition are untraceable. This does not mean that the beneficiary is without a remedy. The beneficiary has an action against the trustee for breach of trust, and this claim can be proven in the bankruptcy of the trustee. In doing so, the beneficiary will share *pari passu* with all the other creditors who have personal claims against the bankrupt.

Trusts can arise through a number of different means. Many come into existence by virtue of an intention to create a trust. These are called express trusts, and the persons who create them are called settlors. Others come into existence by operation of law. These can be either resulting trusts or constructive trusts. Finally, there are some trusts that are created by legislation. These are referred to as statutory trusts. The use of "implied trust" as a category of trust is not recommended because of the ambiguity of the term. It can be used to refer to intentional trusts where the intention is derived from the circumstances, but it can also be used to refer to trusts that arise by operation of law.

a) Express Trusts

In order to create an express trust, there must be a clear intention to create a trust; the subject matter of the trust must be certain; and the persons intended to be the beneficiaries must be clearly indicated.[129] These are referred to as the three certainties. If any one of these conditions is not satisfied, the trust will fail. The trust must also be completely constituted. If the settlor goes bankrupt before the property is transferred to the trustee, the trust will not have been completely constituted and the creditors of the settlor rather than the beneficiaries of the trust will obtain the benefit of the property. A failure of a trust does not necessarily mean that the trustee in bankruptcy will be able to distribute the property to the creditors. If a settlor transfers property to the bankrupt in trust for another and the trust fails, the bankrupt will hold the property under a resulting trust for the settlor. In order

---

129 *Abakhan & Associates Inc (Trustee of) v 554925 BC Ltd* (2004), 7 CBR (5th) 8 (BCSC).

to be recognized in bankruptcy, the trust must also comply with any formalities, such as the *Statute of Frauds*, that are imposed by law in respect of the transaction.

An agent who has the power to sell the property of the principal to a buyer becomes the owner of the sale proceeds. The obligation to pay money to the principal is merely a debt and not a trust. However, if the parties agree that the monies are to be held in trust, the requisite intention to create a trust exists.[130] Disputes will often arise over whether the parties in fact came to such an agreement. The use of the word "trust" is neither necessary nor sufficient in order to show an intention to create it.[131] Customers who make prepayments in respect of future deliveries of goods do not generally intend to create a trust. Despite this, a seller can unilaterally create a trust to protect the customer's prepayments even though the customers may be unaware of its existence.[132]

The subject matter of the trust must be adequately defined. Sometimes there is a problem in identifiability that manifests itself at the outset. A good example of this can be found in cases where a party purports to hold property in trust for another, but the property cannot be ascertained. Investors who have been given certificates that acknowledge their ownership of gold bullion or wine have discovered that they do not have any legal or equitable interest in the inventory of an insolvent dealer who has not set aside and appropriated items to the individual contracts with the investors.[133] In other cases the problem arises when, after a trust is properly constituted, the identity of the property is lost and there is no substitute property into which its value can be traced.[134]

b) Resulting Trusts

There are two situations where a resulting trust will typically arise. The first is where an express trust fails in whole or in part. In this case, the trustee will hold the assets on a resulting trust for the settlor. The

---

130 *Canadian Pacific Airlines Ltd v Canadian Imperial Bank of Commerce* (1987), 71 CBR (NS) 40 (Ont HCJ).

131 *Re Ontario Worldair Ltd* (1983), 45 CBR (NS) 116 (Ont HCJ), aff'd (1983), 8 CBR (NS) 112 (Ont CA).

132 *Re Kayford Ltd*, [1975] 1 All ER 604.

133 *Re London Wine Co (Shippers) Ltd* (1975), [1986] PCC 121; *Re Goldcorp Exchange Ltd*, [1995] 1 AC 74 (PC). But see *Hunter v Moss*, [1994] 1 WLR 452 (CA), which held that a declaration of a trust of 50 of the 950 shares held by the settlor was not uncertain.

134 *Re Graphicshoppe Ltd* (2005), 15 CBR (5th) 207 (Ont CA).

second situation that gives rise to a resulting trust occurs when a person transfers property gratuitously[135] to another or pays the purchase price to a vendor and directs that it be transferred into the name of another.[136] In this case, there is said to be a presumption of a resulting trust. The presumption can be rebutted by evidence that shows that a gift was intended. The presumption of resulting trust does not operate in all cases. It does not apply to a gift from a husband to a wife or from a father to a child. In some provinces, the presumption of advancement between husband and wife has been replaced with a presumption of resulting trust.[137]

It has been said that these two types of resulting trusts arise for essentially different reasons.[138] In the failed trust cases, it is said to arise automatically by operation of law without regard to the intention of the settlor ("automatic resulting trusts"). In the apparent gift cases, it is said to operate on the basis of the donor's presumed intention to create a trust for himself or herself ("presumed intention resulting trusts").

Some commentators argue that a single unifying theory explains both situations. A resulting trust is said to arise in response to the receipt of an asset by someone who was not intended to receive it as a gift.[139] If this theory is accepted as correct, it may mean that all trusts that arise by operation of law as a response to unjust enrichment should be characterized as resulting trusts rather than constructive trusts. The transferor in these cases does not intend that the recipient should become the beneficial owner of the asset, and this activates the resulting trust.[140] This theory has also been used to explain *Quistclose* trusts.[141] This kind of trust arises when a lender makes a loan to a borrower but imposes a

135 *Pecore v Pecore*, 2007 SCC 17.

136 *Nishi v Rascal Trucking Ltd*, 2013 SCC 33.

137 See, for example, *The Family Property Act*, SS 1997, c F-6.3, s 50.

138 *Vandervell v Inland Revenue Commissioners*, [1967] 2 AC 291 (HL).

139 R Chambers, "Resulting Trusts in Canada" (2000) 38 *Alberta Law Review* 378 at 387; P Millett, "Restitution and Constructive Trusts" (1998) 114 *Law Quarterly Review* 399 at 410: "the development of a coherent doctrine of proprietary restitution for subtractive unjust enrichment is impossible unless it is based on the resulting trust as traditionally understood."

140 See M McInnes, *The Canadian Law of Unjust Enrichment and Restitution* (Markham, ON: LexisNexis Canada, 2014) at 1350–364.

141 *Twinsectra Ltd v Yardley*, [2002] 2 AC 164 (HL). However, a majority of the law lords regarded the trust as an express trust. See also W Swadling, ed, *The Quistclose Trust: Critical Essays* (Oxford: Hart, 2004). See also *Cliffs Over Maple Bay Investments Ltd (Re)*, 2011 BCCA 180; *Ontario (Minister of Training, Colleges and Universities) v Two Feathers Forest Products LP*, 2013 ONCA 598.

restriction on the use of the funds.[142] The recipient holds the funds on a resulting trust if the purpose of the loan fails because the lender does not intend to give the recipient the beneficial ownership of the money.

c) Constructive Trusts

Constructive trusts arise by operation of law, but they respond to a number of different events. The constructive trust is used to reverse an unjust enrichment. At one time it was thought that this was its primary function,[143] but it is now accepted that it responds to other events as well.[144] Constructive trusts also arise in order to compel a person to give up property acquired as a result of wrongdoing[145] or in disparate circumstances involving attempts to transfer assets. As an example of the latter, a vendor of land under an agreement for sale holds the land on a constructive trust in favour of the purchaser until its conveyance to the purchaser. Constructive trusts arise, too, as a means of enforcing secret trusts, mutual wills, and oral agreements to sell land where there is non-compliance with writing requirements.[146] In these instances, the purpose of the constructive trust is to perfect the intentions of the person who is attempting to transfer the property. This last category of constructive trusts rarely leads to controversy in bankruptcy. When the necessary facts have been proven, the trust comes into existence and plays its role. Difficulties are more likely to be encountered in respect of constructive trusts that respond to unjust enrichment and wrongdoing. These are sometimes said to be remedial in nature, and there is considerable uncertainty as to when a court will declare their existence in an insolvency setting and the extent to which their creation depends upon the exercise of discretion by the court.

A threshold question concerns the time when the constructive trust comes into existence. Does it arise when the facts essential for its creation have occurred? Or is it a remedy that arises when a court makes an order declaring its existence? Under bankruptcy law, a trust is effective only if it exists at the time of the bankruptcy. The majority of

---

142 *Barclays Bank Ltd v Quistclose Investments Ltd*, [1968] 3 All ER 651 (HL); *Gignac, Sutts v National Bank of Canada* (1987), 5 CBR (4th) 44 (Ont HCJ).

143 *Becker v Pettkus*, [1980] 2 SCR 834.

144 *Soulos v Korkontzilas*, [1997] 2 SCR 217.

145 *Ibid.*

146 See R Chambers, "The Constructive Trust in Canada" (1999) 37 *Alberta Law Review* 173. A secret trust arises when a person is given a testamentary gift but has agreed to use it for the benefit of another. Mutual wills involve wills that mirror each other and that are subject to an agreement between the parties that their wills shall have stipulated provisions in them when they die.

the Supreme Court of Canada in *Rawluk v Rawluk*[147] held that the trust arises when the duty to make restitution arises. The minority took the view that it arises when a court declares it but that it has a retroactive effect.[148] On either view of the matter, the fact that a court has not yet declared a constructive trust to exist does not prevent it from being effective in bankruptcy.

Although a constructive trust is used as a remedy to compel disgorgement of property obtained through wrongdoing, not all breaches of duty are so protected. Constructive trusts can arise where the wrong is a breach of confidence or a breach of fiduciary duty[149] or where the gain is obtained through the deliberate killing of the victim.[150] Uncertainty over the potential availability of the remedy arises because the categories of fiduciary relationship are not closed and have been found in a wide variety of commercial and non-commercial situations.[151] The property obtained by the wrongdoer must be identifiable or traceable into other property.[152] It cannot be imposed on the other assets of the wrongdoer.[153]

The Supreme Court of Canada in *Soulos v Korkontzilas*[154] indicated that, in order for a constructive trust to be imposed as a redress for wrongdoing, the following four conditions should be satisfied. There should be: (1) a breach of an equitable obligation; (2) assets obtained as a result of deemed or actual agency activities of the wrongdoer in breach of the obligation; (3) a legitimate reason for seeking a proprietary remedy; and (4) no factors that would render imposition of a constructive trust unjust, such as prejudice to the interests of intervening creditors.

These four conditions greatly diminish the likelihood of a constructive trust in cases where the gain is not derived from property

---

147 [1990] 1 SCR 70, Cory J.

148 *Ibid*, McLachlin J. See also *Re Croteau* (1985), 47 RFL (2d) 45 (Ont HCJ); *Bedard v Schell*, [1987] 4 WWR 699 (Sask QB).

149 *Lac Minerals Ltd v International Corona Resources Ltd*, [1989] 2 SCR 574.

150 *Schobelt v Barber* (1966), 60 DLR (2d) 519 (Ont HCJ).

151 See J McCamus, "Prometheus Unbound: Fiduciary Obligation in the Supreme Court of Canada" (1997) 28 *Canadian Business Law Journal* 107.

152 *AG for Hong Kong v Reid*, [1994] 1 AC 324 (PC).

153 *Barnabe v Touhey* (1995), 37 CBR (3d) 73 (Ont CA); *Ontario (Director, Real Estate & Business Brokers Act) v NRS Mississauga Inc* (2003), 40 CBR (4th) 127 (Ont CA).

154 Above note 144. This formulation was derived from R Goode, "Property and Unjust Enrichment" in Andrew Burrows, ed, *Essays on the Law of Restitution* (Oxford: Clarendon Press, 1991) 215.

previously held by the plaintiff.[155] The requirement that the asset be obtained as a result of a deemed or actual agency activity means that the gain must have arisen out of the use of the assets, information, or resources that were supposed to be applied for the benefit of the person claiming the remedy.[156] This would rule out its use in cases where a fiduciary accepts a bribe. The requirement that there be a legitimate reason for a proprietary remedy means that the plaintiff must show that a personal right to seek an accounting of the profits is insufficient.[157]

The real knockout blow is in the fourth requirement. A proprietary remedy will almost inevitably have the effect of prejudicing creditors where the wrongdoer is insolvent (unless it involves exempt property or property that is unavailable to creditors), and this makes it highly unlikely that it will be imposed in a bankruptcy context.[158] This does not mean that the person to whom the duty is owed has no recourse in the bankruptcy of the wrongdoer. The right to seek an accounting of the wrongfully gained profit is a claim that can be proven in the bankruptcy. An inability to obtain a proprietary remedy simply means that the claimant will be required to share *pari passu* with the other creditors.

The conditions under which a court will impose a constructive trust to reverse an unjust enrichment are necessarily different from those that apply to wrongdoing, since unjust enrichment is premised on receipt of a gain rather than breach of a duty. In order for a cause of action in unjust enrichment to be made out, it must be shown that: (1) the defendant received an enrichment; (2) the plaintiff suffered a corresponding deprivation; and (3) there is an absence of any juristic reason for the enrichment. If these elements are established, a court must decide upon an appropriate remedy. The usual remedy is for the court to give the plaintiff judgment for the value of the enrichment. If the court determines that a monetary award is inadequate for some reason, it may impose a constructive trust.[159] A classic example of this occurs in the case of a mistaken payment. If the money paid by mistake has been retained or can be traced to other property, a court may impose a

---

155 Goode, *ibid* at 219. In other words, these limitations on availability do not apply where the plaintiff claims a constructive trust on proceeds received by the wrongdoer derived from a dealing with the plaintiff's property.

156 *Ibid* at 239. And see Chambers, above note 146 at 182.

157 Goode, above note 154 at 244.

158 *Ibid* at 240–44.

159 *Peter v Beblow*, above note 18.

constructive trust that compels the recipient to hold it on behalf of the mistaken payor.[160]

It is difficult to predict when a court will impose a constructive trust as a remedy to reverse an unjust enrichment. Courts have been well aware that the declaration of a constructive trust gives a claimant an ability to "jump the queue" over other unsecured creditors in the bankruptcy.[161] Despite this, there are occasions where they are willing to disregard the bankruptcy scheme of distribution.[162]

Academic commentators have attempted to provide a principled framework. Professor Chambers has argued that two minimum conditions must be satisfied: (1) the unjust enrichment must be an asset capable of being the subject matter of a trust; and (2) the defendant did not acquire the full beneficial use of the asset before the unjust enrichment arose.[163] The first requirement means that gains involving services could never give rise to a constructive trust to reverse unjust enrichment.[164] The second requirement restricts the availability of the remedy where the claimant intended that ownership should pass to the recipient but there is a subsequent event that produces the unjust enrichment.[165] For example, a claimant who terminates a contract for breach and seeks to recover the price for failure of consideration is not entitled to a constructive trust, even if the money can be located.

Other commentators have argued that proprietary restitution should not be available when the claimant has accepted the risk of the defendant's insolvency.[166] This involves a determination whether the claimant is analogous to an unsecured creditor who takes this risk or to a secured

---

160 *Chase Manhattan Bank NA v Israel-British Bank (London) Ltd*, [1979] 3 All ER 1025 (Ch D) [*Chase Manhattan*].

161 *Baltman v Coopers & Lybrand Ltd* (1996), 43 CBR (3d) 33 at para 48 (Ont Ct Gen Div) [*Baltman*].

162 *Re Ellingsen* (2000), 19 CBR (4th) 166 (BCCA).

163 Chambers, above note 146 at 208.

164 This would appear to run contrary to the view of the Supreme Court of Canada that a constructive trust may be awarded in respect of services so long as the claimant can demonstrate a link or causal connection between his or her contributions and the acquisition, preservation, maintenance, or improvement of the disputed property. See *Peter v Beblow*, above note 18. In order to accept Professor Chamber's theory, it would be necessary to take the position that constructive trusts in family property are not in response to unjust enrichment, but rather operate as a perfectionary trust in response to the claimant's detrimental reliance and the defendant's intention. See McInnes, above note 140 at 1208–209.

165 See P Birks, *Unjust Enrichment* (Oxford: Oxford University Press, 2003) at 174–78.

166 A Burrows, *The Law of Restitution*, 2d ed (Croydon, UK: Butterworths LexisNexis, 2002) at 69–72. See also DM Paciocco: "The Remedial Constructive Trust: A

creditor who does not. In some cases, the failure of a sophisticated commercial party to take effective security is considered to be a factor in not awarding a proprietary remedy, but in other cases this has not precluded a declaration of a constructive trust.[167]

Richard Calnan has taken the most restrictive view. He argues that *Chase Manhattan*[168] was wrongly decided and that only a personal remedy should be available except in those instances where the claimant is given a right of rescission.[169] In these cases, the claimants remedy is limited to rescission, and there is no role for the constructive trust to expand or augment this right as it undermines bankruptcy law's scheme of distribution, introduces uncertainty, and places courts in the difficult position of having to rank creditors by evaluating their respective worthiness.[170]

Unless and until a principled approach is agreed upon and implemented by courts in Canada, the question as to whether a remedial constructive trust will be awarded will remain perplexing, and outcomes will be uncertain as they will ultimately depend upon the application of vague notions of discretion and remedial flexibility.

d) Statutory Trusts

Statutory trusts are created by federal and provincial legislation as a means of enhancing the claims held by certain classes of claimants. They are most commonly created in respect of claims by the Crown for the remittance of taxes, by workers' compensation boards for unpaid assessments, and by unpaid employees for unpaid wages. The statutes provide that the person owing the obligation is deemed to hold property in trust for the claimant. In most cases, the person will not actually hold the property separate and apart, and therefore the statutes typically contain additional language that deems the property to be kept separate and apart. Although these provisions are effective outside bankruptcy, their effectiveness within bankruptcy has been greatly limited.

The *BIA* provides that trust property is not divisible among the creditors. The Supreme Court of Canada in *British Columbia v Hen-*

Principled Basis for Priorities Over Creditors" (1989) 68 *Canadian Bar Review* 315 at 351.

167 Compare *Re Ellingsen*, above note 162, with *Baltman*, above note 161.

168 Above note 160.

169 R Calnan, *Proprietary Rights and Insolvency* (Oxford: Oxford University Press, 2010) at 150.

170 *Ibid* at 39–40.

frey Samson Belair Ltd[171] held that statutory deemed trusts that lack the common law attributes of a trust are not to be regarded as trusts for the purposes of this provision. The decision only purported to cover deemed trusts that attempted to elevate the ranking afforded by the *BIA* to preferred creditors. On this view, the decision was not inconsistent with the Supreme Court of Canada in *John MM Troup Ltd v Royal Bank of Canada*,[172] which upheld the constitutional validity of a deemed trust created by builders' lien legislation. However, subsequent decisions have since interpreted the decision as applicable to all statutory deemed trusts.[173] As a consequence, courts have held that *Troup* is no longer authoritative and that deemed trusts created by builders' liens legislation are ineffective in bankruptcy unless the ordinary requirements for creation of a trust are satisfied.[174] In most cases, this will render the statutory trust ineffective because the property will either not have been identified from the outset or will have subsequently been commingled so as to be untraceable.[175] As a result, *Henfrey* continues to be relevant in respect of federal and provincial statutes that create statutory trusts in favour of persons other than the Crown. However, the *BIA* was amended in 1992, and the status of statutory trusts in favour of the Crown is now specifically addressed in the Act.

The *BIA* provides that property held in trust for the Crown shall not be regarded as a trust "unless it would be so regarded in the absence of that statutory provision."[176] This merely codifies the decision of the Supreme Court in relation to Crown claims. However, a major exception is carved out in respect of statutory trusts that are created in respect of source deductions[177] (i.e., income tax, Canada Pension Plan [CPP], and Employment Insurance [EI] deductions from the pay of employees that have not been remitted). These statutory trusts are therefore fully effective in bankruptcy and give the Crown the right to take possession or control of the property or their proceeds from the trustee in bankruptcy.

---

171 [1989] 2 SCR 24 [*Henfrey*].

172 [1962] SCR 487 [*Troup*].

173 See *Re Ivaco Inc* (2006), 25 CBR (5th) 176 (Ont CA); *Bassano Growers Ltd v Diamond S Produce Ltd (Trustee of)* (1997), 6 CBR (4th) 188 (Alta CA) [*Bassano*]; *Points of Call Holidays Ltd (Re)* (1991), 5 CBR (3d) 299 (BCSC).

174 *Iona Contractors Ltd (Re)*, 2014 ABQB 347; *Royal Bank of Canada v Atlas Block Co*, 2014 ONSC 3062; *Factory Window and Door Ltd (Re)* (1995), 34 CBR (3d) 196 (Sask QB).

175 *Bassano*, above note 173.

176 *BIA*, s 67(2).

177 *Ibid*, s 67(3).

2) Exempt Property

The *BIA* provides that exempt property is not divisible among the creditors. For the most part, the *BIA* does not create classes of exempt assets but instead incorporates the exemptions that are created by provincial and federal statutes. In respect of certain types of assets, such as an RRSP, the *BIA* creates an exemption for an asset that otherwise might not be exempt under provincial law.

a) Provincial and Federal Exemption Statutes

Provincial judgment enforcement law provides that certain types of property are exempt from seizure or other judgment enforcement remedy. The purpose of the exemption is to permit the debtor to preserve his or her independence and self-sufficiency so that the cost of the continued maintenance of the debtor does not fall to society.[178] For this reason, exemptions are given only to individuals and not to artificial entities such as corporations. There is considerable variation in the list of exempt assets among the various provinces. Provincial law provides an exemption for certain types of goods that are considered necessary for the maintenance of the individual or that are required by the individual to earn a livelihood. The residence is also exempt in the western provinces and the territories. The exemption provisions often contain a monetary limit that defines the maximum exemption that the debtor can claim in respect of the property. Provincial and federal statutes also typically provide an exemption for certain pensions and future retirement plans, although not all such plans are afforded an exemption. Federal law additionally provides an exemption in respect of real and personal property situated on a First Nations reserve.[179]

Some provinces adopt a principle of universal exigibility under which a judgment creditor has an enforcement remedy against all real and personal property of the debtor unless the property is specifically afforded an exemption by legislation. In the other provinces, where a principle of universal exigibility does not operate, there are gaps in the judgment enforcement remedies, with the result that creditors may be unable to proceed against certain types of assets. This failure of provincial law to afford a judgment enforcement remedy against the property does not give it an exempt status under bankruptcy law. In order to be

---

178 *Re Pearson* (1997), 46 CBR (3d) 257 (Alta QB); *Investors Group Trust Co v Eckhoff*, [2008] 8 WWR 306 (Sask CA).

179 *Indian Act*, RSC, 1985, c I-5, s 89.

exempt, the legislation must specifically render the property immune from judgment enforcement measures.[180]

Bankruptcy law provides that property that is exempt from execution or seizure under the laws of a province where the property is situated and within which the bankrupt resides is not available to satisfy the claims of the creditors.[181] This incorporates exemptions created under federal legislation as well as under provincial legislation. Although provincial law also provides an exemption from garnishment in respect of wages or salary earned by a debtor, these exemptions are not available to the bankrupt. Instead, the surplus income provisions of the *BIA* create an alternative means of ensuring that there is sufficient post-bankruptcy income to maintain the bankrupt and his or her dependants.[182]

The time for determining the exempt status of the property is at the date of the bankruptcy; i.e., the date of the bankruptcy order, the date of filing of an assignment, or the date of the event that gives rise to a deemed assignment.[183] The bankrupt may acquire exempt property after the date of bankruptcy. This can occur when the bankrupt uses surplus income to buy exempt property, or when the bankrupt obtains a transfer of a spouse's interest in a residence under a matrimonial property order after the date of bankruptcy but before discharge of the bankrupt. In this case, the exemption will be determined at the date the property is acquired by the bankrupt.[184]

b) Pre-bankruptcy Disposition of Exempt Property

If the bankrupt sold an exempt asset prior to the bankruptcy and received proceeds, the bankrupt's right to claim an exemption in respect of the proceeds will depend upon whether the proceeds are afforded an exempt status under the applicable exemption law.

On this question, exemption laws fall into two patterns. In the first, the exemption statute does not specifically provide for an exemption for proceeds of the property. Here, courts have drawn a distinction between a voluntary sale and a forced sale of the exempt property. If the debtor voluntarily sells the property, the exemption is lost.[185] If the property is sold by virtue of a forced sale, the debtor can claim

---

180 *Ranch des Prairies Ltée (Prairie Ranch Ltd) v Bank of Montreal* (1988), 69 CBR (NS) 180 (Man CA).

181 *BIA*, s 67(1)(b).

182 See Section D(2), below in this chapter.

183 *BIA*, s 2 "time of bankruptcy." And see *Re Neuls* (1985), 56 CBR (NS) 132 (Sask CA); *Re Davis* (1991), 6 CBR (3d) 100 (Alta CA).

184 See *Re Monteith* (2004), 6 CBR (5th) 47 (Sask CA); *Knight (Re)*, 2012 ABQB 759.

185 *Alberta Treasury Branches v Wilson* (1996), 38 CBR (3d) 245 (Alta CA).

an exemption in respect of the proceeds.[186] In the second pattern, the exemption statute specifically provides for an exemption in respect of the proceeds. In Alberta, for example, the proceeds of a sale of exempt property are themselves exempt for sixty days from the day of the sale if the proceeds are not intermingled with other funds of the debtor.[187] The question under either pattern of statute is the same: Were the proceeds exempt under the applicable exemption law at the date of the bankruptcy?

c) Post-bankruptcy Disposition of Exempt Property

The determination of the exempt status of the property is made at the date of the bankruptcy. Thereafter, the provincial or federal exemption law has no further application, and events that would ordinarily result in a loss of an exempt status under the exemption law are no longer relevant. For example, a voluntary sale of exempt property ordinarily results in a loss of the exemption in respect of the proceeds of sale under exemption laws that do not specifically create an exemption for proceeds. Despite this, a post-bankruptcy sale of the exempt asset does not deprive the bankrupt of an exemption in respect of the proceeds. Although the *BIA* is silent on this question, courts have held that, as a matter of bankruptcy law, the proceeds are exempt even though the bankrupt voluntarily entered into the transaction.[188] The rationale for this rule is that the law should facilitate the reorganization of the bankrupt's affairs by permitting the bankrupt to sell exempt property in order to support his or her family or to reduce expenses.[189]

The same analysis is applied in respect of exemption laws that specifically provide for an exemption of the proceeds of sale. Suppose that the bankrupt held an exempt asset at the date of bankruptcy but subsequently sold it. Provincial law provides a sixty-day exemption in respect of proceeds of exempt property so long as the fund is segregated. This provincial exemption rule does not apply. The asset was exempt at the date of the bankruptcy, and the proceeds of a post-bankruptcy disposition of the property are governed by the judicially created bank-

186 *Higgins Co v McNabb* (1979), 33 CBR (NS) 243 (Sask CA). Saskatchewan's *The Enforcement of Money Judgments Act*, SS 2010, c E-9.22, ss 94(7) and (12) has since abrogated the voluntary sale/forced sale distinction in favour of the second pattern. For a discussion of what constitutes a forced sale, see *Royal Bank of Canada v Nguyen*, 2004 BCSC 895.

187 *Civil Enforcement Regulation*, Alta Reg 276/1995, s 37(2).

188 *Re Gruber* (1993), 22 CBR (3d) 262 (Alta QB); *Pannell Kerr MacGillivray Inc v Beer* (1988), 69 CBR (NS) 203 (Man QB); *Pyne (Re)*, 2010 SKQB 201.

189 *Re Gruber*, above note 188.

ruptcy rule that gives the proceeds an exempt status. Suppose that the exempt asset was sold thirty days before the date of bankruptcy and the bankrupt kept the money segregated. The fund would be exempt under provincial law at the date of the bankruptcy, and therefore the fund would not be available to satisfy claims of the creditors in the bankruptcy.[190] A subsequent post-bankruptcy lapse of the sixty-day period would be of no consequence, since the exemption is determined at the date of the bankruptcy and provincial law thereafter does not apply.[191] However, if the sale occurred sixty-one days before the date of bankruptcy, no exemption could be claimed by the bankrupt since the funds would not have been exempt under provincial exemption law at the date of the bankruptcy.

d) Value-Capped Exemptions

Some exemptions are absolute in nature and can be claimed regardless of the value of the property. Other exemptions are subject to a maximum value limitation. Sometimes the exemption is drafted so that the exemption is available only if the value of the property is less than the specified value. In this case, the property is exempt only if the property does not exceed the specified value on the date of the bankruptcy.[192] More often, the exemption law provides that, if the property exceeds the maximum value, it can be sold and the creditor is entitled to any excess after the exempt portion is paid to the debtor from the proceeds of sale.[193] In this case, the trustee is entitled to sell the asset. The exempt portion is paid to the bankrupt and any amount in excess of the maximum exempt value is divisible among the creditors.[194]

---

190 *Re Dunbar* (1997), 47 CBR (3d) 195 (Alta QB).

191 Although there is a statement in *Re Dunbar, ibid* at para 23 that suggests that the exemption might be lost by the post-bankruptcy expiration of the sixty-day period, this conflicts with the position taken in *Re Gruber*, above note 188.

192 See *Re Fields* (2004), 2 CBR (5th) 179 (Ont CA). The Ontario *Execution Act*, RSO 1990, c E.24, s 2.6 provided an exemption for a "motor vehicle not exceeding . . . $5,000 in value." The Ontario Court of Appeal held that the exemption from seizure applies only when the total value of a car is $5,000 or less. The legislation was subsequently altered so that the exemption can be claimed up to the maximum value regardless of the total value of the motor vehicle. See SO 2006, c 19, Sch B, s 6, amending s 3 of the Act.

193 If the exemptions law does not provide for a sale of the exempt asset, the trustee is similarly unable to sell it so long as the bankrupt occupies the property. See *Re Neuls*, above note 183.

194 See *Re Pearson*, above note 178; *R v Crema* (1981), 38 CBR (NS) 18 (Ont Dist Ct); *Atwal (Re)*, 2012 BCCA 46.

A buoyant economy will sometimes produce an increase in the value of the property following the date of bankruptcy. A number of cases from Alberta have considered the effect of this on property that is subject to a value-capped exemption. An issue arose as to whether the value of the property ought to be assessed at the date of the bankruptcy or at the date that the trustee deals with the property. The predominant view is that it is to be assessed at the time that the trustee deals with the property, with the result that a post-bankruptcy increase in value is distributable among the creditors.[195]

This principle is subject to two qualifications. The first deals with the trustee's actions during the estate administration stage, while the second deals with the trustee's actions at the bankruptcy discharge stage. During the estate administration stage following the bankruptcy, the trustee must decide upon the best course of dealing with the property. If the value of the property is below the maximum exempt value, the trustee may decide to disclaim the interest and revest the interest in the bankrupt. If this is done, the trustee is bound by the disclaimer and cannot thereafter seek to recover an increase in value for the creditors.[196] Secondly, a trustee must decide upon a course of action by the time of application for discharge of the bankrupt, and cannot wait indefinitely for the property to increase in value following the bankrupt's discharge.[197] If the value can be realized for the creditors through sale of the property, the trustee should proceed to sale before the discharge of the bankrupt. Alternatively, surplus value in excess of the exemption can be taken into account in making an order for a conditional discharge,[198] or through a sale of the trustee's interest in the property to the bankrupt.[199]

---

195 *ICI Paints v Gazelle* (2001), 24 CBR (4th) 54 (Alta QB); *Re Kaabachi* (2003), 47 CBR (4th) 27 (Alta QB); *Re MacKay* (2002), 35 CBR (4th) 275 (Alta QB); *Re Piraux* (2006), 23 CBR (5th) 247 (Alta QB); *Niekamp (Re)*, 2013 SKQB 288.

196 *Re Dodyk* (2001), 26 CBR (4th) 189 (Alta QB); *Re Prior* (2003), 47 CBR (4th) 129 (BCSC).

197 *Zemlak*, above note 119. In order to pursue a claim to the non-exempt equity in a personal residence in Saskatchewan (where a trustee in bankruptcy does not have a right to sell the property), the trustee must set out the value of the non-exempt equity, indicate an intention to file a caveat, and take specific steps to inform the creditors and the bankrupt. See also *Armbruster v Armbruster (Trustee of)*, 2010 SKCA 125.

198 *Re MacKay*, above note 195.

199 *Re Rassell* (1998), 5 CBR (4th) 97 (Alta QB).

e) Exceptions to Exemptions

Some exemption statutes provide that the exemptions do not apply to certain classes of creditors. For example, exemptions legislation in Alberta provides that a debtor cannot claim an exemption in respect of writ proceedings on a judgment for the payment of support, maintenance, or alimony or arising out of an act for which the enforcement debtor has been convicted of a criminal offence.[200] As a result, the property may be exempt against some but not all of the creditors at the date of bankruptcy. In principle, the property nevertheless should be considered exempt. The exception to the exemption applies only when the excepted claimant brings the enforcement proceedings against the property.[201] This does not occur in a bankruptcy, since enforcement proceedings of all the creditors are stayed. However, to the extent that these claims are ones that are not discharged in bankruptcy,[202] the creditor may proceed against the exempt asset under provincial judgment enforcement law once the stay of proceedings is lifted.

f) GST Credit Payments

The goods and services tax (GST) credit is a tax-free quarterly payment that is directed towards individuals and families with low income. The *BIA* provides that GST tax credit payments are not available for distribution to creditors.[203] Although the payment cannot be distributed to creditors, it can be used to pay the expenses incurred in respect of the bankruptcy (i.e., the payment can be used up to the threshold at which dividends would be paid to the creditors). If there are sufficient other receipts to cover these costs, the value of the credit payment must be paid to the bankrupt.[204] The *BIA* creates an additional exemption in respect of prescribed payments relating to the essential needs of an individual.[205]

g) Registered Retirement Savings Plans

The 2009 amendments to the *BIA* created a new exemption in respect of registered retirement savings plans and registered retirement income

---

200 *Civil Enforcement Act*, RSA 2000, c C-15, s 93.

201 See *Re Harris* (1984), 51 CBR (NS) 112 (Alta QB), which held that the claim that the Crown was not subject to exemptions legislation because of a Crown prerogative did not have any application in a bankruptcy of the debtor.

202 See Chapter 10, Section G. And see *Dudgeon v Dudgeon* (1980), 34 CBR (NS) 308 (Alta QB).

203 *BIA*, s 67(1)(b.1).

204 *Re McGowan* (2003), 44 CBR (4th) 106 (Alta QB).

205 *BIA*, s 67(1)(b.2). This exemption was added in the 2007 amendments.

funds.[206] These plans and funds are designed to provide future retirement income to individuals. The exemption does not cover contributions that are made in the twelve months before the date of bankruptcy. The limitation is designed to prevent the debtor from converting non-exempt assets into an exempt asset immediately before the bankruptcy. The exception covers all contributions during this twelve-month period even if they were of a kind that were ordinarily made by the debtor and not intended to shelter the asset from creditors.

Some provinces do not provide any exemption in respect of RRSPs unless they are in the form of an insurance annuity. In these provinces, the insurance-based product will be fully exempt, while other RRSPs will be exempt only in respect of all contributions made outside the twelve-month period. Most provinces give a debtor an exemption in respect of RRSPs regardless of whether or not an insurance company issues them.[207] Unlike the exemption created by the *BIA*, statutes in those provinces do not provide an exception in respect of contributions made in the twelve-month period before the date of bankruptcy. The provincial exemption will continue to apply and the entire plan or fund will be exempt, including any contributions that are made during the twelve-month period. British Columbia provides an exemption for RRSPs but makes this subject to a one year claw-back of contributions similar to that contained in the *BIA*.[208]

D. POST-BANKRUPTCY PROPERTY

1) After-Acquired Property

The property vesting in a trustee is not limited to the assets in existence at the date of bankruptcy. It extends also to assets that are acquired by the bankrupt following the bankruptcy. The vesting of after-acquired property in the trustee occurs automatically and does not require any intervention or act on the part of the trustee.[209] Where the bankrupt is an individual, the vesting of after-acquired property covers only the assets that are acquired by the bankrupt before he or she obtains a discharge. Post-discharge assets therefore do not vest in the trustee, and creditors will not be able to look to these assets to satisfy their claims

206 *Ibid*, s 67(1)(b.3).

207 See, for example, *Registered Plan (Retirement Income) Exemption Act*, SS 2002, c R-13.01.

208 *Court Order Enforcement Act*, RSBC 1996, c 78, s 71.3.

209 *Wallace*, above note 82.

unless their claims fall within the limited class of claims that survive a bankruptcy discharge.[210]

Because of the difference in treatment between pre-discharge assets that vest in the trustee and post-discharge assets that do not, there are sometimes disputes over precisely when a right arises. A pre-discharge asset that is subject to a contingency that is subsequently satisfied after the bankrupt's discharge is nevertheless caught by the wide definition of property and vests in the trustee. A trustee is therefore entitled to claim lottery winnings that are announced after discharge but that arise out of a ticket acquired before discharge.[211] The fact that the trustee has obtained a discharge does not affect this outcome, since the trustee can apply to be reappointed in order to claim the property.

In one case, an undischarged bankrupt obtained an inheritance on the death of her mother. The testamentary gift was subject to the condition that the beneficiary survive for thirty days following her mother's death. The contingent right vested in the trustee as after-acquired property and was not affected by the discharge of the bankrupt before the determination of the contingency. In the event that the bankrupt survived for thirty days, the money would be available to the trustee.[212] A contingent right must be distinguished from an incomplete gift or a mere expectancy. A beneficiary under a will does not obtain any interest prior to the testator's death and therefore has no right that can vest in the trustee. The possibility of a future inheritance is sometimes a factor that a bankruptcy court will consider in determining the appropriate order of discharge of the bankrupt,[213] but it does not alter the principle that a mere hope to receive an inheritance is not an asset that vests in the trustee.

In appropriate cases, the trustee can rely upon tracing principles to assert a claim against other assets that have been acquired after the bankruptcy by a third party using property that vested in the trustee in bankruptcy. In *FC Jones & Sons v Jones*,[214] Mr. Jones transferred funds that had vested in the trustee in bankruptcy to his wife, who increased its value by five times through trading in the potato futures market.

---

210 *BIA*, s 178(1). And see Chapter 10, Section G.

211 *Re Sindaco* (2003), 47 CBR (4th) 132 (BCSC); *Laserlight Inc v Weise* (2001), 31 CBR (4th) 44 (BCSC).

212 *Re Brausen* (2005), 9 CBR (5th) 1 (Alta QB).

213 See *Re Baker* (1987), 63 CBR (NS) 21 (Ont HCJ).

214 [1997] Ch 159 (CA). The vesting in that case was retroactive to the date that the bankruptcy petition was brought under the relation-back doctrine. This doctrine has been abolished under Canadian bankruptcy law so that the vesting of property now occurs only as of the date of bankruptcy.

The trustee in bankruptcy was able to trace the value to this fund and claim the entire amount as property of the bankrupt estate.

2) Surplus Income

The *BIA* provides a major exception to the principle that assets acquired after the bankruptcy but before discharge of the bankrupt vest in the trustee. The exception applies only to an individual. Unlike corporations or other artificial entities that cease to operate after a bankruptcy, natural persons must carry on with their lives. They must earn income to pay for food, shelter, and other necessary expenses. Bankruptcy law recognizes this need through a special regime that governs income earned by the bankrupt between the date of bankruptcy and the date of the bankrupt's discharge. This regime determines how much of this income can be retained by the bankrupt and how much should be paid over to the trustee for distribution to the creditors.

Before 1966, income earned by an individual bankrupt vested in the trustee as after-acquired income. Provincial law provided that a certain portion of wages was exempt in garnishment proceedings, and this exemption was effective in bankruptcy.[215] This was changed in 1966, when a new provision was introduced that provided a procedure that a trustee could invoke to attach the post-bankruptcy earnings of the bankrupt. Through this mechanism, a trustee could apply to a court for an order directing the payment of a portion of the wages, salary, or other remuneration. This procedure was problematic in that the court was given no guidance regarding the amount to be retained by the bankrupt, other than a direction that it should have regard to the family responsibilities and personal situation of the bankrupt. As a result, there was significant inconsistency in its application.

In 1997 the provision was completely overhauled. The requirement of a court application was eliminated, and the trustee was given a much more limited discretion on whether to proceed against post-bankruptcy income. Instead, the trustee must have regard to a directive established by the superintendent in bankruptcy that sets out the standards for making the determination. The 2009 amendments to the *BIA* provided further clarification as to the operation of the provision.

Surplus income is defined as the portion of the total income of an individual bankrupt that exceeds the amount that is necessary to enable the bankrupt to maintain a reasonable standard of living.[216] Total

---

215 *Industrial Acceptance Corp v Lalonde*, [1952] 2 SCR 109.

216 *BIA*, s 68(2) "surplus income."

income is defined as all of a bankrupt's revenues from whatever nature or source that are received between the date of the bankruptcy and the discharge.[217] The fact that all or part of these amounts might be afforded an exemption by the *BIA* is of no relevance in this determination. The definition of total income includes any amounts received as damages for wrongful dismissal, as a pay-equity settlement, or under a statute that relates to workers' compensation. It does not include amounts received as a gift, a legacy, or an inheritance, or any other windfall.

The superintendent's surplus income directive sets out the standards that are to be used in determining the amount of income that is necessary to enable the bankrupt to maintain a reasonable standard of living. In determining this amount, the trustee must have regard to both the earnings and the expenses of the debtor's family unit.[218] The family unit's available income is determined by calculating the family unit's total income and subtracting from it certain qualifying expenses. The family unit's total income does not include income tax, pension, employment insurance, and other mandatory deductions. The qualifying expenses are limited to things such as support payments, child-care expenses, and medical expenses.

If available income exceeds the amount set out in the standards,[219] which varies according to the number of persons in the family unit, the excess is considered surplus income. The trustee is then required to fix the amount that the bankrupt is required to pay to the bankrupt estate, inform the official receiver and any creditor who has requested the information, and take reasonable efforts to ensure that the debtor complies with the requirement.[220] The trustee is not required to "blindly follow" the guidelines but is directed to consider both the Superintendent's Standards and the personal and family situation of the bankrupt in determining whether or not the bankrupt has surplus income.[221]

The directive sets the calculation that is to be used in fixing the amount to be paid to the bankrupt estate. No payment is required if the surplus income is less than $200. If the surplus income is $200 or more, half of the surplus income must be paid to the trustee. If there is

---

217 *Ibid*, s 68(2) "total income."

218 In *Flostrand (Re)*, 2013 BCSC 1809, it was held that an adult child attending school elsewhere and not financially independent qualifies as part of the family unit.

219 For example, in 2015 the standard was $2,062 for a single person and was $3,831 for a family of four.

220 *BIA*, s 68(4).

221 *Plamondon (Re)*, 2012 ONSC 1379; *Wilson (Re)*, 2012 ONSC 2034; *Dore (Re)*, 2001 SKQB 524.

more than one income earner in the family unit, the amount that the bankrupt is required to pay is adjusted to the same percentage as the bankrupt's portion of the family unit's available monthly income. For example, if the bankrupt earns $30,000 and her spouse earns $20,000, the bankrupt will be required to pay 60 percent of the amount determined through the surplus income calculation. The trustee must make a fresh surplus income determination if the trustee becomes aware of a material change in the debtor's financial situation.[222]

A mediation procedure is provided to resolve disagreements as to the appropriate amount, and the court has the ultimate power to resolve the matter.[223] If the bankrupt fails to pay, the trustee can obtain a court order and serve it on the employer or other person who is obligated to pay the bankrupt. The employer is thereby bound to pay the money to the trustee, and risks having to pay it twice if the funds are instead paid to the bankrupt.[224] The order to pay is enforceable against the debtor's total income.[225] An opposition to an automatic discharge does not result in an extension of the requirement to pay surplus income to the trustee. The obligation comes to an end on the day that the automatic discharge would otherwise have been obtained, but a court may order a conditional discharge if appropriate.[226]

The surplus income procedure is a complete code in the sense that surplus income governed by this procedure does not constitute property that automatically vests in the trustee, as is normally the case with after-acquired property.[227] As a result, the earnings of the bankrupt vest in the trustee only upon actual payment of the money to the trustee. Courts have liberally interpreted the kinds of payments that will be considered income for the purposes of this calculation. Income tax refunds, severance pay, and damages for wrongful dismissal and disability payments were all held to qualify under the pre-1997 provisions that covered "salary, wages or other remuneration." The 2009 amendments have changed

---

222 *BIA*, s 68(3).

223 *Ibid*, ss 68(6)–(12). The mediation is mandatory and a court should adjourn an application until the mediation has been resolved. See *Wilson (Re)*, above note 221. However, a court on application of a trustee may set the amount under s 68(10) if the bankrupt fails to comply with a requirement to pay. See *Kovarcsik (Re)*, 2012 ONSC 3338.

224 *BIA*, s 68(13).

225 *Ibid*, s 68(15).

226 *Ibid*, s 68(16). And see *Gurniak v Royal Bank of Canada*, 2011 SKQB 292 [*Gurniak*].

227 *Marzetti v Marzetti*, [1994] 2 SCR 765; *Re Landry*, above note 82. Section 68 does not, however, modify the principle that a secured creditor who has a security interest in the income or revenue will prevail over the trustee. See *Cargill Ltd v Meyers Norris Penny Ltd*, 2008 MBCA 104.

this in one respect. The *BIA* now provides that an income tax refund owing to the bankrupt automatically vests in the trustee as after-acquired property.[228] An income tax refund will therefore no longer be treated as earnings or income for the purposes of the surplus income provisions. This change reflects the fact that the income tax refund is often the source of funds that is used to pay the fees of the trustee in bankruptcy.

The new provisions refer to "all revenues of a bankrupt of whatever nature or source."[229] This language undoubtedly covers the types of payments covered by the pre-1997 provision and encompasses other types as well, such as pension payments,[230] child- or spousal-support payments,[231] and farm-support payments.[232] If the property is considered income, then provincial exemptions do not apply to the income or revenue.[233] Instead, the surplus income calculation will be used to provide the bankrupt a full or partial exemption. The surplus income provision applies to income that was earned before the bankruptcy but that was not received by the bankrupt at the time of the bankruptcy.[234]

The new language does not sweep in every form of post-bankruptcy payment. The payment of proceeds generated from a sale of real estate that occurred before the bankruptcy is not income or revenue, and therefore it vests in the trustee as after-acquired property.[235] Receipts that are completely unconnected to any personal effort, resource, or other asset also do not qualify as income or revenue.[236] Windfall gains such as lottery winnings,[237] inheritances,[238] or natural resource rebates[239] therefore vest in the trustee as after-acquired property and are divisible among creditors unless the assets are exempt. Military-danger pay or disability pensions are not considered income for the purposes of the surplus income calculation or after-acquired income.[240] The debtor may retain these amounts, and in this respect the payments are akin to amounts received for personal injuries.

---

228 *BIA*, s 67(1)(c).
229 *Ibid*, s 68(2)(a).
230 *Re Byrne* (2003), 41 CBR (4th) 6 (Alta QB).
231 *Re O'Brien* (2005), 11 CBR (5th) 275 (Alta QB).
232 *Kallenberger v Beck* (2005), 18 CBR (5th) 113 (Alta QB).
233 *Re Coates* (2006), 57 Alta. L.R. (4th) 108 (Alta QB).
234 *Re Landry*, above note 82.
235 *Re Millin* (2005), 13 CBR (5th) 91 (BCSC).
236 *Re Coates*, above note 233.
237 *Re Sindaco*, above note 211.
238 *Re Hoff* (2003), 42 CBR (4th) 258 (Alta QB).
239 *Re Coates*, above note 233.
240 *Re Duffney* (2007), 32 CBR (5th) 72 (NBQB); *Smith (Re)*, 2009 NSSC 261.

A personal injury claim for lost earning capacity is not a right of action that is personal to the victim, and therefore it can be used to satisfy the claims of creditors.[241] However, this does not mean that the entire award will be available. The award compensates the victim for lost income and therefore will attract the surplus income calculation. The award potentially compensates the victim for lost income from three different time periods: (1) the period before bankruptcy; (2) the period after bankruptcy and before the debtor's discharge; and (3) the period after discharge. The portion of the award that covers the first and second periods is subject to the surplus income calculation. However, the portion attributable to post-discharge lost wages should not be available to the trustee at all since the creditors have no right to post-discharge earnings of the bankrupt.[242]

E. THE RULE IN *EX PARTE JAMES*

Ex parte James; Re Condon[243] involved a judgment creditor of the bankrupt who had completed execution before the bankruptcy. The judgment creditor was therefore entitled in law to keep the proceeds. The judgment creditor paid the funds to the trustee after the trustee demanded payment and threatened legal proceedings to recover it. At the time, a claim to recover mistaken payments (what is recognized to be a claim in unjust enrichment) was not available in respect of payments made under a mistake of law. Despite the fact an action to recover the money was not then available, the court held that the judgment creditor was entitled to recover the money paid to the trustee. The decision relied upon the principle that the trustee is an officer of the court and is expected to act in accordance with a standard of fairness that prevents the trustee from asserting a legal right if to do so would be inconsistent with natural justice and honesty.[244]

---

241 *Re Bell* (1996), 39 CBR (3d) 236 (BCSC).

242 *Re Anderson* (2004), 2 CBR (5th) 27 (Alta QB). This approach was not adopted in *Re MacLeod* (2008), 45 CBR (5th) 214 (Ont SCJ). Instead, Registrar Nettie held that the award constitutes property rather than income with the result that the full amount of the award is available to satisfy the claims of the creditors. Subsequent cases have not followed *Re MacLeod*, but have treated the award as income and pro-rated it so that amounts associated with post-discharge income is not distributed. See *Gurniak*, above note 226; *Conforti (Re)*, 2012 ONSC 2656.

243 (1874), LR 9 Ch App 609.

244 *Re Tyler*, [1907] 1 KB 865.

Payments made on the basis of a mistake of law are now recoverable in an action for unjust enrichment.[245] However, the rule in *Ex parte James* is not restricted to mistaken payments. Nor is the principle restricted to cases where the trustee's high-handed action has caused the payment to be made. It has been applied where the trustee is passive and the hardship comes about for other reasons. For example, the principle was applied in *Re McDonald*[246] in which a bankrupt had been granted a discharge conditional on payment of $3,300 to the trustee, and the bankrupt had repaid all but one dollar.

The difficulty with the rule is that it is unpredictable and provides little guidance as to its proper application. Often it is possible to achieve the same result through the application of some other established legal principle,[247] and this is likely to produce a more principled and predictable approach than an overreliance on the rule in *Ex Parte James*.

FURTHER READINGS

BURROWS, A. "Proprietary Restitution: Unmasking Unjust Enrichment" (2001) 117 *Law Quarterly Review* 412

CALNAN, R. *Proprietary Rights and Insolvency* (Oxford: Oxford University Press, 2010)

CHAMBERS, R. "The Constructive Trust in Canada" (1999) 37 *Alberta Law Review* 173

———. "Resulting Trusts in Canada" (2000) 38 *Alberta Law Review* 378

DUGGAN, A, & N SIEBRASSE. "Protection of Creators' Rights in Insolvency" (2014) 26 *Intellectual Property Journal* 271

---

245 *Air Canada v British Columbia*, [1989] 1 SCR 1161.

246 (1971), 16 CBR (NS) 244 (Ont HCJ).

247 In *Re McDonald*, *ibid*, an undated cheque for $1 had been given to the trustee with a written authorization permitting it to be dated and applied at any time. The acceptance of this cheque by the trustee could have been regarded as payment, in which case the bankrupt would have been discharged. In *Armadale Properties Ltd v 700 King Street (1997) Ltd* (2001), 25 CBR (4th) 198 (Ont SCJ), the principle was applied to prevent a trustee from disclaiming an agreement for the purchase of a condominium. A much simpler response would be to recognize that the vendor is bound to hold the property under a constructive trust for the purchaser, and that the trustee of the vendor is in no better position.

GOODE R. "Property and Unjust Enrichment" in Andrew Burrows, ed, *Essays on the Law of Restitution* (Oxford: Clarendon Press, 1991) 215

KLOTZ, R. *Bankruptcy, Insolvency and Family Law*, 2d ed (Scarborough, ON: Carswell, 2002) ch 6

MCINNES, M. *The Canadian Law of Unjust Enrichment and Restitution* (Markham, ON: LexisNexis Canada, 2014) ch 32

PALMER, K. *The Law of Set-Off in Canada* (Aurora, ON: Canada Law Book, 1993) 176–207

ROSE, F, ed. *Restitution and Insolvency* (London: Mansfield Press, 2000)

SWADLING, W, ed. *The Quistclose Trust: Critical Essays* (Oxford: Hart, 2004)

TELFER, T. "The Proposed Federal Exemption Regime for the *Bankruptcy and Insolvency Act*" (2005) 41 *Canadian Business Law Journal* 279

———. "Statutory Licences and the Search for Property: The End of the Imbroglio?" (2007) 45 *Canadian Business Law Journal* 224

ZIEGEL, J. "The Unwelcome Intrusion of the Remedial Constructive Trust in Personal Property Security Law: *Ellingsen (Trustee of) v Hallmark Ford Sales Ltd*" (2001) 34 *Canadian Business Law Journal* 460

CHAPTER 5

PROPRIETARY CLAIMS OF THIRD PARTIES

This chapter is the flip side of the previous chapter. Upon bankruptcy, the assets of the bankrupt vest in the trustee. However, the occurrence of bankruptcy does not permit the trustee to confiscate assets belonging to persons other than the bankrupt. A third party who successfully claims an interest in an asset is permitted to withdraw it from the bankrupt's estate. Where the claimant establishes absolute ownership in the property, the asset is entirely removed from the bankrupt's estate. The third party's proprietary right in the asset may be of a more limited nature such that the asset or its value is not completely removed from the estate. For example, a person who owns land jointly with the bankrupt does not have the right to take the land entirely out of the bankrupt's estate. Bankruptcy severs the joint tenancy and converts it into a tenancy in common. The trustee may bring proceedings for partition and sale of the interest, or may sell the bankrupt's interest to a purchaser who will enjoy a similar ability to do so.[1]

An astonishing variety of property interests can be created. Many arise through consensual dealings, but they can also arise through the operation of law in response to other events such as wrongdoing or unjust enrichment.[2] It is beyond the scope of this work to catalogue all the different kinds of property rights. This chapter will limit itself to a consideration of the bankruptcy procedure that is used to determine the

1 See Chapter 4, Section B(1).

2 See Chapter 3, Section C(1).

legitimacy of the third party's claim to the property and to an examination of some of the proprietary claims that are commonly asserted by third parties in the context of bankruptcy proceedings.

As a general rule, proprietary rights that are in existence at the date of the bankruptcy are effective against the trustee in bankruptcy. Conversely, personal rights are converted into a right to prove a claim for a dividend and do not give the claimant a proprietary right in any asset of the debtor. This is subject to a number of important exceptions provided for in the bankruptcy statute. Certain types of proprietary rights, such as deemed trusts, are extinguished upon the occurrence of a bankruptcy. As well, upon bankruptcy a proprietary right is conferred upon certain types of claimants, such as unpaid suppliers of goods, who have only a personal right outside of bankruptcy. These provisions will be examined in detail in this chapter.

A. ASSERTING PROPRIETARY CLAIMS AGAINST THE TRUSTEE

The *BIA* provides a procedural mechanism for the resolution of proprietary claims made by third parties in respect of assets that are under the control of the trustee. The procedure is a complete code and it is not open for a claimant to pursue an alternative avenue to have the claim recognized.[3] Although the procedure is of general application, claims of secured creditors and sellers claiming thirty-day goods are resolved through a different procedure.[4]

A person who claims a proprietary right in an asset in the possession of the trustee must file a proof of claim verified by an affidavit that sets out the basis for the claim and sufficient particulars to enable the property to be identified.[5] The trustee must either admit the claim and deliver possession of the property to the claimant or give notice that the claim is disputed and provide reasons.[6] The onus of proof is on the claimant to establish the claim.[7] This determination must be made within fifteen days from the filing of the proof of claim or fifteen days after the first meeting of creditors, whichever is later. If the claim-

3 *BIA*, s 81(5). And see *Bank of Montreal v XED Services Ltd* (1992), 15 CBR (3d) 112 (BCSC); *Re Bothwell* (2000), 22 CBR (4th) 56 (Ont SCJ).

4 See Sections B(2) and C, below in this chapter.

5 *BIA*, s 81(1).

6 *Ibid*, s 81(2).

7 *Ibid*, s 81(3).

ant does not appeal the trustee's decision to dispute the claim within fifteen days of the sending of the notice, the claimant is deemed to have abandoned all right and interest in the property. A court has the discretion to extend the time for the appeal even after expiry of the fifteen-day period.[8]

B. SECURED CREDITORS

Creditors who have taken the precaution of obtaining a security interest are able to assert a proprietary claim to some or all of the bankrupt's property. The pervasive use of secured credit in modern times has meant that these claims arise routinely. Indeed, it has occurred to such a degree that some commentators have expressed concern that it has permitted most of the bankrupt's assets to be swept out of the bankrupt's estate, leaving nothing at all for the unsecured creditors.[9]

A secured creditor's enforcement remedies against the collateral are not regulated by the bankruptcy system and continue to be governed by non-bankruptcy law principles. Personal property security law generally governs enforcement proceedings against personal property while provincial mortgage foreclosure law generally governs proceedings against land.[10] The exercise of these enforcement remedies results in the removal of the collateral from the bankruptcy estate. The proceeds from the realization of the collateral are not shared among the creditors but are used to satisfy the obligation owed to the secured creditor. If there is a surplus following an enforcement sale, the trustee is entitled to claim the proceeds unless there is another party with a higher right (such as the holder of a subordinate perfected security interest). A secured creditor will typically assert a claim in bankruptcy only if the value of the collateral is not sufficient to satisfy the obligation secured.

1) The Definition of Secured Creditor

The *BIA* defines a "secured creditor" as "a person holding a mortgage, hypothec, pledge, charge or lien on or against the property of the debtor"

8 *Ibid*, s 187(11). *Re St-Pierre* (1963), 5 CBR (NS) 61 (Que Sup Ct).

9 R Goode, "Is the Law Too Favourable to Secured Creditors?" (1984) 8 *Canadian Business Law Journal* 53.

10 Some federal statutes create federal security interest enforcement regimes on certain types of collateral, such as ship mortgages. See R Cuming, C Walsh, & R Wood, *Personal Property Security Law*, 2d ed (Toronto: Irwin Law, 2012) at 709–14.

that secures a debt.[11] This definition covers security interests in both real property and personal property. It encompasses security rights that arise by operation of law or by statute (non-consensual security interests) as well as consensually created security interests. The definition therefore covers a common law possessory lien of a repairer as well as a non-possessory statutory lien given to a garage keeper. Legislation may give the provincial or federal Crown a non-consensual security interest in the debtor's property to secure an obligation owing to the Crown. Although the Crown falls within the definition of a secured creditor, it will not be able to assert its secured creditor status unless an additional registration requirement is satisfied.[12]

If the claim is one that is given the status of a preferred claim in bankruptcy, the holder of the claim is unable to rely upon any provincial law that would confer a secured creditor status upon the claimant.[13] This is illustrated in the treatment afforded landlords who have exercised a right of distress against goods located on the leased premises. Prior to 1949, a distraint claim of a landlord fell within the definition of a secured creditor. In 1949 the bankruptcy legislation was amended so as to provide that the claim for distress was a preferred claim in bankruptcy. Thereafter, landlords who exercised a right to distress were no longer regarded as secured creditors.[14]

Provincial personal property security law deems certain types of transactions to be security interests for the purpose of the legislation. Leases and consignments that do not in substance create a security interest and absolute transfers of accounts are brought within the scope of the legislation. The definition of secured creditor in the *BIA* does not cover lessors, consignors, or assignors who are deemed to be secured parties under provincial legislation.[15] Claims by such parties should be dealt with under the general procedure for resolving proprietary claims, rather than the procedure set out for secured creditors. A failure to register or perfect these interests may nonetheless result in their subordination to the trustee under personal property security legislation.

It is less clear whether conditional sales agreements, leases, and consignment arrangements that would be regarded as true security in-

---

11 *BIA*, s 2 "secured creditor." The definition also identifies with considerable specificity the rights under the *Civil Code of Quebec* that are brought within the definition.

12 *Ibid*, s 87(1). And see Section E, below in this chapter.

13 *Deloitte Haskins & Sells Ltd v Alberta (Workers' Compensation Board)*, [1985] 1 SCR 785.

14 See *Re Profoot Enterprises Ltd* (1981), 39 CBR (NS) 80 (Alta QB) [*Profoot*].

15 *Re Western Express Airlines Inc* (2005), 10 CBR (5th) 154 (BCSC).

terests under personal property security legislation are caught by the definition. These transactions did not create security interests under the common law but were brought within personal property security legislation by virtue of a wider test that looked to the substance and economic realities of the transaction. The definition of secured creditor in the *BIA* does not employ a similar test. Although it brings conditional sales and title-retention devices within the scope of the definition in respect of the *Civil Code of Quebec*, it fails to do so in respect of common law jurisdictions.

In other contexts, the failure to provide language that covers these transactions has meant that federal legislation did not extend to conditional sales agreements and security leases.[16] There is no reason in principle why the *BIA* provisions that relate to secured creditors should not apply to conditional sales agreements, security leases, and security consignments, and incongruous outcomes result if the these transactions are not caught by the definition of security.[17] The real difficulty will be in explaining why the same interpretive approach is not applied to similarly worded legislation.[18] Although the definitional question was not directly addressed, the Supreme Court of Canada in *Re Giffen*[19] seems to have proceeded on the basis that a security lease fell within the definition of a secured creditor.

Unfortunately, the inconsistent approach to the definition of a secured creditor in the federal statutes produces serious problems concerning the determination of priorities in bankruptcy.[20] The statutory deemed trust created by the *Income Tax Act*[21] in respect of source deductions

---

16 *DaimlerChrysler Financial Services (Debis) Canada Inc v Mega Pets Ltd* (2002), 212 DLR (4th) 41 (BCCA); *Canada (Deputy Attorney General) v Schwab Construction Ltd* (2002), 31 CBR (4th) 75 (Sask CA). In these cases, the superpriority given to deemed statutory trusts over security interests was held not to extend to conditional sales agreements and leases.

17 See R Wood, "The Definition of Secured Creditor in Insolvency Law" (2010) 25 *Banking and Finance Law Review* 341.

18 The approach taken in the cases above is criticized by JS Ziegel, "Conditional Sales and Superpriority Crown Claims under *ITA* s. 227" (2003) 38 CRR (4th) 161.

19 [1998] 1 SCR 91. The Court addressed the question whether the British Columbia *Personal Property Security Act* disturbs the federal bankruptcy priority scheme, which is stated to be subject to the rights of secured creditors. This discussion would have been unnecessary if a lessor under a security lease was not within the definition of a secured creditor.

20 See R Wood, "The Structure of Secured Priorities in Insolvency Law" (2011) 27 *Banking and Finance Law Review* 26. See also R Wood & D Bryan, "Creeping Statutory Obsolescence in Bankruptcy Law" (2014) 3 *Journal of the Insolvency Institute of Canada* 1 at 7–10.

21 RSC 1985, c 1 (5th Supp), s 224(1.3) [*ITA*].

ranks ahead of the claim of a secured creditor. Because security leases and conditional sales contracts are not considered to be secured creditors, the proprietary right of the lessor or seller is not affected by the deemed trust.[22] The statutory security created by the *BIA* in favour of unpaid pension contributions also ranks ahead of the claim of secured creditors.[23] But if the definition of secured creditor in the *BIA* covers holders of security leases and conditional sales contracts, the statutory security will have priority over these claims. The problem is that the statutory deemed trust for source deductions is afforded priority over the statutory security in respect of pension contribution. This produces a circular priority system. The conditional sales agreement has priority over the deemed trust for source deductions. The deemed trust has priority over the statutory charge for unpaid pension contributions. The statutory charge has priority over the conditional sales agreement. The best solution is to amend the definition of secured creditor in the *BIA* and in the other federal statutes to ensure that they encompass security leases and conditional sales agreements. Absent that, courts will be forced to devise some theory that will permit it to break the circularity.[24]

2) Asserting Secured Creditor Status against the Trustee

The *BIA* sets out a special procedure that applies when a secured creditor wishes to assert a security interest in property that has vested in the trustee. This special procedure supersedes the general procedure for asserting proprietary claims against the trustee.[25] If the trustee believes that property may be subject to a security interest, the trustee may demand that a person file a proof of security that gives full particulars of it.[26] If the person does not do so within thirty days of service, the trustee, with leave of the court, can sell or dispose of the property free of the security interest.[27] Although a trustee can sell the collateral with-

---

22 Above note 16.

23 *BIA*, s 81.5(2).

24 See R Wood, "Circular Priorities in Secured Transactions Law" (2010) 47 *Alberta Law Review* 823.

25 *R v Ford Credit Canada Ltd* (1990), 78 CBR (NS) 266 (Ont HCJ); *Commcorp Financial Services Inc v Royal Bank of Canada* (1994), 30 CBR (3d) 87 (Sask QB); *Re Shibou* (1982), 42 CBR (NS) 132 (Man QB). But see *Re Kay's Furniture Mart Ltd* (1968), 11 CBR (NS) 279 (NBQB); *Re Stephenson* (1983), 50 CBR (NS) 18 (BCSC), which held that the general procedure in respect of proprietary claims applied to security interests.

26 *BIA*, s 128(1).

27 *Ibid*, s 128(1.1).

out following this procedure, the buyer will not take the interest free of the security interest.[28]

The trustee is required to examine the proof of security and may require further evidence to support the claim.[29] The trustee has the right to inspect the collateral if it is in the possession of the secured party.[30] The trustee may disallow the claim in whole or in part and, upon doing so, must give a notice to the secured creditor setting out reasons.[31] The determination by the trustee is final and determinative unless the secured party appeals the decision to court within thirty days after service of the notice or such other period as the court may order.[32] The bankrupt and the other creditors also have standing to challenge the validity of a security interest if the trustee declines to do so.[33]

If the trustee is dissatisfied with the assessed value of the collateral in the proof of security, the trustee may require that the collateral be offered for sale.[34] Alternatively, the trustee can redeem the security interest by paying to the secured creditor the assessed value of the collateral, or the obligation secured if it is less than the assessed value.[35] A secured creditor can force the trustee to make an election between the right to force a sale and the right to redeem.[36] If the trustee does not respond within one month or such further time ordered by the court, the right to take either action is lost.

3) Non-compliance with Validity and Perfection Requirements

Statutes that govern secured transactions frequently impose registration or other perfection requirements. Non-compliance with these provisions often will result in subordination of the security interest to the interests of a trustee. Except in one instance, this does not arise by virtue of bankruptcy law. Instead, it arises because the law that governs the secured transaction mandates this result. If the statute does

---

28 *Royal Bank of Canada v United Used Auto & Truck Parts Ltd* (2002), 32 CBR (4th) 297 (BCSC).

29 *BIA*, s 135(1).

30 *Ibid*, s 79.

31 *Ibid*, s 135(3). And see *Pyne (Bankruptcy) (Re)*, 2009 SKQB 458.

32 *BIA*, s 135(4).

33 *Ibid*, s 135(5).

34 *Ibid*, s 129(1). If the secured creditor and trustee cannot agree upon the terms of the sale, it will be determined by the court. If the sale is by public auction, both the trustee and the secured creditor are permitted to bid. See s 129(2).

35 *Ibid*, s 128(3). And see *Cutting Edge Foods Inc (Re)*, 2008 ABQB 340.

36 *BIA*, s 130.

not provide for subordination to the trustee, the proprietary right will be fully recognized in the bankruptcy despite non-compliance with the registration requirement.

The *BIA* imposes a registration requirement on assignments of present or future book debts by a person engaged in trade or business.[37] Failure to register renders the assignment void against the trustee. The provision was added to the bankruptcy statute in 1921. At the time, provinces did not impose a registration requirement on assignments of book debts. Following this amendment, provinces introduced legislation that created registry systems for the assignment of book debts, and this feature has been retained in provincial legislation relating to personal property security. The *BIA* does not provide a mandatory registration requirement for any other kind of security interest. The effect of non-compliance with registry requirements therefore falls to be determined by the secured transaction law that governs the security interest. In most cases, it is provincial law that governs this question.

A security interest that is governed by provincial legislation on personal property security must satisfy two conditions in order for it to be effective against a trustee. First, a security interest must satisfy certain formal requirements in order to be effective against third parties. A non-possessory security interest is not enforceable against a third party unless it is in writing and provides an adequate description of the collateral.[38] Second, the security interest must be perfected. In order to be perfected, a security interest must have attached (i.e., come into existence) and a perfection step must have been completed.[39] Registration is the most common perfection step, but a secured creditor can also perfect a security interest by taking possession of the collateral.[40] As well, the legislation in certain limited circumstances provides a temporary perfection period that permits a secured creditor to perfect the security interest by registration or possession.

Personal property security legislation provides that a security interest that is not perfected at the date of bankruptcy is not effective against a trustee.[41] A secured creditor who perfects a security interest after the date of a bankruptcy application but before a bankruptcy order is entitled to priority over a trustee. The perfected status of the

---

37 *Ibid*, s 98.1. Registration is not required in respect of assignments of a specific account or an assignment made in connection with a transfer of a business.

38 *Personal Property Security Act*, RSO 1990, c P.10, s 11(2)(c) [Ont *PPSA*]; RSBC 1996, c 359, s 10(2) [BC *PPSA*].

39 Ont *PPSA*, above note 38, s 19; BC *PPSA*, above note 38, s 19.

40 Ont *PPSA*, above note 38, s 22; BC *PPSA*, above note 38, s 24.

41 Ont *PPSA*, above note 38, s 20(1); BC *PPSA*, above note 38, s 20(b).

security interest is tested at the date of the bankruptcy, which in an involuntary bankruptcy is the date that the court grants the bankruptcy order.[42] Although the secured creditor may have registered before the date of bankruptcy, the registration will be invalid if there was a seriously misleading error in it.[43] A trustee will frequently dispute the effectiveness of a security interest on the ground that the registration contains such an error in the name of the debtor or in the description of the collateral.[44]

The Supreme Court of Canada in *Re Giffen*[45] upheld the validity of provincial legislation that subordinated an unperfected security interest as against a trustee. Although the usual bankruptcy rule is that the trustee merely acquires the bankrupt's interest in the property and acquires no better position against other third-party claims, this does not apply if the provincial legislation subordinates the security interest to the trustee. The priority that the trustee enjoys is not based on a theory that the trustee in any way is misled by the lack of registration. Rather, the trustee is given priority because bankruptcy stays the enforcement remedies of unsecured creditors. If these enforcement remedies had been completed, the unsecured creditors would obtain priority over the secured creditor. The provincial legislation simply confers upon the trustee, as representative of the unsecured creditors, the same priority status that they would enjoy were they able to complete enforcement proceedings.

The position is fundamentally different in respect of security interests in real property. Unlike personal property security legislation, the registry systems that govern land do not give a trustee in bankruptcy priority over an unregistered interest in land.[46] Although land registry systems give priority to a purchaser for value, a trustee does not occupy this status.[47] As a consequence, lack of registration of a mortgage or charge on land does not prevent the secured creditor from asserting the interest and gaining priority over the trustee.

---

42 *BIA*, s 2 "time of the bankruptcy."

43 Ont *PPSA*, above note 38, s 46(4); BC *PPSA*, above note 38, s 43(6).

44 See Cuming, Walsh, & Wood, above note 10 at 363–71.

45 Above note 19.

46 *Citifinancial Canada East Corp v Hurley (Trustee of)* (2006), 20 CBR (5th) 74 (NBQB).

47 *Re Canadian Engineering & Contracting Co* (1994), 28 CBR (3d) 136 (Ont Ct Gen Div). And see R Wood, "The Floating Charge on Land in the Western Provinces" (1992) 20 *Canadian Business Law Journal* 132 at 133–36.

4) Subrogation to the Rights of a Secured Creditor

Subrogation permits a party to exercise the rights of another person. A person who does not have a valid security interest in certain circumstances may be subrogated to rights of a secured creditor. The person is thereby entitled to be substituted for and exercise the rights of the secured creditor. Subrogation to secured creditor status can occur in a number of situations. A surety who has paid the principal debtor's debt is entitled to be subrogated to any security interest that the creditor has in respect of the debt. Suppose that A lends money to B and is given a security interest in B's property. C also guarantees repayment of the money to A. If C pays the debt owed to A, C is entitled to be subrogated to the security interest that A holds against B. If B is bankrupt, C is nevertheless able to assert the security interest against B's trustee.[48]

A right of subrogation also arises where, at the request of a debtor, a lender pays out the loan of a third party. The lender is entitled to be subrogated to any security interest held by the third party. The fact that the lender may have taken security that is ineffective against the trustee is not relevant. So long as the security interest that was taken by the third party is valid and effective against the trustee, the right of subrogation permits the secured party to exercise the rights under that security interest.[49]

A right of subrogation also arises in connection with the equitable doctrine of marshalling of securities. This occurs when a senior secured creditor has a security interest in two funds and a junior secured creditor has a security interest in only one of them. If the senior secured creditor enforces its remedies against the common fund, this will undercut the junior secured party's position. Marshalling of securities permits the senior secured party to enforce its security interest against the common fund, and gives the junior secured party the right to be subrogated to the security held by the senior secured party against the other fund. The right of subrogation that arises in connection with the marshalling of assets is effective against the trustee in bankruptcy of the debtor.[50]

---

48 *Re Windham Sales Ltd* (1979), 31 CBR (NS) 130 (Ont HCJ).

49 *Re N'Amerix Logistix Inc* (2001), 29 CBR (4th) 222 (Ont SCJ). And see R Wood, "Supplementing PPSA Priorities: The Use and Abuse of Common Law and Equitable Principles" (2014) 56 *Canadian Business Law Journal* 31 at 55–70.

50 *Re Bread Man Inc* (1978), 29 CBR (NS) 58 (Ont HCJ); *Canada Trustco Mortgage Co v Wenngatz Construction & Holdings Ltd* (1986), 60 CBR (NS) 270 (BCSC).

5) Security Interests in Post-bankruptcy Property

Security agreements frequently contain after-acquired property clauses that give the secured creditor a security interest in property that is acquired by the debtor after the security agreement is executed. After-acquired property clauses are fully effective in respect of property that is acquired by the debtor after the security agreement is executed but before the date of bankruptcy. They are ineffective in respect of property acquired by the debtor after the debtor obtains a bankruptcy discharge.[51] Their effectiveness is less certain in respect of property that is acquired after the date of bankruptcy but before discharge.

The controversy often arises in connection with a security interest in all present and after-acquired accounts. There is no difficulty if the account arises before the bankruptcy. In this case, the security interest attaches to the account and the secured creditor can claim it in priority to the trustee.[52] It is not necessary that the amount be due and payable at the time of bankruptcy. It is enough that the events that give rise to the obligation to pay have occurred.[53] There is also no difficulty if the account arises after the date of bankruptcy upon the sale by the trustee of some or all of the assets of the bankrupt's estate. The bankrupt's assets vest in the trustee, and the sale of the assets does not produce a debt owing to the debtor.[54] The troublesome cases are those that involve post-bankruptcy property that does not arise from the disposition of property that has vested in the trustee.

The Supreme Court of Canada in *Holy Rosary Parish (Thorold) Credit Union Ltd v Premier Trust Co*[55] held that an assignment of wages given by the bankrupt to a credit union was effective in giving the credit union priority over the trustee in respect of wages earned after the date of bankruptcy but before discharge. As soon as the post-bankruptcy wages were due, the assignment operated in equity to transfer the property to the assignee. The bankruptcy statute was amended in 1992 to reverse this outcome. An assignment of existing or future wages that is made before the bankruptcy is of no effect in respect of wages earned

51 *Holy Rosary Parish (Thorold) Credit Union Ltd v Bye*, [1967] SCR 271.

52 *Irving A Burton Ltd v Canadian Imperial Bank of Commerce* (1982), 41 CBR (NS) 217 (Ont CA).

53 *Re Dominion Used Store Fixtures Ltd* (1939), 20 CBR 325 (Ont HCJ). In *Cliffs Over Maple Bay (Re)*, 2010 BCSC 389 at para 129, the court stated that the claim must be "more than trifling or completely contingent in nature before a security interest may be said to attach."

54 *Re Anderson & Hiltz Ltd* (1985), 57 CBR (NS) 222 (Ont HCJ).

55 [1965] SCR 503.

after the bankruptcy.[56] An assignment of amounts payable as a result of services rendered by a natural person is also of no effect in respect of amounts earned or generated after the bankruptcy.[57]

The bankruptcy provisions do not render after-acquired property clauses ineffective in all cases. In cases that are not covered, it is necessary to determine if the enactment of modern personal property security legislation has altered the analysis.[58] This legislation does not make use of legal and equitable principles in connection with the determination of priorities. Assuming that the secured creditor has properly completed a perfection step where this is required to obtain priority over a trustee, priority should be given to the secured creditor only if the security interest attached to the collateral before the property vests in the trustee. The mechanism by which after-acquired property vests in the trustee is far from clear. It may be that it operates through an initial vesting in the bankrupt followed by an immediate vesting in the trustee. If that is the case, it might be argued that the secured party's security interest attaches to the after-acquired property an instant before it vests in the trustee. Alternatively, it might be that after-acquired property vests directly in the trustee by operation of law without the bankrupt ever acquiring an interest in it. If this is the case, the security interest will not attach to the after-acquired asset.

6) Inversion of Priorities on Bankruptcy

In most cases, the priority that a secured party enjoys against other claimants is unchanged by the occurrence of a bankruptcy. A secured creditor who has a security interest in goods is subordinate to a repairer who claims a possessory lien on those goods. This outcome is unaffected by the debtor's bankruptcy. However, there are a number of instances where the priority status of a secured creditor is improved in bankruptcy over what it would be outside bankruptcy. Bankruptcy therefore produces an inversion or reversal of priorities.

There are four situations where an inversion of priorities is most likely to occur. The first involves creditors who have claims that are given preferred creditor status under bankruptcy law.[59] Provincial statutes give some of these preferred claimants priority over secured creditors. For example, in many provinces a landlord who exercises

---

56 *BIA*, s 68.1(1).

57 *Ibid*, s 68.1(2).

58 For a more detailed discussion of this issue, see Cuming, Walsh, & Wood, above note 10 at 532–38.

59 *BIA*, s 136(1).

a right of distress against goods for unpaid rent has priority over a competing security interest other than a purchase-money security interest.[60] The Supreme Court of Canada has held that provincial statutes that attempt to confer a higher priority status on preferred creditors are inoperative in bankruptcy.[61] Upon bankruptcy, the landlord loses the right to exercise the right of distress and must claim in the bankruptcy as a preferred creditor.[62] As the trustee's right is subordinate to that of the secured creditor, the asset is effectively withdrawn from the bankrupt's estate. The unsecured creditors, including the landlord, will not have any recourse to the asset unless there is a surplus after the secured creditor's enforcement sale.

The second situation arises in relation to Crown claims and workers' compensation bodies. Provincial or federal statutes often give these claimants a proprietary right in the form of a lien, charge, or security interest that has priority over secured creditors. In bankruptcy, these claims are subject to rules that in most cases ensure that the interest is subordinate to that of a secured creditor.[63]

The third situation arises in connection with deemed statutory trusts. Provincial and federal statutes impose a deemed statutory trust on the assets of a debtor who has failed to remit taxes or pay an amount due to a claimant. Under bankruptcy law, these deemed statutory trusts are ineffective, with the result that the claimant is reduced to the status of an unsecured creditor.[64]

The fourth situation arises in connection with a writ or judgment that under provincial law is entitled to priority over a security interest. This can occur if a writ or judgment is registered in a land registry system. The writ or judgment is given priority over a subsequently created security interest.[65] In respect of personal property, a judgment enforcement creditor can obtain priority over a secured creditor who has failed to perfect its security interest. An unperfected security interest is subordinate to a judgment enforcement creditor who has taken certain steps. In some provinces, the creditor must have taken control of the

60 See, for example, *Civil Enforcement Act*, RSA 2000, c C-15, s 104(b).

61 *Husky Oil Operations Ltd v Canada (Minister of National Revenue)*, [1995] 3 SCR 453.

62 *Profoot*, above note 14.

63 See the discussion in Section E, below in this chapter.

64 *British Columbia v Henfrey Samson Belair Ltd*, [1989] 2 SCR 24; *BIA*, ss 67(2)–(3). An exception is made for deemed trusts to secure unremitted source deductions. See the discussion in Chapter 3, Section C(1).

65 The writ does not, however, obtain priority over a prior unregistered interest in the real property. See *Jellett v Wilkie* (1896), 26 SCR 282.

collateral under judgment enforcement proceedings.[66] Other provinces permit registration of a writ or judgment. In these jurisdictions, the judgment enforcement creditor is given substantially the same priority as a secured creditor.[67] Even where the secured party has registered first in time, personal property security legislation subordinates this priority in respect of future advances that are made after the secured creditor is notified of the interest of the judgment enforcement creditor.[68] Any priority that the judgment enforcement has against a secured creditor ceases as soon as a bankruptcy occurs. The writ or judgment ceases to exist, and the secured creditor can therefore withdraw the asset from the bankrupt estate free of the writ or judgment.[69]

Not surprisingly, a secured creditor will often seek to initiate a bankruptcy for the sole purpose of improving its priority ranking as against other competing claimants. The difficulty with this practice is that it produces an additional layer of bankruptcy costs without providing any corresponding benefit for the unsecured creditors for whose benefit the bankruptcy system was intended. In these cases, a receiver-manager appointed by the secured creditor conducts the realization of the assets, and the trustee takes a purely passive role in the liquidation. Despite this, courts have held that it is not improper for a secured creditor to initiate a bankruptcy for the sole purpose of improving its priority, and that such conduct does not provide the court with grounds to exercise its discretion to dismiss the creditor's application for a bankruptcy order.[70]

There is one argument that has the potential in some situations to curtail the strategic use of bankruptcy by secured creditors to improve their priority. Its central premise is that the proprietary right of

---

66 See Ont *PPSA*, above note 38, s 20(1).

67 See, for example, *Civil Enforcement Act*, above note 60, ss 35–36. And see RCC Cuming, "When an Unsecured Creditor is a Secured Creditor" (2003) 66 *Saskatchewan Law Review* 255.

68 Ont *PPSA*, above note 38, s 30(4); BC *PPSA*, above note 38, s 35(6).

69 *Westcoast Savings Credit Union v McElroy* (1981), 39 CBR (NS) 52 (BCSC); *James Hunter & Associates Inc v Citifinancial Inc*, 2007 CarswellOnt 8400 (SCJ). Saskatchewan and Newfoundland and Labrador provide that a trustee in bankruptcy of a judgment debtor succeeds to the interest of a judgment creditor. This allows the trustee to assert the charge of the judgment creditor against the secured creditor, but the distribution of the proceeds would be in accordance with the bankruptcy scheme of distribution. See *The Enforcement of Money Judgments Act*, SS 2010, c E-9.22; *The Land Titles Act, 2000*, SS 2000, c L-5.1, s 173.3(9); *Judgment Enforcement Act*, SNL 1996, c J-1.1, s 48(2).

70 *Bank of Montreal v Scott Road Enterprises Ltd* (1989), 73 CBR (NS) 273 (BCCA); *Harrop of Milton Inc* (1979), 29 CBR (NS) 289 (Ont HCJ).

the subordinated claimant is not destroyed.[71] The claimant cannot assert the non-bankruptcy proprietary right as against the trustee since this would interfere with the scheme of distribution set out in the *BIA*. However, the proprietary right vests in the trustee as representative of the creditors,[72] and the trustee obtains the same priority over the secured creditor as that given to the claimant in a non-bankruptcy context. This argument cannot be used in connection with statutory deemed trust claims held by the Crown, since the *BIA* clearly renders the trust ineffective.[73] Nor can it be used in respect of the provisions dealing with Crown claims since these set out specific priority rules for resolving priority competitions between secured creditors and Crown claimants. Although the argument might still be employed in respect of preferred claims and writ proceedings of unsecured creditors, it was rejected in *Bank of Montreal v Titan Landco Inc.*[74] The British Columbia Court of Appeal held that the claimant's right against the secured creditor ceases to have any force and effect in bankruptcy, and that it was not the intention of Parliament to give the claimant any higher priority.

C. UNPAID SUPPLIERS OF GOODS

A supplier of goods who did not exercise the precaution of taking a security interest in goods that it sold had a very limited ability to claim a proprietary right in the goods at common law. The seller could claim an unpaid seller's lien if the seller remained in possession of the goods.[75] The seller also had the right of stoppage in transit, which permitted the seller to retake possession of goods that had been delivered to a carrier.[76] These limited rights were of no use in cases where the buyer had obtained delivery of the goods.

In 1992 new provisions were added to the bankruptcy statute that enhanced the position of suppliers. Trade suppliers were given a right to repossess recently delivered goods. Suppliers of agricultural products were given a secured charge on all the inventory of the debtor. In both cases, the supplier's right is given priority over any competing

71 See J Williamson, "Statutory Liens: The Trustee's Kick at the Can" (1986) 60 CBR (NS) 97.

72 *Re Giffen*, above note 19.

73 *BIA*, s 67(2).

74 (1990), 78 CBR (NS) 231 (BCCA).

75 See, for example, *Sale of Goods Act*, RSBC 1996, c 410, s 44.

76 *Ibid*, s 47.

security interest in the goods. The provisions have attracted controversy.[77] Some believe they should be scrapped. Others think that they should be redesigned. Despite this, the provisions were not greatly altered by the 2009 amendments to the *BIA*.

1) Thirty-Day Goods

An unpaid supplier who sells and delivers goods for use in the purchaser's business has a right to repossess the goods. The right can be exercised against a trustee in bankruptcy or receiver. There are four conditions that must exist before this right can be exercised.[78] First, the supplier must present a written demand for repossession to the purchaser, trustee, or receiver. The demand must set out the details of the transaction and must be given within a period of fifteen days after the day that the debtor went into bankruptcy or receivership. Second, the goods must have been delivered within thirty days before the day that the debtor went into bankruptcy or receivership.[79] Third, the purchaser must be bankrupt or a receiver must have been appointed at the time of the demand. Fourth, the goods must be in the possession of the purchaser, trustee, or receiver,[80] they must be identifiable as the goods sold, they must be in their same state, and they must not have been sold or agreed to be sold in an arm's length transaction.

If the goods have been partly paid for, the supplier can repossess a portion of the goods proportional to the unpaid amount. Alternatively, the supplier can repay the amount of the partial payment and repossess all of the goods.[81] The purchaser, trustee, or receiver is allowed to retain the goods if their full purchase price is paid to the supplier after the demand is made.[82] The supplier's right to repossess is lost if the right is not

77 See T Buckwold & R Wood, "Priorities" in S Ben-Ishai & A Duggan, eds, *Canadian Bankruptcy and Insolvency Law: Bill C-55, Statute c. 47 and Beyond* (Markham, ON: LexisNexis Canada, 2007) 101 at 129–31.

78 *BIA*, s 81.1(1).

79 The demand does not need to provide a description of the goods sufficient to identify them. It must merely give notice of the claim and provide details of the transaction that gave rise to it. See *Royal Bank of Canada v Stereo People of Canada Ltd (Trustee of)* (1996), 44 CBR (3d) 213 (Alta CA).

80 The requirement of possession is not satisfied if the goods are in the possession of a warehouse keeper or other bailee who is claiming a storage lien in respect of the goods. See *Thomson Consumer Electronics Canada Inc v Consumers Distributing Inc (Receiver of)* (1999), 5 CBR (4th) 141 (Ont CA), aff'g (1996), 43 CBR (3d) 77 (Ont Ct Gen Div) [*Thomson Consumer Electronics*].

81 *BIA*, s 81.1(2).

82 *Ibid*, s 81.1(1)(d).

exercised within the fifteen-day period following the bankruptcy or receivership, unless the time period is extended by the trustee or receiver, or by the court.[83] The supplier is given priority over every other right or claim to goods except for that of a *bona fide* subsequent purchaser of the goods for value without notice of the supplier's right of repossession.[84]

Two justifications were given for the creation of a supplier's superpriority over all other claimants. The first was concerned with the behaviour of debtors who are insolvent or on the eve of insolvency. The provision was intended to undo the harm that would be suffered by suppliers when the debtor orders excessive amounts of inventory immediately before bankruptcy or receivership. The second is that the protection afforded by these provisions will induce suppliers to continue to supply goods to businesses that are encountering financial difficulties.[85]

On its surface, the supplier's right of repossession appears powerful. The reality, however, is that suppliers are often unable to assert it against the goods that they have delivered. The supplier must act swiftly since the notice must be given not later than fifteen days after the bankruptcy or receivership.[86] This feature of the provisions was introduced by the 2009 amendments to the *BIA*. The notice requirement under the original provision was even more onerous: thirty days from the date of delivery. In many instances the time period would have expired or would be on the verge of expiring before the supplier even learned of the bankruptcy or receivership.[87] The right of repossession is lost if the goods have been sold or subject to an agreement for sale,[88] and the supplier has no right to claim the proceeds of sale. It is also lost if raw products that have been supplied to a manufacturer are transformed into work in progress or finished products. The thirty-day goods rule therefore does not provide an effective antidote to the problem

---

83 *Ibid*, s 81.1(5).

84 *Ibid*, s 81.1(6).

85 Senate Standing Committee on Banking, Trade and Commerce, *Debtors and Creditors: Sharing the Burden: A Review of the Bankruptcy and Insolvency Act and the Companies' Creditors Arrangement Act* by Richard H Kroft & David Tkachuk (Ottawa: Standing Senate Committee on Banking, Trade and Commerce, 2003) at 106.

86 The court can extend the time period, but this will be done only in unusual circumstances. See *Keystone Forest Products Ltd v Garibaldi Building Supplies Ltd (Receiver of)* (1995), 32 CBR (3d) 139 (BCSC) (extension of time granted where delay in appointment of receiver caused by Christmas holidays).

87 See R Klotz, "Protection of Unpaid Sellers under the New *Bankruptcy and Insolvency Act*" (1993) 21 *Canadian Business Law Journal* 161.

88 *Re Commercial Body Builders Ltd* (1993), 21 CBR (3d) 218 (BCSC), aff'd (*sub nom Basic Technologies Inc v Price Waterhouse Ltd*) (1994), 29 CBR (3d) 155 (BCCA).

of excessive purchases on the eve of bankruptcy. Furthermore, it is unlikely that any supplier would continue to supply goods on reliance of its right of repossession. This is particularly so in light of the fact that the right is not available in restructuring proceedings under the *CCAA* or under the commercial proposal provisions of the *BIA*.[89]

A supplier's right of repossession is also lost if the goods are no longer identifiable. Some courts have strictly interpreted this requirement. Suppose that a supplier delivers 100 items on 1 September and another 100 items on 1 October. The purchaser goes bankrupt on 15 October and on 30 October the supplier gives the trustee the demand for repossession. There are 80 items in the possession of the trustee; the purchaser sold the rest prior to the bankruptcy. The items are not marked with a serial number or other identifier so that it is not possible to determine their delivery date. Courts that apply a strict test of identifiability will conclude that the supplier cannot assert a right of repossession against any of the goods because the supplier is unable to show which of the goods came from the last delivery.[90] Courts using the strict test are unwilling to apply a presumption — either that the first items to be delivered were the first to be sold, or that sales were to be attributed proportionally out of the two deliveries — that would break the evidentiary impasse.

A greater willingness to apply common law rules to identify mixed goods was shown by the British Columbia Court of Appeal in *Port Alice Specialty Cellulose Inc Estate (Trustee of) v ConocoPhillips Co*.[91] Fuel oil was pumped into a storage tank in which there was fuel oil from earlier deliveries. The amount added to the storage tank and the amount previously in it was known. The court held that the commingling of the goods did not destroy their identity and that the court could properly infer that the fuel was evenly drawn upon. The supplier's right to repossess could be exercised against the same proportion of the remaining fuel oil as the quantity of new oil bears to the total quantity of new oil and old oil.

---

89 Section 81.1(4) of the *BIA* provides that the running of the thirty-day period is suspended during the time in which a commercial proposal is being attempted. The courts have created a similar rule in respect of the *Companies' Creditors Arrangement Act*. See *Re Woodward's Ltd* (1993), 17 CBR (3d) 253 (BCSC). This is of no help to the supplier if the inventory has been sold to customers during the reorganization attempt.

90 *Thomson Consumer Electronics*, above note 80; *Bruce Agra Foods Inc v Everfresh Beverages Inc (Interim Receiver of)* (1996), 45 CBR (3d) 169 (Ont Ct Gen Div); *Re Stokes Building Supplies Ltd* (1994), 30 CBR (3d) 36 (Nfld SC).

91 (2005), 11 CBR (5th) 279 (BCCA).

2) Suppliers of Agricultural Products

A farmer, fisher, or aquaculturalist who has sold products to a purchaser within fifteen days prior to the date of a bankruptcy or receivership of the purchaser has a security on all the inventory of the purchaser to secure the unpaid price.[92] In order to assert the security, the claimant must file a proof of claim within thirty days of the bankruptcy or receivership. The security has priority over any other claim, right, or security, except that it is subordinate to a supplier's right to repossess thirty-day goods. A trustee or receiver who sells the property is liable to the supplier for the net amount realized but is subrogated to the supplier's rights.

The security does not arise in respect of goods that are sold to a buyer prior to the bankruptcy. Because the security interest comes into existence on the date of the bankruptcy and covers all inventory then owned by the debtor, it will not cover inventory that was sold prior to the bankruptcy. Nor can it be claimed against the proceeds of such pre-bankruptcy sales. The security arises only on a bankruptcy or receivership of a debtor. It does not arise if the purchaser attempts to restructure under the commercial proposal provisions of the *BIA* or under the *CCAA*. The security is not subject to the identifiability problems associated with thirty-day goods. Because the supplier does not need to identify or trace the product that was sold to the purchaser, the security can be claimed on inventory even if it is not in any way connected with the product supplied to the purchaser.

D. EMPLOYEE CHARGES

The 2009 amendments to the *BIA* introduced sweeping changes that affect the status of the claims of employees in a bankruptcy of the employer. Under the prior law, an employee was afforded the status only of a preferred claimant. This was of limited use, since in many cases the assets of the employer were subject to a security interest that covered all of the debtor's assets. This effectively gave the secured creditor priority over all preferred creditors. Although employment standards statutes in several provinces gave the employees priority over a prior

92 *BIA*, s 81.2(1). The security is not available to persons who acquire the products from a farmer, fisher, or aquaculturalist. See *St Anne-Nackawic Pulp Company Ltd (Bankruptcy of); Re Forest Products Marketing Boards v Green Jain Wedlake*, 2005 NBQB 291.

secured creditor, these were rendered inoperative in a bankruptcy.[93] An employee also encountered difficulties in recovering unpaid pension contributions and pension liabilities of the employer. Pension legislation often creates a deemed trust in favour of the employees, but this, too, was ineffective in bankruptcy. As a result, the employee was considered to be an ordinary creditor in respect of these claims and was entitled only to share *pro rata* with the other ordinary creditors. The *BIA* has now been amended so as to provide a new charge that secures unpaid wages of employees and a new charge that secures unpaid pension contributions.

1) The Wage-Earner Charge

Employees will usually not need to resort to the wage-earner charge because they are permitted to make a direct claim for compensation with the wage-earner protection program.[94] This is an insurance scheme funded out of general revenues that provides payment to individuals in respect of wages that are owed to them by employers who are bankrupt or in receivership. Once a payment is made to an unpaid employee, the federal government becomes subrogated to any right that the employee has against the bankrupt or insolvent employer, and against any director or officer in the case of a bankrupt or insolvent employer.[95] For this reason, it is likely that the federal Crown rather than the individual employees will be asserting the claim in the bankruptcy of the employer.[96] The claim is made by delivering the prescribed form to the trustee.[97]

The *BIA* gives an employee a statutory secured charge to the extent of $2,000 less any amount paid to the employee by the trustee.[98] It secures wages, salary, commissions, or compensation that was earned during the period that begins six months before the date of the initial bankruptcy event and ends on the date of the bankruptcy.[99] This includes vacation

93 See Section B(6), above in this chapter.

94 *Wage Earner Protection Program Act*, SC 2005, c 47, s 1, as am by SC 2007, c 36 [*WEPPA*].

95 *Ibid*, s 36.

96 The maximum recovery under the *WEPPA* is in excess of $3,000, while the maximum amount secured by the wage-earner charge is $2,000 for each employee. This means that the federal government bears the risk of uncompensated liability for a portion of the claim.

97 *BIA*, s 81.3(8).

98 *Ibid*, s 81.3(1).

99 Commissions that are payable when goods are shipped, delivered, or paid are secured by the charge if the shipment, delivery, or payment occurs within this

pay but not termination or severance pay.[100] Although the charge secures contributions that are directed to third parties from the pay of employees such as union dues or payments to a third-party service provider such as an extended health coverage provider,[101] the third-party service provider is not permitted to assert the charge in respect of amounts owed to it by the employer in respect of benefits that had been provided to the employees.[102] Disbursements to a maximum of $1,000, less any amount paid by the trustee, owing to a travelling salesperson are also secured by a statutory secured charge.[103] A director or officer of a bankrupt corporation is not entitled to claim the charge.[104] A person who is not acting at arm's length with the bankrupt is also not entitled to claim the charge unless the trustee is of the opinion that the parties would have entered into a substantially similar transaction if they had not been dealing with one another at arm's length.[105]

The wage-earner charge attaches to all current assets of the employer. Current assets are defined as cash, cash equivalents (including cheques and demand deposits), inventory or accounts receivable, or the proceeds of dealing of any of these assets.[106] It does not include real property or equipment. Nor does it include intellectual property rights unless the employer holds them as inventory.

The wage-earner charge ranks above every other claim, right, charge, or security against the bankrupt's current assets other than the statutory right to recover thirty-day goods, the statutory charge in favour of suppliers of agricultural products, and source deductions of income tax, CPP, and EI or provincial equivalents that are deemed to be held in trust.[107] If a trustee disposes of currents assets covered by an employee's

---

period. See *BIA*, s 81.3(2).

100 *Ibid*, s 81.3(9) "compensation."

101 *Ted Leroy Trucking Ltd v Century Services Inc*, 2010 BCCA 223.

102 *Ted LeRoy Trucking Ltd (Re)*, 2012 BCCA 511. If the benefit has been provided to the employees by the third-party provider, the employees will have no claim in respect of their contribution since nothing is owed to them and the third-party provider has simply an unsecured claim against the employer. If the employees have not received the benefit from the third-party provider, then they have a secured claim in respect of the contributions owed to them, but the third-party provider will have no claim as it did not supply the benefits.

103 *BIA*, s 81.3(3).

104 *Ibid*, s 81.3(6).

105 *Ibid*, s 81.3(7). In making this determination, the trustee is directed to consider the remuneration for, the terms and conditions of, and the duration, nature, and importance of the services rendered.

106 *Ibid*, s 2 "current assets."

107 *Ibid*, s 81.3(4).

secured charge, the trustee or receiver is liable for the amount realized on the disposition of the current assets.[108]

2) The Pension Contribution Charge

The *BIA* creates a charge that secures unpaid pension contributions in respect of prescribed pension plans.[109] These amounts are not recoverable under the wage-earner protection program.[110] The charge covers pension contribution arrears (amounts deducted from the employee's remuneration that were not paid into the fund), contributions owed by an employer for the normal costs of the plan[111] (the cost of benefits offered under the pension plan that are to accrue during a plan year, excluding amounts payable to reduce an initial unfunded pension liability or solvency deficiency), and contributions owed by an employer to a defined contribution plan.

Unlike the wage-earner charge, the pension-contribution charge is not limited to current assets but extends to all of the debtor's assets. There is no limitation on the amount that can be claimed or on the time period within which it may be claimed. The pension-contribution charge ranks above every other claim, right, charge, or security against the bankrupt's assets other than the statutory right to recover thirty-day goods, the statutory charge in favour of suppliers of agricultural products, the wage-earner charge, and source deductions of income tax, CPP, and EI or provincial equivalents that are deemed to be held in trust.[112] If a trustee disposes of currents assets covered by an employee's secured charge, the trustee or receiver is liable for the amount realized on the disposition of the current assets.[113]

E. CROWN CLAIMS

Prior to 1992, Crown claims and of workers' compensation bodies (hereafter referred to simply as "Crown claims") were afforded the status of a preferred claim in bankruptcy and any provincial devices, such as a statutory charge or deemed trust, were rendered inoperative.

108 *Ibid*, s 81.3(5).
109 *Ibid*, s 81.5(1).
110 *WEPPA*, above note 94, s 2.
111 See *Pension Benefits Standards Regulations, 1985*, SOR/87-19, s 2(1) "normal cost" and "special payment," s 9.
112 *BIA*, s 81.5(2).
113 *Ibid*, s 81.5(3).

In 1992 this regime underwent a fundamental change. Crown claims are now afforded an unsecured creditor ranking in bankruptcy unless the matter falls within either of two exceptions.[114] The first is where the claim is secured by a security conferred by a law of general application. The Crown is therefore able to obtain a consensual security interest in the same manner as any other creditor. The second exception is where the Crown registers the security in the manner provided for in the *BIA*.[115] If either of these exceptions is satisfied, the Crown's claim will enjoy the status of a secured creditor and the bankruptcy provisions that apply to secured creditors will come into play.[116] These provisions do not apply to deemed trusts in favour of the Crown. A different bankruptcy provision invalidates most deemed trusts in favour of the Crown unless they satisfy the legal requirements of an ordinary express trust.[117]

The provisions respecting Crown claims do not apply to the federal statutory garnishment remedy that secures certain types of obligations in respect of income tax, CPP and EI, or to any provincial counterpart.[118] The *Income Tax Act* provides an attachment remedy by which a debt owed by a third party to the debtor can be intercepted. It also provides that the remedy has priority over competing secured creditors who have a security interest in this account.[119] This claim will therefore continue to enjoy priority over secured creditors despite a bankruptcy of the debtor. Although a similar attachment remedy is enacted in the *Excise Tax Act*[120] in respect of GST, this is not within the exception and therefore will be reduced to an unsecured claim unless it is registered before the date of the initial bankruptcy event. If a requirement to pay in respect of unpaid GST has been given before the bankruptcy proceedings are initiated, the Crown will prevail since the statute provides that the Crown becomes the owner of the debt, and therefore the debt will not form part of the bankrupt estate.[121]

---

114 *Ibid*, ss 86(1)–(2).

115 Registration is necessary even in the case of a possessory lien in favour of the Crown, if it is not one that would be ordinarily available to a person other than the Crown. See *Resource Plastics Inc (Trustee of) v W Pickett & Bros. Customs Brokers Inc* (1995), 36 CBR (3d) 231 (Ont Ct Gen Div).

116 See Section C, above in this chapter.

117 Chapter 4, Section C(1)(d). An exception is made for deemed trusts in respect of source deductions of income tax, CPP, and EI.

118 *BIA*, s 87(3).

119 *ITA*, above note 21, s 224(1.2).

120 RSC 1985, c E-15, s 317(3) [*ETA*].

121 *Toronto Dominion Bank v Canada*, 2010 FCA 174.

The *ITA* and *ETA* also create a mechanism through which the minister may certify an amount that is payable in respect of income tax or GST, and when registered in the Federal Court it has the same effect as if it were a judgment.[122] Although a trustee in bankruptcy ordinarily takes precedence over registered or unregistered writs and judgments,[123] the statutes expressly provide that registration gives the Crown the status of a secured creditor.[124]

In order to comply with the registration requirements, the security must be registered before the date that an application for a bankruptcy order is filed in the case of an involuntary bankruptcy or the date of an assignment in the case of a voluntary bankruptcy.[125] Crown claims are registered in the appropriate real or personal property registry,[126] and several provinces have modified their registration rules to specifically accommodate these types of registrations.[127]

The bankruptcy provisions also provide a priority rule to resolve competitions between a Crown claim and the claim of a secured creditor.[128] The rule has two parts to it. First, the Crown's security is subordinate to competing security interests in the same property if the secured creditor completed "all steps necessary to make them effective against other creditors" before registration of the Crown claims. In order to take advantage of the first rule, a secured creditor must comply with the validity and perfection requirements that pertain to the secured transaction regime that governs its security interest.[129] In the case of a security interest that is governed by provincial personal property security law, registration is not sufficient. A security interest is not effective against third parties unless it has attached (i.e., come into existence) and a perfection step (usually registration) is completed.

---

122 *ITA*, above note 21, s 223; *ETA*, above note 120, s 316.

123 See Chapter 6, Section A(4).

124 *ITA*, above note 21, s 223(11.1); *ETA*, above note 120, s 316(10.1). This will mean that the Crown will have a security interest the priority of which is governed by *BIA*, s 87(2) so long as the registration occurs before the bankruptcy or insolvency proceedings are first initiated.

125 *BIA*, s 87(1). And see s 2 "date of the initial bankruptcy event." Other provisions cover the situation where other insolvency were initiated prior to the bankruptcy proceedings.

126 The *Bankruptcy and Insolvency General Rules*, CRC 368, s 111, provides that a "prescribed system of registration" referred to in section 86(2) "is a system of registration of securities that is available to Her Majesty in right of Canada or a province and to any other creditor holding a security, and is open to the public for inspection or for the making of searches."

127 See, for example, *Personal Property Security Regulation*, Alta Reg 95/2001, s 31.

128 *BIA*, s 87(2).

129 *Korchynski v Sparkle Car Wash Ltd* (1998), 8 CBR (4th) 47 (Man QB).

If a secured creditor has not obtained a written security agreement or has not given value at the time of registration of the Crown claim, the secured creditor cannot rely upon this priority rule.[130]

It is unclear if the bankruptcy priority rule gives a secured creditor priority in respect of property acquired by the debtor after registration of the Crown claim. In order for a security interest to attach, a debtor must have rights in the collateral. As one of the conditions for attachment will not yet have occurred, a court might hold that not all steps necessary to make the security effective against other creditors had been taken. If the *BIA* priority rule were held to be inapplicable for this reason, priority would then be determined by giving effect to any priority rule specified in the legislation that creates the Crown's security, or, in the absence of a legislative priority rule, by giving priority to the first interest to attach.[131] On the other hand, a court might interpret the "all steps" requirement to refer to active steps that must be taken by the secured party rather than to the preconditions for attachment. In this event, the *BIA* priority rule would be applicable and the secured creditor would be given priority.

The second part of the bankruptcy priority rule contains the sting. Whereas the first part creates a first-in-time rule of priority, the second part greatly limits the Crown's ability to obtain its benefit. The Crown's security is valid only against amounts owing to the Crown at the time of the registration of the Crown claim.[132] This prevents the Crown from making an effective registration before the obligation owing to it arises. In the vast majority of cases, the Crown claim arises when the debtor is in financial difficulties and failing to pay its creditors. A secured creditor's security interest will usually have been granted to it earlier, during more buoyant times. As a consequence, the secured creditor will usually enjoy priority over the Crown.

F. ENVIRONMENTAL REMEDIATION ORDERS

Provincial and federal environmental protection statutes generally create liability rules rather than priority rules. They provide that a person who is in control of premises is liable for the costs of environmental

130 Ont *PPSA*, above note 38, s 10(2); BC *PPSA*, above note 38, s 12(1).

131 See Cuming, Walsh, & Wood, above note 10 at 512–14.

132 The Crown can only claim as a secured creditor for the amount of the obligation owing, and does not rank as a secured creditor in respect of costs associated with seizure or enforcement of the security. See *Re Gillford Furniture Mart Ltd* (1995), 36 CBR (3d) 157 (BCCA).

remediation.[133] The *BIA* alters this by significantly limiting the liability that would otherwise face a trustee in bankruptcy. The trustee is not liable for environmental damage that occurred prior to the trustee's appointment and is not liable for post-appointment damage unless it occurred as a result of the trustee's gross negligence or wilful misconduct.[134]

In place of a liability rule, the *BIA* creates a new proprietary right in favour of the government in respect of the costs of remediation of the environmentally damaged property. The remediation costs are secured by a security interest on the real property affected by the environmental condition as well as on any contiguous real property.[135] The security interest is given superpriority status over any other claim, right, charge, or security against the property.

G. SALES TRANSACTIONS

A sales transaction involves the passage of property in goods from the seller to the buyer. Whether or not this has occurred at the date of bankruptcy is of fundamental importance in bankruptcy law. If the buyer is bankrupt and title in the goods has not yet passed to the buyer, the seller remains the owner and can assert its proprietary right to the goods against the trustee. The bankruptcy does not terminate the contract of sale, and the trustee can therefore affirm the contact and obtain the goods by tendering the price to the seller.[136] If title has passed to the buyer, the buyer becomes the owner and the property in the goods vests in the trustee on bankruptcy. The seller no longer has an interest in the goods and can prove a claim for the unpaid price only as an unsecured creditor. The situation is otherwise if the seller is entitled to an unpaid seller's lien,[137] is able to assert the right to repossess thirty-day goods,[138] or has reserved a security interest in the goods.

If it is the seller who goes bankrupt, the tables are turned. A buyer will be able to assert a proprietary right against the trustee only if title to the goods has passed to the buyer under the contract of sale. If it has

---

133 See, for example, *Environmental Protection Act*, RSO 1990, c E.19, s 1 "person responsible" and s 124.

134 *BIA*, s 14.06(2).

135 *Ibid*, s 14.06(7).

136 See Chapter 6, Section B(1).

137 The seller in this case falls under the definition of a secured creditor. See Section B(1), above in this chapter.

138 See Section C(1), above in this chapter.

not, the buyer can prove a claim in the bankruptcy only for damages or for recovery of the price paid. A buyer is not given a lien to secure a prepayment of the price under sales law, although in British Columbia a prepaying consumer buyer is given a lien on the seller's inventory and on any account in a savings institution in which the seller usually deposits the proceeds of sales.[139] This consumer lien is effective in bankruptcy and gives the consumer the status of a secured creditor in relation to his or her claim.

Although the crucial question in these cases is whether title has passed to the buyer, it is often difficult to determine if this has occurred. Sale of goods legislation provides rules for determining when property passes. The primary rule is that property in the goods is transferred at the time the parties to the contract intend it to be transferred.[140] The contrary intention does not need to be expressly manifested in words but can be implied from the circumstances. In many instances, the parties do not specify when this is to occur. If the intention of the parties cannot be determined, the issue will be resolved through the application of a set of default rules provided in sale of goods legislation.[141] These rules draw a basic division between specific goods and unascertained goods.

Specific goods are ones that are identified and agreed upon at the time of the contract.[142] If the seller has agreed to sell specific goods to the buyer, that is what must be delivered. It is not open for the seller to substitute similar goods. The usual rule is that the property passes immediately upon making the agreement if the goods are in a deliverable state. If something more needs to be done to put them in a deliverable state, property passes when the thing is done and the buyer has notice of it.

Unascertained goods are those that have not been specifically identified. For example, the contract may call for the sale of 10 cases of wine. The wine merchant may have 100 cases in stock but may not have designated any particular cases to this contract. Or the wine merchant may not be holding any stock at all, intending to acquire it at some later time from a supplier. In order for property in unascertained goods to pass, there must be an irrevocable earmarking of the goods such that it is no longer open to the seller to substitute other goods. The inability to demonstrate an unconditional appropriation of goods to the contract

---

139 *Sale of Goods Act*, RSBC 1996, c 410, s 75.

140 *Ibid*, s 22(1). And see *NEC Corp v Steintron International Electronics Ltd* (1985), 59 CBR (NS) 91 (BCSC).

141 *BIA*, s 23.

142 *Ibid*, s 1 "specific goods."

of sale has dashed the hopes of many buyers despite the fact that the seller may have some or all of the stock on hand. A buyer simply cannot acquire title until the subject matter of his or her claim is known.[143]

Several points should be kept in mind concerning the passage of property rules. First, transfer of title can occur before, after, or at the same time as delivery of possession of the goods. The fact that a buyer has not received possession of the goods does not mean that the buyer cannot claim that title has passed under the contract of sale. Second, the passage of property rules do not depend on payment terms.[144] Property may pass to a buyer even though the buyer has not yet paid for the goods. In this case, the buyer can claim the goods from the trustee, but the bankrupt seller's right to be paid the price of the goods vests in the trustee and the trustee can bring a personal action against the buyer if the price is not paid when due. The trustee may also assert an unpaid seller's lien against goods in the possession of the bankrupt seller to the extent that the seller was entitled to claim this lien against the buyer. Third, a title-retention device that is created by a seller to secure the unpaid purchase price falls within the scope of provincial personal property security legislation. As such, it must be perfected in order to be effective against a trustee.[145]

H. MATRIMONIAL PROPERTY CLAIMS

Provincial matrimonial property legislation gives a spouse the right to apply to court for a matrimonial property order. Although jurisdictions that use an equalization approach give courts the power to make orders creating charges and transferring assets,[146] these powers are used sparingly in situations where non-compliance with the order is reasonably anticipated.[147] In jurisdictions that adopt a division of assets approach, the choice of remedies is discretionary.[148] The court may order that a spouse pay a sum of money to the other spouse or that a security or charge be given on a spouse's property to secure an obligation to pay. A court may also make an order vesting property in a spouse. The nature

---

143 *Ibid*, s 21; *Re London Wine Co (Shippers) Ltd* (1975), [1986] PCC 121; *Re Goldcorp Exchange Ltd*, [1995] 1 AC 74 (PC).

144 *Royal Bank of Canada v Saskatchewan Telecommunications*, [1985] 5 WWR 333 (Sask CA).

145 See Section B(3), above in this chapter.

146 See, for example, *Family Law Act*, RSO 1990, c F.3, s 9.

147 *Thibodeau v Thibodeau* (2009), 97 OR (3d) 618 (SCJ).

148 See, for example, *Matrimonial Property Act*, RSA 2000, c M-8, s 9(2).

of the order granted and the timing of the events are of critical importance when the spouse who owns the assets goes bankrupt.

The Supreme Court of Canada in *Maroukis v Maroukis*[149] examined the proprietary nature of a matrimonial property claim in bankruptcy. The Court held that the wording used in most models of matrimonial property legislation does not give a spouse any proprietary right to the property of the other spouse until the court makes an order vesting the property or creating some other proprietary right.[150] For this reason, the matrimonial property regimes are sometimes called deferred sharing regimes.

If a bankruptcy occurs before a court makes a matrimonial property order, the property of the owning spouse vests in the trustee in bankruptcy, and the court cannot thereafter make an order that gives the other spouse a proprietary right in this property.[151] Although matrimonial property legislation does not give the spouse any proprietary right before an order is made, the spouse may assert a proprietary claim to it on some other basis such as a resulting or constructive trust.[152]

Many matrimonial property orders do not confer a proprietary right on a spouse who is entitled to a share of the property. This depends very much on the nature of order granted by the court. An order that merely requires that a spouse pay a sum of money to the other creates only a personal right that does not give the claimant any right in the other spouse's property.[153] The order will have a proprietary effect only if it vests property in the claimant or if it creates a charge on the property to secure an obligation to pay. An order may transfer property to a spouse while also ordering him or her to pay a sum of money to the other spouse. The transfer in this case is conditional, so that no right is acquired in the property until the money obligation is satisfied. If the spouse given the entitlement to the property goes bankrupt before satisfying the monetary obligation, the condition for transfer of

---

149 [1984] 2 SCR 137. See also *Schreyer v Schreyer*, 2011 SCC 35 [*Schreyer*].

150 A few of the provinces provide for the creation of a proprietary interest at some earlier point. Newfoundland and Labrador gives both spouses an immediate joint interest in the matrimonial home. In British Columbia, legislation creates a one-half interest on the occurrence of a triggering event. See *Walsh v Canadian General Insurance Co* (1989), 60 DLR (4th) 358 (Nfld CA); *Biedler v Biedler*, [1983] 5 WWR 129 (BCSC). And see R Klotz, *Bankruptcy, Insolvency and Family Law*, 2d ed (Scarborough, ON: Carswell, 2002) at 4.2(c).

151 *Burson v Burson* (1990), 4 CBR (3d) 1 (Ont Ct Gen Div); *Menzies v Menzies* (2002), 37 CBR (4th) 98 (Sask QB).

152 See Chapter 4, Sections C(1)(b) & C(1)(c).

153 *Re Coulthard* (2003), 48 CBR (4th) 59 (Alta QB); *Re Torrie* (1993), 21 CBR (3d) 227 (Sask QB).

the property is not met and the property therefore will not vest in the trustee.[154]

This analysis is modified where exempt assets are involved. Exempt property is not divisible amongst the creditors in bankruptcy. In such cases, courts are prepared to lift the stay of proceedings and permit the non-owning spouse to bring an application under matrimonial property legislation.[155] Difficulties can arise if the owning spouse fails to disclose the other spouse as a creditor and then obtains a bankruptcy discharge. A failure to disclose does not give the non-owning spouse the right to treat the claim as an undischarged claim.[156] Courts have addressed this problem by setting aside the bankruptcy discharge.[157]

I. CLAIMS BASED ON TRACING

A claimant who had a proprietary right in an asset prior to the date of bankruptcy may discover that the asset is no longer in the possession or control of the bankrupt or the trustee. The asset may no longer exist or its whereabouts might simply be unknown. The asset might also have been sold to another person under circumstances in which the transferee obtained good title to it. In any of these events, the claimant will not be in a position to assert a proprietary right to the original asset. But this is not necessarily the end of the trail for the claimant. If the claimant can demonstrate that the bankrupt dealt with the original asset and obtained new assets in its place, the claimant may be able to trace the value of the original asset into the new asset and assert a proprietary right to it.

There are two different stages of analysis when a claim based on tracing is raised. The first involves tracing, the second claiming. Tracing is a process that is used to locate the value of the original asset. It is used to identify new assets that were substituted for the original assets. Claiming involves an assessment of the validity and priority of any right that the claimant may enjoy over the new asset. Claims that are asserted as a result of the tracing process often arise in connection with trust property. But tracing is not limited to this context. If a thief steals goods from the owner, sells them, and then goes bankrupt, the

---

154 *Millar v Millar* (1991), 8 CBR (3d) 220 (Alta CA).

155 *Schreyer*, above note 149; *Re Cunningham*, 2009 ABQB 758. And see Chapter 6, Section A(6).

156 *Schreyer*, above note 149.

157 *BIA*, s187(5); *Schreyer (Re)*, 2014 MBQB 44.

owner can elect one of two courses. The owner can follow the goods into the hands of the buyer and seek to recover the goods or their value from the buyer. Alternatively, the owner can claim the traceable proceeds of sale in the hands of the trustee.[158]

In some cases, the tracing exercise is simple. A bankrupt may have sold an automobile and received a cheque in payment of the price. The cheque may still be in the hands of the bankrupt at the time of the bankruptcy. A claimant who has a proprietary right in the automobile may trace the value of the automobile into the cheque and claim a proprietary interest in it. In other cases, the tracing exercise may be more complex. The complexity often arises because the asset is mixed with other assets so that its identification becomes difficult. Such issues would arise if the cheque were deposited into an active bank account, thereby becoming mixed with funds belonging to the bankrupt. The law of tracing provides rules that permit the claimant to resolve the evidential impasse that would otherwise put an end to any claim to substituted assets.

If property is mixed with property that belongs to a wrongdoer, tracing principles will resolve any evidential difficulty against the wrongdoer. Suppose that a thief steals $1,000 from the claimant and deposits it into a bank account that contains $500 of the thief's own money. The thief later withdraws $500 and uses it to buy a bicycle. The thief then goes bankrupt. The claimant can trace the value of the money stolen into the funds remaining in the account and assert a proprietary claim to it against the trustee. This will be the preferred choice if the bicycle has depreciated in value. Alternatively, the claimant can trace the value into the bicycle. This will be the preferred choice if the thief subsequently withdrew and spent the remaining funds in the account. The claimant rather than the thief gets to choose, and the trustee in bankruptcy is in no better position than the thief in this regard.

This rule applies only if there is a factual possibility that the value could have ended up in the new asset. Suppose that the thief drains the bank account of all its funds and loses all of it at a casino. The thief later deposits his paycheque into the account. The claimant's right to trace comes to an end. The claimant can no longer link her money to the funds in the account.[159] This forms the basis of a principle called the "lowest intermediate balance rule." Suppose that $200 of trust money is mixed with $200 belonging to a trustee who has wrongfully mixed the

---

158 The bankrupt will hold the proceeds for the owner under a constructive trust. See *British Columbia Teachers' Credit Union v Betterly* (1975), 61 DLR (3d) 755 (BCSC).

159 See *Re Graphicshoppe Ltd* (2005), 15 CBR (5th) 207 (Ont CA).

funds in breach of trust. The trustee withdraws $300 and then later deposits $100 of the trustee's own money into the account. The claimant has a traceable claim to only $100. That is the maximum amount that could have come from the claimant, and a later deposit of the wrongdoer's money can do nothing to change this fact.

Sometimes there is a mixing of property of several claimants, none of whom has breached any duty owed to the others. The presumption against a wrongdoer cannot be applied. If there is not enough to cover all their claims, some other rule must be used to determine their portion of the fund. The Supreme Court of Canada in *Ontario (Securities Commission) v Greymac Credit Corp*[160] held that it is not appropriate in this case to apply a presumption that the first funds to be deposited are the first to be withdrawn. Instead, it applied a *pro rata* depletion rule that shares the loss in proportion to their respective contributions.

There is one further possibility. Suppose that $200 belonging to A is mixed with $200 belonging to B. The trustee withdraws $300. The *pro rata* depletion rule provides that the loss is shared so that both A and B can claim $50 each. But later $400 belonging to C is added to the mixture. The intermediate balance rule permits C to trace its value to the extent of $400, and A and B are limited to their claims of $50.[161] If the financial records are such that is impossible or impracticable to determine the sequence of events, the courts will apply a *pari passu* approach that shares the end balance in proportion to the original contributions.[162] Under this approach, A and B would recover $125 and C would recover $250.

There is considerable uncertainty on whether tracing is available where a debt is incurred in connection with the acquisition of an asset, and property of the claimant is later used to satisfy that debt.[163] This is sometimes referred to as "backwards tracing." Suppose that D incurs a debt of $100 in order to acquire goods. Property of E is then used to pay the debt. E argues that payment of this debt permits it to trace the

---

160 [1988] 2 SCR 172.

161 *Boughner v Greyhawk Equity Partners Limited Partnership (Millenium)*, 2012 ONSC 3185, aff'd 2013 ONCA 26.

162 *Law Society of Upper Canada v Toronto Dominion Bank* (1998), 169 DLR (4th) 353 (Ont CA).

163 See L Smith, *The Law of Tracing* (Oxford: Clarendon Press, 1997) at 146–52 who argues that tracing through a debt is permissible. But see M Conaglen, "Difficulties with Backwards Tracing" (2011) 127 *Law Quarterly Review* 432 who argues that the caselaw support for it is weaker than suggested, and that there are policy concerns that militate against it.

value of the payment into the goods. Courts in other jurisdictions have held that the payment of the debt signifies the end of the tracing trail.[164]

A claimant may not wish to claim the traceable proceeds as property held in trust by the bankrupt for the beneficiary. It may be advantageous for the claimant to assert a claim to an equitable lien on the proceeds.[165] An equitable lien is a proprietary right in the asset that secures an obligation. Suppose that a trustee takes $20,000 of his own funds and $20,000 of B's funds and uses them to buy an automobile. The automobile depreciates with use and currently has a value of $30,000. A proprietary claim to beneficial ownership would give the claimant a 50 percent interest in the automobile. A claim to an equitable lien would give the claimant a lien on its entire value to secure a personal right to recover $20,000 from the trustee. As against a wrongdoer, the claimant has the option to claim a proportional share or a lien.[166] Upon a bankruptcy, the holder of an equitable lien would fall within the definition of a secured creditor in the *BIA*.[167]

Claims based on tracing also arise when a secured creditor asserts a claim to proceeds of collateral sold by the bankrupt. Personal property security legislation gives the secured creditor a right to claim a security interest in the proceeds.[168] The statutes use the tracing principles to determine which assets are sufficiently connected with the original collateral so as to be considered proceeds. A security interest in proceeds must be perfected in order to have priority over the trustee in bankruptcy.[169]

J. SPECIFIC PERFORMANCE

Under certain circumstances, a court may make an order for the specific performance of an obligation. By virtue of this order, the person against whom the order is made may be directed by the court to transfer property to the other party. The equitable remedy of specific performance is available in cases where damages are inadequate. In order to satisfy this condition, the person seeking the order must demonstrate that the property is unique or irreplaceable so that damages would not provide

164 *Bishopsgate Investment Management Ltd (In Liquidation) v Homan*, [1995] Ch 211 (CA), Leggatt LJ; *Re Registered Securities*, [1991] 1 NZLR 545 at 554 (CA).

165 See Smith, above note 163 at 347–50.

166 *Foskett v McKeown*, [2001] 1 AC 102 (HL), Lord Millett.

167 See Section B(1), above in this chapter.

168 See Cuming, Walsh, & Wood, above note 10 at 556–84.

169 Ont *PPSA*, above note 38, s 20(1); BC *PPSA*, above note 38, s 20(b).

an adequate substitute. Contracts for the sale of land are specifically enforceable, whereas contracts for the sale of personal property generally are not.

A person who could be compelled to transfer property by an order for specific performance may become bankrupt, and it is necessary to determine the effect of bankruptcy on the party who has the right to compel the transfer. If the claimant can assert the right against the trustee, the claimant will obtain a transfer of the property. This will leave less for the other creditors who must satisfy their claims from the remaining assets of the bankrupt. If the right to compel a transfer is not available, the claimant must prove the claim in the bankruptcy and share with the other creditors.

In order to determine the effect of bankruptcy on a claim for specific performance, it is necessary to analyze the proprietary effect of a specifically enforceable contract. As soon as the parties enter into a specifically enforceable contract, an immediate proprietary interest arises in equity even though the contract contemplates that legal title will be conveyed at some future date. The vendor immediately holds the property under a constructive trust, and the beneficial ownership of the property passes to the purchaser.[170] The *BIA* specifically provides that trust property is not divisible among the creditors.[171] For this reason, a claimant who has entered into a specifically enforceable contract for land can compel its transfer.

The analysis is rendered more complex by two difficulties. The first arises out of the decision of the Supreme Court of Canada in *Semelhago v Paramadevan*.[172] The Court held that it was not appropriate to distinguish between land and personal property, and that courts should not assume that the land is unique and that a decree of specific performance should be granted. Unfortunately, the Court did not consider the implications of this conclusion in respect of the proprietary rights of the parties. The constructive trust that is imposed on the vendor arises only if the contract is specifically enforceable. It is now far more difficult to predict whether the vendor will be regarded as holding the land in trust for the purchaser. If the vendor does not hold it in trust for the purchaser, the trustee in bankruptcy will be entitled to retain the property. The purchaser may attempt to claim an equitable lien against the property to secure the refund of the purchase price. However, this right is also linked to the availability of specific performance, and therefore

170 *Lysaght v Edwards* (1876), 2 Ch D 499; *Young v Royal Bank of Canada* (1978), 27 CBR (NS) 244 (Ont HCJ).

171 *BIA*, s 67(1)(a).

172 [1996] 2 SCR 415.

it is uncertain whether the claim to an equitable lien will be recognized if the property is not unique.[173]

The second difficulty concerns specific performance against personal property. Although courts will not usually make a decree for specific performance in respect of goods, they may do so if the goods are unique. Ordinarily, this would attract the same analysis as applied in respect of land. The seller would immediately hold the goods under a constructive trust, and beneficial ownership would pass to the buyer. However, there is considerable uncertainty over whether the enactment of sale of goods legislation displaced the creation of equitable property rights in respect of contracts for the sale of goods. The English Court of Appeal in *Re Wait*[174] held that legislation was intended to codify the passage of property rules in sales contracts and that a failure to make reference to equitable property interests indicated an intention to exclude them. On this view, a claimant who could obtain a decree of specific performance in respect of goods does not have any proprietary right in the goods. The claimant is therefore unable to compel their transfer from the trustee. Even if Canadian courts adopt this view, it is limited to cases dealing with goods and will not extend to other forms of personal property such as shares.[175] Although shares in publicly traded companies would not be regarded as unique since replacements can be purchased, shares in closely held corporations would likely satisfy this condition.[176]

FURTHER READINGS

Baird, D, & R Davis. "Labour Issues" in S Ben-Ishai & A Duggan, eds, *Canadian Bankruptcy and Insolvency Law: Bill C-55, Statute c. 47 and Beyond* (Markham, ON: LexisNexis Canada, 2007) ch 4

---

173 See R Chambers, "The Importance of Specific Performance" in S Degeling & J Edelman, eds, *Equity in Commercial Law* (Sydney: Lawbook, 2005) 431. The High Court of Australia in *Hewett v Court* (1983), 149 CLR 639 held that the purchaser's lien was available even though the contract was not specifically enforceable, and it is possible that Canadian courts would adopt this approach. See *Corse v Ravenwood Homes Ltd* (1998), 226 AR 214 (QB).

174 [1927] 1 Ch 606 (CA), Atkin LJ.

175 *Michaels v Harley House (Marylebone) Ltd*, [1999] 3 WLR 229 (CA).

176 *Connor v MacCulloch* (1974), 18 NSR (2d) 404 (SCTD).

BUCKWOLD, T, & R WOOD. "Priorities" in S Ben-Ishai & A Duggan, eds, *Canadian Bankruptcy and Insolvency Law: Bill C-55, Statute c. 47 and Beyond* (Markham, ON: LexisNexis Canada, 2007) ch 5

CHAMBERS, R. "The Importance of Specific Performance" in S Degeling & J Edelman, eds, *Equity in Commercial Law* (Sydney: Lawbook, 2005) 431

CUMING, R, C WALSH, & R WOOD. *Personal Property Security Law*, 2d ed (Toronto: Irwin Law, 2012) ch 10

GOODE, R. *Proprietary Rights and Insolvency in Sales Transactions* (London, Sweet & Maxwell, 1985)

KLOTZ, R. "Protection of Unpaid Sellers under the New *Bankruptcy and Insolvency Act*" (1993) 21 *Canadian Business Law Journal* 161

———. *Bankruptcy, Insolvency and Family Law*, 2d ed (Scarborough, ON: Carswell, 2002–) ch 4

SARRA, J, & S BOYD. "Competing Notions of Fairness: A Principled Approach to the Intersection of Insolvency Law and Family Property Law in Canada" in J Sarra, ed, *Annual Review of Insolvency Law, 2011* (Toronto: Carswell, 2012) 207

SMITH, L. *The Law of Tracing* (Oxford: Clarendon Press, 1997)

WILLIAMSON, J. "Statutory Liens: The Trustee's Kick at the Can" (1986) 60 *Canadian Bankruptcy Reports (New Series)* 97

WOOD, R. "The Definition of Secured Creditor in Insolvency Law" (2010) 25 *Banking and Finance Law Review* 341

———. "The Structure of Secured Priorities in Insolvency Law" (2011) 27 *Banking and Finance Law Review* 26

CHAPTER 6

PRESERVING THE BANKRUPT ESTATE

The property of the debtor vests in the trustee on bankruptcy, and the trustee will gather in and assemble these assets. To facilitate this process, bankruptcy law provides a set of rules and principles that are designed to preserve the bankrupt estate so that its full value can be realized. Bankruptcy is a collective proceeding through which claimants with personal rights against a debtor can enforce their claims against the debtor's assets. For this to work properly, it is absolutely essential to stop attempts by these creditors to enforce their claims or to recover their debts. To permit them to remove assets from the bankrupt estate would seriously destabilize the bankruptcy system. Ordinary litigation must also come to a stop on the occurrence of a bankruptcy. In its place, bankruptcy law provides a summary method for determining the validity and the value of claims against the bankrupt. Bankruptcy law prevents creditors from interfering with the trustee's administration of the bankrupt estate through an automatic stay of proceedings.

In order to maximize the value of the bankrupt estate, the trustee must also make a number of important decisions. The trustee must decide whether or not to perform contracts that were concluded between the debtor and a third party prior to the bankruptcy. If the debtor's property has been polluted or contaminated and is subject to an environmental remediation order, the trustee must make a choice between retaining and cleaning up the property or abandoning it. Finally, bankruptcy law contains rules and mechanisms that protect against post-bankruptcy conduct or actions of the debtor that would otherwise diminish the value of the bankrupt estate.

A. THE STAY OF PROCEEDINGS

1) Objectives of the Stay

The bankruptcy stay of proceedings serves two fundamental purposes. First, by preventing creditors from commencing or continuing their legal actions, it replaces the normal civil process with a summary method by which the trustee reviews, accepts, or rejects and values claims against the bankrupt estate. This prevents a multiplicity of actions and significantly reduces the costs of adjudication of the various claims.[1] Second, by preventing creditors from enforcing their claims against the bankrupt's property, it replaces a free-for-all — in which creditors attempt to seize assets before other creditors are able to do so — with a more orderly liquidation and *pro rata* sharing that, to the collective benefit of all the creditors, is more likely to enhance the value that will be received for the assets.[2]

Bankruptcy law draws a sharp division between proprietary rights and personal rights held by claimants. Claimants who can establish a proprietary right to an asset are able to take the asset out of the bankrupt estate, since it is only the property of the debtor that is divisible among the creditors. The mechanism by which they assert such claims has been previously examined.[3] Those who have personal rights against the bankrupt must prove their claims within the bankruptcy regime. The bankruptcy claims procedure as well as the trustee's responsibility to liquidate assets and distribute the proceeds by way of a bankruptcy dividend are exclusive processes that replace the normal methods by which creditors establish and enforce their personal rights. The automatic bankruptcy stay of proceedings is the mechanism that ensures the exclusivity of these two processes. For this reason, the automatic bankruptcy stay of proceedings applies only to creditors who have provable claims in bankruptcy. Claimants who have proprietary claims or personal claims that arise after the bankruptcy do not have provable claims, and therefore they must enforce their claims outside the bankruptcy system.

---

1 *382231 Ontario Ltd v Wilanour Resources Ltd* (1982), 43 CBR (NS) 153 (Ont HCJ) [*Wilanour*].

2 *R v Fitzgibbon*, [1990] 1 SCR 1005; *Amanda Designs Boutique Ltd v Charisma Fashions Ltd* (1972), 17 CBR (NS) 16 (Ont CA) [*Amanda Designs*].

3 See Chapter 5, Section A.

2) Scope of the Stay

The stay of proceedings prevents claimants from invoking any remedy against the debtor or the debtor's property. The Supreme Court of Canada has held that this includes both judicial and extra-judicial proceedings, such as a right to recover an overpayment by retention from subsequent benefit.[4] The stay also operates on other remedies, such as a statutory right of distress.[5] The stay of proceedings operates only in respect of proceedings by creditors against the bankrupt. It does not apply in respect of proceedings against third parties.[6]

Although the stay of proceedings that is typically granted by courts in *CCAA* proceedings prevents a contracting party from terminating an agreement between it and the debtor, the automatic stay of proceedings in bankruptcy has never been interpreted as preventing the exercise of this right. The restructuring provisions of the *BIA* contain a separate provision that prevents the termination of executory contracts.[7] This supports the view that the automatic stay of proceedings was not intended to extend to the termination of executory contracts, since the provision would not be needed otherwise.

The stay of proceedings operates only in respect of claims that are provable in bankruptcy. In order to be provable, the claim must be one that was in existence at the date of bankruptcy. Although post-bankruptcy claimants are able to commence action and obtain judgment against the bankrupt without leave of the court,[8] they will encounter difficulties when they attempt to enforce their judgments.[9] Most of the bankrupt's assets will have vested in the trustee on bankruptcy. Post-bankruptcy claimants will not be able to take judgment enforcement proceedings against these assets because the bankrupt no longer owns them. Upon obtaining a bankruptcy discharge, an individual bankrupt thereafter obtains ownership of any newly acquired assets. These new assets will be available to satisfy the claims of post-bankruptcy claimants.

---

4 *Vachon v Canada (Employment & Immigration Commission)*, [1985] 2 SCR 417. The stay of proceedings does not affect contempt proceedings against the debtor. See *Wilson Air v Firth*, 2013 ONSC 4248.

5 *Re Standard Pharmacy Ltd* (1926), 7 CBR 424 (Alta SC).

6 *Gadbois v Stimpson-Reeb Builders Supply Co*, [1929] SCR 587; *Ford Credit Ltd v Crosbie Realty Ltd* (1992), 12 CBR (3d) 282 (Nfld CA).

7 *BIA*, s 65.1(1).

8 *Richardson & Co v Storey* (1941), 23 CBR 145 (Ont HCJ); *Greenfield Park Lumber & Building Supplies Ltd v Zikman* (1967), 12 CBR (NS) 115 (Que Sup Ct).

9 *Firestone Tire & Rubber Co v Douglas* (1940), 21 CBR 343 (Ont Master).

Although family-support obligations are provable in bankruptcy, they are partially excluded from the operation of the stay of proceedings.[10] The family-support claimant is permitted to commence or continue an action against the bankrupt, but not to take any action or proceeding against the property of the bankrupt that has vested in the trustee or in respect of surplus income payments that are made to the trustee.[11]

3) Duration of the Stay

The automatic stay of proceedings commences on the date of bankruptcy[12] and ends when the trustee is discharged.[13] On its face, this might seem to suggest that creditors have a window of opportunity after the discharge of the trustee and before the bankrupt obtains a discharge during which they can sue the bankrupt and enforce their claims against any assets that have not vested in the trustee. Courts initially held that the bankruptcy law could not have been intended to declare an "open season" on undischarged bankrupts.[14] They were also concerned that this would undermine the bankruptcy scheme of distribution by permitting claimants to enforce their claims against the bankrupt's property and to apply the proceeds solely in satisfaction of their own claims. Claimants who had provable claims were therefore unable to take any action against an undischarged bankrupt even after the stay comes to an end.[15]

More recently, several courts departed from this view and held that claimants with provable claims can bring action and enforce their claims against the bankrupt's property after discharge of the trustee.[16] The issue often arose in cases where there had been misconduct or lack of cooperation on the part of the bankrupt. Other courts refused to follow this new line of decisions and defended the view that claimants with provable claims are subject to the stay after the discharge of the trustee unless a court lifts the stay.[17]

---

10 *BIA*, s 69.41(1).

11 *Ibid*, s 69.41(2).

12 *Ibid*, s 69.3(1).

13 *Ibid*, s 69.3(1.1).

14 *Markis v Soccio* (1954), 35 CBR 1 (Que Sup Ct) quoting from a case comment of W Goodman, (1954) 33 CBR 191 at 197.

15 *Ibid*; *Potapoff v Kleef* (1964), 6 CBR (NS) 165 (BCCA).

16 *Canada (Attorney General) v Ramjag* (1995), 33 CBR (3d) 89 (Alta QB); *Re Fraser* (1996), 41 CBR (3d) 33 (Sask QB); *Thiessen v Antifaev* (2003), 41 CBR (4th) 266 (BCSC); *Re Ross* (2003), 50 CBR (4th) 274 (Ont SCJ).

17 *Re Morgan* (1999), 12 CBR (4th) 48 (Man QB); *McKerron v Marshall* (2002), 34 CBR (4th) 244 (Ont SCJ).

The decisions are difficult to reconcile. Moreover, there appears to be an assumption in some of the decisions that the cessation of the stay will necessarily confer upon a creditor the right to enforce its claim against the assets and apply the proceeds solely in satisfaction of its claim. This is open to question. Consider the case of a bankrupt who fails to disclose an asset to the trustee. The undisclosed asset will nevertheless vest in the trustee, and the cessation of the stay should not operate to give a creditor a right to enforce against an asset in which the bankrupt has no interest. Unless the trustee has returned the property to the bankrupt as unrealizable property,[18] title to the asset remains vested in the trustee. The proper course is to seek the reappointment of the trustee who will liquidate the asset and distribute the proceeds according to the bankruptcy scheme of distribution.[19]

The existence of a gap between the discharge of the trustee and the discharge of the bankrupt has given rise to a further controversy concerning limitation periods. The issue is whether a creditor with a provable claim at the time of bankruptcy is entitled to share in a distribution by a trustee if that creditor did not protect its claim by initiating civil proceedings after the discharge of the trustee. Courts have accepted the proposition that the stay ends upon the discharge of the trustee, but have held that this does not mean that the creditor must bring civil proceedings to protect its claim during the gap. Although there is a hiatus in the administration of the estate, the discharge of the trustee does not divest the creditor of the entitlement to share in the distribution of the estate.[20]

4) Incomplete Enforcement by Creditors

The *BIA* gives the bankruptcy order or assignment precedence over all judgment enforcement remedies or processes unless they have been completely executed by payment to the creditor.[21] The fact that a judgment creditor registered in a land registry system or a personal property registry system prior to the bankruptcy does not give the writ or other process the status of a secured creditor.[22] Money that has been paid into court in respect of garnishment proceedings must also be turned over to the trustee if it had not been paid to the judgment creditor at the

18 *BIA*, s 40(1).
19 *Ibid*, s 41(11).
20 *Decker v Canada (Superintendent of Bankruptcy)*, 2010 ABCA 189.
21 *BIA*, s 70(1).
22 *Re Sklar* (1958), 37 CBR 187 (Sask CA); *Laurentian Bank of Canada v Woo* (1994), 29 CBR (3d) 280 (Alta QB).

date of the bankruptcy.[23] A surplus that becomes available following a forced sale of property by a secured creditor also vests in the trustee in bankruptcy.[24] On receiving a copy of the assignment or bankruptcy order from the trustee, an executing officer[25] must turn over to the trustee any property that has been seized or any proceeds that are held following a sale.[26]

The seizing creditor is not entitled to deduct the enforcement costs from proceeds realized. The costs are recoverable as a preferred claim only if the creditor qualifies as the first creditor to have initiated enforcement proceedings.[27] The position is slightly different in the case of a landlord or municipality that has caused the property to be seized. If a sale of the property was completed before the bankruptcy, the landlord or municipality is entitled to retain the proceeds of sale.[28] If the property has been seized but was not sold at the time of the bankruptcy, the property must be turned over to the trustee on production of the bankruptcy order or assignment.[29] The costs form a first charge on the property and are entitled to priority over competing secured creditors.[30]

5) Validity of Proceedings Taken without Leave

A creditor may have commenced action or enforced a claim in ignorance of the existence of a bankruptcy stay of proceedings. A failure to obtain leave does not render the action a nullity; it is an irregularity that a court is able to cure by granting leave *nunc pro tunc* to proceed with the

---

23 *Canadian Credit Men's Trust Assn v Beaver Trucking Ltd*, [1959] SCR 311. And see *BIA*, s 73(3).

24 *Re Radovini* (1983), 45 CBR (NS) 220 (Ont CA).

25 Section 2 of the *BIA* defines an executing officer as a sheriff, bailiff, or other officer charged with the execution of a writ or other process.

26 *BIA*, ss 73(2)–(3).

27 *Ibid*, ss 70(2) and 136(1)(g).

28 *Re Southern Fried Foods Ltd* (1976), 21 CBR (NS) 267 (Ont HCJ). It is unnecessary that the proceeds be paid to the landlord by a private bailiff, since the bailiff acts as agent for the landlord in effecting the seizure and sale. It is unclear if the same principle applies in Alberta, since the exercise of a landlord's right of distress can be carried out only by a civil enforcement agency, and the precise status of such agencies is currently uncertain. It is possible that they will be treated as an executing authority, in which case payment to the landlord would be necessary under the *BIA*, s 70(1). See R Wood, "Enforcement Remedies of Creditors" (1996) 34 *Alberta Law Review* 783.

29 *BIA*, s 73(4).

30 *Burdyny v Dacar Enterprises Ltd (Trustee of)* (1988), 71 CBR (NS) 205 (Man CA).

action.[31] Any judgment enforcement proceedings that are taken after the stay are ineffective to transfer any interest in the property that is seized.[32] If the property is sold pursuant to judgment enforcement proceedings, a good faith buyer of the property acquires a good title,[33] but the proceeds of the sale must be turned over to the trustee.[34]

6) Lifting the Stay

A creditor may apply to court for a declaration that a stay of proceedings should no longer operate in respect of that creditor. The court may make the order if it is satisfied that the creditor is likely to be materially prejudiced by the continued operation of the stay or that it is equitable on other grounds to make such a declaration.[35] In making this assessment, the applicant is not required to show that it has a *prima facie* case in respect of its underlying claim. Instead, the court should determine if there is a sound reason that the automatic bankruptcy stay should be lifted.[36]

The situations where courts have determined it appropriate to lift the stay of proceedings are usually ones where a civil action offers a superior means of determining issues of liability than the bankruptcy claims process, or is advantageous for some other reason. Although there may be good grounds to use the ordinary civil process to assess liability or quantify damages, this does not mean that the claimant should be exempted from the requirement that the creditors share the assets of the bankruptcy estate. Accordingly, the orders that are granted by courts typically provide that no enforcement be taken on any judgment obtained in the action.[37] In any event, enforcement of the judgment would be fruitless since the debtor's property will have automatically vested in the trustee upon the occurrence of the bankruptcy, and there will not be any assets owned by the debtor to satisfy the judgment until after the debtor obtains a bankruptcy discharge.

---

31 *Blais v Bankers' Trust Corp* (1913), 14 DLR 277 (Alta SC); *Trusts and Guarantee Co v Brenner*, [1933] SCR 656; *Preferred Steel Construction Inc v M3 Steel (Kamloops) Ltd*, 2013 BCSC 664.

32 *Amanda Designs*, above note 2.

33 *BIA*, s 73(1). And see *Gobeil v Cie H Fortier*, [1982] 1 SCR 988.

34 *Hudson v Brisebois Brothers Construction Ltd* (1982), 42 CBR (NS) 97 (Alta CA).

35 *BIA*, s 69.4.

36 *Re Ma* (2001), 24 CBR (4th) 68 (Ont CA). This does not preclude a court from considering the merits of the proposed action in appropriate cases.

37 See, for example, *Re Turner* (2006), 19 CBR (5th) 290 (Ont SCJ).

Courts have lifted the stay where there are multiple defendants and the bankrupt is a necessary party to the complete and proper adjudication of the facts.[38] The stay may also be lifted where the action involves issues of a complex nature that cannot be disposed of in any summary fashion,[39] or where the civil proceedings have progressed to a point that it is sensible to permit it to continue to judgment.[40] Another ground for lifting the stay is where the bankrupt is insured and the real purpose of the action is to establish liability so that the injured party can recover from the bankrupt's insurer.[41] Courts have also lifted the stay where the claim is one that is not released by the discharge of the debtor. Because the claimant is able to enforce the judgment against any new post-discharge assets acquired by the debtor, courts have permitted the action to proceed provided that it does not interfere with the administration of the bankrupt estate or give the creditor an unfair advantage over the other creditors.[42]

7) Staying Proceedings against Secured Creditors

The automatic bankruptcy stay does not apply to a secured creditor who is exercising its enforcement remedies against the collateral. A secured creditor's right to seize and sell the collateral or to foreclose upon the debtor's interest is not affected by the bankruptcy unless the trustee actively intervenes by applying to a court for a stay of proceedings.[43] A court cannot postpone a secured creditor's remedies for more than six months. If the collateral is not, or is not expected to be, sufficient to satisfy the obligation secured, a secured creditor may prove a claim for the deficiency. This claim is provable in bankruptcy and is subject to the automatic bankruptcy stay in the same manner as any other provable claim. A different set of rules governs the interface between national insolvency law and the rights of a secured party, lessor, or seller who has an interest in an aircraft object governed by the *Convention on International Interests in Mobile Equipment* and the associated *Protocol on Matters Specific to Aircraft*.[44] The legislation limits the effect of a stay

---

38 *Ibid*; *Re Jenkins* (2005), 13 CBR (5th) 208 (NSSC).

39 *Wilanour*, above note 1; *Re Taylor Ventures Ltd* (2002), 32 CBR (4th) 120 (BCSC).

40 *Re Advocate Mines Ltd* (1984), 52 CBR (NS) 277 (Ont HCJ).

41 *Re Duvall* (1992), 11 CBR (3d) 264 (BCSC).

42 *Re Bookman* (1983), 47 CBR (NS) 144 (Ont HCJ).

43 *BIA*, s 69.3(2).

44 See the *International Interests in Mobile Equipment (Aircraft Equipment) Act*, SC 2005, c 3. This Act, which sets out the text of the Convention and the Protocol,

of proceedings on a creditor who holds a security interest in an aircraft object or a lessor or conditional seller of an aircraft object.[45]

8) Non-application of the Stay to Revenue Authorities

The *BIA* provides that a stay of proceedings in bankruptcy does not prevent the federal or a provincial government from exercising a statutory requirement to pay procedure.[46] The requirement to pay procedure is a statutory garnishment remedy for the recovery of income tax, CPP, and EI contributions or their provincial counterparts. This limitation does not apply in respect of the exercise of enforcement remedies by revenue agencies in respect of the recovery of the Goods and Services Tax (GST).[47]

B. EXECUTORY CONTRACTS

The trustee is under a duty to take possession and control of the assets of the bankrupt estate and dispose of them. The wide definition of property used in the *BIA* sweeps in contractual rights held by the bankrupt. If the bankrupt's side of the bargain has been fully performed, the contractual right is a pure asset that vests in the trustee and permits the trustee to call for the other party's performance. If the other party has fully performed but the bankrupt has not, the other party cannot demand performance from the trustee. Instead, the party is limited to proving a claim for damages for breach of contract or for recovery of the price in the bankruptcy.

---

came into force on 1 April 2013. See also R Cuming, C Walsh, & R Wood, *Personal Property Security Law*, 2d ed (Toronto: Irwin Law, 2012) at 717–31.

45 Aircraft objects are defined as airframes, aircraft engines, and helicopters. Each of these terms is defined in the Protocol, which contains exceptions for smaller aircraft objects. A court-ordered stay of proceedings does not prevent a secured creditor from taking possession of aircraft objects if the trustee defaults in maintaining or preserving them in accordance with the agreement. The stay of proceedings also ceases to operate after a sixty-day waiting period that runs from the day a court order is made unless the trustee has cured all defaults and agrees to perform all future obligations under the agreement. The secured creditor is permitted to take possession of the aircraft object within the sixty-day waiting period if the trustee defaults in performing an obligation under the agreement.

46 *Income Tax Act*, RSC 1985 (5th Supp), c 1, s 224(1.2); *BIA*, s 69.5.

47 *Canada (Minister of National Revenue) v Points North Freight Forwarding Inc* (2000), 24 CBR (4th) 184 (Sask QB).

A more difficult case arises where neither the bankrupt nor the other party has fully performed their contractual obligations. The trustee may want to obtain the third party's performance, but it comes at a price. To obtain it, the trustee must fulfil the bankrupt's part of the bargain. Alternatively, the trustee may decline to perform the contract, thereby giving the other party the right to terminate any future performance and to prove a claim for contractual damages in the bankruptcy. In order to preserve the value of the bankrupt estate, the trustee must move quickly and elect which course to take.

An executory contract, as the term is used in bankruptcy law, is one in which neither party has fully performed and the contractual obligations are linked so that performance by one is not required unless the other is willing and able to perform.[48] Executory contracts are said to have characteristics of both assets and liabilities arising out of the same transaction.[49] The trustee can turn the contract into a pure liability against the bankrupt estate by disclaiming the contract. This gives the other party the right to terminate any future performance and to prove a claim for contractual damages in the bankruptcy.[50] Alternatively, the trustee may affirm the contract by indicating to the other party that the trustee is willing to perform it. The consideration that is earned through this contractual performance is an asset that is divisible among the creditors who prove their claims in the bankruptcy.

Canadian bankruptcy legislation is largely silent when it comes to setting out the rules and principles that govern executory contracts. This task has been left to the judiciary to work out. The one exception is where the executory contract takes the form of a lease of real property. Canadian bankruptcy law expressly incorporates provincial statutes that set out in detail the right of the trustee to affirm or disclaim a real property lease. Here, the discussion will begin with the general principles that govern executory contracts in bankruptcy and will follow with an examination of the special treatment that is afforded to real property leases.

---

48 V Countryman, "Executory Contracts in Bankruptcy, Part I" (1973), 57 *Minnesota Law Review* 439 at 460.

49 T Jackson, "Translating Assets and Liabilities to the Bankruptcy Forum" (1985) 14 *Journal of Legal Studies* 73 at 104.

50 *BIA*, s 121(1) provides that a provable claim includes post-bankruptcy liabilities to which the bankrupt may become subject by reason of a pre-bankruptcy obligation. This obscurely worded provision was intended to cover liabilities that arise after the bankruptcy as a result of a disclaimer of a contract by the trustee. See Roderick J Wood & David J Bryan, "Creeping Statutory Obsolescence in Bankruptcy Law" (2014) 3 *Journal of the Insolvency Institute of Canada* 1 at 13–15.

1) The General Principles Governing Executory Contracts

The occurrence of bankruptcy does not of itself cause the contract to come to an end or constitute a breach of the contract.[51] This is subject to two qualifications. First, the parties to the contract may expressly stipulate events that constitute a breach of the contract or that bring the contract to an end, and these provisions are generally effective in bankruptcy.[52] Second, bankruptcy of an employer has the effect of terminating contracts of employment.[53]

If the contract has not been terminated, the trustee must elect between two courses of action. The trustee can affirm the contract or disclaim it.[54] The choice will very much depend upon whether the contract is a profitable one for the bankrupt estate. If a trustee decides to affirm the contract, the decision to affirm must be communicated to the other party within a reasonable time. If the trustee fails to do so, the other party can treat the contract as having been breached and may refuse further performance under it.[55] If the decision to affirm the contract by calling for performance is communicated within a reasonable time, the other party will be bound to perform it.

There are two exceptions to this rule. First, a trustee is not able to affirm a personal services contract. A person who enters into a contract with an artist to have her portrait painted cannot be forced to accept performance by another person. She contracted for the skill or personal ability of the bankrupt and is not compelled to accept substitute performance from the trustee or anyone else.[56] Second, an affirmation of the contract by the trustee will, in some cases, result in a modification of the contractual obligation owed by the other party. A contracting party who agrees to supply goods on credit to a buyer is not required to extend credit once the buyer is insolvent, but is entitled to demand to be paid cash before the property is delivered.[57] In order to affirm a

---

51 *Ex p Chalmers* (1873), 8 Ch App 289 (CA).

52 An exception is made in respect of contractual provisions that provide for termination upon the insolvency of the party or upon the commencement of insolvency proceedings. See Section B(2), below in this chapter and Chapter 4, Section B(2).

53 *Re Kemp Products Ltd* (1978), 27 CBR (NS) 1 (Ont HCJ).

54 One finds a number of variations in terminology in respect of these two options. The American usage is to refer to assumption or rejection of the contract. Older cases also refer to an approbation of the contract by the trustee. See *Re Thomson Knitting Co* (1925), 5 CBR 489 (Ont SCAD).

55 *Re Thomson Knitting Co, ibid.*

56 *Stead Lumber Company Limited v Lewis* (1958), 37 CBR 24 (Nfld SC).

57 *Grainex Canada Ltd (Trustee of) v Canbra Foods Ltd* (1987), 34 DLR (4th) 646 (BCCA).

contract for the sale of goods in instalments, it is not enough that the trustee pay the price for the post-bankruptcy deliveries. The trustee must also pay for any past deliveries that were made on credit terms.[58] This illustrates the principle that the trustee must affirm the entire contract and cannot cherry-pick its favourable portions.

The trustee may instead choose to disclaim the contract. The trustee will communicate to the other contracting party that the trustee is not prepared to perform the contract. The trustee does not incur any personal liability by doing so. Instead, the contracting party may prove a claim for contractual damages in the bankruptcy.

A disclaimer does not involve a rescission of the contract in the sense that the contract ceases to exist. The contract remains alive. A disclaimer simply notifies the other party that future performance of the contract will not be forthcoming. This distinction is of vital importance. A disclaimer by the trustee does not undo the contract or cause property that has vested under an executory contract to revest in the bankrupt. This is well illustrated in agreements to purchase land in which the vendor has not conveyed the property and the purchaser has not paid the price. Because a contract for the sale of land is specifically enforceable, the purchaser acquires an immediate equitable interest in the land.[59] The vendor's trustee cannot simply disclaim the contract and keep the land. The vendor holds the land for the purchaser under a constructive trust, and the trustee in bankruptcy is in no better position than the vendor.

The situation is different in respect of a contract for the sale of goods. Sale of goods statutes provide a complete codification of rules governing the transfer of proprietary rights to goods under a contract of sale, and this ousts the operation of equitable principles.[60] A buyer cannot obtain a proprietary right in the goods under the contract of sale until legal title passes to the buyer. The buyer has merely a contractual right to call for the delivery of the goods. This is a personal right that is converted into a right to prove for a bankruptcy dividend. Without a proprietary right, the buyer will be able to acquire the goods only if the trustee affirms the contract. If the trustee disclaims the contract, the trustee keeps the goods and the buyer has merely a right to prove a claim in bankruptcy for contractual damages or for the recovery of the purchase price.

---

58 *Ex p Chalmers*, above note 51.

59 *Re Triangle Lumber & Supply Co* (1978), 27 CBR (NS) 317 (Ont HCJ).

60 *Re Wait*, [1927] 1 Ch 606 (CA).

The effect of bankruptcy on technology licensing agreements has been a topic of concern for many licensees.[61] The worry is that a trustee might be able to disclaim a technology agreement and thereby extinguish obligations that bound the bankrupt licensor.[62] This involves a misunderstanding of the trustee's right to disclaim a contract. When a trustee disclaims a contract, the other party is notified that the trustee is not prepared to perform the obligation required under the contract in order to obtain performance by the other party. Upon a disclaimer by the trustee, the other party will often elect to treat the disclaimer as a breach of the contract and treat the contract as terminated. When this occurs, performance of the future obligation is no longer required. The other party has a claim for contractual damages, and this claim can be proved in the bankruptcy. But it does not follow that the other party must elect to treat the contract as terminated. Bankruptcy does not fundamentally change the position of a contracting party following a breach of contract. The party can elect to terminate future performance under the contract but is not compelled to do so. In respect of a technology licence, a licensee can elect not to treat the contract as at an end and may continue to use the technology as permitted by the terms of the licence.[63]

This is not a complete solution to all difficulties arising out of technology licensing agreements. Although the trustee cannot prevent the licensee's use of the property by disclaiming the contract, the trustee may seek to sell the underlying intellectual property right to a third

---

61 See W Adams & G Takach, "Insecure Transactions: Deficiencies in the Treatment of Technology Licences in Commercial Transactions Involving Secured Debt or Bankruptcy" (2000) 33 *Canadian Business Law Journal* 321.

62 This was the approach taken by the Fourth Circuit of the United States Court of Appeal in *Lubrizol Enterprises Inc v Richmond Metal Finishers Inc*, 756 F2d 1043 (1985). The technology licensing agreement imposed a number of obligations on the licensor including the obligation to notify the licensee of any other licences that had been granted and to lower the royalty rate if a lower rate was given to another licensee. The exercise by the trustee of a right of rejection was held to terminate this obligation. The reasoning in this case has been rejected by other courts. See *Sunbeam Products Inc v Chicago American Mfg*, 686 F3d 372 (7th Cir 2012).

63 See A Duggan & N Siebrasse, "The Disclaimer, Affirmation and Assignment of Intellectual Property Licences in Insolvency" (2014) 3 *Journal of the Insolvency Institute of Canada* 163 at 172. See also D Baird, *The Elements of Bankruptcy*, 4th ed (Foundation Press: New York, 2006) at 130–40. The United States *Bankruptcy Code*, 11 USC, was subsequently amended by the addition of § 365(n). This provided that, in the event of rejection of an executory contract under which the debtor is a licensor of a right to intellectual property, the licensee may elect to treat the contract as terminated and prove for damages in the bankruptcy, or to retain its rights pursuant to the agreement.

party. If the licensing agreement does not give the licensee a proprietary right, the third party will acquire the intellectual property right free of any restriction that bound the bankrupt.[64] Although the parties may attempt to draft their agreements so as to confer a proprietary right on the licensee so that third parties would be bound by the terms of the licensing agreement,[65] legislative reform is required in order to produce consistent and predictable outcomes.

2) *Ipso Facto* Clauses and the Statutory Anti-deprivation Rule

The parties to the contract may expressly stipulate events that constitute breach of the contract or that bring the contract to an end. For example, a contract may provide that a party may terminate a contract if work performed by the other party fails to pass an inspection as to its quality. A trustee in bankruptcy occupies the same position as the bankrupt in respect of the operation of these contractual provisions. If the work performed is substandard, the other party is entitled to terminate the contract. This excuses future performance and permits the other party to prove a claim in the bankruptcy for contractual damages.

The 2009 amendments to the *BIA* have modified this principle in respect of one particular kind of contractual provision. These provisions — often referred to as *ipso facto* clauses — stipulate that the commencement of bankruptcy or other insolvency proceedings is of itself an event of default that permits the party to terminate the contract. These had the potential to prevent a trustee from affirming the contract without the consent of the other party, since the other party retained a power to terminate the agreement. The statutory anti-deprivation rule in the *BIA* augments the common law anti-deprivation principle, which restricts the validity of these contractual provisions.[66] The statutory rule prevents a party from terminating, amending, or claiming accelerated payment or forfeiture of the term under any agreement by reason only of the debtor's bankruptcy or insolvency.[67] However, this does not prevent the counterparty from requiring payment to be made in cash for goods, services, or use of leased property provided after the time of the bankruptcy, and does not require the further advance of money or

64 See *Royal Bank of Canada v Body Blue Inc*, 2008 CarswellOnt 2445 (SCJ).

65 See R Gold, "Partial Copyright Assignments: Safeguarding Software Licensees against the Bankruptcy of Licensors" (2000) 33 *Canadian Business Law Journal* 193.

66 See Chapter 4, Section B(2).

67 *BIA*, s 84.2(1).

credit.[68] The provision applies only if the debtor is an individual. If the debtor is a corporation or other artificial entity, the validity of the provision will be determined through the application of the common law anti-deprivation principle. The provision does not apply to an eligible financial contract.[69]

The statutory anti-deprivation provisions are not limited to cases where the trustee wishes to affirm a valuable contract in order to swell the value of the bankrupt estate.[70] The provisions also apply to contracts that cannot be affirmed and performed by the trustee, such as personal services contracts. This prevents the other contracting party from using the bankruptcy as a ground for terminating the contract with the debtor.

Two other provisions further limit the ability of the other contracting party to terminate or otherwise alter the contract on bankruptcy. Both of these are primarily concerned with ongoing contracts between the debtor and the other contracting party rather than with contracts that are likely to be affirmed and performed by the trustee. In the case of a lease, the statutory limitation on the effectiveness of a contractual termination or forfeiture provision extends to non-payment of rent before the time of the bankruptcy.[71] This means that the debtor may continue to occupy the leased premises despite non-payment of pre-bankruptcy arrears of rent so long as post-bankruptcy rental payments are paid. A similar provision prevents a public utility from discontinuing service on the basis of a debtor's failure to pay for services rendered or material provided before the time of bankruptcy.[72] So long as the debtor pays for post-bankruptcy service, the public utility must continue to provide services to the debtor.

If the operation of any of these limitations on *ipso facto* clauses creates significant financial hardship for the other party to the agreement, that party may apply to court for an order declaring that the section does not apply in whole or in part.[73]

---

68 *Ibid*, s 84.2(4).

69 *Ibid*, s 84.2(7). See the discussion in Chapter 13, Section F.

70 The section gives the bankrupt the right to challenge the exercise of a contractual provision notwithstanding that the bankrupt has lost the capacity to deal with the bankrupt's assets. See *Munkittrick (Syndic de)*, 2011 QCCS 239.

71 *BIA*, s 84.2(2).

72 *Ibid*, s 84.2(3).

73 *Ibid*, s 84.2(6).

3) Leases of Real Property

The *BIA* does not contain provisions that govern the affirmation or disclaimer of real property leases, despite the fact that the trustee is given the power to exercise those rights.[74] The *BIA* expressly incorporates the provincial law of the place where the leased premises are situated to govern the rights of landlords.[75] Although there is considerable variation in the wording of the provincial legislation, the provisions typically cover the right of the trustee to occupy the premises for a temporary period of time, and the right of the trustee to affirm or disclaim the lease. The provincial statutes also limit the lessor's right to prove a claim for damages for breach of the lease by restricting the claim to three months of future rent.[76] Because of the wide variation in wording, it is essential to examine and compare closely the wording of the provincial statutes before relying upon cases from another province.

In order for the trustee to obtain these rights, there must have been a subsisting lease in existence at the time of the bankruptcy. If a landlord has exercised a right to terminate the lease for breach of a covenant or condition, the lease is forfeited and the trustee is unable to exercise any of the rights provided under provincial law.[77] If the landlord has not terminated the lease prior to bankruptcy, the provincial law comes into operation. The decision to continue the lease or terminate it no longer rests with the landlord. Upon bankruptcy, it is the trustee who has the power to make this decision. The rights that are given to a trustee apply despite any contractual stipulation in the lease that provides otherwise.[78]

a) Temporary Occupation of the Leased Premises

The trustee is given a right to occupy the leased premises for a temporary period of time. In most provinces, the period cannot extend beyond three months following the bankruptcy.[79] If the trustee elects

---

74 *Ibid*, s 30(1)(k). The trustee must obtain the permission of the inspectors before exercising these rights.

75 *Ibid*, s 146. This approach was adopted after federal bankruptcy provisions that dealt with the rights between landlords and bankrupt tenants were found to be *ultra vires*: See *In re Stober* (1923), 4 CBR 34 (Que Sup Ct).

76 See Chapter 9, Section A(8).

77 *Standard Trusts Co v David Steele Ltd* (1921), 2 CBR 183 (BCSC), aff'd (1922), 3 CBR 141 (BCCA).

78 *Re Karelia Ltd* (1980), 36 CBR (NS) 58 (Ont HCJ); *Re Café La Ronde Ltd* (1984), 50 CBR (NS) 283 (Alta QB), aff'd (1984), 54 CBR (NS) 320 (Alta CA).

79 See, for example, *Commercial Tenancy Act*, RSBC 1996, c 57, s 29(2); *Landlord and Tenant Act*, RSNB 1973, c L-1, s 43(1); *Commercial Tenancies Act*, RSO 1990,

to occupy the leased premises, the trustee must pay rent to the landlord for the period during which the trustee is in actual occupation of the premises, calculated on the basis of the rentals provided for in the lease. In exercising this right, the trustee is not required to pay any arrears of rent that are due under the lease. A payment to be made to the landlord in respect of future rent may be credited towards the amount payable by the trustee for occupation rent.[80] The obligation to pay occupation rent arises only if the trustee actually takes up occupation of the leased premises.[81] It does not accrue simply because the landlord is unable to obtain possession of the leased premises during the three-month period during which the trustee can choose to affirm or disclaim the lease.[82] Even though a trustee does not operate the bankrupt's business on the leased premises, a trustee may be viewed as being in occupation of the premises if the trustee exercises acts of control over the premises.[83]

The question whether the obligation to pay occupation rent is a personal obligation owed by the trustee or merely an expense that must first be paid out of the assets of the bankrupt estate varies from province to province.[84] The answer to this question becomes important if the assets are not sufficient to pay the landlord the amounts due for occupation rent. In some provinces, the provincial legislation imposes an express obligation on the trustee to pay occupation rent.[85] In these jurisdictions, the obligation to pay occupation rent is a personal obligation. In other provinces, the statute provides that the trustee is not personally liable beyond the assets of the debtor in the hands of the trustee.[86] Other provinces, such as Ontario, do not expressly deal with

---

c L.7, s 38(2). And see *Re Limestone Electrical & Supply Co* (1955), 35 CBR 20 (Ont CA). Alberta does not limit the time period but allows the trustee to occupy the premises for so long as required by the trustee. See *Landlord's Rights on Bankruptcy Act*, RSA 2000, c L-5, s 5(1).

80 The provision only covers rent paid by a trustee; rent paid by a receiver cannot be deducted from the preferred claim of the landlord. See *Dancole Investments Ltd v House of Tools Company*, 2011 ABCA 145.

81 *Re Toyerama Ltd* (1981), 37 CBR (NS) 275 (Ont HCJ); *Carpita Corp (Trustee of) v Douglas Shopping Centre Ltd* (1994), 28 CBR (3d) 241 (BCCA).

82 *Re Century 21 Brenmore Real Estate Ltd* (1983), 46 CBR (NS) 72 (Ont HCJ); *Village Shops Centre (Red Deer) Ltd v Thorne Riddell Inc* (1989), 75 CBR (NS) 281 (Alta QB).

83 *Sawridge Manor Ltd v Western Canada Beverage Corp* (1995), 33 CBR (3d) 249 (BCCA).

84 See W Rowe, "The Trustee in Bankruptcy's Liability for Occupation Rent" (1984) 51 CBR (NS) 206.

85 See, for example, *Landlord's Rights on Bankruptcy Act*, above note 79, s 5(2).

86 See, for example, *Commercial Tenancy Act*, above note 79, s 29(9).

the question, and courts have divided on the issue. Some have regarded it as a personal obligation,[87] while others have held that the trustee is simply required to pay this amount as an administrative expense of the bankruptcy.[88]

b) Affirmation or Disclaimer of the Lease

During the three-month period following the bankruptcy, the trustee may choose to retain the lease for the whole or a portion of the unexpired term. In order to do so, the trustee must give written notice to the landlord before the expiration of the three-month period,[89] but cannot do so if the trustee has already given notice of intention to surrender possession of the lease or disclaim it. It is unusual for the trustee to carry on the bankrupt's business for extended periods, and this right is usually invoked if the trustee is planning to assign the lease to another party.

The trustee can also elect to surrender possession of the lease or disclaim the lease. Surrender of possession occurs when possession of the leased premises is given to the landlord by mutual consent; a disclaimer of a lease occurs through a unilateral act on the part of the trustee. Although the statutes distinguish between these two techniques, they both cause the landlord to get back the reversionary interest.[90]

A disclaimer of an executory contract ordinarily does not cause the contractual obligations to disappear. It simply means that the trustee is not prepared to perform and the other party therefore has the right to terminate future performance and prove a claim for damages for breach. However, courts have taken a different view of the effect of disclaimer of a lease; they treated the disclaimer as being akin to a surrender of a lease, which has the effect of extinguishing the obligations under the lease.[91] This difference is based on the wording of the provincial statutes that assimilates surrender of possession with disclaimer and that limits the landlord's claim for future rent.[92] A line of cases concluded

---

87 *1133 Yonge Street Holdings Ltd v Clarke, Henning & Hahn Ltd* (1991), 2 CBR (3d) 11 (Ont Ct Gen Div); *Sasso v D & A MacLeod Co* (1991), 5 CBR (3d) 239 (Ont Ct Gen Div).

88 *Re Listowel Feed Mill Ltd* (1990), 1 CBR (3d) 230 (Ont Ct Gen Div); *Ottawa Elgin Investments Ltd v McKechnie* (1983), 47 CBR (NS) 191 (Ont Co Ct).

89 Alberta does not limit the election to a three-month period.

90 *Berkley Property Management Ltd v Garden City Plaza Ltd* (1995), 32 CBR (3d) 258 (Alta QB).

91 *Re Vrablik* (1993), 17 CBR (3d) 152 (Ont Ct Gen Div); *West Shore Ventures Ltd v KPN Holding Ltd* (2001), 25 CBR (4th) 139 (BCCA) [*West Shore Ventures*].

92 In most jurisdictions, the landlord's claim is expressly limited to the rent that has accrued due and to accelerated (future) rent not exceeding that for three

that a guarantor of the lessee's obligations under a lease was released when the lessee's trustee disclaimed the lease.[93] However, in 2004, the Supreme Court of Canada in *Crystalline Investments Ltd v Domgroup Ltd*[94] expressed the view that a disclaimer of a lease does not discharge the guarantor's liability.[95]

4) Assignment of the Agreement

Instead of performing the agreement, the trustee may wish instead to assign it to another person. The consideration given by that party is then divisible among the creditors who prove their claims in the bankruptcy. A trustee in bankruptcy ordinarily is in no better position than the bankrupt in exercising contractual rights that have vested in the trustee.

This position is modified in respect of the trustee's ability to assign the contract to another person. A trustee may apply to court for an order assigning the rights and obligations of the debtor to a specified person who agrees to the assignment.[96] This power was originally conferred on a trustee by provincial statute and was available only in respect of an assignment of a lease of real property. The 2009 amendments to the *BIA* have superseded these provisions through the addition of an express federal provision that applies to most types of contracts. This power can be exercised notwithstanding a provision in the agreement that prohibits or limits the assignment of the agreement.[97]

---

months. See, for example, *Commercial Tenancy Act*, above note 79, ss 29(6)–(7); *Landlord's Rights on Bankruptcy Act*, above note 79, ss 3–4. This dovetails with *BIA*, s 136(1)(e), which gives a landlord a preferred claim for a maximum of three months future rent. See Chapter 9, Section B(1)(g).

93 *Cummer-Yonge Investments Ltd v Fagot* (1965), 8 CBR (NS) 62 (Ont HCJ); *West Shore Ventures*, above note 91.

94 [2004] 1 SCR 60.

95 The case dealt with the liability of the original tenant following the disclaimer of the lease by an insolvent assignee, but the judgment expressed the view that post-disclaimer assignors and guarantors ought to be treated the same with respect to liability.

96 *BIA*, s 84.1.

97 See the discussion in Chapter 4, Section B(2).

C. ABANDONMENT OF ENVIRONMENTALLY DAMAGED PROPERTY

Federal and provincial environmental protection legislation gives environmental regulators the right to issue remediation orders to compel the clean-up of polluted property. If the environmental damage is extensive, the costs of clean-up may be in excess of the value of the property. Compliance with the remediation order in such cases will diminish the value of the assets available to the other creditors who claim in the bankruptcy. In this respect, the property can be viewed as having a negative value.

The trustee is given the ability to abandon the environmentally damaged property.[98] If this is done, the trustee is not required to comply with a remediation order. The trustee must elect to abandon the property by giving notice to the authority that issued the order. Unless some other period is specified in the order, the election to abandon must occur within ten days after the order is made. If the order was in effect before the trustee's appointment, the trustee is given ten days following the appointment to make an election to abandon the property. Alternatively, the trustee may apply to court within the applicable time period for a stay of the order to allow the trustee to contest the order or to assess the economic viability of complying with it. A decision by the trustee to abandon the property does not mean that the clean-up costs are unrecoverable. The costs of remediation form a charge on the polluted property and any contiguous property, and have priority over any other mortgage or charge.[99] If the costs of remediation exceed the value of this property, the environmental authority can claim the costs as an unsecured creditor in the bankruptcy.[100] If the trustee decides to keep the property and clean it up, the trustee can recover the costs of clean-up as one of the costs of administration of the estate.

D. PREVENTING THE BANKRUPT FROM DEALING WITH THE ESTATE

In order to preserve the bankrupt estate for the benefit of the creditors, it is necessary to prevent the bankrupt from engaging in activities that may result in the loss of property that would otherwise be available to

---

98 *BIA*, s 14.06(4).
99 *Ibid*, s 14.06(7).
100 *Ibid*, s 14.06(8).

the creditors. Two things need to be done. First, it is necessary to acquire control over the assets. Although the bankrupt's assets will have vested in the trustee, this will be of little benefit to the creditors unless the trustee is also able to obtain control over the assets so as to be in a position to dispose of them. Second, it is necessary to take certain legal steps to prevent the bankrupt from selling or otherwise disposing of any of the assets to a third party. Here, the controversy is whether the loss caused by the actions of the bankrupt will be borne by the innocent third party who acquired an asset from the bankrupt or whether it will be borne by the trustee and, ultimately, by the creditors who prove their claims in the bankruptcy.

The *BIA* imposes an obligation on a bankrupt to cooperate with the trustee in identifying assets, disclosing records, and aiding in the realization of assets.[101] The *BIA* also provides that no property of a bankrupt shall be removed from the province in respect of which bankruptcy proceedings were commenced without the permission of the court or the inspectors.[102] These provisions assist the trustee in assembling and preserving the bankrupt estate.

The bankrupt estate is also protected from actions by the debtor that attempt to dispose of or otherwise deal with the assets. Upon the occurrence of a bankruptcy, the bankrupt ceases to have any capacity to dispose of or otherwise deal with the property.[103] Acting mistakenly or fraudulently, a bankrupt may purport to transfer an interest in property to another despite this lack of capacity. The transaction will generally not be effective to transfer any interest to the transferee, since the bankrupt no longer has any interest in the property, and it makes no difference that the transferee took in good faith and for value. The third-party purchaser will usually have a personal action against the bankrupt. As this is a post-bankruptcy claim, it will not be subject to the automatic bankruptcy stay and will not be extinguished upon a discharge of the bankrupt. However, in seeking to recover this claim, the third-party purchaser will be unable to resort to any of the assets that have vested in the trustee. A third-party purchaser can conduct a bankruptcy search prior to entering into the transaction in order to determine if the seller is bankrupt.

This general principle is subject to two statutory exceptions that operate to protect innocent third parties who deal with the bankrupt after the bankruptcy. The first applies only to property acquired by the

101 See Chapter 8, Section D.
102 *BIA*, s 76.
103 *Ibid*, s 71.

bankrupt after the bankruptcy and before intervention by the trustee.[104] Any transaction that is completed between the bankrupt and another person in good faith and for value is valid against the trustee. Although the after-acquired property vests immediately in the trustee,[105] the bankrupt is given the power to pass a good title to a transferee. Knowledge of the bankruptcy on the part of the purchaser or bad faith on the part of the bankrupt does not prevent the application of the provision.[106] After-acquired income governed by the surplus income provisions does not vest automatically in the trustee. The bankrupt can therefore validly transfer the money to a third party, and the transferee therefore does not need to rely upon this protective provision in order to claim a superior title to the property over the claim of the trustee.

The second exception operates in respect of real property that is governed by a land registry system.[107] A transfer of an interest in the land to a *bona fide* purchaser for value is valid and has the same effect under provincial law as if no bankruptcy had occurred. This provision protects the integrity of the land registration system and permits third parties to rely on the registry when acquiring interests in the land. The trustee is able to preserve the property by registering the bankruptcy order or assignment in the land registration system.[108]

FURTHER READINGS

ANDREWS, M. "Executory Contracts in Bankruptcy: Understanding Rejection" (1988) 59 *University of Colorado Law Review* 845

BAIRD, D. *The Elements of Bankruptcy*, 4th ed (New York: Foundation Press, 2006) ch 6 and 9

COUNTRYMAN, V. "Executory Contracts in Bankruptcy, Part I" (1973) 57 *Minnesota Law Review* 439

DUGGAN, A. "Partly Performed Contracts" in S Ben-Ishai & A Duggan, eds, *Canadian Bankruptcy and Insolvency Law: Bill C-55, Statute c. 47 and Beyond* (Markham, ON: LexisNexis Canada, 2007) ch 3

104 *Ibid*, s 99.

105 *Wallace v United Grain Growers Ltd*, [1997] 3 SCR 701.

106 *Re Hord* (1945), 27 CBR 175 (Ont HCJ); *Re Van Pelt* (1984), 53 CBR (NS) 28 (Ont HCJ).

107 *BIA*, s 75.

108 *Ibid*, s 74.

DUGGAN, A, & N SIEBRASSE. "The Disclaimer, Affirmation and Assignment of Intellectual Property Licences in Insolvency" (2014) 3 *Journal of the Insolvency Institute of Canada* 163

GOLD, R. "Partial Copyright Assignments: Safeguarding Software Licensees against the Bankruptcy of Licensors" (2000) 33 *Canadian Business Law Journal* 193

WESTBROOK, J. "A Functional Analysis of Executory Contracts" (1989) 74 *Minnesota Law Review* 227

CHAPTER 7

ENHANCING THE BANKRUPT ESTATE

Anticipating a bankruptcy, a debtor will sometimes transfer assets to another person in a pre-bankruptcy transaction. Gifts of property may be given to friends or relatives. Assets may be sold at a price that is significantly less than their value. Favoured creditors may be selectively paid off, leaving less property to be shared in bankruptcy among the remaining creditors. As the debtor no longer owns these assets at the date of bankruptcy, they cannot vest in the trustee. The possibility that a debtor will engage in such activities threatens the integrity of the bankruptcy process, since the creditors will be prejudiced by these actions. Bankruptcy law gives the trustee extensive powers to impeach pre-bankruptcy transactions. The trustee can use these powers to claw back the asset or its value from the recipient. This will swell and enhance the bankrupt estate, and ensure that more assets will be available for division among the participating creditors.

A. IMPEACHING PRE-BANKRUPTCY TRANSACTIONS

The trustee has a variety of powers that can be used to impeach pre-bankruptcy transactions. There are many different terms that are used to describe the exercise of these powers. Judges and commentators have referred to this process as "avoiding," "annulling," "reversing," "rescinding," "setting aside," "reviewing," "impugning," or "impeaching" the transaction in question. This usage is misleading to the extent that it suggests that the process, when successful, necessarily results in the avoidance of the transaction and a recovery of the property that was transferred. Some of the powers do not have this effect but respond by giving the trustee a personal right against the recipient of the property. In order to capture the full array of outcomes, these powers are referred to collectively as impeachment powers. Below, terms that refer to an avoidance of the underlying transaction will be used only in connection with impeachment powers that specifically provide this type of remedy.

1) The Sources of the Impeachment Powers

Several of the impeachment powers that are available to trustees have their source in provisions of the *BIA*. However, a trustee is not limited to these provisions when seeking to impeach pre-bankruptcy transactions. The *BIA* expressly provides that the trustee may invoke laws or statutes relating to property and civil rights that are not in conflict with the *BIA* "as supplementary to and in addition to the rights and remedies provided by this Act."[1] The Supreme Court of Canada in *Robinson v Countrywide Factors Ltd*[2] held that provincial legislation that gave creditors the right to impeach a transfer of property as a fraudulent preference is not rendered inoperative by the fact that the *BIA* also contains preference provisions. As a result, a trustee may impeach a transaction by using the *BIA* provisions, provincial law, or both.

The *Bankruptcy Act* of 1919 gave the trustee the power to impeach preferences and settlements. In 1961 amendments to the bankruptcy statute gave the trustee additional impeachment powers against distributions to shareholders and against reviewable transactions with related persons or other non–arm's length parties. The 2009 amendments to the *BIA* eliminated the settlement and reviewable transaction provisions and substituted a provision dealing with transfers at undervalue.

There are now four distinct impeachment powers contained in the *BIA*. A pre-bankruptcy transaction may be impeached as:

- a transfer at undervalue;
- a preference;
- a post-initiation transfer; or
- a distribution to a shareholder.

---

1 *BIA*, s 72.
2 [1978] 1 SCR 753.

The first two powers have the widest potential application and therefore are the most significant. The third power is limited in scope, covering only transactions that occur after insolvency proceedings are initiated but before the date of bankruptcy. For example, in an involuntary bankruptcy it would cover transactions that occur after an application for a bankruptcy order is filed by a creditor but before the court grants a bankruptcy order.

Provincial law gives creditors avoidance powers in respect of fraudulent preferences and in respect of fraudulent conveyances. In all provinces, fraudulent preferences law is derived from a provincial statute. The source of the avoidance powers in respect of fraudulent conveyances varies somewhat from one province to another. Fraudulent conveyances law is derived from the *Statute of Elizabeth*[3] of 1571. This Act was received into the law of the various provinces. Some of the provinces have re-enacted its provisions in a provincial statute called the *Fraudulent Conveyances Act*.[4] The matter is complicated by the fact that the provincial fraudulent preferences legislation also contains a single provision covering fraudulent conveyances. Courts have held that this was not intended to impliedly repeal the *Statute of Elizabeth*.[5]

As a result, there are three bases upon which a transfer may be impeached through use of provincial law. First, it may be challenged as a fraudulent conveyance under the *Statute of Elizabeth* or the provincial statutes that re-enact it. There are no substantive differences between these two sources of fraudulent conveyances law, and hereafter references to the *Fraudulent Conveyances Act* will encompass both. Second, a transfer may be challenged as a fraudulent conveyance under the special provision found in provincial fraudulent preference legislation. Third, it may be challenged as a fraudulent preference pursuant to provincial fraudulent preference legislation.

2) The Objectives of the Provisions

The general objectives of the impeachment powers are easy to identify. The provisions are directed against transactions that diminish the value that would otherwise be available for distribution to the creditors, or that undermine the statutory scheme of distribution among the creditors. The first kind of transaction results in less for all creditors. The second kind of transaction does not affect the total amount avail-

3 13 Eliz I, c 5.

4 See, for example, *Fraudulent Conveyance Act*, RSBC 1996, c 163.

5 *Bank of Montreal v Reis*, [1925] 3 DLR 125 (Sask KB); *Bank of Montreal v Crowell* (1980), 34 CBR (NS) 15 (NSSC).

able for creditors but results in a different distribution than would otherwise prevail in bankruptcy. The favoured creditor receives a greater share, and the other creditors receive less.

Although the general objectives are relatively uncontroversial, the means by which bankruptcy law attempts to implement them is highly contested. In particular, there is considerable debate as to precisely what kinds of conduct or transactions should be subject to impeachment. The traditional approach has been to focus upon the intent of the debtor. Avoidance of a transaction is available where a debtor intended to defeat, hinder, or delay creditors or intended to play favourites and prefer one creditor over the others.

The underlying rationale of the law is to prevent the debtor from engaging in conduct that harms some or all of the creditors. However, it does not seek to achieve its objective by punishing the debtor.[6] Instead, the chief impact of the provisions is directed against the person who received the transfer of property from the debtor. This has given rise to a competing objective — that of preserving the finality of legitimate commercial transactions. There is a constant tension between this objective and the objective of protecting creditors against the harmful acts of the debtor. More recently, some of the impeachment powers have shifted their focus away from the bad intentions of the debtor and towards the detrimental effect of the transaction on creditors.

Unfortunately, the various impeachment powers do not adopt a consistent approach. Some look to intent, while others look to effect. Some of them draw distinctions based upon the type of transaction, i.e., whether it involves a payment of money as opposed to a transfer of other kinds of property. Some are triggered by a close relationship between the debtor and the recipient. Some require that the debtor be insolvent at the time of the transaction, while others do not. Some require that the recipient participate in the fraud, while others are satisfied if the recipient has not paid fair value. Each provision also establishes a different time period within which the transaction may be impeached. This produces a distressing degree of complexity in the law. The different provisions all operate under their own special rules, and it is difficult for courts to develop an overarching approach since the provisions frequently adopt contradictory strategies.[7]

---

6 Criminal proceedings under the *Criminal Code*, RSC 1985, c C-46, s 392, and under *BIA*, s 198, fulfil this role.

7 See A Duggan & T Telfer, "Voidable Preferences" in S Ben-Ishai & A Duggan, eds, *Canadian Bankruptcy and Insolvency Law: Bill C-55, Statute c. 47 and Beyond* (Markham, ON: LexisNexis Canada, 2007) 145.

3) The Nature of the Remedies

Two different approaches to remedies are found in the impeachable transaction provisions. The first provides for the avoidance of the transaction. This form of remedy is adopted in the federal and provincial preference provisions, in provincial fraudulent conveyances law, and in the post-initiation transfer provision of the *BIA*. The second approach gives the trustee a right to recover a judgment against the recipient of the transfer. This type of remedy is adopted in the *BIA* provision governing distributions to shareholders. The *BIA*'s provision regarding transfer at undervalue gives the court a discretion to choose between avoidance of the transaction and granting judgment against the recipient.

Statutes that provide for avoidance of the transaction permit the trustee to proceed against the property that was transferred by the debtor to the recipient. The precise legal effect of avoidance under provincial law differs from that under the *BIA*. If a transaction is avoided under provincial law, there is no revesting of property in the debtor. The transaction remains valid as between the parties to the contract.[8] Avoidance of the transaction merely permits a creditor to ignore the transfer and to deal with the property as if it were still owned by the debtor.[9] Avoidance under the *BIA* provisions has a different effect. Courts have held that the avoidance of the transaction causes the property to revest in the trustee. The trustee thereby obtains title to the property by virtue of the avoidance of the transaction.[10]

The trustee cannot exercise the avoidance power if the person who received the transfer from the debtor transferred the property to a purchaser in good faith and for adequate valuable consideration.[11] This is illustrated in the following scenario:

> **The debtor transfers property to T1 under an avoidable transaction. T1 sells the property to T2 at its fair market value. The debtor then goes into bankruptcy and the trustee seeks to impeach the transaction.**

The trustee cannot look to the property in the hands of T2, since T2 is an intervening party who acquired the interest in good faith and for fair value. The trustee would be entitled to proceed against the property

8 *Re Lawrason's Chemicals Ltd* (1999), 87 CPR (3d) 213 (Ont CA) [*Lawrason's Chemicals*]; *Bank of Montreal v Bray* (1997), 50 CBR (3d) 1 (Ont CA).

9 *Adams v Adams* (1961), 38 WWR 54 (Sask QB); *Holmes v Holmes* (1913), 4 WWR 1335 (Sask SCTD).

10 *Re H & L Langille Enterprises* (1986), 72 NSR (2d) 418 (CA) [*Langille*].

11 *BIA*, s 98(3).

in T2's hands if T2 acquired it by way of gift or if T2 was acting in bad faith. The trustee may also recover the property from T2 if the consideration paid by T2 did not constitute "adequate valuable consideration." Unlike consideration in contract law, which does not look to the adequacy of the consideration, this phrase requires the court to consider the fair and reasonable monetary value of the property.[12]

If the trustee is not entitled to recover against property that was transferred to T2, the trustee may recover any property that was received by T1 in connection with the transaction.[13] If T1 has disposed of the proceeds, the recipient is also protected if the proceeds were acquired in good faith and for adequate valuable consideration. If T2 has not paid the full purchase price to T1, the trustee is subrogated to this claim and can compel its payment by T2 to the trustee.[14]

When the avoidance power is invoked, the usual outcome is that the trustee will be entitled to proceed against the property in the hands of the recipient or their proceeds unless they have been disposed of to a *bona fide* purchaser. The cases are less clear on whether the trustee has a personal claim against the recipient for the value of the property that was received from the debtor. The property received by the recipient may no longer be identifiable or traceable. This might occur when the recipient receives money from the debtor. It also may occur where the recipient (T1) receives property from the debtor and then sells it to T2 in exchange for money. In either event, the recipient might then spend the money and not obtain any property in return. The issue is whether the trustee is entitled to a money judgment against the recipient for the value of the funds received.

The *BIA* provides that the trustee may recover the property or its value if the property has been disposed of.[15] This gives the trustee the right to a money judgment against the recipient. There are many cases in which a payment of money to a creditor is avoided as a preference under the *BIA*. The usual remedy is judgment against the creditor for the amount of the payment.[16] Although the courts do not specifically identify the *BIA* provision as the source of this power, the provision offers a statutory basis for ordering a money judgment against the recipient. A

---

12 See *Re KS & D Engineering Ltd* (1992), 9 CBR (3d) 130 (BCSC).

13 *BIA*, s 98(1).

14 *Ibid*, s 98(4).

15 *Ibid*, s 98(2).

16 *Principal Group Ltd (Trustee of) v Anderson* (1994), 29 CBR (3d) 216 (Alta QB), aff'd (1997), 46 CBR (3d) 101 (Alta CA) [*Anderson*].

substantially similar provision is found in provincial fraudulent preference statutes.[17]

If the remedy associated with the impeachment provision involves only the recovery of judgment from the other transacting party rather than avoidance of the transaction, the analysis is much simpler. The trustee has a personal right against the recipient, and this right of action is unaffected by the transfer of the property to a third party or the receipt of proceeds. A potential drawback is that the remedy will result in limited recovery if the recipient is also insolvent.

4) Relationship to the Law of Restitution

The precise relationship between the law governing impeachable transactions and the law of restitution is controversial. In particular, there is debate over whether the impeachable transaction provisions should be regarded as restitutionary in nature so as to attract the general principles that are associated with that body of law. The law of restitution requires a person who has received a benefit to give it or its value back. Unlike compensation, it is measured by the gain to the defendant rather than by the loss to the plaintiff. Restitution encompasses two different kinds of claims. First, it is the remedial response to claims for unjust enrichment. Second, it is a remedial response to certain types of wrongdoing, such as breach of fiduciary duty, that require disgorgement of wrongful gains.

The impeachable transaction provisions are not a response to the wrongdoing of the defendant. The recipient of the gain who is required to give it up is often untainted by any wrongful conduct. Therefore, it would be a mistake to resort to principles of law derived from this source of restitutionary principles. The more difficult question is whether the impeachable transaction provisions attract principles derived from the law of unjust enrichment. The restoration of the property or its value in connection with an impeachable transaction might be thought to be a response to the unjust enrichment of the recipient because the recipient has received something that justly belongs to the creditors.[18]

Although there is a certain attraction to this view, it should be resisted. Canadian cases have made it clear that the principles associated with the law of unjust enrichment do not apply when transactions are

---

17 See, for example, *Fraudulent Preferences Act*, RSA 2000, c F-24, s 11.

18 See S Degeling, "Restitution for Vulnerable Transactions" in J Armour & H Bennett, eds, *Vulnerable Transactions in Corporate Insolvency* (Oxford: Hart, 2003). The author argues that both the reversal of the transactions and the claim by the recipient are restitutionary in pattern.

impeached by the trustee or by the creditors, and have held that the defence of change of position is not available.[19] This analysis recognizes that the policies underlying the two bodies of law differ. The impeachable transactions provisions go to great lengths to define the circumstances under which the creditors can lay claim to property that has been transferred to another. The substantive requirements of these provisions attempt to balance the competing objectives of upholding the integrity of creditors' remedies and protecting the finality of commercial transactions. It is therefore inappropriate to apply general principles of unjust enrichment that would skew this balance.

This is not to suggest that there is no role for the law of restitution in this field. There are situations where the trustee can avoid transactions in which the recipient has paid some consideration to the debtor. Alternatively, the recipient may have improved the property. Unjust enrichment law may be relevant in respect of the recovery of these gains. These are not matters that are governed by the statutes dealing with impeachable transactions, and therefore the issue may be properly resolved through the application of principles of unjust enrichment.

5) Status of the Trustee

The trustee occupies a threefold position. First, the trustee is a successor in interest of the property of the debtor. This is the capacity that courts refer to when they state that a trustee steps into the shoes of a bankrupt. The trustee does not acquire any greater status to impugn a transaction than that held by the debtor. If a debtor was fraudulently induced to transfer property to a third party as a result of a fraudulent misrepresentation, the trustee acquires the debtor's right to rescind the contract and recover the property. When trustees seek to impeach pre-bankruptcy transactions, it is usually not done in this capacity. Instead, trustees will usually seek to impugn the transaction in circumstances where the debtor would be unable to do so. In order to succeed, the powers of the trustee must be derived from one of the other two sources.

Second, the trustee has an independent status in the exercise of certain kinds of powers conferred by federal or provincial law to impugn certain types of transactions.[20] These statutes give the trustee the capacity to challenge a transaction between a debtor and a third party,

19 *Anderson*, above note 16; *Re Titan Investments Ltd Partnership*, 2005 ABQB 637 [*Titan*].

20 A failure to distinguish between these two capacities caused some courts to conclude that the trustee could not subordinate an unperfected security interest under provincial personal property security law because the trustee could not

even though the debtor is bound by that transaction. For example, the *BIA* gives the trustee the power to avoid certain pre-bankruptcy transactions as preferences. As well, provincial personal property security law gives the trustee priority over an unperfected security interest.[21] These rights are conferred on the trustee and are not derived from the rights of the creditors. In other words, a trustee has the right to attack the transaction even if none of the creditors had a right to impugn it.

Third, the trustee has a representative capacity that permits the trustee to exercise rights held by the creditors in relation to avoidable transactions. This may appear similar to the second capacity, but it is conceptually distinct. The difference is that the trustee is not given an independent status to impugn the transaction. Instead, the trustee's right is derived from the right of action held by a creditor against the third party prior to the bankruptcy. The trustee operates in this capacity when seeking to avoid a transaction as a fraudulent conveyance or as a fraudulent preference under provincial law. Provincial law does not give the trustee an independent status to avoid the transaction; however, the trustee, as representative of the creditors, is able to assert the same right as a creditor in avoiding the transaction.[22] Upon bankruptcy, the right to bring action to avoid the transaction vests in the trustee in bankruptcy, and the creditor no longer has the ability to pursue the action.[23]

This difference in status can have important implications. In order for the trustee to impeach a transaction under provincial legislation, the trustee must demonstrate that there was a creditor who had standing to avoid the transaction at the time that it was entered into. Suppose that a debtor transfers property to a third party while insolvent. At the time of the transfer, there was a claimant who had an unliquidated claim against the debtor. Other creditors were also owed money, but these claims were later paid before the bankruptcy occurred. The holder of the unliquidated claim does not have standing to avoid the transaction under provincial fraudulent preference law, since the benefits of the statute are available only to a person who has

---

acquire a better title than that of the bankrupt. This misunderstanding has since been dispelled by the Supreme Court of Canada in *Re Giffen*, [1998] 1 SCR 91.

21 See Chapter 5, Section B(3).

22 *Ex parte Butters; Re Harrison* (1880), 14 Ch D 265 (CA); *Totem Radio Supply Co v Stone* (1959), 38 CBR 112 (BCSC) [*Totem Radio Supply*].

23 *Schlumpf v Corey* (1994), 25 CBR (3d) 297 (Alta QB). The creditor is permitted to prosecute the action by invoking s 38 of the *BIA* if the trustee declines to do so. See Chapter 8, Section A(4).

a debt or liquidated demand at the time of the transfer.[24] The fact that debts owing to creditors may thereafter arise does not change matters. The person who challenges the transaction must have been a creditor at the time of the transfer. The trustee in this situation is not able to avoid the transaction, since there is no claimant participating in the bankruptcy who had the status to do so.

This does not mean that a person who has an unliquidated claim or a subsequent creditor may not share in the proceeds of a transaction impeached under provincial law. If, in the example above, there were unpaid creditors who had debts owing to them by the debtor at the date of the transfer, the trustee would be entitled to impeach the transaction. The proceeds recovered would then be distributed to all claimants with provable claims according to the scheme of distribution set out in the *BIA*.[25]

This leaves an unresolved issue. The value of the property that is transferred may exceed the amount owing to the creditors who have standing to impeach the transaction.[26] Suppose that a debtor transfers property worth $1,000 to a recipient while insolvent. At the time of the transfer, creditors were owed $500 and these creditors remain unpaid. Following the transfer, other creditors extend credit to the debtor. The trustee, as representative of the creditors, acquires the creditors' right to avoid the transaction. However, it does not follow that the full $1,000 that was transferred will be available in the bankruptcy. Under provincial law, the transfer is void only against creditors to whom debts were owed at the date of the transfer (in the above example, the creditors who were owed $500).

The trustee may argue that the exercise of his or her right to avoid the transaction causes a revesting of property in the debtor, which then vests in the trustee as after-acquired property by virtue of the *BIA*.[27] The difficulty with this argument is that it mischaracterizes the effect of the provincial legislation. The statute provides that the transfer is void against the person who has the standing to challenge it. This gives the party who impeaches it the right to ignore its effect and to exercise enforcement remedies against the asset in the hands of the third party. Unlike the avoidance powers in the *BIA*,[28] it does not have the effect of undoing the transaction as between the transferor (the debtor) and

24 See Section B(3), below in this chapter.

25 See *Lawrason's Chemicals*, above note 8 at para 8.

26 This scenario is atypical. In most cases, the claims of creditors with standing to avoid the transaction greatly exceed the value of the property.

27 *BIA*, s 67(1)(c).

28 See *Langille*, above note 10.

the transferee so as to cause a revesting of property in the debtor.[29] The trustee should therefore be entitled to proceed against the property in the hands of the transferee only to the extent that the creditors would have been entitled to do. This issue does not arise in respect of the avoidance of a transfer pursuant to the *Fraudulent Conveyances Act* because holders of unliquidated claims and subsequent creditors have standing to avoid transactions.

6) Exempt Property

The application of the impeachable transaction provisions becomes more complicated when exempt property is involved. Two different situations should be distinguished. The first is where the debtor converts non-exempt assets into exempt assets before the occurrence of the bankruptcy. As the exemptions are determined at the date of the bankruptcy, the property will not be available for distribution among the creditors in the bankruptcy. The trustee in bankruptcy may respond by attempting to use the impeachment powers to attack the exempt status of the property. The second occurs where the debtor transfers an exempt asset to a third party, and the trustee seeks to impeach it. The issue here is whether the exempt status of the asset gives a third party a defence against the action.

a) Conversion of Non-exempt Property to Exempt Property

The Supreme Court of Canada in *Royal Bank v North American Life Assurance Co*[30]dealt with the issue of a pre-bankruptcy conversion of non-exempt property into exempt property. A debtor had used non-exempt assets to acquire an insurance annuity prior to the bankruptcy; he had designated his spouse as beneficiary of the annuity, which gave it an exempt status under provincial law. The trustee sought to avoid the designation of the beneficiary as a settlement, thinking that this would result in a loss of the exempt status of the annuity. The Court held that the trustee's right to avoid transactions at the property passing stage does not affect its exempt status at the estate administration stage. As a result, the exempt status of the asset was not affected by the avoidance of the transaction.

The Court also indicated that, if the transaction were impeached as a fraudulent conveyance under provincial law, this would result in

29 See Springman et al, *Fraudulent Conveyances and Preferences* (Scarborough, ON: Carswell, 1994) (loose-leaf) at para 7(b).

30 [1996] 1 SCR 325.

a loss of the exempt status of the property.[31] The upshot is that a pre-bankruptcy conversion of non-exempt assets to exempt assets can be impeached under provincial law but not under the now repealed settlement provision of federal bankruptcy law. That provision has since been replaced with another provision governing transfer at undervalue. However, where a trustee seeks to avoid the appointment of a beneficiary under this new provision, the same reasoning would presumably apply. Avoidance of the appointment under the *BIA* would not affect the exempt status of the asset conferred under provincial law, whereas avoidance of the appointment under provincial law would destroy its exempt status.

The Supreme Court of Canada's decision can be interpreted in one of two ways. The broader view is that it endorses the general principle that conversions of non-exempt property into exempt property can be successfully impeached under provincial fraudulent conveyance law. On this view, a trustee could invalidate an exemption where prior to bankruptcy a debtor uses funds in a bank account to purchase exempt property. The narrower view is that the conversion of non-exempt assets to exempt assets cannot be avoided as a fraudulent conveyance unless the transfer that is being impeached involves a conveyance, transfer, or disposition of the property to another party.

The broader view cannot be supported, since it is incompatible with the principles of fraudulent conveyance law. When a transaction is avoided as a fraudulent conveyance, the creditor who impugns it is permitted to ignore the transaction. This permits the creditor to exercise its enforcement remedies against the assets in the hands of the recipient. When non-exempt assets are used to acquire exempt assets, there is a transfer of the non-exempt asset to the third party. However, this transaction cannot be avoided as a fraudulent conveyance because the third party has acted in good faith and has provided good consideration for the transfer. This is illustrated in the following example. Suppose that a debtor withdraws $5,000 from her bank account to purchase a motor vehicle that is exempt under provincial law. The transfer of the funds to the seller of the motor vehicle involves a transfer of property, but this transaction is not impeachable because the seller has acted in good faith and has provided good consideration for the transfer of the funds. As the transaction cannot be avoided, the debtor can claim the exemption in respect of the motor vehicle.

The narrower view is consistent with fraudulent conveyance cases that have refused to extend the statute to cases where there has not

31 *Ibid* at para 72. See also *Re Sykes* (1998), 2 CBR (4th) 79 (BCCA).

been a conveyance to a third party.[32] Although the narrower view limits the trustee's ability to use fraudulent conveyance law to attack acquisitions of exempt assets by the debtor, this does not mean that the debtor is free to convert non-exempt assets into exempt assets with impunity. A court may use its power to grant a discharge of the debtor to control this type of conduct.[33]

The ability to use fraudulent conveyance law to attack an exemption has been restricted even further by the creation of a federal RRSP exemption in the 2009 amendments to the *BIA*.[34] The exempt status of an RRSP under the *BIA* does not depend on the designation of a family member or relative as a beneficiary. As a consequence, the avoidance of the designation of a beneficiary under provincial law does not affect its exempt status. However, the issue remains relevant in respect of contributions that are made within the one-year period before the date of the bankruptcy. The *BIA* does not afford an exemption to contributions made during this period. The trustee may therefore attempt to use provincial fraudulent conveyance law to avoid a designation of a beneficiary in respect of insurance-based RRSPs acquired during this period. This will not work in provinces that provide an exemption in respect of all future income plans. In these provinces, the exempt status of the asset does not depend on the designation of a beneficiary, and so avoidance of the designation of a beneficiary is of no legal consequence.

b) Transfers of Exempt Assets

The debtor may have transferred exempt property to another before the bankruptcy. The issue that this raises is whether the transaction can be impeached so as to allow the trustee to recover the asset or its value from the recipient. Courts have held that a transfer of exempt property cannot be impeached.[35] The transfer does not have any preferential effect because the asset is not one that would be divisible among the creditors. The granting of a security interest in favour of an unsecured creditor in exempt property cannot be impeached for similar reasons.[36]

---

32 A disclaimer of a benefit under a will cannot be impeached since it does not involve a conveyance. See *Sembaliuk v Sembaliuk* (1984), 15 DLR (4th) 303 (Alta CA).

33 See Chapter 10, Section F(3).

34 See Chapter 4, Section C(2)(g).

35 *Banque canadienne nationale v Tencha*, [1928] SCR 26 [*Tencha*]; *Hamm v Metz* (2002), 209 DLR (4th) 385 (Sask CA) [*Hamm*]; *Royal Bank of Canada v Laughlin* (2001), 277 AR 201 (CA). And see CRB Dunlop, *Creditor-Debtor Law in Canada*, 2d ed (Scarborough, ON: Carswell, 1995) at 484–89.

36 See, for example, *Robin Hood Milling Co v Maple Leaf Milling Co* (1916), 9 WWR 1453 (Man KB); *Canadian Credit Men's Trust Assn v Umbel* (1931), 13 CBR 40 (Alta SC).

A transfer of an exempt asset may have a preferential effect where successive transactions are involved. This is illustrated in the following scenario:

> **The debtor owns a motor vehicle that is subject to a $5,000 exemption and also has $5,000 in cash. The debtor transfers the motor vehicle to his mother by way of gift. The debtor later acquires another motor vehicle and pays for it with the cash. The debtor subsequently goes bankrupt.**

The trustee in bankruptcy cannot proceed against the motor vehicle in the hands of the debtor's mother because the property was exempt at the time of the transfer. Nor can the trustee avoid the conversion of the non-exempt property into exempt property. One possible response to this problem would be to limit the principle that a transfer of exempt property cannot be impeached to cases where the debtor does not claim the same exemption in respect of other assets that are subsequently acquired by the debtor. An alternative response is to make an order for a discharge of the debtor conditional on payment of the exempt asset that was transferred to the third party.[37]

7) Recovery by Secured Creditors

In the event that the impeachment powers are employed and property or its value is recovered by a trustee in bankruptcy, it may be necessary to consider whether a secured creditor may assert its security interest in relation to these assets. If a secured creditor continues to have rights in the collateral following the transfer, the impeachment of the transfer by the trustee will not affect the secured creditor's right to enforce its security interest against the collateral. If its security interest has been lost by virtue of the transfer, the secured creditor merely has a right to prove its claim in bankruptcy and share with the other unsecured creditors.[38] If the collateral is insufficient to satisfy the secured obligation and the security interest is not cut-off, the best course is for the secured creditor assert to its rights in respect of its security interest against the transferee rather than seeking to have a trustee impeach the transfer. Indeed, it may be difficult for the trustee to demonstrate that

---

37 See Chapter 10, Section F(5).

38 *Tucker v Aero Inventory (UK) Limited*, 2011 ONSC 4223; *In Re Yagerphone Ltd*, [1935] 1 Ch 392 (Ch D).

the transfer can be impeached, since the unsecured creditors will not have been prejudiced by it.[39]

8) Time Periods

All of the *BIA* impeachment provisions set out time periods within which the transaction can be challenged. Some but not all of the impeachment provisions governed by provincial law do so as well. There is a fundamental difference in structure between the federal and the provincial provisions.

The federal provisions are primarily backward looking. The anchor is the date of the initial bankruptcy event.[40] This is not the date of the bankruptcy but the date of the initial proceedings that ultimately resulted in a bankruptcy. In a voluntary bankruptcy, it is the date the assignment is filed with the official receiver; in an involuntary bankruptcy, it is the date of the filing of the application for a bankruptcy order; and in a proposal, it is the date of the filing of the proposal or the notice of intention to file a proposal.[41] The time period runs backward from that event for the specified time period. The period also contains a forward component, namely, the period from the date of the initial bankruptcy event up to the date of the bankruptcy. The federal provisions do not cover transactions that are entered into by the bankrupt after the date of bankruptcy.[42]

The operation of the *BIA* time periods is illustrated in the following scenario:

> **D makes a preferential payment to a creditor (C) on 1 January and again on 1 March. On 1 May, other creditors of D bring an application for a bankruptcy order. On 1 June, D makes another preferential payment to C. On 10 July, D becomes bankrupt by virtue of a bankruptcy order granted by the court.**

---

39 For example, a transfer of an asset will not constitute a preference in these circumstances because the asset would not have been divisible in the bankruptcy. Had the transfer not occurred, the secured creditor would have realized on it and there would have been no surplus available for the unsecured creditors. The position would be different if the value of the collateral exceeded the secured obligation as the unsecured creditors would have been entitled to share in the surplus.

40 *BIA*, s 2 "date of the initial bankruptcy event."

41 If a proposal is unsuccessful and a bankruptcy ensues, the date of filing of an application for a bankruptcy order is used if there was an application for a bankruptcy order that preceded the filing of a proposal or a notice of intention.

42 *Montaldi (Re)*, 2011 BCSC 565.

The date of the application for the bankruptcy order is the date of the initial bankruptcy event. A three-month time period runs backwards from this date (1 May). The first payment falls outside this time period and therefore cannot be impeached. The second payment falls within this time period and therefore the trustee can impeach the payment. The time period extends forwards to the date of bankruptcy (10 July). The third payment falls within the time period, so it too can be impeached.

The provincial statutes use a different formulation. The anchor date is the date of the impeachable transaction, and the time period runs forward from that date. The general limitations statue defines the length of this time period in most cases,[43] but the fraudulent preference statutes provide a shorter time period for actions in which it is not necessary to prove preferential intent on the part of the debtor. In most provinces, a sixty-day time period is used, but in some provinces, such as Alberta, the period is one year. A trustee who wishes to use provincial law to impeach the transaction must bring an action against the recipient before the expiration of this time period. The date of the initial bankruptcy event and the date of the bankruptcy are irrelevant. The relevant date is the initiation of the action or proceeding to impeach the transaction. A failure on the part of the trustee to commence an action to impeach the transaction within the relevant time period will not be fatal to the claim if an action has been commenced by one of the creditors within the period. The trustee acts as representative of the creditors and acquires their right to impeach transactions. The trustee can therefore bring an application to be substituted as plaintiff in the action.[44]

In some provinces, such as British Columbia and Ontario, the event that must occur before the special time period expires is either the commencement of the proceedings to impeach the transaction or an assignment for the general benefit of creditors.[45] A voluntary bankruptcy therefore has the effect of preserving a right to impeach a transaction that has occurred during the sixty-day time period immediately prior to the assignment. In other provinces, such as Alberta and Saskatchewan, no special provision is made for assignments so that the trustee must commence an action before the requisite time period expires.

---

43 *Re Abco Asbestos Co* (1981), 40 CBR (NS) 250 (BCSC).

44 *Totem Radio Supply*, above note 22.

45 *Fraudulent Preference Act*, RSBC 1996, c 164, s 4(b); *Assignments and Preferences Act*, RSO 1990, c A.33, s 4(4).

9) Arm's Length Transactions

The *BIA*'s preference provision and the transfers at undervalue provision of the *BIA* use the concept of an arm's length transaction. An arm's length transaction is not defined in the *BIA*. Courts have interpreted the term to mean a situation where the parties are not influenced in their bargaining by something other than individual self-interest.[46] It means that there are "no bonds of dependence, control or influence" between the parties.[47] Whether or not that state of affairs exists is a question of fact.[48] In making this determination the court may consider if there was a common mind directing the bargaining of both parties, if the parties were acting in concert without separate interests, and if there was de facto control.[49] The *BIA* creates a list of related persons for the purposes of the Act.[50] Persons who fall within one of these categories of related persons are deemed not to be acting at arm's length with one another in the absence of evidence to the contrary.[51]

In the case of an individual, related persons are those connected by blood relationship, marriage, common law partnership, or adoption.[52] Further provisions refine precisely what is meant by these terms.[53] In the case of corporations, related persons include persons who control the corporation.[54] The concept of control has been interpreted to mean *de jure* control rather than *de facto* control; it therefore requires a majority of the voting shares even though less is often needed to exercise effective control.[55] Two corporations that are controlled by the same person are related as well.[56] The provisions regarding individuals can also interact with the provisions governing corporations. For example, two corporations are related to one another if a brother controls one

---

46 *Piikani Energy Corporation (Re)*, 2013 ABCA 293 [*Piikani*]; *Skalbania (Trustee of) v Wedgewood Village Estates Ltd* (1989), 74 CBR (NS) 97 (BCCA).

47 *Galaxy Sports Inc (Re)*, 2004 BCCA 284.

48 *BIA*, s 4(4).

49 *Canada v McLarty*, 2008 SCC 26 at para 62.

50 *BIA*, ss 4(2) & (3).

51 *Ibid*, s 4(5). The presumption that related parties do not deal with each other at arm's length can be rebutted only in respect of the impeachment powers. Elsewhere, when the *BIA* imposes a requirement of arm's length dealing, the presumption is irrebuttable.

52 *Ibid*, s 4(2)(a).

53 *Ibid*, ss 4(3)(e)–(g).

54 *Ibid*, s 4(2)(b).

55 *Re Green Gables Manor Inc* (1998), 4 CBR (4th) 273 (Ont Ct Gen Div); *Re Panfab Corp* (1970), 15 CBR (NS) 20 (Ont HCJ).

56 *BIA*, s 4(2)(b).

and a sister controls the other.[57] The provisions are structurally complex since it is necessary to work out a myriad of different corporate relationships. The fact that a party is a director and key employee of a corporation is not sufficient in itself to lead to the conclusion that they were not acting at arm's length.[58] This relationship does not attract a presumption that the parties were not acting at arm's length, and therefore the trustee must establish through evidence that the parties were not acting at arm's length.

B. PREFERENCES

Anti-preference provisions are legislated by federal and provincial statute. The provincial provisions refer to the impeachable transactions as fraudulent preferences, while the *BIA* provisions merely refer to them as preferences. The latter usage is superior in that it more accurately describes the policy that is being pursued. A preference does not involve an intention to defraud in the same sense that the term usually carries in the law. Rather, a preference is unjust because it prefers one creditor over the others and thereby undermines the statutory scheme of distribution mandated by bankruptcy law.[59]

1) Distinction between Fraudulent Conveyances and Preferences

A distinction is often drawn between a fraudulent conveyance and a preference. A fraudulent conveyance involves a transfer or other disposition of property that defeats, hinders, or delays the efforts of persons having claims against the debtor. A debtor may transfer property on the understanding that the property will be returned to the debtor once the financial difficulties come to an end, or once the creditors tire from their pursuit of the debtor. This transfer is designed to hinder the collection efforts of the creditors. The debtor might also transfer property to a friend or relative without any expectation of sharing in the use of the property transferred. This transfer prejudices the claimants since there are fewer assets available to them to satisfy their claims.

A preference does not involve an attempt to defeat creditors. Rather it is a selective transfer of property made to a creditor. Ordinarily, the

57 *Ibid*, s 4(2)(c)(ii).

58 *Piikani*, above note 46.

59 *Orion Industries Ltd v Neil's General Contracting Ltd*, 2013 ABCA 330 [*Orion*].

payment of creditors by debtors is considered to be a good thing. However, if the debtor does not have sufficient assets to satisfy all claims against the debtor, a transfer of property will have the effect of giving that creditor a preference over the other creditors. This is considered unfair because it undermines the scheme of distribution that would otherwise prevail under bankruptcy law or under provincial judgment enforcement law.

A preference requires a transfer of property to a creditor. A fraudulent conveyance does not. A transfer that involves a transfer of property to a creditor will not generally be impeachable as a fraudulent conveyance.[60] The problem associated with a preference is not that it defeats, hinders, or delays creditors; rather, the problem is that a preferred creditor obtains a greater share of the assets, leaving less for the other creditors.[61] There are some instances where a transfer to a creditor may nevertheless be impeached as a fraudulent conveyance.[62] This can occur where the transaction is a sham. For example, a mortgage document might be prepared under which a debtor grants a mortgage to a lender to secure of debt of $100,000. In fact, the debtor owes only $20,000 to the lender. The document is prepared in the hopes that it will dissuade other claimants from attempting to enforce against the property. Alternatively, property valued at $100,000 may be transferred to a creditor in satisfaction of a debt of $20,000. In both instances, the transaction may be impugned as a fraudulent conveyance despite the fact that both involve a transfer to a creditor.

2) Preferences under the *BIA*

A trustee may attempt to avoid a transaction as a preference under the *BIA*. The Act provides a general rule for the avoidance of a preference. The general rule is modified if the person receiving the preference is not acting at arm's length with the debtor. The general rule will be examined first.

Under the general rule, a transaction can be avoided as a preference under the *BIA* if the following conditions are satisfied:[63]

---

60 *Anderson Lumber Co v Canadian Conifer Ltd* (1977), 25 CBR (NS) 35 (Alta CA); *First Royal Enterprises Ltd v Armadillo's Restaurant Ltd*, [1996] 3 WWR 622 (BCCA).

61 *Perkins Electric Co v Orpen* (1922), 70 DLR 397 (SCC).

62 *Optical Recording Laboratories Inc v Digital Recording Corp* (1990), 2 CBR (3d) 64 (Ont CA).

63 *BIA*, s 95(1).

- the debtor has transferred property, provided services, given a charge on property, made a payment, incurred an obligation, or suffered judicial proceedings;
- the transaction is in favour of a creditor;
- the transaction has the effect of giving the creditor a preference;
- the debtor intended to prefer the creditor over other creditors;
- the debtor was insolvent at the time of the preference; and
- the transaction occurred within a period beginning three months before the date of the initial bankruptcy event and ending on the date of the bankruptcy.

Each of these elements will be separately discussed below.

a) Transactions That Constitute a Preference

A preference will usually take one of three forms. First, it may involve a full or partial payment to a creditor. Second, it may involve the granting of a security interest by the debtor to a creditor to secure a previously unsecured debt. Third, it may involve the transfer of property to the creditor in satisfaction of a debt or other liability. An example of this third category of preference is where a debtor returns inventory that had been sold to it by a seller in cancellation of the purchase price.

The preference provision of the *BIA* is not limited to these usual situations but also covers a number of less common cases. A creditor who recovers money pursuant to legal proceedings may discover that its recovery is subject to impeachment by a trustee. The *BIA* provision is not limited to consensual transfers by the debtor but extends to judicial proceedings suffered by the debtor. This will cover a landlord who exercises a right of distress against the debtor's property.[64] It will also cover a debtor who consents to a judgment in order to permit a creditor to recover the claim through judgment enforcement proceedings before any of the other creditors can enforce their claims.

An interesting issue arises in connection with the operation of an after-acquired property clause in a security agreement where the secured creditor is not fully secured. This is illustrated in the following scenario:

> A secured creditor S is given a security interest in all of D's present and after-acquired personal property to secure a loan. The security is properly registered and was given while D was solvent. D later becomes insolvent. The value of D's assets is less than the amount owed to S. D makes unusually large purchases of goods from suppliers on

64 *Re Early Canadian Furniture Ltd* (1984), 50 CBR (NS) 300 (BCSC).

credit. D's intention in doing so is to reduce the amount of S's indebtedness.

Although there are no cases on point, the transaction in principle should be capable of being impeached as a preference. The transfer to S occurred when D acquired the property rather than when the security interest is executed, since this is the time when the security interest attaches to the new goods. The impeachment of this transaction by a trustee would not result in the complete avoidance of the security interest. The security interest could be avoided only in respect of the new assets acquired by the debtor during the relevant time period. Although the trustee has the benefit of a statutory presumption that the debtor intended to give a preference, a secured creditor could rebut this by showing that the acquisition of inventory occurred in the ordinary course of business of the debtor.

b) In Favour of a Creditor

The preference must be in favour of a creditor. The definition of creditor is not restricted to persons who are owed a debt or liquidated demand but includes any person who has a provable claim.[65] This is sufficient to cover claimants who have unliquidated or contingent claims against the debtor. The definition of creditor is further expanded for the purposes of the preference provision to include a surety or guarantor for the debt due to the creditor.[66] This covers the situation where a debtor makes a payment to a creditor with the intention of giving a preference to a guarantor.[67] For example, a bank may have made a loan to a debtor and obtained a personal guarantee from the debtor's mother. The debtor may decide to repay the loan in order to release his or her mother from liability under the personal guarantee. The expanded definition of creditor ensures that the trustee can recover from the bank even though the debtor's intention was to prefer the guarantor rather than the bank.[68]

---

65 *BIA*, s 2 "creditor."

66 *Ibid*, s 95(3) "creditor."

67 *Re Speedy Roofing Ltd* (1987), 66 CBR (NS) 213 (Ont HCJ), aff'd (1990), 79 CBR (NS) 58 (Ont CA).

68 The trustee has a remedy only against the creditor who received the payment or transfer and not against the guarantor. See *Re Mendelson-Luke-Ennis Galleries Ltd* (1963), 5 CBR (NS) 134 (Ont HCJ).

c) Preferential Effect

The transaction must have the effect of giving a creditor a preference.[69] Some courts refer to this as a requirement that there be a "preference in fact."[70] The test for preferential effect is whether it has improved a creditor's position from that which would have prevailed under the statutory scheme of distribution in bankruptcy. Payment of a creditor does not have preferential effect if the creditor ranks as a preferred creditor under the statutory scheme of distribution in the bankruptcy and if there would have been sufficient assets to pay the preferred claim in full.[71] A payment to a fully secured creditor does not have preferential effect since it reduces the obligation secured by the security interest. The value of the payment lost by the bankrupt estate is matched by the gain in the unencumbered value of the collateral. However, a payment to a secured party can be impeached if the payment exceeds the value of the collateral, or if the security interest is subordinate to the trustee.[72]

Although a payment to a fully secured creditor does not have the effect of preferring the secured creditor, it may in some circumstances prefer a subordinate secured creditor. This is illustrated in the following scenario:

> A senior secured creditor (S1) has first priority to an asset valued at $10,000 that secures an obligation of $5,000. A junior secured creditor (S2) has second priority to the asset that secures an obligation of $10,000. The debtor pays $5,000 to S1.
>
> S2 has first priority to the asset upon the satisfaction of S1's claim. The payment has improved S2's position to the extent of $5,000, since S2 will now recover $10,000 (100 percent of its claim). Before the payment to S1, S2 would have recovered only the surplus of $5,000 (50 percent of its claim).

A transaction that involves a simultaneous exchange of value will not generally constitute a preference because the position of the other creditors is not prejudiced. The value transferred by the debtor will be equalled by the exchange value that is gained.[73] A debtor who gives a security interest in collateral to secure a new advance of credit does not

---

69 *Re Van der Liek* (1970), 14 CBR (NS) 229 (Ont HCJ).

70 See *Burns v Royal Bank of Canada* (1922), 2 CBR 241 (Ont HCJ).

71 *Kisluk v BL Armstrong Co* (1982), 44 CBR (NS) 251 (Ont HCJ) [*Kisluk*].

72 *Re Royal City Chrysler Plymouth Ltd* (1995), 30 CBR (3d) 178 (Ont Ct Gen Div).

73 *Re Reliable Gutter Shop on Wheels Ltd (Reliable Exteriors)* (1985), 58 CBR (NS) 156 (BCSC).

constitute a preference.[74] The transaction can, however, be impeached if the security interest that is granted secures past unsecured loans as well as the new advances of credit.[75] Granting a security interest to a creditor will not have preferential effect if it simply replaces an earlier valid security interest on the same property that had been created outside the relevant time period.[76]

A transaction that gives a creditor a right of set-off can also be impeached as a preference under the *BIA*.[77] Ordinarily, a sale of property by the debtor in consideration of a promise to pay its fair value would not constitute a preference. Although the bankrupt estate no longer has the property, the trustee may recover the price from the transferee. However, the transaction may operate as a preference if the transferee is a creditor. The transaction gives rise to a new cross-obligation against which the creditor can exercise a right of set-off. This permits the creditor to reduce the amount it owes to the debtor on the new obligation by the value of the creditor's claim against the debtor. The result is that the creditor's position is greatly improved. This is illustrated in the following scenario:

> **The debtor (D) owes $1,000 to a creditor (C). D's assets on a bankruptcy are sufficient to afford ordinary unsecured creditors with a dividend of 10 cents on the dollar. C would therefore be entitled to recover $100. D enters into a contract with C under which D sells and delivers goods to C for $1,000 with payment to occur within thirty days. D then goes into bankruptcy. C can set-off one cross-obligation against the other. C no longer can prove for a dividend in the bankruptcy but has acquired goods worth $1,000 from D. The net effect is that C's position has been improved by $900.**

d) Intention to Prefer

The debtor must have entered into the transaction "with a view to giving that creditor a preference over the other creditors." This means that the debtor must have intended to give a preference.[78] This element has given rise to the most litigation. Early cases divided on the question whether the concurrent intention of both the debtor and the creditor was required. The Supreme Court of Canada resolved this issue in

74 *Re Goldstein* (1923), 3 CBR 404 (Ont SCAD); *Re Aboud* (1940), 22 CBR 121 (Ont HCJ). These decisions also hold that there is no intention to prefer in such cases.

75 See Section B(2)(c)(ii), below in this chapter.

76 *Rahemtulla v Kushwaha*, 2013 ABQB 136.

77 *BIA*, s 97(3) makes the exercise of a right of set-off subject to the provisions of the *BIA* respecting frauds or fraudulent preferences.

78 *Re McIntosh-Marshall Equipment Ltd* (1968), 12 CBR (NS) 60 (Alta SCAD).

Hudson v Benallack.[79] The Court held that it is only the intention of the debtor that is relevant.

The *BIA* gives the trustee the benefit of an evidentiary presumption. If it is shown that the transaction had a preferential effect, it will be presumed, in the absence of evidence to the contrary, that the debtor intended to give the creditor a preference.[80] The shift in the evidential burden means that the creditor will need to adduce evidence to show that the debtor's dominant intention was not to prefer the creditor but was directed to some other purpose. Courts have applied an objective rather than a subjective test in determining the debtor's intention.[81] In other words, it is "that intention which the conduct of the parties bears when reasonably construed"[82] that is determinative rather than the debtor's "personal ruminations."[83]

Although much will depend upon the particular facts of the case at hand, it is nonetheless possible to identify certain recurring patterns in the cases where the presumption of intent has been rebutted. Four major categories of cases are discussed below, each of which contain a number of variations and subpatterns.

i) Ordinary Course Transactions

The presumption of preferential intent can be rebutted if it is shown that the payment or transfer was an ordinary course transaction.[84] In such a case, it is easy to draw the conclusion that the debtor simply intended to carry on business in the usual way and had no intention to prefer a creditor. In order to establish this ground, it is necessary to show that the usual pattern of payments has not been altered. A debtor who makes regular payments to suppliers, a landlord, or employees will be covered. Payments may be found to be in the ordinary course of business even if some payments are late so long as it can be shown that the supplier was receiving payment reasonably promptly for each shipment and the debtor was regularly paying for each as received.[85] This

79 [1976] 2 SCR 168.

80 *BIA*, s 95(2). This rebuttable presumption does not apply to a margin deposit made by a clearing member with a clearing house. See *BIA*, s 95(2.1).

81 *Re Holt Motors Ltd* (1966), 9 CBR (NS) 92 (Man QB). And see the discussion in Springman et al, above note 29 at para 20(j).

82 *Coast Wire Rope & Supply Ltd (Trustee of) v Trans Pacific Hardware Inc*, 1999 BCCA 217 at para 8.

83 *St. Anne-Nackawic Pulp Co (Trustee of) v Logistec Stevedoring (Atlantic) Inc* (2005), 13 CBR (5th) 125 at para 6 (NBCA).

84 *Deloitte & Touche Inc v White Veal Meat Packers Ltd* (2000), 16 CBR (4th) 74 (Man QB).

85 *Re Checkout Foodmarts Ltd* (1977), 24 CBR (NS) 286 (Ont HCJ.).

ground is not limited to the payment of creditors but can also be made out where it is the regular practice that unsold inventory be returned to the supplier for a credit.[86]

ii) Transactions Necessary to Stay in Business

The presumption that the debtor intended to prefer a creditor can be rebutted if it is shown that the dominant intent of the debtor was to complete the transaction in order to remain in business. This might occur where a supplier refuses to supply any further goods unless the past debts for previous orders have been paid.[87] This argument will not succeed if the supplies can be easily obtained elsewhere[88]or if there is not a reasonable prospect that the transaction would allow the debtor to continue in business.[89] But it will apply where it is necessary to pay out a judgment enforcement creditor in order to sell property free of a writ.[90] Lenders who are given a security interest in refinancing transactions also employ the argument when the trustee attempts to impeach a security interest that was given to secure a past unsecured indebtedness as well as a present advance.[91] If the transaction was a genuine attempt by the debtor to keep the business afloat, it will not be avoided as a preference.[92] In order to succeed, there must be a reasonable prospect that the refinancing will permit the debtor to remain in business.[93]

iii) Pre-existing Agreements to Transfer

The presumption can also be rebutted if it is shown that the transfer occurred pursuant to an agreement that was concluded outside the relevant time period for avoiding the transaction.[94] The leading decision concerned a debtor who gave a security interest in a sawmill to a

---

86 This was rejected in *SR Petroleum Sales Ltd v Arlyn Enterprises Ltd* (2000), 21 CBR (4th) 296 (Alta QB) because the return of inventory was a single transaction that covered the bulk of the inventory.

87 *Davis v Ducan Industries Ltd* (1983), 45 CBR (NS) 290 (Alta QB); *Re Kovalcik* (1973), 18 CBR (NS) 69 (Ont HCJ).

88 *Sinco Trucking Ltd (Trustee of) v Western Tire Service Ltd* (1992), 11 CBR (3d) 291 (Sask QB).

89 *Re Spectrum Interiors (Guelph) Ltd* (1979), 29 CBR (NS) 218 (Ont HCJ).

90 *Re Partington* (1971), 15 CBR (NS) 147 (Ont HCJ).

91 *Re D Elkind Clothing Inc* (1978), 26 CBR (NS) 240 (Ont HCJ).

92 *Orion*, above note 59.

93 *IBL Industries Ltd (Trustee of) v White Oaks Welding Supplies Ltd* (1991), 4 CBR (3d) 286 (Ont Ct Gen Div).

94 See G Levine & A Flouris, "Rebutting the Presumption Prior Agreements and Section 95 of the BIA," in J Sarra, ed, *Annual Review of Insolvency Law, 2008* (Toronto: Carswell, 2009) 529.

creditor.[95] The execution of the security document was delayed because a fire had destroyed many of the assets. Execution of the documents ultimately occurred within the time period for avoiding preferences. The transaction, as originally contemplated, would have fallen outside this period. The court held that the intention to prefer was rebutted since the debtor's intention was not to prefer a creditor but to fulfil a pre-existing contractual obligation. The pre-existing agreement cannot have been made at a time when the debtor was insolvent and cannot have been made with the intention of giving a creditor a preference.[96] There must be a concrete agreement to give security — incomplete negotiations or expressions of willingness to give security in the future are not enough.[97]

iv) Diligent Creditors

If the transfer to a creditor came about because the creditor was pressuring the debtor for payment, courts in England and Canada concluded that the debtor's intention was not to prefer the creditor but to relieve the pressure being applied by the creditor. This was known as the doctrine of pressure, and it was notoriously easy to satisfy. A simple demand for payment was often enough without the need for any threat of legal proceedings.[98] In 1920 Canadian bankruptcy legislation was amended to abolish the doctrine of pressure.[99]

Yet the doctrine appears to have been reincarnated, perhaps in a weaker form, through the diligent creditor defence. Courts have held that, if the transfer is made in response to the efforts of a creditor to collect, the presumption of preferential intent can be rebutted.[100] In doing so, courts have sometimes focused on the conduct of the creditor. They state that, although dishonest creditors should be punished, the law does not punish creditors for diligence.[101] This is puzzling since it is the intention of the debtor rather than the creditor that is significant. Some courts have required a higher threshold in respect of the pressure applied, and have held that the diligence of a creditor is relevant

95 *Re Blenkarn Planer Ltd* (1958), 37 CBR 147 (BCSC).

96 *Re Thunder Moon Investments Ltd* (1993), 20 CBR (3d) 195 (BCSC).

97 *Re Carpet Warehouse (Saskatoon) Ltd* (1983), 49 CBR (NS) 220 (Sask QB); *Re Penner Motor Products (1969) Ltd* (1972), 18 CBR (NS) 32 (Man QB).

98 *Stephens v McArthur* (1891), 19 SCR 446.

99 SC 1920, c 34, s 8. See now *BIA*, s 95(2).

100 *Re Houston and Thornton* (1973), 18 CBR (NS) 102 (Ont HCJ); *Keith G Collins Ltd, as Trustee of the Estate of Dubois-Vandale, a Bankrupt v MBNA Canada Bank*, 2006 MBQB 258.

101 See *Re Totem Painting Co* (1960), 1 CBR (NS) 38 (BCSC).

only if the creditor's actions cause an imminent business or commercial crisis.[102] On this view, the creditor diligence ground is essentially a subvariant of transactions that are necessary to stay in business.

Even more puzzling is a line of cases that involve diligent landlords who actually cause the goods of the debtor to be seized and sold under a right to distress prior to the bankruptcy. Courts have held that this constitutes a preference in the form of the suffering of a judicial proceeding.[103] These cases focus upon the intention of the creditor in taking enforcement steps, rather than upon the intent of the debtor. It is not clear what steps the debtor could have taken to prevent the enforcement, and so it is difficult to understand how the debtor could be said to have suffered or intended it. The situation would be different if there had been some form of collusion between the parties. If the debtor informed the landlord of the imminent bankruptcy and the landlord responded by exercising its right of distress, this would certainly be covered. However, the cases do not reveal this kind of conduct.

e) Insolvency of the Debtor

The onus is on the trustee to prove that the debtor was insolvent at the date of the alleged preference.[104] The *BIA* contains a definition of an insolvent person;[105] Chapter 1 contains a discussion of this definition and the concept of insolvency.[106] If a balance sheet test of insolvency is being applied, it is calculated after the transfer of the property to the creditor.

f) Within the Relevant Time Period

The preference must have occurred within the period that begins three months before the date of the initial bankruptcy event and ends on the date of the bankruptcy. The parameters of this time period are described earlier in this chapter.[107]

---

102 *Krawchenko (Trustee of) v Canada (Minister of National Revenue)* (2005), 11 CBR (5th) 238 (Man QB); *Re Norris* (1994), 28 CBR (3d) 167 (Alta QB), rev'd on other grounds (1996), 44 CBR (3d) 218 (Alta CA); *Re Advent Sales & Marketing Corp* (2003), 46 CBR (4th) 163 (Ont SCJ).

103 *Re Early Canadian Furniture Ltd*, above note 64; *Re KS & D Engineering Ltd*, above note 12.

104 *Re Van der Liek*, above note 69.

105 *BIA*, s 2 "insolvent person."

106 See Chapter 1, Section E.

107 See Section A(7), above in this chapter.

g) Non–Arm's Length Dealings

The *BIA* contains a special rule for preferences that are made to a creditor who is not dealing at arm's length with the debtor. This rule was added by the 2009 amendments to the *BIA*.[108] If the transfer occurred within a period beginning one year before the date of the initial bankruptcy event and ending on the date of the bankruptcy, it may be avoided if the preference has the effect of giving the creditor a preference over other creditors. This represents a marked departure from the general rule, since the focus is no longer upon the intent of the debtor but simply on the preferential effect of the transaction.

Some concerns have been raised concerning the trustee's ability to avoid support payments that are made pursuant to separation agreements during the relevant time period. There are two countervailing principles that lessen the likelihood that this will occur. Although persons are caught by the definition of related persons despite the fact of the breakdown of their marital or other personal relationship, they are able to introduce evidence to rebut the presumption that their dealings were not at arm's length.[109] It may be relatively easy to overcome this hurdle if the relationship has indeed broken down. As well, the payments will usually not be considered to be preferential in effect because the support payments will often qualify as a preferred claim in the bankruptcy.[110]

3) Fraudulent Preferences under Provincial Law

Although there are many commonalities between the preference provisions in the *BIA* and the provincial fraudulent preference statutes, there are also many differences. The provincial provisions are similar to the federal provisions in that a transaction cannot be avoided unless the following conditions are satisfied:

- the debtor has transferred property;[111]
- the transfer is to a creditor;

---

108 The special rule that it replaced simply extended the time period from ninety days to one year where the preference was made to a related person.

109 *BIA*, s 4(5).

110 See Section B(2)(c), above in this chapter.

111 The *BIA* provisions are somewhat wider in that they are not restricted to a transfer of property but also cover the incurring of an obligation or the suffering of judicial proceedings. It is unclear whether the more limited language of the provincial statutes covers these types of transactions.

- the debtor was insolvent at the time of the preference;[112] and
- the transaction has the effect of giving the creditor a preference.

There are four major differences between the *BIA* provisions and the provincial statutes. The first concerns proof of intent. The provincial statutes provide a two-track approach. If the transfer is impeached within a specified time period, it is easier to avoid. This rule will be referred to as the "effects rule." A major limitation of the effects rule is that the sixty-day time period that is adopted in most provinces is relatively short, and in the result many transfers will not be caught by the rule. A transfer that falls outside the time period may still be impeached, but the hurdles that must be overcome are far greater since proof of intent is required. This rule will be referred to as the "intent rule."

The second major difference is that the provincial statutes, unlike the *BIA*, provide a list of protected transactions. Despite the fact that the conditions of the effects rule or the intent rule have been satisfied, the transaction cannot be avoided if it falls within one of these categories of protected transactions. The list therefore provides a safe harbour for a creditor who receives a transfer of property from the debtor.

The third major difference is in the operation of the time period. This has been discussed earlier in this chapter. The fourth major difference is that the provincial statutes do not generally provide a special rule for a preference that is made to a non–arm's length or related party.[113]

a) Standing to Bring the Action

Only persons who are creditors at the time of the transfer can bring proceedings to have the transfer avoided as a fraudulent preference under the provincial statutes. Claimants who have an unliquidated claim[114] are therefore excluded as well as those who do not become

---

112 The test of insolvency under the provincial statutes is not the one found in the *BIA*. It must be shown that the debtor was insolvent, on the eve of insolvency, or unable to pay debts in full. See *Stihl Ltd v Motion Engine Services Ltd* (1990), 106 AR 118 (QB). Both the cash flow test and the balance sheet test can be used to establish insolvency under this formulation. Older decisions sometimes refer to the former as "commercial insolvency" and the latter as "legal insolvency." See *Rae v MacDonald* (1886), 13 OR 352 (CP).

113 The exception is the Yukon *Fraudulent Preferences and Conveyances Act*, RSY 2002, c 95, which extends the time period from three months to twelve months in the case of a related person.

114 *Huss v Lakin*, [1924] 3 WWR 841 (Sask KB).

creditors until after the transfer has been completed.[115] Secured creditors who are fully secured at the time of the transfer also do not have standing to impeach a transfer as a preference.[116] A trustee who wishes to impeach a transaction as a fraudulent preference under provincial law must demonstrate that the trustee represents claimants who were creditors at the time of the fraudulent preference.[117]

b) The Effects Rule

In some provinces it is unnecessary to show preferential intent on the part of the debtor or the creditor if the transaction is impeached within the requisite time period. In other words, it is sufficient to show that the transfer operated as a preference. This is sometimes referred to as an irrebuttable presumption of intent, but this terminology is really not helpful since intent is irrelevant. This formulation is used in the four western provinces and the Yukon.

In Ontario and Prince Edward Island, the effects rule simply operates as a presumption of intent. The recipient can therefore attempt to rebut the presumption by introducing evidence that demonstrates that the debtor did not have the intent to prefer. However, the statutes and the caselaw have made it clear that the doctrine of pressure has been abolished.[118] In these provinces, the effects rule therefore operates much like the rebuttable presumption contained in the *BIA*.

Some of the other statutes are unclear on this point. The statutes in New Brunswick and Nova Scotia simply provide that the intent to prefer is presumed within the sixty-day period. Some courts have held that the presumption will not be interpreted as being capable of being rebutted unless the statute contains language that indicates that the presumption is only *prima facie* or can be rebutted by evidence to the contrary.[119]

c) The Intent Rule

If proceedings to impeach the transfer have not been commenced within the time period available for the effects rule, it may be impeached pursuant to the more generous time period associated with the intent rule. There are three major hurdles facing the trustee. The first is that the trustee must show that the debtor intended to prefer a creditor. Unlike

---

115 *Raynel Mortgage Corp v Candela Development Ltd* (1979), 31 CBR (NS) 157 (BCSC).

116 *Ehattesaht Co-operative Enterprises Assn v Vancouver Equipment Corp Ltd* (1977), 3 BCLR 117 (SC).

117 See Section A(5), above in this chapter.

118 See, for example, *Assignments and Preferences Act*, above note 45, s 4(3).

119 *Shediac Boot & Shoe Co v Buchanan* (1903), 35 NSR 511 (SC).

the preference provisions of the *BIA*, the trustee does not obtain the benefit of a rebuttable presumption.

The second difficulty concerns the concurrent intent doctrine. Despite the fact that the provincial statutes refer only to intent on the part of the debtor to give a preference, most courts have interpreted this to mean that the creditor who receives the property must also have the intention to receive a preference.[120] The trustee will generally attempt to prove that this was so by showing that the creditor had knowledge of the debtor's insolvency at the time of the transfer.[121] Concurrent intent of both the debtor and the creditor is often easier to demonstrate where the transfer is to a related party.[122]

The third difficulty concerns the doctrine of pressure. The provincial statutes do not generally abolish the doctrine of pressure as was done in the preference provisions of the *BIA*. If the transfer occurred in response to pressure for payment that was being applied by a creditor, the debtor will not have an intention to prefer. It is not necessary to show that the creditor was in a position to enforce the claim immediately or to precipitate a crisis in the business, or that there was even a threat to resort to legal proceedings in the demand.[123] An honest demand for payment is sufficient.

d) Protected Transactions

The provincial statutes protect the following transactions from impeachment as a fraudulent preference:[124]

- a *bona fide* sale or payment made in the ordinary course of trade to an innocent party;
- a payment of money to a creditor;

---

120 *Benallack v Bank of British North America* (1905), 36 SCR 120; *Van Duzen v Van Duzen* (2001), 23 RFL (5th) 401 (BSSC). The doctrine of concurrent intent has been abolished in PEI, so that it is only the intent of the debtor that must be proven. See *Frauds on Creditors Act*, RSPEI 1988, c F-15, s 2(5). In Alberta, there is a division of opinion. Some courts have required concurrent intent. See *Burton v R & M Insurance Ltd* (1977), 81 DLR (3d) 455 (Alta QB); *Alberta (Director of Employment Standards) v Sanche* (1992), 15 CBR (3d) 58 (Alta QB). However, more recently courts have indicated that only the intent of the debtor is relevant. See *Christensen (Trustee of) v Christensen* (1994), 30 CBR (3d) 271 (Alta QB); *Titan*, above note 19. And see CRB Dunlop & T Buckwold, *Debt Recovery in Alberta* (Toronto: Carswell, 2012) at 1112–119.

121 *Re Webb* (1921), 2 CBR 16 (Ont HCJ).

122 *Canadian Imperial Bank of Commerce v Grande Cache Motor Inn Ltd* (1977), 25 CBR (NS) 207 (Alta SCTD).

123 *Stephens v McArthur*, above note 98.

124 See, for example, *Fraudulent Preference Act*, above note 45, s 6.

- a transfer of property in consideration of a present actual *bona fide* sale; and
- a transfer by way of security for a present actual *bona fide* advance of money.

The transactions are protected only if the consideration obtained in respect of the transfer bears a fair and reasonable relative value to the consideration. The protection of payments of money to creditors constitutes the most significant limitation to the application of the provincial provisions, since it insulates a major form of preference from impeachment.[125] A payment of money can therefore only be impugned by use of the *BIA* preference provisions.

The protection of ordinary course sales and payments functions in much the same manner as the ordinary course transaction rule under the *BIA* preference provisions. The return of inventory to a supplier in return for a credit against the unpaid price can fall within the ordinary course exception if it can be shown that the transaction was a normal practice in the industry. In one case, this was proven by showing that it was expressly provided for in the distributorship agreement.[126]

Transfers that are in consideration of a present and actual *bona fide* sale or transfers by way of security for present advances cannot be avoided as preferences. This protection does not add much. Such transactions would not constitute a preference in any event, since the creditor does not obtain any advantage over the other creditors. The value of the property transferred to the creditor is matched by the value of the consideration received by the debtor. The same holds true for the granting of a security interest by the debtor. The transaction is protected only if there has been a present advance of money to the debtor.[127] The protection, therefore, only covers security that is given to secure new advances of credit to the debtor.

Further provisions in the provincial statutes protect the following types of transactions that involve security interests:[128]

- a payment of money to a creditor that results in a loss of the security;
- a substitution of one security for another in good faith that does not lessen the value to other creditors; and

---

125 *Kisluk*, above note 71; *Christensen (Trustee of) v Christensen* (1996), 40 CBR (3d) 152 (Alta CA).

126 *Canadian Commercial Bank v Prudential Steel Ltd* (1986), 66 CBR (NS) 172 (Alta QB).

127 *Grep Properties (II) Ltd v 371154 Alberta Inc* (1995), 34 Alta LR (3d) 210 (QB).

128 See, for example, *Fraudulent Preferences Act*, RSA 2000, c F-24, s 9.

- a security for a pre-existing debt that is given for an advance made by the creditor to the debtor in the belief that it will enable the debtor to continue in business and fully pay all debts.

The first enumerated situation is redundant, since any payment to a creditor will be protected. The second situation also adds little, since a creditor is not preferred if the position of the creditor is not improved by the transaction. It is the third situation that is of greatest significance. The position of a creditor who takes a security to cover both a past indebtedness as well as a present advance obtains a preference, since that creditor's position is improved over that of other creditors. So long as the creditor believes that the refinancing will solve the financial difficulties experienced by the debtor, both the past indebtedness as well as the present advance will be protected. If this cannot be established, the security can be avoided in relation to the past advance but not in respect of the present advance.[129]

C. FRAUDULENT CONVEYANCES

The impeachment of a transaction as a fraudulent conveyance is governed by provincial law. There are two different fraudulent conveyances provisions that can be found in most provinces. The first is through use of the *Statute of Elizabeth* or the provincial *Fraudulent Conveyances Acts* that have re-enacted it. The second is through a provision found in provincial fraudulent preferences legislation. On the surface, the two types of provisions seem very similar; however, there are a number of subtle but important differences in their operation. The former are subject to less restrictive conditions, and thus they usually offer a better route for impugning a transaction as a fraudulent conveyance. Yet there is one situation where the latter may offer a superior means of impeachment.

1) The *Fraudulent Conveyances Act*

A conveyance or other disposition of property may be avoided under the *Fraudulent Conveyances Act* if it was made with intent to defeat, hinder, delay, or defraud creditors or others. The classic example of a fraudulent conveyance is a gift by the debtor to a friend or relative that was made with the intention of defeating the claims of creditors. Unlike

---

129 *Re Candie Maid Ltd* (1975), 20 CBR (NS) 106 (Ont HCJ).

many of the other impeachment provisions, it is not necessary to show that the debtor was insolvent at the time of the transaction. The focus of the inquiry is on the intent of the debtor and, in certain cases, on the intent of the recipient as well.

a) Standing to Bring the Action

The statute confers its benefits on "creditors and others" who are defeated, hindered, delayed, or defrauded of their just and lawful actions. This wording has been interpreted broadly so as to include persons who had unliquidated claims at the date of the transaction.[130] It also covers subsequent creditors — claimants whose claims were not in existence at the time of the transaction.[131] A secured creditor whose obligation was fully secured at the date of the transaction is also given standing to avoid the transaction, since its unsecured claim for a deficiency is considered to be equivalent to a claim by a subsequent creditor.[132]

b) Voluntary Transactions

Fraudulent conveyances law draws a distinction between voluntary transactions — i.e., transactions for no consideration or for nominal consideration — and transactions for valuable consideration. A transaction is referred to as voluntary because the transfer is to a volunteer who has not given good consideration for it. A voluntary transaction typically takes the form of a gift to the recipient. A more stringent set of conditions is imposed when seeking to impeach a transaction for valuable consideration. The law is more protective of good faith purchasers for value in order to produce stability and finality in commercial dealings between parties.

In order to avoid a voluntary transaction as a fraudulent conveyance, it is only necessary to inquire into the intent of the debtor. The knowledge or intent of the recipient of the property is irrelevant. The treatment of voluntary transactions can be subdivided into two classes of cases. The first is when the debtor is insolvent before or immediately after the disposition of the property. Courts have held that there is a legal presumption that the debtor intended to defraud his or her creditors. Whether the presumption is rebuttable or not is a matter that has attracted considerable debate.

---

130 *Hamm*, above note 35; *Petryshyn v Kochan*, [1940] 3 DLR 796 (Sask KB) [*Petryshyn*].

131 *McGuire v Ottawa Wine Vaults Co* (1913), 48 SCR 44.

132 *Canadian Imperial Bank of Commerce v Boukalis* (1987), 65 CBR (NS) 66 (BCCA).

The controversy began with two English decisions. The first was *Freeman v Pope*,[133] which appeared to support an irrebuttable presumption. The second was *Re Wise; Ex parte Mercer*,[134] which held that the presumption was rebuttable. The Supreme Court of Canada in *Sun Life Assurance Co v Elliott*[135] held that, if the debtor was insolvent, the transaction was void regardless of the intent of the debtor. The decision therefore seems to support an irrebuttable presumption. Some Canadian courts have interpreted this to be *obiter* because there appeared to be evidence that the debtor possessed the required intent.[136] Other courts have held that the statement of law forms the *ratio* of the decision and is therefore binding authority.[137]

The second class of cases involves a debtor who is solvent both before and immediately after the disposition of the property. In such cases, the person who is impeaching the transaction must adduce evidence to show that the debtor intended to defeat, hinder, delay, or defraud creditors or others.

c) Transactions for Good Consideration

The *Fraudulent Conveyances Act* does not apply to a disposition of property for good consideration and in good faith to a person who did not know of the fraud at the time of the transfer.[138] There are three elements that the purchaser of the property must satisfy in order to shelter within this protection.

The first is that the transaction must be for good consideration. Courts frequently refer to this as a requirement for valuable consideration. This is not the same as a requirement for adequate consideration. Many courts have confirmed that it is not necessary to show that the full value of the property has been given, though it must be more than nominal or entirely inadequate.[139]

The second element is the requirement for good faith. Because the third element directly deals with the concurrent fraudulent intent of both the debtor and the purchaser, the requirement of good faith does not add anything more in respect of the honesty or intent of the parties. Some

133 (1870), 5 Ch App 538.

134 (1886), 17 QBD 290.

135 (1900), 31 SCR 91.

136 *Mandryk v Merko* (1971), 15 CBR (NS) 246 (Man CA); *Mutual Trust Co v Stornelli* (1995), 43 CBR (3d) 221 (Ont Ct Gen Div) [*Mutual Trust*].

137 *Pigeon Lake Park Maintenance Ltd v Foley* (1997), 48 CBR (3d) 66 (Alta QB).

138 See, for example, *Fraudulent Conveyances Act*, RSO 1990, c F.29, s 3.

139 *Meeker Cedar Products Ltd v Edge* (1968), 12 CBR (NS) 49 (BCCA) [*Meeker Cedar Products*]; *Bank of Montreal v Horan* (1986), 54 OR (2d) 757 (Ont HCJ).

courts have treated the reference to good faith as relating to the genuineness of the transaction — i.e., that the transaction is not a sham.[140]

The third element concerns the knowledge and intent of the purchaser of the property. The statute provides that the purchaser must not have knowledge of the fraud. Despite this language, courts have held that something more than mere knowledge on the part of the purchaser is required. The Supreme Court of Canada in *Mulcahy v Archibald*[141] held that mere knowledge on the part of the purchaser of the motive or design of the debtor is not sufficient. There must be some further evidence that the purchaser was privy to the fraud.[142] In other words, there must be concurrent intent on the part of both the debtor and the purchaser to carry out the fraudulent purpose.

d) Proof of Fraudulent Intent

In order to impeach a transaction as a fraudulent conveyance, the plaintiff must show that the debtor intended to defeat, hinder, delay, or defraud creditors or other claimants. Intent will be presumed if the debtor was insolvent at the time of the transaction, but there is debate over whether this presumption is rebuttable. If the transaction was for valuable consideration, fraudulent intent on the part of the purchaser must also be proven. Rarely will there be direct evidence as to fraudulent intent, such as an admission by the debtor. Intent must usually be proven by circumstantial evidence. The process by which this is done in fraudulent conveyances law has an ancient lineage that dates back to *Twyne's Case*[143] in 1601. Courts since that time have kept a catalogue of suspicious circumstances or indicia of fraud, referred to as the "badges of fraud." Once a badge of fraud is established, the evidential burden of persuasion shifts to the defendant to provide some explanation of the transaction that shows that it was not made with any fraudulent intent. Badges of fraud can be grouped into a number of larger categories, which are discussed below.

i) Secrecy and Untruthfulness

Secrecy may take the form of attempts to hide or cover up a transaction. It is sometimes established when the transferee fails to register a conveyance of land or a security interest in a public registry.[144] Untruthfulness may take the form of misstatements to creditors to the effect that

---

140 *Chan v Stanwood* (2002), 216 DLR (4th) 625 (BCCA).

141 (1898), 28 SCR 523.

142 *Meeker Cedar Products*, above note 139.

143 (1601), 76 ER 809 (Star Chamber).

144 *Niemyt v Commertec Capital Corp* (1999), 11 CBR (4th) 66 (BCSC).

the debtor still owns the property after the conveyance of property has occurred.[145] It can also occur in misstating consideration or backdating an agreement.[146] The most extreme case of untruthfulness is where the transaction is a complete sham that is intended to make creditors think that the debtor no longer owns the property when that is not in fact the case.

ii) *Continued Use or Benefit of the Property*

The continued use or possession of the property by the debtor after the conveyance of property is considered evidence of fraudulent intent.[147] This often occurs where a transfer is to a family member and the debtor continues to use the property.[148]

iii) *Generality of the Conveyance*

A conveyance of all or substantially all the assets of the debtor is a situation where the courts will view the transaction with suspicion.[149] A transfer of only a small portion of the debtor's assets is obviously less likely to arouse suspicion.

iv) *Anticipated Liabilities*

A transfer that is made while litigation is ongoing or anticipated raises a suspicion that the transfer was designed to defeat the claim of the plaintiff.[150] Unusual haste in carrying out the transaction is also a suspicious circumstance when it is associated with action by claimants to recover their claims, or when it occurs immediately before a voluntary bankruptcy.[151]

v) *Inadequate Consideration*

Courts will not inquire into the adequacy of the consideration when deciding if a conveyance is for valuable consideration. This means that the fraudulent intent of both the debtor and the recipient must be proven. However, grossly inadequate consideration may arouse a suspicion that the transaction was intended to defeat creditors.[152]

---

145 *Northland Bank v Smetaniuk* (1986), 62 CBR (NS) 113 (BCSC).
146 *Meeker Cedar Products*, above note 139.
147 *Bank of Nova Scotia v Zgurski* (1970), 14 CBR (NS) 185 (Alta SCTD).
148 *Chow v Pearson* (1992), 12 CBR (3d) 226 (BCSC).
149 *Bank of Montreal v Vandine*, [1953] 1 DLR 456 (NBSCAD).
150 *Petryshyn*, above note 130.
151 *Wilson v Gill* (1995), 33 CBR (3d) 21 (BCSC).
152 *Mutual Trust*, above note 136.

vi) Related Parties

A conveyance to a relative or to a related corporation has been characterized as a badge of fraud in many cases.[153] Some courts have gone so far as to characterize it as a legal presumption, but the better view is that it operates to shift the burden of adducing evidence to rebut a *prima facie* case to the debtor in circumstances where the existence of the relationship creates a suspicion of fraud.[154]

2) Impeachment of Conveyances under Fraudulent Preferences Legislation

Although provincial fraudulent preferences statutes primarily deal with fraudulent preferences, they also contain a provision covering fraudulent conveyances.[155] For convenience, this will be referred to as the FPA provision. A transfer of property that is made when the debtor is insolvent and with intent to defeat, hinder, delay, or prejudice creditors can be avoided by the creditors. This formulation is narrower than the *Fraudulent Conveyances Act* in two respects. First, it requires that the debtor be insolvent at the time of the transfer. The *Fraudulent Conveyances Act* contains no equivalent requirement. Second, only persons who are creditors at the time of the transaction have standing to impeach the transaction. The *Fraudulent Conveyances Act* uses a wider formulation that confers standing on persons with unliquidated claims and subsequent creditors.

Although the *Fraudulent Conveyances Act* has an advantage over the FPA provision on these two scores, there is one situation where the FPA provision may be more favourable. A transaction for valuable consideration is more difficult to impeach under the *Fraudulent Conveyances Act* because it must be shown that the transferee was privy to the fraud. A purchaser can qualify for this protection even though the transaction was for an undervalue — i.e., the consideration given by the transferee did not reflect the full value of the property transferred.

The FPA provision does not contain a similar limitation. Instead, the provision is subject to the same exceptions as those in respect of fraudulent preferences under provincial legislation. In order to fall within the relevant protective provision, it must be shown that the property received by the debtor bears a fair and reasonable relative value to the consideration given for it. The FPA provision therefore

---

153 The leading decision is *Koop v Smith* (1915), 51 SCR 554.

154 *Krumm v McKay* (2003), 47 CBR (4th) 38 (Alta QB).

155 See, for example, *Assignments and Preferences Act*, above note 45, s 4(1).

offers a more effective means of impeaching a transaction at an undervalue. If the consideration is inadequate, the protective provision will not apply. Thus, only proof of the debtor's fraudulent intent will be required.[156]

D. TRANSFER AT UNDERVALUE

The provisions regarding transfer at undervalue were added by the 2009 amendments to the *BIA*. They replace both the settlement provisions and the reviewable transactions provisions that formerly provided the means through which certain types of gifts and transfers at undervalue were impeachable. The wording and structure of the new provisions are similar to the reviewable transaction provisions in some respects, and so some of the caselaw under the older provision remains relevant when interpreting the new provisions.

The provisions regarding transfer at undervalue cover two different situations. The first involves cases where the debtor and the recipient are dealing at arm's length; the second involves cases where the debtor and the recipient are not dealing at arm's length. In both cases, the transaction that is being impeached must constitute a transfer at undervalue.

1) Definition of a Transfer at Undervalue

The *BIA* defines a transfer at undervalue as a disposition of property or provision of services for no consideration or for which the consideration received by the debtor is conspicuously less than the fair market value of the consideration given by the debtor.[157] The automatic vesting of an interest pursuant to a right of survivorship upon the death of the other joint tenant does not constitute a transfer at undervalue. There is no transfer; rather the interest of the other joint tenant is extinguished upon death.[158] The provision does not apply where the transfer does not convey the beneficial interest and the transferee holds the asset as a bare trustee for the debtor.[159] The provision covers a wide range of

---

156 *Leighton v Muir* (1962), 34 DLR (2d) 332 (NSSC).

157 *BIA*, s 2 "transfer at undervalue."

158 *Cameron (Re)*, 2011 ONSC 6471. The court noted that even if it were considered a transfer, the other joint tenant did not obtain it at an undervalue as both were presumed to have contributed equally towards the acquisition of the asset.

159 *Anderson (Re)*, 2013 BCSC 317 at para 22: [Section 96 of the *BIA*] "was not intended simply to punish a participant in a transfer at undervalue . . . but was

dealings. The following transactions are examples of transactions that are potentially caught by the definition:

- the debtor makes a gift of an asset;
- the debtor sells an asset at a price less than its fair market value;
- the debtor buys an asset at a price greater than its fair market value;
- the debtor enters into a lease agreement as lessor at a rent less than its rental value;
- the debtor enters into a lease agreement as lessee at a rent greater than its rental value;
- the debtor supplies services for less than their fair market value;
- the debtor pays for services at greater than their fair market value;
- the debtor settles a claim against the debtor for more than its recoverable value; or
- the debtor agrees to accept a lesser sum in satisfaction of a claim owed to the debtor.

2) Conspicuous Disparity in Value

The definition of transfer at undervalue indicates that there must be a conspicuous disparity between the fair market value of the property or services and the amount given or received for it. The lack of any consideration at all flowing to the debtor is also covered. The trustee in bankruptcy must state his or her opinion as to the fair market value of the property or services and the value of the actual consideration given or received.[160] In the absence of any evidence to the contrary, the values stated by the trustee will be used. The recipient therefore carries the onus of establishing that some other value ought to be used.

The disparity must be such as to be plainly evident and attracting notice. This determination will depend upon all the facts of the case, and it is not subject to exact quantification. With this limitation in mind, some guidance can be obtained from cases that applied a substantially similar conspicuous disparity test under the now repealed reviewable transaction provisions. A 17 percent difference was held to constitute a conspicuous disparity,[161] whereas a 6 percent difference was not.[162]

---

intended to bring the real value of assets transferred at undervalue back into the bankrupt's estate for the benefit of creditors."

160 *BIA*, s 96(2).

161 *Henfrey Samson Belair Ltd v Wedgewood Village Estates Ltd* (1987), 65 CBR (NS) 48 (BCCA).

162 *Peoples Department Store Inc (Trustee of) v Wise*, [2004] 3 SCR 461 [*Peoples Department Store*].

3) Arm's Length Dealings

If the debtor and the recipient are dealing with one another at arm's length, the transfer can be impeached only if the debtor was insolvent at the time of the transfer or was rendered insolvent by it and if the debtor intended to defraud, defeat, or delay a creditor. The time period for impeaching the transfer begins one year from the date of the initial bankruptcy event and ends on the date of the bankruptcy.[163]

This portion of the provision covers much of the same ground as fraudulent conveyance law. The provisions regarding transfer at undervalue are more restrictive than the *Fraudulent Conveyances Act* in two respects. First, the trustee must prove that the debtor was insolvent at the time of the transfer. This is not a requirement under fraudulent conveyances law. Second, the definition of "creditor" in the *BIA* covers persons with unliquidated claims.[164] As is the case under fraudulent conveyances law, a transfer that was intended to defeat an unliquidated claim can therefore also be impeached under the provision. However, unlike fraudulent conveyances law, the *BIA* provisions do not cover cases where the intent was to defraud, defeat, or delay a future creditor.

These provisions are broader than fraudulent conveyances law in one respect. They give less protection to a transferee who has given valuable consideration. Under fraudulent conveyances law, both the debtor and the transferee must be privy to the fraud if the transferee gave good consideration. The *BIA* provisions do not look to the knowledge or intent of the transferee.[165]

4) Non–Arm's Length Dealings

The second kind of case covered by the transfer at undervalue provisions involve non–arm's length dealings. No proof of fraudulent intent and no proof of insolvency are needed if the transfer for undervalue occurred within the period that begins one year from the date of the initial bankruptcy event and ends on the date of the bankruptcy.[166] This portion of the provisions is substantially similar to the reviewable transactions provisions that it replaces.

---

163 *BIA*, s 96(1)(a).

164 *Ibid*, s 2 "creditor" and s 121(1).

165 In this respect, the transfer at undervalue provisions are similar to the fraudulent conveyance provision found in the provincial fraudulent preferences statutes. See Section C(2), above in this chapter.

166 *BIA*, s 96(1)(b)(i).

If the transfer at undervalue falls outside the one-year period, it may nevertheless fall within an extended five-year period. In order to impeach the transfer, the trustee must show either that the debtor was insolvent at the time of the transfer or that the debtor intended to defraud, defeat, or delay a creditor.[167] Impeachment of a transaction as a transfer at undervalue in the extended period offers two advantages over fraudulent conveyances law. First, no proof of fraudulent intent was needed if the debtor is insolvent at the time of the transfer or rendered insolvent by it. Under fraudulent conveyances law, there is currently a division of opinion on whether the insolvency of the debtor gives rise to a rebuttable or irrebuttable presumption of fraudulent intent.[168] Second, if the debtor was not insolvent at the time of the transfer, it is only necessary to prove fraudulent intent on the part of the debtor. Unlike fraudulent conveyances law, it is not necessary to prove that a purchaser who gave value was also privy to the fraudulent intent.

5) Remedies

The remedies available pursuant to the provisions governing transfer at undervalue are significantly different from those found in the other *BIA* provisions. The court is given an option. The court may declare the transfer void or it may order a money judgment for the difference in value against the transferee or a person who is privy to the transfer. Although the statute is silent on the matter, a transferee likely would be entitled to recover the value of the property that it gave as consideration if a court elects to avoid the transfer.[169] A judgment for the difference is less useful in cases where the party dealing with the debtor is also insolvent. Avoidance of the transaction will be less useful in cases where property that has been transferred has been destroyed, has depreciated in value, or can no longer be located.

The remedy is not limited to a judgment against the party who entered into the transaction with the debtor. The court may also award a judgment against any other person who is privy to the transaction. The *BIA* contains a new definition that clarifies the meaning of a person who is privy to the transfer.[170] The term covers a person who is not dealing at arm's length with a party to a transfer and who by reason of

167 *Ibid*, s 96(1)(b)(ii).

168 See Section C(1)(b), above in this chapter.

169 See Section A(4), above in this chapter.

170 *BIA*, s 96(3). This substantially incorporates the view expressed by the Supreme Court of Canada in *Peoples Department Store*, above note 162, in relation to the meaning of the term "privy to the transaction" in the reviewable transactions

the transfer directly or indirectly receives a benefit or causes a benefit to be received by another person. The Supreme Court of Canada in *Peoples Department Store Inc v Wise*,[171] in interpreting a similar provision in the now repealed reviewable transaction provisions, indicated that this person must have some degree of knowledge or control of one of the parties to the transaction. The directors and officers of a corporation are prime candidates for the application of the privy provision. This might occur where a corporation obtains an asset at undervalue and then makes a distribution of the value to its directors, officers, or controlling shareholders.[172]

6) Judicial Discretion

The provisions regarding transfer at undervalue use the permissive "may" in relation to the remedies. The question that is raised by this use of language is whether this was intended to confer discretion on a court to decide whether to grant a remedy in any given case. The reviewable transactions provision shared a somewhat similar structure. It provided that a court "may" give judgment to the trustee for the difference in value.[173] The Nova Scotia Court of Appeal held that this did not give the court the discretion to withhold the remedy.[174] The Ontario Court of Appeal[175] took the opposite view and held that the court may decide not to grant the remedy having regard to factors such as the good faith, the intentions of the parties, and the fact that fair value may have been given. The Supreme Court of Canada has endorsed this view and indicated that "equitable considerations" should be taken into account when deciding whether to exercise it.[176]

The difficulty with this approach is that it appears to jumble together all the different elements used in the various impeachment powers without providing any guidance as to which of the factors will be relevant. It is not clear whether it is the debtor's intent, the recipient's intent, or both that is relevant. Even if these additional factors are established, they are not determinative of the issue. They are merely factors that may

---

provisions of the *BIA*. See *Bank of Montreal v EL04 Inc (Just Between Us and Pink Elephant)*, 2012 ONCA 80.

171 Above note 162.

172 *Rustop Ltd v White* (1979), 32 CBR (NS) 25 (NSCAD) [*Rustop*].

173 The reviewable transactions provisions were contained in s 100 of the *BIA* and were repealed by the 2009 amendments.

174 *Rustop*, above note 172.

175 *Standard Trustco Ltd v Standard Trust Co* (1995), 36 CBR (3d) 1 (Ont CA).

176 *Peoples Department Store*, above note 162.

be considered by a court in exercising its discretion once the required elements of the provision have been proven. It is exceedingly difficult to predict how courts in future cases will exercise this discretion.

On the other hand, it can be argued that the use of the term "may" in the provision regarding transfer at undervalue has a different function from its use in the reviewable transactions provision, and that the caselaw decided under the latter should not be applied. The provision governing transfer at undervalue gives a court a choice between two remedies — avoiding the transfer or granting a judgment against the party to the transfer. The reviewable transaction provision did not give a court this choice. The permissive term "may" might have been included because a court is given discretion to choose between these two alternative remedies. On this view, the discretion is limited to a choice between one of two kinds of orders. It was not intended to permit a court to decline to do either on the basis of other unarticulated factors.

E. POST-INITIATION TRANSFERS

Canadian bankruptcy law originally used a relation-back doctrine borrowed from English bankruptcy law. Under this doctrine, an involuntary bankruptcy was deemed to occur at the time that proceedings were first initiated by the creditors, rather than at the date that a bankruptcy court granted a bankruptcy order. One consequence of this doctrine was that the debtor's property was deemed to have vested in the trustee at the date of the filing of the creditor's application. Persons who dealt with the debtor during the period following initiation of the proceedings but before the granting of a bankruptcy order were therefore placed in a very difficult position. Any transfer or transaction that occurred in this period would be liable to be invalidated by virtue of the relation-back doctrine. The property of the debtor was deemed to have vested in the trustee, and the debtor lacked the capacity to dispose of the assets. The severity of this rule was tempered by a provision in the bankruptcy legislation that protected *bona fide* transactions that occurred during this period.[177]

The relation-back doctrine was eventually abolished in 1992. The protective provision was then transformed into an impeachment provision.[178] The reformulated provision starts by stating that no transaction entered into between the date of the initial bankruptcy event

177 See *Re Pic-N-Save Ltd* (1972), 19 CBR (NS) 42 (Ont HCJ).
178 *BIA*, s 97(1).

and the date of the bankruptcy is valid. The provision then provides a very wide exception that validates the following transactions if they are made in good faith:

- a payment to a creditor;
- a payment or delivery to a bankrupt;
- a conveyance or transfer by the debtor for adequate valuable consideration; and
- a contract, dealing, or transaction, including the giving of security, for adequate valuable consideration.

A transaction is considered to be for adequate valuable consideration if it is for fair and reasonable money value with relation to the known or reasonably anticipated benefits of the contract, dealing, or transaction.[179] It is unnecessary to show intent to defraud on the part of either the debtor or the party dealing with the debtor. If the transfer or transaction is not for adequate valuable consideration, it will not be protected and therefore will be invalid as against the trustee.

The trustee is not limited to a judgment for the difference between the consideration paid and the fair value in the case of a transfer of property to a person for less than fair value. Since the transaction is invalid, the trustee is treated as being vested with the title to the property. As a result, the trustee is entitled to the property and any increase in value in it or its proceeds that may have thereafter occurred.[180]

The provision makes it clear that it operates as an additional ground for impeaching a transaction that occurs after the date of the initial bankruptcy event. A transaction that occurs during this period may also be impeached using any of the other powers.

F. DISTRIBUTION TO SHAREHOLDERS

The *BIA* permits a trustee to impeach distributions to shareholders that occur when the debtor corporation is insolvent. The distribution may have taken the form of a declaration of dividends or a share repurchase or redemption. A dividend in the form of additional shares is not impeachable since the creditors are not prejudiced by the creation of additional equity claims. In order to impeach the corporate distribution, the following conditions must be satisfied:[181]

---

179 *Ibid*, s 97(2).

180 *FC Jones & Sons v Jones*, [1996] 3 WLR 703 (CA).

181 *BIA*, ss 101(1) & (2).

- money has been paid to a shareholder pursuant to a declaration of dividends, a share repurchase, or share cancellation;
- the transaction occurred within a period beginning one year before the date of the initial bankruptcy event and ending on the date of the bankruptcy;
- the transaction occurred when the corporation was insolvent; and
- the directors did not have reasonable grounds to believe that the transaction was occurring at a time when the corporation was solvent.

The onus of proving the first two elements falls upon the trustee, while the onus of disproving the last two elements falls upon the directors.[182]

If these conditions are satisfied, the court may give judgment to the trustee against the directors in the amount of the dividend or redemption or purchase price. In making a determination that the directors knew of the insolvency, the court is directed to consider whether the directors acted as prudent and diligent persons and whether they in good faith relied on financial or other reports prepared by the officers of the corporation, the auditor, or by outside professionals.[183] A director is exonerated from liability if he or she protested against payment.[184] The court may also give judgment against a shareholder if the shareholder is related to one or more of the directors or to the corporation.[185]

Business corporations legislation also provides for director's liability in respect of corporate distributions.[186] Since the right of recovery is in the corporation, the trustee will acquire this right of action upon a bankruptcy of the corporation. There are two advantages of these types of provisions over the *BIA* provisions. The first is that a different financial test is applied. In place of the usual balance sheet test, the business corporations statutes provide that the assets must exceed the aggregate of liabilities and stated capital. The stated capital is the amount received by the corporation as consideration for the issue of the shares.[187] This provides an extra cushion for the benefit of the creditors of the corporation. The time period associated with the right of action under

---

182 *Ibid*, s 101(5).

183 *Ibid*, s 101(2.1).

184 *Ibid*, s 101(3).

185 *Ibid*, s 101(2.2). The court may also give judgment against a shareholder who is related to a director who is not to be liable because of lack of knowledge of the insolvency, or because the director protested against the payment. The shareholder has the onus of proving that the corporation was not insolvent. See *BIA*, *ibid*, s 101(6).

186 See, for example, *Canada Business Corporations Act*, RSC 1985, c C-44, ss 34–36, 42, and 118.

187 *Ibid*, s 26(2).

business corporations legislation also may prove advantageous if the time period in the *BIA* provision has expired.[188]

The *BIA* provisions are limited to distributions by corporations to their shareholders. It does not cover distributions made by non-corporate business entities to their investors. Courts have sometimes struggled to use the other available impeachment powers to provide a remedy to the creditors in respect of these distributions. In *Titan*,[189] the court held that a distribution to investors in respect of a limited partnership qualified as a payment to a creditor so as to fall under fraudulent preferences legislation. This argument would usually fail on the ground that investors do not qualify as creditors. However, in this case, the investors had been the victims of a fraudulent Ponzi scheme and therefore qualified as creditors by virtue of their having an action for the return of their money.

FURTHER READINGS

ARMOUR, J, & H BENNETT. *Vulnerable Transactions in Corporate Insolvency* (Oxford: Hart, 2003)

BRITISH COLUMBIA LAW REFORM COMMISSION. *Report on Fraudulent Conveyances and Preferences*, Report No 94 (Vancouver: British Columbia Law Reform Commission, 1988)

CLARK, R. "The Duties of the Corporate Debtor to Its Creditors" (1977) 90 *Harvard Law Review* 505

CUMING, R. "Transfers at Undervalue and Preferences under the *Bankruptcy and Insolvency Act*: Rethinking Outdated Approaches" (2002) 37 *Canadian Business Law Journal* 5

DUGGAN, A, & T TELFER. "Gifts and Transfers at Undervalue" in S Ben-Ishai & A Duggan, eds, *Canadian Bankruptcy and Insolvency Law: Bill C-55, Statute c. 47 and Beyond* (Markham, ON: LexisNexis Canada, 2007) ch 7

———. "Voidable Preferences" in S Ben-Ishai & A Duggan, eds, *Canadian Bankruptcy and Insolvency Law: Bill C-55, Statute c. 47 and Beyond* (Markham, ON: LexisNexis Canada, 2007) ch 6

188 Section 118(7) of the *Canada Business Corporations Act*, *ibid*, provides that the action may not be commenced after two years from the date of the resolution authorizing the action complained of.

189 Above note 19.

DUNLOP, C. *Creditor-Debtor Law in Canada*, 2d ed (Scarborough, ON: Carswell, 1995) ch 18

KERR, R. "Fraudulent Conveyances and Unjust Preferences," in M Springman & E Gertner, eds, *Debtor-Creditor Law: Practice and Doctrine* (Scarborough, ON: Butterworths, 1985)

SPRINGMAN, M, ET AL. *Frauds on Creditors: Fraudulent Conveyances and Preferences* (Scarborough, ON: Carswell: 1994) (loose-leaf)

WEISBERG, R. "Commercial Morality, the Merchant Character, and the History of the Voidable Preference" (1986) 39 *Stanford Law Review* 1

CHAPTER 8

ADMINISTERING THE BANKRUPT ESTATE

Many decisions need to be made when administering the bankrupt estate. A right of action that vests in the trustee may have an uncertain value if the person alleged to owe the obligation contests liability. Someone must decide whether to pursue the legal action or attempt to settle. Someone must decide whether pre-bankruptcy transactions should be impugned. Someone must decide whether the price offered by buyers for bankruptcy assets is adequate. Bankruptcy legislation identifies those who are entitled to make decisions on these and other matters, and defines the avenues for recourse available to those who may disagree with these decisions. The governance structure that is established is particularly important because it is designed to limit potential conflict of interest and abuse that arises in the absence of any checks and balances on the exercise of power.

A. THE ROLE OF THE CREDITORS

1) The Creditor Control Model

Insolvency regimes vary considerably as to the administrative model that is used to govern this decision-making process. Three models of administrative decision making within insolvency regimes can be identified: the judicial control model, the creditor control model, and the official control model. Under the judicial control model, a bankruptcy judge occupies a central role in making decisions. In the creditor control model, it is the creditors who make the important decisions. And, in the official control model, a state official takes on this role.

The bankruptcy regime in Canada uses a modified creditor control model that contains some elements of official control.[1] A model that promotes the participation of creditors seems sensible on first impression. After all, it is the creditors who have a direct financial interest in the outcome. The administrative decisions that are made directly affect the size of the bankruptcy dividend that the creditors will receive. However, the reality is that creditors rarely have an adequate incentive to carry out these responsibilities. This phenomenon is sometimes called rational apathy. The amount that is recovered by an unsecured creditor by way of a bankruptcy dividend is often only a small fraction of the original claim. In many cases, it simply does not make economic sense for a creditor to expend time and effort given the small return. Moreover, creditors who choose not to involve themselves at all obtain the same recovery as those who participate in the decision making.

Bankruptcy systems that are based upon a creditor control model are susceptible to abuse if the creditors do not take an interest in the administration of the bankrupt estate. Although a trustee's primary legal duty is to act for the benefit of the creditors, the reality is that most bankruptcies are voluntary ones that have been initiated by the debtor. In practice, it is debtors rather than creditors who choose the trustee. One need only look to the Yellow Pages under the bankruptcy trustee heading to see that the advertising is directed to debtors and not to creditors. Even in involuntary bankruptcies, the creditor who initiates the bankruptcy often is a secured creditor wishing to obtain a more favourable priority for its claim.[2] Having attained this objective, the secured creditor often has no further interest in the administration of the bankruptcy. Under these circumstances, there exists a potential for abuse. A trustee may engage in conduct that is not in the interests of the creditors but that benefits the debtor, a secured creditor, or the trustee. Indeed, a perception of dishonest administration contributed to the wholesale repeal of Canadian insolvency legislation in 1880.

Canadian bankruptcy law departs from a pure creditor control model in order to curb the potential for conflict of interest and abuse that arises out of creditor indifference. It does so by regulating, licensing, and supervising those who are permitted to act as trustee. This

---

1 This model is not adopted in all of the Canadian insolvency regimes. Most notably, the reorganization regime of the *CCAA* adopts the judicial control model.

2 See Chapter 5, Section B(6).

has created a professionalized group of bankruptcy trustees. Canadian bankruptcy law also contains conflict-of-interest rules that restrict a trustee's ability to act in certain cases.

Despite the problems inherent in the creditor control model, it undoubtedly provides a powerful means through which a creditor can legitimately influence the administrative decision making in a bankruptcy. In those cases where a creditor's claim is sufficiently large and there are adequate assets to justify participation, engagement in the process can be effectively invoked to advance the interests of the creditors.

2) The First Meeting of Creditors

The trustee[3] calls the first meeting of creditors by determining the names and addresses of the creditors and notifying them of the meeting.[4] The notice must be sent within five days of the trustee's appointment, with the meeting held within twenty-one days of the appointment.[5] The notice must be accompanied by a list of the creditors and the amount of their claims, a proof of claim, and a proxy. In the case of an individual bankrupt, the notice must also provide information about the bankrupt's financial situation and, if applicable, the bankrupt's obligation to make payments of post-bankruptcy surplus income.[6] A first meeting of creditors is not required in a summary administration bankruptcy unless there is a request for one by the official receiver or creditors holding 25 percent of the proven claims.[7]

The official receiver or nominee chairs the first meeting of creditors.[8] If the official receiver has conducted an examination of the debtor before the first meeting of creditors, he must give a report to the creditors on the debtor's responses to the questions.[9] Two formal matters are carried out at the first meeting of creditors: the affirmation of the

---

3 The trustee is appointed by the court in the case of an involuntary bankruptcy, and by the official receiver in the case of a voluntary bankruptcy. See Chapter 3, Sections C(7) and D.

4 *BIA*, s 102(1). The notice must also be published in a local newspaper. See *BIA*, s 102(4). A newspaper advertisement is not required in respect of summary administration bankruptcies. See *BIA*, s 155(c).

5 The official receiver may extend this period by ten days, or by up to thirty days where there are special circumstances. See *BIA*, s 102(1.1).

6 *Ibid*, s 102(3).

7 *Ibid*, s 155(d.1).

8 *Ibid*, s 105(1). The meeting is usually held in the offices of the official receiver of the debtor's locality.

9 See *ibid*, ss 161(1) and (2.1). The official receiver must examine the debtor with respect to the bankrupt's conduct, the causes of the bankruptcy, and the dis-

appointment of the trustee or substitution of another, and the appointment of inspectors.[10] The trustee will give a report on the preliminary administration of the estate.[11] The meeting provides creditors with a forum in which they can communicate with one another as well as with the trustee. The bankrupt is required to attend the meeting and is required to answer questions asked by the creditors.[12] The meeting also affords the creditors the opportunity to give instructions to the trustee on matters relating to the administration of the estate.

A single creditor entitled to vote constitutes a quorum for a meeting of creditors.[13] Only creditors who have filed proof of claims with the trustee are permitted to vote at a meeting of creditors,[14] although creditors who have not done so may attend the meeting.[15] Proxy voting is permitted, except that the debtor cannot be appointed a proxy to vote.[16] Votes on ordinary resolutions are calculated by counting one vote for each dollar of every claim that is not disallowed.[17] A person who acquires the claim of another creditor either before or after the bankruptcy is permitted to prove the claim and vote. The only limitation to this principle is that a person who acquires a portion of a claim after the bankruptcy cannot vote that claim.[18]

The chair has the power to admit or reject a proof of claim for the purposes of voting at a meeting, and this decision may be appealed to

---

position of the bankrupt's property. A prescribed form (Form 26) sets out the questions that the official receiver must ask the bankrupt.

10 *Ibid*, s 102(5).

11 See Office of the Superintendent of Bankruptcy Directive No 32. The trustee at the meeting will table the questionnaire completed by the bankrupt, the long statement of affairs, and the examination of the bankrupt.

12 *BIA*, s 158(h). A failure to attend constitutes a bankruptcy offence. See *BIA*, s 198(2). In the case of a corporation, the official receiver can specify an officer or person in control of the corporation who is required to attend.

13 *Ibid*, s 106(1). If there is no quorum at the first meeting of creditors, the appointment of the trustee is deemed to be confirmed and the meeting is adjourned to a specified time and place or is adjourned without setting the time and place of the next meeting. See *BIA*, s 106(2).

14 *Ibid*, s 109(1). The filing of a proof of claim before the first meeting of creditors is only a requirement for voting at the meeting. A proof of claim can be filed thereafter in order to permit the creditor to participate in a dividend.

15 *Re McCoubrey* (1924), 5 CBR 248 (Alta SC).

16 *BIA*, ss 109(3) & (4). Often the trustee is appointed a proxy to vote for a creditor. See *ibid*, s 113(1). The trustee, however, cannot vote as proxy for a creditor on any resolution affecting the conduct or remuneration of the trustee. See *ibid*, s 113(2).

17 *Ibid*, s 115.

18 *Ibid*, s 110(1).

the court.[19] However, the chair has no discretion to admit a claim for voting if the trustee has disallowed the claim.[20] Unliquidated or contingent claims do not permit the claimant to vote until the trustee has valued the claim.[21] Secured creditors can assess the value of their security and prove for the balance.[22] In determining the outcome of a vote, the chair must exclude the vote of a creditor who did not deal at arm's length with the debtor in the year prior to the initial bankruptcy event up until the date of bankruptcy, unless a court directs otherwise.[23] Certain creditors who are related to the debtor are also not permitted to vote on the appointment of a trustee or inspectors.[24]

Although affirmation of the trustee requires an ordinary resolution carried by a majority, a decision to substitute another trustee is a matter that requires a special resolution.[25] A special resolution is defined as a dual majority in which there is both a majority in number of the creditors and three-fourths of the value of the proven claims in favour of the resolution.[26]

The first meeting of creditors is usually also the last, but it is possible to call further meetings of creditors. A trustee may call a meeting of creditors at any time, and must do so when directed by the court, or when requested in writing by a majority of inspectors or by 25 percent of the number of the creditors holding 25 percent of the value of the proved claims.[27]

3) The Appointment and Duties of the Inspectors

At the first meeting of creditors or at a subsequent meeting, the creditors may appoint up to five inspectors of the estate of the bankrupt or agree not to appoint any inspectors.[28] A person need not be a creditor

---

19 *Ibid*, s 108(1). In cases of doubt, the chair may mark the proof as objected to and allow the creditor to vote subject to its being declared invalid should the objection be sustained. See *BIA*, s 108(3).

20 *Northstone Power Corp v RJK Power Systems Ltd* (2002), 33 CBR (4th) 261 (Alta QB).

21 *BIA*, s 121(2). And see *Re Arthur Fuel Co* (1926), 8 CBR 46 (Man KB).

22 *BIA*, s 112.

23 *Ibid*, s 109(6). And see *Re Galaxy Sports Inc* (2003), 42 CBR (4th) 211 (BCSC), rev'd on other grounds 2004 BCCA 284 [*Galaxy Sports*].

24 *BIA*, s 113(3).

25 *Ibid*, s 14.

26 *Ibid*, s 2 "special resolution."

27 *Ibid*, s 103.

28 *Ibid*, s 116(1). A vacancy may be filled by the inspectors or by resolution at a meeting of creditors. See *ibid*, s 116(4). The creditors at a meeting of creditors

to be appointed as an inspector,[29] but a party to a contested action by or against the bankrupt estate cannot be appointed.[30] Inspectors do not need to be appointed in summary administration bankruptcies.[31]

Meetings of the board of inspectors are usually called by the trustee but may also be called on the request of a majority of the inspectors.[32] The powers of the inspectors are exercised by a majority vote.[33] If there is a tie, the trustee casts the deciding vote.[34] The meetings can be carried out in whole or in part by telephone or via other means if all the inspectors consent.[35] Inspectors are entitled to recover their travel expenses and a prescribed fee for meetings, but the fees are very modest.[36]

The inspectors must authorize most of the significant decisions concerning the administration of the estate. In particular, the permission of the inspectors is required in respect of the following matters:

- the sale, lease, or other disposition of the assets of the bankrupt estate, the carrying on of the business of the bankrupt, and an election to retain, disclaim, or assign a lease;[37]
- the institution or continuation of legal proceedings relating to the property of the bankrupt and the compromise or settlement of claims by or against the bankrupt estate;[38]

---

or the court may revoke an appointment of an inspector. See *ibid*, s 116(5). The court has no power to appoint inspectors in the first instance or to replace them if they fail to act. The proper procedure is for the trustee to call a meeting of creditors under *BIA*, s 118. See *Re Laughy* (1995), 38 CBR (3d) 71 (BCSC). But see *Re Monahan* (2006), 26 CBR (5th) 220 (NBQB), which held that a court may appoint some other third party as an inspector if the creditors are unwilling to meet and appoint inspectors.

29 *Re F & W Stereo Pacific Ltd* (1975), 22 CBR (NS) 84 (BCSC).

30 *BIA*, s 116(2).

31 *Ibid*, s 155(e).

32 *Ibid*, s 117(1).

33 *Ibid*, s 116(3).

34 *Ibid*, s 117(2). The trustee must first seek the opinion of any absent inspector to resolve the difference. If the matter concerns the personal conduct or interest of the trustee, the matter must be referred to the court or to a meeting of creditors.

35 *Ibid*, s 117(1.1).

36 *Ibid*, s 120(5). Section 135 of the *Bankruptcy and Insolvency General Rules*, CRC, c 368, provides a range of fees from $10 per meeting for estates with net receipts of less than $10,000 to a maximum of $40 per meeting for estates with net receipts of $100,000 or more.

37 *BIA*, ss 30(1)(a), (b), (c), (f), and (k).

38 *Ibid*, ss 30(1)(d), (e), (h), and (i).

- the borrowing of money or incurring of other obligations and the granting of security on the bankrupt assets in priority to the claims of the creditors;[39]
- the division *in specie* among the creditors of property that from its peculiar nature or other special circumstances cannot be readily or advantageously sold;[40]
- the appointment of the bankrupt to aid in administering the estate;[41]
- the divesting of any real property by a notice of quit claim or disclaimer;[42]
- the amount for which and the hazards against which the property of the bankrupt is to be insured;[43]
- the return of unrealizable property to the bankrupt;[44]
- the withdrawal of funds from the trust account of the estate except for the payment of dividends or charges incidental to the administration of the estate;[45]
- the timing of the declaration and distribution of dividends;[46] and
- the examination of the bankrupt or other persons.[47]

If no inspectors are appointed, the trustee is given the power to make these decisions.[48]

Courts have indicated that the function of the inspectors is to supervise the trustee and to instruct the trustee on steps that they consider appropriate to protect the interests of the creditors.[49] The inspectors are under a statutory obligation to satisfy themselves that all the property has been accounted for, the administration of the estate has been completed, the disbursements and expenses are proper and authorized, and the fees and remuneration are just and reasonable.[50] They are also obligated to verify the bank balance of the estate, examine the

---

39 *Ibid*, s 30(1)(g).
40 *Ibid*, s 30(1)(j).
41 *Ibid*, s 30(1)(l).
42 *Ibid*, s 20(1).
43 *Ibid*, s 24.
44 *Ibid*, s 40.
45 *Ibid*, s 25(1.3).
46 *Ibid*, s 148(1).
47 *Ibid*, s 163(1).
48 *Ibid*, s 30(3).
49 *Re Fishman* (1985), 56 CBR (NS) 316 (Ont HCJ); *Impact Tool & Mould Inc (Trustee of) v Impact Tool & Mould (Windsor) Inc (Interim Receiver of)* (2006), 20 CBR (5th) 220 (Ont CA) [*Impact Tool & Mould*].
50 *BIA*, ss 120(4) and 151–52.

trustee's accounts, and approve the trustee's final statement of receipts and disbursements.[51]

The inspectors stand in a fiduciary relation to the general body of creditors.[52] This imposes a number of obligations on the inspectors. A creditor who has been appointed inspector must not act in his or her own self-interest but in the interests of the creditors generally.[53] An inspector is also under an obligation to make full disclosure of information to the trustee and the other inspectors where there is a potential conflict of interest.[54] A breach of this obligation may result in the revocation by the court of the decision of the inspectors[55] or the removal of the inspector by the court[56] in addition to any civil action that the creditors may have against the inspector. An inspector is not permitted to purchase property of the bankrupt estate without the prior approval of the court.[57] It is a bankruptcy offence for an inspector to accept an additional fee from the bankrupt or the trustee.[58] In order to carry out their duties, the inspectors must be given complete and unrestricted access to the books, records, and documents of the bankrupt.[59] The inspectors must not use this information for purposes not connected to the administration of the bankrupt estate.[60]

If there is a conflict between a decision of the inspectors and directions given by the creditors, the directions of the creditors prevail.[61] Although a court may review a decision of the inspectors and revoke or vary it, it is inappropriate for a court to do so unless the inspectors are not acting in good faith and in the interests of the creditors.[62]

4) Proceedings by Creditors

Upon bankruptcy, causes of action available to the bankrupt against third parties vest in the trustee.[63] The trustee may also have a right to bring an action against a third party to impeach a pre-bankruptcy

---

51 *Ibid*, s 120(3).
52 *Re Bryant, Isard & Co* (1923), 4 CBR 41 (Ont HCJ).
53 *Re Global Plastic Packaging Ltd* (2004), 2 CBR (5th) 217 (Ont SCJ).
54 *Re Shannon & Co* (1931), 13 CBR 291 (Alta SC).
55 *BIA*, s 119(2).
56 *Ibid*, s 116(5).
57 *Ibid*, s 120(1).
58 *Ibid*, s 201(2).
59 *Re Taylor Ventures Ltd* (1999), 9 CBR (4th) 136 (BCSC).
60 *Impact Tool & Mould*, above note 49.
61 *BIA*, s 119(1).
62 *Re Feldman* (1932), 13 CBR 313 (Ont CA).
63 See Chapter 4, Section B(7).

transaction or to subordinate an unperfected security interest in personal property. The trustee may decide not to prosecute the action in light of the likelihood of success of the action and the potential for recovery from the third party in the event of success. Alternatively, the trustee may be unwilling to act because the expected value of the bankrupt estate is not sufficient to cover the costs of the action.[64]

The *BIA* creates a mechanism by which the creditor can take proceedings against a third party if the trustee is unwilling to do so.[65] The creditor must first request that the trustee take the proceedings. If the trustee refuses or neglects to do so, the creditor may apply to the court for an order authorizing the creditor to take proceedings in the creditor's own name and at its own expense and risk.[66] The creditor must demonstrate a *prima facie* case, which must be supported by evidence and not mere allegations.[67] When this procedure is invoked, the creditor stands in the shoes of the trustee and pursues the trustee's cause of action rather than a right of action held by the creditor.[68] This procedure is not available if the trustee and third party have agreed to a settlement of the claim[69] or if the trustee has assigned the right of action to another person.[70]

The order granted by the court must notify the other creditors of the intended proceedings. This gives them the opportunity to decide whether or not to participate in the action. If they choose to do so, they will share the benefit of gain but also the risk of loss. If they choose not to participate in the action, they are not entitled to share in the proceeds but are also not responsible for any costs. If there is a surplus after the claims of the participating creditors are satisfied, it is to be paid to the bankrupt estate.[71] A failure to give notice to all of the creditors before commencing the action does not invalidate the action or prevent them from later joining it.[72] The court order may also authorize the

64 The trustee will usually be personally liable for costs if the action is unsuccessful. See *Touche Ross Ltd v Weldwood of Canada Sales Ltd* (1984), 49 CBR (NS) 284 (Ont HCJ).

65 *Toyota Canada Inc v Toronto-Dominion Bank*, 1994 ABCA 261; *Shaw Estate v Nicol Island Development Inc*, 2009 ONCA 276.

66 *BIA*, s 38(1).

67 *Smith v Pricewaterhousecoopers Inc*, 2013 ABCA 288.

68 *Indcondo Building Corp v Sloan*, 2012 ONCA 502.

69 *Re Krezeks Motors Ltd* (1977), 23 CBR (NS) 93 (Ont HCJ).

70 *Kay Motors Ltd v Canadian Imperial Bank of Commerce* (1983), 48 CBR (NS) 78 (BCSC).

71 *BIA*, s 38(3).

72 *Toyota Canada Inc v Imperial Richmond Holdings Ltd* (1993), 20 CBR (3d) 102 (Alta QB).

creditors to invoke the powers conferred on a trustee to examine the bankrupt and others.[73]

If the action is successful, the proceeds are shared among the creditors who participated in the action. This distribution is not affected by the scheme of distribution that governs proceeds of property realized by the trustee. As a result, a creditor who is entitled to claim as a preferred creditor in the bankruptcy does not obtain a preference over the claims of the other creditors in respect of the proceeds of an action brought by the creditors.[74]

A curious feature of this procedure is that a creditor can participate in an action brought against itself by the other creditors. By contributing to the costs of the action, the defendant creditor hedges its bets. If it wins, it keeps the property or funds. If it loses, it shares them *pro rata* with the other participating creditors.[75]

A trustee is not permitted to set up a scheme under which the trustee brings the action and the fruits of the litigation are distributed only among the creditors who funded the litigation, since this interferes with the bankruptcy scheme of distribution.[76] The trustee, with the approval of the inspectors, can borrow funds to prosecute the action or proceed on the basis of indemnifications given by the creditors. Any amounts recovered must be distributed according to the bankruptcy scheme of distribution. Alternatively, the trustee may decide not to proceed with the action, and the creditors may obtain a court order permitting them to prosecute the action.

5) The Creditors' Right to Information

The trustee is required to report to the creditors at the first meeting of creditors and when directed to do so by the inspectors.[77] Individual creditors also have a right to require the trustee to report. The report must disclose the condition of the bankrupt's estate, the money on hand, and the particulars of any unsold property. The trustee must keep proper books and records of the bankrupt estate and allow access

---

73 *371890 Alberta Ltd v Gray Beverage Inc* (1991), 7 CBR (3d) 78 (Alt CA).

74 *Re Ontario Metal Importers Ltd* (1992), 15 CBR (3d) 8 (Ont Ct Gen Div).

75 The defendant creditor who participates in the proceedings is not permitted to participate in the strategy and prosecution of the action. See *Manitoba Capital Fund Ltd Partnership v Royal Bank of Canada* (2001), 27 CBR (4th) 265 (Man QB). See also *Isabelle v The Royal Bank of Canada*, 2008 NBCA 69.

76 *Re Keele-Wilson Supermarkets Ltd* (1990), 78 CBR (NS) 189 (Ont HCJ).

77 *BIA*, s 27(1).

to them for inspection by any creditor.[78] The trustee must also prepare a final statement of receipts and disbursements that contains a complete account of all monies received by the trustee out of the property of the bankrupt, the amount of interest received, all monies disbursed and expenses incurred, the remuneration claimed by the trustee, and the particulars of all property of the bankrupt that has not been sold and the reasons why it was not sold.[79] A right of examination under oath of the bankrupt, trustee, or other party is also given to the creditors, but they must first obtain a court order authorizing it.[80]

B. THE ROLE OF THE TRUSTEE

1) Appointment of the Trustee

A trustee in bankruptcy is an officer of the court. The conduct of trustees is regulated by a Code of Ethics in the General Rules.[81] They must carry out their duties in a timely manner and carry out their functions with competence, honesty, integrity, and due care.[82] They must be honest and impartial and shall provide to interested parties full and accurate information.[83] They are given a broad discretion as to how best to carry out their duties and courts will not lightly interfere with their business judgment unless there is obvious error.[84]

A trustee is not bound to act in any particular bankruptcy, but, having accepted an appointment, a trustee must perform the duties required of the office until discharged or another is appointed.[85] The creditors by a special resolution at a meeting may replace the trustee.[86] The court on application of any interested person may for cause replace the trustee.[87] The existence of a conflict of interest often forms the grounds for removal and replacement of a trustee by a court.[88]

---

78 *Ibid*, ss 26(1) and (3).
79 *Ibid*, s 152
80 *Ibid*, s 163(2).
81 *Bankruptcy and Insolvency General Rules*, above note 36, ss 34–53.
82 *Ibid*, s 36. And see *Dubyk (Re)*, 2009 SKQB 426.
83 *Bankruptcy and Insolvency General Rules*, above note 36, s 39.
84 *Graves, (Re)* (2000), 17 CBR (4th) 72 (Sask QB).
85 *Bankruptcy and Insolvency General Rules*, above note 36, s 14.06(1).
86 *Ibid*, s 14. And see Section A(2), above in this chapter.
87 *Ibid*, s 14.04.
88 See *Re Commonwealth Investors Syndicate Ltd* (1986), 61 CBR (NS) 147 (BCSC).

The *BIA* specifically enumerates the following situations in which a trustee is not qualified to act as such in relation to the estate of a debtor unless the trustee obtains the permission of the court:[89]

- the trustee was a director or officer of the debtor, or was related to or in an employment relationship with the debtor or a director or officer of the debtor during the past two years;
- the trustee was the auditor, accountant, or solicitor or a partner or employee of the auditor, accountant, or solicitor during the past two years; and
- the trustee is a trustee under a trust indenture issued by the debtor or a person related to the debtor or is related to the trustee under a trust indenture.

The trustee is not permitted to act as a trustee in relation to an estate of a debtor in the following situations unless the trustee provides full disclosure at the time of appointment as well as at the first meeting of creditors:[90]

- the trustee is acting as trustee in a bankruptcy or proposal of a person related to the debtor; and
- the trustee is acting as receiver or liquidator of the property of any person related to the debtor.

A trustee who acts for an estate is not permitted to act for or assist a secured creditor to realize or otherwise deal with the security unless the trustee has obtained a written opinion from independent legal counsel that the security is valid and enforceable against the estate.[91] This requirement is often invoked when a secured creditor appoints a receiver in respect of the assets of a debtor and then forces or persuades a debtor to go into bankruptcy in order to obtain a more favourable priority status.[92] The trustee has a limited role since the realization is conducted primarily through the receivership. The trustee who acts in this dual capacity must notify the superintendent and the creditors or inspectors that the trustee is acting for the secured creditor and inform them of the basis of any remuneration from the secured creditor and of the legal opinion.[93]

---

89 *BIA*, s 13.3(1).

90 *Ibid*, s 13.3(2).

91 *Ibid*, s 13.4(1).

92 See Chapter 5, Section B(6).

93 *BIA*, s 13.4(1.1). A copy of the legal opinion must be provided on request. See *BIA*, s 13.4(2).

2) Taking Possession or Control of the Bankrupt Estate

One of the primary duties of the trustee is to take possession or control of the property of the bankrupt. Although the property of the bankrupt vests in the trustee upon the occurrence of the bankruptcy, the taking of possession or control over the asset is a practical necessity. A trustee will find it difficult to sell or otherwise dispose of the asset if the trustee is unable to deliver possession or control of it to the purchaser. The powers conferred on the trustee to obtain and realize property can be exercised anywhere,[94] but it may be necessary to seek the assistance of a foreign court if the property is located in another country. The trustee is required to open a separate trust account for the bankrupt estate and deposit all funds received from the estate into it.[95]

As soon as possible, the trustee must take possession of the books and records of the bankrupt as well as all property of the bankrupt and make an inventory.[96] The trustee is empowered to enter premises in order to make an inventory but must first obtain a warrant if a person other than the bankrupt occupies the premises, unless that person consents to the entry.[97] No person is permitted to assert a lien or right of retention of the records against the trustee.[98] A solicitor's lien is therefore ineffective against a trustee in respect of documents in the possession of the solicitor.[99]

Persons who are in possession of property of the bankrupt are required to deliver the property to the trustee unless they have a right to retain it as against the bankrupt.[100] Secured creditors are therefore not required to surrender possession so long as they have priority against the trustee. A lessee who has a right to retain the goods as against the owner is also not required to surrender possession of the property to the trustee. The trustee can bring an action for conversion against a person who wrongfully fails to surrender property of the bankrupt to the trustee.[101] The trustee can also obtain a search warrant authorizing the

94 *Ibid*, s 17(2).

95 *Ibid*, s 25.

96 *Ibid*, s 16(3). The trustee must permit authorized persons to inspect the books and records. See *BIA*, s 23.

97 *Ibid*, ss 16(3), 16(3.1), and 189.

98 *Ibid*, s 16(5).

99 *Re 422686 Ontario Ltd* (1980), 36 CBR (NS) 41 (Ont HCJ).

100 *BIA*, s 17(1).

101 *Re Kostiuk* (2001), 27 CBR (4th) 249 (BCSC).

trustee to enter and search premises and to seize the property of the bankrupt.[102]

The trustee, if authorized by the creditors or inspectors, may conduct an examination of the bankrupt or of any other person who is reasonably believed to have knowledge of the affairs of the bankrupt.[103] The person to be examined is required to attend and answer questions.[104] The trustee is not required to obtain a court order before conducting the examination.

The trustee can also obtain legal advice and take legal proceedings necessary for the recovery or protection of property of the bankrupt prior to the first meeting of creditors and thereafter on an emergency basis when the necessary authority cannot be obtained from the inspectors in time.[105] The trustee has the power to insure the assets temporarily until the appointment of the inspectors, at which time they are to authorize the insurance coverage.[106] The trustee also has the power to request the redirection of the bankrupt's mail, but must obtain a court order in the case of mail addressed to the residence of an individual bankrupt.[107]

3) Carrying on the Business of the Bankrupt

A trustee may carry on the business formerly conducted by the bankrupt if the trustee thinks that this may be advantageous for the administration of the bankrupt estate.[108] A wider set of powers is given to a trustee in respect of a bankruptcy of a securities firm to permit the effective operation of the business.[109] A decision to carry on the business carries certain risks. Prior to 1949, the courts recognized that post-bankruptcy transactions entered into by the trustee were personal obligations owed by the trustee to the other contracting party, unless the contract expressly excluded this liability.[110] Although the trustee, if authorized to carry on the business by the inspectors, had a right to claim these expenses as a cost of administration of the estate, this

---

102 *BIA*, s 189(1). The trustee must satisfy the court that there are reasonable grounds for the belief that property of the bankrupt is located on the premises. Use of force is not permitted unless authorized by the order and the trustee is accompanied by a peace officer. See *BIA*, s 189(2).

103 *Ibid*, s 163(1).

104 *Ibid*, ss 166–67.

105 *Ibid*, ss 19(1)–(2).

106 *Ibid*, s 24(1).

107 *Ibid*, s 35.

108 *Ibid*, ss 18(b) and 30(1)(c).

109 *Ibid*, s 259.

110 *Re Smith & Son* (1929), 10 CBR 393 (Ont HCJ).

did not protect the trustee if the assets were insufficient to cover these obligations. Because of this potential for personal liability, a trustee is not required to carry on the business of the bankrupt if the trustee is of the opinion that the realizable value of the assets of the estate are insufficient to protect the trustee against loss and the creditors fail to provide the trustee with an appropriate indemnity.[111]

The personal liability of the trustee in respect of post-bankruptcy transactions has apparently been altered by a statutory provision that was added in 1949. The *BIA* provides that debts incurred in carrying on the business of a bankrupt are deemed to be debts of the estate.[112] In *Transalta Utilities Corp v Hudson*,[113] it was held that this provision reversed the presumption that the trustee was personally liable. The debt is that of the estate only, unless the supplier or creditor can show that the trustee incurred personal liability on the transaction. In light of this provision, post-bankruptcy creditors who deal with the trustee should recognize that, unless they expressly provide that the trustee is to be personally liable on the contract, they are exposed to a potential risk of loss should the assets of the bankrupt estate be insufficient to cover the expenses of administration. The provision protects the trustee from personal liability for debts. It does not extend to liability for wrongful conduct.[114] Nor will it apply if the trustee has failed to obtain authorization from the inspectors or the court to carry on the business of the bankrupt.[115]

A trustee may be authorized to borrow money in order to raise sufficient funds to operate the business. The authorization must be given by the inspectors but can also be granted by a court on application by the trustee before the appointment of the inspectors.[116] The borrower may be granted a security interest on the assets of the bankrupt estate to secure this obligation. Although this will give the creditor priority over the claims of the unsecured creditors of the estate, it will not give the creditor priority over secured creditors who were granted security interests by the debtor before the bankruptcy. The credit grantor must therefore take care to ensure that the unencumbered assets are sufficient to cover the amount borrowed.

111 *BIA*, s 32.

112 *Ibid*, s 31(4).

113 (1982), 44 CBR (NS) 97 (Alta QB).

114 *Glick v Jordan* (1967), 11 CBR (NS) 70 (Ont HCJ).

115 *Re Tremblay; Faust v Trustee* (1922), 3 CBR 488 (Que Sup Ct).

116 *BIA*, ss 30(1)(g) and 31(1).

4) Sale or Other Disposition of the Assets

After taking possession and control over the property of the bankrupt, the next primary duty of the trustee is to sell or otherwise dispose of the property. This produces a fund out of which bankruptcy dividends can be paid to participating creditors. The inspectors must authorize the sale.[117] Although normally the trustee will not sell the property before the first meeting of creditors and the appointment of inspectors, the trustee is permitted to dispose of property that is perishable or likely to depreciate rapidly in value and may carry on the business of the bankrupt until the first meeting of creditors.[118] The trustee is not required to obtain a court order approving the sale but may apply to court for directions if it appears that a proposed sale is likely to be contested.[119]

The trustee is permitted to sell by any commercially reasonable manner, including private sale, tender, or public auction.[120] There is no single, best method of sale, since the preferred method will depend upon the nature of the property and the nature of the market for it.[121] The choice among the methods should be made with a view to maximizing the yield for the assets of the bankrupt estate and obtaining the fair market value for the asset if possible.[122] In this respect, the trustee must act in good faith and not take into consideration extraneous factors such as the desire of some creditors that a particular purchaser should not obtain the property.[123] The trustee is under a duty to sell the property in an expeditious manner.[124]

Finally, the trustee must have regard for the integrity of the sale process that has been established, and should not engage in conduct that will undermine it. For this reason, it is not appropriate in a sale by tender to use the highest bid to attempt to obtain an even higher bid

---

117 *Ibid*, s 30(a). See *Re MacKenzie* (1998), 4 CBR (4th) 314 (Alta QB). *BIA*, s 33 provides a mechanism by which a trustee can obtain an order for the sale of the property to reimburse the costs of the trustee. It can be invoked if permission of the inspectors cannot be obtained.

118 *BIA*, s 18. See *Re Near North Home Health Care Ltd* (1998), 5 CBR (4th) 249 (Ont Ct Gen Div).

119 *BIA*, s 34. And see *Re Fantasy Construction Ltd* (2006), 22 CBR (5th) 108 (Alta QB) [*Fantasy Construction*].

120 *Re Assaf & Dabous* (1926), 7 CBR 689 (Ont HCJ).

121 *Re Katz* (1991), 6 CBR (3d) 211 (Ont Ct Gen Div).

122 *Re Rassell* (1999), 12 CBR (4th) 316 (Alta CA).

123 *Fantasy Construction*, above note 119.

124 *Re Gray* (1992), 16 CBR (3d) 251 (BCCA).

from other prospective purchasers[125] or to accept non-conforming tenders.[126] The property cannot be sold to an inspector without the prior approval of the court.[127]

A trustee is not permitted to sell or otherwise dispose of the bankrupt's property to a person who is related to the bankrupt unless authorized to do so by the court.[128] The Act sets out a list of factors that a court is to consider in deciding whether to grant the authorization.[129] The code of ethics for trustees prohibits trustees from purchasing property of a bankrupt for whom they act.[130] Nor can they sell the property to their employees or to related persons unless it is purchased at the same time and at the same price and on the same conditions as it is offered to the public. The code also prohibits trustees from purchasing property from bankrupt estates for which they do not act in private sale transactions.

A sale by the trustee vests in the purchaser all the legal and equitable interest of the bankrupt estate in the property.[131] The purchaser therefore acquires the interest subject to the interest that some other person may have in the property. The trustee will generally sell the property on an "as is" basis and will exclude express and implied terms concerning title and freedom from encumbrances.[132]

Where the asset is a right of action, the trustee has a number of options. The trustee may commence or continue the action and recover judgment if successful.[133] The trustee may also negotiate a settlement or compromise of the claim.[134] The trustee can transfer the right of action back to the bankrupt or other person on the condition that the bankrupt pay a portion of the judgment to the trustee if successful.[135] The trustee can also conduct a sale of the right and can accept a bid from the defendant in the action.[136] If the trustee is not prepared to take any

125 *Re Pretty Fashion Inc* (1951), 31 CBR 217 (Que Sup Ct).

126 *Re Ashcroft Steel Co* (1962), 5 CBR (NS) 239 (Que Sup Ct).

127 *BIA*, s 120(1).

128 *Ibid*, ss 30(4) & (5).

129 *Ibid*, s 30(6). These factors include whether the process was reasonable, the extent to which creditors were consulted, the effect of the sale on interested parties, the adequacy of the consideration received, whether good faith efforts were made to sell to a non-related party, and whether any better offers were received.

130 *Bankruptcy and Insolvency General Rules*, above note 36, ss 42–43.

131 *BIA*, s 84.

132 See A Lando, "Sale of Assets by a Trustee: The Fundamental Pragmatics" (1991) 3 CBR (3d) 179.

133 *BIA*, s 30(d).

134 *Ibid*, ss 30(h) & (i).

135 *Kay Motors Ltd v Canadian Imperial Bank of Commerce* (1983), 48 CBR (NS) 78 (BCSC).

136 *Re Geler* (2005), 12 CBR (5th) 15 (Ont SCJ).

of these options, the creditors can obtain a court order for the assignment of the action to them.[137]

C. THE ROLE OF THE OFFICIAL RECEIVER

The official receiver is a federal government employee in the Office of the Superintendent of Bankruptcy. Each of the provinces constitutes one bankruptcy district, but some are further subdivided into bankruptcy divisions.[138] An official receiver is an officer of the court and performs the duties and responsibilities specified by the *BIA* and the General Rules.[139]

The duties of the official receiver include:

- receiving assignment and associated documents in respect of voluntary bankruptcies;[140]
- appointing trustees in voluntary bankruptcies;[141]
- reviewing surplus income calculations to determine if they are substantially in accordance with the applicable standards;[142]
- receiving requests for mediation concerning surplus income disputes;[143]
- chairing the first meeting of creditors;[144]
- examining the debtor under oath as to the debtor's conduct, the causes of the bankruptcy, and the disposition of the debtor's property;[145] and
- receiving requests for mediation concerning the recommendations of the trustee.[146]

137 See Section A(4), above in this chapter.
138 *BIA*, s 12(1).
139 *Ibid*, s 12(2).
140 *Ibid*, s 49(3).
141 *Ibid*, s 49(4).
142 *Ibid*, s 68(5).
143 *Ibid*, s 68(7).
144 *Ibid*, s 105(1).
145 *Ibid*, s 158(c).
146 *Ibid*, s 170.1(1).

D. THE ROLE OF THE BANKRUPT

The bankrupt is obligated to assist in the administration of the bankrupt estate in several ways. The bankrupt must:

- prepare a statement of affairs;[147]
- meet with the official receiver and answer his or her questions, and attend the first meeting of creditors and, when required, any other meeting of creditors or inspectors or with the trustee;[148]
- submit to any examinations under oath as may be required;[149]
- disclose all records, documents, and property and deliver them to the trustee, and assist the trustee in making an inventory of the assets;[150]
- disclose to the trustee the details concerning pre-bankruptcy gifts or dispositions of property in order to permit the trustee to determine if they can be set aside or otherwise challenged;[151]
- aid in the realization of property and execute any instruments as may be required;[152]
- examine all proofs and inform the trustee of any false claims;[153]
- inform the trustee of any material change in the bankrupt's financial situation and any change in residence or address;[154] and
- disclose to the trustee particulars of property acquired after a court grants a conditional discharge.[155]

The bankrupt may be convicted of a bankruptcy offence and fined or imprisoned for failing to perform these duties without reasonable excuse.[156] A failure to perform these duties is also a factor that a bankruptcy court will consider in granting or refusing an order of discharge of a bankrupt.[157]

---

147 *Ibid*, s 158(d). The trustee ordinarily assists the bankrupt in the preparation of the statement of affairs.
148 *Ibid*, ss 158(c) and (h).
149 *Ibid*, ss 158(j) and 163.
150 *Ibid*, ss 158(a), (b), and (e).
151 *Ibid*, s 158(g).
152 *Ibid*, ss 158(k) & (l).
153 *Ibid*, ss 158(m) & (n).
154 *Ibid*, ss 158(n.1) and (p).
155 *Ibid*, s 176(1).
156 *Ibid*, s 198(2).
157 *Ibid*, s 173(1)(o). See also *ibid*, s 176(2).

E. THE ROLE OF THE BANKRUPTCY COURT

1) Jurisdiction of the Bankruptcy Court

It is common to speak of the bankruptcy court as if it were a separately constituted court. This usage is misleading. There is no separate bankruptcy court. Instead, the *BIA* confers jurisdiction on the superior court in each province.[158] When the *BIA* makes reference to a court, this means a court having jurisdiction in bankruptcy.[159] The procedure is governed by the rules and procedures set out in the General Rules[160] as well as the various prescribed forms. A bankruptcy registrar can also perform a number of judicial functions.[161]

The bankruptcy court will often become involved when disputes arise as to legal rights of the bankrupt, of creditors, or of other third parties. A contest may arise over whether the debtor or a third party owns a particular asset. The trustee may seek to impeach pre-bankruptcy transactions or to subordinate security interests[162] in personal property that were not properly perfected. A dispute may also arise as to whether a person has a provable claim in bankruptcy. All of these matters are properly brought before a bankruptcy court.

Although the Canadian bankruptcy system is based upon a creditor control model rather than a judicial control model, the *BIA* provides that aggrieved parties have recourse to the courts in appropriate cases. The court on application of the trustee may give directions to the trustee concerning the administration of the bankrupt estate.[163] This gives the trustee the ability to seek the direction of the court if the trustee is uncertain about the proper procedure to follow. A bankrupt, creditor, or an aggrieved party is also given the right to have a decision of a trustee reviewed by the court, and the court may confirm, reverse, or modify the act or decision.[164]

These provisions are not intended to override the ordinary rules of governance that apply to the administration of the bankrupt estate. An application to court does not permit the court to substitute its own

---

158 *Ibid*, s 183(1).

159 *Ibid*, s 2 "court."

160 Above note 36.

161 *BIA*, s 192. These matters include making bankruptcy orders if unopposed, granting orders of discharge, making interim orders in cases of urgency, determining matters relating to proofs of claims, and determining any matter with the consent of all parties.

162 See *Re MB Greer & Co* (1953), 33 CBR 69 (Ont HCJ).

163 *BIA*, s 34(1).

164 *Ibid*, s 37.

business judgment for that of the trustee or the inspectors.[165] A trustee is not entitled to use an application for directions as a means of overturning the decision of the inspectors unless it is shown that they were not acting in good faith and in the interests of the creditors.[166] Similarly, a bankrupt, creditor, or other person will not be able to obtain a variation of a decision of the trustee unless there is a lack of authority, bad faith, or unreasonableness in the conduct of the trustee or inspectors.[167]

A person who brings an application before a bankruptcy court to review the decision of a trustee cannot obtain a judgment for damages against the trustee or an accounting of profits if it is found that the trustee has caused loss to another through a breach of duty. In order to pursue this type of claim, the person must bring an action against the trustee and must obtain leave of the bankruptcy court before doing so.[168] The threshold for obtaining leave is not high, since the provision was designed to protect the trustee against frivolous or vexatious actions.[169]

2) Appeals from the Decision of a Trustee

The *BIA* provides for an appeal from the decision of a trustee in connection with the acceptance or disallowance of proof of claims of creditors,[170] proof of security,[171] proof of claims to property in the possession of a bankrupt,[172] as well as on matters arising at a meeting of creditors.[173] There is considerable uncertainty as to whether this is an appeal on the record or an appeal *de novo*.[174] The original view was that it was an appeal *de novo*.[175] The British Columbia Court of Appeal in *Galaxy Sports Inc (Re)*[176] rejected this view and held that it was a true appeal on the record. The court was concerned that there would be a loss of efficiency

---

165 *Re Pachal's Beverages Ltd* (1969), 13 CBR (NS) 160 (Sask CA).

166 *Re Feldman* (1931), 13 CBR 95 (Ont HCJ).

167 *Re Groves-Raffin Const Ltd (No 2)* (1978), 28 CBR (NS) 104 (BCSC).

168 *BIA*, s 215.

169 *GMAC Commercial Credit Corp - Canada v TCT Logistics Inc* (2006), 22 CBR (5th) 163 (SCC).

170 *BIA*, s 134(4).

171 *Ibid*, s 135(1). And see *Pyne (Bankruptcy) (Re)*, 2009 SKQB 458.

172 *BIA*, ss 81(2) and 81.1(8). And see *Hertz v 1593658 Ontario Inc*, 2011 SKQB 379; *Sran (Re)*, 2010 BCSC 937.

173 *BIA*, s 51(3).

174 See A Brown, "Bankruptcy Claims after *Re Galaxy Sports* and *Re Lin*: No Longer a Businessperson's Statute?" in Janis P Sarra, ed, *Annual Review of Insolvency Law, 2011* (Scarborough, ON: Thomson Carswell, 2012) 833.

175 *Eskasoni Fisheries Ltd (Re)* (2000), 16 CBR (4th) 173 (NSSC); *Alberta Permit Pro Inc (Re)*, 2011 ABQB 141.

176 Above note 23 (BCCA). And see *Lin (Re)*, 2010 BCSC 264.

if fresh evidence were allowed to be introduced. A hybrid position has emerged in which a "more flexible, case by case approach" is applied, and an appeal *de novo* has been permitted where there is no discernable record,[177] if a meaningful appeal were not possible without such evidence,[178] or if there is an allegation of serious wrongdoing.[179] Under both the *Galaxy* approach as well as the hybrid approach, the standard of review is correctness on matters or law and reasonableness where there is a factual determination or the exercise of discretion.[180]

F. THE ROLE OF THE SUPERINTENDENT OF BANKRUPTCY

The Office of the Superintendent of Bankruptcy was created in 1932 as a response to cases involving the appointment of incompetent or dishonest trustees.[181] The superintendent is responsible for supervising the administration of all estates and matters to which the *BIA* applies.[182] One of the primary duties of the superintendent is to license trustees. The superintendent determines the qualifications and the criteria to be applied in determining if a trustee's licence is to be issued to a person.[183] These include successful completion of qualifying courses and exams. The superintendent has the power to investigate complaints concerning potential wrongdoing in the administration of a bankrupt estate.[184] Following an investigation, the superintendent may cancel or suspend the licence of a trustee or place conditions on it if it appears that the trustee has not properly performed the duties of a trustee or has failed to comply with the provisions, rules, or directives governing trustees or if it is in the public interest to do so.[185]

---

177 *Erdman, Re (Bankrupt)*, 2005 SKQB 515.

178 *San Juan Resources Inc (Re)*, 2009 ABQB 55.

179 *JJ Lacey In Re Bankruptcy & Insolvency Act*, 2008 NLTD 9.

180 *Galaxy Sports*, above note 23 (BCCA); *Able Automotive Ltd v Cameron – Okolita Inc*, 2009 SKQB 476.

181 Canada, Study Committee on Bankruptcy and Insolvency Legislation, *Report of the Study Committee on Bankruptcy and Insolvency Legislation* (Ottawa: Study Committee on Bankruptcy and Insolvency Legislation, 1970) at 17.

182 *BIA*, s 5(2).

183 *Ibid*, s 5(4)(d). And see Office of the Superintendent of Bankruptcy Directive 13R: Trustee Licensing.

184 *BIA*, ss 5(3)(e) & (f), 6, and 10.

185 *Ibid*, s 14.01(1).

The superintendent issues directives on the powers, duties, and functions of trustees.[186] Several directives have been issued on matters such as the preparation of the inventory of estate assets and surplus income and on standards for recommending conditions of discharge for first-time bankrupts. The superintendent also maintains a record of all bankruptcies and has established a registry system that permits interested persons to search by individual or debtor name to determine if insolvency proceedings have been initiated.[187]

FURTHER READINGS

ANDERSON, H. "Insolvency Practitioners: Professional Independence and Conflict of Interest" in A Clarke, ed, *Current Issues in Insolvency Law* (London: Stevens, 1991) 1

BROWN, A. "Bankruptcy Claims after *Re Galaxy Sports* and *Re Lin*: No Longer a Businessperson's Statute?" in Janis P Sarra, ed, *Annual Review of Insolvency Law, 2011* (Scarborough, ON: Thomson Carswell, 2012) 833

CANADA, STUDY COMMITTEE ON BANKRUPTCY AND INSOLVENCY LEGISLATION. *Bankruptcy and Insolvency: Report of the Study Committee on Bankruptcy and Insolvency Legislation* (Ottawa: Study Committee on Bankruptcy and Insolvency Legislation, 1970) ch 6 (*Tassé Report*)

LALONDE, L. "Fairness and Due Process: Update on the Disciplinary Powers of the OSB over Trustees" in Janis P Sarra, ed, *Annual Review of Insolvency Law, 2007* (Scarborough, ON: Carswell, 2008) 295

———. "It All Began With *Galaxy*: Appeals and Trials De Novo in Insolvency Revisited" in Janis P Sarra, ed, *Annual Review of Insolvency Law, 2013* (Scarborough, ON: Carswell, 2014) 875

LANDO, A. "Sale of Assets by a Trustee: The Fundamental Pragmatics" (1991) 3 *Canadian Bankruptcy Reports* (3d) 179

NEVILLE, W. "Faithful Watchman or Trojan Horse???" (2006) 23 *National Insolvency Review* 39

---

186 *Ibid*, s 5(4)(c).
187 *Ibid*, s 11.1.

ZIEGEL, J. "The Personal Liabilities of Insolvency Practitioners under Insolvency Legislation: A Comparative Analysis of Canadian, English and American Positions" in Janis P Sarra, ed, *Annual Review of Insolvency Law, 2006* (Scarborough, ON: Thomson Carswell, 2007) 277

CHAPTER 9

THE PROOF, VALUATION, AND PAYMENT OF CLAIMS

After the property of the bankrupt estate has been assembled and liquidated, the proceeds are distributed to the participating creditors. The bankruptcy claims process involves two fundamental questions: Who is eligible to participate in the proceeds of the bankruptcy estate? How will these funds be distributed among the participating claimants? The first question is addressed in the provisions of the *BIA* that deal with the proof of claims. The second question is dealt with in provisions that address the scheme of distribution in bankruptcy.

The right to prove a claim against a bankrupt estate is "based upon the theory that the debtor's business has come to an end and that all obligations whether already incurred or merely contingent are to be disposed of and cleared off in the bankruptcy proceedings."[1] This allows as many claimants as possible to participate in the process and share in the liquidation proceeds.[2] This means that creditors will be entitled to share in the bankrupt estate even though the debtor may not have been in default of a contractual obligation at the date of the bankruptcy and even though a debt was not due until some future date.

The right to prove a claim in bankruptcy is subject to the principles that govern executory contracts.[3] A claimant cannot prove a claim if the trustee affirms the contract, since the claimant will receive the

1 *Re McKay* (1922), 2 CBR 462 (Ont HCJ).

2 *Newfoundland and Labrador v AbitibiBowater Inc*, 2012 SCC 67 at para 35 [*AbitibiBowater*].

3 See Chapter 6, Section B.

agreed-upon performance. If the trustee disclaims the contract, the claimant is entitled to prove a claim for breach of contract in the bankruptcy.

A. PROVABLE CLAIMS

A creditor must file a proof of claim with the trustee in order to participate in the distribution of the assets of a bankrupt estate.[4] The filing of a proof of claim also permits the creditor to vote at meetings of creditors.[5] A failure to file a proof of claim before the first meeting of creditors does not preclude the creditor from participating in the distribution of assets. However, it is unwise for a creditor to wait too long before filing a proof of claim, since that creditor will not be entitled to disturb the dividends that have already been paid out to other creditors.[6]

The concept of a provable claim is significant in a number of other respects. First, a provable claim is subject to the automatic bankruptcy stay of proceedings. This prevents the creditor from commencing or continuing any action or enforcing any remedy against the bankrupt or the bankrupt's property.[7] If the claim is not provable, the stay of proceedings does not affect it. Second, the discharge of an individual bankrupt ordinarily releases the bankrupt from claims provable in bankruptcy.[8] These events do not depend upon whether or not the creditor has filed a proof of claim. Rather, they arise if the claim falls within the definition of a provable claim.

Possessing a claim that is provable in bankruptcy against an individual bankrupt is not necessarily a good thing from the point of view of a creditor. Although the creditor is able to participate in a bankruptcy dividend, the creditor's claim will usually be extinguished upon the discharge of the bankrupt. If there are few or no assets in the bankrupt estate, the creditor may be better off with a non-provable claim. A creditor with a non-provable claim cannot enforce it against the property of the bankrupt estate, since the debtor no longer holds title to the property. However, the creditor will be able to enforce it against future, post-discharge assets of the debtor, since a non-provable claim is not released when the debtor obtains a discharge.

---

4 *BIA*, s 124(1).

5 See Chapter 8, Section A(2).

6 *BIA*, s 150.

7 *Ibid*, s 69.3(1) and see Chapter 6, Section A.

8 *BIA*, s 178(2). Certain types of claims listed in s 178(1) are not released. See Chapter 10, Section G.

The situation is different if the bankrupt is a corporation. Bankruptcy signals the end of the line for the corporation, unless all of the claims of the creditors are satisfied.[9] Without a provable claim, a creditor will recover nothing. The corporation will cease to carry on operations and all of its assets will be distributed to creditors who have proven their claims in the bankruptcy.

1) The Proof of Claim Procedure

A bankrupt is required to submit to the trustee a statement of affairs that sets out the names and addresses of all the creditors.[10] The trustee uses this information to identify the creditors in order to send them the prescribed proof of claim form together with the notice of the first meeting of creditors.[11] The trustee also publishes a notice of the bankruptcy in a local newspaper[12] and will provide the proof of claim forms to creditors who respond to the advertisement.

The proof of claim must make reference to a statement of account showing the particulars of the claim and make reference to vouchers or other evidence by which it can be substantiated.[13] The statement of account and supporting evidence must be sufficient to enable the trustee to make an informed decision as to whether the claim has merit.[14] The creditor also gives particulars of any security held by the creditor and indicates any payments received by the creditor in the past three months.[15] Proof of claims for unpaid wages owing to workers can be made in a single proof by a union, a federal or provincial labour department, or other person acting on behalf of the creditors.[16]

Once the proof of claim is completed, the creditor delivers it to the trustee.[17] After examining it, the trustee may admit the claim or

9 *BIA*, s 169(4).

10 *Ibid*, s 158(d).

11 *Ibid*, s 102(2).

12 *Ibid*, s 102(4). It is not necessary to do so in summary administration bankruptcies. See *BIA*, s 155(c).

13 See *Re Port Chevrolet Oldsmobile Ltd* (2004), 49 CBR (4th) 146 (BCCA).

14 *Re Norris* (1988), 67 CBR (NS) 246 (Ont HCJ), rev'd on other grounds (1989), 75 CBR (NS) 97 (Ont CA).

15 The period is twelve months in the case of a related party. This information is relevant for the purposes if any of the payments might be avoided as preferences. See Chapter 7, Section B.

16 *BIA*, s 126(2).

17 *Ibid*, s 124(2).

disallow it in whole or in part.[18] The trustee may also allow the claim but disallow a right to priority provided by the *BIA*. Alternatively, the trustee may request that the creditor provide further evidence in support of the claim.[19] If the claim is a contingent claim or an unliquidated claim, the trustee must determine if it is provable, and, if it is, the trustee is required to value it.[20] If the trustee disallows a claim in whole or part or makes a determination in respect of a contingent or liquidated claim, the trustee must notify the creditor of the reasons. A notice of disallowance or notice of valuation must be served or sent by registered mail or courier.[21] The disallowance or valuation of the trustee is final unless the creditor appeals the trustee's decision to the court within a thirty-day period after service of the notice.[22]

An appeal by a creditor from a notice of disallowance or on the valuation of a contingent or liquidated claim is usually before a registrar.[23] Every creditor who has filed a proof of claim is entitled to examine the proofs of other creditors.[24] Even if a trustee chooses not to disallow a claim, a bankrupt or another creditor may apply to court for an order expunging or reducing it.[25]

2) The Definition of a Provable Claim

The Supreme Court of Canada in *Newfoundland and Labrador v AbitibiBowater Inc*[26] set out the following three conditions that must be satisfied in order for a claim to be provable in bankruptcy: (1) a debt, liability, or obligation must be owed to a creditor; (2) the debt, liability, or obligation must be incurred before the debtor becomes bankrupt; and (3) it must be possible to attach a monetary value to the debt, liability, or obligation.

---

18 *Ibid*, s 135(2). The allowance of a liquidated claim does not prevent trustees from changing their minds in light of new information that comes to light. See *Herman v First Capital Management Ltd*, 2012 ABCA 299.

19 *BIA*, s 135(1).

20 *Ibid*, s 135(1.1).

21 *Bankruptcy and Insolvency General Rules*, CRC, c 368, s 113.

22 *BIA*, ss 135(3) & (4). Although a court may extend this period, the application for an extension must be brought within the thirty-day period.

23 *Ibid*, ss 192(1)(h) and (n). See Chapter 8, Section E(2) dealing with whether it is an appeal on the record or *de novo*.

24 *BIA*, s 126(1).

25 *Ibid*, s 135(5). And see *Royal Bank of Canada v Insley*, 2010 SKQB 17; *Roberts v E Sands & Associates Inc*, 2013 BCSC 902.

26 Above note 2 at para 26.

In order to bring involuntary bankruptcy proceedings against a debtor, a creditor must be owed a debt.[27] If these proceedings are successful, the court will make a bankruptcy order. However, the persons who are able to share the proceeds of the bankrupt estate are not limited to creditors who are owed debts. The *BIA* uses a wider meaning of "creditor" than that ordinarily denoted by the term. Any person who has a claim provable under the *BIA* falls within the definition of a creditor.[28] Provable claims are not limited to debts but include all liabilities to which the bankrupt was subject on the day of the bankruptcy.[29]

Provable claims therefore encompass debts that are presently due as well as unmatured debts that will become due sometime in the future. Provable claims also include unliquidated claims against the debtor, i.e., rights of action that, if successful, will result in a judgment or order for the payment of money. The claim may be founded in contract, tort, unjust enrichment, or some other source of obligation.[30] The fact that the debtor disputes the debt or liability does not in itself alter its characterization as a provable claim, but it will likely be a factor in the trustee's allowance or disallowance of the claim or the trustee's valuation of it.

The status of contingent claims is more controversial. A contingent claim is one where the obligation may or may not arise in the future depending upon the occurrence of specified future events. For example, a contract under which a person agrees to guarantee the debt of another person is a contingent liability. The liability depends upon whether there is a default by the principal debtor, and this is something that may be unknowable at the date of the bankruptcy. The formulation used by the *BIA* to identify provable claims is broken into two branches.[31] The first branch covers "all debts and liabilities, present and future, to which the bankrupt is subject on the day on which the bankrupt becomes bankrupt." The second branch is expressed as an alternative to the first. It covers all debts or liabilities "to which the bankrupt may become

27 See Chapter 3, Section C(2).

28 *BIA*, s 2 "creditor."

29 *Ibid*, s 121(1). And see s 2 "claim provable in bankruptcy," "provable claim," and "claim provable."

30 The original *Bankruptcy Act* of 1919 provided that unliquidated damages arising otherwise than by reason of a contract, promise, or breach of trust were not provable claims. This restriction was removed in 1949 with the result that unliquidated claims arising in tort became provable claims. See *Letovsky v Mutual Motor Frieght Ltd* (1958), 37 CBR 83 (Man QB).

31 *BIA*, s 121(1).

subject before the bankrupt's discharge by reason of any obligation incurred before the day on which the bankrupt becomes bankrupt."

In *Ontario New Home Warranty Program v Jiordan Homes Ltd*,[32] the court held that the liability of a bankrupt under a contract of indemnity is not a provable claim if the event that gives rise to the liability (the payment by the creditor who is claiming the indemnity) occurs after the discharge of the bankrupt. In reaching this conclusion, the court applied the second branch of the test, which appears to draw a distinction between contingent liabilities that crystallize before discharge and those that crystallize after discharge. As a consequence of this interpretation, the liability of the bankrupt under the contract of indemnity was not released by virtue of the bankruptcy discharge.

The interpretation of the second branch in *Jiordan* misconstrues the original purpose of the provision. The language was included to ensure that a claimant whose contract is disclaimed by a trustee will have a provable claim in the bankruptcy.[33] Bankruptcy does not by itself constitute a repudiation of an executory contract. The trustee has the option of affirming the contract, in which case the counterparty will not have a provable claim. It is only when the trustee disclaims that contract that the counterparty obtains the right to prove a claim, and this will typically arise after the date of bankruptcy.[34]

The *Jiordan* decision was considered in two Alberta decisions. One followed it,[35] the other did not.[36] The latter held that a contingent liability that had been incurred by contract before the day of bankruptcy fell within the first branch of the test. This interpretation has the benefit of producing an outcome that does not undermine the fresh start principle that is fundamental to bankruptcy law.[37]

3) The Timing of the Claim

The claim's time of creation is of crucial significance in determining if it is provable in bankruptcy. Bankruptcy law draws a sharp line between

---

32 (1999), 10 CBR (4th) 1 (Ont Ct Gen Div) [*Jiordan*].

33 See L Duncan, *The Law and Practice of Bankruptcy in Canada* (Toronto: Carswell, 1922) at 428–29.

34 See R Wood & D Bryan, "Creeping Statutory Obsolescence in Bankruptcy Law" (2014) 3 *Journal of the Insolvency Institute of Canada* 1 at 13–15.

35 *Peters v Remington* (2001), 28 CBR (4th) 82 (Alta QB), aff'd on other grounds (2004), 49 CBR (4th) 273 (Alta CA). See also *ERI Engine v MacEachern*, 2011 PECA 2.

36 *Auctioneers' Association (Alberta) v Hunter* (2002), 31 CBR (4th) 178 (Alta QB).

37 See S Bomhof, "Case Comment: *Ontario New Home Warranty Program v Jiordan Homes Ltd.*" (1999) 10 CBR (4th) 5.

debts and liabilities that were in existence on the date of the bankruptcy and those that are created thereafter. The former are provable, the latter are not. If the debtor negligently operates an automobile and strikes a pedestrian on the day following the bankruptcy, the claimant does not have a provable claim. Similarly, any debts or contractual liabilities that are incurred following the bankruptcy are not provable claims. An exception is made in the case of the costs of remedying environmental damage on the debtor's land. The clean-up costs, to the extent that they are not secured by the statutory security created by the *BIA*, are provable in the bankruptcy even though the environmental damage may have occurred after the date of the bankruptcy.[38]

The formulation of the test for provable claims was devised at a time when tort claims were not provable in bankruptcy. This restriction was later removed from the statute, but the test for provable claims was not changed. The test does not make it clear what events must occur in order for a tort claim to be considered a provable claim, merely referring to the time when the obligation is incurred. This language is better suited to contractual claims and is less easy to apply where a claim for negligence is involved. In order for the claim to arise, three things must be established. There must be a duty of care, there must be a breach of that duty, and there must be damage caused by the breach of duty. There are many instances, often involving the manufacture of defective products, in which the damage occurs sometime after the breach of duty. In these cases, it is possible that the breach of duty occurs before the bankruptcy but the damage occurs afterwards. The issue is whether the plaintiff has a claim provable in the bankruptcy.

A court may decide that all three elements must occur before the bankruptcy. If so, plaintiffs who suffer post-bankruptcy losses will not have provable claims and so will not share with the other creditors and will recover nothing. The difficulty with this interpretation is that it assumes that the cause of action must accrue at the time of bankruptcy. However, the accrual of a cause of action is not a prerequisite for a provable claim. A cause of action in contract does not arise until there has been a breach. A contracting party has a provable claim even though the bankrupt was not in breach of the contract at the date of the bankruptcy.[39] Future liabilities are provable claims so long as the obligation that gives rise to the future liability was incurred at the date of bankruptcy.

38 *BIA*, s 14.06(8). And see *AbitibiBowater*, above note 2 at paras 28–29.

39 *Re McKay* (1922), 2 CBR 462 (Ont HCJ).

A court might instead conclude that the defendant incurs an obligation when the defendant breaches a duty of care, even though the identity of the plaintiffs will not be known until they suffer damage. If this view is adopted, the claims will be provable so long as the breach of duty did not occur after the date of bankruptcy. Claimants who suffer loss after the date of bankruptcy would therefore have provable claims and would be entitled to participate in the bankruptcy so long as they deliver a proof of claim to the trustee before the final distribution is made. But once all the assets have been distributed, future victims will be out of luck. Unlike restructuring law that can be used to permit recovery by future claimants,[40] there is no mechanism in Canadian bankruptcy law that would permit the trustee to withhold some of the assets of the bankruptcy estate in order to satisfy the claims of future victims.

A provable claim must be one recoverable by legal process.[41] The time for determining the validity or enforceability of the claim is at the date of bankruptcy. If the claim is time-barred by a limitation statute at the date of bankruptcy, the creditor will not be entitled to prove the claim in bankruptcy.[42] If the claim was not time-barred at the date of bankruptcy, it is provable even if the limitation period expires before the creditor files a proof of claim with the trustee.[43]

4) Interest and Claims Payable at a Future Time

A creditor who has a right to interest on a debt can prove only for the interest that has accrued up to the date of the bankruptcy.[44] No post-bankruptcy interest can be recovered.[45] Bankruptcy courts developed this rule[46] to respond to a concern that, if different claims carried different interest rates, the *pro rata* sharing calculation would constantly change and a recalculation of interest would be needed every time a dividend was declared.[47]

40 See Chapter 15, Section A(3).

41 *Farm Credit Corp v Holowach (Trustee of)* (1988), 68 CBR (NS) 255 (Alta CA).

42 *Re Morton* (1922), 3 CBR 114 (Sask KB).

43 See *Re Crosley* (1887), 35 Ch D 266 (CA).

44 *Re Belleville Milling Co* (1930), 12 CBR 505 (Ont HCJ). This principle does not apply where there is a surplus in the bankrupt estate.

45 If the parties did not agree upon a rate of interest, an interest rate of 5 percent per annum will be used to calculate interest up to the date of the bankruptcy. See *BIA*, s 122(2).

46 *In re Browne and Wingrove*, [1891] 2 QB 574 (CA); *In re Humber Ironworks and Shipbuilding Company* (1869), LR 4 Ch App 643.

47 Note, "Post-Bankruptcy Interest in Chapter X Reorganizations" (1958) 67 *Yale Law Journal* 1131. And see *Re Nortel Networks Corporation*, 2014 ONSC 4777 at paras 9–18.

This principle does not apply where the debt is due sometime in the future. Claims for debts that are payable at a future time are provable in respect both of the principal and of the interest. However, the amount is discounted at the rate of 5 percent per annum from the declaration of the dividend to the date that the future debt would have been payable.[48]

5) Family Support Claims

Family support claims did not qualify as provable debts under traditional bankruptcy law principles.[49] This characterization extended to payments that were due after the bankruptcy as well as to payments that were in arrears on the date of the bankruptcy.[50] The support order was subject to variation by a court, and therefore it was not considered to be capable of valuation. Although support claims based on contract as opposed to court order were provable in bankruptcy,[51] the ability of a court to vary the agreement later resulted in these being considered non-provable claims as well.[52] This meant that, although family support claims were not released by the discharge of the bankrupt, the family support claimants were unable to share in the division of assets in the bankruptcy.

Legislative amendments were introduced in 1997 to reverse this outcome. Family support claims that are payable under an order or agreement made before the date of the initial bankruptcy event and at the time when the spouse, common law partner, or child was living separate and apart from the bankrupt are now provable.[53] These claims are given a preferred creditor status in the bankruptcy scheme of distribution and are not subject to release on the discharge of the debtor.[54]

Support claims are provable only if the order is made before the date of the initial bankruptcy event. Amounts payable under an agreement or order made after the creditors file an application for a bankruptcy order are not provable. It is also necessary for the claimant to be living apart from the recipient. If these conditions are not satisfied, the support claim will not qualify as provable.

In order to qualify as a provable claim, the family support obligation must also be payable. Although some commentators had argued

---

48 *BIA*, s 121(3). And see *In re Browne and Wingrove*, above note 46.

49 *Linton v Linton* (1885), 15 QBD 239 (CA); *Kerr v Kerr*, [1897] 2 QB 439.

50 *Re Freedman* (1924), 5 CBR 47 (Ont SCAD).

51 *Speal v Moore* (1960), 38 CBR 193 (Ont HCJ).

52 *Re Burrows* (1996), 42 CBR (3d) 89 (Ont Ct Gen Div).

53 *BIA*, s 121(4).

54 *Ibid*, s 136(d.1) and ss 178(1)(b) & (c).

that this meant that support claims that arose after the date of bankruptcy were not provable, this argument was rejected in *Bukvic v Bukvic*.[55] The court held that a claim for future support was provable in bankruptcy.

6) Claims by Secured Creditors

When considering the position of a secured creditor in bankruptcy, it is necessary to distinguish between a proof of claim made by the secured creditor and a proof of security. A secured party may file a proof of claim with the trustee if the value of the collateral is or is expected to be less than the value of the collateral. This permits the secured creditor to participate in the proceeds of the bankrupt estate in respect of the deficiency on a *pro rata* basis with the ordinary unsecured creditors. A proof of security is requested by a trustee in order to provide the trustee with details of the security so that the trustee can assess the validity of the security and decide whether to redeem it or require its sale.[56] A secured creditor can be required to provide a proof of security whether or not the secured creditor has filed a proof of claim. A secured creditor who fails to comply with the provisions of the *BIA* relating to the proof and valuation of security is not entitled to participate in a bankruptcy dividend.[57]

If the secured creditor has already realized the collateral, the amount of the deficiency claim is known and the secured party need prove only for the balance.[58] The secured creditor may prove for the entire amount by surrendering the security to the trustee.[59] If a secured creditor has not realized the security or surrendered it, the secured creditor may nevertheless prove a claim for an expected deficiency by estimating the value of its security in a proof of claim. The secured creditor can then participate in the distribution of the bankruptcy estate to the extent of the balance due after subtracting the assessed value of the security.[60] If the collateral is thereafter sold, the net amount realized must be substituted for the estimated value.[61] A secured creditor may amend its valuation of the security on showing, to the satisfaction

---

55 (2007), 86 OR (3d) 297 (SCJ). For a critique of this decision, see R Klotz, "Case Comment on *Bukvic v. Bukvic*" (2007) 46 R.F.L. (6th) 145.

56 The proof of security procedure is described in Chapter 5, Section B(2).

57 *BIA*, s 133.

58 *Ibid*, s 127(1).

59 *Ibid*, s 127(2).

60 *Ibid*, s 128(2).

61 *Ibid*, s 131.

of the trustee or court, that it was made in good faith on a mistaken estimation.[62]

7) Claims by Guarantors

A third party may have guaranteed a debt owed by a principal debtor to a creditor. The claim of the guarantor is a contingent liability and the guarantor is entitled to file a proof of claim in the bankruptcy of the principal debtor, even if the guarantor has not been called upon to pay or has not paid.[63]

The creditor also has a provable claim in the bankruptcy of the principal debtor. If the creditor files a proof of claim in the bankruptcy, the guarantor will not be able to prove a claim for its right of indemnity against the bankrupt estate in competition with the claim of the creditor.[64] The right of the guarantor to do so is limited by a principle referred to as the rule against double proofs. This rule prevents more than one proof of claim being made in respect of a debt, even though there may be two separate contracts relating to the debt.[65]

If the guarantor has guaranteed only part of a debt, the guarantor may prove the claim in the bankruptcy after paying that part to the creditor, and the creditor's claim is correspondingly reduced.[66] However, a different rule applies if the guarantor has guaranteed the whole debt subject to a limit. In this case, the guarantor cannot prove a claim in competition with the creditor until the creditor is paid in full.[67] The creditor is thereby permitted to get as much as possible out of the debtor's estate and then look to the guarantor for the shortage.

The creditor is not required to reduce the claim against the bankrupt estate by amounts that have been received from the guarantor so long as the creditor does not recover more than one hundred cents on

62 *Ibid*, s 132(1). If the valuation was too high, the secured creditor must pay the excess dividend back to the trustee. If it was too low, the secured creditor is entitled to be paid from any amount remaining in the bankrupt estate before the ordinary creditors receive any future dividend, but the secured creditor is not entitled to disturb the distribution of a dividend that has already been declared before the amendment. See *ibid*, s 132(3).

63 *Re Froment* (1925), 5 CBR 765 (Alta SC); *McCrie v Gray* (1940), 22 CBR 390 (Ont HCJ).

64 *Kaupthing Singer and Friedlander Ltd, (Re)*, [2011] UKSC 48.

65 *Re Coughlin & Co* (1923), 4 CBR 294 (Man CA); *Re Olympia & York Developments Ltd.* (1998), 4 CBR (4th) 189 (Ont Ct Gen Div).

66 *Re Sass*, [1896] 2 QB 12.

67 *Re Coughlin & Co*, above note 65.

the dollar.[68] Once the guarantor pays the full amount of the guaranteed debt to the creditor, the guarantor is subrogated to any security held by the creditor[69] and the creditor is accountable for any dividends that are thereafter received.[70]

If both the principal debtor and the guarantor are bankrupt, the creditor can prove a claim against both bankrupt estates. The creditor's proof of claim must be reduced by amounts that are received from the principal debtor prior to the proof of the creditor's claim against the estate of the guarantor. Amounts that are received after the proof of claim is submitted do not need to be deducted so long as the creditor does not receive more than one hundred cents on the dollar.[71]

8) Claims by Landlords

When a trustee disclaims an executory contract, the other party has the right to prove a claim for damages for breach of contract. If the bankrupt is a lessee under a real property lease, the lessor's right to claim damages on a disclaimer of the lease is limited by provincial statute.[72] The *BIA* provides that the rights of lessors shall be determined according to the laws of the province where the leased premises are situated. Although the landlord may prove a claim for any arrears of rent that were due at the date of bankruptcy, claims for future rent are curtailed. The provincial statutes limit the claim to three months of accelerated rent.[73] If the trustee elects to occupy the premises and pay occupation rent, the trustee may deduct this amount from the claim for accelerated rent.

The limitation on recovery of future rent applies only if a landlord tenant relationship is in existence at the date of the bankruptcy.[74] If the lease has been validly terminated before bankruptcy, the lessor may

---

68 *Re Houlder* (1929), 1 Ch 205. This principle does not apply if the contract of guarantee deems the guarantor to be the principal debtor for the performance of the obligations, since these payments will be treated as those of the principal debtor. See *Re Olympia & York Developments Ltd* (1998), 6 CBR (4th) 254 (Ont CA).

69 *Routley v Gorman* (1920), 55 DLR 58 (Ont CA).

70 *Re Sass*, above note 66.

71 *Re J LeBar Seafoods Inc* (1981), 38 CBR (NS) 64 (Ont HCJ).

72 *Re Vrablik* (1993), 17 CBR (3d) 152 (Ont Ct Gen Div); *West Shore Ventures Ltd v KPN Holding Ltd* (2001), 25 CBR (4th) 139 (BCCA).

73 See, for example, *Landlord's Rights on Bankruptcy Act*, RSA 2000, c L-5, ss 3–4; *Commercial Tenancy Act*, RSBC 1996, c 57, ss 29(6)–(7). See also Chapter 6, Section B(3).

74 *Standard Trusts Co v David Steele Ltd* (1921), 2 CBR 183 (BCSC), aff'd (1922), 3 CBR 141 (BCCA).

claim for damages for losses incurred over the full term of the lease. A repudiation of a lease by a lessee does not result in termination of the lease. The lessor must accept the termination and communicate this to the lessee.[75]

9) Valuation of Contingent and Unliquidated Claims

The trustee determines if contingent and unliquidated claims are provable, and if so the trustee will value the claim. Thereafter, the claim is considered to be a proved claim to the amount of the valuation.[76] The valuation exercise often requires a trustee to estimate the value of a claim on the basis of limited information. The harsh reality of insolvency is that the investment of the time and effort needed to produce the kinds of valuations that would be expected in the course of ordinary civil litigation is often not feasible, since such an investment would severely diminish the already inadequate assets available to satisfy the claims of the creditors. A streamlined process is needed.

In valuing a contingent claim, a trustee must estimate the probability of the occurrence of the future event that transforms the obligation from a potential liability to a present liability. For example, the bankrupt may have given a personal guarantee to a creditor and the principal debtor may be in a sound financial position at the time that the claim is valued by the trustee. That does not mean that the claim will be valued at zero, since there exists the possibility that things may worsen sometime in the future. This is illustrated in the case of *Re Wiebe*.[77] A dentist had entered into an agreement with a health unit under which a loan of $94,458.58 was advanced to the dentist. The agreement provided that the loan would be forgiven if the dentist remained employed by the health unit until 1998. The dentist went bankrupt and the health unit lodged a proof of claim in 1994. Although there was currently satisfaction on the part of both parties with their relationship, the court considered the possibility that it might end in the future either because of a desire to move to private practice or relocation or by virtue of dismissal for misconduct. The court estimated that the contingency of this occurring was approximately 10 percent, and the claim was valued at $9,500.

Courts are more reluctant to use this methodology where the expected claim is very high but the probability of the event giving rise to it is very low. Suppose that the expected claim is estimated to be $10

75 *TNG Acquisition Inc (Re)*, 2011 ONCA 535.
76 *BIA*, s 135(1.1).
77 (1995), 30 CBR (3d) 109 (Ont Ct Gen Div).

million but the probability of the event is estimated to be 10 percent. If the same approach were employed, the claim would be valued at $1 million. The valuation of the claim at this amount may mean that the bulk of the assets of the bankrupt estate will be distributed to a claimant who had a claim that was unlikely to materialize.

In order to prevent this from occurring, some courts have decided that some claims are simply too remote and speculative to be considered provable. In *Claude Resources Inc (Trustee of) v Dutton*,[78] the court held that there must be "some element of probability" about the claim before it can be considered a provable claim. The Ontario Court of Appeal in *Re Confederation Treasury Services Ltd*,[79] although recognizing that highly speculative claims might be excluded, suggested that the test articulated in *Claude Resources* imposes too high a threshold to the extent that it requires some probability of success.

The valuation of unliquidated claims raises somewhat different considerations. If liability is undisputed, the matter usually involves the assessment of damages. In a claim for personal injuries, it is necessary to place a value on the pecuniary loss suffered by the victim as well as non-pecuniary loss such as pain and suffering and loss of amenity. If liability is disputed, in order to value the claim it is necessary to estimate the probability of success of the action in the event that the matter had been litigated. In this instance, it is more likely that the claim will be valued at its full amount so long as the probability of success on the merits is estimated to be greater than 50 percent.

The Supreme Court of Canada in *Schreyer v Schreyer*[80] held that matrimonial property claims in provinces that have enacted an equalization approach are provable in bankruptcy. There is less certainty as to whether such claims are provable in provinces that have adopted a division of property approach. The Saskatchewan Court of Appeal in *Walton v Walton*[81] held that such claims were not provable because the judge has a high degree of discretion on whether to make the award and also on the nature of the remedy that can be awarded. The decision has been criticized on the basis that it exaggerates the degree of discretion that can be exercised by the court.[82] More recent cases from

---

78 (1993), 22 CBR (3d) 56 (Sask QB).

79 (1997), 43 CBR (3d) 4 (Ont CA).

80 2011 SCC 35.

81 (1993), 23 CBR (3d) 315 (Sask CA).

82 R Klotz, *Bankruptcy, Insolvency and Family Law*, 2d ed, (Scarborough, ON: Carswell, 2001) (loose-leaf), ch 5.1(b).

Saskatchewan have not applied the decision and have held that such claims are provable in bankruptcy.[83]

10) Environmental Remediation Claims

If an environmental protection order is issued and the government then cleans up the pollution, the government has an unliquidated claim that can be proved and valued in the bankruptcy. If the government has not commenced to clean up the site but it is sufficiently certain that it will do so, it will also constitute a contingent claim that is provable in bankruptcy. If it is not sufficiently certain that the government will clean up the site, then it is not a provable claim. In this case, the trustee in bankruptcy may decide to clean up the site and the costs will constitute a cost of administration. Alternatively, the trustee may elect to abandon the property. In determining if the cleanup is "sufficiently certain," it is not necessary to demonstrate "likelihood approaching certainty."[84]

B. THE BANKRUPTCY SCHEME OF DISTRIBUTION

The *BIA* recognizes three categories of unsecured claims among those entitled to participate in the proceeds of realization of the bankrupt estate: preferred claims, ordinary claims, and postponed claims. Secured creditors do not form a class of claims that participate in the proceeds of the bankrupt estate. Secured creditors enforce their security outside the bankruptcy system. If the value of their collateral is insufficient to satisfy the obligation secured, they may prove for the deficiency in bankruptcy. The claim for a deficiency is merely an unsecured claim that does not provide the claimant with any right of priority over other claimants.

1) Preferred Claims

The *BIA* sets out a hierarchy of thirteen subclasses of preferred claims. Each subcategory must be fully paid out to the extent of the preference before the claimants in the next subclass are entitled to receive anything. In several instances, the amount of the preference is subject to a monetary limit or a time limit. In these cases, the claimant has a

83 *Bellamy v Hill*, 2005 SKQB 333; *Charles v Becerra*, 2012 SKQB 27.

84 *AbitibiBowater*, above note 2 at paras 59–61.

preferred claimant status only up to the limitation but is permitted to claim the balance as an ordinary claimant.[85]

If there are insufficient funds to pay all preferred creditors, the result may be that the higher ranking subclasses of preferred claims are paid in full, the next ranking subclass is entitled to a partial payment, and the lower subclasses receive nothing. In this case, the claimants who fall within the subclass entitled to a partial payment will participate in the available funds on a *pro rata* basis, unless some other order of distribution is specified.[86]

Two of the subclasses are unlikely to have any application to current bankruptcies.[87] Prior to 1992, Crown claims and claims of workers' compensation bodies were designated as preferred. The position of these types of claims was then altered so that they would have the status of either a secured or an ordinary unsecured claim.[88] The preferred status of these claims is recognized, but only in respect of bankruptcies that occurred before the prescribed date of 30 November 1992.[89] The other nine subclasses are discussed below in the descending order of their priority.

a) Funeral and Testamentary Expenses

If the bankrupt is deceased, the reasonable funeral and testamentary expenses incurred by the legal representative of the deceased person constitute a preferred claim.[90] This covers the situation where the legal representative of a deceased person makes an assignment in bankruptcy in respect of the estate, as well as the situation where a bankrupt dies after the occurrence of the bankruptcy.[91]

b) Administrative Costs

The costs of administration are designated as preferred claims.[92] The costs of administration are subdivided into three further classes for the purposes of determining priority of payment. First priority is given to a person who takes over the administration of a bankrupt estate after

---

85 *BIA*, s 136(3).

86 The subcategory of administrative costs in *BIA*, s 136(1)(b) is the only subcategory that provides further rules for priority of payment among the claims falling within the subcategory.

87 *BIA*, ss 136(1)(h) and (j).

88 See Chapter 5, Section E.

89 *Bankruptcy and Insolvency General Rules*, above note 21, s 137.

90 *BIA*, s 136(1)(a).

91 *Re Bertram* (1972), 18 CBR (NS) 64 (Ont HCJ).

92 *BIA*, s 136(1)(b).

a trustee is unable to do so because of death, incapacity, removal, or other cause.[93] Second priority is given to the expenses and fees of the trustee. Third priority is given to legal costs. A further set of priorities in respect of legal costs is set out in the *BIA* as follows:[94]

1. Commissions on collections.
2. Costs incurred after the bankruptcy but before the first meeting of creditors.
3. Costs of the bankruptcy assignment or of the costs incurred by an applicant creditor up to the issue of a bankruptcy order.
4. Costs awarded against the trustee or a bankrupt estate.
5. Costs of other legal services rendered to the trustee.

Expenses that were incurred by the debtor before the occurrence of a bankruptcy do not enjoy the status of administrative costs even though they may save the trustee from having to incur similar costs. Thus, a real estate agent who earned a commission for finding a buyer for the debtor's home can claim only as an ordinary creditor despite the fact that this effort saved the trustee the expense of doing so.[95] Although the general rule is that pre-bankruptcy costs cannot be claimed as administrative costs,[96] courts have sometimes departed from this position. In *Re Canada 3000 Inc*,[97] a creditor was required to provide services to a debtor company under a *CCAA* order. The company abruptly ceased operation and went into bankruptcy, leaving the creditor unpaid. The court used the principle in *Ex parte James*[98] to justify its decision to treat the costs as an administrative cost. In *Tri Technology Resource Inc v Lamford Forest Products Ltd.*,[99] the court held that environmental assessment costs that were incurred after the date of the bankruptcy but before appointment of a trustee qualified as administrative costs.

It is difficult to extract from these decisions a principle that describes when pre-bankruptcy or pre-appointment costs can be claimed as administrative costs. The fact that such costs save the trustee from incurring the expense is clearly not enough to engage the principle. There must be some further element of essential service or necessity such that the trustee is obliged to pay for the services.

---

93 *Ibid*, s 14.03.

94 *Ibid*, s 197(6).

95 *Re Bertrand* (1981), 40 CBR (NS) 64 (Que Sup Ct).

96 *Re Claymore Development Ltd* (1983), 50 CBR (NS) 312 (Alta QB).

97 (2002), 36 CBR (4th) 17 (Ont SCJ).

98 See Chapter 4, Section E.

99 (1995), 36 CBR (3d) 279 (BCSC).

c) Superintendent's Levy

The levy payable to the Superintendent of Bankruptcy is given the status of a preferred claim. The *BIA* provides for payment of a levy on all payments made by the trustee by way of dividend or otherwise on account of the claims of creditors.[100] An exception is made for the costs of the first-seizing creditor, which is not subject to the levy. The levy is used to defray the expenses of the Office of the Superintendent of Bankruptcy in supervising the bankruptcy system. The levy is charged proportionately against all payments of claims that rank below that of the levy, and is deducted and remitted to the superintendent by the trustee.[101] The levy is payable only in respect of payments to creditors of proceeds of the bankrupt estate. It does not apply to payments by the trustee of property that belongs to a third party or to property that is not distributable to creditors such as exempt property and property held by the debtor in trust.[102]

The levy is currently set at a rate of 5 percent. If the distribution to creditors is more than $1 million, the rate drops to 1.25 percent on the portion over $1 million and not more than $2 million, and to 0.25 percent on anything above $2 million.[103]

d) Unpaid Wages and Pension Contributions

Employee claims were at one time afforded the status of a preferred claim to the extent of $2,000. This preferred status did not ensure that employees would receive payment of their wages, since the preferred claim was often defeated by the claim of a secured creditor. The introduction of the *Wage Earner Protection Program Act*[104] and the creation of superpriority charges in favour of employee claims and pension contributions[105] have significantly improved the position of claims of employees in a bankruptcy of the employer.

The preferred creditor status of unpaid employees has been modified to reflect these changes. An unpaid employee may claim as a preferred creditor to the extent that there are insufficient current assets to satisfy the obligation that is secured by the employee charge.[106] In other cases, the superpriority that is afforded the employee's charge or the

---

100 *BIA*, s 147(1).

101 *Ibid*, s 147(2).

102 *Re Walter Davidson Co (No 2)* (1958), 37 CBR 81 (Ont HCJ).

103 *Bankruptcy and Insolvency General Rules*, above note 21, s 123.

104 SC 2005, c 47, s 1, as am SC 2007, c 36 [*WEPPA*]. And see Section D, below in this chapter.

105 *BIA*, s 81.3. And see Chapter 5, Section D.

106 *Ibid*, s 136(1)(d).

pension charge may mean that some or all of the assets will no longer be available as security in respect of the secured creditor's claim. The secured creditor can prove a claim as a preferred creditor in respect of the amount lost as a result of the superpriority.[107]

e) Family Support Claims

Family support claims are designated as preferred claims to the extent that the arrears are provable.[108] A distinction is drawn between periodic amounts and lump-sum amounts. The preferred status is conferred in respect of periodic amounts only if they have accrued in the year before the date of the bankruptcy. A similar time limitation is not imposed in respect of lump-sum amounts that are payable.

f) Municipal Taxes

Municipal taxes that are secured against real property by provincial law have the status of a secured claim.[109] Municipal taxes that are not secured against real property are given the status of a preferred claim.[110] There are two limitations associated with the preferred claim to municipal taxes.[111] First, the taxes must have been assessed or levied within a two-year period before the bankruptcy. Second, the claim for taxes cannot exceed the value of the interest of the bankrupt in the property in respect of which the taxes were imposed.[112] It is the value of the debtor's interest in the property and not the value of the property itself that is used. If the debtor has merely a leasehold interest in the property, it is the value of this interest that limits the preferred claim. If the interest has no value, there will be no preferred claim in respect of the municipal taxes. The amount due must be in respect of a municipal tax.

---

107 *Ibid*, ss 136(1)(d.01) & (d.02).

108 *Ibid*, s 136(1)(d.1). For a discussion of the provability of family support claims, see Section A(5), above in this chapter.

109 Municipal taxes that are a secured charge against land are not subject to an inversion of priorities on bankruptcy. If they are entitled to priority over other secured parties under provincial law, they retain this priority on bankruptcy. Such charges are not subject to the two-year time limitation that pertains to municipal taxes that are afforded only a preferred claim. See *Donalda (Village) v Toronto Dominion Bank* (1990), 4 CBR (3d) 212 (Alta QB).

110 Any other priority afforded the claim by provincial law is lost upon the occurrence of a bankruptcy. See *Re Pinestone Resort & Conference Centre Inc* (1999), 9 CBR (4th) 159 (Ont CA).

111 *BIA*, s 136(1)(e).

112 See *Re Harrison's Ltd* (1953), 33 CBR 182 (BCSC). See also *Re Spartacus Pizza & Spaghetti House (1978) Ltd* (1992), 9 CBR (3d) 187 (Alta QB) and *Re Midland Book Centre Ltd* (1976), 22 CBR (NS) 70 (Man QB), which declined to follow earlier Alberta and Manitoba decisions that reached the opposite conclusion.

In order to qualify, the amounts collected must be earmarked for municipal purposes. It is not sufficient that the provincial legislation deems the sums to be municipal taxes.[113]

g) Landlord's Claim for Rent

A landlord's claim for rent qualifies as a preferred claim.[114] The claim is limited in two ways. First, the rent must be in respect of arrears during the three-month period immediately preceding the bankruptcy. A claim for accelerated rent also qualifies as a preferred claim but is limited to a three-month period following the bankruptcy.[115] Second, the preferred claim is limited to the amount realized from the disposition of the property on the premises. The landlord loses the right to distrain for rent and must turn over any seized property to the trustee on production of a copy of the assignment or bankruptcy order.[116] Secured creditors often initiate a bankruptcy in order to prevent a landlord from exercising a right of distress, which ordinarily has priority over most security interests under non-bankruptcy law.[117]

h) Fees of the First-Enforcement Creditor

Any enforcement proceedings that are brought by an enforcement creditor that have not been fully executed by payment to the creditor at the date of bankruptcy are rendered ineffective against the trustee, and any property or funds must be paid over to the trustee.[118] Despite this, the *BIA* provides for payment of the costs of the first creditor to have attached by way of garnishment or who has filed an attachment, execution, or other process against the property of the bankrupt.[119] The costs that are recoverable include a lawyer's bill of costs,[120] an executing officer's fees, and land registration fees. These costs are afforded the status of a preferred claim.[121] The preferred claim is limited to the amount realized from the disposition of the property that was subject to the enforcement proceeding instituted by the creditor.

---

113 *Re Westline Ranch Ltd* (1987), 65 CBR (NS) 16 (BCCA).

114 *BIA*, s 136(1)(f).

115 The trustee is entitled to credit any payments made in respect of accelerated rent against amounts payable by the trustee for occupation rent. See also Chapter 6, Section B(3)(a).

116 See Chapter 6, Section A(4).

117 See Chapter 5, Section B(6).

118 See Chapter 6, Section A(4).

119 *BIA*, s 70(2).

120 *Walker (Re)*, 2010 BCSC 489, held that this includes the entirety of a litigant's taxable costs including appeal proceedings.

121 *BIA*, s 136(1)(g).

It is not clear what steps need to be taken by the creditor in order to recover the costs of enforcement under this provision. Judicial decisions are divided on whether it is sufficient if the judgment enforcement creditor registered the writ or other process in a land registration system.[122] Provinces that have modernized their judgment enforcement law also permit the registration of writs or other process in the provincial personal property security registries. In most cases, this step is undertaken immediately after judgment is obtained. Registration has the effect of encumbering the exigible property of the debtor. The language used in the *BIA* may suggest that something more than registration is needed. There must be an attachment by way of garnishment. This will typically occur when a garnishee summons is served on the garnishee. Alternatively, there must be an execution or other process filed with an executing officer. An executing officer is defined as any officer charged with the execution of a writ or other process.[123] This does not appear to encompass a creditor's unilateral act of registering a financing statement in a personal property registry. It is not necessary that the enforcement activity be completed or that a seizure be effected.[124]

i) Funds for Injured Workers

The *BIA* confers a preferred status on claims resulting from injuries to employees that are not covered by workers' compensation, but only to the extent of "moneys received from persons guaranteeing the bankrupt against damages resulting from those injuries."[125] This was likely intended to cover insurance payments. In the absence of a statutory or contractual provision that gives the injured party a direct right of recovery against the insurer, the insurance monies are payable to the bankrupt estate.[126] The preferred status given to such claims ensures that the insurance money will not be shared with ordinary creditors. However, injured workers will not receive these monies if there are insufficient funds in the bankruptcy estate to satisfy higher-ranking preferred claims.

---

122 *Re Yawoski* (1921), 2 CBR 181 (Man KB) (registration alone is not sufficient); *Re Drysdale* (1938), 19 CBR 324 (BCSC) (registration alone is sufficient). *Walker (Re)*, above note 120, accepted the view that registration of a writ in the land registration system is sufficient.

123 *BIA*, s 2 "executing officer."

124 *Re Ferguson* (1935), 16 CBR 261 (Ont HCJ); *Re LeSuir*, [1948] 2 WWR 974 (BCSC).

125 *BIA*, s 136(1)(i).

126 See Chapter 4, Section B(7).

2) Ordinary Claims

Once all the preferred claims are paid, the residue of the bankrupt estate is distributed rateably among the ordinary creditors.[127] Preferred claimants who do not obtain full payment of their claims because of a monetary or other limit associated with their preferred claim may share in this distribution for the balance of their claim. Secured creditors may also participate in the fund to the extent of a deficiency between the value of their collateral and the secured obligation.[128]

3) Postponed Claims

Certain classes of claims are postponed until the ordinary claims are paid in full. In most cases, this will mean that the postponed claimants will recover nothing. In the unlikely event that all the ordinary claims are satisfied and there is more than one postponed claim, the postponed claimants will share *pro rata* in the residue.[129]

a) Non–Arm's Length Transactions

The *BIA* provides for the postponement of a creditor who entered into a non–arm's length transaction with the debtor. This complements the *BIA*'s treatment of transfers at undervalue.[130] If the third party has received a transfer of property from the debtor, the appropriate response is to recover the asset or its value from the third party. This remedy is not available if the debtor incurs an obligation to the third party but no property is transferred in connection with it. Here, the appropriate response is to postpone the obligation until the claims of the other creditors are satisfied. For example, the third party may have sold goods to the bankrupt for $500 even though their fair market value is only $50. If the third party received $500 in payment of the price, the trustee can recover the $450 difference in value by bringing an action against the third party. If the third party did not receive payment, the trustee can postpone the third party's claim.[131] In this event, the third party will not participate in the *pro rata* distribution of the bankruptcy estate. If the trustee or a court is of the opinion that the transfer was not at undervalue, the claim should be allowed as a proper transaction.[132]

---

127 *BIA*, s 141.
128 See Section A(6), above in this chapter.
129 *BIA*, s 141.
130 See Chapter 7, Section D.
131 *BIA*, s 137(1).
132 *Re Provost Shoe Shops Ltd* (1993), 21 CBR (3d) 108 (NSSCTD).

The effect of disallowance is that the entire claim is postponed, and not merely the portion of the claim that is in excess of its fair value.

The trustee may be able to use this provision to postpone the claim of a person who was given a guarantee by the debtor if the parties were not dealing at arm's length and the debtor received a benefit that was conspicuously less than the value of the guarantee. Determining the value of a guarantee and the value of the benefits received by the guarantor can be a particularly difficult exercise.[133]

b) Claims of Profit-Sharing Lenders

A lender who advances money to a borrower under a contract in which the lender receives a share of the profits or in which the rate of interest varies with the profits is postponed until all the ordinary creditors are paid in full.[134] A lender who obtains a security interest in the debtor's property is not prevented from asserting the security interest in the bankruptcy and thereby obtaining priority over unsecured creditors.[135] However, the lender cannot share *pro rata* with the other creditors for any deficiency.

A shareholder may make a loan to the corporation that issued the shares. So long as the loan agreement does not provide for a sharing of profits, the shareholder will be entitled to claim as a creditor in respect of the loan.[136] If the shareholder purports to make a loan to the corporation but does not keep records as to the terms of repayment or rate of interest, the advances may be characterized as capital contributions that are not entitled to share until all the claims of the creditors have first been satisfied.[137]

A profit-sharing lender who also exercises a sufficient degree of control in the operation of the business takes the risk that the relationship between the lender and the borrower will be characterized as that of partners.[138] This will result in the lender becoming personally liable for the business debts and obligations of the borrower.

---

133 These difficulties are discussed in R Goode, *Principles of Corporate Insolvency Law*, 4th ed (London: Thomson/Sweet & Maxwell, 2011) at 547–51.

134 *BIA*, s 139. And see *Canada Deposit Insurance Corp v Canadian Commercial Bank*, [1992] 3 SCR 558, which held that a participation agreement that is primarily a loan transaction but that has some incidental "investment features" does not lose its characterization as a loan transaction.

135 *Sukloff v AH Rushforth and Co Ltd*, [1964] SCR 459.

136 *Re GMD Vending Co* (1994), 27 CBR (3d) 77 (BCCA); *Re Emarc Contracting Ltd* (1992), 17 CBR (3d) 279 (BCCA).

137 *Laronge Realty Ltd v Golconda Invt Ltd* (1986), 63 CBR (NS) 74 (BCCA).

138 *Pooley v Driver* (1876), 5 Ch Div 458.

c) Equity Claims

Claims by shareholders for the return of equity are of a fundamentally different nature from claims of creditors. If the true nature of the claim is that of a shareholder for recovery of the capital invested in the corporation, it is not one that can be proven as a debt or liability in the bankruptcy of the corporation.[139] This does not preclude a shareholder from making a separate loan to the corporation. In this event, the shareholder may claim as a creditor in the bankruptcy of the corporation to the extent of the loan.

A shareholder may have a claim for damages against a corporation for fraudulent misrepresentation or a claim for the recovery of money or other property on the rescission of a contract for the purchase of shares. Courts held that these claims did not rank with the claims of ordinary creditors but were postponed by virtue of the doctrine of equitable subordination.[140]A shareholder may also have a claim for the payment of money against a corporation in connection with some right associated with the share. Although a declared dividend was recoverable as a debt,[141] other forms of distributions did not permit the shareholder to claim as a creditor in relation to the distribution. Preferred shareholders who exercised a retraction right that permitted the shareholders to be paid the redemption price of their shares prior to the bankruptcy were not permitted to claim as creditors in an insolvency.[142] However, a minority shareholder who obtained a money judgment against a corporation as a remedy for the oppressive conduct of other shareholders, directors, or officers was ranked as an ordinary creditor and permitted to share *pro rata* with the other creditors.[143]

The 2009 amendments to the *BIA* have added new provisions that specifically deal with the position of shareholder claims. These claims, defined as "equity claims," are not entitled to a dividend in bankruptcy until all non-equity claims have been fully satisfied.[144] Equity claims include claims for the payment of dividends, return of capital, a redemption or retraction obligation, and a monetary loss resulting from the ownership, purchase, or share of an equity interest or from the rescission of

---

139 *Re Central Capital Corp* (1996), 38 CBR (3d) 1 (Ont CA) [*Central Capital*].

140 *National Bank of Canada v Merit Energy Ltd* (2001), 28 CBR (4th) 228 (Alta QB), aff'd (2002), 96 Alta LR (3d) 1 (CA); *Re Blue Range Resource Corp* (2000), 15 CBR (4th) 169 (Alta QB) [*Blue Range*].

141 See *Re I Waxman & Sons Ltd*, 2008 CarswellOnt 1245 (SCJ) [*Waxman*].

142 *Central Capital*, above note 139.

143 *Waxman*, above note 141.

144 *BIA*, ss 2 "equity claim," and 140.1. And see *Nelson Financial Group Ltd (Re)*, 2010 ONSC 6229.

a purchase or sale of shares. Equity claims retain their postponed status even if the claimant became a judgment creditor before the commencement of the insolvency proceedings.[145] The definition of an equity claim focuses on the nature of the claim rather than the identity of the claimant.[146] Claims by auditors or underwriters against a debtor for contribution and indemnity fall within the definition of equity claims.[147]

4) Equitable Subordination

At one time, the conventional view in Canadian bankruptcy law was that the statutory scheme of distribution could not be altered on equitable or other grounds. If a claim were proven, it was entitled to participate according to the bankruptcy scheme of distribution.[148] Adherence to this principle by the court appears to be less strong than it once was, and the source of uncertainty is due to a bankruptcy principle that emerged in the United States.

Bankruptcy courts in the United States developed a doctrine of equitable subordination through which a court could subordinate a claim of a creditor on equitable grounds. The claim was thereby postponed until all of the ordinary claims were satisfied in full. A three-part test sets out the prerequisites for equitable subordination. The court must be satisfied that: (1) the claimant engaged in some type of inequitable conduct; (2) the misconduct must have caused harm to the creditors or given an unfair advantage to the claimant; and (3) the equitable subordination must not be inconsistent with the express provisions of the bankruptcy statute.[149]

The Supreme Court of Canada in *Canada Deposit Insurance Corp v Canadian Commercial Bank*[150] specifically referred to the doctrine of equitable subordination but declined to rule on its applicability in Canada. Four Canadian decisions have subsequently indicated that the doctrine of equitable subordination should be imported into Canadian

---

145 *Bul River Mineral Corporation (Re)*, 2014 BCSC 1732.

146 *Sino-Forest Corporation (Re)*, 2012 ONCA 816.

147 *Ibid.*

148 *Re Orzy* (1923), 3 CBR 737 (Ont SCAD); *Re Keele-Wilson Supermarkets Ltd* (1990), 78 CBR (NS) 189 (Ont HCJ).

149 *Re Mobile Steel*, 563 F.2d 692 (5th Cir 1977).

150 Above note 134.

bankruptcy law.[151] Some courts have indicated that it should not have application.[152] Others have simply left the matter open.[153]

It is difficult to predict when courts will invoke the doctrine or even if it is applicable at all on the basis of the existing Canadian decisions.[154] The three-part test holds little promise of illuminating matters. The third part of the test would appear to rule out its application completely. Under Canadian bankruptcy legislation, ordinary creditors are given a statutory right to share rateably in the bankrupt estate unless the statute postpones their claims. A judicial subordination of a claim on grounds other than those permitted by the statute would appear to interfere with the bankruptcy scheme of distribution. Furthermore, some courts have questioned whether a requirement of inequitable conduct (the first part of the test) is a necessary precondition for the application of equitable subordination in Canada.[155]

5) Contracting Out of the Statutory Scheme of Distribution

The statutory scheme of distribution mandated by bankruptcy legislation cannot be overridden by contract.[156] This is sometimes referred to as the *pari passu* principle or the fraud on the bankruptcy law principle.[157] Both of these monikers are slightly misleading. The principle protects the entire statutory scheme of distribution and not simply the *pari passu* sharing amongst unsecured creditors, and intentional misconduct is not required to be proven. The principle is not engaged when the contract gives the creditor a security interest in an asset. The

151 *Re Christian Brothers of Ireland in Canada* (2004), 49 CBR (4th) 12 (Ont SCJ); *General Chemical Canada Ltd* (2006), 22 CBR (5th) 298 (Ont SCJ); *Blue Range*, above note 140; *Oppenheim v JJ Lacey Insurance Limited*, 2009 NLTD 148.

152 *AEVO Co v D & A MacLeod Co* (1991), 7 CBR (3d) 33 (Ont Ct Gen Div); *Pioneer Distributors Ltd v Bank of Montreal* (1994), 28 CBR (3d) 266 (BCSC).

153 *Olympia & York Developments Ltd v Royal Trust Co* (1993), 19 CBR (3d) 1 (Ont CA); *Unisource Canada Inc v Hongkong Bank of Canada* (1998), 43 BLR (2d) 226 (Ont Ct Gen Div).

154 See T Telfer, "Transplanting Equitable Subordination: The New Free-Wheeling Equitable Discretion in Canadian Law?" (2001) 36 *Canadian Business Law Journal* 36.

155 *Blue Range*, above note 140. But see *Waxman*, above note 141, which upheld the requirement of inequitable conduct.

156 *British Eagle International Air Lines Ltd v Compagnie Nationale Air France*, [1975] 1 WLR 758 [*British Eagle*].

157 See R Wood, "Direct Payment Clauses and the Fraud upon the Bankruptcy Law Principle: *Re Horizon Earthworks Ltd (Bankrupt)*" (2014) 52 *Alberta Law Review* 171.

principle has been applied in respect of direct payment clauses in construction contracts and to contractual rights of set off.[158] The clause is contained in a contract between the owner and the general contractor, and it permits the owner to pay the subcontractors amounts that would otherwise be payable to the general contractor upon a bankruptcy or insolvency of the contractor. These provisions are ineffective in a bankruptcy as it is not lawful for the parties to contractually stipulate a scheme of distribution under which they are entitled to a greater share. It is, however, open for a party to contractually subordinate or postpone their claim.[159]

6) Allocation of Payments

A bankrupt may owe two obligations to a creditor, one of which is a preferred claim and one of which is an ordinary claim. For example, a landlord may be owed rent, which qualifies as a preferred claim, as well as another debt that is not rent. If the bankrupt has made payments to the creditor prior to the bankruptcy, it may be necessary to determine which of the pre-bankruptcy payments were directed towards the preferred claim and which were directed towards the ordinary claim. In other instances, one of the obligations owed to the creditor may be an ordinary claim while the other obligation may be a postponed claim. Here, as well, it may be necessary to determine the allocation of pre-bankruptcy payments.

The allocation of payments may also be significant in respect of preferred claims that are subject to a time limitation. For example, claims for arrears of family support are preferred to the extent that the arrears did not accrue more than one year prior to the date of the bankruptcy. Because of this time limitation, the amount of the preferred claim is affected by the manner in which payments are allocated prior to the bankruptcy. If payments are allocated first towards arrears and then towards current amounts due, the preferred status of the claim will be preserved. If the payments are allocated first to the most recent obligations and then to arrears, the outstanding claim will pertain to arrears. If the arrears are for periodic payments that accrued more than

158 *AN Bail v Gingras*, [1982] 2 SCR 475; *Horizon Earthworks Ltd (Re)*, 2011 ABQB 799; *British Eagle*, above note 156.

159 *In re Maxwell Communications Corporation Plc*, [1993] 1 WLR 1402 (Ch); *Re Air Canada* (2004), 2 CBR (5th) 4 (Ont SCJ).

a year before the date of the bankruptcy, a preferred claim will not be available.[160]

Bankruptcy law does not provide any special rules for the allocation of payments. The issue must therefore be resolved by applying non-bankruptcy principles. The common law rule for allocation of payments gives the payor the choice as to allocation in the absence of an agreement as to the appropriation of payments. If the payor does not make an allocation at the time of the payment, the payee is given the right to allocate the payment.[161] The allocation does not need to be express but may be implied from the conduct of the parties.[162] If neither party has made an allocation of the payment, the courts will allocate the payment towards the earlier debt.[163]

Sometimes the rules governing allocation of payments are modified by statute in specific situations. For example, most Canadian provinces have adopted a different allocation of payments rule in respect of family support payments that are enforced by government officials. These statutes provide that payments are allocated first to the current amounts due and thereafter to arrears.[164] In some provinces, the statutory allocation of payments rule can be varied by an agreement between the parties.[165] This will diminish the amount of the preferred claim if there are support payments that accrued prior to the one-year period before the bankruptcy.

7) Distribution of Surplus

In the rare but happy event that there is a surplus, the debtor is entitled to receive payment of it.[166] If there is a surplus, the rule that payment of interest stops on bankruptcy[167] does not apply, and the claimants are

---

160 Alternatively, the debtor may owe obligations that relate both to the division of property and to the payment of support. Here, too, the allocation of payments can be significant. If payments are allocated to the matrimonial property division, a preferred claim in respect of family support is preserved.

161 *Barrett-Lennard v Hood Point Estates Ltd* (1952), 5 WWR (NS) 24 (BCCA).

162 *Cory Bros & Co Ltd v "The Mecca,"* [1897] AC 286 (HL).

163 *Polish Combatants' Assn Credit Union Ltd v Machnio* (1984), 9 DLR (4th) 60 (Man CA).

164 See, for example, *Maintenance Enforcement Act*, RSA 2000, c M-1, s 36(2).

165 See, for example, *Enforcement of Maintenance Orders Act, 1997*, SS 1997, c E-9.21, s 58.

166 *BIA*, s 144.

167 See Section A(4), above in this chapter.

entitled to recover interest before the surplus is paid to the debtor.[168] However, they cannot recover out of the surplus the superintendent's levy, which is deducted from their claim by the trustee.[169]

C. PAYMENT OF DIVIDENDS

After retaining sufficient funds to cover the costs of administration of the bankrupt estate, the trustee is required to pay the claims of the preferred creditors as soon as funds are available.[170] If there are insufficient funds to pay them all, they are paid in order of their priority. The residue, if any, forms the fund out of which dividends are paid to ordinary creditors. The trustee may declare interim dividends if directed to do so by the inspectors.[171] If a claim is being disputed, the trustee should withhold sufficient funds to pay it in the event that it is admitted.[172] A creditor may prove a claim after an interim dividend has been made but before payment of a final dividend. The late-filing creditor is entitled to receive payment of the missed dividend before the other creditors are entitled to any further dividends.[173]

If the trustee knows of a creditor who has not proved a claim, the trustee may notify that creditor that a final dividend will be made without regard to their claim unless they prove it within thirty days of the sending of the notice.[174] If they do not do so within the thirty-day period or such other period ordered by a court, they are excluded from sharing in the final dividend.[175]

Once the bankrupt estate is fully administered, the trustee can declare a final dividend. The trustee must prepare a final statement of receipts and disbursements and a dividend sheet and divide the remaining property among the creditors who proved their claims.[176] These must be submitted to the inspectors for approval and a copy must

---

168 *Canada (Attorney General) v Confederation Trust Co* (2003), 44 CBR (4th) 198 (Ont SCJ).

169 *Re Cameron* (2002), 32 CBR (4th) 176 (Alta QB).

170 *BIA*, s 136(2).

171 *Ibid*, s 148(1). If a trustee disagrees with a direction to declare dividends, the trustee may apply to court under s 119(2) to overrule the decision of the inspectors. A court may also order a trustee to pay a dividend if the trustee fails to pay it after being directed to do so by the inspectors. See *BIA*, s 148(3).

172 *Ibid*, s 148(2).

173 *Ibid*, s 150.

174 *Ibid*, s 149(1).

175 *Ibid*, s 149(2).

176 *Ibid*, s 151.

be sent to the Superintendent of Bankruptcy, who may comment on the trustee's account.[177] The taxing officer then reviews the trustee's accounts. Following the taxation of the account, the trustee sends a copy of the documents to the bankrupt, the superintendent, and creditors whose claims have been proved.[178] A creditor who wishes to object to the statement of receipts and disbursement or to the proposed dividend must file notice of the objection with the registrar within fifteen days of the sending of the notice.[179] If a creditor does not claim a dividend or if there are undistributed funds, the trustee is required to forward them to the superintendent.[180]

D. PAYMENT OF EMPLOYEE CLAIMS

The most recent amendments to the *BIA* have significantly enhanced the treatment of employee claims in a bankruptcy of the employer. Prior to the amendments, the employees were given the status of a preferred creditor in respect of their unpaid wages. A creditor who had been given a security interest in the assets of the employer was afforded a higher-ranking claim. This often meant that the employees recovered little or nothing in the bankruptcy.[181] Although employment standards legislation in some provinces gave claims of employees priority over a prior secured creditor, these provincial statutes were rendered inoperative in a bankruptcy.[182]

This was recognized as a problem in Canada for many years, but the federal government was unable to arrive at a politically acceptable solution to it. A proposal for a simple superpriority for the claims of secured creditors and another for an insurance scheme funded out of payroll deductions were both withdrawn after receiving a hostile reception from parties negatively affected by the proposals.[183]

---

177 *Ibid*, ss 152(2)–(4).

178 *Ibid*, s 152(5).

179 *Ibid*, s 152(6).

180 *Ibid*, s 154. The Office of the Superintendent in Bankruptcy maintains an unclaimed dividends search system on its website. There are currently over $18 million dollars in unclaimed dividends.

181 The government estimated that between 10,000 to 15,000 workers annually had unpaid wage claims when employers went bankrupt. The majority of these workers (79 percent) received no payment at all and in total only 13 cents on the dollar was recovered in respect of wage claims.

182 See Chapter 5, Section B(6).

183 See Senate Standing Committee on Banking, Trade and Commerce, *Debtors and Creditors: Sharing the Burden: A Review of the Bankruptcy and Insolvency Act and*

Ultimately, a hybrid of these two approaches was chosen. The insurance portion of the scheme is implemented in the *Wage Earner Protection Program Act*.[184] The *WEPPA* provides a program for payment to individuals in respect of wages that are owed to them by employers who are bankrupt or in receivership. The claim is limited to a maximum of $3,000 or an amount that is four times the maximum weekly insurable earnings under the *Employment Insurance Act*, whichever is greater.[185] The funding of the program is from the general revenues of the federal government. However, the federal Crown becomes subrogated to any right that the employee has against the employer or against a director and can sue in either the name of the federal Crown or the name of the individual on payment of the amount to the employee.[186] An unpaid employee is given a secured charge on the current assets of the employer to the maximum of $2,000.[187] This charge has priority over the claim of a secured creditor. As a result, the burden of the program is shared partly by the secured creditor and partly by the federal government.

The program covers claims for wages, which includes salaries, commissions, compensation for services rendered, and vacation pay but not severance or termination pay.[188] The wages that are owed must have been earned during the six months before the date of the bankruptcy.[189] An individual is ineligible to receive a payment in respect of wages earned during a period in which the individual was an officer or director of the employer, had a controlling interest in the employer, occupied a managerial position with the employer, or was not dealing at arm's length with a person acting in any of those capacities.[190] The *WEPPA* sets out procedures for the review and appeal of determinations of eligibility for payment.[191]

A trustee is under a statutory obligation to identify each individual who is owed wages by a bankrupt or insolvent employer earned during the six-month period immediately before the bankruptcy, to determine

---

the Companies' Creditors Arrangement Act by Richard H. Kroft & David Tkachuk (Ottawa: Standing Senate Committee on Banking, Trade and Commerce, 2003) at 87–91 for a brief history of wage-protection proposals.

184 Above note 104.

185 *Ibid*, s 7(2).

186 *Ibid*, s 36.

187 *BIA*, s 81.3. And see Chapter 5, Section D.

188 *WEPPA*, above note 104, s 2(1) "wages."

189 *Ibid*, ss 5 and 7.

190 *Ibid*, s 6. The Act contemplates that the regulations will set out the criteria for determining if a person has a controlling interest in the business or if a person occupies a managerial position.

191 *Ibid*, ss 11–20.

the amount owing to them, and to inform them of the program and the conditions for eligibility.[192] The trustee or receiver is entitled to charge reasonable fees and disbursements for the performance of the duties, which are paid out of the bankrupt estate.[193]

E. BANKRUPTCY OF SECURITIES FIRMS

In the past, bankruptcies of securities firms usually led to protracted litigation as each investor sought to argue that the value of their property was traceable into the assets of the securities firm. This difficulty was further compounded by the rise of the system of indirect securities holdings. Most investors are not registered holders of the securities they purchase. Instead, they rely upon the fact that they are reflected as having an entitlement to the security in the records of the securities firm. In this environment, tracing becomes extraordinarily difficult, if not impossible. The *BIA* was amended in 1997 by the addition of special rules relating to the bankruptcy of securities firms.

On the bankruptcy of a securities firm, the assets are placed into three categories: (1) customer name securities; (2) the customer pool fund; and (3) the general fund. Customer name securities are those that are held on behalf of the customer and registered or recorded in the name of the customer.[194] The fact that the securities firm may have internally allocated some of the securities to certain customers is not sufficient to make them customer name securities.[195] These assets belong to the customers and therefore do not vest in the trustee.[196] The customer is entitled to delivery of the security, but the trustee may sell sufficient securities to discharge an obligation owed by the customer to the securities firm if the customer fails to pay it.[197]

Cash and securities, other than customer name securities, are used to establish a customer pool fund.[198] The customer pool fund is distributed first towards the costs of administration if these cannot be satisfied out of the general fund.[199] The balance is then distributed to

---

192 *Ibid*, s 21.

193 *Ibid*, s 22.

194 *BIA*, s 253 "customer name securities."

195 *Ashley v Marlow Group Private Portfolio Management Inc* (2006), 22 CBR (5th) 126 (Ont SCJ).

196 *BIA*, s 261(1).

197 *Ibid*, s 263.

198 *Ibid*, s 261(2)(a).

199 *Ibid*, s 262(1).

the customers in proportion to their net equity. If there is anything remaining, it is paid to the general fund.

All of the remaining property is used to form the general fund.[200] The general fund is distributed first to satisfy the claims of preferred creditors. Once these claims are satisfied, any remaining funds are distributed rateably to the eligible claimants.[201] The claimants who are entitled to participate include the customers to the extent of any deficiency claims after payment received from the customer pool fund, the claim of any customer compensation body that has paid or compensated customers, and ordinary creditors of the firm. Creditors who have entered into non–arm's length transactions that are not found to be proper transactions are postponed. The trustee or a customer compensation body may seek to have a claimant classified as a deferred customer on the basis that the conduct of the customer caused or materially contributed to the insolvency of the securities firm. If such a ruling is made, the claim is postponed until all other claims are paid in full.[202]

F. BANKRUPTCY OF PARTNERSHIPS

Although partners are personally liable for debts and obligations that are incurred by other partners in connection with the business of the firm, a distinction is drawn between the separate property of a partner and the joint property of the partnership and between the separate debts of a partner and the joint debts of the partnership. If all the partners are bankrupt, the distribution of the joint estate is kept separate from the distribution of the separate estates of the partners.[203] The joint property of the partnership is distributed first towards payment of the partnership debts. Once these are paid in full, the surplus is paid towards the separate debts of a partner. The separate property of a partner is distributed first towards payment of the separate debts of the partner. Once these are paid in full, any surplus is paid towards the joint debts of the partnership. If both joint and separate properties are administered, the dividends can be declared together and the trustee can apportion the expenses between the two estates.[204] If there is no

200 *Ibid*, s 261(2)(b).

201 *Ibid*, s 262(3).

202 *Ibid*, ss 253 "deferred customer" and 258.

203 *Ibid*, s 142.

204 *Ibid*, s 153.

joint property of the partnership, these rules do not apply and the joint creditor ranks *pari passu* with the separate creditors.[205] The anomalous feature of this rule is that any joint estate, regardless of how small, will postpone the claims of the joint creditors to those of the separate creditors in the bankruptcy of an individual partner.[206]

A creditor may be owed two separate obligations under distinct contracts: one owed personally by the individual and one owed jointly by the partners. The common law rule was that the creditor had to elect to prove either as a creditor of the separate property of the partner or as a creditor of the joint property of the partnership, and could not lodge a proof of claim in both bankrupt estates.[207] This rule has been abrogated by statute. A creditor can now prove a claim in both estates if both the individual and the partnership have incurred distinct obligations.[208]

FURTHER READINGS

ANAND, A. "Should Shareholders Rank with Unsecured Creditors in Bankruptcy?" (2008) 24 *Banking and Finance Law Review* 169

BAIRD, D, & R DAVIS. "Labour Issues" in S Ben-Ishai & A Duggan, eds, *Canadian Bankruptcy and Insolvency Law: Bill C-55, Statute c. 47 and Beyond* (Markham, ON: LexisNexis Canada, 2007) ch 4

BÉLIVEAU, L, & G MICHAUD. "Insolvency and Environmental Law following the *AbitibiBowater* Case: Still a Murky Intersection" (2013) 2 *Journal of the Insolvency Institute of Canada* 247

BOMHOF, S. "Case Comment: *Ontario New Home Warranty Program v Jiordan Homes Ltd.*" (1999) 10 *Canadian Bankruptcy Reports* (4th) 5

GOODE, R. *Legal Problems of Credit and Security*, 3d ed (London: Sweet & Maxwell, 2003) ch 8

KLOTZ, R. *Bankruptcy, Insolvency and Family Law*, 2d ed (Scarborough, ON: Carswell, 2001) (loose-leaf), ch 2

SARRA, J. "From Subordination to Parity: An International Comparison of Equity Securities Claims in Insolvency Proceedings" (2007) 16 *International Insolvency Review* 181

---

205 *Re Budgett*, [1894] 2 Ch 557.

206 *Ex p Kennedy; In re Entwistle* (1852), 42 ER 859.

207 *Ex parte Honey, In re Jeffrey* (1871), LR 7 Ch 178.

208 *BIA*, s 123.

TELFER, T. "Transplanting Equitable Subordination: The New Free-Wheeling Equitable Discretion in Canadian Law?" (2001) 36 *Canadian Business Law Journal* 36

WOOD, R. "Direct Payment Clauses and the Fraud upon the Bankruptcy Law Principle: *Re Horizon Earthworks Ltd. (Bankrupt)*" (2014) 52 *Alberta Law Review* 171

CHAPTER 10

DISCHARGE OF THE BANKRUPT

For many individuals, the prospect of a bankruptcy discharge is the light at the end of the tunnel. Through discharge, a debtor is given a fresh start and is freed from the burdens of pre-existing indebtedness. However, the right to obtain a discharge is not absolute. A discharge may be made conditional, suspended, or denied completely in appropriate cases. Furthermore, not all debts are released on discharge, and the debtor may find that discharge has rejuvenated debts that otherwise would have been released. Discharge on bankruptcy remains a controversial subject, as is attested by the frequent shifts in bankruptcy policy that attempt to find the appropriate balance between the objective of economic rehabilitation of the debtor and that of maintaining public confidence in the credit system.

A. THE POLICY BEHIND DISCHARGE

The bankruptcy discharge is one of the primary mechanisms through which bankruptcy law attempts to provide for the economic rehabilitation of the debtor. However, it is not the only means by which bankruptcy law seeks to meet this objective. The exclusion of exempt property from distribution to creditors, the surplus income provisions, and mandatory credit counselling also are directed towards this goal. The goal of debtor rehabilitation applies only to natural persons and not to artificial entities, and for this reason a corporation cannot obtain a discharge unless it has satisfied the claims of its creditors in full.[1]

The "honest but unfortunate debtor" occupies a station in bankruptcy law akin to that of the "reasonable person" in negligence law. The phrase is used again and again throughout the Canadian caselaw, as well as that of the United States.[2] In the case of the individual, the purpose of the bankruptcy discharge is to permit the honest but unfortunate debtor to reintegrate into the business life of the country as a useful citizen free from the crushing burden of his or her debts.[3] This marks a change from earlier attitudes towards bankruptcy that viewed all debtors as dishonest and that did not care to draw distinctions among reasons for financial distress.[4]

Debtor rehabilitation was not the original objective of the bankruptcy discharge when it was first enacted in 1705. Its purpose was to provide an incentive to cooperate, and it operated in tandem with the death penalty as a disincentive for non-cooperative behaviour. The use of the discharge as a reward for cooperative conduct still exists in modern bankruptcy law. A bankrupt who fails to cooperate with the trustee or to comply with the duties of a bankrupt may result in the suspension[5] or refusal[6] of a discharge. Although the prospect of a bankruptcy discharge continues to be used for the purpose of inducing cooperation, it is no longer viewed as its primary purpose.

The Supreme Court of Canada in several of its decisions has expressly recognized that the economic rehabilitation of the debtor is one of the central objectives of bankruptcy law.[7] This objective proceeds from the idea that a debtor who has acquired an unserviceable debt load is in a hopeless situation. Lacking any real prospect that the debts can ever be repaid, a debtor will become discouraged and will cease to participate in the economic life of society. The concern is not only with the well-being of the individual. There is recognition that unserviceable debt imposes hardship on the debtor's family and also on society

---

1 *BIA*, s 169(4).

2 See, for example, *Local Loan Co v Hunt*, 292 US 234 (1934).

3 See *Holy Rosary Parish (Thorold) Credit Union Ltd v Premier Trust Co* (1965), 7 CBR (NS) 169 (SCC).

4 Chapter 2, Section A(1).

5 *Re Jefferson* (2004), 1 CBR (5th) 209 (BCSC).

6 *Re Rahall* (1997), 49 CBR (3d) 268 (Alta QB); *Mancini (Trustees of) v Mancini* (1987), 63 CBR (NS) 254 (Ont HCJ) [*Mancini*].

7 See *Industrial Acceptance Corp v Lalonde*, [1952] 2 SCR 109; *Vachon v Canada (Employment & Immigration Commission)*, [1985] 2 SCR 417.

at large. A debtor who is given a fresh start through the release of past debts can once more become a productive member of society.

The honest but unfortunate debtor was originally idealized as an individual who suffered financial setbacks due to events beyond his control. In earlier times, one contemplated the merchant whose ship was lost in a storm or through enemy action during wartime. Honesty alone was not enough. The loss had to result from misfortune, and the misfortune had to result from external events. There has been a marked shift in the meaning of the phrase in modern times. Certainly there are many instances where the financial loss results from external factors over which the debtor has no control, such as sickness or loss of employment. However, the notion of the honest but unfortunate debtor now encompasses individuals whose financial distress is attributable to poor financial management as well. This shift in meaning occurred during a time of unparalleled growth in the consumer credit market during the twentieth century, and coincided with a steep increase in the number of consumer bankruptcies.

The easy availability of consumer credit has made it much easier for debtors to get themselves into a financial crisis. Some scholars have argued that the principal motivation for a bankruptcy discharge should be recognized as the protection of a debtor from ill-considered borrowing decisions.[8] On this view, a bankruptcy discharge operates as a kind of insurance against losses caused by debtors who fail to properly assess the risks associated with the over-consumption of consumer credit.[9]

Although debtors who have made poor financial decisions can nevertheless obtain the benefits of a bankruptcy discharge, the same does not hold true for a debtor who is guilty of dishonest conduct.[10] Furthermore, it is not only intentional dishonesty that can result in the denial of an absolute discharge. The *BIA* establishes certain standards of commercial morality that must be maintained. If the bankruptcy is brought on by rash and hazardous speculations, by unjustifiable extravagance in living, by gambling, or by culpable neglect, a bankruptcy court is directed to refuse, suspend, or make conditional any order of

8 T Jackson, *The Logic and Limits of Bankruptcy Law* (Cambridge, MA: Harvard University Press, 1986) at 232–41.

9 See D Baird, "Discharge, Waiver and the Behavioral Undercurrents of Debtor Creditor Law" (2006) 73 *University of Chicago Law Review* 17.

10 *Bank of Montreal v Giannotti* (2000), 51 OR (3d) 544 (CA).

discharge.[11] A failure to keep proper books and records also prevents the court from granting the debtor an absolute discharge.[12]

B. PROCEDURE FOR DISCHARGE

The procedure that governs the granting of bankruptcy discharges is divided into four streams. The first stream is available to first-time bankrupts and will result in an automatic discharge unless an interested party actively takes steps to object to it. The second stream applies to debtors who have been bankrupt once before. It shares a similar structure to the first, except that longer time periods are imposed before the debtor obtains an automatic discharge. The third stream applies to debtors who have previously been bankrupt more than twice as well as to first-time and second-time bankrupts who do not obtain an automatic discharge because a valid notice of opposition to the discharge has been given. No automatic discharge is available. Instead, a bankruptcy court hears the matter and determines the terms of discharge of the bankrupt. The fourth stream applies to debtors who owe substantial amounts of income tax indebtedness.

1) The Trustee's Report

In order to make an assessment on whether to object to a discharge, interested parties must have sufficient information about the circumstances of the bankruptcy. The report of the trustee partly fulfils this function. The report sets out the causes of the bankruptcy and the conduct of the debtor, and describes any circumstances that would justify the court in refusing an unconditional order of discharge.[13] It is accompanied by a resolution of the inspectors declaring whether or not they approve or disapprove of the report. The trustee must send a copy of the report to the Superintendent of Bankruptcy, to the bankrupt, and to creditors who request it.[14]

---

11 *BIA*, ss 173(1)(e) and 172(2).

12 *Ibid*, s 173(1)(b).

13 *Ibid*, s 170(1).

14 *Ibid*, s 170(2).

2) Automatic Discharge

The automatic discharge provisions were designed to cut down on the number of discharge applications that came before bankruptcy courts.[15] If the debtor is a first-time bankrupt and no surplus income payments have been required,[16] the debtor is given the benefit of a procedure that will, in most cases, result in an automatic discharge without the need for a court order.[17] The automatic discharge comes into effect nine months after the date of bankruptcy if it is not opposed.[18] If surplus income payments have been required in respect of a first-time bankrupt, there is an automatic discharge after twenty-one months unless an opposition to the discharge has been filed.

If the debtor was bankrupt one time before under the laws of Canada or any prescribed jurisdiction, a longer time period comes into effect.[19] In the absence of any opposition, the automatic discharge comes into effect twenty-four months after the date of bankruptcy. If the debtor has been required to make surplus income payments, the automatic discharge comes into effect after thirty-six months.

The trustee must give the superintendent, the bankrupt, and the creditors a notice of an impending discharge at least fifteen days before an automatic discharge comes into effect.[20] The superintendent, a creditor, or the trustee can oppose the discharge by giving notice of the intended opposition to the discharge. The notice must set out the grounds for opposition and must be given to the other parties.[21] If

---

15 *Re Snow* (2001), 27 CBR (4th) 157 (Alta QB). The automatic discharge provisions were first added to the *BIA* in 1992. The 2009 amendments to the *BIA* added a means test that extended the period where the debtor was required to make surplus income payments, and also added rules covering the automatic discharge of second-time bankrupts.

16 See Chapter 4, Section D(2).

17 *BIA*, s 168.1(1).

18 The running of the nine-month period is suspended if there is an appeal from the making of a bankruptcy order. See *Re Lee* (2001), 24 CBR (4th) 209 (BCSC).

19 *BIA*, s 168.1(1)(b).

20 *Ibid*, s 168.1(4). An inadvertent failure by the trustee to send these notices to the creditors can result in the setting aside of the automatic discharge if the creditors can establish that the debtor would not suffer prejudice and that a court would have arrived at an appreciably different result. See *Re Cameron* (1995), 36 CBR (3d) 272 (Ont Ct Gen Div).

21 *BIA*, s 168.2(1). A failure by a creditor to notify the bankrupt invalidates the opposition, with the result that the debtor will obtain an automatic discharge. See *Haywood Securities Ltd v Witwicki* (1995), 32 CBR (3d) 103 (BCCA). See also *Re Murray* (1995), 35 CBR (3d) 264 (NBQB), which holds that, if the trustee is notified in time but the debtor is not, there is no automatic discharge. The trustee

there is opposition to the automatic discharge, the trustee must apply to court for a hearing, unless the matter goes to mediation.[22] If no opposition is made, the debtor obtains a discharge automatically upon the expiration of the relevant time period, and the trustee will issue a certificate of discharge to the debtor.[23] The discharge is absolute and takes effect immediately.[24] The automatic bankruptcy provisions do not preclude a debtor from applying to court for discharge before the expiration of the time period for automatic discharge.[25]

3) Compulsory Mediation

If the discharge of a bankrupt is opposed by a creditor or by the trustee solely on the ground that the debtor failed to comply with a requirement to pay surplus income to the trustee or that the debtor could have made a viable proposal but instead chose bankruptcy, the trustee is required to apply for mediation to the official receiver.[26] If the mediation does not resolve the disagreement, the trustee must apply to court for a discharge hearing.[27]

4) Application to Court for Discharge

If there has been a valid opposition to an automatic discharge or if the debtor has previously been bankrupt more than twice, discharge can be granted only by a bankruptcy court. The bankruptcy order or assignment operates as an application by the debtor for a discharge.[28] The trustee must apply to court for a discharge hearing no sooner than three months and no later than one year after the bankruptcy.[29] The trustee must give notice at least fifteen days before the day appointed

---

must make an appointment for a hearing at which time the question of notification can be raised.

22 *BIA*, s 168.2(2). The hearing must be within thirty days from the day the appointment for a hearing is made unless the court fixes a later time.

23 *Ibid*, s 168.1(6).

24 *Ibid*, s 168.1(5). The creditors cannot oppose the automatic discharge after the relevant time period has expired. See *Turcotte v Jensen* (1998), 9 CBR (4th) 312 (Alta QB).

25 *BIA*, s 168.1(2).

26 *Ibid*, s 170.1(1). The application for mediation must be sent within five days after the day that the debtor would otherwise have obtained an automatic discharge.

27 *Ibid*, s 170.1(3).

28 *Ibid*, s 169(1). The debtor can waive the application by filing a written notice of waiver of application.

29 *Ibid*, s 169(2).

for the hearing to the superintendent, the debtor, and creditors who have proved their claims.[30]

C. THE COURT'S POWER TO GRANT OR REFUSE DISCHARGE

On a hearing of an application for a discharge, a bankruptcy court is given the power to make the following orders:[31]

- grant an absolute discharge;
- grant a conditional discharge;
- suspend the operation of the order for a specified time; and
- refuse a discharge.

The conditions attached to a conditional order must relate to the debtor's post-discharge earnings or income or after-acquired property. A conditional order can be also subject to a suspension.[32]

A court cannot make an absolute discharge if there has been proof of any of the following facts:[33]

- the debtor's assets are not of a value equal to fifty cents on the dollar unless this has arisen from circumstances for which the debtor cannot justly be held responsible;[34]
- the debtor has failed to kept proper business books and records;[35]
- the debtor continued to trade after becoming aware of being insolvent;[36]
- the debtor has failed to account satisfactorily for any loss of assets;
- the debtor contributed to the bankruptcy by rash and hazardous speculations, by unjustifiable extravagance in living, by gambling, or by culpable neglect of the bankrupt's business affairs;
- the debtor put creditors to unnecessary expense by frivolous or vexatious defence;

30 *Ibid*, s 169(6).

31 *Ibid*, s 172(1).

32 *Ibid*, s 172(4).

33 *Ibid*, ss 172(2) and 173.

34 In calculating the value of the debtor's assets, the court must use the value of the property when properly realized. See *BIA*, s 174.

35 This does not apply to a person whose principal occupation and means of livelihood on the date of the initial bankruptcy event was farming. See *BIA*, s 173(2).

36 This also does not apply to farmers. See *ibid*.

- the debtor brought a frivolous or vexatious action;[37]
- the debtor made an undue preference to a creditor when unable to pay debts as they became due;[38]
- the debtor incurred liabilities in order to make the bankrupt's assets equal to fifty cents on the dollar;[39]
- the debtor was previously bankrupt or made a proposal to creditors;
- the debtor has been guilty of any fraud or fraudulent breach of trust;
- the debtor committed a bankruptcy offence;
- the debtor failed to comply with an order to pay surplus income;
- the debtor could have made a viable proposal to creditors but chose bankruptcy; or
- the debtor failed to perform the duties imposed on the bankrupt under the *BIA* or pursuant to a court order.

Upon proof of any of these facts, the court may refuse the discharge, suspend it, or make an order for a conditional discharge. Although a court may make an order for a conditional discharge even if one of these facts is not proven,[40] there is less latitude given to the kinds of orders that can be made. In such cases, the condition must relate to post-bankruptcy earnings or income or after-acquired property. The power given to a court to make a conditional order for discharge is wider when one of the listed facts is proven. The court may in addition require the debtor to perform such acts, consent to such judgments, or comply with such other terms as the court may direct.[41]

---

37 The action must have been brought within the period beginning three months before the date of the initial bankruptcy event and ending on the date of the bankruptcy. See *BIA*, s 173(1)(g).

38 The preference must have been given within the period beginning three months before the date of the initial bankruptcy event and ending on the date of the bankruptcy. See *BIA*, s 173(1)(h).

39 The liabilities must have been incurred within the period beginning three months before the date of the initial bankruptcy event and ending on the date of the bankruptcy. See *BIA*, s 173(1)(j).

40 *Re Henderson* (1992), 24 CBR (3d) 245 (Ont Ct Gen Div).

41 *BIA*, s 172(2)(c).

D. THE NATURE AND CHARACTERISTICS OF THE ORDERS

1) Absolute Discharge

An absolute discharge is effective on the date that it is made. However, its effect is suspended until the expiration of the time period for appeals or, if an appeal is entered, until the appeal has been finally disposed of.[42] This has the effect of maintaining the status quo until any appeal is determined.[43]

2) Conditional Discharge

Several different types of conditions may be attached to a discharge order. The court may make it a condition of the order that a certain sum of money must be paid to the trustee. Often this order also specifies the time period within which these payments must be made, as in the case of an order for payment of $75,000 over a period of three years from the date of the order.[44] The order can provide for periodic payments or establish minimum monthly payments.[45] The order can also make the discharge conditional upon the performance of some act, such as consent to a judgment,[46] making an assignment of an interest in a legacy or bequest,[47] or cooperating with the trustee in pursuing litigation.[48] The condition must be certain and capable of ascertainment: an order for payment of a certain amount after which the matter is to be reviewed is not permissible.[49] The order must provide for payment of the funds to the trustee.[50] The court cannot order that the debtor or the trustee make the payment to a specified creditor since this would undermine the scheme of distribution set out in the *BIA*.[51]

---

42 *Ibid*, s 182(1).

43 *Canada (Attorney General) v Moss* (2001), 29 CBR (4th) 37 (Man CA).

44 See, for example, *Nelson v Nelson* (1995), 33 CBR (3d) 292 (Sask QB).

45 See, for example, *Re Varma* (1995), 30 CBR (3d) 263 (Man QB).

46 See, for example, *Re Fingold* (1991), 3 CBR (3d) 241 (Ont Ct Gen Div).

47 See, for example, *Re Rosenblatt* (1982), 45 CBR (NS) 170 (BCSC). Although such rights may vest automatically in the trustee as contingent future property, the assignment by the debtor of the right may assist the trustee in the administration of the estate.

48 *Re Wyssling* (1989), 75 CBR (NS) 296 (Ont HCJ).

49 *Patterson v Royal Bank of Canada* (1984), 57 CBR (NS) 6 (BCCA).

50 *BIA*, s 176(3).

51 *Re Milad* (1984), 50 CBR (NS) 113 (Ont CA); *Re Palmer* (1989), 79 CBR (NS) 52 (Sask QB).

The discharge is effective on the date that the term or condition is satisfied.[52] If the condition is for the payment of money, then this occurs when the money is paid to the trustee. If the debtor acquires non-exempt property after the bankruptcy but before the condition is satisfied, it vests in the trustee and is divisible among the creditors even if it exceeds the amount that was required to be paid by the conditional discharge.[53]

If the condition is that the debtor consents to a judgment in favour of the trustee, the condition is satisfied when the consent to judgment is given rather than when the judgment is satisfied. However, the trustee is able to enforce the judgment against the assets of the debtor following the discharge of the bankrupt. The court may also annul the discharge or rescind the order of discharge for failure to satisfy the consent judgment.[54]

The court may modify the terms of the order or of any substituted order if, after one year from the date of the order, the debtor satisfies the court that there is no reasonable probability that the debtor will be in a position to comply with its terms.[55] Courts have looked to the following four factors when deciding whether to modify the terms of an order:[56]

- changes in circumstances that have occurred since the order was made, and whether they were within the debtor's control;
- evidence that the debtor is unable to comply with the order;
- the credibility of the debtor, which will typically require the debtor to be present at the hearing; and
- evidence that the debtor has made efforts to comply with the terms of the order.

3) Suspension of Discharge

A court may suspend the operation of an order for discharge for a specified period of time. The discharge takes effect once the period of time has elapsed. An order that suspends discharge is often made when one of the listed facts has been proven, but this is not a requirement for suspension of the order.[57] In general, a conditional discharge is preferred

52 *Re Gray* (1988), 67 CBR (NS) 161 (Ont HCJ).

53 *Re Harrison* (1996), 39 CBR (3d) 304 (Man QB).

54 *Re Benigno* (1999), 14 CBR (4th) 173 (NSSC).

55 *BIA*, s 172(3).

56 *Re Whyte* (1980), 35 CBR (NS) 194 (Ont HCJ); *Re Estrin* (2005), 10 CBR (5th) 176 (Alta QB).

57 *Re Babiy* (1991), 3 CBR (3d) 8 (Sask QB).

where there is a real prospect that the debtor will have the assets available to satisfy the condition. However, where this is not the case, the court may wish to show its disapproval of the debtor's misconduct by suspending the order for a period of time.[58]

Often an order is suspended where the debtor is bankrupt for the second time, and the issue that arises in these cases concerns the appropriate length of the suspension. This question was considered in *Re Walterhouse*.[59] The court held that extremely long suspension periods (such as those between ten and twenty-five years) are akin to a refusal of a discharge. Refusal may be appropriate where there is no chance of rehabilitation of the debtor, where it is likely that the debtor will abuse the process again, or in the case of three-time bankrupts. However, if some residual prospect of rehabilitation exists, the suspension should not exceed five years. A suspension of a discharge can also be used where one of the enumerated facts has been proven but the breach is of a minor or technical character and the debtor is not guilty of misconduct. Under these circumstances, courts have suspended the discharge for short periods, such as for one month.[60]

4) Refusal of Discharge

A refusal of a discharge is the most severe order that can be imposed on the debtor at a discharge hearing. The effect of the refusal is that the debtor remains in bankruptcy. This means that the duties and disabilities that are imposed on a bankrupt continue to apply into the indefinite future. As well, future assets of the debtor will continue to be available to satisfy the claims of creditors either as surplus income to be paid to the trustee or as after-acquired property that automatically vests in the trustee. For this reason, an outright refusal of a discharge is appropriate in cases where the debtor is guilty of extreme or flagrant misconduct or where the prospect of rehabilitation is remote.[61]

In many cases, a refusal of a discharge is tempered by an order that permits the debtor to reapply to court after a period of time. This type of order can be used to provide the debtor with an incentive to cooperate with the trustee[62] or to demonstrate a renewed interest in rehabilitation

---

58 *Re MacLean* (1980), 35 CBR (NS) 261 (Ont HCJ); *Re Tanner* (1993), 21 CBR (3d) 244 (BCSC).

59 (2002), 43 CBR (4th) 295 (Alta QB).

60 *Re Stafford* (1959), 37 CBR 206 (Ont HCJ).

61 *Re Messier* (1980), 36 CBR (NS) 118 (Alta QB); *Re Resnick* (1990), 80 CBR (NS) 223 (Ont HCJ).

62 *Mancini*, above note 6.

by taking steps to put his or her financial affairs in order.[63] Although courts will often refuse discharge in the case of three-time bankrupts on the basis that three times are too many,[64] a court is not required to do so and may make some other order if the debtor has behaved responsibly.[65]

E. PERSONAL INCOME TAX DEBTS

The 2009 amendments to the *BIA* added new discharge rules where substantial amounts of personal income tax debt are owed. A bankrupt cannot obtain an automatic discharge if the bankrupt has $200,000 or more of personal income tax debt and if the personal income tax debt represents 75 percent or more of the bankrupt's total unsecured proven claims.[66] The application for the discharge cannot be brought before the expiry of nine months after the date of bankruptcy in the case of a first-time bankrupt if no surplus income payments have been required. If surplus income payments have been required in respect of a first time bankrupt, the application cannot be brought before the expiry of twenty-one months from the date of bankruptcy. If the bankrupt has been bankrupt one time before, the application cannot be brought until the expiry of twenty-four months from the date of bankruptcy if no surplus income payments have been required. In any other case, the application cannot be brought until the expiry of thirty-six months from the date of bankruptcy.

On the hearing of the application, the court is not permitted to order an absolute discharge. The court is directed to make an order suspending the discharge, refusing the discharge, or requiring the bankrupt, as a condition of her discharge, to perform any acts, pay any monies, consent to any judgments, or comply with any other terms that the court may direct.[67] In doing so, the court must consider:

63 *Re Plante* (1996), 43 CBR (3d) 265 (Ont Ct Gen Div).

64 *Re Hardy* (1979), 30 CBR (NS) 95 (Ont HCJ); *Re Boivin*, 2008 CarswellBC 349 (SC).

65 *Re Willier* (2005), 14 CBR (5th) 130 (BCSC); *Re Deley* (1998), 2 CBR (4th) 289 (Man QB).

66 *BIA*, s 172.1(1). The $200,000 amount includes any interest, penalties, or fines but not amounts payable by an individual by virtue of an obligation of the corporation for which the director is liable in his capacity as director. See *BIA*, s 172.1(8).

67 *Ibid*, s 172.1(3). If the court makes an order suspending the discharge, the court shall, in the order, require the bankrupt to file income and expense statements with the trustee each month and to file all returns of income required by law to

- the circumstances of the bankrupt at the time the personal income tax debt was incurred;
- the efforts, if any, made by the bankrupt to pay the personal income tax debt;
- whether the bankrupt made payments in respect of other debts while failing to make reasonable efforts to pay the personal income tax debt; and
- the bankrupt's financial prospects for the future.

A tax debtor who has failed to pay income tax as part of a deliberate and persistent course of conduct is a scofflaw who leaves other Canadians to pay for the benefits that the tax debtor enjoys.[68] Courts have required such debtors to pay a larger portion of the indebtedness when making an order for a conditional discharge.[69] Some courts are inclined to take a more lenient approach where the tax debtor has acted honestly such as in instances where the tax debt is imposed upon disallowance of a tax shelter that was widely believed to be acceptable to the CRA,[70] but other courts are "unsympathetic to the bankrupt's plea of ignorance or reliance on the advice of others in entering into the schemes."[71] Against these factors, a court also balances the future financial prospects of the tax debtor. Courts consider such matters as the tax debtor's age, health, earning capacity, and family responsibilities.[72]

The bankrupt may apply to the court after one year if there is no reasonable probability that he will be in a position to comply with the terms of the order.[73]

F. OTHER FACTORS CONSIDERED BY THE COURTS

Most of the factors that are listed in the *BIA* are directed towards dishonesty, non-cooperation in the bankruptcy process, or some other

be filed. See *ibid*, s 172.1(5). The powers of suspending and of attaching conditions to the discharge of a bankrupt may be exercised concurrently. See *ibid*, s 172.1(7).

68 *Tjelta (Re)*, 2012 BCSC 984 at para 14.

69 *Lebeau (Re)*, 2012 BCSC 638; *Newson (Re)*, 2014 SKQB 106.

70 *Usher (Re)*, 2014 ONSC 925; *Desai (Re)*, 2014 ONSC 136; *Stanzel (Re)*, 2014 SKQB 187.

71 *Foerster (Re)*, 2014 BCSC 1565 at para 57; *Gelpke (Re)*, 2012 BCSC 1770.

72 *Suggitt (Re)*, 2013 MBQB 149; *Farr (Re)*, 2014 SKQB 214; *Baran (Re)*, 2013 ONSC 7501.

73 *BIA*, s 172.1(6).

misconduct, although the list also covers some facts that may relate to a lack of financial management skills.[74] Courts have indicated that there is a need to send a "strong message of condemnation" where the debtor is guilty of fraud or dishonesty, since this will undermine the integrity of the insolvency system.[75]

A court cannot grant an order for an absolute discharge if there has been proof of one of the enumerated facts. A court is not restricted to a consideration of these facts, and there are many cases in which the court considers factors that are not contained on the list. The analysis usually begins with the observation that an effort must be made to balance the interests of the bankrupt and her creditors and to preserve the integrity of the bankruptcy system.[76] The discussion that follows examines some of the major ideas and approaches that are revealed in the caselaw in relation to other factors that a court will look to in attempting to achieve this balance.

1) Future Earning Capacity

Upon bankruptcy, the debtor's non-exempt assets are available to satisfy the claims of creditors, but the post-discharge assets are not. The impact of this rule on debtors differs depending on the extent to which a debtor has invested in his future earning capacity. Debtors who have increased the value of their human capital are better off than those who have directed their efforts to the acquisition of assets. Courts have taken this into account in at least two contexts. First, in bankruptcies of professionals, such as doctors and lawyers, courts have made the discharge conditional on payment of a substantial portion of future income.[77] It might be argued that the *BIA* now takes into account the enhanced earning capacity of the debtor by requiring surplus income to be paid before an automatic discharge is obtained, and that there is no further scope for considering the future income capacity of the debtor. However, it is by no means clear that courts will regard this as a limitation on their power to consider future income earning capacity.

---

74 In particular, s 173(1)(a), *ibid*, covers instances where the debtor's assets are not sufficient to produce a dividend of at least fifty cents on the dollar, and s 173(1)(k), *ibid*, covers repeat bankrupts.

75 *Re Mathew* (2007), 39 CBR (5th) 21 at para 18 (Ont SCJ); *Montalban (Re)*, 2013 BCSC 683.

76 See, for example, *Re Johnson* (1987), 62 CBR (NS) 108 (Ont HCJ).

77 *Westmore v McAfee* (1988), 67 CBR (NS) 209 (BCCA) (discharge conditional on payment of $80,000); *Re Fingold*, above note 46 (discharge conditional on payment of $100,000).

Courts have viewed the existence of the superintendent's standards for surplus income as a reason for not following an older line of cases that gave special consideration to the debtor's "station in life" in determining how much of the future income should be made available to the creditors.[78]

This approach to enhanced future earning capacity can also be observed in student loan cases involving private lenders or that otherwise are not covered by the provision that makes government student loans non-dischargeable.[79] Courts have made orders of discharge conditional on the repayment of substantial amounts where the earning capacity of the debtor has been enhanced for the future by the education paid for by the loans.[80] They do so on the theory that education should be treated as a capital asset that brings benefits throughout the debtor's working life.[81]

Courts will also consider the potential earning capacity of a bankrupt in cases where the debtor deliberately refrains from obtaining employment or does not utilize his or her full earning potential.[82]

2) Involuntary Creditors

Courts will also consider the nature of the claim held by the creditor. A creditor who extends credit in an ordinary commercial transaction will generally contemplate the possibility of non-payment. The creditor chooses whether or not to extend credit to the debtor and is able to diversify any loss caused by non-payment by charging a rate of interest that reflects this risk. An involuntary creditor does not have these options. Courts frequently look at the involuntary nature of the claim in connection with judgments or claims of persons who are injured by the wrongful acts of the debtor. Courts have held that it is inappropriate to use bankruptcy as a process to avoid liability on personal injury claims.[83] In such cases, courts have made orders that span much longer

78 *Re Morgan* (1999), 12 CBR (4th) 48 (Man QB). Cases such as *Bayliss v Doerksen* (1982), 40 CBR (NS) 16 (Ont HCJ) are representative of the view that the court should take into account the lifestyle appropriate to a professional person.

79 *BIA*, s 178(1)(g).

80 *Re Bialek* (1994), 25 CBR (3d) 271 (Ont Ct Gen Div); *Re Coffey* (2004), 2 CBR (5th) 121 (NLSCTD); *Insley (Re)*, 2007 SKQB 383.

81 *Re Bodner* (2008), 39 CBR (5th) 293 (Man QB).

82 *Re Swerid*, 2007 MBQB 173.

83 *Kozack v Richter*, [1974] SCR 832; *Osatchoff v Pinder Bueckert & Associates Inc*, 2010 SKQB 171.

periods than would be the case with ordinary debts.[84] A claim for unpaid taxes has also been characterized as a debt owing to an involuntary creditor, thereby justifying less scope for leniency.[85] Courts are not permitted to make an order that the payments be directed towards the claim of a particular creditor. This means that other creditors will share in any amounts recovered if there are other substantial creditors involved in the bankruptcy.[86]

Courts have also afforded special consideration for costs awards arising out of litigation. They have noted that the costs awards will be ineffective if a plaintiff is able to escape from the consequences of ill-advised litigation through bankruptcy.[87]

3) Recovery of Funds Justly Due in Bankruptcy

Courts have used a conditional order of discharge in several different situations to ensure that creditors receive amounts that are justly due to them in the bankruptcy. One class of case involves payments or transfers to family members who reside outside Canada. Often it is not feasible to attempt to impeach such transactions, and therefore the conditional discharge provides a method by which creditors can recover amounts that would otherwise have been available to satisfy their claims.[88]

Another class of case arises when a trustee determines that it is not worthwhile to force a sale of property that is subject to an exemption. For example, suppose that the debtor's equity in the residence is $45,000 and the value of the debtor's exemption in the property is $40,000. In such cases, a court may take into account the $5,000 in surplus value by making it a condition that this amount be paid to the trustee for distribution to the creditors. In other cases, the debtor may have disposed of post-bankruptcy property that ought to have been given to the trustee. Courts have responded by requiring repayment of this value as a condition of the discharge.[89]

---

84 *Re Heinonen* (1990), 3 CBR (3d) 1 (BCCA); *Re Hubbard* (1999), 10 CBR (4th) 295 (Sask QB).

85 *Re Silbernagel* (2006), 20 CBR (5th) 155 (Ont SCJ).

86 Although the 2005 amendment to the *BIA* contained a provision that permitted a court to direct that, as a condition of discharge, the bankrupt pay money to a particular creditor or a class of creditors, the provision was repealed in the 2007 amendment to the *BIA*.

87 *Re Berry*, 2008 CarswellOnt 1945 (SCJ).

88 *Re Fida*, 2008 CarswellOnt 387 (SCJ).

89 *Re Pottayil* (2000), 20 CBR (4th) 275 (Ont Ct Gen Div); *Re Missal* (1999), 14 CBR (4th) 123 (Alta QB).

Prior to bankruptcy, the debtor may have converted non-exempt property into exempt property. The trustee is unable to set aside such transactions using the usual methods for impeaching pre-bankruptcy transfers if the exempt assets are owned outright by the debtor, since there is no transfer that can be set aside.[90] Courts can take account of this conduct by making an order for discharge conditional on paying the value of the exempt property that was acquired in connection with the eleventh-hour conversion of assets.[91]

4) Programs for the Benefit of the Public

Courts also take a different approach when the amount owing is to a program that is of benefit to the general public. This approach was displayed in respect of government student loans before they were made non-dischargeable debts. Courts indicated that there is a public interest in maintaining these programs and that wiping out the student loan through bankruptcy could undermine them. This rationale was reinforced by the further argument that the purpose of the loan was to enhance the borrower's future earning capacity. The same approach is seen in the treatment of income tax debts. Courts have treated debts differently because the taxes are an obligation of citizenship, and if a taxpayer does not pay her income tax, the burden falls on the other members of the community.[92] Although the *BIA* now contains provisions that set out a special procedure for bankrupts who have significant income tax indebtedness, the courts have considered this factor in cases where large amounts of income tax are owing but the amounts fall outside the threshold that triggers the application of the special procedure.[93] In cases that involve a person who persistently ignores his or her tax obligations, the principle of deterrence rather than rehabilitation comes to the forefront.[94]

5) Exempt Property

Despite the fact that some of the debtor's property may be exempt and therefore not divisible among the creditors, a court may nevertheless consider the existence of the exempt property in deciding whether a

---

90 See Chapter 7, Section A(6).

91 *Hagerman (Re)*, 2014 SKQB 185.

92 *Re Johnson* (1987), 62 CBR (NS) 108 (Ont HCJ); *Re Mintz* (1998), 7 CBR (4th) 217 (Man QB).

93 *R v Wutzke*, 2011 SKQB 270.

94 *Pinc (Re)*, 2007 BCSC 380; *Fiddler (Re)*, 2014 SKQB 231.

conditional order should be made. Some courts have taken the view that the conditional order should take into account the availability of exempt assets if the size of the exemption is such that it would offend a reasonable person and undermine the integrity of the bankruptcy system.[95] Other courts have been more reluctant to consider the existence of exempt property on the ground that to do so would circumvent the intention of Parliament that such assets should not be divisible among the creditors.[96] For this reason, they will not consider exempt assets unless there is some compelling reason such as misconduct on the part of the debtor.

6) Multiple Bankruptcies

Although the primary objective of the bankruptcy discharge is the economic rehabilitation of the honest but unfortunate debtor, a countervailing consideration — that of protecting the public and maintaining the integrity of the bankruptcy system — is engaged when the debtor enters into bankruptcy three times or more.[97] Although these are sometimes viewed as competing objectives, some courts have attempted to reconcile them on the basis that multiple bankruptcies demonstrate that the debtor has failed to demonstrate any real effort to break the pattern of conduct that has produced the problem and therefore the possibility of economic rehabilitation is unrealistic.[98] Instead of refusing the discharge outright, courts have afforded the debtor the opportunity to reapply in two years to demonstrate that the debtor has made appropriate changes in his or her life to prevent another bankruptcy from occurring.[99]

G. NON-DISCHARGEABLE CLAIMS

The *BIA* sets out a list of claims that are not released by a bankruptcy discharge.[100] An exception is made in these cases in order to recognize that the fresh start policy of bankruptcy law must yield to certain over-

95 *Nelson v Nelson* (1995), 33 CBR (3d) 292 (Sask QB); *Re Fredette* (2003), 45 CBR (4th) 34 (Man QB).

96 *Re Cole* (2001), 28 CBR (4th) 19 (NSSC); *Re Poettcker* (2007), 38 CBR (5th) 259 (Alta QB).

97 *Bankruptcy of Willier*, 2005 BCSC 1138; *Pitre (Re)*, 2009 SKQB 280.

98 *Kusch (Re)*, 2007 BCSC 618; *Hiebert, Re (Bankrupt)*, 2008 SKQB 153.

99 *Pitre (Re)*, above note 97; *Kusch (Re)*, above note 98.

100 *BIA*, s 178(1).

riding social policy objectives that require that certain claims be protected against the discharge.[101] Non-dischargeable claims are subject to the automatic stay of proceedings[102] and are entitled to participate with the other creditors in a bankruptcy distribution in the ordinary manner.[103] A failure to file a proof of claim in the bankruptcy does not prevent a creditor from pursuing a non-dischargeable claim against the debtor, although it will prevent the claimant from participating in a bankruptcy distribution.[104] Any interest associated with non-dischargeable claims is also recoverable from the debtor.[105] If a judgment was obtained before the bankruptcy, the costs associated with the award are recoverable following the bankruptcy discharge.[106]

There are a number of different ways in which a claimant can establish that his claim falls within one of the categories of non-dischargeable claims. If the claimant obtained a judgment before the bankruptcy that contains a finding of facts sufficient to bring the claim within one of the categories of non-dischargeable claims, nothing else need be done.[107] If the judgment does not expressly make a finding of the necessary elements, the claimant can seek a declaration of the court that the claim was not discharged by the bankruptcy of the debtor.[108] If no judgment has been obtained, the claimant can bring an action against the debtor, and, if the alleged facts are proven, the existence of a bankruptcy discharge will be no defence to the action.[109]

---

101 *Martin v Martin* (2005), 9 CBR (5th) 235 (NBCA).

102 Because the claim is not discharged on bankruptcy, a court may be willing to lift the stay of proceedings to allow the action to proceed, provided that it does not interfere with the administration of the bankruptcy estate. See *Re Bookman* (1983), 47 CBR (NS) 144 (Ont HCJ).

103 *Algoma Steelworkers Credit Union Ltd v Kennedy* (1973), 18 CBR (NS) 51 (Ont Dist Ct).

104 *Turner v Midland Doherty Ltd* (1992), 13 CBR (3d) 16 (BCSC).

105 *BIA*, s 178(1)(h).

106 *Re Hayton* (2005), 17 CBR (5th) 278 (Ont SCJ).

107 *Re Smith* (1985), 43 Sask R 27 (QB), aff'd (1986), 45 Sask R 240 (CA).

108 The court can then look to the pleadings to determine if the relevant facts are established. Some courts have indicated that a bankruptcy court that hears an application for discharge can make such a declaration. See *Berthold v McLellan* (1994), 25 CBR (3d) 45 (Alta CA). However, other courts have taken the view that a bankruptcy court has no jurisdiction to make such a declaration and that it ought to be made by the ordinary courts. See *Re Mathieu* (1998), 7 CBR (4th) 214 (Sask QB); *Re Kierdorf* (1990), 80 CBR (NS) 6 (Ont HCJ).

109 See, for example, *Moose Jaw Credit Union Ltd v Kennedy* (1981), 41 CBR (NS) 132 (Sask QB).

A determination of whether the claim falls within one of the categories of non-dischargeable claims must be made by a court.[110] A decision of an administrative tribunal is not sufficient.[111] Opinion is divided on whether a default judgment obtained before the bankruptcy constitutes proof of the alleged facts. Some hold that it does not, since the entry of a default judgment is a ministerial act that does not involve a finding by a court.[112] Others have held that it constitutes proof of the facts alleged in the pleadings.[113]

1) Fines, Penalties, and Restitution Orders

The first category of non-dischargeable claims covers fines, penalties, and restitution orders. These are not restricted to penalties associated with criminal law but also include fines imposed for regulatory offences and for violations of municipal bylaws.[114] It does not cover civil penalties, such as an award for punitive damages.[115] The category encompasses penalties that are imposed by a judge in a criminal or quasi-criminal context in which the court engaged in the exercise of sentencing the offender considers factors such as the ability of the accused to pay the fine, penalty, or restitution as well as the rehabilitation of the offender. It therefore does not cover statutes that provide for mandatory orders for repayment of tax.[116] Increasingly, government agencies are using administrative monetary penalties to ensure regulatory compliance. These do not fall within the category of non-dischargeable claims, since the courts have held that the fine or penalty must be one that relates to a criminal or quasi-criminal proceeding.[117]

---

110 A consent judgment that does not contain a declaration that it is for a claim that survives a discharge is nevertheless sufficient if the relevant facts are alleged in the pleadings. See *Re Demitor* (1993), 17 CBR (3d) 132 (Alta QB).

111 *Canada (Attorney General) v Bourassa (Trustee of)* (2002), 36 CBR (4th) 181 (Alta CA).

112 *Re Page*, 2006 ABQB 430.

113 *Perciasepe v Smith* (2003), 50 CBR (4th) 241 (Ont SCJ).

114 *Vancouver (City) v Alliston* (2003), 47 CBR (4th) 142 (BC Prov Ct).

115 *Buland Empire Development Inc v Quinto Shoes Imports Ltd* (1999), 11 CBR (4th) 190 (Ont CA) [*Buland*].

116 *R v Manzioros* (2004), 3 CBR (5th) 91 (Man QB).

117 *Buland*, above note 115; *Re Air Canada* (2006), 28 CBR (5th) 317 (Ont SCJ).

2) Damages Awards for Intentional Bodily Harm or Sexual Assault

The second category of non-dischargeable claims covers damages awards for bodily harm that was intentionally inflicted, for sexual assault, or for wrongful death caused by either.[118] It is not necessary that the debtor have actually inflicted the harm, so long as the debtor is a joint tortfeasor who acted in concert with a person who intentionally caused the harm.[119] It does not cover physical harm that results from defamation or malicious prosecution where there is no finding that the act was done with the intent of causing injury to the victim.[120]

3) Family Support Claims

The third and fourth categories of non-dischargeable claims covers claims for alimony[121] and claims arising under a judicial decision establishing affiliation or respecting support or maintenance, or under an agreement for maintenance and support of a spouse, former spouse, former common law partner, or child living apart from the bankrupt.[122] Claims for support were not formerly provable in bankruptcy but were made provable and given a preferred creditor ranking by amendments to the *BIA* in 1997.[123]

The difference in treatment in bankruptcy between family support obligations and obligations that relate to the division of property often makes characterization of the obligation a critical issue. If the obligation is for support, it survives. If it relates to the division of property, it is released. The difficulty is that a separation agreement may not make it clear how the obligation is to be characterized, with the result that this task falls to a court to decide. In making this determination, a court must look to the nature of the liability, the words of the agreement, and the circumstances surrounding the negotiation of the agreement.[124]

118 *BIA*, s 178(1)(a.1). And see *Dickerson v 1610396 Ontario Inc (Carey's Pub & Grill)*, 2013 ONCA 653.

119 *Martin v Martin*, above note 101.

120 *Re Marshall* (2001), 32 CBR (4th) 74 (Ont SCJ); *Floros v Mueller* (2003), 2 CBR (5th) 189 (Sask QB).

121 *BIA*, s 178(1)(b).

122 *Ibid*, s 178(1)(c).

123 See Chapter 9, Sections A(5) and B(1)(e).

124 *Moore v Moore* (1988), 72 CBR (NS) 50 (Ont HCJ); *Shea v Fraser* (2007), 32 CBR (5th) 196 (Ont CA). And see R Klotz, *Bankruptcy, Insolvency and Family Law*, 2d ed (Scarborough, ON: Carswell, 2001) (loose-leaf), ch 3.

4) Fraud or Misappropriation by a Fiduciary

The fifth category of non-dischargeable claims covers claims arising out of fraud, embezzlement, misappropriation, or defalcation while acting in a fiduciary capacity.[125] The requirement that the debtor act in a fiduciary capacity applies to all of the types of conduct listed in the provision.[126] Fiduciary relationships are ones in which a person must act with loyalty and in good faith for the interests of another. Fiduciary relationships are not restricted to the classic categories, such as between a trustee and a beneficiary or between a corporation and its directors and officers. They may also arise outside the established categories when there is a "mutual understanding that one party has relinquished its own self-interest and agreed to act solely on behalf of the other party."[127]

Although the relationship between an employer and employee is not by its nature a fiduciary relationship, the employee may be found to be acting in a fiduciary capacity when he or she is responsible for handling money belonging to the employer.[128] A fiduciary relationship has been found to exist when a claimant advances funds to permit the borrower to acquire an asset on behalf of the claimant and the recipient fails to use the funds for this purpose.[129]

A breach of a fiduciary relationship alone is not sufficient to fall within the category of claim. There must also be an act of fraud, embezzlement, misappropriation, or defalcation on the part of the debtor. Some courts have held that a defalcation might occur simply from a failure to account when called upon to do so.[130] Other courts have held that the association of those terms with fraud and embezzlement indicates that there must be an element of dishonesty.[131] This latter view better accords with the fresh start policy of bankruptcy law. A breach of

---

125 *BIA*, s 178(1)(d).

126 *166404 Canada Inc v Coulter* (1998), 4 CBR (4th) 1 (Ont CA); *Ross & Associates v Palmer* (2001), 22 CBR (4th) 140 (Man CA).

127 *Hodgkinson v Simms*, [1994] 3 SCR 377 at para 33.

128 *Re McNabb* (1995), 31 CBR (3d) 90 (Alta QB); *Re Petrasuk* (1990), 78 CBR (NS) 290 (QB).

129 *Re Kitnikone* (1999), 13 CBR (4th) 76 (BCSC).

130 *Smith v Henderson* (1992), 10 CBR (3d) 153 (BCCA); *Confederation Life Insurance Co v Waselenak* (1997), 57 Alta LR (3d) 38 (QB). Subsequent cases have indicated that "misappropriation" requires wrongdoing and "defalcation" requires a minimum of negligence or incompetence. See *Valastiak v Valastiak*, 2010 BCCA 71; *Armstrong v Lang*, 2011 BCCA 205.

131 *Simone v Daley* (1999), 8 CBR (4th) 143 (Ont CA); *Ironwood Investments Joint Venture v Leggett* (1996), 38 CBR (3d) 256 (Ont Ct Gen Div); *Garlicki (Bankrupt), Re*, 2010 MBCA 73.

fiduciary obligation can occur without any intentional wrongdoing,[132] and there is little justification for making these types of claims non-dischargeable in the absence of moral misconduct on the part of the debtor.

5) Obtaining Property or Services by False Pretences or Fraudulent Misrepresentation

The sixth category of non-dischargeable claims covers claims for obtaining property or services by false pretences or fraudulent misrepresentation.[133] Unlike the previous category, it does not require the existence of a fiduciary obligation. In order for a representation to be fraudulent, it must be shown that: (1) the statement is untrue in fact; (2) the maker knew it to be untrue or was indifferent to its truth; (3) the maker intended to induce the plaintiff to act upon it; and (4) the plaintiff acted upon it and suffered damage.[134] It is not necessary that the debtor receive the property from the claimant; it is sufficient if the fraudulent misrepresentation induces the claimant to give the property to some other person.[135]

The misrepresentation may relate to only part of the claim. This can occur when two separate loans are involved, only one of which was induced by a fraudulent misrepresentation. In this case, it is necessary to determine whether subsequent loan repayments were directed towards the discharged loan or the non-dischargeable loan. A court, in this situation, must apply the common law rules that govern allocation of payments.[136]

A different analysis is applied where there is a refinancing or consolidation of a new loan and old loan. For example, a borrower may make a fraudulent misrepresentation to a lender that induces the creditor to provide an additional loan of $100. The lender cancels the old loan (which was not tainted by a misrepresentation) and makes a new loan of $200. Some courts have held that the full amount of the

---

132 The case of *Boardman v Phipps*, [1967] 2 AC 46 (HL) is the classic illustration of this principle.

133 *BIA*, s 178(1)(e).

134 *Derry v Peek* (1888), 14 App Cas 337 (HL).

135 *McAteer v Billes*, 2006 ABCA 312; *Toronto-Dominion Bank v Merenick*, 2007 CarswellBC 1922 (SC).

136 See CRB Dunlop, *Creditor-Debtor Law in Canada*, 2d ed (Scarborough, ON: Carswell, 1995) at 23–26. And see Chapter 9, Section B(6).

new loan is a non-dischargeable claim.[137] Other courts have held that only the portion of the loan that represents new value qualifies as a non-dischargeable claim.[138] This latter view better accords with the law in other areas of commercial law.[139] It also is more consistent with the fresh start policy underlying bankruptcy law, since it limits the exception to the value obtained by the debtor as a result of her dishonesty.

6) Undisclosed Claims

The seventh category of non-dischargeable claims covers claims to a bankruptcy dividend that a creditor would have been entitled to receive on a provable claim that was not disclosed by the debtor to the trustee.[140] The debtor is required to disclose the names and addresses of the creditors.[141] If the debtor fails to do so, whether intentionally or inadvertently, the entire claim is not rendered non-dischargeable. Following a bankruptcy discharge, the debtor will be liable only for the amount that the creditor would have received if the claim had been proven in the bankruptcy. If the other creditors did not receive any dividends, then the undisclosed creditor will not be entitled to recover anything from the debtor.[142] Moreover, a creditor cannot recover from the debtor if the creditor knew or had notice of the bankruptcy and failed to take reasonable action to prove the claim.[143]

7) Student Loans

The eighth category of non-dischargeable claims covers student loans made under the *Canada Student Loans Act*, the *Canada Student Financial Assistance Act*, or any provincial statute that provides for loans or guarantees of loans to students.[144] The student loan is non-dischargeable if the date of the bankruptcy occurred while the debtor was a full-time or

---

137 *Beneficial Finance Corp v Anderson* (1963), 5 CBR (NS) 177 (Ont Co Ct); *Seaboard Securities Canada Ltd v Durand* (1969), 13 CBR (NS) 276 (Sask Dist Ct).

138 *Beneficial Finance Co of Canada v Scime* (1968), 2 DLR (3d) 176 (Ont Co Ct); *Moose Jaw Credit Union Ltd v Kennedy* (1981), 41 CBR (NS) 132 (Sask QB).

139 A refinancing or consolidation does not generally destroy or transform the status of an obligation associated with a purchase-money security interest. See R Cuming, C Walsh, & R Wood, *Personal Property Security Law*, 2d ed (Toronto: Irwin Law, 2012) at 456–60.

140 *BIA*, s 178(1)(f).

141 *Ibid*, s 158(1)(d).

142 *Negus v Oakley's General Contracting* (1996), 40 CBR (3d) 270 (NSSC).

143 *Schreyer v Schreyer*, 2011 SCC 35.

144 *BIA*, s 178(1)(g).

part-time student or during a seven-year period after the debtor ceased to be a full-time or part-time student. The category covers only government student loans and does not extend to loans by private lenders that permit the borrower to acquire education.[145] A government student loan is released by a bankruptcy discharge if the bankruptcy occurs after the expiration of the seven-year period. Once it becomes dischargeable, courts have held that there must be evidence of misconduct in addition to evidence of an ability to pay before the court should order a condition of payment.[146] Student loans that were incurred outside the seven-year period are not rendered undischargeable by the fact that the debtor obtains an additional student loan in respect of a new program of study within the seven-year period.[147]

If a person who has a government student loan goes bankrupt before the seven-year period has elapsed, the bankruptcy will release the ordinary debts including any non-government student loans, but it will not release the government student loan. The bankrupt may apply to a court at any time after five years from the cessation of studies and request an order that the non-dischargeable claims provisions not apply to the debt.[148] The court is not given the power to discharge only part of the student loan; it is an all-or-nothing proposition.[149] To qualify, the debtor must satisfy the court that he or she has acted in good faith and has and will continue to experience financial difficulty to the extent of being unable to pay the liabilities under the loan.[150] The good faith requirement means that the debtor must have acted honestly both in the bankruptcy and in obtaining the student loan. A debtor who intentionally made false statements in completing the loan documentation does not satisfy the good faith requirement.[151]

This category of non-dischargeable claims has caused considerable controversy in its brief history.[152] No special treatment was originally given to student loans. However, student loans as Crown claims qualified for preferred creditor status until 1992. This created a strong

---

145 *Re Ledoux* (2005), 8 CBR (5th) 225 (Sask QB).

146 *Funk (Re)*, 2014 SKQB 236.

147 *McNutt (Re)*, 2008 NSSC 166; *Hildebrand (Re)*, 2010 SKQB 321; *Dreger (Re)*, 2013 BCSC 200. But see *Québec (PG) c NP*, 2011 QCCA 726.

148 *BIA*, s 178(1.1).

149 *Re Lowe* (2004), 2 CBR (5th) 277 (Alta QB).

150 See *Re Pyke* (2005), 8 CBR (5th) 308 (NSSC). And see *Lundrigan (Re)*, 2012 NSSC 231 for an enumeration of the factors that a court will consider.

151 *Re Dustow* (1999), 14 CBR (4th) 186 (Sask QB); *Re Kelly* (2000), 20 CBR (4th) 251 (Ont SCJ).

152 See S Ben-Ishai, "Government Student Loans, Government Debts and Bankruptcy: A Comparative Study" (2006) 44 *Canadian Business Law Journal* 1.

incentive for the student loan administrators to object to the discharge of the debtor since the funds recovered did not need to be shared with other creditors. The result was a very large number of cases that considered the status of student loans. This activity slowed considerably when Crown claims lost their preferred creditor status. In 1997 student loans were designated as non-dischargeable claims with a two-year period for the hardship hearing, a time frame that was changed to ten years in 1998 upon the introduction of the federal millennium scholarship program. This has been widely criticized as too harsh, and both the Personal Insolvency Task Force and a Senate report recommended that the time period be reduced to five years.[153]

H. THE LEGAL CONSEQUENCES OF DISCHARGE

1) The Release of Provable Claims

A bankruptcy discharge releases the debtor from all claims provable in the bankruptcy. The release of debts is not effective in respect of all debts or liabilities of the debtor that exist at the date of the discharge. Only those claims provable at the date of the bankruptcy are released.[154] This means that debts or liabilities that arise after the date of the bankruptcy are unaffected by the discharge. Such claims are released only if the debtor undergoes a subsequent bankruptcy and obtains another discharge. A bankruptcy discharge operates to release a claim whether or not the creditor actually proved the claim in the bankruptcy. This holds true even where the debtor fails to disclose the claim to the trustee.[155]

The concept of a provable claim therefore plays a dual role in bankruptcy law. It identifies which claims are permitted to share in the distribution of the bankrupt estate, and it also operates to extinguish these claims once the debtor obtains a discharge. Claims that are not provable in bankruptcy do not share in a bankruptcy distribution, but they are not released upon discharge of the debtor. For this reason, the

---

153 Personal Insolvency Task Force, *Final Report* (Ottawa: Personal Insolvency Task Force, 2002) at 17; Senate Standing Committee on Banking, Trade and Commerce, *Debtors and Creditors: Sharing the Burden: A Review of the Bankruptcy and Insolvency Act and the Companies' Creditors Arrangement Act* by Richard H. Kroft & David Tkachuk (Ottawa: Standing Senate Committee on Banking, Trade and Commerce, 2003) at 56.

154 *BIA*, s 178(2).

155 *Scotia Mortgage Corp v Winchester* (1997), 46 CBR (3d) 314 (Alta QB).

principles that are used to determine if a claim is provable for the purposes of distribution are equally applicable to issues concerning release of the claim on discharge of the debtor.[156]

A debtor may have entered into a contract that contains a non-competition clause prior to the bankruptcy. The claim of the other contracting party is clearly a provable claim since it is a liability to which the bankrupt may become subject before the bankrupt's discharge and which arose out of a pre-bankruptcy obligation.[157] In essence, it is a contingent claim that is subject to the valuation procedure provided for in the *BIA*.[158] A bankruptcy discharge operates to release the debtor from claims provable in bankruptcy. This releases the debtor from any liability for contractual damages in connection with the non-competition clause. However, the other contracting party may argue that the discharge releases the debtor only from the obligation to pay the debt, and does not affect the ability of the contracting party to obtain a prohibitive injunction to prevent the debtor from breaching the non-competition clause. The difficulty with this argument is that it erodes a central policy of bankruptcy law by tying the debtor to pre-bankruptcy obligations. Courts in the United States have held that a rule that would force the debtor to perform pre-bankruptcy employment contracts violates the fresh start policy of bankruptcy law.[159] The release of claims should therefore also extinguish claims for injunctive relief.

2) Discharge and After-Acquired Property

A second legal consequence of discharge is that assets thereafter acquired by the debtor are not available for distribution to the creditors but may be kept and used by the debtor. Property that is acquired by the debtor after the date of the bankruptcy, other than property governed by the surplus income provisions, vests automatically in the trustee. This automatic vesting comes to an end once the debtor obtains a bankruptcy discharge.[160]

A discharge of the debtor has no effect on the administration of the bankrupt estate and the distribution of assets to creditors by a

156 See Chapter 9, Section A(3).

157 *BIA*, s 121(1).

158 See Chapter 9, Section A(9).

159 *All Blacks BV v Gruntruck*, 199 BR 970 (WD Wash 1996). The analysis employed by US courts to reach this conclusion is based upon the executory contracts provisions of United States bankruptcy law. See *Delightful Music Ltd v Taylor*, 913 F2d 102 (3d Cir 1990).

160 *BIA*, s 67(1)(c). And see Chapter 4, Section D.

trustee.[161] So long as the assets were acquired by the debtor before the date of the discharge, the trustee is unaffected by discharge of the bankrupt and can administer the bankrupt estate in the usual way. A discharge of the debtor from bankruptcy should not be confused with a discharge of the trustee. The discharge of a trustee simply means that the trustee has completed the task of administering the bankrupt estate. This may occur before the date that a bankrupt obtains a discharge or after that date. It sometimes happens that an undischarged bankrupt unexpectedly acquires property through a gift or inheritance, a lottery win, or other such event after the trustee has been discharged. In such a case, the trustee can be reappointed or a new trustee can be appointed to liquidate and distribute these new assets.[162]

3) The Effect of Discharge on Secured Creditors

A bankruptcy discharge extinguishes pre-bankruptcy claims against the debtor. However, a creditor who has been given a security in the debtor's property does not lose the benefit of the security upon discharge of the debtor. The discharge extinguishes the debts owed by a bankrupt at the time of bankruptcy,[163] but it does not release the security of a creditor that existed at the time of bankruptcy.[164] A secured creditor may therefore enforce its security by sale, foreclosure, or other disposition of the collateral after the debtor obtains a discharge from bankruptcy, but the secured creditor cannot sue on the underlying debt for any deficiency. Often a security covers after-acquired property. Property that is acquired by the debtor after the discharge of the debtor does not become subject to the secured creditor's security.[165] The extinction of the secured obligation prevents the after-acquired property clause from attaching to any post-discharge assets. The effectiveness of after-acquired property clauses in relation to assets acquired by the debtor after bankruptcy but before discharge is a controversial question and is discussed elsewhere in this book.[166]

---

161 *Re Hood* (1975), 21 CBR (NS) 128 (Ont HCJ).

162 *BIA*, s 41(11). And see *Carriere v PJ Kelleher Ltd* (1994), 26 CBR (3d) 297 (Man CA).

163 *Bowes v Foster* (1858), 27 LJ Ex 262; *Tildesley v Weaver* (1998), 7 CBR (4th) 313 (BCSC).

164 *Pelyea v Canada Packers Employees' Credit Union Ltd* (1969), 13 CBR (NS) 284 (Ont CA); *Andrew v FarmStart* (1988), 71 CBR (NS) 124 (Sask CA).

165 *Holy Rosary Parish (Thorold) Credit Union Ltd v Bye*, [1967] SCR 271; *Pelyea v Canada Packers Employees' Credit Union Ltd*, *ibid*.

166 See Chapter 5, Section B(5).

Although a secured creditor can enforce a security interest in pre-bankruptcy assets of the debtor following the discharge of the debtor, matters become more complicated when there has been a post-discharge increase in the value of the collateral. This can occur when the collateral increases in value because of market forces, which is particularly likely when the collateral is land or investment property. It can also occur when the security interest of a senior secured creditor is paid out, thereby promoting the priority of junior secured creditors. The issue is whether the secured creditor obtains the benefit of this increase in value, or whether the trustee in bankruptcy obtains the benefit of post-discharge increases in value.

There is a division of opinion in the caselaw on this question. In *Patrie v Royal Bank of Canada*,[167] the value of the collateral was less than the obligation secured by the security interest of the senior secured creditor. After the discharge of the debtor, the debtor paid out the senior secured creditor. The court held that the equity in the property that was acquired by the debtor should be treated as post-discharge assets and therefore the junior secured creditor's security interest did not attach to it. *Andrew v FarmStart*[168] involved essentially similar facts. The court held that the post-discharge increase in value accrued to the junior secured creditor. There is a similar division of opinion in academic commentary.[169]

A rule that gives the benefit of post-discharge increases in value to a secured party interferes with the fresh start policy of bankruptcy law. It creates a hidden trap for unsophisticated debtors, and forces bad choices on debtors who happen to understand the technicalities of the rule. It is highly unlikely that the debtor in *FarmStart* would have paid out the senior secured creditor if he knew the consequences of this action. A knowledgeable debtor would be forced to abandon the property and instead acquire some other property in order to prevent a rejuvenation of the junior secured party's claim.

---

167 (1994), 27 CBR (3d) 89 (Ont Ct Gen Div).

168 Above note 164.

169 See T Buckwold, "Post-Bankruptcy Remedies of Secured Creditors: As Good as It Gets" (1999) 31 *Canadian Business Law Journal* 436; and "Post-Bankruptcy Remedies of Secured Creditors: A Reply to Professor J. Ziegel" (2000) 33 *Canadian Business Law Journal* 128; J Ziegel, "Post-Bankruptcy Remedies of Secured Creditors: Comments on Professor Buckwold's Article" (1999) 32 *Canadian Business Law Journal* 142; and "Post-Bankruptcy Remedies of Secured Creditors: A Brief Rejoinder" (2000) 33 *Canadian Business Law Journal* 144.

4) Effect of Discharge on Third Parties

A third party may have entered into a contract of guarantee with a creditor. The discharge of the principal debtor under the contract of guarantee does not affect the liability of the guarantor.[170] Nor does the discharge of a person who is jointly liable with another affect the liability of that other party.

5) Claims by Trustees for Fees

Ordinarily, an agreement between a trustee and a debtor for payment of the trustee's fees that are entered into before the bankruptcy constitutes a provable claim and therefore cannot be recovered by a trustee.[171] Although the trustee is given a preferred creditor ranking, this is of no use when there are little or no assets available to satisfy the claims of creditors. The debtor may choose to voluntarily pay this amount, but, if the debtor does not do so, the agreement is unenforceable in law.[172] Courts have generally been unprepared to make orders for discharge conditional on payment to the trustee of the amount of the trustee's fees where the circumstances of the bankrupt do not justify it.[173] If the parties enter into the fee agreement after the bankruptcy, it will not constitute a provable claim and therefore will not be released on the discharge of the debtor.[174] The 2009 amendments have modified this position. A first-time bankrupt who is not required to make any surplus income payments can now enter into a binding pre-bankruptcy agreement if the total amount is not more than the prescribed amount and is to be paid within one year of the bankrupt's discharge.[175]

---

170 *BIA*, s 179. And see *Agricultural Credit Corp of Saskatchewan v Clarkson* (1990), 4 CBR (3d) 176 (Sask QB).

171 *Re Berthelette* (1999), 11 CBR (4th) 1 (Man CA). See also J Ziegel, "Financing Consumer Bankruptcies; *Re Berthelette* and Public Policy" (2000) 33 *Canadian Business Law Journal* 294.

172 *Re Clark* (1998), 8 CBR (4th) 2 (Alta QB).

173 *Re Weatherbee* (2001), 25 CBR (4th) 133 (NSSC); *Re Alderdice* (2001), 24 CBR (4th) 176 (Alta QB).

174 *Re Pelletier* (2001), 25 CBR (4th) 313 (NBQB). But see *Re Cole*, above note 96, which expressly declined to follow this case.

175 *BIA*, s 156.1. *Bankruptcy and Insolvency General Rules*, CRC, c 368, s 58.1 sets the prescribed amount at $1,800.

6) Payment of Released Claims as a Condition for Some Other Benefit

Some government services or programs provide that a benefit will not be available if a debt or liability has not been paid. For example, legislation that governs student loans may provide that a bankrupt is not eligible to obtain a new provincial student loan until student loans that had been discharged by the bankruptcy are paid in full.[176]

Some statutes prohibit a person who has an unsatisfied judgment arising out of a motor accident or who has failed to pay highway tolls from receiving a licence to operate a motor vehicle. Recent cases from Alberta and Ontario have held that these statutes are inoperative as they conflict with federal bankruptcy legislation.[177] Professional associations that regulate doctors, lawyers, or other professionals may require the payment of fines or penalties as a condition for obtaining a licence. A statutory power given to a professional association under provincial law to suspend a licence for non-payment of fines or penalties does not conflict with the federal insolvency legislation. Suspension of a licence is not being used to enforce payment of a debt but rather is a consequence of not paying the fine.[178]

I. REVIVAL OF RELEASED CLAIMS

An agreement by the debtor to waive the benefit of the bankruptcy discharge is unenforceable, since it violates the fresh start policy of bankruptcy law.[179] For this reason, a debtor cannot revive a discharged debt by giving the creditor a promissory note following the discharge.[180] However, a revival of a claim released by a bankruptcy discharge can be effected if the creditor gives fresh consideration for the promise to pay the discharged debt.[181] The fact that the new promise to pay is on

---

176 *Williams v Alberta (Alberta Learning)*, 2002 ABQB 974.

177 *Moloney v Alberta (Administrator, Motor Vehicle Accident Claims Act)*, 2014 ABCA 68, appeal to SCC heard 15 January 2015; *Ontario (Finance) v Clarke and Superintendent of Insurance for Ontario*, 2013 ONSC 1920. See also *Canada (Superintendent of Bankruptcy) v 407 ETR Concession Company Limited*, 2013 ONCA 769, appeal to SCC heard 15 January 2015.

178 *Re Hover* (2005), 10 CBR (5th) 19 (Alta CA).

179 *Halliday v Kennedy* (1997), 50 CBR (3d) 281 (Ont Div Ct); *Cleve's Sporting Goods Ltd v Jones* (1986), 58 CBR (NS) 304 (NSCA).

180 *Tildesley v Weaver* (1998), 7 CBR (4th) 313 (BCSC); *Trans Canada Credit Corp v Wolfe* (1994), 28 CBR (3d) 237 (Man QB).

181 *Jakeman v Cook* (1878), 4 Ex D 26; *Halliday v Kennedy*, above note 179.

easier terms than the original obligation is not sufficient, since the original obligation is extinguished by the discharge. The fresh consideration requirement is satisfied if the creditor advances new credit to the debtor on the condition that the debtor also pays the discharged debt. A post-bankruptcy agreement for the revival of a debt that is supported by new consideration will not be enforceable if its effect is to undermine the integrity of the bankruptcy as a collective proceeding for the benefit of all the creditors. Courts have therefore invalidated secret side deals under which a debtor agrees to pay a pre-bankruptcy debt if a creditor agrees not to object to the debtor's discharge.[182]

It is not uncommon for a debtor to continue to make payments to a secured creditor after the debtor obtains a discharge. A debtor will frequently do so in order to retain the property and prevent the secured creditor from repossessing it. The problem arises when the debtor subsequently defaults and the secured creditor repossesses the property. After disposing of the property, the secured creditor may also seek to sue the debtor for any deficiency. Ordinarily, the secured creditor would be unable to sue the debtor for the deficiency since the debt would have been discharged. However, the result would be different if there had been a post-bankruptcy agreement between the secured creditor and the debtor under which the debtor agreed to revive the discharged debt and the secured party agreed not to repossess the collateral. A similar controversy arises in connection with a lessor's action to recover damages for breach of a lease of goods following a post-bankruptcy continuation of the relationship.

Canadian cases have permitted recovery by secured creditors and lessors under these circumstances.[183] A difficulty with these decisions is that they do not employ the concept of a new post-discharge contract described above but are instead based on the idea that there is a continuation of the original contract. It is very difficult to understand how continuation of the contract can be reconciled with the discharge of pre-bankruptcy claims.[184] Other cases have departed from this view and justify the outcome on the existence of a new contractual bargain that is entered into following the discharge.[185] The new contract theory does not explain all cases. It cannot apply if the secured party is unaware of

182 *Engels v Merit Insurance Brokers Inc* (2000), 17 CBR (4th) 209 (Ont SCJ). See also *Chamandy Brothers Ltd v Albert*, [1928] 2 DLR 577 (Ont SCAD).

183 *Seaboard Acceptance Corp v Moen* (1986), 62 CBR (NS) 143 (BCCA); *Manulife Bank of Canada v Planting* (1996), 43 CBR (3d) 305 (Ont Ct Gen Div).

184 See Buckwold, "Post-Bankruptcy Remedies of Secured Creditors: As Good as It Gets," above note 169 at 445–49.

185 *Scotia Mortgage Corp v Winchester* (1997), 46 CBR (3d) 314 (Alta QB).

the bankruptcy of the debtor. In such a case, it has been argued that the debtor's failure to comply with the disclosure obligation imposed by bankruptcy law gives rise to an estoppel that permits recovery by the secured party.[186]

If the courts accept a new contract theory, they will directly need to confront the issue of the contractual intention of the parties. It was not necessary to do so under the explanation based on continuation of the agreement, since the original contract was somehow viewed as continuing in effect despite the discharge of any claim based on it. A new contract theory recognizes that the original contractual obligation has been extinguished by the discharge. It must therefore look to the intentions of the parties in respect of a new post-bankruptcy contract. Where there is a written agreement, the intentions of the parties will be clear. The task is more difficult where a debtor has simply continued to make payments and there is no express agreement that the original debt should be revived. A court might imply an intention to revive the original debt, but it is by no means clear that this is appropriate in all cases. The debtor, if informed that a continuation of payments would result in the revival of a discharged debt, might very well have decided not to make these payments.

Agreements for the revival of discharged debts are referred to as reaffirmation agreements in the United States, and are regulated by provisions in the United States Bankruptcy Code.[187] The debtor is given a right to rescind the agreement within sixty days and there is a mechanism for ensuring that the agreement does not impose undue hardship on the debtor. Although there have been proposals to regulate reaffirmation agreements in Canada, no legislation has yet been enacted. In the absence of statutory regulation, courts must attempt to further work out the principles of law governing such agreements.

J. ANNULMENT OR RESCISSION OF THE DISCHARGE

A court may annul a discharge if a debtor has failed to perform the obligations imposed on a bankrupt by the *BIA* or if the debtor has obtained the discharge by fraud.[188] If a court annuls a discharge, property that

---

186 See Ziegel, "Post-Bankruptcy Remedies of Secured Creditors: Comments on Professor Buckwold's Article," above note 169 at 144–47.

187 11 USC § 524(c).

188 *BIA*, ss 180(1) & (2).

was acquired by the debtor after the discharge will vest in the trustee and will be available for distribution to the creditors. An order annulling the discharge does not affect the validity of any transfer, payment, or other thing done prior to the annulment.[189] Third parties who receive post-discharge transfers of such property are therefore unaffected by the annulment of the discharge. In cases where there has been a considerable passage of time from the date of the discharge to the date that an application for annulment of the discharge is brought, courts may be reluctant to order an annulment of the discharge that would give the creditors the ability to satisfy their claims from assets acquired over a lengthy period of time. The court may instead order that the discharge be retroactively suspended for a specified period following the discharge.[190]

A court may also rescind a discharge under its more general power to review, rescind, or vary any order made by it under its bankruptcy jurisdiction.[191] Although courts are inclined to use this power sparingly,[192] they have been prepared to do so in cases of wilful non-disclosure.[193] Although a long delay in seeking rescission of the discharge would ordinarily militate against its award, courts are prepared to do so where the non-disclosure is in respect of a matrimonial property claim with the result that the claimant loses the ability to enforce its claim against an exempt asset.[194]

FURTHER READINGS

BAIRD, D. "Discharge, Waiver, and the Behavioral Undercurrents of Debtor-Creditor Law" (2006) 73 *University of Chicago Law Review* 17

BEN-ISHAI, S. "Discharge" in S Ben-Ishai & A Duggan, eds, *Canadian Bankruptcy and Insolvency Law: Bill C-55, Statute c. 47 and Beyond* (Markham, ON: LexisNexis Canada, 2007) ch 14

189 *Ibid*, s 180(3).

190 *Re Bardyn* (2005), 14 CBR (5th) 163 (Ont SCJ).

191 *BIA*, s 187(5).

192 *Vince v Cinezeta Internationale Filmproduktionsgesellschaft MHB & CO KG*, 2013 SKQB 423.

193 *Carlson v Carlson*, 2012 ABCA 173.

194 *Schreyer (Re)*, 2014 MBQB 44.

———. "Government Student Loans, Government Debts and Bankruptcy: A Comparative Study" (2006) 44 *Canadian Business Law Journal* 211

BUCKWOLD, T. "Post-Bankruptcy Remedies of Secured Creditors: As Good as It Gets" (1999) 31 *Canadian Business Law Journal* 436

GROSS, K. *Failure and Forgiveness* (New Haven, CT: Yale University Press, 1997) Part II.

HONSBERGER, J. "Philosophy and Design of Modern Fresh Start Policies: The Evolution of Canada's Legislative Policy" (1999) 37 *Osgoode Hall Law Journal* 171

HOWARD, M. "A Theory of Discharge in Consumer Bankruptcy" (1987) 48 *Ohio State Law Journal* 1047

JACKSON, T. *The Logic and Limits of Bankruptcy Law* (Cambridge, MA: Harvard University Press, 1986) ch 10

TELFER, T. "Access to the Discharge in Canadian Bankruptcy Law and the New Role of Surplus Income: A Historical Perspective" in C Rickett & T Telfer, eds, *International Perspectives on Consumers' Access to Justice* (Cambridge: Cambridge University Press, 2003)

———. "Repeat Bankruptcies and the Integrity of the Canadian Bankruptcy Process" (2014) 55 *Canadian Business Law Journal* 231

ZIEGEL, J. "Philosophy and Design of Contemporary Consumer Bankruptcy Systems: A Canada-United States Comparison" (1999) 37 *Osgoode Hall Law Journal* 205

———. "Post-Bankruptcy Remedies of Secured Creditors: Comments on Professor Buckwold's Article" (1999) 32 *Canadian Business Law Journal* 142

PART TWO

COMMERCIAL RESTRUCTURING LAW

CHAPTER 11

THE FOUNDATIONS OF COMMERCIAL RESTRUCTURING LAW

The creation of a bankruptcy system has naturally given rise to a parallel phenomenon — arrangements between debtors and creditors under which the creditors agree to accept something less than full and timely payment of their debts. These arrangements, which in a commercial context are referred to as restructurings or reorganizations, are negotiated within a statutory framework created by federal insolvency legislation. If approved by the creditors, the arrangement operates as an alternative to bankruptcy or receivership. A successful restructuring will often permit a debtor to continue in business, although sometimes it will result in the sale of a going concern to an outside party.

The growth of restructuring law in Canada in the past three decades has been an astonishing phenomenon on several levels. It has eclipsed bankruptcy law and has become the insolvency proceeding that is used by the very largest business enterprises. It has also stimulated an unforeseen creativity on the part of the judiciary in formulating new kinds of orders, many of which have had the effect of altering pre-existing contractual and property rights of third parties. Restructuring law continues to be in a state of rapid evolution, and its proper role as well as its relationship with other commercial insolvency regimes continues to be controversial.

A. A SHORT HISTORY OF RESTRUCTURING LAW

1) Voluntary Arrangements

Originally, voluntary arrangements operated in the absence of a statutory framework. A variety of different agreements were possible, and a number of different terms were used to describe the various types of agreements. An agreement under which a creditor agreed to accept a lesser amount in full satisfaction of the debt was referred to as a composition agreement. An agreement under which the time for payment of debts was postponed was called a moratorium. A deed or scheme of arrangement was employed in a wide range of situations. It could be used where the claims of the creditors were partially released or converted into other kinds of claims. In many instances, the arrangement provided for the transfer of some or all of the debtor's assets to a trustee. Agreements between debtors and creditors that are concluded outside a statutory framework are commonly referred to as workouts or private arrangements.

It became increasingly common for such agreements to be concluded within a statutory framework. These statutory regimes addressed one or more of the following four problems associated with the negotiation of a private arrangement. First, there was no method through which the debtor could prevent creditors from enforcing their claims through judicial or extra-judicial seizure of the debtor's assets while the debtor was attempting to negotiate with the creditors. This made negotiations more difficult, since each creditor had a strong incentive to attempt to join in the race to grab assets.[1] Second, the agreement bound only the creditors who agreed to the arrangement and could not be imposed on dissenting creditors.[2] This gave dissenting creditors the opportunity to make strategic threats to derail the whole arrangement by instituting bankruptcy proceedings against the debtor unless their claims were given preferred treatment. This type of holdout threat has a corrosive effect, since it lessens the likelihood that any arrangement will be negotiated. Third, creditors generally lacked sufficient information concerning the affairs of the debtor and therefore were unable to make informed decisions. Fourth, there were concerns that private arrangements might not be properly administered and that, through

1 See Chapter 1, Section A(2).

2 See I Treiman, "Majority Control in Compositions: Its Historical Origins and Development" (1938) 24 *Virginia Law Review* 507.

fraud or neglect, amounts properly due to the creditors would not be accounted for or distributed.

2) The Emergence of Canadian Restructuring Law

In common with English bankruptcy legislation of the Victoria era, both the *Insolvent Act*[3] of 1869 and the *Insolvent Act*[4] of 1875 permitted a debtor to enter into a deed of composition with creditors. The deed was binding on all creditors if approved by a majority of creditors holding three-quarters of the value of debts. After the repeal of federal insolvency legislation in 1880, the only arrangements were those governed by provincial law. This state of affairs persisted until the enactment of the *Bankruptcy Act* of 1919.

The *Bankruptcy Act* of 1919 reintroduced a statutory scheme that permitted an insolvent debtor to make a proposal for a composition, extension, or scheme of arrangement.[5] Concern over fraudulent proposals led to amendments to Canadian bankruptcy legislation in 1923 which allowed a debtor to make a proposal only if the debtor first went into bankruptcy.[6] Although this afforded creditors better information concerning the financial affairs of the debtor and curbed opportunities for abuse by fraudulent trustees, the stigma of bankruptcy cast a pall over the debtor's ability to carry on business. In 1949 this restriction was eliminated so that debtors were again able to make proposals without having to go into bankruptcy.[7] However, the proposal provisions were afflicted with another critical weakness: secured creditors were left unaffected. The inability to stay the rights of secured creditors pending consideration of the proposal by the creditors severely curtailed the effectiveness of these provisions in a commercial context.

In 1933, in the midst of the Great Depression, the Parliament of Canada enacted the *Companies Creditors' Arrangement Act* (*CCAA*),[8] which provided a mechanism through which a company could attempt to negotiate an arrangement with its creditors. Unlike the proposal provisions in the bankruptcy legislation, the *CCAA* permitted a court to stay enforcement proceedings of secured creditors. In 1953 amendments to the *CCAA* restricted its application to companies that had

---

3 32–33 Vict, c 16, s 49.
4 38 Vict, c 16, s 94.
5 SC 1919, c 36, s 13.
6 SC 1923, c 11.
7 SC 1949, c 7.
8 SC 1933, c 36.

issued bonds or debentures under a trust indenture.[9] This restriction seriously limited the availability of the statute, with the result that it was on the verge of being rendered a dead letter.

The *CCAA* was resuscitated in the early 1980s during an economic recession. The courts, aware of the unavailability of an effective regime for corporate restructuring, breathed new life into the *CCAA* by recognizing "instant trust deeds" issued by corporations to secure a nominal sum that were issued for the sole purpose of qualifying the corporation to restructure under the *CCAA*.[10] The *CCAA* rapidly became the primary vehicle through which cooperate restructurings were attempted.[11] Although the original statute was sparsely worded, the fundamental legal principles of restructuring law were articulated and developed in the decisional law.

In 1992 the proposal provisions of the *Bankruptcy and Insolvency Act* (*BIA*)[12] were amended to permit an insolvent debtor to make a proposal to both secured and unsecured creditors.[13] The threshold for acceptance of the proposal by creditors was also reduced so that it was necessary to obtain the consent only of a majority of creditors holding two-thirds the value of the claims. Although it was anticipated that the proposal provisions of the *BIA* would become the primary vehicle for restructuring financially distressed enterprises, this prediction turned out to be incorrect. The *CCAA* was not repealed, and it continued to be employed to restructure corporations and was the vehicle of choice in respect of large corporate enterprises.

This has given rise to a highly distinctive feature of Canadian insolvency law — the existence of dual commercial restructuring regimes. Because of this duality, an insolvent debtor corporation will usually need to make an assessment of the advantages and disadvantages of attempting to restructure under each regime in order to choose the one that will maximize the chances of success. The reform of commercial insolvency law has since adopted a deliberate strategy of convergence under which the rules and principles pertaining to each restructuring regime have been increasingly aligned.[14] Despite this process, there

9 SC 1952–53, c 3.

10 See *United Maritime Fishermen Co-operative* (1988), 67 CBR (NS) 44 (NBQB); *Elan Corp v Comiskey* (1990), 1 CBR (3d) 101 (Ont CA). The requirement for the issue of a trust indenture was subsequently removed from the *CCAA* in 1997.

11 For a history of this development, see R Jones, "The Evolution of Canadian Restructuring Law: Challenges for the Rule of Law" in Janis P Sarra, ed, *Annual Review of Insolvency Law, 2005* (Toronto: Thomson/Carswell, 2006) 481.

12 RSC 1985, c B-3 [*BIA*].

13 SC 1992, c 27.

14 For example, in 1997 the threshold for acceptance of an arrangement by creditors under the *CCAA* was reduced from 3/4 to 2/3 of the value of the claims in

are still many significant differences between the two regimes, and it remains necessary for legal advisors to conduct a careful evaluation of each before making a choice in those cases where both restructuring regimes are available.

The 2009 insolvency reforms proceeded on the basis that the two general commercial restructurings regimes should be kept separate. This was based in part on the view that the *CCAA* was more flexible and better suited for resolving the multitude of issues that arise in connection with restructuring larger businesses. The rule-based approach of the *BIA* was regarded as more suitable for small- and medium-sized enterprises. Fewer court applications were needed, thereby reducing the cost of restructuring.[15] The reforms continued to adhere to the policy of convergence under which differences between the two restructuring regimes were to be minimized. Although this policy has brought the two regimes even closer together, the process is incomplete. Many significant differences between the two restructuring regimes remain.

B. THE OBJECTIVES OF RESTRUCTURING LAW

At one time, the objectives of restructuring law were relatively uncontroversial. Courts had consistently maintained that the purpose of restructuring law was to provide an insolvent debtor with a limited but reasonable period of time within which to develop a plan or proposal and to put it before the creditors who must then decide to accept or reject it.[16] However, the task has become more complicated because restructuring proceedings are increasingly employed as a mechanism for selling the business as a going concern. In a "liquidation *CCAA*" or "liquidation commercial proposal," it is often the case that a plan is never developed and the creditors never vote.

---

order to bring it in line with the proposal provisions of the *BIA*.

15 See Senate Standing Committee on Banking, Trade and Commerce, *Debtors and Creditors: Sharing the Burden: A Review of the Bankruptcy and Insolvency Act and the Companies' Creditors Arrangement Act* by Richard H Kroft & David Tkachuk (Ottawa: Standing Senate Committee on Banking, Trade and Commerce, 2003) at 171–74.

16 See, for example, *Re Lehndorff General Partner Ltd* (1993), 17 CBR (3d) 24 at para 6 (Ont Ct Gen Div) [*Lehndorff*].

1) Rescuing Financially Distressed Firms

The traditional justification for restructuring law was that it permitted the rescue of financially distressed businesses. The recognition of this objective represented a significant shift in commercial insolvency law. Although the idea of debtor rehabilitation was of fundamental importance in respect of bankrupt individuals, bankruptcy of a corporation or other artificial entity represented the cessation of its commercial activities. The emergence of restructuring law in the 1980s therefore represented a shift in favour of insolvency proceedings that sought to restructure the affairs of a financially distressed enterprise so as to avoid liquidation.

This did not mean that bankruptcy was regarded as a bad thing and that it was always desirable to rescue a firm from liquidation. There are many reasons why firms become financially distressed. It may result from incompetent management or the inefficient use of assets. It may be due to a temporary downturn in markets. It may be that the firm has taken on too much debt or has embarked on projects that turn out to be less profitable than anticipated. Depending on the nature of the problem, the solution may be to replace the management of the firm, to get rid of unprofitable portions of the business, to cut costs, or to reschedule debt or convert some of it to equity.[17] However, it may be that there is no longer a realistic prospect that the firm can be made economically efficient. In that case, it is not an appropriate candidate for rescue. The best outcome is for its assets to be liquidated so that others may put them to higher-valued uses.

The traditional view of rescue centred upon the survival of the legal entity. The normal expectation was that an enterprise that underwent restructuring proceedings would continue to operate the business in some restructured or reorganized form. It was therefore the debtor corporation that was rehabilitated and which survived to carry on operations. This view has been displaced to a large degree by a new view that regards the rescue of the ongoing business rather than the legal entity as the legitimate goal of the restructuring effort. On this view, a going-concern sale of the business to a third party can satisfy the rehabilitation objective as it preserves the economic relationships with the employees, suppliers, and other stakeholders.

---

17 See *Re 843504 Alberta Ltd* (2003), 4 CBR (5th) 306 at para 14 (Alta QB).

2) Maximizing the Value of Assets for Creditors

Traditional restructurings were thought to be desirable because they provided a process through which creditors could obtain a higher recovery than otherwise would be available to them through bankruptcy or other liquidation proceedings. The reason for enhanced recoveries by creditors in restructuring proceedings is due to the preservation of the value of the firm as a going concern. The value of a business as a going concern is generally higher than the value that would be obtained by breaking it up and selling off the assets to individual buyers. If there is not a reasonable prospect that a restructuring will give creditors more than they would receive in a bankruptcy, the case is not considered to be appropriate for restructuring, and the proceedings should be terminated.[18]

One difficulty with this explanation is that it does not adequately explain why the same value cannot be obtained for the creditors through a liquidation in which the business is sold to a buyer as a going concern. As a liquidation process does not involve the additional costs associated with the negotiation of the arrangement with creditors, it is not obvious why restructuring proceedings are the preferred method of retaining the going-concern value of a firm through a sale of the business.

In some instances, particularly where a smaller firm is involved, the reason may be that an owner/manager has firm-specific skills and knowledge that would be lost on a sale of the business.[19] Alternatively, it may be that there are few potential outside buyers or that it is too costly for them to obtain accurate information about the business.[20] In other instances, bankruptcy proceedings or receivership proceedings may simply not be a viable option. Because bankruptcy does not stay the enforcement remedies of secured creditors, a going-concern sale may not be possible where a creditor has a security interest in certain key assets. Receivership proceedings are typically available only where a creditor has a security interest on the entire undertaking.

Sometimes the causes of the financial distress and the best method of redressing the difficulty may not be immediately apparent. Restructuring proceedings provide an opportunity to evaluate the nature of the problem and to propose strategies designed to achieve a turnaround.

---

18 See Chapter 12, Section E.

19 See T Jackson & D Baird, "Bargaining After the Fall and the Contours of the Absolute Priority Rule" (1988) 55 *University of Chicago Law Review* 738 at 742–43.

20 See R Clark, "The Interdisciplinary Study of Legal Evolution" (1981) 90 *Yale Law Journal* 1238 at 1252.

After the parties have been given an opportunity to assess the various options, it may turn out that a going-concern liquidation of the enterprise is the best alternative. If so, the firm can be liquidated within the restructuring regime. The longer time frames associated with restructuring proceedings may also provide more time within which to search for potential buyers. In other cases, the expertise and assistance of the debtor's management team may be needed in order to obtain the best possible price from potential buyers.[21] The restructuring process might also involve a dual track in which both liquidation and restructuring are put forward as possibilities, with the ultimate choice depending on the best offer that is obtained.[22]

The growth in liquidating *CCAA*s and liquidating commercial proposals may signify a change in the economic environment. Some believe that the traditional restructuring is no longer able to outperform a going-concern liquidation of the business.[23] It is argued that asset sales are now much more likely able to yield more than can be obtained through keeping the firm intact. Assets have become more fungible and less firm-specific so that there is less going-concern value. Markets are more liquid so that even when there is going-concern value, the whole enterprise can be sold off.[24] The increase in the number of liquidating *CCAA*s and commercial proposals does not in itself vindicate this argument. Some of the increase may be due to the fact that a liquidation that would formerly be carried out through a receivership is now carried out through restructuring proceedings. Moreover, it cannot be assumed that a liquidation will necessarily maximize the value obtained by the creditors. It may be that senior secured creditors have

---

21 See W Bodoh, J Kennedy, & J Mulligan, "The Parameters of the Non-Plan Liquidating Chapter Eleven: Refining the Lionel Standard" (1992) 9 *Emory Bankruptcy Developments Journal* 1 at 12–13.

22 See K McElcheran, *Commercial Insolvency in Canada*, 2d ed (Markham, ON: LexisNexis Canada, 2011) at 289–91. See also D Baird & R Rasmussen, "Chapter 11 at Twilight" (2003) 56 *Stanford Law Review* 673 at 675, who conclude that "corporate reorganizations today are the legal vehicles by which creditors in control decide which course of action — sale, prearranged deal, or a conversion of debt to controlling equity stake — will maximize their return."

23 D Baird & R Rasmussen, "The End of Bankruptcy" (2002) 55 *Stanford Law Review* 751; D Baird, "The New Face of Chapter 11" (2004) 12 *American Bankruptcy Institute Law Review* 69.

24 D Baird, "Bankruptcy's Undiscovered Country" (2008) 25 *Emory Bankruptcy Developments Journal* 1 at 7.

developed more effective strategies to prevent a beneficial restructuring that would yield greater value to creditors as a group.[25]

3) Protecting the Public Interest

The idea that the creditors in a restructuring must receive at least as much as they would receive in bankruptcy does not mean that courts should take into account only the interests of creditors.[26] Canadian courts on a number of occasions have considered the effect of bankruptcy of the enterprise on employees, suppliers, and the larger community.[27] Justice Deschamps in *Century Services Inc v Canada (AG)*[28] recognized that restructurings may serve the public interest by serving stakeholders beyond the employees and creditors who have contractual relationships with the debtor company.

Some commentators have questioned why this subject should be the exclusive concern of insolvency law. The closure of a plant that occurs outside insolvency may have precisely the same consequences on employees and the community.[29] In any event, one should not overstate the role of non-creditor stakeholders in restructuring proceedings. Although courts may consider such stakeholder interests when deciding whether to permit restructuring proceedings to go ahead and when deciding whether the plan should be sanctioned by the court, the decision whether or not to accept the plan ultimately is one that is made by the creditors. If the creditors do not consent to the plan, then it will fail and there is nothing that a court can do to reverse this outcome.

4) The Appropriateness of Restructuring Proceedings for Liquidation

The initial shift from receivership proceedings to liquidating *CCAA*s and commercial proposals occurred because of a concern over the potential

---

25 See R Wood, "Rescue and Liquidation in Restructuring Law" (2013) 53 *Canadian Business Law Journal* 407.

26 Review Committee of Insolvency Law and Practice, *Report of the Review Committee of Insolvency Law and Practice*, Cmnd 8558 (London: HMSO, 1982) at 56 [*Cork Report*].

27 See *Re Algoma Steel Inc* (2002), 30 CBR (4th) 1 (Ont SCJ); *Re Canadian Airlines Corp* (2000), 20 CBR (4th) 1 (Alta QB). And see J Sarra, *Creditor Rights and the Public Interest* (Toronto: University of Toronto Press, 2003).

28 2010 SCC 60 at para 18 [*Century Services*].

29 See D Baird, "Bankruptcy's Uncontested Axioms" (1998) 108 *Yale Law Journal* 573 at 588.

liability of the receiver.[30] Because a monitor or proposal trustee does not take control of the business, it is less likely that the insolvency professional will be liable for employment obligations under successor liability provisions of labour and employment legislation. Although the 2009 *BIA* amendments limited the liability of receivers under such statutes,[31] the restructuring regimes continued to be used for liquidations.

There are a number of reasons why a senior secured creditor might prefer to liquidate under a restructuring regime. Some of these reasons may be consistent with the objectives described above, while some of these reasons may undermine these goals. A major difference between restructuring proceedings and receivership proceedings is that the debtor remains in control of the business in the former, and an insolvency professional takes control in the latter. To the extent that it can be shown that value can be maximized by having the debtor remain in control, a liquidation that is carried out through restructuring proceedings may not be objectionable.

The use of restructuring regimes to liquidate will undercut the goals if it permits a creditor to force a sale under circumstances in which some other process would yield a higher return to creditors as a group. A senior secured creditor has a strong preference to conduct a quick sale of the assets if the expected value of the sale proceeds are sufficient to pay out its claim. A secured creditor may opt for a liquidation under restructuring proceedings because it gives the creditor a better ability to control the process. There are two mechanisms by which this control can be exercised.[32] The first is through the use of contractual provisions in the financing agreements that are entered into after the restructuring proceedings are commenced. A secured lender can influence the direction of the insolvency proceedings by the use of negative and positive covenants in the interim financing agreement. These may set strict timelines that make it less likely that a traditional restructuring can be achieved or that will limit access and use of cash flow. The agreements may also include events of default that effectively impose onerous financial stress tests that are difficult to satisfy.[33] The second is through devices that give the creditor power over the selection or compensation of the managers.

---

30 *GMAC Commercial Credit Corporation - Canada v TCT Logistics Inc*, 2006 SCC 35.

31 *BIA*, s 14.06. And see Chapter 19, Section E(1).

32 See Kenneth M Ayotte & Edward R Morrison, "Creditor Control and Conflict in Chapter 11" (2009) 1 *Journal of Legal Analysis* 511.

33 D Skeel, Jr, "The Past, Present and Future of Debtor-in-Possession Financing" (2004) 25 *Cardozo Law Review* 1905 at 1916–919; G Kuney, "Hijacking Chapter 11" (2004) 21 *Emory Bankruptcy Developments Journal* 19 at 52–59.

Although receivership proceedings provide a secured creditor with the means to liquidate the firm, a senior creditor may prefer to use restructuring proceedings as a vehicle for liquidation because of the ability to assert influence on the process and may have access to the monitor and to financial information that is not made available to other creditors. This is in stark contrast to a court appointed receiver who is under an obligation to act fairly and consider the interests of all the stakeholders. This access to information may be particularly important if the secured creditor is a potential bidder in the sale process.

The use of restructuring proceedings to carry out a going-concern sale may also be problematic because many of the features of the process were designed for a traditional restructuring and may not be well-suited for a liquidation. For example, interim financing is of critical importance in the case of a traditional restructuring. The extraordinary terms associated with such financing is more difficult to justify if the process is primarily for the benefit of the senior secured creditors.[34] Other attributes of the restructuring process may similarly be ill-suited for carrying out a liquidation. Suppliers are given super-priority rights over recent deliveries (thirty-day goods) and agricultural inputs in bankruptcy and receivership.[35] A similar right was not conferred in respect of restructuring proceedings because it was thought to interfere with the rescue objective. Unpaid employees are also treated differently in restructuring proceedings. Unpaid employees may make an immediate claim against the *Wage Earner Protection Program Act*[36] (WEPPA) insurance scheme in the bankruptcy and receivership proceedings. In restructuring proceedings, they must wait. These provisions were designed when a sharp division existed between rescue and liquidation. The use of the restructuring process as a liquidation vehicle permits a secured creditor to nullify the rights of employees and suppliers that would otherwise be available to them.

---

34 See D Bish, "The Plight of Receiverships in a CCAA World" (2013) 2 *Journal of the Insolvency Institute of Canada* 221 at 242–43.

35 See Chapter 5, Section C.

36 SC 2005, c 47, s 1.

C. THE FUNDAMENTAL PRINCIPLES OF RESTRUCTURING LAW

1) The Debtor's Control of the Assets

In bankruptcy, the assets of the debtor vest in a bankruptcy trustee. In receivership proceedings or winding-up proceedings, the assets remain vested in the debtor but a receiver or administrator obtains control over the management of the business. Restructuring proceedings in Canada diverge from both of these models in that the debtor retains both ownership and control of the business assets. The debtor therefore has the ability to operate the business while the restructuring proceedings are under way.

In order to create an environment in which negotiation with creditors is facilitated, it is necessary to impose a stay of proceedings on the creditors and prevent them from engaging in manoeuvres during this period that would give them an advantage over other creditors. This prevents creditors from seizing assets or otherwise enforcing their claims against the debtor's assets. Unlike bankruptcy, the stay of proceedings applies to both secured and unsecured creditors. The stay also prevents legal actions from being commenced or continued. This permits the managers of the firm to direct their undiverted attention to the restructuring attempt.

2) The Maintenance of Business Operations

Although creditors are prevented from enforcing their claims against the business assets or from wresting managerial control from the existing managers, this alone is not enough to maintain the business as a going concern while the restructuring plan is being developed. Because the debtor continues to operate the business, it is necessary to distinguish between pre-filing and post-filing creditors.

The plan that will be negotiated and voted on affects only the pre-filing creditors — i.e., creditors who were owed obligations on or before the date that restructuring proceedings were commenced. Post-filing creditors expect to receive full payment of their claims. They will often refuse to extend any further credit, and suppliers will frequently insist on being paid cash on delivery. The insolvent business also is faced with the prospect of paying sizeable fees to insolvency professionals and lawyers. The obligations incurred by the enterprise following the initiation of restructuring proceedings must be paid, and a source of interim financing is needed in order to meet these interim expenses. In addition, performance of contractual obligations incurred by the enterprise prior to the initiation of the proceedings may impair the ability of the enterprise to restructure successfully. Restructuring law provides mechanisms by which interim financing can be obtained and onerous contractual obligations can be disclaimed.[37]

3) The Creditors' Right to Information

Restructuring proceedings provide the debtor an opportunity to devise a restructuring plan and place it before the creditors for acceptance or rejection. Because the debtor retains control over the management of the enterprise during this period, it is critically important that the creditors are supplied with full and accurate information to permit them to make an informed decision on the merits of the proposed plan. For this reason, Canadian restructuring law ensures the flow of relevant information to creditors. A salient feature of Canadian restructuring law is the use of independent insolvency professionals to act as monitors or trustees. These persons are officers of the court and are under an obligation to act in the best interests of all the creditors. Their primary role is to ensure that creditors obtain accurate information about the financial condition of the firm.[38]

4) The Need for Creditor Approval

In a traditional restructuring, a plan is developed by the debtor and a meeting of creditors is called so that the creditors can vote on whether to accept or reject it. This requirement for creditor approval of the plan is of critical importance, and it shapes the dynamics of the negotiations among the debtor and the creditors. Where restructuring proceedings are used to liquidate the business, it is often the case that a plan is never developed and a vote is never conducted. The requirement for creditor approval of a plan is therefore only a fundamental characteristic in relation to a traditional restructuring where the debtor survives the process and thereafter continues business operations.

In a traditional restructuring, there must be a viable business plan as well as a restructuring plan. The business plan is largely within the control of management. The managers of the debtor must come up with a plan that will produce a turnaround in the fortunes of the business. This may involve decisions to downsize operations by eliminating units

37 See Chapter 13, Sections A and D.
38 See Chapter 14, Section B.

or product lines and reducing the workforce. The creditors do not vote upon the business plan, although it will influence the decision of the creditors in voting on the restructuring plan. The restructuring plan involves the deal that is presented to the creditors. It describes how the claims of the creditors will be treated. The restructuring plan is not binding on the creditors unless they approve it.

The restructuring plan does not require unanimous consent in order to be binding on the creditors. In other words, dissenting creditors who vote against the plan may nevertheless find that they are bound by its terms. In order to bind creditors to a plan, a head count as well as a dollar count is undertaken for each class of affected creditors. The plan must be approved by a majority in number of the creditors who hold at least two-thirds of the value of the claims for each class of claimant.[39]

The ability of a majority to bind a minority to a modification of contractual or other claims represents a marked departure from ordinary private law principle. It is considered necessary because of a complex dynamic that comes into play when multiparty negotiations are involved. Opportunistic creditors may adopt "hard-line" bargaining positions in the hopes that their threat to upset the applecart will induce the debtor to agree to give preferred treatment to their claims. This is undesirable for two reasons. First, it results in similarly situated creditors being afforded different treatment and rewards non-cooperative behaviour over cooperative behaviour on the part of creditors. Second, it makes it much less likely that any agreement will be concluded among the creditors. Creditors will naturally prefer to obtain the greater rewards afforded by non-cooperative behaviour, but, if all creditors behave in this fashion, no agreement will be reached. A dual-majority requirement is imposed in order to curtail the power of creditors who adopt value-reducing holdout strategies.

A second element of the rules for creditor approval governs the classification of claims.[40] Claimants hold a variety of different kinds of rights, and a voting regime under which the majority could impose their will on a dissenting minority can result in the unfair confiscation of value by the majority from the minority. Suppose that secured creditors who are fully secured are placed into the same class as unsecured creditors. There are five secured creditors who have claims that total $1 million; there are also one hundred unsecured creditors whose total claims amount to $4 million. If they are all placed in the same class, there is a strong incentive for the unsecured creditors to gang up

39 See Chapter 16, Section C(2).

40 See Chapter 16, Section D.

against the secured creditors and agree to a plan that unfairly prejudices the latter. For example, the plan might provide that all creditors, whether secured or unsecured, be treated equally under the plan and receive fifty cents on the dollar. This is patently unfair, since secured creditors have a higher priority ranking that entitles them to be paid in full in a bankruptcy of the debtor. Restructuring law prevents claimants who have different legal rights from being included in the same class if their claims are so dissimilar that it prevents them from voting on the plan with a common interest. Each separate class of creditors must approve the plan by a dual majority.

5) The Supervisory Role of the Court and Its Officers

The two restructuring regimes differ from one another in that the *CCAA* relies more heavily upon involvement of courts in framing the parameters of the restructuring attempt, while the commercial proposal provisions in the *BIA* rely more upon statutory rules in doing so. Despite this difference, the courts perform a unique and crucial role under both restructuring regimes. It is said that the courts play a supervisory role in commercial restructurings. In fact, there are several distinct functions that they undertake in restructuring proceedings.[41]

Courts serve a gatekeeping function in that they screen out ineligible or inappropriate applications.[42] Ineligible applications are ones that do not meet the conditions imposed by the governing statute concerning availability of the proceedings. Inappropriate applications are ones where the court is of the view that the restructuring attempt is unlikely to succeed because the debtor is not acting diligently or in good faith or because it is anticipated that creditors who have the ability to veto the plan will vote against its approval or that a viable plan is unlikely to be developed.

Courts also have an important role in ensuring that there is a framework within which negotiations between the parties is possible. In order to achieve this, it is necessary to maintain the status quo and prevent parties from engaging in manoeuvres that seek to undermine the legal position of other parties. Therefore, courts will often make rulings to ensure procedural fairness. For example, courts will review

---

41 See Chapter 14, Section C.

42 See L LoPucki & G Triantis, "A Systems Approach to Comparing US and Canadian Reorganization of Financially Distressed Companies" in J Ziegel, ed, *Current Developments in International and Comparative Corporate Insolvency Law* (Oxford: Clarendon Press, 1994) 109 at 125.

the classification scheme of a plan in order to ensure that it does not unfairly prejudice certain of the creditors.

In a traditional restructuring, courts have the responsibility to decide whether or not to give their approval to a plan that has been accepted by the creditors. This is an essential final step, since the plan is not binding on creditors until the court has approved it. In a liquidating CCAA or commercial proposal, the court oversees the sale process.

D. JURISDICTION OF THE COURT TO MAKE ORDERS

1) Development of the Judicial Powers

Prior to 2009, although courts routinely exercised wide powers in making a variety of different types of orders in connection with restructuring proceedings, there was considerable controversy concerning the source of and limits on these powers. The powers that were exercised by the courts in restructuring matters under the *CCAA* greatly exceeded the powers expressly conferred on the courts by the statute.[43]

On several matters, the *CCCA* and the *BIA* expressly confer power upon the courts to make certain kinds of orders. For example, both the *CCAA* and the commercial proposal provisions of the *BIA* give a court the power to approve the plan or proposal. The *CCAA* also gives a court the power to stay proceedings. This power is not needed under the commercial proposal provisions, since a statutory stay of proceedings arises automatically upon the initiation of the restructuring proceedings.[44] There are many other matters in respect of which courts found that they had jurisdiction to make orders under the *CCAA* despite the absence of express power-conferring provisions. These include the following types of orders:

- orders that authorize the debtor to obtain interim financing and that give the interim financer superpriority over existing secured creditors;[45]

---

43 See K. Yamauchi, "The Courts' Inherent Jurisdiction and the *CCAA*: A Beneficent or Bad Doctrine?" (2004) 40 *Canadian Business Law Journal* 250.

44 See Chapter 12, Section D.

45 *Skydome Corp v Ontario* (1998), 16 CBR (4th) 118 (Ont Ct Gen Div).

- orders that create charges that secure the extension of credit by post-filing creditors and that give the post-filing creditors superpriority over existing secured creditors;[46]
- orders that create a charge for administrative expenses such as the monitor's fees and disbursements and that give the charge superpriority over existing secured creditors;[47]
- orders that permit the debtor to terminate contractual obligations owed to a third party;[48]
- orders that authorize the assignment of a contract notwithstanding that it contains an anti-assignment clause and the other contracting party does not consent to the assignment;[49]
- orders that authorize the debtor to pay arrears in payment to a supplier in order to ensure that the supplier will continue to supply the critical goods or services that cannot be obtained from another supplier;[50]
- orders that prevent a person from exercising a remedy or taking proceedings against a third party (as opposed to the debtor) where the exercise of the remedy would detrimentally affect the success of the restructuring proceedings;[51]
- orders that authorize a sale of substantially all the business assets before a plan has been put before the creditors for approval;[52] and
- orders that authorize the use of a claims bar procedure that will bar a claimant from making a claim unless the claim is filed within a particular date after the claimants are notified.[53]

Courts struggled to explain the jurisdictional basis for such orders. In many of the cases, the courts stated that the orders were made pursuant to their "inherent jurisdiction." The Supreme Court of Canada in *Century Services Inc v Canada (AG)*[54] ultimately rejected this view and held that in most instances the statute itself confers these powers.

---

46 *Re Smoky River Coal Ltd* (2001), 28 CBR (4th) 127 (Alta CA).

47 *Re United Used Auto & Truck Parts Ltd* (2000), 16 CBR (4th) 141 (BCCA).

48 *Re Skeena Cellulose Inc* (2003), 43 CBR (4th) 187 (BCCA).

49 *Re Playdium Entertainment Corp* (2001), 31 CBR (4th) 302 (Ont SCJ).

50 *Re Air Canada* (2003), 47 CBR (4th) 163 (Ont SCJ).

51 *Lehndorff*, above note 16; *ATB Financial v Metcalfe & Mansfield Alternative Investments II Corp* (2008), 45 CBR (5th) 163 (Ont CA).

52 *Re Canadian Red Cross Society* (1998), 5 CBR (4th) 299 (Ont Ct Gen Div).

53 *Re Blue Range Resource Corp* (1999), 251 AR 1 (QB).

54 Above note 28. And see R Wood, "Priorities and Judicial Authority under the *CCAA*: *Century Services Inc v Canada (Attorney General)* (2011) 51 *Canadian Business Law Journal* 118.

The ability to make these types of orders under the *CCAA* was one of the reasons why the *CCAA* emerged as the dominant restructuring regime for larger corporations. It was far less clear whether courts had the same latitude to make similar orders in the context of commercial proposals under the *BIA*. If the ability to make such orders were derived from the court's inherent jurisdiction, there would be no reason in principle why similar orders could not be made in respect of *BIA* restructurings.[55] The rejection of inherent jurisdiction as the source of authority for the orders means that it is unlikely that similar orders can be made under the *BIA*. The greater detail and framework of rules provided by the commercial proposal provisions in the *BIA* indicate that Parliament exhaustively dealt with the matters and that supplementation of these rules by the courts was not intended.

2) Statutory Reform

To a large extent, these jurisdictional worries about the source of the court's powers have been resolved by the 2009 amendments to the *BIA* and *CCAA*. The amendments expressly confer jurisdiction on the courts to make the kinds of orders that were routinely granted in *CCAA* proceedings. Similarly worded provisions were introduced into both the *CCAA* and the *BIA*. These give the court the power to make a wide variety of orders, including:

- the power to authorize the debtor to obtain interim financing that gives the interim financer priority over existing secured creditors;[56]
- the power to create a charge for administrative expenses that has priority over existing secured creditors;[57]
- the power to authorize a sale of substantially all the business assets before a plan has been put before the creditors for approval;[58]
- the power to authorize the assignment of a contract notwithstanding that it contains an anti-assignment clause and the other contracting party does not consent to the assignment;[59]
- the power to approve a disclaimer of a contract;[60] and
- the power to remove a director.[61]

---

55 *Re Bearcat Explorations Ltd* (2004), 3 CBR (5th) 167 (Alta QB); *Re FarmPure Seeds Inc*, 2008 SKQB 381.

56 *CCAA*, s 11.2(1); *BIA*, s 50.6(1).

57 *CCAA*, s 11.52; *BIA*, s 64.2.

58 *CCAA*, s 36; *BIA*, s 65.13.

59 *CCAA*, s 11.3; *BIA*, s 84.1.

60 *CCAA*, s 32; *BIA*, s 65.11.

61 *CCAA*, s 11.5(1); *BIA*, s 64(1).

In addition to these powers, a court is given a general power under the *CCAA* to make any other order it thinks appropriate, subject to the restrictions contained in the legislation.[62] A similar power is not conferred on a court in respect of *BIA* restructuring proceedings.

These statutory reforms are highly significant for a number of different reasons. First, they greatly enhance the kinds of orders that are available in *BIA* restructurings. A court now has jurisdiction in *BIA* restructurings to make the kinds of orders that were formerly thought to be available only under the *CCAA*. Whether this will cause debtors to choose to restructure under the *BIA* instead of the *CCAA* remains to be seen. Although the statutory reforms have resulted in a greater similarity in the kinds of orders that can be made under the *CCAA* and the *BIA*, the reforms have not produced a complete convergence. The stay of proceedings in *CCAA* proceedings has a potentially wider scope. It can be used to stay proceedings against parties other than the debtor,[63] and it covers both pre-filing and post-filing creditors.[64] The *CCAA* has been amended by a new provision that permits a court to make an order in respect of a critical supplier.[65] A similar provision was not included in the *BIA*. As well, there are a number of important differences in the rules pertaining to executory contracts.[66] In deciding which restructuring regime is more appropriate, insolvency lawyers must continue to give close attention to the potential consequences of these dissimilarities.

Second, in some instances, the reforms impose a stricter rule in respect of *CCAA* restructurings than was formerly the case. For example, courts are not permitted to make orders that disturb the priority ranking of secured creditors unless the secured creditors are notified of the application. As well, certain features, such as cross-collateralization provisions in DIP ("debtor-in-possession") loans, may no longer be approved.[67]

Third, the existence of the new statutory provisions appears to put to rest the uncertainty over the source of the court's power to make orders under the *CCAA*. It is no longer necessary for courts to attempt to justify their exercise of power on the basis of inherent jurisdiction, equitable

62 *CCAA*, s 11.

63 *Re T Eaton Co* (1997), 46 CBR (3d) 293 (Ont Ct Gen Div).

64 *ICR Commercial Real Estate (Regina) Ltd v Bricore Land Group Ltd* (2007), 33 CBR (5th) 50 (Sask CA). The stay under the *BIA* restructuring provisions covers only pre-filing creditors. See Chapter 12, Section D(10).

65 *CCAA*, s 11.4. And see Chapter 13, Section B.

66 See Chapter 13.

67 See Chapter 13, Section A(2).

jurisdiction, or implied statutory power based on notions of gap filling.[68] The statute now expressly confers upon the court the power to make orders. Given the history of the *CCAA*, it seems likely that courts will not hesitate to engage in further innovations when appropriate.[69] However, the failure to include a similar general power on courts under the *BIA* means that it is unlikely that the court will be able to make similar orders. There are two reasons supporting this view. The first is that the inclusion in 2009 of a general power in the *CCAA* but not in the *BIA* indicated that Parliament intended that such powers should be available to a court only in *CCAA* proceedings. Secondly, the decision of the Supreme Court of Canada in *Century Services*[70] indicates that the powers are conferred by statute and not by virtue of the principle of inherent jurisdiction. In determining whether to exercise this power, the requirements of appropriateness, good faith, and due diligence are baseline considerations.[71]

The statutory reforms will not resolve all controversies concerning the powers of the court in *CCAA* restructuring proceedings. Where the legislation has specifically addressed a matter, the courts may be asked to decide if it was intended as an exhaustive codification of the court's power, or if the court may issue some other order under its general power to address the matter in a different manner. For example, the statutory provision that governs critical suppliers under the *CCAA* sets out a legislative approach to the problem of suppliers who refuse to deal with the debtor unless pre-filing obligations are satisfied. The provision permits a court to order the critical supplier to continue to supply the critical goods or services to the debtor. It is unclear if the provision is to be an exhaustive source of authority in respect of critical supplier orders, or if a court is able to make other types of critical supplier orders based upon the more general authority to make orders.[72]

---

68 See G Jackson & J Sarra, "Selecting the Judicial Tool to Get the Job Done: An Examination of Statutory Interpretation, Discretionary Power and Inherent Jurisdiction in Insolvency Matters" in Janis P Sarra, ed, *Annual Review of Insolvency Law, 2007* (Toronto, Thomson/Carswell, 2008) 41.

69 See J Sarra, "Judicial Discretion" in S Ben-Ishai & A Duggan, eds, *Canadian Bankruptcy and Insolvency Law: Bill C-55, Statute c. 47 and Beyond* (Markham, ON: LexisNexis Canada, 2007) 199 at 224–25.

70 Above note 28 at paras 64–67.

71 *Ibid* at para 70.

72 See *Canwest Global Communications Corp (Re)*, (2009) 59 CBR (5th) 72 at para 43 (Ont SCJ).

FURTHER READINGS

BAIRD, D. "Bankruptcy's Uncontested Axioms" (1998) 108 *Yale Law Journal* 573

BISH, D. "The Plight of Receiverships in a CCAA World" (2013) 2 *Journal of the Insolvency Institute of Canada* 221

EDWARDS, S. "Reorganizations under the *Companies' Creditors Arrangement Act*" (1947) 25 *Canadian Bar Review* 587

JACKSON, G, & J SARRA. "Selecting the Judicial Tool to Get the Job Done: An Examination of Statutory Interpretation, Discretionary Power and Inherent Jurisdiction in Insolvency Matters," in Janis P Sarra, ed, *Annual Review of Insolvency Law, 2007* (Toronto: Thomson/Carswell, 2008) 41

JONES, R. "The Evolution of Canadian Restructuring Law: Challenges for the Rule of Law" in Janis P Sarra, ed, *Annual Review of Insolvency Law, 2005* (Toronto: Thomson/Carswell, 2006) 481

LOPUCKI, L, & G TRIANTIS. "A Systems Approach to Comparing US and Canadian Reorganization of Financially Distressed Companies" in J Ziegel, ed, *Current Developments in International and Comparative Corporate Insolvency Law* (Oxford: Clarendon Press, 1994) 109

NOCILLA, A. "The History of the Companies' Creditors Arrangement Act and the Future of Restructuring Law in Canada" (2014) 56 *Canadian Business Law Journal* 73

———. "Is 'Corporate Rescue' Working in Canada?" (2013) 53 *Canadian Business Law Journal* 382

SARRA, J. *Creditor Rights and the Public Interest* (Toronto: University of Toronto Press, 2003)

———. "Judicial Exercise of Inherent Jurisdiction under the *CCAA*" (2004) 40 *Canadian Business Law Journal* 280

STUDY COMMITTEE ON BANKRUPTCY AND INSOLVENCY LEGISLATION. *Report of the Study Committee on Bankruptcy and Insolvency Legislation* (Ottawa: Study Committee on Bankruptcy and Insolvency Legislation, 1970) Part I, c 2 (*Tassé Report*)

WOOD, R. "Rescue and Liquidation in Restructuring Law" (2013) 53 *Canadian Business Law Journal* 407

ZIEGEL, J. "New and Old Challenges in Approaching Phase Three Amendments to Canada's Commercial Insolvency Laws" (2002) 37 *Canadian Business Law Journal* 75

CHAPTER 12

COMMENCING RESTRUCTURING PROCEEDINGS

A decision to initiate a restructuring is not taken lightly. The debtor will usually explore a number of alternatives, such as the injection of additional equity by the shareholders, to avert the financial difficulties of the business, and will engage in discussions with the key stakeholders, such as the principal lenders. If the debtor concludes that it is not possible to resolve the problems through other measures, the debtor must decide whether a restructuring should be attempted. The debtor must also determine which restructuring regime can be used. If both the *Companies' Creditors Arrangement Act* (*CCAA*) and the *Bankruptcy and Insolvency Act* (*BIA*) are available, a choice will need to be made. The commencement of restructuring proceedings is accompanied by a stay of proceedings. This gives the debtor a short respite from the enforcement activities of creditors and the opportunity to develop a plan to put before the creditors for their approval. Some creditors may take the view that an immediate liquidation of the debtor is the preferred option, and they may attempt to convince a court that the restructuring attempt should be terminated. If they are successful in their arguments, the court will terminate the restructuring proceedings and the debtor will likely be liquidated through bankruptcy or receivership proceedings or through a liquidating *CCAA* or commercial proposal.

A. ELIGIBLE PERSONS

Before commencing restructuring proceedings, it is necessary to determine if the debtor meets the statutory eligibility requirements imposed by the insolvency regime. Sometimes both of the restructuring regimes will be available and the debtor must make a choice between them. In other instances, only one of them will be available. Both regimes require that the debtor be bankrupt or insolvent.[1] The meaning of insolvency and whether a different conception of it is used in restructuring proceedings is examined in Chapter 1.[2] Banks, insurance companies, and trust companies cannot use either restructuring regime[3] but must instead restructure pursuant to the meager restructuring provisions contained in the *Winding-up and Restructuring Act* (*WURA*).[4]

Both the *CCAA* and the *BIA* exclude railway companies.[5] This exclusion only applies to railway companies that are incorporated pursuant to special federal or provincial legislation.[6]

1) Eligibility under the *CCAA*

The *CCAA* has the stricter statutory eligibility requirements. In order to qualify, the debtor must be a "debtor company" and the total claims against it and any affiliated debtor companies must exceed $5 million.[7] The Act defines "debtor company" as a company that is bankrupt or insolvent.[8] The definition of "company" covers federal and provincial

---

1 *CCAA*, s 2(1) "debtor company"; *BIA*, s 50(1).

2 See Chapter 1, Section E(5).

3 *CCAA*, s 2(1) "company"; *BIA*, s 2 "corporation." It may, however, be feasible to replace a non-eligible entity with an eligible entity prior to the restructuring in order to comply with the eligibility conditions of the *CCAA*. See *ATB Financial v Metcalfe & Mansfield Alternative Investments II Corp* (2008), 42 CBR (5th) 90 (Ont SCJ).

4 RSC 1985, c W-11 [*WURA*].

5 *CCAA*, s 2 "company"; *BIA*, s 2 "corporation."

6 *Montréal, Maine & Atlantique Canada Co (Arrangement relatif à)*, 2015 QCCS 3236. And see Chapter 21, Section B.

7 *CCAA*, s 3(1).

8 *Ibid*, s 2(1) "debtor company." An application made by a bankrupt company must be made with the consent of the inspectors. See *CCAA*, *ibid*, s 11.6. The definition also extends to companies that are being wound up under the *WURA* as well as companies that have committed an act of bankruptcy under the *BIA* or that are deemed insolvent under the *WURA* whether or not insolvency proceedings have been commenced.

corporations as well as any foreign corporation having assets or doing business in Canada.[9] The *CCAA* therefore adopts an eligibility requirement that depends upon the legal form of the business entity. Non-corporate business entities, such as partnerships, cannot restructure under the *CCAA*. The 2009 amendments expanded the scope of the *CCAA* by bringing income trusts into the definition of a "company."[10]

The second component of the eligibility conditions relates to the amount of total claims outstanding against the company. The $5-million threshold limits the availability of the *CCAA* to larger companies. However, in determining this amount, claims against all affiliated companies are combined. Companies are affiliated if one is a subsidiary of the other, if both are subsidiaries of another company, or if the same person controls both companies.[11] Claims are defined as any indebtedness, liability, or obligation that would be provable in bankruptcy.[12] This permits the inclusion of unliquidated or contingent claims into the determination.[13] Although the statute makes it clear that these claims must be considered in calculating whether the total claims exceed $5 million, there is controversy over whether unliquidated or contingent claims should be taken into account when determining if the debtor is insolvent under the balance sheet test.[14]

2) Eligibility under the *BIA*

The commercial proposal provisions in the *BIA* adopt less restrictive eligibility conditions. The provisions are not limited to corporations but apply to persons generally.[15] Individuals[16] and non-corporate business entities can therefore restructure under this regime. A trustee in

---

9 *Re Global Light Telecommunications Inc* (2004), 2 CBR (5th) 210 (BCSC) held that a court will not inquire as to the relative quantity of assets held in Canada by a foreign corporation. It is sufficient for the purposes of the eligibility requirements that there was a nominal amount held in a Canadian bank account.

10 *CCAA*, s 2(1) "company" and "income trust." And see Chapter 3, Section A for a discussion of the difficulties associated with treating an income trust as a legal person.

11 *CCAA*, s 3(2). And see *Re Long Potato Growers Ltd* (2008), 45 CBR (5th) 29 (NBQB).

12 *CCAA*, s 2(1) "claim." See also Chapter 9, Section A(2).

13 See, for example, *Re Muscletech Research & Development Inc* (2006), 19 CBR (5th) 54 (Ont SCJ).

14 See Chapter 1, Section E(4).

15 *BIA*, ss 2 "person" and 50(1).

16 An individual cannot make a commercial proposal if a consumer proposal has been filed and the administrator has not been discharged. See *BIA*, s 50(1.1).

bankruptcy, a receiver, or a liquidator of the debtor may also initiate the proceedings.[17] Unlike the *CCAA*, the *BIA* does not impose a financial threshold based on the value of outstanding claims against the debtor.

B. CONSOLIDATION OF PROCEEDINGS

A distinction must be drawn between procedural consolidation and substantive consolidation of restructuring proceedings. In procedural consolidation, the court directs that restructuring proceedings against two or more related persons be consolidated in a single proceeding. This is merely an administrative convenience that reduces the time and expense involved in maintaining separate proceedings. Procedural consolidation does not alter the substantive rights of claimants against their respective debtors.

Substantive consolidation involves a pooling of assets and a pooling of claims. Instead of recognizing the separate assets and separate liabilities of each business entity, the assets and the claims are treated as if they were all held by or against a single entity. As with substantive consolidation of bankruptcy proceedings, an order for substantial consolidation may prejudice creditors who have claims against an entity with a higher assets-to-liabilities ratio and benefit creditors who have claims against a related entity with a lower assets-to-liabilities ratio.[18]

Canadian courts have demonstrated a willingness to consider United States caselaw that sets out the conditions that need to exist in order to justify an order for substantive consolidation.[19] The leading decision from the United States on substantive consolidation is *In re Owens Corning*.[20] The court held that the general expectation of the laws and the markets is that entity separateness is to be maintained. Substantive consolidation is appropriate only when the conduct of the debtor has made it inappropriate to recognize the separateness of the entities, and only when more precise remedies have been considered and rejected. In order to succeed, the party asking for substantive consolidation must show that (1), before the commencement of restructuring proceedings, the entities had disregarded separateness so significantly that their creditors relied on the breakdown of entity

17 *Ibid*, s 50(1).

18 *Re Snider Bros*, 18 BR 230 (Bkrtcy D Mass 1982).

19 *Re Northland Properties Ltd* (1988), 69 CBR (NS) 266 (BCSC); *Re Atlantic Yarn Inc* (2008), 42 CBR (5th) 107 (NBQB); *Bacic v Millennium Educational & Research Charitable Foundation*, 2014 ONSC 5875.

20 419 F3d 195 (3d Cir 2005).

borders and treated them as one legal entity; or that (2), after the commencement of restructuring proceedings, these entities' assets and liabilities were so scrambled that separating them would be prohibitively expensive and would hurt all creditors.[21]

C. COMMENCEMENT OF PROCEEDINGS

1) Commencing Proceedings under the *CCAA*

Restructuring proceedings under the *CCAA* are commenced through an application to a court for an initial order.[22] The application may be made to a court in the province within which the company has its head office or chief place of business.[23] If the company has neither, then the application may be made in the province within which any of the assets of the company are situated.[24] Although the statute does not require that the debtor company bring the application,[25] it is nearly always the case that the debtor company will initiate the proceedings.

An application for an initial order under the *CCAA* can be made on an *ex parte* basis.[26] This may be useful if there is a real prospect that creditors will attempt to exercise their enforcement remedies against the debtor's assets before the court hears the matter. Sometimes the initial application is made only with notice to the major creditors if it is impracticable to identify and notify all the creditors.[27] A projected cash-flow statement and copies of financial statements prepared in the prior year must be submitted with an application for an initial order.[28]

The initial application will usually request an order that does the following things:

---

21 *Ibid* at 211.

22 *CCAA*, s 11.02(1).

23 *Ibid*, s 9(1).

24 See *Re Oblats de Marie Immaculée du Manitoba* (2002), 34 CBR (4th) 76 (Sask QB), in which the Saskatchewan court concluded that it did not have jurisdiction to hear a *CCAA* application where a provincially incorporated company had its head office and chief place of business in Manitoba.

25 *CCAA* restructuring proceedings have been initiated by secured creditors; see *Re 1078385 Ontario Ltd* (2004), 16 CBR (5th) 152 (Ont CA). However, the initiation of *CCAA* proceedings by creditors is rare.

26 *CCAA*, ss 11 and 11.02(1). The applicant must make full and fair disclosure of all relevant facts. See *Re Hester Creek Estate Winery Ltd* (2004), 50 CBR (4th) 73 (BCSC).

27 *Re Royal Oak Mines Inc* (1999), 6 CBR (4th) 314 (Ont Ct Gen Div).

28 *CCAA*, s 10(2).

- abridges service of notice of the application;
- declares the debtor company to be one to which the *CCAA* applies;
- authorizes the debtor company to continue its business operations and continue in possession of its property;
- stays proceedings against the debtor company;
- appoints a monitor;
- authorizes the debtor company to obtain interim financing (DIP financing);
- requires the debtor company to indemnify its directors and officers for any liability that they incur following the date of the initial order;
- creates charges against the property that secure the administrative expenses, the interim financing, and the indemnification of directors and officers, and that gives the charges priority over all other security interests and encumbrances;
- authorizes the debtor company to file a plan of arrangement; and
- permits interested parties to apply to the court for variation or amendment of the order (a "comeback" clause).

The stay of proceedings provided for in the initial order cannot exceed thirty days. The applicant will therefore need to bring a subsequent application before the court for a stay of proceedings of a longer duration.[29] This permits parties affected by the initial order to have an opportunity to express their views concerning the eligibility of the debtor or the appropriateness of the order. The monitor must notify every known creditor who has a claim of more than $1,000 against the company and advise them of the order.[30]

2) Commencing Proceedings under the *BIA*

There are two routes through which restructuring proceedings under the *BIA* can be initiated. Unlike the *CCAA*, neither route requires the intervention of a court in order to commence the proceedings. The first route is the simplest. If the debtor has already developed a commercial proposal, the restructuring proceedings can be initiated by filing it with a licensed trustee.[31] The trustee then files the proposal together with a cash-flow statement and associated documents with the official receiver.[32]

29 *Ibid*, s 11.02(2).
30 *Ibid*, s 23(1)(a).
31 *BIA*, s 50(2).
32 *Ibid*, ss 62(1) and 50.4(2).

Most business organizations will find that they are unable to file a proposal in the first instance, since they need time to negotiate its terms with their creditors. For this reason, most commercial entities that restructure under the *BIA* take the second route. This permits the debtor to initiate proceedings by filing a notice of intention to make a proposal with the official receiver.[33] The trustee is required to notify every known creditor of the notice of intention within five days of its filing.[34] The debtor must file a cash-flow statement and associated documents with the official receiver within ten days of the filing of the notice of intention.[35] If the debtor fails to file the cash-flow statement within this time, the debtor will be deemed to have made an assignment in bankruptcy.[36]

3) Switching Restructuring Regimes

Some corporations are eligible to commence proceedings under either restructuring regime. In this case, the corporation will typically elect one or the other. The corporation may subsequently decide that it would prefer to attempt the restructuring under the other regime. Both the *CCAA* and the *BIA* contain provisions that prevent a debtor from invoking the other restructuring regime if the plan or proposal has failed under the regime initially chosen. Proceedings under the *CCAA* are considered to have failed if the creditors have voted against accepting the arrangement or if a court has refused to sanction it.[37] Proceedings under the *BIA* are considered to have failed if there has been a deemed bankruptcy or if there has been a refusal or deemed refusal by the creditors or if the proposal has been annulled.[38]

Although a debtor cannot invoke the alternative regime after the restructuring attempt under the original regime has ended in failure, mid-stream jumps between regimes are permissible.[39] The *BIA* provides that proceedings commenced under the *CCAA* shall not be dealt with or continued under the *BIA*.[40] This does not mean that a switch is

33 *Ibid*, s 50.4(1).
34 *Ibid*, s 50.4(6).
35 *Ibid*, s 50.4(2).
36 *Ibid*, s 50.4(8).
37 *Ibid*, s 66(2)(b).
38 *CCAA*, s 11.6(b).
39 In *Royal Oak Mines Inc (Re)* (1999), 14 CBR (4th) 279 (Ont SCJ), the switch was from the *CCAA* to the *BIA*. In *Re Mega Bleu Inc/Mega Blue Inc* (2003), 39 CBR (4th) 80 (NBQB), the switch was from the commercial proposals provisions of the *BIA* to the *CCAA*.
40 *BIA*, s 66(2)(a).

not possible. Rather, it means that the *BIA* proceedings must be commenced afresh through the filing of a notice of intention or a proposal. The *CCAA* provides that restructuring proceedings under the *BIA* may be continued under the *CCAA*.[41] This means that the *CCAA* initiation proceedings do not need to be commenced afresh and that therefore the initial application/subsequent application procedure is not invoked. If a proposal is filed under the *BIA*, continuation of the proceedings under the *CCAA* is no longer possible.

D. THE STAY OF PROCEEDINGS

A major difference between the stay of proceedings under the *CCAA* and the stay of proceedings under the *BIA* is that the former is derived from a court order while the latter arises automatically upon the commencement of the proceedings. As a consequence, a court in *CCAA* proceedings is able to tailor the stay of proceedings to address specific problems associated with the particular business. Both Acts provide that the Crown is bound.[42]

Courts have held that the stay of proceedings under the *CCAA* serves four different purposes, namely: (1) it maintains the status quo by preventing a creditor from seizing assets; (2) it prevents the business from being disrupted through the termination of contracts; (3) it relieves the debtor corporation of the burden of dealing with litigation so that it can focus its efforts on the restructuring; and (4) it can be used to prevent the frustration of the restructuring after its implementation on the basis of pre-filing defaults or breaches in respect of unaffected creditors whose claims are not compromised by the plan.[43]

1) The Stay of Proceedings under the *CCAA*

The *CCAA* provides that a court may make an order staying proceedings under the *BIA* or the *WURA*, restraining further proceedings in any action or suit or proceeding against the debtor company or prohibiting the commencement of any proceeding with any other action, suit, or proceeding against the company.[44]

---

41 *CCAA*, s 11.6(a).

42 *Ibid*, s 40; *BIA*, s 4.1.

43 *Doman Industries Ltd (Trustee of) (Re)*, 2003 BCSC 376 at para 22.

44 *CCAA*, ss 11.02(1) & (2).

The stay of proceedings that is typically granted by a court in *CCAA* proceedings is very broad in its scope. It prevents any commencement or continuation of proceedings before a court or a tribunal.[45] This covers judicial, extra-judicial, and self-help remedies, and is effective against secured and unsecured creditors.[46] The stay of proceedings does not apply to the prosecution of criminal or quasi-criminal proceedings against the debtor,[47] but it will apply to enforcement proceedings that are brought to recover a fine or penalty.[48] It also covers proposed arbitration,[49] grievances under collective agreements,[50] and warning notices issued by foreign pension administrators pursuant to long arm pension legislation that allows pension regulators to pursue assets in other jurisdictions.[51]

The stay of proceedings created by the initial order has a maximum duration of thirty days. In order to extend the length of the stay, a subsequent application must be brought. In seeking an initial order staying proceedings as well as any subsequent order, the applicant must satisfy the court that circumstances exist that make such an order appropriate. In seeking a subsequent order, the applicant must also satisfy the court that the applicant is acting in good faith and with due diligence.[52]

2) The Stay of Proceedings under the *BIA*

The stay of proceedings under the *BIA* arises automatically upon the filing of a proposal with a trustee[53] or upon filing of a notice of intention with the official receiver.[54] The automatic stay of proceedings prevents a creditor from exercising a remedy against the debtor or the debtor's property and prevents a creditor from commencing or continuing any action, execution, or proceeding for the recovery of any claim provable

45 *Re Smoky River Coal Ltd* (1999), 12 CBR (4th) 94 (Alta CA).

46 *Quintette Coal Ltd v Nippon Steel Corp* (1990), 2 CBR (3d) 303 (BCCA).

47 *Milner Greenhouses Ltd v Saskatchewan* (2004), 50 CBR (4th) 214 (Sask QB).

48 *Re Air Canada* (2006), 28 CBR (5th) 317 (Ont SCJ).

49 *Luscar Ltd v Smoky River Coal Limited*, 1999 ABCA 179.

50 *Canwest Global Communications Corp*, 2011 ONSC 2215.

51 *Nortel Networks Corporation (Re)*, 2010 ONSC 1304. And see M Zigler & B Walancik "Some Reflections on the Benefits and Limitations of Long-Arm Pension Legislation" in Janis P Sarra, ed, *Annual Review of Insolvency Law, 2014* (Toronto: Carswell, 2015) 269.

52 *CCAA*, s 11.02(3).

53 *BIA*, s 69.1(1).

54 *Ibid*, s 69(1).

in bankruptcy. This has been interpreted as encompassing proceedings for injunctive relief.[55]

Unlike the automatic stay of proceedings in bankruptcy, the automatic stay that operates in *BIA* restructuring proceedings binds secured creditors as well as unsecured creditors. This is subject to an important limitation. The stay of proceedings does not operate against a secured creditor if the secured creditor has taken possession of the secured assets. Nor does it apply if the secured creditor has given a notice of intention to enforce a security[56] more than ten days before filing of a proposal or a notice of intention to make a proposal, or if the debtor consented to enforcement after receiving the notice of intention.[57] It is therefore crucial that the debtor commence *BIA* restructuring proceedings before the ten-day period expires. Because of the intense time constraints involved, this will normally be through the filing of a notice of intention to make a proposal.

When restructuring proceedings are initiated under the *BIA* through a notice of intention, the automatic stay of proceedings ends upon the filing of the proposal.[58] Upon filing of the proposal, a second stay of proceedings automatically comes into operation and ends when the trustee is discharged or the debtor has become bankrupt.[59] If the restructuring fails and an automatic bankruptcy ensues,[60] the stay of proceedings that governs a commercial proposal comes to an end and the automatic bankruptcy stay of proceedings is activated. When this happens, secured creditors are entitled to enforce their remedies against the collateral, since the bankruptcy stay does not cover secured creditors.[61]

3) Staying Proceedings against Third Parties

The statutory provisions in both the *CCAA* and the *BIA* provide a court only with the power to stay proceedings brought against the debtor. In

55 *Golden Griddle Corp v Fort Erie Truck & Travel Plaza Inc* (2005), 29 CBR (5th) 62 (Ont SCJ).

56 *BIA*, s 244 provides that a notice of intention to enforce a security interest must be given at least ten days before enforcement of a security taken on all or substantially all of the debtor's inventory, accounts receivable, or other property.

57 *Ibid*, ss 69(2) and 69.1(2). The consent must be given after the notice of intention to enforce is given. A contractual consent or waiver provision in a security agreement is not sufficient. See *BIA*, s 244(2.1).

58 *Ibid*, s 69(1). The stay also comes to an end if the debtor becomes bankrupt.

59 *Ibid*, s 69.1(1)(a).

60 *Ibid*, ss 50(12.1), 50.4(8)(a), 57(a), and 61(2)(a).

61 See Chapter 6, Section A(7).

some cases, courts have been asked to grant a stay of proceedings in respect of actions or remedies brought by a claimant against a person other than the entity that is attempting to restructure. This is usually done where the proceedings against the third party would significantly undermine the possibility of a successful restructuring.

In some cases, the need for this type of order arises because of the restricted scope of the *CCAA*. In *Re Lehndorff General Partner Ltd*,[62] the court granted a stay of proceedings in respect of a limited partnership. A restructuring of a corporate group had been initiated. The corporations within this group were able to restructure under the *CCAA*, but one of the entities within the group was a limited partnership. Justice Farley granted a stay of proceedings in respect of actions and remedies against the limited partnership despite the fact that the limited partnership was not a company within the meaning of the *CCAA*. A stay of proceedings under the *CCAA* can be made only in respect of proceedings against a company; however, Justice Farley held that the source of the jurisdiction to grant the stay in respect of a third party was not the *CCAA* but rather the inherent jurisdiction of the court to grant such an order where just and convenient to do so.

In *Re T Eaton Co*,[63] the court made an order that prevented third parties from asserting their contractual rights against landlords that owned shopping malls in which Eaton's was the anchor store. The co-tenancy clauses gave smaller tenants the right to reduce the rent payable or to terminate the lease if an anchor store closed. The court held that the order was properly granted since the court had jurisdiction to make the order either under the statutory power to stay proceedings in respect of a company under the *CCAA* or under the inherent jurisdiction of the court.

A debtor may prefer to use the *CCAA* if it is necessary to obtain a stay of proceedings against a third party. The automatic stay of proceedings under the *BIA* operates only in respect of actions and remedies against the debtor. Although a debtor who commences restructuring proceedings under the *BIA* might apply to a court for a stay of proceedings in respect of proceedings against a third party, there is significant uncertainty over the court's jurisdiction to grant such orders under the *BIA*.[64]

---

62 (1993), 17 CBR (3d) 24 (Ont Ct Gen Div). See also *Re Calpine Canada Energy Ltd* (2006), 19 CBR (5th) 187 (Alta QB).

63 (1997), 46 CBR (3d) 293 (Ont Ct Gen Div). See also *Target Canada Co (Re)*, 2015 ONSC 303.

64 See Chapter 11, Section D. The orders could now be made pursuant to the *CCAA*, s 11. There is no equivalent provision in the *BIA*.

The *CCAA* limits the ability of a court to stay proceedings brought by a creditor against certain types of third parties. For example, a stay of proceedings cannot affect proceedings that are brought against a third party who is obligated under a letter of credit or guarantee.[65]

4) Staying Proceedings against Directors

Both the *CCAA* and the *BIA* provide for a stay of proceedings against directors.[66] Both Acts permit the compromise of claims against directors in respect of claims that arose before the commencement of restructuring proceedings and that relate to the obligations of the corporation where the directors are by law liable in their capacity as directors for the payment of such obligations.[67] In order to prevent any future compromise from being undermined by post-filing manoeuvres by creditors, actions against directors are stayed until the plan or approval is approved by the court or upon failure of the restructuring attempt.[68] The stay of proceedings under the *BIA* is automatic and arises upon the filing of a proposal or the filing of a notice of intention to make a proposal. The stay of proceedings under the *CCAA* is derived from the court order, and therefore the initial and subsequent orders must contain a provision staying proceedings against directors in order to be effective. If all the directors have resigned or have been removed, a person who manages or supervises the management of the business affairs of the corporation is deemed to be a director for the purposes of these provisions.[69]

5) Staying Proceedings of Regulatory Bodies

If a regulatory body is simply attempting to enforce a claim as a secured or unsecured creditor, the stay of proceedings affects the regulatory body in the same manner as any other creditor. Different considerations apply if the proceedings are not for the recovery of a claim but

---

65 *CCAA*, s 11.04. Prior to the enactment of this provision, some courts stayed proceedings against a third party under a guarantee. See *Quintette Coal Ltd v Nippon Steel Corp*, above note 46. But see, *contra*, *Re Fairview Industries Ltd* (1991), 11 CBR (3d) 37 (NSSCTD).

66 *CCAA*, s 11.03; *BIA*, s 69.31.

67 *CCAA*, s 5.1; *BIA*, ss 50(13)–(18).

68 *CCAA*, s 11.03(1); *BIA*, s 69.31(1). The stay of proceedings does not apply in respect of an action against a director who has given a guarantee in respect of the obligations of the corporation or a suit for injunctive relief against a director. See *CCAA*, s 11.03(2); *BIA*, s 69.31(2).

69 *CCAA*, s 11.03(3); *BIA*, s 69.31(3).

are connected to the regulatory mandate of the agency. For example, a regulatory body may have launched an investigation into the conduct of the debtor and may be threatening to suspend or revoke a licence that permits the debtor to carry on business. Although the issue is now governed by statutory provision, it is useful to review the development of the law in order to understand the effect of the legislation.

Prior to the 2009 amendments, the automatic stay of proceedings under the *BIA* was not sufficiently wide to prevent a regulatory body from carrying out these types of proceedings since the stay was effective only in respect of proceedings for the recovery of a claim provable in bankruptcy.[70] The language used in many of the orders granted under the *CCAA* was sufficiently wide to cover proceedings brought by the agency to ensure regulatory compliance.[71] In *Toronto Stock Exchange Inc v United Keno Mines Ltd*,[72] the stay covered any proceedings brought by a creditor or other entity exercising regulatory or administrative functions. The Toronto Stock Exchange (TSE) brought a motion to lift the stay to permit it to bring proceedings that would suspend trading in the shares of the debtor company. The court declined to lift the stay on the ground that the TSE failed to show how the public was harmed given that the *CCAA* proceedings were public knowledge and the price had fallen to nine cents a share. In making its decision, the court engaged in an exercise in which it weighed the public interest. It concluded that there was little likelihood of harm to public investors and that there was grave potential harm to employees, suppliers, shareholders, landlords, and customers if the restructuring attempt were to fail.

This position has been altered by the 2009 amendments to both the *CCAA* and the *BIA*.[73] Under these provisions, a stay of proceedings does not affect the rights of a regulatory body[74] with respect to any investigation or any proceeding taken against the debtor except when it is seeking to enforce a right to payment.[75] A regulatory agency that

---

70 *BIA*, ss 69(1) & 69(1.1).

71 See *Re Anvil Range Mining Corp* (1998), 3 CBR (4th) 93 (Ont Ct Gen Div).

72 (2000), 19 CBR (4th) 299 (Ont SCJ).

73 *CCAA*, s 11.1; *BIA*, s 69.6.

74 A regulatory body is defined in the provision as a person or body that has powers, duties, or functions relating to the enforcement or administration of an Act of Parliament or the legislature of a province. See *CCAA*, s 11.1(1); *BIA*, s 69.6(1).

75 *CCAA*, s 11.1(2); *BIA*, s 69.6(2). *CCAA*, s 11.1(4) and *BIA*, s 69.6(4) provide that, if there is a dispute over whether a regulatory body is seeking to enforce its rights as a creditor, a court may make an order declaring that the regulatory body is seeking to enforce its rights as a creditor and that the enforcement of the regulatory body is stayed.

is regulating ongoing activities or that is investigating or prosecuting a debtor is not, at that stage, seeking to enforce payment. Thus, the prosecution of offences under health and safety legislation does not fall within the exception despite the fact that debtor may well choose to expend considerable resources defending the action.[76] The stay of proceedings will prevent the issuance of an assessment under forestry legislation that gives rise to lien rights and rights to recover a penalty as these are concerned with the financial consequences of past actions, not the regulation of ongoing conduct.[77]

A court is permitted to stay the proceedings of a regulatory body if the court, on notice to the regulatory body, makes an order declaring that a viable plan or proposal could not be made in the absence of a stay of proceedings.[78] The court shall not make such an order if it is of the opinion that it is contrary to the public interest to do so.

The new provisions therefore alter the law in three ways. First, the provisions give a court the jurisdiction to stay regulatory compliance proceedings in respect of restructuring proceedings under the *BIA*. Second, the regulatory body must now receive notice of the stay. This was not necessarily the case under the *CCAA*. Third, the stay will be granted only if it can be demonstrated that it is essential to the success of the restructuring. This was not a prerequisite under the *CCAA*.

6) Staying Proceedings of Revenue Agencies

Under both the *BIA* and *CCAA*, the stay of proceedings prevents the federal or a provincial government from exercising its statutory requirement to pay procedure[79] (a statutory garnishment remedy for the recovery of income tax, CPP, and EI contributions). In order to keep this stay of proceedings in effect, the debtor must ensure that all post-filing revenue obligations are kept in good standing. The stay of proceedings will automatically terminate against the government if the debtor defaults in payment of the amount that becomes due after the commencement of the restructuring proceedings or if another creditor becomes entitled to realize a security against any property in respect of which the statutory garnishment remedy could be exercised.[80]

A court cannot sanction a plan or proposal unless it provides for payment in full of these amounts within six months of court approval,

---

76 *Terrace Bay Pulp Inc (Re)*, 2013 ONSC 5111.

77 *Lemare Holdings Ltd (Re)*, 2012 BCSC 1591.

78 *CCAA*, s 11.1(3); *BIA*, s 69.6(3).

79 *BIA*, ss 69(1)(c) and 69.1(1)(c); *CCAA*, s 11.09(1).

80 *BIA*, ss 69(3) and 69.1(3); *CCAA*, s 11.09(2).

unless the Crown agrees to compromise its claim.[81] The Crown therefore has a veto right in respect of these claims. Although the recovery of these claims can be delayed, they cannot be denied, unless the Crown agrees to something other than full recovery. The stay of proceedings against a revenue agency comes to an end six months after court approval of the plan. A failure to pay these amounts in full within the six-month period will therefore result in the revival of the Crown's collection remedies against the debtor. The stay of proceedings will also terminate if the restructuring fails because either the creditors or the court refuses to approve it.[82]

These statutory provisions apply only to the collection of income tax, CCP, and EI. The stay of proceedings under both the *BIA* and the *CCAA* is effective in staying the exercise of enforcement remedies in respect of the recovery of the GST.[83]

7) Staying Proceedings against Aircraft Objects

The effect of a stay of proceedings under the *CCAA* or *BIA* is limited in respect of the enforcement remedies of secured creditors and lessors against an aircraft object that is governed by the *Convention on International Interests in Mobile Equipment* and the associated *Protocol on Matters Specific to Aircraft*.[84] The stay of proceedings does not prevent a creditor, lessor, or conditional seller from taking possession of aircraft objects if the debtor defaults in maintaining or preserving them in accordance with the agreement. The stay of proceedings also ceases to operate after a sixty-day waiting period that runs from the commencement of the proceedings unless the debtor has cured all defaults and agrees to perform all future obligations under the agreement. The creditor, lessor, or conditional seller is permitted to take possession of the aircraft object within the sixty-day waiting period if the debtor defaults in performing an obligation under the agreement.

81 *BIA*, s 60(1.1); *CCAA*, s 6(3).

82 *BIA*, s 69.1(1)(d); *CCAA*, s 11.09(1). Under the *BIA*, the stay also comes to an end if the trustee has been discharged or if the debtor becomes bankrupt. Under the *CCAA*, the stay also comes to an end on the expiry of the order, the default of the company on any term of a compromise or arrangement, or on performance of the compromise or arrangement.

83 *Canada (Minister of National Revenue) v Points North Freight Forwarding Inc* (2000), 24 CBR (4th) 184 (Sask QB).

84 See the *International Interests in Mobile Equipment (aircraft equipment) Act*, SC 2005, c 3. This Act sets out the text of the Convention and the Protocol. See also R Cuming, C Walsh, & R Wood, *Personal Property Security Law*, 2d ed (Toronto: Irwin Law, 2012) at 717–31.

8) Enforcement against Financial Collateral

Although the remedies of secured creditors in a restructuring are subject to the stay of proceedings under both the *BIA* and the *CCAA*, an exception is made in respect of a secured creditor who enforces a security interest against certain kinds of collateral that secures an obligation under an eligible financial contract.[85] Both Acts provide a definition of financial collateral.[86] This includes cash or cash equivalents, securities, a securities account, a securities entitlement or a right to acquire securities, and a futures agreement or futures account. Both Acts provide that the stay of proceedings does not prevent the secured creditor from enforcing the security interest against the collateral.[87] They also provide that a court may not make an order that has the effect of subordinating financial collateral.[88]

9) Registration of Security Interests

Unlike bankruptcy, the commencement of restructuring proceedings does not result in a subordination of an unperfected security interest.[89] The secured creditor may wish to perfect its security interest through registration in order to prevent its subordination against other parties. However, the secured creditor may be unable to do so if the stay of proceedings prevents registration of the security interest. The position under the *CCAA* depends upon the terms of the order.[90] In some cases, the wording of the order prevents a secured creditor from registering; in other cases, it does not.[91] The stay of proceedings under the *BIA* will prevent registration only if it is regarded as a proceeding for the recovery of a claim. Registration is a step that is needed to protect the priority ranking of a security interest against competing third-party interests. It is not required in order to assert the security interest against the debtor. On this basis, it may be argued that the *BIA* stay of proceedings does not prevent registration of a security interest. If a stay of proceedings

---

85 An eligible financial contract is the term used to encompass derivative contracts. The treatment of eligible financial contracts is discussed in Chapter 13, Section F.

86 *BIA*, s 2 "financial collateral"; *CCAA*, s 2(1) "financial collateral."

87 *CCAA*, ss 34 (8) & (9); *BIA*, s 65.1(9).

88 *CCAA*, s 34(11); *BIA*, s 88.

89 *Re PSINet Ltd* (2002), 30 CBR (4th) 226 (Ont SCJ); *Re TRG Services Inc* (2006), 26 CBR (5th) 203 (Ont SCJ); *Pioneer Grain Co v Sullivan & Associates Inc* (2007), 36 CBR (5th) 179 (Sask CA).

90 *Re PSINet Ltd*, above note 89; *Re TRG Services Inc*, above note 89.

91 The template initial orders of the provinces now expressly provide that the order does not prevent registration.

prevents a secured creditor from registering, the secured creditor may apply to court to lift the stay in order to permit registration.

10) Post-filing Creditors

A debtor that is restructuring proposes a plan to its pre-filing creditors. The post-filing creditors are not affected by the plan. However, whether or not the stay of proceedings affects the post-filing creditors is a different issue. Under the *CCAA*, the court is given the power to stay, restrain, or prohibit any proceedings against the company. The orders that are ordinarily made by the courts do not distinguish between pre-filing claims and post-filing claims, and courts have held that both kinds of claims are subject to the stay.[92]

The position under the *BIA* is unclear. The automatic stay of proceedings arises upon the filing of the proposal or a notice of intention and stays any proceeding for a claim provable in bankruptcy.[93] A post-bankruptcy claim is not provable in bankruptcy and therefore is not subject to the stay.[94] This may suggest by analogy that the date of the filing of the proposal or the notice of intention should be treated as the day of the bankruptcy for the purposes of determining which claims are subject to the stay.[95] On this view, the stay would not affect post-filing creditors. However, the provision may also be interpreted as covering both pre-filing and post-filing creditors. On this view, the statutory reference to claims provable in bankruptcy was simply intended to define the kinds of claims that are subject to the stay, not to differentiate the claims on the basis of when they arose. This latter interpretation is more consonant with the underlying policy of restructuring law: the purpose of the stay is to give the debtor the breathing space within which to develop a proposal to put before the creditors for their consideration, and this objective will be undermined if litigation and enforcement activity is permitted regardless of when the claim arose. This interpretation also has the advantage of producing a common approach to the matter in *BIA* and *CCAA* restructurings.

---

92 *ICR Commercial Real Estate (Regina) Ltd v Bricore Land Group Ltd* (2007), 33 CBR (5th) 50 (Sask CA). Although post-filing creditors are bound by the stay of proceedings, a court does not have the power to stay proceedings in respect of obligations that arise subsequent to the implementation of the plan. See *Re Doman Industries Ltd* (2003), 41 CBR (4th) 29 (BCSC).

93 *BIA*, ss 69(1) and 69.1(1).

94 *Kidd v Flad* (2006), 19 CBR (5th) 282 (Sask QB).

95 See *Wescraft Manufacturing Co* (1994), 27 CBR (3d) 28 (BCSC).

E. LIFTING THE STAY OF PROCEEDINGS

In some cases, creditors will bring a motion to lift a stay of proceedings in an attempt to terminate the restructuring and replace it with some other insolvency regime, such as bankruptcy or receivership. This "showstopper" tactic will be examined in the next section dealing with termination of restructuring proceedings. In other cases, a creditor will bring a motion to lift a stay of proceedings on a more limited basis. The aim of the creditor is not to terminate the restructuring attempt. Instead, the creditor simply seeks to obtain an exception from the operation of the stay on the basis that it is causing some special hardship to the creditor and that it would be just and equitable to lift or modify the stay in respect of that particular creditor. The factors that a court will consider fall within three general headings: (1) the relative prejudice to parties; (2) the balance of convenience; and (3) the merits (chances of success) of any proposed litigation.[96] The courts have taken the view that a party seeking to lift a stay bears a heavy onus of persuading a court to do so.[97]

Where a restructuring is attempted under the *CCAA*, a creditor can bring an application to lift a stay pursuant to the comeback provision that is typically found in the initial order or subsequent order.[98] This provision gives an interested person the right to apply to the court to vary or amend the order. The motion can also be brought before the court when the debtor company makes a subsequent application to obtain an extension of the stay beyond the period granted by the initial order.

Where a restructuring is attempted under the *BIA*, a creditor may apply to a court for a declaration that the stay of proceedings no longer applies to that creditor.[99] The court may make the declaration, subject to any qualifications it thinks appropriate, if the court is satisfied that the creditor is likely to be materially prejudiced and that it is equitable on other grounds to do so. Although the *CCAA* does not articulate the grounds for lifting the stay, the courts apply a similar approach in deciding if a stay of proceedings should be amended or varied in relation to a particular creditor.

96 *ICR Commercial Real Estate (Regina) Ltd v Bricore Land Group Ltd*, 2007 SKCA 72.
97 *Timminco Limited (Re)*, 2012 ONSC 2515.
98 See Chapter 14, Section C(3).
99 *BIA*, s 69.4.

1) Prejudicial Effect of the Stay

In order to convince a court to lift the stay of proceedings, a creditor may attempt to show that the stay has had a materially prejudicial effect on the creditor. In deciding whether to amend or vary the stay, the court is said to balance the interests of all parties by weighing the harm to the creditor against the harm to the other claimants.[100] Courts have also referred to this as a weighing of the relative prejudice to the parties.[101] Applicants are more likely to succeed if they can convince the court that the lifting of the stay will ameliorate its prejudicial effect and that it will not be construed as an open invitation for other creditors to seek similar treatment. To this end, they will need to show that their position is in some sense unique from that of the other creditors who remain subject to the stay. The creditors must therefore establish that they will suffer material prejudice in that they will be treated differently or some way unfairly, or that they will suffer worse harm than other creditors.[102] Courts sometimes state that the prejudicial effect must be objective rather than subjective.[103] The idea that this is meant to convey is that the harm must be measured by the prejudicial effect on the right of action, interest, or security held by the creditor, and not on the basis of the financial health or other characteristic of the creditor. It may be appropriate to lift the stay in respect of a project that has not been disclaimed by the debtor but which is not subject to the sales process as the continuation of the stay will prejudice the other party by preventing it from finding a replacement contractor.[104]

2) Proceedings to Protect an Action or Interest

A lifting of the stay is appropriate where the proceeding is intended merely to preserve or protect the interest of the creditor. These proceedings will generally have little impact on the success of the restructuring, but they will have a severe impact on the position of the claimant if the proceeding or step is not permitted. For example, a claimant may face a limitation period for bringing an action, filing an appeal,[105] or filing a

100 *Icor Oil & Gas Co v Canadian Imperial Bank of Commerce* (1989), 102 AR 161 (QB).

101 *Timminco Limited (Re)*, above note 97; *Re Dylex Ltd* (1995), 31 CBR (3d) 106 (Ont Ct Gen Div).

102 *Golden Griddle Corp v Fort Erie Truck & Travel Plaza Inc*, above note 55.

103 *Re Cumberland Trading Inc* (1994), 23 CBR (3d) 225 (Ont Ct Gen Div); *Toronto-Dominion Bank v Ty (Canada) Inc* (2003), 42 CBR (4th) 142 (Ont SCJ).

104 *Comstock Canada Ltd (Re)*, 2013 ONSC 6043.

105 *Timminco Limited (Re)*, above note 97.

lien that is about to expire.[106] The court may lift the stay in order to permit the action to be commenced, but maintain the stay of proceedings in respect of any further step in relation to the prosecution of the action. The stay has also been lifted in order to permit a secured creditor to register a financing statement in respect of its security interest.[107] The initial or subsequent order under the *CCAA* will often anticipate this issue by permitting the filing of liens or the registration of a financing statement in respect of security interests or by providing that any limitation period is extended by a period of time equal to the duration of the stay of proceedings.[108]

Courts have also lifted the stay in order to permit a creditor to make an application for a bankruptcy order in respect of the debtor. This was done in order to preserve the right to impeach pre-bankruptcy transactions and payments under the *BIA* in the event that the restructuring attempt ended in failure.[109] This step is no longer required, since the 2009 amendments extend the application of the preference and other impeachment provisions of the *BIA* to *CCAA* proceedings.[110]

3) Undersecured Secured Creditors

A secured creditor may also seek to have a stay of proceedings modified or varied when it is suffering disproportionate prejudice as a result of the operation of the stay. This will most often occur if the collateral is diminishing in value because of depreciation caused by the use of equipment or because of declining levels of inventory or accounts.

The Canadian law on this point is less well developed than that of the United States. American bankruptcy law has adopted the concept of adequate protection in relation to secured creditors.[111] Under this doctrine, the value of a secured creditor's rights must be protected in the insolvency proceedings in order for the stay of proceedings to be maintained against the secured creditor. Adequate protection may involve the making of cash payments to the secured creditor to the extent that the value of the collateral diminished in value, the giving of a se-

---

106 *Re Anvil Range Mining Corp*, above note 71. If no action is taken to lift the stay, the limitation will come into effect and the proceeding will be time-barred. See *Re Smoky River Coal Ltd*, above note 45.

107 *Re PSINet Ltd*, above note 89. And see Section D(9), above in this chapter.

108 See *Re Scaffold Connection Corp* (2000), 15 CBR (4th) 289 (Alta QB).

109 *Re JTI-Macdonald Corp* (2004), 5 CBR (5th) 233 (Ont SCJ).

110 *CCAA*, s 36.1. And see Chapter 15, Section C.

111 See C Tabb, *The Law of Bankruptcy* (Westbury, NY: Foundation Press, 1997) at 189–203.

curity interest on other collateral, or the giving of some other collateral of equivalent value. There is no need to provide adequate protection to a secured creditor who is oversecured (i.e., the value of the collateral exceeds the obligation secured) since the secured creditor has an "equity cushion" that protects the secured creditor from suffering loss due to the declining value of the collateral.

Under the *CCAA* and the *BIA*, the stay of proceedings does not operate so as to prevent a person from requiring immediate payment for goods, services, or use of leased or licensed property.[112] Although this will give lessors under true lease agreements the right to demand payment for the continued use of the asset by the debtor, it does not limit the operation of the stay of proceedings in respect of secured creditors.[113]

Despite the dearth of Canadian authority on this point, the idea that a secured creditor should be entitled to some degree of protection is consistent with the underlying principles of Canadian restructuring law. A foundational principle is that a creditor should not be required to accept less in restructuring proceedings than the creditor would have obtained from liquidation of the debtor's assets on bankruptcy or receivership.[114] An undersecured secured creditor who is required to wait as its collateral declines in value is thus prejudiced by the stay of proceedings and suffers loss while the other claimants gain from the restructuring proceedings. Against this, the court must weigh the consequences of lifting the stay on the viability of the restructuring attempt.[115] If the collateral is not essential to the business operations, a court will be more inclined to grant the relief. The court may also consider other forms of relief that balance the interests of both parties. For example, it might authorize payments to the secured party that are designed to cover the diminished value of its collateral.[116]

To satisfy the court that some modification of the stay of proceedings is necessary, a secured creditor must do more than adduce evidence that its collateral is worth less than the amount of the obligation secured. The secured creditor must lead evidence to show the projected amount by which the value of the secured creditor's interest is expected

---

112 *CCAA*, s 11.01; *BIA*, s 65.1(4)(a).

113 See Chapter 13, Section A(5).

114 *Re Woodward's Ltd* (1993), 20 CBR (3d) 74 (BCSC).

115 *505396 BC Ltd (Re)*, 2013 BCSC 1580.

116 See *Clayton Construction Co Ltd (Re)*, 2009 SKQB 397. Section 11 of the *CCAA* provides the authorization for this exercise of power by the court. It is questionable whether a similar power is available under the commercial proposal provisions of the *BIA*.

to decline in value. In other words, it is not enough to show that the secured creditor is undersecured. There must be evidence that demonstrates that the value of the collateral will decline over the course of the restructuring proceedings.[117]

4) Balance of Convenience

In considering balance of convenience, a court may be influenced by the appropriateness of available remedies. The claims process in restructuring proceedings monetizes an employee's right of reinstatement under a collective agreement. Although, as a general rule, grievances should be adjudicated along with other claims in the claims process of the restructuring proceedings, a court may conclude that the balance of convenience and the interests of justice favour the lifting of stay to permit the grievance to proceed through arbitration in order to give a terminated employee the opportunity to seek reinstatement as an employee in the restructured entity.[118] The balance of convenience may also favour lifting the stay when the action seeks a declaration of a constructive trust that would give the claimant priority over secured claimants.[119]

F. TERMINATING RESTRUCTURING PROCEEDINGS

Both the *CCAA* and the *BIA* permit creditors to seek to terminate the restructuring proceedings. It is costly to attempt a restructuring, and creditors may end up worse off if the restructuring is allowed to proceed and ends in failure. The court is therefore given the ability to "pull the plug" on the restructuring attempt if it appears that the restructuring is unlikely to succeed. Courts will terminate the restructuring if the debtor is not acting diligently in moving the process forward or is acting in bad faith. They will also terminate the proceedings if it is probable that it will end in failure because the creditors will reject the plan or if the creditors will suffer prejudice by virtue of that attempt (i.e., the creditors will not gain anything from a successful restructuring).

---

117 *Re Cumberland Trading Inc*, above note 103.

118 *Canwest Global Communications Corp*, above note 50.

119 *Re Puratone*, 2013 MBQB 171. This is particularly the case in a liquidating *CCAA* where there is no restructuring plan that is put at risk.

The legal effect of a termination of restructuring proceedings differs under the two restructuring regimes. Under the *CCAA*, a general lifting of the stay terminates restructuring proceedings. All of the creditors are thereby entitled to exercise their ordinary remedies against the debtor. This will usually result in the liquidation of the debtor through bankruptcy or receivership. However, these proceedings do not arise automatically by virtue of the termination of the restructuring but must be initiated by the creditors following the termination. Despite the termination of the *CCAA* proceedings, a court has the authority under the *CCAA* to maintain the stay until bankruptcy proceedings are commenced.[120] If this were not permitted, the gap between the termination of restructuring proceedings and the commencement of bankruptcy proceedings could produce a race to grab assets. The continuation of the stay subject to a partial lifting of it to allow the debtor company to make an assignment in bankruptcy provides an orderly transition from restructuring proceedings to bankruptcy proceedings and curtails the incentive of a creditor to frustrate a rescue attempt for fear of losing a priority afforded to it in bankruptcy.[121]

Under the *BIA*, a failure of the restructuring proceedings automatically results in the bankruptcy of the debtor.[122]

1) Timing and Procedure

a) Procedure under the *CCAA*

There are three methods by which the creditors can bring a request for termination of the restructuring proceedings before the courts under the *CCAA*. The first is to wait until the debtor applies to court for a renewal of the stay of proceedings. A challenge by creditors is most likely to be brought at the hearing of the debtor company's subsequent application for a stay immediately following the end of the period specified in the initial order.[123] There is no limit on the length in time or the number of subsequent extensions to the stay of proceedings that can be granted by a court. Creditors may also choose to seek termination of restructuring proceedings at one of these later extension applications.[124] However, there is often a significant increase in costs after the initial period comes to an end and the restructuring proceedings gain momentum. It is therefore advisable for the creditors to bring their

120 *Century Services Inc v Canada (AG)*, 2010 SCC 60.

121 *Ibid* at paras 47, 77, and 80.

122 See Chapter 3, Section E.

123 See, for example, *Re 843504 Alberta Ltd* (2003), 4 CBR (5th) 306 (Alta QB).

124 See, for example, *Re San Francisco Gifts Ltd* (2005), 10 CBR (5th) 275 (Alta QB).

challenge at the earliest opportunity if it is clear from the outset that they are opposed to the restructuring attempt.

The second method by which creditors may seek to terminate the stay of proceedings is to bring an application to the court pursuant to a comeback clause that is typically included in the court order.[125] The creditors are thereby able to bring the matter before the court at a time of their choosing. The third method of challenging the stay of proceedings is to appeal the order. This route is more difficult than the other two because of the high threshold that is applied in respect of appeals of orders made in restructuring proceedings.[126]

b) Extension of Time under the *BIA*

Although the *BIA* imposes an automatic stay of proceedings, the termination of the restructuring proceedings is not brought about by a termination of the stay but through a separate process that terminates the proceedings and replaces them with an automatic bankruptcy of the debtor. A debtor who files a notice of intention to make a proposal is given a thirty-day period within which to make a proposal.[127] The debtor may apply to court for an extension, but any extension granted by a court cannot exceed forty-five days.[128] An application for an extension of the time period must be made before the initial or extended time period has expired. Further extensions can be granted, but the total length of the extensions following the initial thirty-day period cannot exceed five months. A restructuring under the *BIA*, therefore, should not be attempted unless there is a realistic possibility that the proposal can be developed no later than six months after the commencement of the proceedings. A failure to file a proposal within these time periods results in an automatic bankruptcy of the debtor. Creditors who wish to challenge the restructuring proceedings are not required to wait until the debtor makes an application for an extension of the time period. Instead, they may apply to court for an order terminating the time period, which will result in the automatic bankruptcy of the debtor.[129]

If the debtor has filed a proposal with the trustee, the creditors are not required to wait until a meeting is called and then vote down the proposal. Instead, they may make an application to court for a declara-

---

125 See, for example, *Re Algoma Steel Inc* (2001), 25 CBR (4th) 194 (Ont CA). And see Chapter 14, Section C(3).

126 See Chapter 14, Section C(5).

127 *BIA*, s 50.4(8).

128 *Ibid*, s 50.4(9).

129 *Ibid*, s 50.4(11).

tion deeming the proposal to be refused by the creditors,[130] and this will result in the automatic bankruptcy of the debtor.[131]

2) Grounds for Terminating Restructuring Proceedings

The *BIA* sets out the following four grounds for termination of restructuring proceedings: (1) lack of due diligence of the debtor; (2) bad faith of the debtor; (3) unlikelihood of a viable proposal being made; and (4) material prejudice to the creditors.[132] The grounds set out in the *CCAA* are less precise. Lack of due diligence and bad faith on the part of the debtor are grounds for termination. However, the remaining ground is that there are circumstances that make the granting of the order appropriate.[133] An earlier version of the 1997 amendments to the *CCAA* adopted a formulation identical to that contained in the *BIA*.[134] However, there was a concern among some insolvency experts that this change would narrow the broad discretion given to courts and deprive the *CCAA* of some of its flexibility as a restructuring vehicle for large, complex corporate restructurings. Because of this concern, the more specific language was dropped.

The absence of specific language in the *CCAA* concerning the likelihood of a viable proposal and material prejudice to a creditor does not mean that these are not relevant factors. Clearly these are significant matters that will be considered by a court when requested to exercise its discretion to terminate restructuring proceedings. Rather, the difference between the two statutes appears to be that a court is given somewhat more latitude under the *CCAA* to permit restructuring proceedings to continue despite the fact that it may cause prejudice to a creditor. Justice Blair in *Skydome Corp v Ontario* stated:[135]

---

130 *Ibid*, s 50(12). This provision clearly covers situations where the restructuring proceedings are commenced by filing the proposal with a trustee. However, there is nothing in the wording of this provision that would prevent it from applying as well to a situation where the proceedings are commenced by filing a notice of intention and a proposal is subsequently filed with the trustee. In *Re Triangle Drugs Inc* (1993), 16 CBR (3d) 1 (Ont Ct Gen Div) the court came to the same result by the more convoluted route of importing *CCAA* principles into the *BIA*.

131 *BIA*, s 57.

132 *Ibid*, ss 50(12), 50.4(9), and 50.4(11).

133 *CCAA*, s 11.02(3).

134 The proposed amendment and the reaction to it is discussed in *ICR Commercial Real Estate (Regina) Ltd v Bricore Land Group Ltd*, above note 92 at paras 52–54.

135 (1998), 16 CBR (4th) 125 at para 11 (Ont Ct Gen Div) [emphasis in original]. The statement must be characterized as *obiter*, since the court held that the objecting creditor did not in fact suffer material prejudice.

> I do not think it follows that if a creditor would be "materially prejudiced" by the refusal to lift the stay it would necessarily be *in*appropriate to extend the *CCAA* proceedings, or that if there would be no prejudice it necessarily follows that it would be appropriate to do so. Insolvency proceedings, by their nature, involve a balancing of prejudices — even, at times, of "material" prejudices.

a) Lack of Due Diligence

It is generally easy for a debtor to qualify for an initial order. Under the *BIA*, it is given automatically upon the filing of a notice of intention. Under the *CCAA*, there is a very strong predisposition to grant the initial order as a matter or course. Thereafter, on applications by the debtor for an extension of the time period, the debtor must show that it is making reasonable progress in moving the restructuring forwards. A failure to show sufficient progress can result in termination of the restructuring proceedings.[136]

b) Lack of Good Faith

A lack of good faith on the part of the debtor will justify a termination of restructuring proceedings. Evidence that the debtor has attempted to mislead the other parties[137] or the court or that the debtor is attempting to use the restructuring for an ulterior purpose are factors that may cause the court to use this ground to terminate restructuring proceedings. For example, an attempt by the debtor to negotiate management employment contracts with unconscionable termination provisions has been considered to be evidence of bad faith.[138]

In *Re San Francisco Gifts Ltd*,[139] the debtor was alleged to have acted dishonestly in respect of some of its dealings with the public through the sale of consumer goods with counterfeit safety-certification labels. The creditors argued that this lack of honesty constituted a lack of good faith. The court held that there is an obligation on the part of the debtor to act honestly in relation to the restructuring proceedings, and that the primary focus of the good faith requirement is on the conduct of the debtor vis-à-vis the court and its officers and the creditors in the context of the restructuring proceedings.[140] In its view, the prosecution

---

136 *Timber Lodge Ltd v Imperial Life Assurance Co* (1992), 17 CBR (3d) 126 (PEIS-CTD); *Re SLMSoft Inc*, 2003 CarswellOnt 4402 (Ont SCJ).

137 See *Re Hayes Forest Servies Ltd*, 2008 BCSC 1256.

138 *Re SLMSoft Inc*, above note 136.

139 Above note 124.

140 See also *Worldspan Marine Inc (Re)*, 2011 BCSC 1758 in which the court indicated that unproven allegations of fraud and misappropriation of funds prior to the

did not preclude the debtor from attempting to restructure, although there might be some circumstances where the business practices were so offensive that a court should terminate the proceedings order to maintain public confidence in the insolvency system.

c) Viability of the Plan

There is no point in incurring the expenses of restructuring proceedings if there is no reasonable prospect that the attempt will succeed. In the *BIA* this is referred to as the viability or acceptability of the proposal. In the *CCAA*, it is more colourfully referred to as the "doomed to failure" ground.[141]

In order for a plan to be accepted by the creditors, it must be approved by a majority of the creditors who have two-thirds of the value of the outstanding claims. A creditor or block of creditors who have more than one-third of the value of the claims or a majority in number of creditors within a particular class have a veto and are able to defeat the plan. Often creditors who possess a veto will seek termination of the restructuring on the basis that they will be unwilling to vote in favour of the plan regardless of its terms. Under the CCAA, courts have held that the mere assertion that no future plan will be acceptable to the creditors is premature and not determinative of the issue when no plan has yet been developed.[142]

The position under the *BIA* is less clear. The difficulty stems from the drafting of the legislation. In order to obtain an extension of time, the debtor must show that it would likely be able to make a viable proposal.[143] But if a creditor applies to terminate, the creditor must show that the debtor will not be able to make a viable proposal or that the debtor will not be able to make a proposal that is accepted by the creditors.[144] Some courts have held that this latter ground is satisfied when creditors who have a veto position indicate they will not support any proposal.[145] Other courts have held that the acceptability of a proposal

---

commencement of restructuring proceedings does not constitute a lack of good faith in their dealings with stakeholders in the course of the *CCAA* process.

141 See, for example, *Re Rio Nevada Energy Inc* (2000), 283 AR 146 (QB) [*Rio Nevada*].

142 *Re Bargain Harold's Discount Ltd* (1992), 10 CBR (3d) 23 (Ont Ct Gen Div); *Re Philip's Manufacturing Ltd* (1992), 9 CBR (3d) 25 (BCCA).

143 *BIA*, s 50.4(9).

144 *Ibid*, s 50.4(11).

145 *Re Cumberland Trading Inc*, above note 103; *Re Triangle Drugs Inc*, above note 130.

to the creditors should not be determined by the mere assertion by creditors with a veto position that no proposal will be supported.[146]

A debtor is not required to show that acceptance of a plan by the creditors is probable; it is enough to establish that it is a reasonable possibility.[147] The lack of support of key creditors together with other evidence such as inadequate financing or loss of faith in management may cause a court to terminate the proceedings on the ground that it has no reasonable chance of success.[148]

d) Material Prejudice

A fully secured creditor cannot immediately realize against the collateral but must wait until the plan is developed and put before the creditors. The fact that the secured creditor's remedies are temporarily stayed is not considered to be material prejudice that would justify a termination of the restructuring proceedings.[149] There must be material prejudice in the sense that the proceedings are resulting in a loss of value of the underlying assets so that the creditors will receive less than if the assets were immediately liquidated. This might occur when no interim financing is available and the debtor is seeking to pay the ongoing expenses from the proceeds of inventory or accounts that are not being replaced.[150] The fact that creditors would be afforded a priority in bankruptcy or receivership proceedings that is not afforded to it in restructuring proceedings does not constitute material prejudice.[151]

FURTHER READINGS

CUEVAS, C. "Good Faith and Chapter 11: Standard That Should Be Employed to Dismiss Bad Faith Chapter 11 Cases" (1993) 60 *Tennessee Law Review* 525

KORS, M. "Altered Egos: Deciphering Substantive Consolidation" (1998) 59 *University of Pittsburgh Law Review* 381

146 *In the Matter of the Proposal of Cantrail Coach Lines Ltd*, 2005 BCSC 351; *Andover Mining Corp (Re)*, 2013 BCSC 1833.

147 *Rio Nevada*, above note 141; *In Re Entegrity Wind Systems Inc*, 2009 PESC 25.

148 *Re Baldwin Valley Investors Inc* (1994), 23 CBR (3d) 219 (Ont Ct Gen Div); *In Re Entegrity Wind Systems Inc*, 2009 PESC 33; *Scanwood Canada Ltd (Re)*, 2011 NSSC 306; *1252206 Alberta Ltd v Bank of Montreal*, 2009 ABQB 355.

149 *Re H & H Fisheries Ltd* (2005), 18 CBR (5th) 293 (NSSC).

150 *Re Bargain Harold's Discount Ltd*, above note 142.

151 *Quality Meat Packers Limited (Re)*, 2014 ONSC 2296.

LOPUCKI, L, & G TRIANTIS. "A Systems Approach to Comparing US and Canadian Reorganization of Financially Distressed Companies," in J Ziegel, ed, *Current Developments in International and Comparative Corporate Insolvency Law* (Oxford: Clarendon Press, 1994) 109

MACNAUGHTON, M, & M ARZOUMANIDIS. "Substantive Consolidation in the Insolvency of Corporate Groups: A Comparative Analysis," in Janis P Sarra, ed, *Annual Review of Insolvency Law, 2007* (Toronto, Carswell, 2008) 525

YAMAUCHI, K. "The UNCITRAL Model Cross-Border Insolvency Law: The Stay of Proceedings and Adequate Protection" (2004) 13 *International Insolvency Review* 87

ZIEGEL, JS. "Corporate Groups Crossborder Insolvencies: A Canada-United States Perspective" (2002) 7 *Fordham Journal of Corporate and Finance Law* 367

CHAPTER 13

OPERATING THE BUSINESS

Restructuring law imposes a stay of proceedings on the actions and remedies of the creditors. It does so in order to keep the assets intact and the business ongoing while the debtor attempts to develop a plan to put before the creditors for their approval (in the case of traditional restructuring proceedings) or while a sales process is being devised (in the case of a liquidating restructuring proceedings). During this interim period, the debtor will continue to carry on business. However, a dramatic change occurs when restructuring proceedings are commenced. Suppliers of goods and services may no longer be prepared to extend credit to the insolvent firm. Significant administrative costs are incurred in a restructuring, and insolvency professionals will not be prepared to provide their services unless payment of their fees is assured. The restructuring plan may involve a downsizing in which only the more profitable portions of the business are retained. It may be necessary to reduce the workforce, break leases, and terminate other contractual arrangements. Restructuring law provides a number of devices to address these and other difficulties that arise during this interim period.

A. INTERIM FINANCING

1) The Position of Post-filing Creditors

There is a fundamental difference between creditors who extend credit prior to the commencement of the restructuring proceedings (pre-filing creditors) and those who extend credit after its commencement (post-filing creditors). The claims of pre-filing creditors are subject to the plan,[1] and these creditors are given an opportunity to vote to accept it or reject it.[2] If the plan is accepted, their claims will be compromised or otherwise affected in the manner specified in the plan. The post-filing creditors are not affected by the plan. In the event that the restructuring is successful, their claims will be fully enforceable against the debtor. Claimants who have entered into pre-filing contracts that are later disclaimed by the debtor after the commencement of restructuring proceedings are treated as pre-filing creditors in respect of their damages claims against the debtor for breach of contract.[3]

This does not mean that post-filing creditors should blithely extend credit to the debtor without a worry or care. The fact remains that the debtor is insolvent and the success of the restructuring is by no means assured. If the restructuring fails, the post-filing creditors will be in the same position as the pre-filing creditors.[4] They will share *pari passu* with all the other unsecured creditors after the secured creditors have withdrawn their collateral or its value from the pot of realizable assets. For this reason, post-filing creditors are often unwilling to grant credit to the debtor. The post-filing creditor has four options in this situation: (1) refuse to supply the goods or services; (2) supply the goods and services on a cash-on-delivery basis; (3) negotiate a post-filing trade creditor's charge on the debtor's assets to secure the payment obligation; or (4) take the risk of supplying goods or services on credit.[5]

Some of the earlier orders granted under the *CCAA* required post-filing creditors to continue to supply goods or services to the debtor

---

1 *CCAA*, s 19(1); *BIA*s 121(1).

2 It is possible to leave some of the pre-filing creditors out of the plan or proposal. When this occurs, their rights are unaffected. See Chapter 16, Section C(3).

3 *BIA*, s 65.11(8); *CCAA*, s 32(7).

4 See Chapter 16, Section H for a discussion of the position of post-filing creditors where a proposal is approved and later annulled by reason of a default in its performance.

5 *ICR Commercial Real Estate (Regina) Ltd v Bricore Land Group Ltd* (2007), 33 CBR (5th) 50 (Sask CA). Under the *CCAA*, a court will sometimes create a fund in favour of post-filing suppliers who extend credit to the debtor. See *Molson Canada v O-I Canada Corp* (2003), 43 CBR (4th) 172 (Ont CA).

while restructuring proceedings were under way.[6] The legislation was subsequently amended to make it clear that a creditor could not be compelled to do so.[7] Both the *CCAA* and the *BIA* now provide that a post-filing creditor is not prevented from requiring immediate payment for goods, services, use of leased property, or other valuable consideration, and neither statute requires a creditor to make a further advance of money or credit.[8] The supplier may exercise this right even if the agreement provides a later date for payment.[9]

A debtor who is contemplating restructuring proceedings must therefore devise a strategy to ensure that it will be able to operate the business and pay post-filing obligations during the restructuring proceedings. A failure by the debtor to put into place some means of financing the operations of the business during the restructuring proceedings may result in the termination of the proceedings by a court.[10]

Once restructuring proceedings are commenced, the debtor will suspend any further payment to the pre-filing creditors.[11] The claims of these creditors will be compromised or otherwise affected in the manner specified in the plan. The suspension of these payments is sometimes sufficient to free up sufficient cash flow to pay the post-filing creditors and the insolvency professionals. However, often it is not enough, and the debtor must search out some other source of financing for these expenses.

2) Interim (DIP) Financing

The term "debtor-in-possession" (DIP) financing has been used to describe the interim financing required for the ongoing operations of the business during restructuring proceedings. The term originates in the United States and is used in American bankruptcy law to describe a debtor who remains in possession of the property under Chapter 11

6 See L Lopucki & G Triantis, "A Systems Approach to Comparing US and Canadian Reorganization of Financially Distressed Companies" in J Ziegel, ed, *Current Developments in International and Comparative Corporate Insolvency Law* (Oxford: Clarendon Press, 1994) 109 at 132.

7 The change was first introduced in 1997.

8 *CCAA*, ss 11.01 and 34.4; *BIA*, s 65.1(4). And see *Re 728835 Ontario Ltd* (1998), 3 CBR (4th) 211 (Ont Ct Gen Div), aff'd (1998), 3 CBR (4th) 214 (Ont CA).

9 *Re Cosgrove-Moore Bindery Services Ltd* (2000), 17 CBR (4th) 205 (Ont SCJ).

10 *Re Bargain Harold's Discount Ltd* (1992), 10 CBR (3d) 23 (Ont Ct Gen Div); *Re SLMSoft Inc*, 2003 CarswellOnt 4402 (SCJ).

11 Under the *CCAA*, the initial order will usually prohibit the debtor from paying pre-filing creditors. See *New Skeena Forest Products Inc v Kitwanga Lumber Co* (2007), 34 CBR (5th) 94 at para 50 (BCSC).

restructuring proceedings. Although Canadian insolvency law does not make use of this legal concept, the term has been widely used in reference to interim financing.[12]

In some cases, the interim (DIP) lender is a new lender that has had no past dealings with the debtor. In other cases, the interim financing loan is obtained from an existing creditor. A pre-filing lender may extend funds to the debtor in order to gain a greater ability to influence the direction of the restructuring.

a) Judicial Development

Neither the *CCAA* nor the *BIA* originally addressed the issue of interim financing. The gap was filled by the courts, which began to exercise their inherent jurisdiction or equitable jurisdiction to grant orders authorizing the debtor to obtain interim financing.[13] The courts also began to grant charges against the assets of the debtor to secure the interim financing. At first, these orders simply gave the interim lender priority over existing unsecured creditors.[14] However, this was not sufficient to induce an interim lender to advance funds to an insolvent debtor who had given a security interest in all of its present and future assets to an earlier lender. Courts then began to make orders that gave the charge priority over existing secured creditors.[15] When this type of order is made, the DIP charge is said to prime the other secured loans. Some courts took the view that they can also give the DIP charge priority over statutory liens,[16] while others held that they were unable to do so.[17] Courts also made orders creating a superpriority for a DIP lender under the *BIA* on the basis of their inherent jurisdiction.[18]

Although notice to secured creditors affected by the order was viewed as desirable, it was not strictly insisted upon where the application was made on an urgent and interim basis.[19] As the availability of

---

12 It may be that Canadian courts will eventually retire the "DIP" terminology in favour of "interim" financing terminology, but at present the terminology is used interchangeably.

13 M Rotsztain, "Debtor-in-Possession Financing in Canada: Current Law and a Preferred Approach" (2000) 33 *Canadian Business Law Journal* 283.

14 *Re Westar Mining Ltd* (1992), 14 CBR (3d) 88 (BCSC).

15 *Skydome Corp v Ontario.* (1998), 16 CBR (4th) 118 (Ont Ct Gen Div).

16 *Re Sulphur Corp of Canada Ltd* (2002), 35 CBR (4th) 304 (Alta QB); *Re Temple City Housing Inc*, 2007 CarswellAlta 1806 (QB).

17 *Re Royal Oak Mines Inc* (1999), 7 CBR (4th) 293 (Ont Ct Gen Div).

18 *Re Bearcat Explorations Ltd* (2004), 3 CBR (5th) 167 (Alta QB); *Re FarmPure Seeds Inc*, (2008) SKQB 381.

19 *Re Algoma Steel Inc* (2001), 25 CBR (4th) 194 (Ont CA); *Re Hunters Trailer & Marine Ltd* (2001), 27 CBR (4th) 236 (Alta QB).

a comeback provision provided only a limited check on overreaching orders, courts took the position that the initial order should be limited to terms that are reasonably necessary for a brief time on an urgency basis.[20] The initial order should give the debtor the ability to "keep the lights on" and more extensive provisions should be introduced in the subsequent order when all interested parties have been notified and given the opportunity to consider their positions. The priority afforded to the DIP lender was also extended to amounts advanced prior to the making of the initial order so long as it was connected to the restructuring proceedings.[21] Courts attempted to contain the potential prejudicial effect of DIP financing orders by placing a monetary cap on the amount secured by the charge.

In determining whether it is appropriate to give a DIP lender priority over existing secured creditors, courts considered the extent to which the secured creditors would be adversely affected. They indicated that there should be "cogent evidence that the benefit of DIP financing clearly outweighs the potential prejudice to the lenders whose security is being subordinated."[22] To make this assessment, the court must be given information as to the value of the collateral and the amount of the secured obligations.

b) Statutory Reform

The 2009 amendments specifically address interim financing in both *CCAA* and *BIA* restructurings. The legislative provisions empower a court to make an order declaring that all or part of the debtor's property is subject to a security or charge in an amount that the court considers appropriate.[23] The court may also order that the security or charge shall rank in priority over the claim of any secured creditor.[24] Although these provisions have been said to codify the approaches previously developed by the courts,[25] the statute also limits the powers of the court in three important respects. In particular, it imposes three prerequisites, namely: (1) a requirement that notice be given to secured creditors

---

20 *Re Royal Oak Mines Inc*, above note 17.

21 *Re Hunters Trailer & Marine Ltd*, above note 19.

22 *Re United Used Auto & Truck Parts Ltd* (1999), 12 CBR (4th) 144 at para 28 (BCSC), aff'd (2000), 16 CBR (4th) 141 (BCCA); *Re Tuan Development Inc* (2007), 38 CBR (5th) 71 (BCSC).

23 *CCAA*, s 11.2(1); *BIA*, s 50.6(1).

24 *CCAA*, s 11.2(2); *BIA*, s 50.6(3).

25 See K Atlas & K Andersen, "DIP Super-Priorities and the Secured Creditor's Dilemma," in Janis P Sarra, ed, *Annual Review of Insolvency Law, 2009* (Toronto: Carswell, 2010) 171.

who are likely to be affected by an interim financing charge; (2) a requirement that the amount to be granted under the interim financing facility is appropriate and required having regard to the debtor's cash-flow statement; and (3) a restriction that prevents the interim financing charge from securing an obligation that exists before the order is made.[26] The latter restriction would appear to prevent the charge from securing advances made by the lender prior to the interim financing even if they were connected with the expenses of the restructuring proceedings.[27] Notice to secured creditors is not required if the interim financing charge does not give the DIP charge priority over their security interests.[28] The notice requirement may be difficult to satisfy where the debtor is a construction company, as there may be a large number of construction liens that have arisen and it may be difficult to identify all the lien claimants. In such cases, courts have held that the notice requirement is satisfied through substituted service combined with the availability of a comeback provision in the initial *CCAA* order.[29]

In deciding whether to make such an order, the statute directs the court to consider the following non-exhaustive factors:[30]

- the period during which the debtor is expected to be subject to restructuring proceedings;
- how the debtor's business and financial affairs are to be managed during the proceedings;
- whether the debtor's management has the confidence of its major creditors;
- whether the loan will enhance the prospects of a viable plan or proposal being made in respect of the debtor;
- the nature and value of the debtor's property;

---

26 *CCAA*, s 11.2(1); *BIA*, s 50.6(1). The courts have adopted the approach of first confirming that these three prerequisites are satisfied and, in the event that they are, then considering the specific factors enumerated in the statute. See *Canwest Global Communications Corp (Re)* (2009), 59 CBR (5th) 72 (Ont SCJ) [*Canwest*].

27 In this respect, the legislation would alter the result in *Re Hunters Trailer & Marine Ltd*, above note 19.

28 See *Canwest*, above note 26, in which the DIP charge was granted priority over secured creditors except for those who had perfected purchase money security interests or specified statutory encumbrances in respect of source deductions. Notice did not need to be given to the excepted secured creditors as their interests were unaffected.

29 *Comstock Canada Ltd (Re)*, 2013 ONSC 4756.

30 *CCAA*, s 11.2(4); *BIA*, s 50.6(5). And see *Pacific Shores Resort & Spa Ltd (Re)*, 2011 BCSC 1775, and *OVG Inc (Re)*, 2013 ONSC 1794, in which the courts considered each of these factors.

- whether any creditor will be materially prejudiced as a result of the security or charge; and
- the report of the monitor or trustee as to the reasonableness of the debtor's cash-flow statement.

In addition to these factors, courts have considered the reasonableness of the financing terms and associated fees;[31] and the fact that it will provide to the suppliers and employees a reassurance of payment sufficient to allow the debtor to continue business operations.[32] Courts have also taken into account the fact that the terms of the charge's priority had been negotiated to minimize prejudice to other creditors.[33]

An interim lender obtains an enhanced ability to control the direction of the restructuring proceedings.[34] This may be beneficial to the creditors as a group if the interests of the interim lender and the other creditors are aligned. However, it may also permit the interim lender to use this control in order to steer the restructuring in a direction that is favourable to the interim lender but unfavourable to the other creditors. For example, it may permit the interim lender to force a sale of the business or to allow the interim lender to obtain an advantage over other bidders on an auction of the business.[35]

c) Roll-Ups

Although the 2009 *CCAA* amendments prohibit the interim financing charge from securing pre-filing obligations, a further question is whether the use of a "roll-up" contravenes this restriction. In a simple roll-up, a portion of the new money advanced by the interim lender is used to pay off some or all the pre-filing obligation owed to that lender. In a creeping roll-up, the old loan is repaid from the revenue generated from the ongoing business operations. The obligation is thereby progressively diminished. It can be argued that simple roll-ups and creeping roll-ups do not constitute a prohibited cross-collateralization, since the old loan is paid out and is therefore not secured by the interim financing charge. The counterargument is that roll-ups frustrate the policy behind the legislative provision by permitting through indirect means that which cannot be accomplished directly. Although roll-ups

---

31 *Canwest Publishing Inc*, 2010 ONSC 222 at para 45.

32 *US Steel Canada Inc (Re)*, 2014 ONSC 6145 at para 9.

33 *Re PJ Wallbank Manufacturing Co Limited*, 2011 ONSC 7641.

34 See Chapter 14, Section D(3).

35 See D Skeel, "The Past, Present and Future of Debtor-in-Possession Financing" (2004) 25 *Cardozo Law Review* 1905; J Sarra, "Governance and Control: The Role of Debtor-in-Possession Financing under the *CCAA*" in Janis P Sarra, ed, *Annual Review of Insolvency Law, 2004* (Toronto: Carswell, 2005) 119.

have been authorized in Canada, the issue has not been definitively addressed in the judicial decisions to date.[36]

3) Administrative Charges

Although the *CCAA* was originally silent as to the treatment of the administrative costs of the restructuring proceedings, courts began to make orders that created charges that secured these amounts and gave them priority over pre-existing secured parties. The charge is typically afforded priority over a charge in favour of an interim (DIP) lender. The courts relied on their inherent jurisdiction or alternatively on their equitable jurisdiction to make such orders.[37]

The 2009 amendments to the *CCAA* and *BIA* expressly empower courts to make such orders.[38] Notice must be given to secured creditors who are affected by the order. The administrative charge may cover the costs of the monitor including the fees and expenses of any financial, legal, or other experts engaged by the monitor, experts engaged by the debtor, and any experts engaged by other interested persons if the court is satisfied that the security or charge is necessary for their effective participation in the restructuring proceedings. Courts have considered the following non-exhaustive list of factors in determining whether the amounts are appropriate and whether the charges should extend to the proposed beneficiaries: (a) the size and complexity of the businesses being restructured; (b) the proposed role of the beneficiaries of the charge; (c) whether there is an unwarranted duplication of roles; (d) whether the quantum of the proposed charge appears to be fair and reasonable; (e) the position of the secured creditors likely to be affected by the charge; and (f) the position of the monitor.[39]

---

36 In *Hartford Computer Hardware, Inc (Re)*, 2012 ONSC 964 the court proceeded on the basis that a partial roll-up violated the restriction in *CCAA*, s 11.2. Other courts have authorised creeping roll-ups. See R Rutman, A Macfarlane, A North, & A Khokhar, "Creeping Roll-Up DIP" (2012) 1 *Journal of the Insolvency Institute of Canada* 161 at 175–78.

37 *Re United Used Auto & Truck Parts Ltd*, above note 22.

38 *CCAA*, s 11.52; *BIA*, s 64.2.

39 *Canwest Publishing Inc (Re)*, 2010 ONSC 222; *Timminco Limited (Re)*, 2012 ONSC 106.

4) Other Court Ordered Charges

The *BIA* and *CCAA* contain express statutory provisions that govern the granting of court ordered charges in respect of interim financing,[40] administrative expenses,[41] and claims against directors.[42] The *CCAA* also has an express provision governing court ordered charges in respect of the claims of critical suppliers.[43] In addition to these charges, courts have granted charges in respect of other types of claims. The earliest instance was the granting of court ordered charges in respect of post-filing trade creditor claims. Instead of using cash to pay suppliers for goods and services provided after commencement of restructuring proceedings, a debtor may ask the court to sanction the creation of a charge against the debtor's assets to secure payment of such obligations.[44] Court ordered charges have also been granted in respect of key employee retention plan claims.[45] These other charges typically confer priority on the claims, not exceeding a fixed amount, over the claims of existing secured creditors. It is unclear whether courts will be willing to make similar orders in *BIA* restructuring proceedings.[46]

5) Characterization of Leases of Personal Property

The characterization of a transaction as a true lease as opposed to a disguised security interest (a security lease) is highly significant in restructuring proceedings for two reasons. First, if the transaction is characterized as a true lease, the lessor will not be postponed to any interim (DIP) financing, administrative, or directors' charges. The superpriority that is given to these charges is available only against a secured creditor, and a lessor under a true lease does not fall within this definition.[47] Second, the characterization of the transaction is of crucial importance in determining the nature of the debtor's obligation to the lessor during the restructuring proceedings. If the transaction is characterized as a true lease, the lessor is able to demand payment of lease obligations that become due after the commencement of the re-

---

40 See Section A(2), above in this chapter.

41 See Section A(3), above in this chapter.

42 See Chapter 14, Section A(4).

43 See Section B(1), below in this chapter.

44 *Re Westar Mining Ltd*, above note 14; *Re Smoky River Coal Ltd*, 2001 ABCA 209.

45 *Target Canada Co (Re)*, 2015 ONSC 303.

46 See Chapter 11, Section D(2).

47 *Re Western Express Airlines Inc* (2005), 10 CBR (5th) 154 (BCSC). And see Chapter 5, Section B(1).

structuring proceedings.[48] The lessor is therefore treated as a post-filing creditor in respect of lease payments that arise after the commencement of restructuring proceedings. If the transaction is characterized as a security lease, the lessor will be treated in the same manner as a secured creditor. The debtor can retain possession of the property and suspend payment of the lease obligations.

The test for determining if a transaction is a true lease or a security lease is essentially the same one that is used to determine if a transaction is in substance a security interest under personal property security legislation.[49] A substance test is used to characterize a lease as a true lease or a security lease.[50] The test looks to the substance of the transaction and not to the form of the transaction or the location of title. If the transaction is structured such that the lessee is under an obligation to pay the equivalent of the lessor's capital investment and the cost of the funds invested, the transaction is likely to be characterized as a security interest.

A transaction is also likely to be characterized as a security interest if it takes the form of a lease combined with an option to purchase for a price that is significantly below the expected residual value of the property at the end of the lease term.[51] Open-end leases are also characterized as security interests.[52] These provide for the sale of the property at the end of the lease term. If the sale proceeds are greater than a predetermined amount set out in the contract, the lessee is entitled to the surplus. If they are less, the lessee must pay the deficiency to the lessor.

A true lease that falls within the definition of a "lease for a term of more than one year" is a deemed security interest that is brought within the scope of the registration and priority rules of the PPSA. This has no bearing on the characterization of the transaction as a true lease.[53] Therefore, the lessor is not affected by the superpriority charges and can demand payment of lease obligations that become due after the commencement of restructuring proceedings.

---

48 The lessor will be classified as an unsecured creditor in respect of any lease payments in arrears at the date of the filing of restructuring proceedings.

49 *Royal Bank of Canada v Cow Harbour Construction Ltd*, 2012 ABQB 59; *Smith Brothers Contracting Ltd (Re) (Trustee of)* (1998), 53 BCLR (3d) 264 (SC).

50 See R Cuming, C Walsh, & R Wood, *Personal Property Security Law*, 2d ed (Toronto: Irwin Law, 2012) at 125–33.

51 See, for example, *Canadian Western Bank v Baker* (1999), 15 CBR (4th) 199 (Sask QB).

52 See, for example, *Crop & Soil Service Inc v Oxford Leaseway Ltd* (2000), 186 DLR (4th) 85 (Ont CA).

53 *Re Western Express Airlines Inc*, above note 47.

B. CRITICAL SUPPLIERS AND PAYMENT OF PRE-FILING CLAIMS

Pre-filing claims are generally not entitled to receive payment of their claims while the restructuring proceedings are ongoing. A court may decide that it is appropriate under the *CCAA* to order that some of the pre-filing creditors should be afforded special treatment by having some or all of the value of their claims paid to them. Such orders were commonly made in favour of critical suppliers who were able to threaten to refuse to provide critical supplies in the future unless past amounts were paid. The 2009 amendments have provided courts with a wider range of responses in respect of critical suppliers in restructuring proceedings under the *CCAA*. Courts have also authorized payment of some pre-filing claimants to prevent hardship. It is questionable whether such orders can be authorized in restructuring proceedings under the *BIA*, since that statute has no counterpart to the general power conferred on courts under the *CCAA* to make any order that it considers appropriate in the circumstances.[54]

1) Critical Suppliers

A supplier may hold a monopoly on goods or services critical to the operation of the debtor's business. It may be impossible to restructure the business without an assurance that the product or service will continue to be made available. A supplier is not compelled to extend credit to a debtor in restructuring proceedings but is entitled to demand cash on delivery.[55] However, a critical supplier may take the position that this is not enough. The supplier may be unwilling to furnish any further goods or services unless some or all of the pre-filing arrears are paid. In this respect, the critical supplier is adopting the same strategy as a DIP lender who seeks to cross-collateralize. The supplier is attempting to use its bargaining power to avoid having to participate in the plan as an unsecured creditor in respect of its pre-filing claims.[56]

There are two approaches to the problem of the critical supplier. The first involves a stick; the second involves a carrot. The first approach is put into operation by ordering the supplier to continue to supply goods or services to the debtor. The second involves negotiating a deal with the critical supplier under which some or all of its pre-filing

54 *CCAA*, s 11.

55 *Ibid*, ss 11.01 and 34(4); *BIA*, s 65.1(4).

56 See *Re Canadian Red Cross Society*, 1999 CarswellOnt 3123 (SCJ).

claim is satisfied in order to assure the future availability of the critical goods or services. Prior to the 2009 amendments, the first approach had never been employed in Canada. Although a supplier cannot terminate a pre-filing supply contract, courts have not gone so far as to force the supplier to enter into new contracts where none exist.[57]

The second approach had occasionally been employed in Canada. Courts designated certain suppliers as critical to the success of the restructuring and approved payment of their pre-filing obligations in order to ensure the continuation of the supply of goods or services. In *Re Air Canada*,[58] the court approved an agreement between Air Canada and Lufthansa under which pre-filing obligations were satisfied in order to maintain a strategic alliance with a key international partner that was vital to Air Canada's business. The court concluded that it would not be feasible to enter into a similar arrangement with some other airline, and that the future benefit was in excess of the pre-filing debt that was to be paid. The court also took into account the fact that the agreement had the general support of a majority of the creditors, and that the pre-filing claims owed to the critical supplier were to be paid from post-restructuring profits. The critical supplier issue has created difficulties for courts in other jurisdictions as well. There is considerable controversy over the appropriateness of critical supplier orders in the United States.[59]

The 2009 amendments to the *CCAA* added a new provision that directly addresses the critical supplier question. A similar provision was not included in the *BIA*. A court has the power to declare that a person is a critical supplier if the goods or services it supplies are critical to the continued operation of the business.[60] The court may compel a critical supplier to supply goods or services to the debtor on terms that are consistent with the supply relationship or that the court considers appropriate.[61] A court may not make such an order unless it also makes an order that declares that all or part of the debtor's property is subject to a charge or security in favour of the critical supplier in an amount equal to the value of the goods or services supplied under the terms of the order.[62] The court may specify in the order that the critical

---

57 See P Shea, "Dealing with Suppliers in a Reorganization" (2008) 37 CBR (5th) 161.

58 *Re Air Canada* (2003), 47 CBR (4th) 163 (Ont SCJ).

59 See *In re Kmart Corp* 359 F3d 866 (7th Cir 2004); *In re CoServ, LCC*, 273 BR 487 (BkrtcyNDTex 2002). And see C Hunt, "Not-So-Critical Vendors: Redefining Critical Vendor Orders" (2005) 93 *Kentucky Law Journal* 915.

60 *CCAA*, s 11.4(1).

61 *Ibid*, s 11.4(2).

62 *Ibid*, s 11.4(3).

supplier's charge ranks in priority over that of any secured creditor.[63] Notice must be given to secured creditors if their rights are affected by the order.[64]

The provision significantly alters the position of a critical supplier. The court may now order a critical supplier to supply goods or services to the debtor. This prevents a critical supplier from using its bargaining power to require payment of its pre-filing obligations.[65] An odd feature of section 11.4 is that it appears to assume that a critical supplier order will always require a critical supplier to supply goods or services on credit terms, since a court is required to create a charge that secures the value of the goods or services supplied under the terms of the order. On the face of it, this seems to exclude the possibility that a court may order the critical supplier to supply the goods or services but require the debtor to pay for them on delivery. It is one thing to force a supplier to continue to supply. It is quite another matter to insist that they extend credit. In principle, the supplier should not be required to extend credit unless this is absolutely essential — the financing of the extraordinary restructuring expenses should ordinarily be borne by lenders who specialize in interim (DIP) financing and who are adequately compensated for their involvement.

Another issue that arises is whether a critical supplier order can be made against a supplier who is already under a contractual obligation to supply future goods or services. The supplier is not permitted to terminate the contractual arrangement and will violate the terms of the initial or subsequent CCAA order if it attempts to do so. The issue is whether a critical supplier order can be made under section 11.4 to require a critical supplier to provide credit to the debtor different from the terms provided for in the original contractual arrangement between the parties. There appears to be nothing in the statute that prevents this order from being made, but this power should be used sparingly as it forces an involuntary extension of credit by a supplier.[66] Some commentators have argued that a court should rank a critical supplier charge above a DIP charge to take into account the fact that the critical supplier, unlike the DIP lender, is being compelled to extend credit.[67]

63 *Ibid*, s 11.4(4).

64 *Ibid*, s 11.4(1).

65 *Priszm Income Fund (Re)*, 2011 ONSC 2061.

66 See K Jackson, D Toigo, & M Arlette, "Critical Thinking: Supply, Credit and Other Critical Supplier Considerations in *CCAA* Proceedings" in Janis P Sarra, ed, *Annual Review of Insolvency Law, 2012* (Toronto: Carswell, 2013) 139.

67 See S Dvorak & H Sevenoaks, "Section 11.4 *CCAA* and Beyond: A 'Critical' Look at Critical Supplier Orders and the Payment of Pre-Filing Claims" in Janis P Sarra, ed, *Annual Review of Insolvency Law, 2012* (Toronto: Carswell, 2013) 167.

Courts have also held that the availability of the power to order a critical supplier to supply does not preclude a court from making an order authorizing a payment to a critical supplier in respect of pre-filing claims. There is considerable controversy concerning the source of this authority. One view is that it is not derived from section 11.4 but rather is founded upon the more general power given to courts to make orders under the *CCAA*. Although some courts have suggested that this represents an exercise of the inherent jurisdiction of the court, it seems more likely that this power is derived from section 11 of the *CCAA*. There are two conclusions that follow from the proposition that an order directing payment of critical suppliers is not an order authorized by section 11.4 of the *CCAA*. The first is that it is not necessary to obtain an order designating a person to be a critical supplier. The second is that it is not necessary to grant a charge in favour of the designated critical suppliers. The contrary view is that the source of the authority is section 11.4 as a court may order a critical supplier to supply on such terms as the court thinks appropriate. This could include an order that the supply occur on condition that the pre-filing amounts are paid. This implies that the court must specifically designate persons as critical suppliers and must also create a charge to secure their claims. The fact these steps are usually not taken when a court authorizes pre-filing claims suggests that the former view is to be preferred.[68]

In deciding whether to order the payment of the pre-filing claims of critical suppliers, a number of factors may come into play. The practical reality may be that it is not possible to force a critical supplier that resides outside of Canada to provide the goods.[69] If the critical suppliers are individuals, it would be inappropriate to order them to supply their labour as this would force them to work without their consent.[70] There is little justification for authorizing the payments of the pre-filing claims of suppliers who are contractually bound to make future deliveries except in cases of real necessity, as in instances where a court order cannot be readily enforced against a foreign supplier.[71]

Many court orders that authorize payments delegate to the debtor and monitor the ability to determine which suppliers are critical. There are a number of reasons why great caution should be exercised when

---

68 In *Canwest Global Communications Corp (Re)* (2009), 59 CBR (5th) 72 (Ont SCJ) the court purported to make an order authorizing payments pursuant to s 11.4 but indicated that it was necessary to grant a charge only in cases where a court is compelling a person to supply.

69 *Northstar Aerospace, Inc (Re)*, 2012 ONSC 4546.

70 *Brainhunter Inc (Re)*, 2009 CanLII 67659 (Ont SCJ).

71 Dvorak & Sevenoaks, above note 67.

authorizing payment of critical suppliers. These payments are inherently unfair in that they give the supplier a payment and therefore violate the principle that like creditors should be treated alike. Moreover a threatened refusal to supply is often not a credible threat because the supplier loses the opportunity to make sales on cash on delivery terms.[72] Giving the debtor the power to determine who is a critical supplier can be a dangerous practice as the choice may be motivated by considerations other than the continued supply of essential goods and services. The payment may be made to remove a vocal and obstreperous creditor from the negotiations on the plan or it may be made simply to confer an underserved preference on a favoured party.

2) Other Payment of Pre-filing Claims

Courts have authorized payment of pre-filing claims in situations beyond that of a critical supplier. The template initial *CCAA* order permits the debtor to pay amounts payable to employees that are owing prior to the commencement of the proceedings.[73] These payments are thought to be necessary in order to preserve the business as a going concern since the non-payment of the workforce produces a risk of "wholesale disruption among the employee ranks."[74] Similarly, courts have authorized payment of pre-filing credits of important customers in respect of the purchase of loyalty rewards where a failure to pay would cause major disruption of the business of the debtor.[75] In *EarthFirst Canada Inc (Re)*,[76] the court authorized the creation of a "hardship fund" that permitted the discretionary payment of pre-filing claims by EarthFirst's chief restructuring officer with the approval of the monitor. The payments were justified on the basis that local contractors were dependent on these payments to meet their payroll and to fund critical supplies, and that a failure to pay could have a domino effect jeopardizing the success of the restructuring. An ameliorating feature of the order was that payments were considered interim distributions under a future plan of arrangement so as to reduce the unfairness to creditors whose pre-filing obligations were not paid. The source of authority for

---

72 *In re Kmart Corp*, above note 59.

73 See P Bélanger, "Critical Suppliers: What Does Section 11.4 *CCRA* Mean?" (2010) 26 *Banking and Finance Law Review* 1 at 13–15.

74 M McDermott "Critical Vendor and Related Orders: Kmart and the Bankruptcy Abuse Presentation and Consumer Protection Act of 2005" (2006) 14 *American Bankruptcy Institute Law Review* 409 at 422.

75 *Futura Loyalty Group Inc (Re)*, 2012 ONSC 6403.

76 2009 ABQB 78.

making such order is the general power contained in section 11 of the *CCAA*.[77]

C. SET-OFF

Courts long took the view that their power to stay proceedings under the *CCAA* extended to extra-judicial remedies including the exercise of a right of set-off.[78] Orders granted under the *CCAA* usually contained a provision that prevented parties from exercising a right of set-off against the debtor company. An amendment to the *CCAA* in 1992 changed the law on this point. The *CCAA* now provides that the law of set-off applies to all claims made against a debtor company and to all actions instituted by it for recovery of debts due to the company.[79] No amendment to the commercial proposal provisions of the *BIA* was required, since the right to exercise set-off was already recognized in the statute.[80]

A creditor who owes an obligation to the debtor is therefore able to set-off obligations that are owed to it by the debtor if the ordinary conditions for exercising the right of set-off have been satisfied.[81] In *Re Blue Range Resource Corp*,[82] a purchaser suffered damages as a result of a termination by the debtor company of a long-term supply contract after the commencement of restructuring proceedings. The purchaser was able to set-off this claim against debts that it owed to the debtor in respect of goods that it purchased both before and after the commencement of restructuring proceedings. Legal set-off was not available because the claim for damages was not a debt. However, equitable set-off was available, since an unliquidated claim can be set-off against a debt so long as the two claims are closely connected.

The matter becomes more problematic when legal set-off is asserted in respect of claims between the parties that arise after the commencement of restructuring proceedings. In order to exercise a right of set-off, the cross-claims must be between the same parties in the same right. In bankruptcy proceedings, post-bankruptcy debts cannot be set-off

---

77 *Futura Loyalty Group Inc (Re)*, above note 75.

78 *Quintette Coal Ltd v Nippon Steel Corp* (1990), 2 CBR (3d) 303 (BCCA).

79 *CCAA*, s 21.

80 *BIA*, s 97(3). This provision is made applicable to restructurings under the *BIA* by s 66(1).

81 See Chapter 4, Section B(6) for a discussion of the governing principles.

82 [2000] 11 WWR 117 (Alta CA).

against pre-bankruptcy debts.[83] In *Re Air Canada*,[84] the court held that the same reasoning does not hold true in restructuring proceedings. Unlike bankruptcy or winding-up proceedings, there is no vesting of property in the debtor or other alteration in the legal status of the debtor. As a consequence, debts that arise after the commencement of restructuring proceedings can be set-off against pre-existing debts.

The ability to exercise a right of set-off in restructuring proceedings can operate to improve greatly the position of one creditor at the expense of the other creditors. This is illustrated in the following example. Suppose that the debtor company owes $1,000 to a creditor. The debtor company then initiates restructuring proceedings. While the proceedings are under way, the debtor company sells and delivers goods to the creditor for $1,000. By exercising its right of set-off, the creditor obtains full recovery of its claim at the expense of the other unsecured creditors whose claims will be compromised or otherwise affected by the plan. There is a further difficulty. Although the transaction may constitute a preference in favour of the party who is enabled to exercise a right of set-off, the *BIA* impeachment powers cannot be used to impugn post-filing transactions.[85]

The position under the commercial proposal provisions of the *BIA* is different from that under the *CCAA*. Although the right of set-off is legislatively preserved,[86] it has been held that pre-filing obligations cannot be set-off against post-filing obligations. Two reasons are cited for this conclusion. The first is that most proposals contain an express provision to this effect.[87] The second is that to permit set-off in this situation would amount to a fraud on the bankruptcy system.[88]

D. EXECUTORY CONTRACTS

Executory contracts, as the term is used in an insolvency context, are contracts where neither party has fully performed and where the contractual obligations are linked so that performance by one party is

---

83 *Coopers & Lybrand Ltd v Lumberland Building Materials Ltd* (1983), 50 CBR (NS) 150 (BCSC); *Re Kryspin* (1981), 40 CBR (NS) 67 (Ont HCJ).

84 (2003), 45 CBR (4th) 13 (Ont SCJ).

85 See Chapter 7, Sections B(2)(c) & (d) and Chapter 15, Section C.

86 *BIA*, s 97(3).

87 *Re 728835 Ontario Ltd* (1998), 3 CBR (4th) 211 (Ont Ct Gen Div).

88 *Re Cobourg Felt Co* (1925), 5 CBR 622 (Ont HCJ).

not required unless the other party is willing and able to perform.[89] Contracts that have been fully performed by the debtor or by the counterparty are not covered by this discussion, since they are largely unproblematic. If the debtor has performed its part of the bargain, the debtor is entitled to call for performance from the other party and may resort to its contractual remedies in the event that the counterparty fails to perform. If the counterparty has fully performed and the debtor has obtained the benefits of this performance, the counterparty has a claim against the debtor that has the status of an unsecured claim in the plan along with all the other pre-filing unsecured creditors.

Three issues arise in relation to executory contracts. The first concerns contracts that the debtor wishes to perform in order to obtain the performance of the counterparty. Problems arise if the counterparty has a right to terminate the agreement. Restructuring law prevents the counterparty from exercising its right to terminate the contract in certain instances. The second concerns contracts that the debtor does not wish to perform. Restructuring law permits the debtor to disclaim contracts and specifies the consequences of doing so. The third concerns contracts that the debtor wishes to assign to third parties. Restructuring law permits a debtor to assign a contract even if the contract contains an anti-assignment clause that prohibits such action.

Originally, the *CCAA* was largely silent on the treatment of executory contracts. Provisions governing executory contracts were added to the *BIA* restructuring provisions in 1992. The 2009 amendments have expanded the executory contract provisions in the *BIA* and have introduced a similar set of statutory provisions into the *CCAA*. The *BIA* provisions respecting disclaimer of contracts and assignment of contracts apply to individuals who make commercial proposals, but only to the extent that the contract pertains to their business activity.[90] The rules respecting disclaimer and assignment of contracts under both the *CCAA* and *BIA* do not apply to eligible financial contracts or to collective agreements.[91]

1) Termination of Contracts

No difficulty arises if the debtor has not breached the agreement with the counterparty. There is no need to affirm the contract, as is the case in bankruptcy. The commencement of restructuring proceedings does

89 V Countryman, "Executory Contracts in Bankruptcy, Part I" (1973) 57 *Minnesota Law Review* 439 at 460.

90 *BIA*, s 84.1(2).

91 *CCAA*, ss 32(9) and 11.3(1); *BIA*, ss 65.11(10) and 84.1(3).

not change the relationship between the parties. The contract can be kept in good standing simply by performance of the debtor's contractual obligations. Problems are more likely to arise where the debtor is in breach of the contract but nevertheless wishes to obtain its future benefits.

The *BIA* and the *CCAA* initially adopted two fundamentally different approaches to this problem. Under the *CCAA*, the stay of proceedings granted by the court was used to prevent counterparties from terminating their agreements with the debtor. The initial and subsequent orders typically contain a provision that prevent the counterparty from terminating or ceasing to perform any contract with the debtor. The stay of proceedings under the *BIA* is not as wide in that it does not prevent termination of contracts by counterparties.[92] Instead, the matter is expressly dealt with by a statutory provision that limits a counterparty's ability to terminate a contract or exercise other contractual remedies for breach.

Contracts entered into by the debtor prior to the commencement of restructuring proceedings would sometimes contain contractual provisions that gave the counterparty the right to terminate the contract if the debtor were insolvent or subject to insolvency proceedings. These kinds of terms are referred to as *ipso facto* clauses in the United States. The *BIA* expressly limited the effectiveness of such clauses by preventing a person from terminating or amending an agreement or calling for accelerated payment or forfeiture of the term under an agreement by reason only that the debtor is insolvent or has commenced restructuring proceedings.[93] A similar provision was added to the *CCAA* by the 2009 amendments.[94] The common law anti-deprivation rule can also be invoked to invalidate provisions that trigger the loss of an asset upon the occurrence of insolvency proceedings.[95]

This statutory provision does not prevent the counterparty from terminating the agreement for other grounds. Consider the example of a debtor who has entered into a long-term supply contract but has failed to pay for several deliveries prior to the commencement of restructuring proceedings. Although the supplier would be unable to terminate the agreement because of the insolvency of the debtor or

92 *Canadian Petcetera Limited Partnership v 2876 R Holdings Ltd*, 2010 BCCA 469.

93 *BIA*, s 65.1(1). And see *1183882 Alberta Ltd (Sok's Contracting) v Valin Industrial Mill Installations Ltd*, 2012 ABCA 62; *853571 BC Ltd v Spruceland Shopping Centre Inc*, 2009 BCSC 1187.

94 *CCAA*, s 34(1).

95 *Aircell Communications Inc (Trustee of) v Bell Mobility Cellular Inc*, 2013 ONCA 95. And see Chapter 4, Section B(2).

the commencement of insolvency proceedings, the supplier is not prevented from terminating future performance to the extent that this right is available to the supplier under ordinary contract or sales law principles. Unless a right to cure is provided by the contract or other applicable law, the debtor is not able to put the contract back into good standing by curing the default.

Both the *BIA* and the *CCAA* contain additional statutory provisions that prevent a counterparty from invoking a contractual right to terminate a contract. A lessor is not permitted to terminate a lease by reason that the debtor has not paid rent in respect of periods prior to the commencement of restructuring proceedings.[96] Although the *BIA* provides a similar rule for a failure to pay royalties under a licensing agreement,[97] the *CCAA* does not contain an equivalent provision. Public utilities are also prevented from discontinuing service by reason of a failure to pay for services rendered before the commencement of restructuring proceedings.[98] The debtor is required to pay only amounts that become due after the commencement of the restructuring proceedings in order to keep the contract in good standing. These statutory provisions override any contractual provision to the contrary.[99] The counterparty or a public utility may apply to court and obtain a complete or partial exemption from the operation of this rule if it can show that it would otherwise suffer significant financial hardship.[100]

The introduction of the new provisions has not been viewed as replacing the court's ability to order a stay of proceedings that prevents a counterparty from terminating contracts under the *CCAA* since courts continue to include the same wide provisions governing termination that were used before the 2009 amendments. As a consequence, courts have a significantly greater ability to prevent the termination of agreements under the *CCAA* than under the *BIA*. The absence of a critical supplier provision in the *BIA* means that a court is unable to prevent a counterparty from terminating a contract on the basis of a default that occurred before the commencement of proceedings despite the fact that the goods or services are essential to the business operations.

---

96 *BIA*, s 65.1(2); *CCAA*, s 34(2). This provision does not affect the right of a lessor to take possession of an aircraft object. See *BIA*, s 65.1(4)(c); *CCAA*, s 34(4)(c).

97 *BIA*, s 65.1(2).

98 *BIA*, s 65.1(3); *CCAA*, s 34(3).

99 *BIA*, s 65.1(5); *CCAA*, s 34(5).

100 *BIA*, s 65.1(6); *CCAA*, s 34(6). And see *Toronto-Dominion Bank v Ty (Canada) Inc* (2003), 42 CBR (4th) 142 (Ont SCJ).

2) Disclaimer of Contracts

A debtor who is attempting to restructure may not wish to perform all of the contracts that it entered into prior to the commencement of restructuring proceedings. The debtor may intend to downsize its operations. It may be necessary for a retail chain to abandon several of its outlets in less profitable locations. This will require it to breach its agreements with some of its employees, lessors, and suppliers. Or it may simply be that the contracts are not favourable ones, and the debtor would be better off by entering into new contracts with other suppliers.

a) The Statutory Disclaimer Provisions

The *CCAA* and the *BIA* originally had little to say about the disclaiming of contracts by a debtor. The *CCAA* did not deal with the issue at all. This lacuna was filled by courts that used their inherent jurisdiction or statutory discretion under the *CCAA* to authorize the disclaimer of agreements by the debtor.[101] The *BIA* provided for disclaimer of leases but not for any other transaction.

The *BIA* gives the debtor the right to disclaim a commercial lease of real property by giving the lessor thirty days' notice.[102] The lessor may challenge the disclaimer of the lease by asking the court for a declaration that the provision does not apply in respect of the lease.[103] To do so, the lessor must apply to a court within fifteen days of receiving notice of the disclaimer. A court may not make a declaration exempting the lessor if it is satisfied that the debtor would be unable to make a viable proposal without the disclaimer.[104] This has been interpreted to mean that the debtor has the onus of showing that the proposal would not be viable without the repudiation of that lease.[105] This sets a relatively high threshold. It is not enough to show that the disclaimer of the lease would enhance the proposal. It must be shown that the proposal will be unworkable unless disclaimer of the lease is permitted.

The 2009 amendments to the *CCAA* and the *BIA* have added provisions that specifically govern disclaimer of executory contracts. A debtor is given the right to disclaim agreements by giving notice to the

101 *Re Skeena Cellulose Inc* (2003), 43 CBR (4th) 187 (BCCA).

102 *BIA*, s 65.2(1).

103 *Ibid*, s 65.2(2).

104 *Ibid*, s 65.2(3).

105 *Re Carr-Harris & Co* (1993), 23 CBR (3d) 74 (BCSC). The debtor was able to satisfy this test in *Re Superstar Group of Companies* (2001), 25 CBR (4th) 119 (BCSC).

counterparty.[106] The right to disclaim can be exercised only in respect of contracts that were in existence before restructuring proceedings were commenced. The debtor cannot give a notice of disclaimer unless the trustee or monitor approves the proposed disclaimer. The counterparty may object to the disclaimer if it applies to court within fifteen days of receiving notice of the disclaimer,[107] and it may also require the debtor to provide written reasons for the disclaimer.[108] The debtor, for its part, may apply to court if the trustee or monitor does not approve a proposed disclaimer.[109] In making the order, the court must consider whether the monitor or trustee approved the disclaimer, whether the disclaimer would enhance the prospects of a viable plan or proposal, and whether the disclaimer would likely cause significant financial hardship to the counterparty.[110] The disclaimer provisions are available even in liquidation proceedings that do not involve the development and approval of a plan.[111] Although there is no mechanism for requiring the debtor to disclaim a contract, a court has the power to lift the stay of proceedings in connection with a particular contract.[112]

Under the *CCAA*, the new rules for disclaimer apply to commercial leases. However, under the *BIA*, the new rules do not apply. Instead, the older provision that governs disclaimer of commercial leases continues to apply.[113] This means that, in a commercial proposal under the *BIA*, it will be more difficult for the debtor to disclaim a commercial lease, since it is necessary to show that the debtor is unable to make a viable proposal without the disclaimer. Under the *CCAA*, it is merely enough to show that a disclaimer will enhance the viability of the plan.

b) The Legal Consequences of Disclaimer

A disclaimer of an agreement does not result in a rescission of the contract.[114] It simply means that the debtor is electing not to perform the contract. The counterparty has the right to treat this as a breach of contract and prove a claim for contractual damages.[115] This claim will participate with the other unsecured claims in the plan or proposal. There

106 *BIA*, s 65.11(1); *CCAA*, s 32(1).
107 *BIA*, s 65.11(3); *CCAA*, s 32(2).
108 *BIA*, s 65.11(9); *CCAA*, s 32(8).
109 *BIA*, s 65.11(4); *CCAA*, s 32(3).
110 *BIA*, s 65.11(5); *CCAA*, s 32(4).
111 *Aveos Fleet Performance Inc/Aveos Fleet performance aéronautique inc (Arrangement relatif à)*, 2012 QCCS 6796.
112 *Comstock Canada Ltd (Re)*, 2013 ONSC 6043.
113 *BIA*, s 65.2.
114 See Chapter 6, Section B(1).
115 *BIA*, s 65.11(8); *CCAA*, s 32(7).

is a difference between the *CCAA* and the *BIA* in the manner in which claims arising out of a disclaimer of commercial leases of real property are handled. Under the *CCAA*, there is no statutory limitation on the lessor's claim following a disclaimer of the lease by the debtor.[116] Under the *BIA*, there is a potential limitation on the claim. The proposal may give the lessor the right to make a claim for the full loss suffered. Alternatively, the proposal may limit the claim to the lesser of (1) the rent for the one-year period following the disclaimer plus 15 percent of the rent for the remainder of the term, or (2) three years' rent.[117]

Both the *CCAA* and the *BIA* contain a provision that deals with the effect of a disclaimer on the counterparty's right to use intellectual property.[118] It provides that a disclaimer of the contract by the debtor (the licensor) does not affect the right of the counterparty (the licensee) to use the intellectual property during the term of the agreement as long as the licensee continues to perform its obligations under the agreement.

This provision should not be regarded as changing the law in any respect. The principle embodied in it is one of more general application, and it is based on the idea that disclaimer does not of itself terminate or rescind the contract. It simply operates as a notification that the debtor does not intend to perform the contract. The counterparty may choose to treat this breach as a reason to terminate its future performance, but is not compelled to do so. Instead, the counterparty may continue to perform the obligations under the agreement. The same analysis holds true in the case of a debtor who leases property. The debtor cannot disclaim the contract and demand the return of the property. The lessee can retain the property by making the monthly payments and performing the lessee's obligations under the agreement.

Both the *CCAA* and the *BIA* provide that the disclaimer provisions do not apply to a financing agreement if the debtor is the borrower or to a lease if the debtor is the lessor.[119] The inclusion of these transactions also appears to be based on a concern that courts might interpret the disclaimer provisions as giving the debtor the power to terminate the agreement.

---

116 *Re Alternative Fuel Systems Inc* (2004), 47 CBR (4th) 1 (Alta CA).

117 *BIA*, s 65.2(4).

118 *BIA*, s 65.11(7); *CCAA*, s 32(6).

119 *CCAA*, s 32(9); *BIA*, s 65.11(10).

3) Assignment of Contracts

As part of the restructuring effort, the debtor may wish to assign some of its contractual rights to other parties. An agreement may contain an anti-assignment clause that prevents one party from assigning the contract to another. While the *CCAA* and the *BIA* did not originally contain provisions for the assignment of contracts, courts held that they had the jurisdiction under the *CCAA* to assign agreements over the objection of the counterparty.[120]

New provisions have been added to both the *CCAA* and the *BIA* governing the assignment of agreements.[121] The assignment transfers both the rights and the obligations of a party under an agreement.[122] Unlike ordinary assignments of contract rights that transfer only the benefits of the contract to the transferee, these provisions transfer the performance obligation as well. This means that the counterparty will have no recourse against the debtor in the event of a default by the assignee.

A court cannot make an order assigning the rights and obligations unless it is satisfied that all monetary defaults in respect of the agreement will be remedied before a date it fixes.[123] In deciding whether to make the order, the court must consider whether the party to whom the rights and obligations were assigned would be able to perform the obligations and whether it would be appropriate to assign the obligations to that party. Under the *CCAA*, it is also necessary to consider if the monitor approved the proposed assignment.

Under the *CCAA*, the debtor company brings the application on notice to the monitor and the counterparty.[124] Under the *BIA*, it is the trustee who brings the application. However, the provision is to be applied "with such modifications as the circumstances require" to commercial proposals under the *BIA*. The role of a trustee in a restructuring differs from that of a trustee in a bankruptcy. The former is much closer in nature to a monitor under the *CCAA*. It is possible that a court would be prepared to modify the operation of the *BIA* provision by treating the trustee under a commercial proposal in the same way as a monitor. If this were done, the debtor could bring the application and the court

---

120 *Re Playdium Entertainment Corp* (2001), 31 CBR (4th) 302 (Ont SCJ); *Re Canadian Red Cross Society* (1998), 5 CBR (4th) 299 (Ont Ct Gen Div).

121 *CCAA*, s 11.3; *BIA*, s 84.1. The *BIA* provision that operates in bankruptcy proceedings is made applicable to *BIA* restructuring proceedings by virtue of s 66(1) of the *BIA*.

122 *CCAA*, s 11.3(1); *BIA*, s 84.1(1).

123 *CCAA*, s 11.3(4); *BIA*, s 84.1(5).

124 *CCAA*, s 11.3(1).

could consider as a factor whether the trustee had given approval to the proposed assignment.

E. COLLECTIVE AGREEMENTS

If the debtor's workforce is unionized, the relations between the debtor and the employees will be governed by a collective agreement negotiated between the debtor and the employee's bargaining agent. In the absence of any other statutory provision, this agreement would potentially be subject to the ordinary principles that govern executory contracts in insolvency proceedings, and the debtor would have the power to disclaim the agreement. The 2009 amendments to the *CCAA* and the *BIA* introduced new provisions that govern collective agreements. The executory contract provisions of the *CCAA* and *BIA* do not apply to collective agreements.[125]

A collective agreement remains in force and cannot be altered except as specifically provided in the agreement or in accordance with the laws of the jurisdiction governing collective bargaining.[126] A court cannot use the concept of inherent jurisdiction or some other source of power to make an order that permits the debtor to disclaim a collective agreement or that alters its terms. This limitation applies only in situations where member employees of a bargaining unit continue to perform work after an initial order has been issued, and does not have the effect of requiring immediate payment in relation to former employees.[127] Although the collective agreement cannot be unilaterally disclaimed, the terms can be amended by the agreement of the debtor and the bargaining agent. In many restructurings, the employer seeks concessions from the employees' union. The new statutory provisions attempt to facilitate a process for the renegotiation of the terms of the collective agreement when other attempts at renegotiation have ended in failure.

If attempts to renegotiate the terms of a collective agreement have been unsuccessful, the debtor can apply to court for an order authorizing service of a notice to bargain pursuant to the laws of a jurisdiction governing collective bargaining. The order can be issued only if the court is satisfied that a viable plan or proposal could not otherwise be made, that the debtor has made good faith efforts to renegotiate the

---

125 *CCAA*, s 32(9); *BIA*, s 65.11(10).

126 *CCAA*, ss 33(1) and (8); *BIA*, ss 65.12(1) and (6).

127 *White Birch Paper Holding Company (Arrangement relatif à)*, 2010 QCCS 2590.

terms of the collective agreement, and a failure to issue the order is likely to result in irreparable damage to the debtor.[128] This mechanism can be used to force the employee's union to meet and bargain with the employer even though the collective agreement has not come to an end. The applicable collective-bargaining legislation defines the rules and processes that govern these negotiations. If an order is issued, the bargaining agent has the right to apply to court to request an order requiring the disclosure of information relating to the debtor's business or financial affairs.[129]

If the parties agree to revise the collective agreement, the bargaining agent is deemed to have a claim as an unsecured creditor equal to the value of the concessions granted.[130] The right to make such a claim applies whether or not an order to bargain is issued by a court. However, a vote by the creditors on a plan or proposal cannot be delayed solely because the time period governing collective bargaining has not come to an end.[131]

F. ELIGIBLE FINANCIAL CONTRACTS

Derivatives are financial contracts whose value is derived from the value of some other thing, such as a commodity, currency, stock, bond, index, or interest rate. They may take many forms, including futures contracts, options, and swaps. Derivatives are used to manage risk by taking the opposite position in the futures market against the value of the underlying asset. For example, an exporter may use derivatives to protect itself against currency fluctuations. In order for "over-the-counter"[132] derivatives to work efficiently, there must be certainty as to the rights and the liabilities of the parties. Insolvency risk — the risk that the counterparty will not be able to satisfy the obligation pursuant to the derivative contract — must be minimized. The rights associated with derivative contracts are designed to achieve this goal. A counterparty is required to provide security if the party is "out of the money." If this is not forthcoming, the party may terminate the contract. This permits the party to enter into a new contract with some

128 *CCAA*, s 33(3); *BIA*, s 65.12(2).

129 *CCAA*, s 33(6); *BIA*, s 65.12(5).

130 *CCAA*, s 33(5); *BIA*, s 65.12(4).

131 *CCAA*, s 33(4); *BIA*, s 65.12(3).

132 These are derivative contracts that are negotiated directly between two parties as opposed to exchange-traded derivatives that are traded through specialized exchanges and guaranteed by a clearing organization.

other counterparty. Often the parties enter into a master agreement that provides for a netting of all "in the money transactions" against all "out of the money" transactions.

The termination and netting out of financial obligations is considered to be of fundamental importance to the efficient operation of capital markets, and a failure to ensure that the legal framework governing derivatives is in accord with international standards would put Canadian financial markets at a competitive disadvantage. The global financial crisis in 2008 highlighted the need for regulation in order to reduce systemic risk — the danger that an insolvency of a counterparty will trigger the insolvency of another counterparty and set off a chain reaction. Insolvency legislation has been amended to ensure that parties are able to exercise their right to terminate and net out in respect of these obligations despite the fact that the counterparty is subject to insolvency proceedings.

In the absence of any special statutory provision, the principles governing executory contracts would apply to derivatives contracts and would interfere with a party's ability to terminate or net out financial obligations under derivatives contracts. The *CCAA* and *BIA* have been amended to ensure that this will not occur. The legislation creates a class of contracts referred to as "eligible financial contracts." The provisions in the *CCAA* and the *BIA* governing executory contracts do not apply to an eligible financial contract.[133] The statutes further provide that the stay of proceedings does not interfere with a party's ability to enforce a security interest against financial collateral that secures an obligation under an eligible financial contract.[134]

The definition of an eligible financial contract (EFC) is of crucial importance since it determines whether a contract will be exempt from the ordinary insolvency rules that limit a party's ability to assert their contractual rights and remedies. The definition was first added to the insolvency statutes in 1992 and produced some litigation. The issue was whether the reference to commodity contracts in the definition should be restricted to those that were financial in nature or whether it should also include contracts that were physically settled by delivery of the commodity. The courts rejected any distinction based on whether the contract was financially or physically settled. Instead they indicated that the definition should encompass contracts dealing with

133 *BIA*, ss 65.1(7) and 65.11(10); *CCAA*, ss 32(9) and 34(7).

134 *BIA*, s 65.1(9); *CCAA*, ss 34(8)–(9). And see Chapter 12, Section D(8).

fungible commodities that trade in a volatile market where the contracts are used as financial hedges and risk-management tools.[135]

The definition of an EFC was amended by the *Budget Implementation Act, 2007*.[136] The legislation did not enumerate the various types of contracts but simply provided that it means an agreement of a prescribed kind. Regulations promulgated under the various insolvency statutes set out the substantive provisions.[137] This permits the legislation to be more easily updated to encompass new financial products. In order to fall within the definition, the derivatives agreements must be traded on regulated markets or be subject to recurrent dealings in the markets. The definition of an EFC in the regulation also covers securities and commodities loans, securities repos, and margin loans in respect of securities accounts or future accounts held by a financial intermediary.

The appropriate treatment of EFCs continues to be controversial. There is presently a debate concerning the proper balance between the goal of reducing systemic risk and the goals of restructuring law.[138]

G. SALE OF THE ASSETS

1) The Statutory Framework

It has become increasingly common in restructurings for the debtor to sell some or all of its assets outside the ordinary course of business. In many cases, this has involved a going-concern sale of substantially all the assets of the debtor. In such instances, it is most often the case that a plan of arrangement is never developed or voted on by the creditors. The *CCAA* has also been used to effect a winding down of the business

---

135 *Re Blue Range Resource Corp* (2000), 20 CBR (4th) 187 (Alta CA); *Re Androscoggin Energy LLC* (2005), 8 CBR (5th) 11 (Ont.CA).

136 SC 2007, c 29.

137 *Eligible Financial Contract General Rules (Bankruptcy and Insolvency Act)*, SOR/2007-256.

138 See the competing views in the Insolvency Institute of Canada, *Task Force on Derivatives Report* (14 November 2013), online: www.insolvency.ca/en/iicresources/resources/IIC_Derivatives_Task_Force_Report_November_2013.pdf and the International Swaps and Derivatives Association, *Comment letter on the Industry Canada's discussion paper "Statutory Review of the Bankruptcy and Insolvency Act and the Companies' Creditors Arrangement Act"* (15 July 2014), online: www.ic.gc.ca/eic/site/cilp-pdci.nsf/vwapj/International_Swaps_and_Derivatives_Association_July_15_2014.pdf/$FILE/International_Swaps_and_Derivatives_Association_July_15_2014.pdf.

operation through an orderly sale of the assets that does not involve a going-concern sale of the business. The sheer magnitude and complexity of the business and the number of stakeholder may weigh in favour of using the more flexible framework of the *CCAA*.[139] Courts have confirmed that the same holds true in respect of commercial proposals — a court may authorize a sale even if it is clear that the debtor is unable to present a proposal to its creditors.[140] The 2009 amendments to the *CCAA* and *BIA* provide for judicial supervision of such sales. They lay out a set of rules that must be followed when a debtor that is undergoing restructuring proceedings proposes to sell assets outside the ordinary course of its business. The provision does not address the broader policy question as to when it is appropriate to use restructuring proceedings rather than bankruptcy or receivership proceedings to effect a liquidation. This question may arise if the creditors challenge the restructuring proceedings and argue that alternative insolvency proceedings would better serve the interests of the parties.[141]

A debtor is not permitted to sell or otherwise dispose of its assets outside the ordinary course of its business unless a court approves the sale or other disposition.[142] Approval by the shareholders of a debtor corporation is not needed notwithstanding any federal or provincial legislation that requires shareholder approval. If the debtor is an individual, the rule only applies to his or her business assets.[143] Secured creditors who may be affected by the order must be given notice of the application.[144] A court may authorize a sale of the assets free and clear of any security, charge, or other restriction, but, if it does so, it must also impose a security, charge, or restriction on the other assets of the debtor or on the proceeds of the sale or other disposition.[145]

In determining whether to authorize the transaction, the court is directed to consider the following non-exhaustive set of factors:[146]

- whether the process leading to the proposed sale or disposition was reasonable in the circumstances;
- whether the monitor or trustee approved the process leading to the proposed sale or other disposition;

139 *Target Canada Co. (Re)*, above note 45.
140 *Komtech Inc (Re)*, 2011 ONSC 3230.
141 See Chapter 11, Section B(4).
142 *CCAA*, s 36(1); *BIA*, s 65.13(1).
143 *BIA*, s 65.13(2).
144 *CCAA*, s 36(2); *BIA*, s 65.13(3).
145 *CCAA*, s 36(6); *BIA*, s 65.13(7).
146 *CCAA*, s 36(3); *BIA*, s 65.13(4).

- whether the monitor or trustee filed with the court a report stating that, in their opinion, the sale or other disposition would be more beneficial than a sale or disposition under a bankruptcy;
- the extent to which the creditors were consulted;
- the effects of the proposed sale or disposition on the creditors or other interested parties; and
- whether the consideration to be received for the assets is reasonable and fair, taking into account their market value.

These factors would appear to encompass the principles set out in *Royal Bank of Canada v Soundair Corp*[147] that were developed to evaluate the reasonableness of a sale by a receiver, but which were subsequently used in connection with liquidations under the *CCAA*.[148]

Often the court is asked to approve the sale process in advance of obtaining any offers. Courts have applied a somewhat different set of factors in connection with the authorization of the sale process.[149] They will consider (a) Is a sale transaction warranted at this time? (b) Will the sale benefit the whole "economic community"? (c) Do any of the debtor's creditors have a *bona fide* reason to object to a sale of the business? (d) Is there a better viable alternative?[150]

If the proposed sale is to a related person, the court may authorize the transaction only if good faith efforts were made to sell the assets to someone other than a related party and the consideration that is received is superior to any other made in accordance with the process leading to the proposed sale or other disposition.[151] The court cannot authorize the transaction unless it is satisfied that the debtor can and will make the payments to employees in respect of unpaid wages or to pension funds that would have been required for court sanction of the plan or proposal.[152]

---

147 (1991), 7 CBR (3d) 1 (Ont CA). The court is to consider: (1) whether the receiver has made a sufficient effort to get the best price and has not acted improvidently; (2) the interests of all parties; (3) the efficacy and integrity of the process by which offers are obtained; and (4) whether there has been unfairness in the working out of the process.

148 *Re Canadian Red Cross Society* (1998), 5 CBR (4th) 299 (Ont Ct Gen Div).

149 *Re Brainhunter Inc* (2009), 62 CBR (5th) 41 (Ont SCJ) [*Brainhunter*].

150 These factors were originally developed in *Nortel Networks Corporation (Re)* (2009), 55 CBR (5th) 229 (Ont SCJ) before the 2009 amendments, but were subsequently applied in *Brainhunter*, above note 149.

151 *CCAA*, s 36(4); *BIA*, s 65.13(5). A related person includes (a) a director or officer of a debtor corporation, (b) a person who has or did have direct or indirect *de facto* control of the debtor, or (c) a person related to a person described in (a) or (b). See *CCAA*, s 36(5); *BIA*, s 65.13(6).

152 *CCAA*, s 36(7); *BIA*, s 65.13(8).

In *Canwest Global Communications Corp (Re)*,[153] the court considered the scope of these provisions. An internal corporate reorganization was proposed that would disentangle the shared services arrangements of two related companies. The difficulty was that if the transaction was regulated by section 36 of the *CCAA*, it would be necessary to demonstrate that good faith efforts were made to sell the assets to someone other than a related party.[154] The court held that certain types of internal reorganizations could qualify as transactions in the ordinary course of business of the company. It did not endorse the view that all internal reorganizations were exempt, and gave the example of a "phoenix corporation" as an example of a transaction that would fall within the scope of the provision.[155]

Section 36 covers going-concern sales of all or part of the business as well as non-ordinary course sales of redundant assets. Prior to the 2009 amendments, initial *CCAA* orders typically authorized the disposal of redundant or non-material assets below a specified monetary value. The template initial orders of some jurisdictions continue to include such provisions except that they require court approval in respect of sales to related parties.[156] Others are more equivocal on the basis that the list of factors indicates that pre-approval is not permitted and that in any event notice would need to be given to affected secured creditors.[157]

2) The Sales Process

The court has considerable latitude in the sale process that it authorizes. The traditional Canadian sales process relied upon the efforts of the court appointed insolvency professional. More recently, auction based sales processes similar to those that were developed in the United States have been used. Regardless of the type of process that is chosen, an overarching principle is that the court must consider the efficacy and integrity of the sales process. This means that a court should not view the maximization of the sale proceeds in the particular case at hand as the sole or primary consideration. Changing the process

153 2009 CanLII 63368 (Ont SCJ).

154 *CCAA*, s 36(4)–(5).

155 In a phoenix transaction, the owners use a new company to purchase the assets free of the claims of the creditors and thereafter carry on the former business.

156 See the Alberta initial *CCAA* order, para 10, online: www.albertacourts.ab.ca/CourtofQueensBench/CommercialPractice/tabid/324/Default.aspx.

157 See the Ontario initial *CCAA* order, para 11, online: www.ontariocourts.ca/scj/practice/practice-directions/toronto/#Notices_and_Guides.

rules midstream in order to permit the acceptance of a higher bid has a detrimental effect on future transactions since a prospective purchaser will be less willing to expend the time and effort to participate if the process can be disrupted after these expenses have been incurred.[158]

The traditional sales process is adapted from that employed by a court appointed receiver. The court typically authorizes the sales process, and the monitor or trustee supervises the tender process and devises a marketing plan. Prospective purchasers are identified and given access to sensitive information upon signing confidentiality agreements. After conducting their due diligence, the prospective purchasers will submit their offers and the court officer will select what is considered to be the best offer. The process therefore does not involve a series of escalating bids, but encourages each prospective purchaser to make its most competitive offer in the first instance. Further negotiations will produce a definitive agreement that will then be submitted to the court for approval.

As an alternative to the traditional approach, a private auction process rather than the more usual process of tendering bids may be proposed. A difficulty with an auction is that a potential buyer will be reluctant to go to the considerable expense of investigating the business affairs only to have the fruit of its efforts scooped by a later bidder that takes advantage of its research. In order to ameliorate this problem, the debtor may enter into a stalking horse agreement that contains a set of provisions that create the incentive for the bidder to act as a stalking horse. These typically take the form of break-up fees and expense reimbursement, minimum overbids, and mandatory bid increments. A break fee remunerates the stalking horse bidder if the business is sold to some other bidder. A minimum overbid defines the amount by which a bid must exceed the stalking horse bid. A mandatory bid increment defines that amount by which a subsequent bid must exceed the prior bid.[159]

In evaluating the reasonableness of a stalking horse bid process, courts must be alert to the fact that the stalking horse bidder has a strong incentive to negotiate the terms of the stalking horse agreement in such a way to stifle competitive bidding so that its stalking horse bid is accepted and used to negotiate the definitive agreement.[160] The court

---

158 See *Terrace Bay Pulp Inc (Re)*, 2012 ONSC 4247 at para 59.

159 See A Taylor & Y Katirai, "An Analysis of Stalking Horse Processes in Canadian Insolvency Proceedings" (2013) 2 *Journal of the Insolvency Institute of Canada* 95.

160 See D Dowdall & J Dietrich, "Do Stalking Horses Have a Place in Intra-Canadian Insolvencies" in Janis P Sarra, ed, *Annual Review of Insolvency Law, 2005* (Toronto: Carswell, 2006) 1.

must assess the reasonableness of the time period (too short a period will dissuade bidders) as well as the magnitude and reasonableness of the break-up fee, minimum overbid, and bid increments. Other contractual provisions also need to be assessed, such as those that unduly restrict the identity of qualified bidders. In deciding whether or not to approve the sale process and the break-up fee, Canadian courts may wish to consider the more extensive caselaw from the United States. Break-up fees will be authorized if the court is of the opinion that they will facilitate an auction and result in an enhanced price.[161] However, courts will scrutinize the terms of the agreement and the size of the fee to ensure that it was not designed to benefit a favoured purchaser over other bidders by increasing the cost to other bidders.[162] Break-up fees in bankruptcy are generally limited to 1 to 4 percent of the purchase price.[163]

3) Credit Bids

Credit bidding occurs when a secured creditor uses some or all of its secured obligation to fund its bid for the purchase of the assets. If successful, the purchase price is paid through a corresponding reduction of the secured obligation. There is no statutory limitations on the use of credit bids in Canada. Courts have held that the secured creditor can bid the full amount of the secured obligation and is not limited to the fair market value of the assets.[164] Credit bidding gives a secured creditor an ability to ensure that the assets are not sold for an unacceptably low price. If the other bids are too low, the secured creditor can step in and acquire the assets through a credit bid. A credit bid can only be made in respect of property that is collateral for the secured debt. If there are other, unencumbered assets that are being sold as well, the secured creditor must pay cash for these assets. If there are claims that rank in priority to the secured creditor, these claims must be paid out. The allocation of value between encumbered and unencumbered assets may become controversial — if the encumbered and unencumbered assets are sold together and the unencumbered assets are assigned only

---

161 *In re Integrated Resources, Inc*, 147 BR 650 (SDNY 1992).

162 *In re O'Brien Environmental Energy, Inc*, 181 F3d 527 (3d Cir 1999).

163 See *In re Tama Beef Packing, Inc*, 321 BR 496 (8th Cir BAP 2005). And see *Brainhunter*, above note 149 in which the court approved a break fee of 2.5 percent.

164 *White Birch Paper Holding Company (Arrangement relatif à)*, 2010 QCCS 4915 at para 34. See *also In re SubMicron Systems Corp*, 432 F3d 448 (3d Cir 2006).

their liquidation value, this may result in the confiscation of value by the secured creditors.[165]

As in the case of a stalking horse bid, there is a concern that the credit bidder may seek to influence the sale process to discourage other prospective purchasers from making bids. A secured creditor will ordinarily be strongly motivated to obtain the best possible price on an asset sale in order to reduce its secured debt. However, a secured creditor who bids on a sale operates under a different incentive — to acquire the assets at the lowest possible price — and this will prejudice junior creditors who might otherwise have a claim to the surplus value in the event that a competitive sales process yielded sufficient funds to fully satisfy the secured debt of the senior creditor. For this reason, the monitor and the court play an important role in ensuring the transparency and integrity of the sale process.

FURTHER READINGS

BELANGER, P. "Critical Suppliers: What Does Section 11.4 CCRA Mean?" (2010) 26 *Banking and Finance Law Review* 1

BEN-ISHAI, S. "Derivatives and the *CCAA*" in S Ben-Ishai & A Duggan, eds, *Canadian Bankruptcy and Insolvency Law: Bill C-55, Statute c. 47 and Beyond* (Markham, ON: LexisNexis Canada, 2007) ch 3

CARHART, J. "Air Canada and the Treatment of Set-Off in Initial *CCAA* Orders" (2004) 21 *National Insolvency Review* 17

DOWDALL, D, & J DIETRICH. "Do Stalking Horses Have a Place in Intra-Canadian Insolvencies" in Janis P. Sarra, ed, *Annual Review of Insolvency Law, 2005* (Toronto: Carswell, 2006) 1

DUGGAN, A. "Partly Performed Contracts" in S Ben-Ishai & A Duggan, eds, *Canadian Bankruptcy and Insolvency Law: Bill C-55, Statute c. 47 and Beyond* (Markham, ON: LexisNexis Canada, 2007) ch 3

HAYES, E. "Executory Contracts and Proposals under the *Bankruptcy and Insolvency Act* (Canada): A Comparative Analysis with the *Companies' Creditors Arrangement Act* (Canada)" in J Ziegel, ed, *Current Developments in International and Comparative Corporate Insolvency Law* (Oxford: Clarendon Press, 1994) 267

165 See M Rosenthal, "Sales Process Dynamics The Monitor's Perspective" in Janis P Sarra, ed, *Annual Review of Insolvency Law, 2012* (Toronto: Carswell, 2013) 123.

HUNT, C. "Not-So-Critical Vendors: Redefining Critical Vendor Orders" (2005) 93 *Kentucky Law Journal* 915

MCDERMOTT, M. "Critical Vendor and Related Orders: Kmart and the Bankruptcy Abuse Presentation and Consumer Protection Act of 2005" (2006) 14 *American Bankruptcy Institute Law Review* 409

ROTSZTAIN, M. "Debtor-in-Possession Financing in Canada: Current Law and a Preferred Approach" (2000) 33 *Canadian Business Law Journal* 283

RUTMAN, R, A MACFARLANE, A NORTH, & A KHOKHAR. "Creeping Roll-Up DIP" (2012) 1 *Journal of the Insolvency Institute of Canada* 161

SHEA, P. "Dealing with Suppliers in a Reorganization" (2008) 37 *Canadian Bankruptcy Reports* (5th) 161

TAYLOR, A, & Y KATIRAI. "An Analysis of Stalking Horse Processes in Canadian Insolvency Proceedings" (2013) 2 *Journal of the Insolvency Institute of Canada* 95

WASSERMAN, M, & C FELL. "Credit Bidding in Canadian Insolvency Proceedings — A Useful Tool for Secured Creditors Requiring Checks and Balances" (2014) 3 *Journal of the Insolvency Institute of Canada* 21

CHAPTER 14

GOVERNANCE AND SUPERVISION

The debtor does not usually lose control over the management of the business during the period in which restructuring proceedings are ongoing. In this respect, restructuring proceedings are unlike other commercial insolvency proceedings, such as bankruptcy and receivership, in which an insolvency administrator assumes control of the business. However, it would be a grave mistake to think that this means that the debtor will simply carry on business as usual. The initiation of commercial restructuring proceedings radically alters the environment within which the debtor manages and operates the business. The debtor must work closely with insolvency professionals and expert legal advisors and must engage in a series of negotiations with claimants in order to develop an acceptable plan or to implement a sales process.

There are a multitude of decisions that must be made, and there inevitably will be parties who are unhappy about some of these decisions. The governance rules establish the legal framework within which the decision making occurs, and the recourse available to those who wish to contest the decisions that are made. In order to make properly informed decisions, the participants in the process must have accurate and timely information available to them. Therefore, it is also necessary to put mechanisms in place that provide for the free flow of reliable information.

A. THE ROLE OF THE DEBTOR

If the debtor is an individual or a partnership, the governance issues are relatively straightforward. The individual or partner is both the owner and the manager of the business and is subject to unlimited liability for claims arising out of the operation of the business. The debtor will attempt to negotiate a deal in which the outcome for both the debtor and the creditors is better than if the debtor's assets were liquidated in bankruptcy proceedings.

The matter is often more complex when the debtor is a corporation. In many instances, the corporation is closely held. In these corporations, a single person or a small group of persons holds a controlling interest in the corporation. The controlling shareholders manage the business and the shares they hold are not traded on an exchange. These individuals sometimes possess firm-specific knowledge and expertise, which makes it necessary to retain them as participants in the restructured business.

In other instances, the shares of the corporation are publicly traded and professional managers are responsible for the management of the business. Here, there is a division between ownership and control. The shareholders are the residual owners of the firm, but they do not actively participate in its management. It is often the case that the total value of the creditors' claims exceeds the going-concern value of the financially distressed firm. The shareholders' interests will usually be wiped out and they will not be participants in the restructured firm.[1] During the restructuring proceedings, the corporate directors must recognize that it is no longer appropriate for them to focus upon the interests of shareholders when making their decisions. It may also be advisable to replace or augment the existing management team. This may be necessary if the creditors have lost trust in the managers, if some or all of the managers have left the firm, or if the managers are thought to lack the expertise necessary to carry out a turnaround of the business.

1) The Duties of Directors of Financially Distressed Corporations

The various stakeholders in a corporation will often have divergent views as to the preferred direction and outcome of the restructuring. Claimants such as secured creditors with higher-ranking claims may press for an immediate sale of the assets. Claimants with lower-ranking

1 *Re Stelco Inc* (2006), 17 CBR (5th) 78 (Ont SCJ).

claims who believe that a sale would result in their recovering little or nothing may push for a restructuring in which their claims are preserved in some form in the hope that the prospects for the business will improve in the future.[2] The corporate directors make decisions on the appropriate course of action, although the court in many instances will be called upon to review the fairness and appropriateness of these decisions. The principles of corporate governance provide the legal structure for this decision-making process by defining the nature of the obligations owed by the directors and identifying the parties to whom these obligations are owed.

The leading Canadian decision on the obligations of the directors of a financially distressed corporation is that of the Supreme Court of Canada in *Peoples Department Stores Inc (Trustee of) v Wise*.[3] The Court held that the corporate directors owe a duty of care to their creditors but that this does not rise to the level of a fiduciary duty. In determining the best interests of the corporation, the directors may legitimately consider the interests of shareholders, employees, suppliers, creditors, consumers, governments, and the environment.[4] The best interests of the corporation are not the same as the best interests of the shareholders.[5] The nature and content of the fiduciary duty does not change when the corporation is in the vicinity of bankruptcy.[6] The directors do not owe separate fiduciary duties to the creditors. Their fiduciary duty continues to be owed only to the corporation. When the corporation is financially distressed, the directors must act in its best interests by creating a "better" corporation and must not favour the interests of any one group of stakeholders.[7]

This might appear to suggest that, in deciding between a going-concern sale and a restructuring in which the debtor continues to conduct the business, the directors should choose the one that maximizes the value of the firm. However, the matter is not clear-cut because the Supreme Court of Canada also indicated that the directors are entitled to consider other factors such as the effect of the decision on the employees, the community, and other stakeholders. It is not obvious how

2 See *Re Anvil Range Mining Corp* (2001), 25 CBR (4th) 1 at para 4 (Ont SCJ) in which Farley J stated: "[H]uman nature may often lead those who have suffered great losses (as the unsecured creditors and shareholders of Anvil certainly have) to hope for a miracle to happen or to present hope as fact and speculation as a firm foundation and to ignore probability in opting for (remote) possibility."

3 [2004] 3 SCR 461.

4 *Ibid* at para 42.

5 *Ibid*.

6 *Ibid* at para 43.

7 *Ibid* at para 47.

directors and courts are expected to balance the competing claims of the stakeholders where there are irreconcilable divergences in interest.

2) Replacement of Corporate Directors

The power to remove a corporate director is normally exercised by the shareholders of a corporation.[8] In *Re Stelco Inc*,[9] the Ontario Court of Appeal discussed the extent to which a court has the power to remove a director. The corporation had initiated proceedings under the *CCAA*, and its corporate board had been depleted by resignations. The board appointed two individuals to fill the vacancies. These individuals had acquired 20 percent of the publicly traded shares following the commencement of the restructuring proceedings. The employee stakeholders objected to the appointment because of the perceived unfairness of giving one stakeholder group a privileged access to the capital-raising process and a say in the corporate decision making. Justice Farley concluded that he had the power to rescind the appointment on the basis of the inherent jurisdiction of the court and the statutory discretion given to the court under the *CCAA*. His decision was appealed.

The Ontario Court of Appeal held that neither the concept of inherent jurisdiction nor the statutory discretion conferred upon a court by the *CCAA* confers a power to remove directors. The court drew a distinction between the role of the court and the role of the corporation in restructuring proceedings. The role of the court is to establish the boundaries of the playing field and to act as referee. In exercising this role, the court is not to usurp the role of the directors in conducting the corporation's restructuring efforts. Although the *CCAA* did not provide for the removal of directors, complainants could request the removal of directors through use of the statutory oppression remedy contained in business corporations legislation.[10] In order to exercise the remedy, there must be some conduct that is oppressive or that unfairly disregards the interests of the complainant. A mere apprehension that such conduct might occur in the future is not sufficient.

8 See, for example, *Canada Business Corporations Act*, RSC 1985, c C-44, s 109(1).

9 (2005), 9 CBR (5th) 135 (Ont CA).

10 Section 42 of the *CCAA* provides that the Act may be applied conjointly with other legislation that provides, authorizes, or makes provision for the sanction of compromises or arrangements between a company and its shareholders. The Ontario Court of Appeal held that this provided a gateway through which a court may utilize the oppression remedy.

Both the *CCAA* and the *BIA* have been amended to give a court the power to remove directors in restructuring proceedings.[11] The court may, on the application of any interested party, make an order removing a director if it is satisfied that the director is unreasonably impairing or is likely to unreasonably impair the possibility of a viable plan from being made, or if the director is acting or is likely to act inappropriately as a director. It is not entirely clear from the language of the provision whether the prospect of unreasonable impairment of the plan must flow from some actual or anticipated conduct on the part of the director or whether it is sufficient to show that the success of the restructuring proceedings is threatened because of the other stakeholders' distrust of the director. The principles enunciated by the Ontario Court of Appeal in *Re Stelco Inc* seem to suggest that the former interpretation is to be preferred.

3) Appointment of a Chief Restructuring Officer

The restructuring environment within which the directors and officers of a financially distressed corporation must operate is very different from the ordinary commercial activities of the business. They must come up with a strategy for achieving long-term viability of the business, which may involve a program of cost cutting and downsizing. They must negotiate with multiple constituencies of creditors and other stakeholders, and often they must procure interim financing from lenders that specialize in loans to financially distressed companies. The existing corporate managers will be knowledgeable about their particular industry, but they are unlikely to have expertise in turnaround management.

For this reason, a financially distressed corporation may decide to appoint a chief restructuring officer (CRO) in order to obtain the services of a turnaround specialist to coordinate its financial restructuring efforts. The appointment of a CRO can also go some way in placating creditors or other stakeholders where there is a perception that the company's financial distress was caused by the incompetence of the existing managers. The CRO may be appointed either before or after the restructuring proceedings are commenced. Although the court appoints or affirms the appointment of the CRO, this does not mean that the CRO undertakes a role similar to that of a monitor or trustee. Unlike a monitor or trustee, the CRO is an officer of the debtor

---

11 *CCAA*, s 11.5(1); *BIA*, s 64(1).

corporation and is expected to take a lead role in the negotiations with creditors and other stakeholders.[12]

4) Directors and Officers Charges

Courts frequently make orders under the *CCAA* that provide for the indemnification of corporate directors and officers for acts done after the commencement of the restructuring. These provisions are designed to retain the services of the directors and officers while the restructuring proceedings are under way.[13] The 2009 amendments to the *CCAA* and the *BIA* codified the court's power to create charges to secure the indemnification of directors and officers for obligations and liabilities that they may incur after the commencement of restructuring proceedings.[14] Notice must be given to secured creditors who are affected by the order. The court may order that the charge rank in priority over the claim of a secured creditor.[15] A court may not make the order if the debtor is able to obtain adequate indemnification insurance for the director or officer at a reasonable cost.[16] The charge is not available in respect of liabilities that involve gross negligence or wilful misconduct.[17]

5) Retention of Key Employees

The issue of director and officer retention can be a contentious one in restructuring proceedings. On the one hand, the retention of key employees may be vital to the success of the restructuring; on the other, creditors and other stakeholders may look askance at the prospect of attractive compensation packages being given to a managerial team that they view as responsible for the business failure. Key employee retention plans (KERPs) may be structured so as to provide additional salary, success bonuses, or termination benefits (golden parachutes). Given the obvious opportunities here for self-dealing by executives, it is important that these plans be reviewed by a court to ensure that they are fair and that they are designed to achieve appropriate object-

12 *Re Ivaco Inc* (2004), 3 CBR (5th) 33 (Ont SCJ).

13 On the interpretation of director and officers charges, see *Re Afton Food Group Ltd* (2006), 21 CBR (5th) 102 (Ont SCJ).

14 *CCAA*, s 11.51(1); *BIA*, s 64.1(1).

15 *CCAA*, s 11.51(2); *BIA*, s 64.1(2).

16 *CCAA*, s 11.51(3); *BIA*, s 64.1(3). And see *Dessert & Passion inc (Proposal)*, 2009 QCCS 4669.

17 *CCAA*, s 11.51(4); *BIA*, s 64.1(4).

ives.[18] In deciding whether to approve a KERP, courts have considered whether the retention of the employees is required, the likelihood that the employees or officers will look for other employment, the length and terms of the plan, and whether the secured creditors and the monitor support the plan.[19] In some instances, the courts have authorized a charge to secure the KERP and granted it priority over existing secured creditors.[20]

6) Appointment of an Interim Receiver

In some cases, it may be prudent to appoint a receiver to manage the business. This may occur where there is a loss of confidence in management[21] or where the directors have resigned.[22] In some cases, the court may give the monitor the power to carry on the business.[23] However, this can sometimes lead to the perception that the monitor is acting in a conflict of interest if the monitor makes application for an extension of time in respect of the restructuring proceedings. If a receiver is appointed because of deficiencies in or resignations of directors or officers, a successful restructuring will need to make provision for new management of the business.

7) Conflicting Duties as a Pension Plan Administrator

The Supreme Court of Canada in *Sun Indalex Finance, LLC v United Steelworkers*[24] considered a conflict of interest where a debtor acts both as the business decision maker and pension plan administrator. An employer that chooses to act as a pension plan administrator owes a fiduciary obligation to the beneficiaries of the pension plan. This means that the directors are subject to two different sets of fiduciary duties: one is owed to the corporation while the other is owed to the pension plan beneficiaries. A conflict of interest does not arise simply because the directors, exercising their management power in the best interests of the corporation, make decisions that have the potential to affect the plan beneficiaries. The commencement of restructuring proceedings

---

18 *Grant Forest Products Inc (Re)* (2009), 57 CBR (5th) 128 (Ont SCJ).
19 *Cinram International Inc (Re)*, 2012 ONSC 3767.
20 *Timminco Limited (Re)*, 2012 ONSC 506.
21 *General Electric Capital Canada Inc v Euro United Corp* (1999), 25 CBR (4th) 250 (Ont SCJ).
22 See *Re 843504 Alberta Ltd* (2003), 4 CBR (5th) 306 (Alta QB).
23 *Ibid.*
24 2013 SCC 6.

and a failure to notify the beneficiaries will not give rise to a conflict of interest if these steps are necessary to preserve the *status quo* for the benefit of all the stakeholders. However, difficulties are more likely to arise when the debtor seeks authorization of an interim financing (DIP) charge or a sale process that may make it impossible to satisfy the claims of the plan beneficiaries. A failure to take steps to ensure that the plan beneficiaries are afforded the opportunity to be represented in the restructuring proceedings can result in the directors breaching their fiduciary duty to the plan beneficiaries. It will not typically be sufficient simply to include the plan beneficiaries in the list of creditors who receive notice. The court should be advised of the conflict so that it can determine an appropriate response. A judicially ordered constructive trust was not an appropriate remedy for the breach of duty in this case as there was no evidence that acquisition of the property was connected to the breach.

B. THE ROLE OF THE MONITOR AND THE TRUSTEE

A monitor under *CCAA* proceedings and a trustee under *BIA* restructuring proceedings fulfil a similar though not identical role. They are both officers of the court and one of their primary obligations is to ensure that accurate and timely information is provided to the creditors and to the court. They owe a fiduciary duty to the stakeholders; they must act independently; and they must treat all parties reasonably and fairly.[25] The *CCAA* and the *BIA* contain provisions that set out eligibility requirements and define the scope of their duties. The *CCAA* originally did not provide for the appointment of a monitor. Monitors were appointed by courts through the exercise of their inherent or equitable jurisdiction. In 1997 the practice was codified in the *CCAA*, and the appointment of a monitor was made a mandatory feature of a *CCAA* restructuring.

1) Eligibility

The *CCAA* did not originally impose any qualification requirements on the appointment of a monitor. The *BIA* contained stricter requirements; the trustee had to be a person qualified to act as a trustee under the *BIA*.[26] The 2009 amendments have now imposed a similar qualifi-

25 *Winalta Inc (Re)*, 2011 ABQB 399.

26 *BIA*, s 2 "trustee."

cation requirement on a monitor under the *CCAA*[27] The appointment process differs in that a monitor is always appointed by court order whereas a trustee is not.

A person who acted as the debtor's auditor during the past two years may be appointed as monitor only if permitted by the court.[28] The appointment of an auditor as monitor often involves a trade-off between fairness and efficiency. The auditor is generally the accounting professional who is most knowledgeable about the business affairs of the company and best able to assemble the financial information required in connection with the commencement of restructuring proceedings.[29] The appointment of the auditor as monitor also helps in reducing costs. This is particularly important where the debtor is a small- or medium-sized firm that is less able to bear the considerable administrative costs of restructuring proceedings. Yet the appointment of the auditor as monitor is not without its problems. It may create a perception that the auditor will not be able to act in an independent role but will be biased in favour of the wishes of the debtor corporation.[30] It may also not be feasible in larger corporations because of the restrictions placed on the activities of auditors by the *Sarbanes-Oxley Act of 2002*[31] in the United States.

2) Statutory Duties

The primary duty of the monitor and the primary duty of the trustee are expressed in somewhat different terms. The monitor is under a statutory obligation to monitor the business and financial affairs of the company.[32] The trustee is under a statutory obligation to make an appraisal and investigation of the affairs and property of the debtor so as to enable the trustee to estimate with reasonable accuracy the financial situation of the debtor and the cause of the debtor's financial difficulties or insolvency and report the result to the creditors.[33] The monitor and the trustee are given a right of access to and examination of the debtor's property, including premises, books, records, and other financial documents, for the purpose of monitoring the debtor's business

---

27 *CCAA*, s 11.7(1).

28 *CCAA*, s 11.7(2)(a)(iii); *BIA*, s 13.3(1)(a)(iv).

29 *Re Hickman Equipment (1985) Ltd* (2002), 34 CBR (4th) 203 (NLSC).

30 See *Re Stokes Building Supplies Ltd* (1992), 13 CBR (3d) 10 (Nfld SC) in which an application to appoint the auditor as monitor was dismissed.

31 PL 107-204, 116 Stat 746, s 201.

32 *CCAA*, s 11.7(1).

33 *BIA*, s 50(5).

and financial affairs.[34] In carrying out their duties, a monitor and a trustee must act honestly and in good faith and must comply with the code of ethics that governs the conduct of trustees.[35]

The *BIA* restructuring proceedings were originally conceived as having much less court involvement than the *CCAA*. The 2009 amendments give the bankruptcy court a much wider ability to make the kinds of orders that were typically made in *CCAA* proceedings. Given these changes, it is likely that the trustee's financial investigation into the debtor's affairs will also be regarded as essential in assisting the court in making such orders.

A key feature in both restructuring regimes is that the names and addresses of creditors are made publicly available. This gives the creditors the opportunity to communicate with one another in order to share information and develop a common strategy in negotiations where possible. It also creates the potential for an outside party to offer to purchase the claims of the creditors.

a) Specific Statutory Duties of the Monitor

The 2009 amendments to the *CCAA* set out a detailed enumeration of the duties and functions of a monitor. The monitor is under a statutory obligation to:[36]

- publish a notice in one or more newspapers, send a copy of the order to every known creditor who has a claim of more than $1,000, and make a list of their names and addresses publicly available within five days of the making of the order, unless otherwise ordered by the court;
- review the company's cash-flow statement as to its reasonableness and file a report with the court;
- investigate and file a report with the court on the state of the company's business and financial affairs and the causes of its financial difficulties;
- file a report with the court on the state of the company's business and financial affairs (1) without delay after ascertaining any material change in the company's projected cash flow or financial circumstances; (2) at least seven days before a meeting of creditors; (3) not later than forty-five days or any longer period specified by the

34 *CCAA*, s 24; *BIA*, ss 50(10) and 50.4(7)(a).

35 *CCAA*, s 25; *BIA*, s 13.5; *Bankruptcy and Insolvency General Rules*, CRC, c 368, ss 34–53.

36 *CCAA*, s 23(1).

court at the end of the company's fiscal quarter; and (4) at any other times ordered by the court.

- advise the creditors of the filing of any reports;
- file with the superintendent a copy of documents specified in the regulations;
- attend court proceedings or meeting of creditors if necessary for the fulfilment of the monitor's duties or functions;
- advise the court immediately if the monitor is of the opinion that bankruptcy proceedings would be more beneficial to the company;
- advise the court on the fairness or reasonableness of any proposed plan;
- make all prescribed documents publicly available and provide information to creditors on how they can be accessed; and
- carry on any other function that the court may direct.

These statutory duties are routinely supplemented by additional duties that are specified in the initial order. The order will typically provide that the monitor is authorized to advise the debtor in its development of a plan and in the administration of meetings of creditors. A monitor is permitted to provide non-confidential information provided to it by the debtor to a creditor, but this does not authorize a monitor, without the knowledge of the debtor, to provide a secured creditor with estimates of the realization values obtained and the professional fees that would be incurred if receivership proceedings were commenced.[37]

Courts have occasionally given a monitor the power of management over the business or carriage of a going-concern sale of the business.[38] The power given to the monitor may be limited or it may involve the monitor being appointed as an interim receiver. The creation of a "supermonitor" creates its own set of problems. The monitor is expected to act in an impartial and even-handed manner. When the monitor becomes involved in the making of business decisions that have a differential impact on the various stakeholders, there may be a perception that the monitor has entered the fray and can no longer carry out an objective and impartial analysis.

b) Specific Statutory Duties of the Trustee

A trustee in *BIA* restructuring proceedings is under a statutory obligation to:

---

37 *Winalta Inc (Re)*, above note 25.

38 *Re Royal Oak Mines Inc* (1999), 11 CBR (4th) 122 (Ont Ct Gen Div).

- investigate the state of the company's business and financial affairs and the causes of the financial difficulties;[39]
- file a cash-flow statement indicating the projected cash flow of the debtor and a report on the reasonableness of the cash-flow statement, both signed by the trustee, and a report containing representations signed by the debtor;[40]
- file a report on the state of the company's business and financial affairs (1) with the official receiver without delay after ascertaining any material change in the company's projected cash flow or financial circumstances; (2) with the court at such times as may be ordered by the court;[41]
- send to every known creditor a copy of a notice of intention to make a proposal (which contains the names and addresses of creditors with claims greater than $250) within five days after the filing;[42]
- advise on and participate in the preparation of the proposal, including negotiations after the filing of a notice of intention;[43]
- call a meeting of the creditors, to be held within twenty-one days after the filing of the proposal with the official receiver, and send every known creditor the relevant documents;[44]
- apply to the court for an appointment for a hearing of the application for the court's approval of the proposal within five days after its acceptance;[45] and
- prepare and file a report with the court that sets out the debtor's realizable assets and liabilities, the causes of the insolvency, the conduct of the debtor, and an opinion on whether the proposal is an advantageous one for the creditors.[46]

3) Breach of Duty

A monitor or trustee must act honestly and in good faith and comply with the Code of Ethics prescribed by the *BIA*.[47] A monitor or trustee who fails to act fairly and impartially is in breach of this duty. This will

---

39 *BIA*, s 50(5).
40 *Ibid*, ss 50(6) and 50.4(2).
41 *Ibid*, ss 50(10) and 50.4(7).
42 *Ibid*, s 50.4(1).
43 *Ibid*, s 50.5.
44 *Ibid*, s 51.
45 *Ibid*, s 58.
46 *Ibid*; Form 40.
47 *CCAA*, s 25; *BIA*, s 13.5. The Code of Ethics is contained in *Bankruptcy and Insolvency General Rules*, above note 35, ss 34–53.

occur if a monitor or trustee favours the interest of one of the creditors over the interests of the debtor or the other creditors. If a breach of duty or excess of authority is established, the court should then determine if damage is attributable to the monitor's conduct, including damage to the integrity of the insolvency system, and ascertain the appropriate fee reduction.[48] A breach of duty may also justify a removal and replacement of a monitor.

4) Relationship with the Debtor

The selection of a person to act as monitor under the *CCAA* or as trustee under the *BIA* is usually made by the debtor in the first instance. However, once that person is appointed, he or she becomes an officer of the court and the debtor has no power to terminate the appointment. Only the court can do so.[49]

The *CCAA* expressly gives the court the power to direct a monitor to carry out other functions.[50] The initial order will usually give the monitor the power to advise the debtor company in the development of its plan and in respect of its meeting with its creditors. Although the *BIA* does not contain a provision that permits a court to confer additional powers on a trustee, the trustee is expressly given the power to advise the debtor and participate in the preparation of the proposal, including negotiations with creditors.

The monitor or trustee therefore undertakes two essential functions, and there is an ever-present danger that these will come into conflict with one another. The first is to provide an independent assessment of the business and financial affairs of the debtor that can be relied upon by the court and by the creditors. The second is to assist the debtor in navigating through the complexities of restructuring proceedings. The monitor or trustee must attempt to guide the debtor through the process without becoming an advocate or mouthpiece for the debtor.

Since they are officers of the court, a monitor's and a trustee's reports do not need to be sworn, and neither a monitor nor a trustee is generally subject to cross-examination on these reports.[51] However, courts are wary of debtors who attempt to hide behind a report of a monitor or trustee. If the matter is contentious, the debtor will be expected

48 See *Winalta Inc (Re)*, above note 25.
49 *CCAA*, s 11.7(3); *BIA*, s 14.04.
50 *CCAA*, s 23(1)(k).
51 *Re Bell Canada International Inc*, 2003 CarswellOnt 4537 (SCJ).

to swear an affidavit in respect of the motion so as to permit cross-examination on the matter.[52]

5) Liability of the Monitor and Trustee

Monitors and trustees are afforded statutory protection from liability. A monitor is not liable for loss caused by a party who relies on a monitor's report if the monitor acts in good faith and takes reasonable care in its preparation.[53] A trustee is not liable for loss to any party resulting from that party's reliance on the cash-flow statement if the trustee acts in good faith and takes reasonable care in reviewing the cash-flow statement.[54]

Monitors and trustees are also afforded protection from personal liability, including liability as a successor employer, in respect of claims of employees that exist before the appointment of the monitor or trustee.[55] Monitors and trustees are protected, too, from liability that arises out of environmental conditions that occurred before their appointment, and from post-appointment liability for environmental damage unless that damage was caused by their wilful conduct or gross negligence.[56] Because these kinds of liabilities are imposed on a party who operates the business, the protections from liability will be most significant in respect of monitors who are given additional powers to act in this capacity.

C. THE ROLE OF THE COURTS

1) The Enhanced Jurisdiction of Courts under the *BIA*

The conventional view of the difference between *CCAA* and *BIA* restructuring proceedings is that the former has a much higher degree of court involvement and a greater degree of judicial discretion or "flexibility." The *BIA* is characterized as being more rule-driven and correspondingly less able to be adapted in larger and more complex restructurings. This view will likely need to be modified in light of the legislative amendments that have been made to both regimes.

---

52 *Ibid* at para 10.
53 *CCAA*, s 23(2).
54 *BIA*, ss 50(9) and 50.4(5).
55 *CCAA*, s 11.8(1); *BIA*, s 14.06(1.2).
56 *CCAA*, s 11.8(3); *BIA*, s 14.06(2).

The amendments to the commercial proposal provisions of the *BIA* give the courts the same kinds of powers as those that have been available to the courts under the *CCAA*. These include:

- the power to authorize DIP financing and to create charges securing such loans ranking in priority over secured creditors;[57]
- the power to authorize the creation of a directors' and officers' charge ranking in priority over secured creditors;[58]
- the power to authorize the creation of an administrative charge ranking in priority over secured creditors;[59]
- the power to review the disclaimer of contracts by the debtor;[60]
- the power to authorize the assignment of contracts;[61]
- the power to authorize the sale of assets outside the ordinary course of business of the debtor;[62] and
- the power to impose a stay of proceedings in respect of regulatory proceedings.[63]

In addition to these new powers, the court in *BIA* restructuring proceedings continues to exercise a critical role in granting extensions in time,[64] terminating proceedings,[65] lifting the stay,[66] and approving the proposal after creditors have approved it.[67] Because of these changes, the court will exercise a role that is much closer to that being undertaken by courts in *CCAA* proceedings. Therefore, the discussion of the court's role that has developed largely under *CCAA* jurisprudence should, in principle, be applicable to bankruptcy courts in the exercise of their new powers in *BIA* restructuring proceedings.

2) Judicial Supervision and Case Management

A court that supervises restructuring proceedings undertakes a role that is significantly different from that exercised in ordinary commercial litigation. Commercial litigation looks backward into the past whereas litigation in restructuring proceedings involves a review of proposed

57 *BIA*, s 50.6.
58 *Ibid*, s 64.1.
59 *Ibid*, s 64.2.
60 *Ibid*, ss 65.11(3)–(4).
61 *Ibid*, s 84.1.
62 *Ibid*, s 65.13.
63 *Ibid*, s 69.6.
64 *Ibid*, s 50.4(9).
65 *Ibid*, s 50.4(11).
66 *Ibid*, s 69.4.
67 *Ibid*, s 59(2).

transactions and ongoing conduct. Justice Farley has described the former as "autopsy litigation" and the latter as "real time litigation."[68]

There are a number of different aspects to the courts' supervisory role in restructuring proceedings. The first element concerns judicial case management of the restructuring proceedings. The litigation is iterative and cannot be separated into discrete parcels that can be decided by different judges. It is therefore important that the same supervising judge be involved in the various court applications. The complexities and the time constraints are such that it would be highly inefficient to have a succession of different judges involved in the restructuring. However, the case management approach is not simply driven by considerations of judicial economy. The supervising judge must be familiar with the immediate past history and future trajectory of the proceedings in order to assess the progress that is being made and to identify the source of difficulties if there is a lack of progress or loss of momentum.

The second element involves judicial specialization. In some jurisdictions, such as Ontario and Quebec, this is achieved on a formal and institutionalized basis through the use of a Commercial List. In others, such as British Columbia and Alberta, it is achieved on an informal basis by assigning supervision of restructuring proceedings to judges who have had past experience in these kinds of proceedings.

The third element involves timing and access to the court. Since the litigation generally involves the review of proposed transactions or directions on a host of interim matters, there is a pronounced need for speedy access to the courts. Significant delay on time-sensitive matters threatens the success of the restructuring. Supervising courts have introduced case management approaches that provide speedy access to courts.

The fourth element involves the use of negotiation and dispute resolution as an integral part of the judicial role. Justice Farley has described this as involving an adherence to the "3Cs" of communication, cooperation, and common sense. It is characterized in part by a reluctance to permit the restructuring proceedings to be sidetracked by procedural wrangling or delays. However, more controversially, it sometimes involves the application of considerable pressure by the supervising judge in order to force disputing parties to come to an agreement.

---

68 *Re Cadillac Fairview Inc* (1995), 30 CBR (3d) 17 at para 7 (Ont Ct Gen Div); *Re Bakemates International Inc* (2001), 25 CBR (4th) 24 at para 16 (Ont SCJ).

3) Comeback Clauses

The time-sensitive nature of restructuring proceedings has given rise to the use of comeback clauses by courts in *CCAA* proceedings. In many cases, the initial order granted by the court is made on an *ex parte* basis or is made on the basis of only limited notice to major creditors. The potential prejudice of such an order is ameliorated to a degree by the inclusion of a comeback clause. Persons who are affected by the order are permitted to bring an application to vary or amend it. On a comeback application, the onus is on the original applicant (the debtor company) to demonstrate why the original or initial order should stand.[69] Appellate courts have recognized that restructuring proceedings are "often urgent, complex and dynamic"[70] and have regarded an appeal from an initial order as premature. The appropriate procedure is for aggrieved parties first to bring their concerns before the supervisory court pursuant to the comeback clause.

The 2009 amendments have somewhat lessened the need for creditors to resort to comeback clauses under the *CCAA*. Orders that create charges that have priority over secured parties[71] and that authorize the sale of assets outside the ordinary course of business[72] can be made only on notice to affected secured parties. There is also less scope for the use of comeback clauses in *BIA* restructuring proceedings, since the stay of proceedings comes into operation automatically upon the filing of the proposal or the filing of a notice of intention.

Courts have recognized that the use of the comeback provision in an initial order under the *CCAA* is not a panacea. Justice Blair in *Re Royal Oak Mines Inc*[73] indicated that there is an inherent disadvantage to the affected party even if that party does not bear the onus of proof in the comeback application, since the restructuring proceedings may have taken on a momentum of their own that is difficult to overcome on the comeback application.

4) Initial Orders under the *CCAA*

Applications for initial orders under the *CCAA* presented courts with two additional difficulties. The first had to do with overreaching initial orders. The initial order requested by the debtor would often put into

69 *Re General Chemical Canada Ltd* (2005), 7 CBR (5th) 102 (Ont SCJ).

70 *Re Algoma Steel Inc* (2001), 25 CBR (4th) 194 at para 7 (Ont CA).

71 *CCAA*, ss 11.2, 11.51, & 11.52; *BIA*, ss 50.6, 64.1, and s 64.2.

72 *CCAA*, s 36(2); *BIA*, s 65.13(3).

73 (1999), 6 CBR (4th) 314 at para 28 (Ont Ct Gen Div).

place the administrative apparatus of the restructuring process. The danger was that considerable costs could be incurred before creditors were notified and afforded the opportunity to object. The second was that the judge hearing the application was faced with a complex document with very little time to review its provisions to ensure that they were not excessive or unusual in comparison with orders normally granted in similar circumstances.

Justice Blair expressed concern over these matters in *Re Royal Oak Mines Inc.*[74] He was of the opinion that the provisions contained in the initial order should be limited to those that are "reasonably necessary for the continued operation of the debtor company during a brief but realistic period of time, on an urgency basis."[75] This principle of minimizing the scope and effect of the order is captured in the idea that the order should be limited to what is necessary to "keep the lights on" until the creditors have had an opportunity to consider their position and prepare their response.

One response to these problems has been the creation of template *CCAA* initial orders in Ontario, Quebec, Alberta, British Columbia, and Saskatchewan. These are intended to provide guidance to counsel and to promote the standardization of *CCAA* provisions.

5) The Role of the Appellate Courts

The real-time nature of restructuring proceedings also has significant implications in respect of the role of the appellate courts in reviewing the decisions of the supervising court. Because the restructuring proceedings are ongoing, an appeal has the potential to delay them and thereby endanger their success. The appellate courts have responded to this problem in two ways. First, they have expedited the appeal process in order to minimize the delay associated with the appeal. Secondly, they have expressed a reluctance to interfere with the exercise of discretion by the supervising court. The appellate courts have recognized that the supervising judge is in the best position to balance the competing factors at play in the restructuring proceedings.[76]

In determining whether to grant leave to appeal, there must be serious and arguable grounds that are of real and significant interest to the parties. In making this determination, the appellate court will consider the following four factors: (1) whether the point on appeal is of signifi-

---

74 *Ibid.*

75 *Ibid* at para 21.

76 *Re Doman Industries Ltd* (2004), 2 CBR (5th) 141 (BCCA).

cance to the practice; (2) whether the point raised is of significance to the action itself; (3) whether the appeal is *prima facie* meritorious or frivolous; and (4) whether the appeal will unduly hinder the progress of the action.[77]

Appellate courts are generally unwilling to intervene where the controversy concerns the weight or degree of importance to be given to particular factors. They have taken the view that the supervising judge makes discretionary decisions in a constantly changing environment and therefore these decisions should be afforded a high degree of deference.[78] However, they are prepared to intervene if the supervising court has failed to apply correct principles.[79]

An appellate court may also refuse to allow an appeal to be heard on the ground that the matter is moot because no merit, substance, or prospective benefit will accrue to the appellant.[80] This may be invoked where it is impossible to "unscramble the egg" because DIP financing has already been extended and used to pay suppliers and employees[81] or if essential elements of the plan have been implemented and are now irreversible.[82]

D. THE ROLE OF THE CREDITORS

1) Creditor Bargaining, Litigation, and Approval

The creditors play a less direct role in the governance of business during the restructuring proceedings. Their proceedings and remedies are stayed until such time as they vote on the plan. Yet, despite an absence of a direct governance role, the creditors can strongly influence the direction of the restructuring through bargaining, through the use of actual or threatened litigation, and through voting on the plan. In extreme cases, creditors may bring application to terminate the restructuring proceedings or to lift the stay of proceedings. They may also attempt to block some action proposed by the debtor company, such as a disclaimer of a contract or a sale of assets outside the ordinary course of business. Finally, the creditors may threaten to vote against the plan if their concerns are not met.

---

77 *Re Canadian Airlines Corp* (2000), 20 CBR (4th) 46 (Alta CA).

78 *Canada v Temple City Housing Inc*, 2008 ABCA 1.

79 *Re New Skeena Forest Products Inc* (2005), 9 CBR (5th) 278 (BCCA).

80 *Re Canadian Airlines Corp*, above note 77.

81 *Canada v Temple City Housing Inc*, above note 78.

82 *Re Canadian Airlines Corp*, above note 77.

The role of creditors has been diminished to a significant extent by the use of *CCAA* and *BIA* restructuring proceedings to achieve a going-concern sale of the assets of the business.[83] Unlike a bankruptcy in which creditors have a major role in the governance of the liquidation proceedings through the appointment of inspectors, creditors have little influence in the sale process. The deference given by the court to the monitor's opinion as to the preferred course of action means that it is often difficult for the creditors to convince a court to take a contrary view of matters, and approval of the plan by the creditors becomes largely irrelevant or is dispensed with altogether.

2) Appointment of a Creditors' Committee

In the United States, the appointment of creditors' committees to represent the interests of creditors in the restructuring is common. The practice is less common in Canada.[84] There is considerable controversy over whether the appointment of a monitor is an adequate substitute for direct creditor representation in the process. Proponents of creditors' committees argue that monitors are unable to fulfil their role as watchdog and instead become proponents of the plan that they have helped the debtor to develop.[85] They also point to the fact that it is far less likely that improper transactions concluded before the commencement of restructuring proceedings will be reviewed and challenged in Canada because of the lack of a creditors' committee that would safeguard the interests of creditors. Others commentators take a more sceptical view of the benefits of creditors' committees. They point out that the appointment of such committees adds an additional layer of cost and may produce unwarranted delays, and that creditors' committees are themselves beset with governance problems because of the inevitable divergence of interests among the various groups of creditors.[86]

---

83 See Chapter 13, Section G.

84 See *Re 4519922 Canada Inc*, 2015 ONSC 124. And see R Chadwick & D Bulas, "Ad Hoc Creditors' Committees in *CCAA* Proceedings: The Result of a Changing and Expanding Restructuring World" in Janis P Sarra, ed, *Annual Review of Insolvency Law, 2011* (Toronto: Thomson Carswell, 2012) 119.

85 See Cassels Brock, *Business Reorganization Group e-COMMUNIQUÉ*, Vol 9, No 5 (June 2005).

86 See K McElcheran, *Commercial Insolvency in Canada*, 2d ed (Markham, ON: LexisNexis Canada, 2011) at 246–50.

3) Appointment of Representative Counsel

The court has the authority to appoint representative counsel in relation to employees, retirees, or other stakeholders. Courts have considered the following factors when granting these orders: (1) the vulnerability and resources of the group sought to be represented; (2) the benefit to the companies under *CCAA* protection; (3) any social benefit to be derived from representation of the group; (4) the facilitation of the administration of the proceedings and efficiency; (5) the avoidance of a multiplicity of legal retainers; (6) the balance of convenience and whether it is fair and just including to the creditors; (7) whether representative counsel has already been appointed for those who have similar interests; (8) the position of other stakeholders and the monitor.[87]

4) Creditor Control through DIP Financing

Another method through which a creditor may attempt to influence the decision making in a restructuring is by providing DIP financing to the debtor. Often an existing lender will provide this financing. Sometimes a new lender that specializes in loans to financially distressed businesses enters the picture. In most cases, the terms of the DIP financing will have been negotiated with the DIP lender before the commencement of the restructuring, and the debtor will make an application for its approval by the court at the earliest opportunity.

These financing arrangements can contain terms that give the DIP lender considerable control over the direction of the restructuring. This can occur in a number of ways. A prospective DIP lender may be in a position to insist upon a number of changes, such as the appointment of a chief restructuring officer, before entering into any loan agreements with the debtor. The terms of the DIP loan may limit the available options that are open to the debtor in connection with the restructuring. For example, they may impose time limits on the debtor in developing a plan. In doing so, they may make it more likely that the restructuring will involve a going-concern sale or liquidation plan rather than a plan in which the debtor will continue to operate the business.[88] The negative covenants in the loan agreement may restrict a variety of operating expenses and operating activities. This has the effect of steering the restructuring in a direction favoured by the lender.

---

87 *Canwest Publishing Inc*, 2010 ONSC 1328; *US Steel Canada Inc (Re)*, 2014 ONSC 6145.

88 See D Skeel, "The Past, Present and Future of Debtor-in-Possession Financing" (2004) 25 *Cardozo Law Review* 1905. See also Chapter 13, Section A(2).

E. THE ROLE OF THE OFFICE OF THE SUPERINTENDENT OF BANKRUPTCY

The *CCAA* was originally outside the purview of the Office of the Superintendent of Bankruptcy. The superintendent had no role in establishing licensing requirements in respect of monitors, in investigating complaints, or in maintaining statistical records of *CCAA* proceedings. This is no longer the case. The 2009 amendments have given the Superintendent of Bankruptcy administrative oversight in the conduct of insolvency professionals in respect of *CCAA* proceedings. The superintendent now has the same broad powers in respect of the licensing and investigation of monitors as exercised by trustees under the *BIA*.[89] In addition, the superintendent is under an obligation to maintain a public record of *CCAA* proceedings.[90]

FURTHER READINGS

KENT, A, & W ROSTOM. "The Auditor as Monitor in *CCAA* Proceedings: What Is the Debate?" in Janis P Sarra, ed, *Annual Review of Insolvency Law, 2003* (Toronto: Carswell, 2004) 197

KENT A, W ROSTOM, A MAEROV, & T WEERASORRIYA. "Canadian Business Restructuring Law: When Should a Court Say 'No'?" (2008) 24 *Banking and Finance Law Review* 1

LOPUCKI, L, & W WHITFORD. "Corporate Governance in the Bankruptcy Reorganization of Large, Publicly Held Companies" (1993) 141 *University of Pennsylvania Law Review* 669

MORAWETZ, G. "Under Pressure: Governance of the Financially Distressed Corporation" in J Sarra, ed, *Corporate Governance in Global Capital Markets* (Vancouver: University of British Columbia Press, 2003) 275

MYERS, F. "Justice Farley in Real Time" in Janis P Sarra, ed, *Annual Review of Insolvency Law, 2006* (Toronto: Carswell, 2007) 197

SANDRELLI, J. "The Role of Court-Appointed Officers in the Governance of Financially Distressed Corporations" in J Sarra, ed, *Corporate*

89 *CCAA*, ss 27–31.
90 *Ibid*, s 26.

Governance in Global Capital Markets (Vancouver: University of British Columbia Press, 2003) 345

SARRA, J. "Ethics and Conflicts: The Role of Insolvency Professionals in the Integrity of the Canadian Bankruptcy and Insolvency System" (2004) 13 *International Insolvency Review* 167

———. "Governance and Control: The Role of Debtor-in-Possession Financing under the *CCAA*" in Janis P Sarra, ed, *Annual Review of Insolvency Law, 2004* (Toronto: Carswell, 2005) 119

SKEEL, D. "The Past, Present and Future of Debtor-in-Possession Financing" (2004) 25 *Cardozo Law Review* 1905

CHAPTER 15

CLAIMS AND PRIORITIES

A creditor who wishes to participate in the restructuring proceedings must establish its claim through a proof of claim process. The claims process ensures that the claims asserted by creditors are valid and that the amounts are not inflated. If a creditor holds a claim that is compromised or otherwise affected by the plan, the creditor is given the right to vote for or against it. If the plan is approved by the creditors and sanctioned by the court, the creditors are bound by its terms whether or not they proved their claims or voted on the plan.

Unlike bankruptcy proceedings, the distribution of assets to creditors is not governed by a statutory scheme of distribution. The distribution to creditors in a restructuring is determined by the terms of the plan, and these terms are negotiated between the debtor and the creditors. Despite this difference, priorities play an important role in restructurings. The negotiations occur in the shadow of the law. The legal entitlements of the parties and their expected recoveries in the event of a bankruptcy affect their relative bargaining power in the negotiations concerning the terms of the plan.

When restructuring proceedings are used to liquidate the business, the claims procedure is truncated since it is often the case that no plan is developed and the creditors do not vote. The courts are then required to determine the process and the priorities associated with the distribution of the proceeds of sale. In many instances, the court will authorize the initiation of bankruptcy proceedings following the sales process so that the proceeds will be distributed in accordance with the bankruptcy scheme of distribution.[1]

A. PROVABLE CLAIMS

1) The Claims Process

There are significant differences between the claims process under the *BIA* and the claims process under the *CCAA*. The *BIA* adopts the claims process applicable to bankruptcy proceedings.[2] The trustee will contact the creditors, provide them with a proof of claim form, and take delivery of the forms once they are completed. The trustee then examines the proof of claims and may accept them or disallow them in whole or in part. If the claim is a contingent claim or an unliquidated claim, the trustee must value it.[3]

The *CCAA* provides very little guidance about the claims process. The rules that govern the claims process are established by the court and set out in a claims procedure order. These orders specify the manner in which creditors are to be given notice. They typically provide for notice to creditors by regular mail and through publication of an advertisement in newspapers. Sometimes the monitor is designated as the person responsible for supervising the claims process, including the determination of the validity and amounts of the claims. It is also common for the claims procedure order to appoint a claims officer who is responsible for determining the validity of the claims and quantifying them if they are unliquidated or contingent claims. In some cases, a reverse claims procedure is employed in which the creditors are notified as to the amounts of their claims based on the debtor's records.[4] This eliminates the need for creditors to file a proof of claim unless they disagree with the amount proposed by the debtor.

Class proceedings can be settled in *CCAA* proceedings, but a court order is necessary.[5] In assessing a proposed settlement, the court should consider (a) whether the settlement is fair and reasonable; (b) whether

---

1 *Ivaco Inc (Re)* (2006), 25 CBR (5th) 176 (Ont CA).

2 *BIA*, s 66(1).

3 See Chapter 9, Section A(1).

4 See, for example, *Re Quality Dino Entertainment Ltd* (1998), 3 CBR (4th) 314 (Ont Ct Gen Div).

5 *Labourers' Pension Fund of Central and Eastern Canada v Sino-Forest Corporation*, 2013 ONSC 1078; *Robertson v ProQuest Information and Learning Co*, 2011 ONSC 1647.

it provides substantial benefits to other stakeholders; and (c) whether it is consistent with the purpose and spirit of the *CCAA*.[6]

2) The Definition of a Provable Claim

The *BIA* and the *CCAA* adopt a similar approach to defining provable claims in restructuring proceedings. The same provision of the *BIA* that is used to define a provable claim in bankruptcy proceedings is employed to define a provable claim in *BIA* restructuring proceedings.[7] This means that unliquidated and contingent claims are provable claims. In bankruptcy proceedings, the existence of the claim is determined at the date of the bankruptcy. In *BIA* restructuring proceedings, the relevant date for determining the existence of the claim is the date of the initiation of the restructuring proceedings — i.e., the filing of the notice of intention or the filing of the proposal with the trustee.[8]

The *CCAA* adopts a similar approach. The *CCAA* defines a claim as any indebtedness, liability, or obligation that would be debt provable in a bankruptcy under the *BIA*.[9] This incorporates the same definition of provable claim that is used in the *BIA*. At one time it was thought that the incorporation of the bankruptcy definition of a claim was only for the purpose of determining the amount of the claim.[10] Contingent claims were not provable since the claimant did not fall within the ordinary meaning of the term "creditor." As a result, a claimant was not affected by the plan. Later cases departed from this view on the basis of a slight legislative rewording of the provision, and held that contingent claims were provable under the *CCAA*.[11] This view has now been codified in the current version of the *CCAA*, which makes it clear that contingent liabilities are provable claims under the statute.[12]

The relevant date for determining the existence of the claim is the date that the initial application was made.[13] However, the date of the initial application under the *CCAA* is not used if insolvency proceedings had been initiated under the *BIA* but later switched to *CCAA* proceedings.

---

6 *Ibid.*

7 *BIA*, s 121(1). And see Chapter 9, Section A(2).

8 *BIA*, s 62(1.1).

9 *CCAA*, s 2(1) "claim."

10 *Quebec Steel Products (Industries) Ltd v James United Steel Ltd*, [1969] 2 OR 349 (HCJ).

11 *Re Quintette Coal Ltd* (1991), 7 CBR (3d) 165 (BCSC). And see A Kulidjian, "Potential Creditors under the *Companies' Creditors Arrangement Act*" (1996) 13 *National Insolvency Review* 51.

12 *CCAA*, s 19(1).

13 *Ibid*, s 19(1)(a).

This can occur if the debtor files a notice of intention to make a proposal. It can also occur if the debtor is bankrupt and the company, with the consent of the inspectors, makes the *CCAA* application. In these situations, the date of the initial bankruptcy event is used. The relevant date will therefore be the date that the notice of intention is filed, the date that an application for a bankruptcy order is made, or the date of an assignment in bankruptcy.

Both the *BIA* and the *CCAA* make an exception for claims for environmental clean-up costs. The claim is provable in the restructuring even though the environmental condition or damage occurs after the commencement of restructuring proceedings.[14]

3) The Timing of the Claim

Although contingent claims are provable in restructuring proceedings, there is uncertainty concerning the status of tort claims where the debtor had breached a duty before the initiation of restructuring proceedings but the plaintiff has not yet suffered damage.[15] Under the *BIA*, a claim is provable if it arises by reason of any obligation incurred before the bankruptcy and if the bankrupt becomes subject to that liability before the bankrupt's discharge. If this formulation were strictly applied to *BIA* restructuring proceedings, all claims associated with a pre-filing breach of duty would be provable regardless of when the damage actually occurs, since the debtor will not ordinarily obtain a bankruptcy discharge. The *CCAA* adopts a slightly different formulation. The claim is provable if it results from a pre-filing obligation and the debtor becomes subject to the liability before the court sanctions the plan.[16] If the plaintiff suffers the damage after the court sanctions the plan, the claim is not considered to be provable and the claimant will not be affected by the plan.

Despite the difference in language, a court may decide that it is more appropriate to adopt the *CCAA* approach to unmanifested tort claims in *BIA* restructuring proceedings. In other words, a court might take the view that, in order for the claim to be provable, the liability must arise before the court approves the *BIA* proposal. The *BIA* provides that the bankruptcy provisions are to apply "with such modifications as the circumstances require."[17] It might credibly be argued that

---

14 *BIA*, s 14.06(8); *CCAA*, s 11.8(9). And see *Newfoundland and Labrador v Abitibi-Bowater Inc*, 2012 SCC 67.

15 See Chapter 9, Section A(3).

16 *CCAA*, s 19(1)(b).

17 *BIA*, s 66(1).

the substitution of the date of court approval for the date of the bankruptcy discharge is an appropriate modification. This would have the benefit of bringing into alignment the rules under both restructuring regimes.

Although tort claims that manifest themselves after court sanction of the plan are not provable and are not affected by the plan, the position of the plaintiff will depend upon the nature of the restructuring. If the debtor continues to operate the business following the plan, the plaintiff will have full recourse against the assets of the restructured business to satisfy the claim. If the business assets have been sold to another entity, the claim will be valueless since the proceeds will have been distributed to the other claimants and the debtor will no longer have any assets available to satisfy the claim.

One solution to this conundrum would be to authorize the sale of the business as a going concern but require that a portion of the proceeds be used to create a trust in favour of future tort claimants. A court could refuse to sanction a plan that did not provide such a feature on the basis that the plan is unfair to future claimants. This would be similar in the result to the approach used in the United States under Chapter 11 in respect of mass torts that cause the insolvency of the defendant.[18]

4) Time Limitations on Making a Claim

a) Claims Bar Orders under the *CCAA*

The court order that establishes the claims process in *CCAA* restructurings will typically provide a claims bar date. This sets a date by which proof of claims must be made, and its purpose is to ensure that all legitimate creditors come forward on a timely basis.[19] The claims bar date prevents claimants from asserting a claim against a debtor or amending a claim that has been made after that date. It thereby provides an assurance to creditors who participate in the plan that there are no other creditors waiting outside the process who are able to assert their claims in full against the debtor.[20] This procedure was an invention of the courts, since earlier versions of the *CCAA* were silent as to the claims process. The 2009 amendments to the *CCAA* codify the judicial practice. The *CCAA* now gives a court the power to make an order fixing deadlines for the purpose of voting on the plan and for the purposes of distributions under the plan.[21]

---

18 See *Kane v Johns-Manville Corp*, 843 F2d 636 (2d Cir 1998).

19 *Re Blue Range Resource Corp* (2000), 193 DLR (4th) 314 (Alta CA) [*Blue Range*].

20 *Re Noma*, 2004 CarswellOnt 5033 (SCJ).

21 *CCAA*, s 12.

The claims bar date does not operate as a rigid limitation period. Courts have retained the discretion to permit late claimants to file claims after the claims bar date. The Alberta Court of Appeal has identified the following factors that should be considered by a court in deciding whether it should exercise its discretion to permit the late filing of a claim:[22]

1) Was the delay caused by inadvertence and if so, did the claimant act in good faith?
2) What is the effect of permitting the claim in terms of the existence and impact of any relevant prejudice caused by the delay?
3) If relevant prejudice is found can it be alleviated by attaching appropriate conditions to an order permitting late filing?
4) If relevant prejudice is found which cannot be alleviated, are there any other considerations which may nonetheless warrant an order permitting late filing?

If the restructuring involves a going-concern sale or other liquidation, it will generally be easier to satisfy a court of a lack of prejudice.[23] In these types of cases, it is appropriate to apply a similar approach to that used in bankruptcy. A creditor will be permitted to file a late claim. By doing so, the creditor is not permitted to upset any distribution that has already been made, but the creditor can call for the missed payment out of funds that have not yet been distributed.[24]

This discretion to permit late filing of claims may be exercised even if the wording of the claims bar order provides that a failure to comply with the claims procedure results in the claim being deemed to be "forever barred." In order to inform claimants of their rights, the wording of the claims bar order should make it clear that their claims will be barred unless they are granted leave by a court.[25] A failure by a claimant to file a proof of claim before the expiration of the claims bar date will not prevent the assertion of the claim if the debtor has failed to comply with the claims procedure order in notifying a known existing creditor.[26]

---

22 *Blue Range*, above note 19 at para 26; *Re Canadian Red Cross Society/Société Canadienne de la Croix-Rouge*, 2008 CarswellOnt 6105 (SCJ).

23 *Timminco Limited (Re)*, 2014 ONSC 3393.

24 *BIA*, s 150.

25 *Blue Range*, above note 19 at para 10.

26 *Ivorylane Corp v Country Style Realty Ltd*, 2004 CarswellOnt 2567 (SCJ). The result may be otherwise if the creditor knows of the insolvency proceedings but files to assert a claim in order to gain an advantage over the other creditors. See *Lindsay v Transtec Canada Ltd* (1994), 28 CBR (3d) 110 (BCSC).

A claimant does not need to file a proof of claim if the claimant is not affected by the plan.[27]

b) The Approach under the *BIA*

The *BIA* does not create a separate claims procedure for *BIA* restructurings. Instead, the bankruptcy claims procedure is used. If the trustee knows of a creditor who has not proved a claim, the trustee may notify that person that a final dividend will be made without regard to their claim unless they prove it within thirty days of the sending of the notice.[28] If they do not do so within the thirty-day period or such other period ordered by a court, they are excluded from sharing in the final dividend.[29] If the creditor is not notified, the creditor is entitled to file a proof of claim at any time prior to the distribution of the funds by way of dividend to the creditors. The late-filing creditor is not permitted to disturb dividends that have been paid. If not all funds have been distributed, the late-claiming creditor may call for payment out of the undistributed funds.[30]

The *BIA* claims procedure may be appropriate for a liquidation-style restructuring, but it may be unsuitable where the debtor continues to carry on business after approval of the proposal. There is a greater risk that the future prospects of the business may be threatened by unexpected liabilities resulting from late claims. One method of dealing with this risk is to include a claims bar date in the proposal itself.[31] It is uncertain, however, if the courts will treat a claims bar date in a proposal in the same manner as a claims bar date in a *CCAA* claims procedure order.[32]

The *BIA* restructuring provisions create a special procedure for proving secured claims.[33] If the proposal made to a secured creditor includes a proposed assessed value of the security, the secured creditor must claim the lesser of the amount of the claim and the assessed value of the security.[34] However, if the secured creditor is dissatisfied with

---

27 *Ibid*. And see Chapter 16, Section C(3).

28 *BIA*, s 149(1).

29 *Ibid*, s 149(2).

30 *Ibid*, s 150.

31 See *Re Roman Catholic Episcopal Corp of St George's* (2007), 31 CBR (5th) 61 (NLCA).

32 *Ibid*.

33 See *BIA*, s 50.1. This section sets out the entire regime governing the proof of secured claims and therefore displaces the more general procedure set out in *BIA*, s 135. See *Re WorkGroup Designs Inc*, 2008 CarswellOnt 1656 (CA).

34 *BIA*, s 50.1(2). The secured creditor may prove for any deficiency as an unsecured creditor. See *BIA*, s 50.1(3).

the proposed assessed value of the security, the secured creditor must apply to court within fifteen days from the date that the proposal is sent to have the value revised.[35] If the proposal does not include a proposed assessed value, the secured creditor may prove for the full value of its claim.[36]

c) Disputed Claims

The same dispute mechanism that operates in bankruptcy proceedings is used to resolve disputed claims in a *BIA* restructuring.[37] A trustee may decide to disallow a claim in whole or in part.[38] If the claim is a contingent claim or an unliquidated claim, the trustee must determine if it is a provable claim, and, if it is, the trustee is required to value it.[39] If the trustee disallows a claim in whole or part or makes a determination in respect of a contingent or liquidated claim, the trustee must notify the creditor of the reasons. The disallowance or valuation of the trustee is final unless the creditor appeals the trustee's decision to the court within a thirty-day period after service of the notice.[40]

Under the *CCAA*, the claims procedure order establishes the procedure that will be used for the adjudication of disputed claims. Some claim procedure orders provide that the decision to allow or disallow a claim is made by the monitor, and, if this decision is disputed, it is to be determined by a claims officer or by a court. Where a court hears the matter, it will be determined by a trial *de novo* in the same manner as an appeal from the decision of a trustee to disallow or value a claim under the *BIA*.[41] Where a claims officer hears the dispute, the court will apply the usual standard of review in appellate proceedings and accord substantial deference to the findings of the claims officer.[42] Other orders set up an alternative dispute resolution mechanism to resolve disputes within *CCAA* proceedings. This may involve the appointment of a mediator. The court in appropriate circumstances may

---

35 *Ibid*, s 50.1(4).

36 *Ibid*, s 50.1(1).

37 See Chapter 9, Section A(1).

38 *BIA*, s 135(2).

39 *Ibid*, s 135(1.1).

40 *Ibid*, ss 135(3) & (4). Although a court may extend this period, the application for an extension must be brought within the thirty-day period.

41 *Re Pine Valley Mining Corp*, 2008 CarswellBC 579 (SC).

42 *Re Triton Tubular Components Corp* (2005), 14 CBR (5th) 264 (Ont SCJ); *Re 1587930 Ontario Inc* (2006), 25 CBR (5th) 264 (Ont SCJ). The law in Alberta differs from that in Ontario. In Alberta, the courts will not defer decisions of court-appointed claims officers but will determine the matter in an appeal *de novo*. See *Re Canadian Airlines Corp*, [2001] 7 WWR 383 (Alta QB).

make an order requiring a stakeholder to participate in the mediation if the stakeholder refuses voluntarily to do so.[43]

5) Post-filing Interest and Expenses

The stop-interest rule that was first formulated by the courts in bankruptcy proceedings[44] is applicable in *CCAA* proceedings whether or not the proceedings are being used to liquidate the company.[45] This prevents a creditor from proving a claim in respect of post-filing interest. The rationale is that the policy of maintaining the status quo is violated if some creditors' claims are permitted to grow disproportionately to others during the stay period, and that this would encourage creditors whose interests are being disadvantaged to immediately initiate bankruptcy proceedings.[46] The parties are, however, free to include post-filing interest payments in a plan. Contractual provisions that permit a creditor to recover post-filing fees and expenses are similarly ineffective in *CCAA* proceedings.[47] It is likely that courts will require notification of affected secured creditors in the same manner as the court ordered charges expressly provided for in the *CCAA*.

B. PRIORITIES

Although priority rules are important in true restructurings, they do not operate in precisely the same manner as they do under liquidation regimes such as bankruptcy and receivership. In a liquidation, the assets are sold and the proceeds are distributed according to the priority ranking of the various claimants. Matters are less clear-cut in a restructuring. A creditor's recovery is not determined by the application of a statutory scheme of distribution or a set of priority rules. Instead, the recovery is determined by the terms of the plan.

Priority rules nevertheless play a crucial role in the restructuring process. Creditors are usually divided into different classes. Each class is afforded different treatment under the plan, and each class votes on whether to approve it. The appropriateness of the classification scheme

---

43 *Re Stelco Inc* (2005), 11 CBR (5th) 164 (Ont SCJ).

44 See Chapter 9, Section A(4). And see J Carfagnini & C Costa, "Claims for Post-Filing Interest and Prepayment Premiums in a *CCAA* Proceeding" in J Sarra, ed, *Annual Review of Insolvency Law, 2011* (Toronto: Thomson Carswell, 2012) 165.

45 *Re Nortel Networks Corporation*, 2014 ONSC 5274.

46 *Ibid* at para 34.

47 *Homberg Invest Inc (Arrangement relatif à)*, 2014 QCCS 980.

depends upon a comparison of the legal rights held by the claimants within a class.[48] The classification scheme that is employed in a plan is therefore directly influenced by the background priority rules. In deciding whether to accept the plan, each class of creditors will compare what they are offered under the terms of the plan against what they would obtain in the event of a liquidation.[49] Creditors will not vote for the plan and courts will not approve it unless the plan gives the creditors at least as much as they would in a bankruptcy. Priority rules also provide each class of creditors with a basis for comparing the deal they are offered with the deal that is offered to each of the other classes of creditors.

1) Secured Claims

The priority status of secured claims is governed by the ordinary rules and principles that establish the validity and priority of security interests in real and personal property. A failure to perfect a security interest in personal property does not result in a loss of priority in restructuring proceedings. Although personal property security legislation subordinates an unperfected security interest against a trustee in bankruptcy, this provision does not apply in respect of a restructuring.[50]

Although a failure to perfect a security will not result in its subordination to a monitor or trustee in restructuring proceedings, it may cause a loss of priority in respect of a claimant who asserts a competing interest in the collateral. This may reduce or obliterate the value of the secured creditor's security interest. For example, suppose that both SP1 and SP2 take a security interest in a piece of equipment. The value of the equipment is $100,000. SP1's security interest secures an obligation in the amount of $50,000, and SP2's security interest secures an obligation in the amount of $150,000. Although SP1 was the first to enter into a security agreement with the debtor, SP1 failed to perfect its security interest. As a result, SP1 is subordinate to SP2. Although SP1 has an enforceable security interest, it is rendered valueless because of SP2's prior ranking security interest. SP1 should therefore be afforded the status of an unsecured creditor in any restructuring proceedings.

---

48 See *Re Woodward's* (1993), 20 CBR (3d) 74 (BCSC); *Re San Francisco Gifts Ltd* (2004), 5 CBR (5th) 92 (Alta QB). And see Chapter 16, Section D.

49 *Century Services Inc v Canada (AG)*, 2010 SCC 60 at para 77.

50 *Re TRG Services Inc* (2006), 26 CBR (5th) 203 (Ont SCJ); *Re PSINet* (2002), 30 CBR (4th) 226 (Ont SCJ).

2) Unsecured Claims

Unlike secured creditors, unsecured creditors have no proprietary right in the assets of the debtor, and therefore they have no right to claim priority over other claimants who are able to assert proprietary rights in the debtor's assets. The situation can change once the unsecured creditor obtains a judgment and pursues judgment enforcement measures. A writ or judgment that is registered in a provincial land registry system will typically have priority over a subsequently created interest in the land. Personal property security legislation in some of the provinces provides for registration of a writ in the personal property security registry.[51] The judgment enforcement creditor obtains a priority status that is similar to that of a secured creditor. The judgment enforcement creditor will thereby obtain priority over a prior unperfected security interest and subsequent security interests. There is nothing in either the *BIA* or the *CCAA* that alters the priority status of judgment enforcement creditors in restructuring proceedings. If the application of these provincial priority rules results in the subordination of a secured creditor to a judgment enforcement creditor, this subordination should continue in the restructuring proceedings.[52]

3) Subordinated Claims

It is not uncommon for creditors to enter into subordination agreements under which they agree to postpone their claims until the claim of some other creditor or class of creditors is paid.[53] It is also possible for a creditor to postpone its claim until all other creditors are paid. The fact that a creditor subordinates its interest to only some of the other creditors does not give the creditors who did not receive the benefit of the subordination any right to demand that their claims should also obtain the benefit of the subordination.[54] It is not necessary to place the subordinated claims in a separate class or exclude them from voting.[55] The contractual subordination that they agreed to is simply given effect, and the amount that they would have received in the absence of

51 R Cuming, C Walsh, & R Wood, *Personal Property Security Law*, 2d ed (Toronto: Irwin Law, 2012) 494–504.

52 See R Cuming, "When an Unsecured Creditor Is a Secured Creditor" (2003) 66 *Saskatchewan Law Review* 255 at 271–73.

53 See P Wood, *The Law of Subordinated Debt* (London: Sweet & Maxwell, 1990); R Wood, "Subordination Agreements, Bankruptcy and the *PPSA*" (2010) 49 *Canadian Business Law Journal* 66.

54 *Re Air Canada* (2004), 2 CBR (5th) 4 (Ont SCJ).

55 See Chapter 16, Section C(8).

the subordination is turned over to the parties who were entitled to the benefit of the subordination.

4) Crown Claims

The same approach to the priority of Crown claims[56] in bankruptcy is applied in respect of restructurings under both the *CCAA* and the *BIA*.[57] The Crown is able to assert a security interest if it is of a kind that is ordinarily available to other creditors. This condition is satisfied if the Crown enters into a security agreement with the debtor. If the Crown relies upon a non-consensual interest created by statute that confers an interest in the debtor's assets to secure the liability owing to the Crown, the Crown claim will be afforded only the status of an unsecured claim unless it is registered under the appropriate provincial real or personal property registry system. An exception is made in respect of the federal statutory garnishment device that is used to recover source deductions of income tax, CPP, and EI. These enjoy a secured creditor status without the need for registration. The statutes governing these devices give them priority over most competing security interests.

In the case of a *BIA* restructuring, the operative date for testing the validity of the registration of a Crown claim is the date of filing of a proposal or a notice of intention to make a proposal.[58] In the case of a *CCAA* restructuring, the operative date for testing the validity of the registration of the Crown claim is the date of the initial application for an order.[59] A Crown claim that is properly registered so as to give it the status of a secured claim may come into competition with a consensual security interest. The Crown's claim is subordinate to competing security interests in the same property if the secured creditor completed all steps necessary to make them effective against other creditors before registration of the Crown claim.[60] The secured status of the Crown claim is limited to amounts that are owed at the time of registration of the Crown claim.[61] This prevents the Crown from pre-registering its

---

56 See Chapter 5, Section E.

57 *CCAA*, ss 38–39; *BIA*, ss 86–87.

58 *BIA*, s 87(1).

59 *CCAA*, s 39(1).

60 See Chapter 5, Section E for a discussion of this requirement in respect of property that is acquired by the debtor after the Crown claim is registered.

61 The Crown can claim as a secured creditor only for the amount of the obligation owing and does not rank as a secured creditor in respect of costs associated with seizure or enforcement of the security. See *Re Gillford Furniture Mart Ltd* (1995), 36 CBR (3d) 157 (BCCA).

claim before the creation of its interest, and usually results in the subordination of the Crown claim to competing secured creditors.[62] It also means that the Crown must make multiple filings to secure any new obligations that arise after the registration of its initial claim.

5) Deemed Trusts

The *BIA* contains special rules that govern deemed trusts in favour of the Crown.[63] These rules apply to both bankruptcy proceedings and restructurings under the *BIA*. A similar set of provisions is found in the *CCAA*.[64] These rules provide that property deemed to be held in trust for the Crown pursuant to federal or provincial legislation shall not be regarded as held in trust unless it would be so regarded in the absence of that statutory provision. An exception to this rule is made for statutory deemed trusts in respect of source deductions (i.e., unremitted income tax and CPP and EI premiums deducted from the pay of employees).

At one time it was thought that the statutory deemed trust in respect of unremitted GST was effective in *CCAA* proceedings. There appeared to be a conflict in the federal legislative provisions. The *CCAA* provided that deemed trusts in favour of the Crown (other than in respect of source deductions) were ineffective despite any federal law to the contrary. However, the *Excise Tax Act*[65] provided that the statutory trust for unremitted GST ranked ahead of any other interest notwithstanding any federal provision except the *BIA*. Some courts applied the interpretive principle of implied repeal to conclude that the later enactment (the *Excise Tax Act*) should prevail over the earlier enactment (the *CCAA*).[66] This view was rejected by the Supreme Court of Canada in *Century Services Inc v Canada (AG)*.[67] The priority provision in the *Excise Tax Act* was interpreted to be a more general provision that yielded to the special rule in the *CCAA* that governed the priority of the deemed trust

---

62 Most security interests are created and perfected when the debtor is in good financial health, while the non-consensual security interests securing Crown claims generally arise when the debtor is in financial distress and failing to meet the obligations due to its creditors. Because pre-registration of Crown claims is ineffective, the registration of the Crown claim will most often occur after secured creditors have created and perfected their security interests.

63 *BIA*, ss 67(2)–(3). See Chapter 4, Section C(1)(d).

64 *CCAA*, s 37.

65 RSC 1985, c E-15, s 222(3).

66 *Re Ottawa Senators Hockey Club Corp* (2005), 6 CBR (5th) 293 (Ont CA); *Re Gauntlet Energy Corp* (2003), 49 CBR (4th) 213 (Alta QB).

67 Above note 49.

in *CCAA* proceedings.[68] The deemed trust in respect of GST is therefore ineffective under both the *CCAA* and *BIA* restructuring proceedings.

These statutory provisions apply only in respect of deemed trusts in favour of the Crown. The deemed trust device is sometimes used to secure payment of other non-Crown claims. For example, pension benefits statutes often create deemed trusts in respect of unpaid pension contributions.[69] The *BIA* provides that property that is held by the bankrupt in trust for another person is not divisible among the creditors. The Supreme Court of Canada in *British Columbia v Henfrey Samson Belair Ltd*[70] held that statutory deemed trusts lacking the common law attributes of a trust are not to be regarded as trusts for the purposes of this provision. The decision was concerned with the interplay between bankruptcy law and provincial devices that create deemed statutory trusts and has no application in *CCAA* reorganization proceedings.[71] The position is less certain in respect of *BIA* restructuring proceedings. The bankruptcy rules are made applicable to *BIA* restructurings proceedings, and therefore it might be argued that the *Henfrey* decision should govern. On the other hand, it might be argued that the decision is inapplicable because it dealt with the divisibility of property amongst the creditors and as such is inapplicable to a restructuring where there is no statutory scheme of distribution. The significance of this issue is diminished to a degree by the fact that courts have permitted claimants to seek a bankruptcy order following restructuring proceedings.[72] This has the effect of activating the bankruptcy rule and invalidating the deemed trust.

6) Environmental Claims

The *CCAA* and *BIA* restructuring regimes incorporate rules governing environmental claims that are substantively the same as those applicable in bankruptcy.[73] The usual liability rules in federal and provincial environmental legislation that make those in control of the premises

68 The reason that the *Excise Tax Act* specifically mentioned the *BIA* and not the *CCAA* in establishing the pre-eminence of the federal provisions was likely to ensure that the statutory charges in ss 81.1, 81.2, 81.4, and 81.6 of the *BIA* are afforded priority over the deemed trust for GST in receivership proceedings. See R Wood, "Priorities and Judicial Authority under the *CCAA*: *Century Services Inc v Canada (Attorney General)*" (2011) 51 *Canadian Business Law Journal* 118.

69 See, for example, *Pension Benefits Act*, RSO 1990, c P.8, s 57.

70 [1989] 2 SCR 24.

71 *Re Ivaco Inc*, above note 1.

72 *Ibid*. See also *Grant Forest Products Inc (Re)*, 2013 ONSC 5933.

73 See Chapter 5, Section F.

liable for the costs of clean-up are modified. A trustee or monitor is not liable for environmental damage that occurred prior to the appointment and is not liable for post-appointment damage unless it occurred as a result of gross negligence or wilful misconduct on the part of the trustee or monitor.[74] The remediation costs are secured by a security interest on the real property affected by the environmental condition as well as on any contiguous real property. The security interest is given superpriority status over any other claim, right, charge, or security against the property.[75]

The Supreme Court of Canada in *Newfoundland and Labrador v AbitibiBowater Inc*[76] held that remediation costs are provable claims if it is possible to attach a monetary value to the debt, liability, or obligation. A regulatory body is able to prove a claim if it has already incurred the costs of remediation or has moved to clean up the pollution. It is able to prove a claim even if it has not yet incurred such costs or moved to clean up the pollution if there is sufficient certainty that it will do so or if the event is too remote or speculative. In making this determination the court may consider the following factors: (1) whether the activities are ongoing; (2) whether the debtor is in control of the property; (3) whether the debtor has the means to comply with the order; and the effect that an order to comply with the order would have on the insolvency process.[77] The impact of this approach will depend upon whether the company will emerge from the restructuring or if liquidating proceedings are involved. If the claim is not provable, it will not be compromised in the plan and the regulatory body will be able to assert it against the company once the plan is approved. If there is no plan and the assets of the company are sold, the claim will effectively be lost as the defunct company will not have any assets to proceed against.

7) Thirty-Day Goods and Suppliers of Agricultural Products

The *BIA* gives a supplier a right to repossess goods that were delivered to the debtor within a thirty-day period.[78] It also gives a supplier of agricultural products a security on all inventory held by the purchaser.[79] These provisions apply only in bankruptcy proceedings and

74 *BIA*, s 14.06(2); *CCAA*, s 11.8(3).
75 *BIA*, s 14.06(7); *CCAA*, s 11.8(8).
76 Above note 14.
77 *Ibid* at para 38.
78 *BIA*, s 81.1. And see Chapter 5, Section C(1).
79 *BIA*, s 81.2. And see Chapter 5, Section C(2).

receivership proceedings; they have no operation in restructuring proceedings. If a bankruptcy or receivership occurs following the filing of a notice of intention or a proposal, the period between the initiation of the *BIA* restructuring proceedings and the initiation of bankruptcy or receivership proceedings is not counted for the purposes of calculating the thirty-day period.[80] Although the statutory provisions do not create a similar rule where bankruptcy or receivership proceedings ensue after *CCAA* restructuring proceedings are initiated, courts have achieved this result by making an order preserving the suppliers' rights.[81] This will be of no assistance to the supplier if the goods have been sold or transformed after the commencement of restructuring proceedings, since the supplier will thus lose the right to repossess the goods. Because these rights have no application in restructuring proceedings, the suppliers may claim only the status of an unsecured creditor and have no right to demand that the proceeds of sales of inventory be placed in trust for their benefit.[82] For similar reasons, the suppliers also have no right to demand to be placed in their own separate class for purposes of voting on the plan or proposal.

8) Wage-Earner Claims

The wage-earner charge that operates in bankruptcy and receivership proceedings does not arise in restructuring proceedings. Instead of creating a priority charge in favour of workers, the *BIA* and the *CCAA* provide a limitation on a court's ability to sanction or approve a plan or proposal. A court may do so only if the employees and former employees receive no less than the amount secured by their statutory security for unpaid wages.[83]

Many provincial statutes give employees a non-consensual security interest to secure unpaid wages.[84] There is nothing in the legislation that suggests that these provincial devices are rendered inoperative in restructuring proceedings. The issue may be significant because the

80 *BIA*, s 81.1(4).

81 See *Thomson Consumer Electronics Canada Inc v Consumers Distributing Inc (Receiver-Manager of)* (1996), 43 CBR (3d) 77 (Ont Ct Gen Div), aff'd (1999), 5 CBR (4th) 141 (Ont CA); *Re Woodward's Ltd* (1993), 17 CBR (3d) 253 (BCSC).

82 *Re Woodward's Ltd, ibid*; *Agro Pacific Industries Ltd* (2000), 76 BCLR (3d) 364 (SC); *Re Henry Birks & Sons Ltd* (1993), 22 CBR (3d) 235 (Que Sup Ct).

83 *CCAA*, s 6(5); *BIA*, s 60(1.3).

84 See, for example, *Employment Standards Code*, RSA 2000, c E-9, s 109. And see G England & R Wood, *Employment Law in Canada*, 4th ed (Markham, ON: LexisNexis Canada, 2005) (loose-leaf), vol 2, ch 19.

availability of the provincial device would in some cases permit unpaid employees to recover more than the $2,000 maximum provided for in the federal provisions. The Supreme Court of Canada has held that these devises are rendered inoperative in bankruptcy. The *BIA* creates a scheme of distribution that gives unpaid employees the status of a preferred claim, and it is not possible for the provinces to give them a higher priority. The doctrine of paramountcy resolves an operational conflict between the federal and provincial statutes in favour of the federal provisions.

This reasoning does not extend to restructuring proceedings. The *CCAA* and the *BIA* restructuring provisions do not set out a scheme of distribution. Therefore, there is no operational conflict between the federal and provincial legislation that would render the provincial provisions inoperative. However, the invocation of bankruptcy proceedings following the implementation of a liquidation restructuring plan would have the effect of invalidating the claims of employees to a secured creditor.[85]

9) Pension Contribution Claims

The pension contribution charge that operates in bankruptcy and receivership proceedings does not arise in restructuring proceedings. Instead of a creating a priority charge in respect of unpaid pension contributions, the *BIA* and the *CCAA* provide a limitation on a court's ability to sanction or approve a plan or proposal. A court may do so only if the employee pension contributions have been paid in full.[86] However, a court may approve a proposal or sanction a plan that does not provide for payment in full if the parties have entered into an agreement, approved by the relevant pension regulator, respecting the payment of those amounts.[87] Pension statutes provide additional protection for unpaid pension contributions through the creation of deemed statutory trusts.[88]

10) Priority of Court Ordered Charges

The initial order will typically specify the ranking of court ordered charges. Although this is left to the discretion of the court, the usual ranking is (1) the administrative charge; (2) the interim financing (DIP)

---

85 *Re Ivaco Inc*, above note 1.

86 *CCAA*, s 6(6); *BIA*, s 60(1.5).

87 *CCAA*, s 6(7); *BIA*, s 60(1.6).

88 See Section B(5), above in this chapter.

charge; (3) the director's charge.[89] It is usual for other court ordered charges such as a critical suppliers charge or KERP charge to be ranked below these charges, but this matter is similarly in the discretion of the supervising judge. The court ordered charges are almost invariably subject to a specified maximum amount. A court is not permitted in a subsequent interim financing order to make a new security or charge that ranks in priority over one made in a previous order unless the lender in respect of the earlier order consents to it.[90]

The court ordered charges are typically afforded priority over all other secured creditors, although in some cases an interim financing charge may be ranked behind specified priority interests such as purchase money security interests.[91] As the definition of secured creditor in both the *CCAA* and the *BIA* encompasses non-consensual liens and charges, a court ordered charge that is granted priority over secured creditors will rank ahead of these non-consensual security interests.[92] The court ordered charge will also rank ahead of provincial deemed trusts even though these do not fall within the definition of a secured creditor. The Supreme Court of Canada in *Sun Indalex Finance, LLC v United Steelworkers*[93] held that deemed trusts in favour of persons other than the Crown are effective subject to the principle of federal paramountcy. A court ordered priority made pursuant to the *CCAA* is treated the same as a statutory priority in this regard. The federal and provincial laws are inconsistent, as they give rise to different, and conflicting, orders of priority. As a consequence, the court ordered charge supersedes the deemed trust. There is presently uncertainty whether court ordered charges have priority over holdbacks under builder's liens statutes. The argument is that these amounts are not property of the debtor as they are not yet owing.[94]

There is also uncertainty whether a court ordered charge will rank ahead of a statutory deemed trust that secures source deductions. A

---

89 This is the ranking that is provided in the model or template initial *CCAA* orders.

90 *CCAA*, s 11.2(3); *BIA*, s 50.6(4).

91 *US Steel Canada Inc (Re)*, 2014 ONSC 6145.

92 *CCAA*, s 2(1) "secured creditor"; *BIA*, s 2 "secured creditor." And see Chapter 5, Section B(1).

93 2013 SCC 6.

94 The matter was raised in the Comstock restructuring but was not resolved by the court as the parties ultimately agreed to a lien regularization order that provided a claims process overseen by the monitor that replicated the builder's liens priority structure but which ranked below the court ordered charge. See A MacFarlane, C Stanek, & T Gertner, "Lien on Me: The Comstock Story, Creative Approaches to Restructurings in the Construction Sector" in Janis P Sarra, ed, *Annual Review of Insolvency Law, 2014* (Toronto: Carswell, 2015) 387.

holder of a deemed trust is likely to make two arguments against an extension of the superpriority of the charge. First, a deemed trust does not fall within the definition of a secured creditor and therefore the priority does not extend over the subject matter of the trust. Second, the statute creating the deemed trust in respect of source deductions expressly provides that the deemed trust has priority over all other security interests.[95] Despite this language, some courts have held that a DIP charge has priority over the deemed trust on the theory that the deemed trust creates something akin to a floating charge that allows the creation of the DIP charge.[96]

Finally, there is some uncertainty whether a court ordered charge will rank ahead of lessors under true leases of personal property. Although it is likely that lessors under financing leases that secure payment or performance of an obligation will be treated as secured creditors,[97] a true lessor can argue that it is not affected by the court ordered charge because the charge only affects the property of the debtor, and the leased property is owned by the lessor.[98]

11) Allocation of Restructuring Costs

Different secured creditors may have security interests in different assets of the debtor. As these secured creditors are subordinate to the court ordered charge, it may become necessary for the court to allocate the costs among the secured creditors. The monitor will usually formulate a cost allocation plan, and the supervising court will review it. Courts are reluctant to interfere with the allocation methodology proposed by the court officer unless the opposing creditors can establish that it is unfair or prejudicial.[99] The courts have developed the following principles in relation to the allocation of restructuring costs:[100]

- The allocation of costs ought to be fair and even-handed upon an objective basis of allocation;
- The fairest basis of allocation is generally a uniform percentage of the sale price received for the asset;

---

95 *Income Tax Act*, RSC 1985 (5th Supp), c 1, en SC 1998, c 19, s 226(1).
96 See *Re Temple City Housing Inc*, 2007 ABQB 786.
97 See Chapter 13, Section A(5).
98 See R Wood, "The Structure of Secured Priorities in Insolvency Law" (2011) 27 *Banking and Finance Law Review* 25 [Wood, "Structure"].
99 *Hunjan International Inc (Re)* (2006), 21 CBR (5th) 276 (Ont SCJ).
100 *Hickman Equipment (1985) Ltd (Re)*, 2004 NLSCTD 164; *Winnipeg Motor Express Inc (Re)*, 2009 MBQB 204; *Respec Oilfield Services Ltd (Re)*, 2010 ABQB 277.

- Costs are not limited to the cost of realization alone but relate to all costs whether direct sales cost or indirect cost;
- Exceptions to a uniform application of cost to creditors ought not to be lightly granted and should only be made where the requirement for such variation is reasonably articulable.

Courts have recognized that it may be appropriate in some cases to take into account distinctions based on the type of collateral held by the secured party and the degree of potential benefit derived by the secured party. In one instance, a court held that a smaller proportion should be allocated to a secured creditor with a first ranking charge on real property since the bulk of the court ordered charge was used to fund ongoing operations and this conferred a greater benefit on operating lenders who are less than fully secured.[101] In assessing the allocation a court should consider the potential benefits of the restructuring even if these were not ultimately realized.[102]

Although the allocation of costs is generally imposed on subordinate secured creditors, there may be some instances where it is appropriate to allocate costs to a higher ranking claimant. This might be justified where the expenses have saved the creditor an expense that it would otherwise have had to incur.[103]

C. IMPEACHABLE TRANSACTIONS

The provisions of the *BIA* that permit a court to impeach transactions[104] are fully applicable in *BIA* restructuring proceedings.[105] The provisions are modified by using the date of the filing of the notice of intention or the proposal instead of the date of the debtor's bankruptcy. If a proposal is annulled, the date of the initial bankruptcy event is used.[106]

The *CCAA* originally did not contain a comparable provision. As a result, parties who wished to challenge a transaction had to seek leave to lift the stay of proceedings in order to apply for a bankruptcy order. This would allow the applicant to preserve the remedies available under the *BIA* in respect of impeachable transactions. The *CCAA* has now

---

101 *Hunters Trailer & Marine Ltd (Re)*, 2001 ABQB 1094.

102 *Medican Holdings Ltd (Re)*, 2013 ABQB 224.

103 *Father & Son Investments Inc v Maverick Brewing Corporation*, 2007 ABQB 651. And see Wood, "Structure," above note 98.

104 *BIA*, ss 95–101. And see Chapter 7.

105 *BIA*, s 101.1(1).

106 *Ibid*, s 101.1(3).

been brought into alignment with the *BIA* restructuring proceedings in respect of the automatic application of the impeachable transactions provisions.[107] The provisions are modified by using the date of the commencement of *CCAA* proceedings and by giving the monitor the same impeachment powers that can be exercised by a trustee.

The impeachment powers set out in the *BIA* can be used to impugn transactions that took place before restructuring proceedings were commenced. For example, the trustee or monitor may seek to avoid a transaction under which assets were transferred to a related party before the commencement of restructuring proceedings. Although the trustee or monitor may also want to use the impeachment powers against transactions that occur after the commencement of restructuring proceedings, there is an impediment in the way of doing so. The impeachment powers contained in the *BIA* permit a trustee to impugn a transaction that occurs within a specific window of time. These time periods end on the date of the bankruptcy. In restructuring proceedings, the date of bankruptcy is to be read as the date on which the restructuring proceedings are commenced.[108] This means that the impeachment powers are not available in respect of transactions that occur after the commencement of restructuring proceedings.

Provincial law also gives creditors the right to avoid transactions as fraudulent preferences or conveyances. The *BIA* permits a trustee in bankruptcy to invoke these provincial powers,[109] and it would follow that a trustee under *BIA* restructuring proceedings would also enjoy the ability to do so.[110] The *CCAA* does not contain an express statutory provision that gives a monitor a similar ability to invoke provincial law to impeach transactions. However, a court may be prepared to make an order that gives the monitor a right to exercise these powers as a representative of the creditors pursuant to its general power to make orders.[111]

If the monitor or the trustee does not choose to prosecute the action, a creditor may apply to court for an order authorizing the creditor to take proceedings in the creditor's own name and at its own expense and risk. The rules and procedure that govern this process are the same as those that apply in bankruptcy proceedings.[112]

---

107 *CCAA*, s 36.1.

108 *BIA*, s 101.1(2)(a); *CCAA*, s 36.1(2)(a). And see P Shea, "Dealing with Suppliers in a Reorganization" (2008) 37 *Canadian Bankruptcy Reports* (5th) 161.

109 *Robinson v Countrywide Factors Ltd*, [1978] 1 SCR 753.

110 *BIA*, s 66.

111 *CCAA*, s 11.

112 *BIA*, s 38; *CCAA*, s 36.1(1). And see Chapter 8, Section A(4).

The creditors may agree in the plan or proposal that they will not attempt to impeach transactions entered into between the debtor and a third party. Both the *BIA* and the *CCAA* contain additional safeguards in respect of these types of terms. The monitor or trustee must provide an opinion on the reasonableness of a term in a plan or proposal that excludes operation of the impeachable transactions provisions of the *BIA* in its report on the state of the debtor's business.[113] The creditors and the court are given this report, and they can use it to decide if they should approve the plan or proposal.

FURTHER READINGS

BUCKWOLD, T, & R WOOD. "Priorities" in S Ben-Ishai & A Duggan, eds, *Canadian Bankruptcy and Insolvency Law: Bill C-55, Statute c. 47 and Beyond* (Markham, ON: LexisNexis Canada, 2007) ch 5

DARE, V. "The Treatment of Late Claims under the *CCAA*" (2001) 26 *Canadian Bankruptcy Reports* (4th) 142

LEE, J. "Rooted in Equity: The Jurisdiction of Canadian Courts to Allocate Restructuring and Realization Costs in Insolvency Proceedings" (2012) 1 *Journal of the Insolvency Institute of Canada* 67

MCKENZIE, T. "Toward a Bankruptcy Model for Non-Class Aggregate Litigation" (2012) 87 *New York University Law Review* 960

SHEA, P. "Dealing with Suppliers in A Reorganization" (2008) 37 *Canadian Bankruptcy Reports* (5th) 161

WOOD, R. "The Structure of Secured Priorities in Insolvency Law" (2011) 27 *Banking and Finance Law Review* 26

113 *BIA*, s 50(10); *CCAA*, s 23(1)(d.1).

CHAPTER 16

DEVELOPING AND APPROVING THE PLAN

The objective in a traditional commercial restructuring is to come up with an agreement that will be approved by the creditors. The agreement is referred to as a plan of compromise or arrangement in *CCAA* proceedings and as a commercial proposal in *BIA* proceedings. For convenience, it will simply be referred to here as the plan when the discussion relates to both restructuring regimes. The plan often separates the creditors into two or more classes. It is not binding on any class of creditors unless the class of creditors approves it. Unanimous consent of all the creditors within a class is not needed in order to bind the creditors. It is sufficient if a majority of creditors who hold at least two-thirds the value of the claims vote in favour of it. A court must then review the plan to ensure that it is not unfair. If the court approves it, the plan becomes binding on all the creditors who are affected by its terms. The creditors relinquish their former claims against the debtor and obtain in their place the rights specified in the plan.

A. DEVELOPING THE PLAN

A debtor who enters into restructuring proceedings encounters two immediate difficulties. First, the debtor must attempt to maintain business operations in a vastly different environment. Extensive negotiations with lenders may be required. Worried suppliers must be reassured. Steps to terminate contracts, close units, and reduce the workforce must be taken. (The problems associated with the preservation and operation of the business have been discussed in Chapter 13.) Second, the debtor must attempt to negotiate and develop an acceptable plan. The debtor often will not have had an opportunity to hammer out a plan with the creditors before initiating restructuring proceedings. The debtor therefore is faced with the considerable challenge of negotiating a deal under severe time constraints and pressure. The process is made more difficult by the fact that the creditors do not speak with one voice and their interests are often in conflict with one another.

1) Bargaining over Surplus Value

Restructurings are feasible when the going-concern value of a firm exceeds its liquidation value. Creditors who participate in a restructuring can therefore obtain a higher recovery than they could if the firm were liquidated in bankruptcy. Although restructuring law provides a process that permits the interested parties to capture this surplus value, it does not give much guidance on how surplus value is to be distributed among the interested parties. The division of the surplus value is a matter that is left to the parties to negotiate among themselves.

Several kinds of disagreements may arise in the course of these negotiations. Disagreements may arise between the debtor and the creditors. The debtor may propose to pay the creditors a certain percentage of their claims. The creditors may take the view that they ought to recover a higher percentage than that which is offered. Disagreements may arise between different classes of creditors over the respective amounts that should be given. Creditors in one class may believe that their class is receiving too little and that another class is being given too much. Conflicts may also occur within a class of creditors over the amount or kind of property that they should receive. Some creditors may prefer to be paid cash, while others might be satisfied with a distribution of shares in satisfaction of their claims.

The decision whether to implement a liquidation plan is also highly significant in the negotiation process. Liquidation settles uncertainty over the going-concern value of the firm. When liquidation is avoided and the firm continues in business, junior classes of claimants are able to use uncertainty over the value of the firm to argue for more favourable treatment. The uncertainty over value explains why classes of claimants that have a lower priority ranking are often able to recover something under a plan despite the fact that higher-ranking classes do not fully recover their claims.[1]

2) Pre-packaged Plans

Very often a business commences restructuring proceedings in order to give it the necessary breathing room to negotiate a deal with its creditors. But this is not always the case. The debtor may have been able to work out the major terms and conditions of the plan with its creditors prior to the initiation of restructuring proceedings. Sometimes the plan can be implemented as a private workout without any need to initiate restructuring proceedings. But sometimes it may be necessary to invoke restructuring proceedings even though the terms of the deal have been settled. It may be necessary to do so in order to bind dissenting creditors to the plan. It may also be necessary to invoke restructuring proceedings in order to obtain some advantage that is not available outside restructuring law. For example, it may be necessary to invoke restructuring proceedings in order to disclaim or assign certain contracts.

A "pre-packaged" plan is one in which the debtor obtains the consent and support of the major creditors before restructuring proceedings are commenced. Courts have taken the view that the use of pre-packaged plans is a healthy and effective practice that should be encouraged.[2] Pre-packaged plans have the advantage of shortening the time needed to complete the restructuring and reducing the costs of restructuring. However, the use of pre-packaged plans does not provide a justification for running roughshod over the interests of those creditors who have not been consulted.

3) Amendment of the Plan

Many restructurings involve intense negotiations between the debtor and the creditors. During the course of these negotiations, the draft plan may be significantly modified. There is no limitation on the amendments or modifications that can be made during the negotiation stage, since this is essentially a matter of contractual bargaining. Once the plan is sufficiently developed, a meeting of creditors is called and the creditors have the opportunity to vote on the plan.[3] Further amendments

---

1 D Baird & D Bernstein, "Absolute Priority, Valuation Uncertainty, and the Reorganization Bargain" (2006) 115 *Yale Law Journal* 1930.

2 *Re Royal Oak Mines Inc* (1999), 6 CBR (4th) 314 (Ont Ct Gen Div).

3 *CCAA*, ss 4–5; BIA, s 51(1).

or modifications to the plan may be proposed at this stage.[4] Both the *CCAA* and the *BIA* contemplate that amendments may be made at the meeting of creditors.[5] Under the *CCAA*, the court has only a very limited ability to amend a plan after the creditors and the court have approved it.[6] Under the *BIA*, the court may do so if it involves correcting an error or omission that does not entail a matter of substance.[7]

4) Exclusivity

In most cases, the debtor takes on the responsibility of developing the restructuring plan that will be placed before the creditors for their approval. Instead of simply waiting until the debtor develops the plan and then voting for or against it, an interested party may wish to propose a rival plan for consideration of the creditors. Under the *BIA*, a creditor cannot develop a competing proposal. The Act restricts the persons who are permitted to make a proposal to the debtor or a receiver, liquidator, or trustee in bankruptcy of the debtor.[8]

The *CCAA* does not restrict the persons who are entitled to propose a plan, and occasionally *CCAA* proceedings have been invoked by a creditor rather than by a debtor.[9] Occasionally, the initial order contains a provision that gives the debtor the exclusive right to prepare and file a plan.[10] Despite the granting of an exclusive order, a creditor could nevertheless apply to court to have it revoked in order to permit the creditor to develop a rival plan. Courts should not be too quick to permit competing plans. Negotiations on a single plan are difficult enough. Having two sets of negotiations in play greatly increases the chances of bargaining failure. However, in appropriate cases it may be useful to permit the development of a rival plan as an alternative to a more drastic measure such as termination of restructuring proceedings if negotiations conducted by the debtor have come to a standstill.

---

4 See *Re Wandlyn Inns Ltd* (1992), 15 CBR (3d) 316 (NBQB).

5 *CCAA*, s 6(1); *BIA*, s 54(1).

6 *Algoma Steel Corp v Royal Bank of Canada* (1992), 11 CBR (3d) 11 (Ont CA); *Ontario v Canadian Airlines Corp* (2001), 29 CBR (4th) 236 (Alta QB).

7 *Bankruptcy and Insolvency General Rules*, CRC, c 368, s 92. And see *Re Cosmic Adventures Halifax Inc* (1999), 13 CBR (4th) 22 (NSSC); *Re Hover* (2000), 21 CBR (4th) 263 (Alta QB).

8 *BIA*, s 50(1).

9 *Re 1078385 Ontario Ltd* (2004), 16 CBR (5th) 152 (Ont CA).

10 See, for example, the initial *CCAA* order in *Re Stelco Inc*, [2004] OJ No 549 (SCJ).

B. MANDATORY FEATURES OF THE PLAN

Both the *BIA* and *CCAA* set out a number of mandatory features that must be included in a plan. A failure to include them will necessarily result in its failure, since a court has no power to approve it if the feature is absent. First, the plan must provide for the payment in full to Her Majesty within six months after court approval of all amounts in respect of amounts that could be subject to a demand under subsection 224(1.2) of the *Income Tax Act*.[11] This feature does not need to be present if the Crown has agreed to waive its inclusion. Second, the plan must provide for payment to the employees of no less than the amount that the employees would be qualified to claim as a preferred creditor in the event of a bankruptcy together with all amounts earned after the commencement of restructuring proceedings.[12] Third, the plan must provide for the payment of unremitted pension contributions.[13] This requirement may be omitted from the plan if the parties have entered into an agreement approved by the relevant pension regulator respecting payment of those amounts.[14] The *BIA* also provides that a proposal must provide for payment in priority to other claims of all proper fees and expenses of the trustee.[15]

C. APPROVAL BY THE CREDITORS

1) The Meeting of Creditors

The *BIA* contains a set of rules that govern the calling of a meeting of creditors. The trustee must call the meeting within twenty-one days from the filing of the proposal with the official receiver.[16] The official receiver or his or her nominee chairs the meeting.[17] The rules contained in the

11 *CCAA*, s 6(3); *BIA*, s 60(1.1).

12 *CCAA*, s 6(5); *BIA*, s 60(1.3). *BIA*, s 136(1)(d) sets this amount at $2,000 for each unpaid employee. See Chapter 9, Section B(1)(d).

13 *CCAA*, s 6(6); *BIA*, s 60(1.5).

14 *CCAA*, s 6(7); *BIA*, s 60(1.6).

15 *BIA*, s 60(1).

16 *Ibid*, s 51(1). Notice of the meeting must be sent to the creditors at least ten days before the meeting.

17 *Ibid*, s 51(3).

BIA governing meetings of creditors are applicable.[18] The chair may adjourn the meeting to permit further investigation or examination.[19]

The *CCAA* provides that a court may order a meeting of the creditors but provides very little guidance on the process. The detail is supplied by the court in a meeting and approval order that establishes the procedure for the calling and holding of a meeting of the creditors to vote on the plan. The *CCAA* provides that the court may adjourn a meeting of creditors if an alteration or modification of the plan has been proposed after the court has ordered a meeting.[20]

2) The Threshold for Creditor Approval

The *CCAA* and the *BIA* set out the rules that govern creditor approval of the plan. Both statutes provide that the plan must be approved by a majority of the creditors representing two-thirds of the value of the claims.[21] Where creditors are classified into different classes of creditors, each class of creditors must approve it by this dual majority in order for the plan to be binding on that class of creditors. This means that, within a class of creditors, a majority of creditors of that class may bind a dissenting minority to the terms of the plan.

The percentage requirements are calculated using the number of creditors within the class who voted on the plan, as opposed to the total number of creditors in the class. Suppose that there are ten creditors within the class and that the total value of the claims is $1 million. At the meeting, seven of the creditors vote on the plan. Four vote in favour and three against. The four who voted in favour have claims that amount to $600,000. The three who voted against have claims of $200,000. The dual-majority threshold is satisfied in this case. The creditors have a majority in number of those who voted (four out of seven) even though they do not have a majority of the total number of creditors within the class. They also have more than two-thirds of the amount of claims of those who voted (75 percent of the value) even though they have less than two-thirds of the value of all the claims within the class.

The ability to bind dissenting creditors to a plan operates only within each class of creditor. Suppose that a plan has three classes of creditors. Two approve the plan by a dual majority, while the other does not. The vote of the two classes that approved cannot bind the class that did

---

18 See Chapter 8, Section A(2).

19 *BIA*, s 52.

20 *CCAA*, s 7.

21 *Ibid*, s 6(1); *BIA*, ss 54(2) and 62(2)(b).

not.[22] Nor does it matter if, in the aggregate, the creditors who approve the plan possess a majority in number representing two-thirds of the value of all claims.[23] Each class has a veto and cannot be forced to accept the plan.[24] There is nothing equivalent to the "cram down" power that permits a court in the United States to bind a dissenting class to a plan even though the class has voted to reject the plan.[25]

3) Unaffected Creditors

A plan does not need to embrace all creditors. Some creditors may be left outside it. These creditors are unaffected by the plan and therefore do not have any right to vote on it. Unaffected creditors enjoy their full legal rights once the restructuring is complete and the stay of proceedings is lifted.

Under the *BIA*, a proposal must be made to all unsecured creditors, either as a mass or divided into classes.[26] It is therefore not possible to leave a class of unsecured creditors outside a proposal as unaffected parties. The *BIA* provides that a proposal may be made to secured creditors. This means that some or all of the secured creditors may be excluded from the proposal.[27] If they are left outside the proposal, their rights are unaffected and they do not vote on the plan.[28] If they are affected by the proposal, they will be placed into one or more classes of affected secured creditors, and each class must approve the proposal by a dual majority in order for the proposal to be binding on that class of secured creditor.[29] The *CCAA* does not contain an equivalent restriction on the kinds of parties who may be designated as unaffected parties under a plan.

Both the *CCAA* and the *BIA* provide that certain types of claims, such as fines, awards for damages for bodily harm intentionally inflicted, and

---

22 *Olympia & York Developments Ltd v Royal Trust Co* (1993), 17 CBR (3d) 1 (Ont Ct Gen Div) [*Olympia & York*].

23 *Re Wellington Building Corp* (1934), 16 CBR 48 (Ont HCJ).

24 *UTI Energy Corp v Fracmaster Ltd* (1999), 11 CBR (4th) 230 at para 14 (Alta CA).

25 See C Tabb, *The Law of Bankruptcy* (Westbury. NY: Foundation Press, 1997) at 854–56.

26 *BIA*, s 50(1.2).

27 Section 50(1.3), *ibid*, provides that, if a proposal is made to one or more of the secured creditors of a particular class, it must be made to all secured creditors in respect of secured claims of that class. It may be difficult to determine when secured creditors are to be viewed as being of the same class. See Section D(1)(c), below in this chapter.

28 *BIA*, ss 50.2 and 53.

29 *Ibid*, s 62(2)(b).

liability for fraud while acting in a fiduciary capacity are not affected unless the plan explicitly provides for the claims compromise and the creditor votes in favour of acceptance.[30]

4) The Effect of Partial Approval

Some but not all classes of affected creditors may have given their approval to the plan. Classes that did not vote to approve the plan cannot be bound by it. However, it is also necessary to consider the effect of their rejection on the other classes of creditors who voted to approve it. If the plan is viewed as severable, it will nonetheless bind those classes who voted in favour of it. If it is viewed as an entirety, no class of creditor is bound unless all classes of creditors agree to approve it.

Under the *BIA*, all classes of unsecured creditors must approve the proposal.[31] A vote against the proposal by any class of unsecured creditor will cause it to fail, and a court will be unable to approve the proposal. The *BIA* does not require the approval of secured creditors. It provides that the proposal is binding only on secured creditors if they approve it by a dual majority. A proposal may therefore satisfy the statutory requirements for creditor approval even if one or more classes of secured creditors have voted against it. Although approval by secured creditors is not essential, a court may decide not to approve a proposal if the rejection by the dissenting class of secured creditors renders the proposal unviable.

The *CCAA* is silent on the question of partial acceptance. In *Olympia & York Developments Ltd v Royal Trust Co*,[32] the plan specifically provided that if a class of creditors voted against the plan that class would drop out of the plan and become unaffected creditors. The court held that the unanimity of all classes was not required in order to bind the consenting classes to the plan. Therefore, the classes of creditors who voted in favour of the plan were bound, while the classes of creditors who did not approve it were not bound. The matter was made easier because the plan expressly dealt with the effect of partial approval. The more difficult case is where the plan is silent on this question and the court must determine the intention of the parties.

The *Olympia & York* case involved a restructuring of a massive real estate empire. The company's viability was not intractably tied to any one piece of property, so that the failure of some of the classes of

30 *Ibid*, s 62(2.1); *CCAA*, s 19(2).

31 *BIA*, s 54(2)(d).

32 Above note 22.

creditors to approve the plan did not result in an overall loss of viability of the plan. The situation may well be different where the assets are integrated so that a failure to bind a class of creditors to the plan would threaten the plan's viability. A court could respond by refusing to approve the plan because of its non-viability. Alternatively, a court under these circumstances might conclude that the parties would have intended that approval by all classes was needed before any class was bound by the plan.

5) Voting by Related Parties

A debtor may have entered into intercorporate transactions with related corporations. These related parties have claims against the debtor that entitle them to vote on the plan. The non-related parties may be concerned that the related party will vote in favour of the plan and thereby swing the vote in favour of approval, whereas the exclusion of the related-party votes would result in a rejection of the plan.

The *BIA* establishes a set of relationships that are defined to be between related persons.[33] If a creditor is related to the debtor, the creditor may vote against but not for the acceptance of the proposal.[34] The restriction against related person voting does not apply if the claim of the related person has been assigned to a non-related party, so long as the assignment is *bona fide* and the assignee is under no obligation to vote in favour of the proposal. But if the assignment is simply a device to evade the restriction against voting and the assignee is merely voting according to the wishes of the assignor, the courts will not permit the votes to be counted in favour of the proposal.[35]

The *CCAA* did not originally contain a similar prohibition on voting by related parties. The matter was therefore left to the courts to decide upon the appropriate treatment of related-party voting. Courts permitted the related person to vote on the plan but directed that the votes be separately tabulated so that the court would be able to determine the outcome of unrelated-party voting on the plan.[36] The 2009 amendments

---

33 *BIA*, s 4(2).

34 *Ibid*, s 54(3).

35 *Re Oulahen* (2000), 16 CBR (4th) 262 (Ont SCJ), aff'd (2001), 24 CBR (4th) 119 (Ont CA).

36 *Re Canadian Airlines Corp* (2000), 19 CBR (4th) 12 (Alta QB), leave to appeal refused (2000), 19 CBR (4th) 33 (Alta CA). However, if the related party is not treated similarly, a court may conclude that there is no commonality of interest and require the related party to be placed in a separate class. See *Re San Francisco Gifts Ltd* (2004), 5 CBR (5th) 92 (Alta QB).

have brought the *CCAA* into alignment with the *BIA* by the inclusion of a rule that prevents a related party from voting in favour of a plan.[37]

6) Disputed Claims

A dispute over the amount of a claim held by a creditor does not simply affect the distribution that will be obtained by the creditor. It also affects the number of votes that can be cast in favour or against the plan by that creditor. Success or failure in obtaining the approval of the creditors may turn on the determination of the amount of a disputed claim. The *CCAA* does not address this issue. Instead, the matter is left for the court to deal with in a claims procedure order. Some orders permit a creditor with a disputed claim to vote on the plan before a final resolution of the amount, and require resolution of the amount for voting purposes only if it would be relevant to the outcome of the vote.

7) The Use of Secret Side Deals

During the course of negotiations with the creditors, the debtor may discover that some of the creditors within a class support the plan while others do not. If those who support the plan do not have sufficient voting power to approve it by a dual majority, the restructuring plan is liable to be defeated. The debtor may be tempted to "sweeten the pot" in favour of some of the dissenting creditors in order to obtain sufficient votes to bind the class to the plan.

The use of secret side deals to buy the consent of dissenting creditors is not permitted since they are unfair to creditors who do not obtain their benefit and undermine the integrity of restructuring proceedings.[38] The British Columbia Court of Appeal in *Northland Properties Ltd v Excelsior Life Insurance Co of Canada*[39] indicated that "side deals are a dangerous game and any arrangement made with just one creditor endangers the appearance of the *bona fides* of a plan." It is fundamentally important that there be transparency in the terms of the deal that is being struck with the creditors. The use of secret side deals strikes at the heart of the negotiating process in insolvency. Such contracts constitute a fraud on the others creditors and are therefore unenforceable.[40] Any payment or transfer of property to the creditor pursuant to

---

37 *CCAA*, s 22(3).

38 *Re Cobourg Felt Co* (1925), 5 CBR 622 (Ont HCJ).

39 (1989), 73 CBR (NS) 195 (BCCA) [*Northland v Excelsior Life*].

40 *Re Cicoria* (2000), 21 CBR (4th) 232 (Ont CA); *Hochberger v Rittenberg* (1916), 54 SCR 480.

the secret side deal may also be set aside.[41] The existence of a secret deal may result in a court refusing to approve the plan.[42]

8) The Status of Subordinated Claims

Some of the creditors may have agreed to subordinate or postpone their claims until the claims of other specified creditors have been satisfied. Several potential issues arise out of this fact pattern. In *Re Stelco*,[43] the subordinated creditors attempted to use their postponed status as a ground for arguing they should be placed in their own separate class for the purposes of voting on the plan. The court rejected this argument on the basis that classification of creditors is determined by their legal rights in relation to the debtor company and not on their rights as creditors in relation to each other. Placing subordinated creditors in a separate class would give the subordinated creditors the ability to threaten to veto the plan in order to obtain a concession in the form of a release from the obligation to turn over funds to the benefiting creditors.

It is therefore appropriate to include the postponed creditors and the benefiting creditors in the same class. If the plan is approved, the turnover provision will be given effect, and the subordinating creditor will be required to surrender any funds to which it is entitled to the benefiting creditor. If there is anything left after the benefiting creditors' claims are satisfied, it is given to the postponed creditor. The turnover provision operates in favour only of parties who receive the benefit of the postponement. In *Re Air Canada*,[44] the court held that the other creditors who were not a party or a beneficiary of the subordination had no right to object to the subordinated party voting on or receiving any distribution under the plan. The subordination operated between the postponed creditor and the benefiting creditor, and did not purport to subordinate the claim to the other creditors.

A second issue that was not discussed in the *Air Canada* decision is whether the beneficiary of the subordination may demand that it be given the postponed creditor's right to vote on the plan. The benefiting creditor may justify this result on the basis that it has obtained the economic benefit of the postponed creditor's claim by virtue of the subordination agreement. However, the matter is complicated by the

41 *McKewan v Sanderson* (1873), LR 15 Eq 229 at 234; *Newlands Textiles Inc v Carrier* (1983), 47 CBR (NS) 148 (Ont HCJ).

42 *Northland v Excelsior Life*, above note 39.

43 (2005), 15 CBR (5th) 307 (Ont CA).

44 (2004), 2 CBR (5th) 4 (Ont SCJ).

fact that the existence of a subordination agreement does not necessarily mean that the subordinated creditor is entitled to receive nothing. Suppose that A postpones its claim to B. Both A and B hold claims for $100,000, and the plan provides for recovery by unsecured creditors of sixty cents on the dollar. If the plan is approved, B will recover $100,000 and A will recover $20,000. A rule that prevents the subordinated creditor from voting prevents A from acting to protect its own interest.

The general approach to subordination agreements in Canada is to treat them as private contracts between the parties. The status of the subordinated creditor's claim in the insolvency is not changed. Rather, the subordinated creditor is required to abide by the terms of the agreement and give up its share to the benefiting creditor.[45] This suggests that the right of the creditor to vote should not be affected unless the creditor has also agreed to vote the shares for the benefit of the senior creditor. There is some judicial support for this view in the form of statements to the effect that subordinated creditors should not be deprived of their right to vote on a plan.[46]

9) The Acquisition of Claims

An investor may seek to acquire the claims of creditors or shareholders after the commencement of restructuring proceedings. This practice, referred to as "claims trading" or, more negatively, "vulture investing,"[47] can dramatically change the dynamics of bargaining in restructuring proceedings. The investor may wish to acquire the claims because it is a sophisticated commercial party that can better assess the true value of the creditors' claims. This is not necessarily a bad thing for the creditors or other claimants. They are under no obligation to sell their claims to the investor, and the fact that there is a willing buyer for their claims provides them with a liquidity that would not otherwise be available.[48]

The ability to acquire claims also gives the investor greater leverage in the bargaining that occurs within restructuring proceedings. The investor may acquire a block of claims within a class sufficient to permit it to veto the plan. This veto power, and the fact that the investor is a repeat player who has a sophisticated understanding of restructuring proceedings, may permit the investor to obtain a better deal than

---

45 *Ibid.*

46 See *Re Uniforêt inc* (2003), 43 CBR (4th) 254 (Que Sup Ct).

47 See R Lieb, "Vultures Beware: Risks of Purchasing Claims against a Chapter 11 Debtor" (1993) 48 *Business Lawyer* 915.

48 See *Re Stelco Inc* (2005), 7 CBR (5th) 310 at para 13 (Ont SCJ), rev'd on other grounds (2005), 9 CBR (5th) 135 (Ont CA).

could be obtained by the creditors whose claims have been acquired. The acquisition of claims might even be motivated by a desire to obtain control over the business by pressing for a restructuring that involves the issuance of equity claims to the creditors.

By acquiring the claims, the investor obtains the same right to vote on the plan as that possessed by the claimant.[49] This is subject to five potential limitations. First, a claimant who acquires the claims of several other creditors is counted only as a single creditor for the purposes of determining whether a majority in number have voted in favour of the plan.[50] The acquisition of claims, therefore, influences only the dollar value of the claims voted by that creditor.

Second, the *BIA* provides that a person is not entitled to vote on a claim acquired after the initiation of restructuring proceedings under the *BIA* unless the entire claim is acquired.[51] A similar restriction is not contained in the *CCAA*.[52]

Third, a transfer of a subordinated claim will not free the claim of its subordinated status. Under the *BIA* and the *CCAA*, creditors who enter into certain types of transactions are postponed until the other creditors are paid. The acquisition of the postponed claim will not free the transferee of the subordinated status connected with the claim.[53]

Fourth, a related party who acquires a claim of a non-related person is unable to use that claim to vote in favour of a plan. The restriction on voting by related parties applies to the person voting on the plan, and not on the nature of the claims that give rise to the voting right.[54] No restriction is placed on a related party's right to vote against a plan.

Fifth, a court may decide to exclude the investor from voting on the plan if the court is of the opinion that the acquisition was motivated by bad faith.[55] Some courts in the United States have held that the acquisition of claims in order to obtain a veto position may amount to bad faith. *In re Allegheny International, Inc*[56] concerned a debtor who had proposed

---

49 *Re Canadian Airlines Corp*, above note 36.

50 *Re Laserworks Computer Services Inc* (1998), 6 CBR (4th) 69 (NSCA); *Toia v Cie de Cautionnement Alberta* (1989), 77 CBR (NS) 264 (Que Sup Ct).

51 *BIA*, s 54(6).

52 Although a similar provision was initially added to the *CCAA* in the 2005 amendments, the provision was removed by the 2007 amendments before it ever came into force. It is unclear why this provision was not thought to be appropriately included in the *CCAA*.

53 *In re Enron Corp*, 333 BR 205 (Bkrtcy SDNY 2005).

54 See Section C(5), above in this chapter.

55 *Minco-Division Construction Inc v 9170-6929 Québec Inc* (2007), 29 CBR (5th) 165 (Que Sup Ct).

56 118 BR 282 (Bkrtcy WD Pa 1990).

a plan that was supported by a majority of the creditors. The investor wished to propose a competing plan that would give it ownership and control of the debtor, and therefore purchased sufficient claims in a number of the classes to defeat the plan put forward by the debtor. Other courts have distinguished this case on the basis that the acquisition of claims by the investor in *Allegheny* was for an ulterior motive. The acquisition of a blocking position has been upheld where it is undertaken to enhance the investor's interests as creditor, rather than to promote a competing restructuring plan of which it is the chief beneficiary.[57] The British Columbia Supreme Court in *Blackburn Developments Ltd (Re)*[58] declined to adopt this approach, and favoured instead a test that would disallow voting of the acquired claims only if the conduct amounts to an abuse of process or other tortious or near tortious character and that that conduct has resulted in a substantial injustice.

Canadian courts have prevented abuse of the bankruptcy system by persons who seek to use it for an improper purpose. For example, courts have prevented an assignee of claims from voting on a proposal where the claims were acquired in order to defeat a plan and thereby get rid of a competitor.[59] However, it is less easy to determine precisely where the line will be drawn in determining what other kinds of conduct will be regarded as improper.

D. CLASSIFICATION OF CREDITORS

Both the *BIA* and the *CCAA* provide for the creation of classes of creditors for the purposes of voting on the plan. The legislation originally provided little guidance on the principles that were to be used in determining the appropriateness of the classification scheme. The governing principles emerged from an important series of judicial decisions dealing with disputes over the classification of creditors. The statutes have since been amended to provide additional classification rules. The *BIA* contains rules that govern the classification of secured creditors[60] but is silent as to the classification of unsecured creditors. Rules governing the classification of secured and unsecured creditors have been added to the *CCAA*.[61] These statutory rules are largely codifications

57 *In re Marin Town Center*, 142 BR 374 (ND Cal 1992).

58 2011 BCSC 1671.

59 *Re Laserworks Computer Services Inc* (1998), 6 CBR (4th) 69 (NSCA).

60 *BIA*, s 50(1.4).

61 *CCAA*, s 22.

of the judicially created principles, and it is necessary to review the caselaw on classification to comprehend fully the logic and rationale behind them.

1) The Judicial Approach

a) The General Principles

An applicant who objects to the proposed scheme of classification may want to be placed in a separate class for the purposes of voting on the plan. Courts are wary about creating additional classes for voting purposes. The creation of a separate class greatly enhances the leverage available to a creditor in its negotiations with the debtor. The creditor obtains a veto power, and this can be used to bargain for more favourable treatment in the plan.[62] The creation of a multitude of classes would defeat one of the underlying principles of restructuring law.[63] A majority-approval rule is used to prevent creditors from using holdout bargaining strategies. Creditors who employ these strategies threaten to defeat bargains that enhance value for all creditors unless their claims are afforded special treatment. A majority-approval principle limits a creditor's ability to adopt such strategies, but this objective is undermined if too many creditors are given the power to block the plan unilaterally.

Courts are also conscious that the classification scheme, like any voting system, is capable of being gerrymandered and abused. The classification scheme proposed by the debtor may have been deliberately devised as a means of swamping the vote of a dissenting creditor by placing that creditor in a class with other claimants that are not similarly affected by the plan. The task of the court is therefore to uphold the majoritarian principle for creditor approval of restructuring plans while at the same time preventing it from being used as an instrument to abuse minority interests.

The classic statement on the principles that are to be applied by a court in reviewing a classification scheme is found in *Sovereign Life Assurance Co v Dodd*.[64] The rationale for placing creditors into different classes is that "the creditors composing the different classes have different interests; and, therefore, if we find a different state of facts existing among different creditors which may differently affect their minds

---

62 See, for example, *Re Canadian Airlines Corp*, above note 36 at para 31.

63 *Norcen Energy Resources Ltd v Oakwood Petroleums Ltd* (1988), 72 CBR (NS) 20 at para 46 (Alta QB).

64 [1892] 2 QB 573 (CA).

and their judgment, they must be divided into different classes."[65] The following test has been devised to determine if a classification scheme is fair and reasonable:

> It seems plain that we must give such a meaning to the term "class" as will prevent the section being so worked as to result in confiscation and injustice, and that it must be confined to those persons whose rights are not so dissimilar as to make it impossible for them to consult together with a view to their common interest.[66]

The problem with placing creditors with different legal interests in the same class for voting purposes is illustrated in a simple example. Suppose that there are three creditors, each of whom has a claim for $100,000 against the debtor. A and B have unsecured claims, while C has a fully secured claim. A liquidation of the debtor's assets would produce $240,000 for distribution among the creditors. C would recover $100,000, while A and B would each recover $70,000. The debtor develops a restructuring plan that avoids a liquidation and proposes that each creditor be paid $80,000 in compromise of the claims they hold. The three creditors are placed in the same class for the purposes of voting on the restructuring plan. A and B have sufficient voting power to impose the plan on C, since together they have a majority of votes representing two-thirds of value of the claims. This represents a transfer of $20,000 from the secured creditor to the unsecured creditors. The restructuring plan therefore results in confiscation and injustice to C, and a court should require that C be placed in a separate class for voting.

Courts will not endorse a classification scheme unless there exists a sufficient commonality of interest among members of the same class. Canadian courts have developed a set of principles for determining when there is a sufficient commonality of interest, and they have also rejected the idea that the legal rights of claimants must be identical.[67] In the latter respect, the Canadian approach differs from that in the United States. In the United States, claimants can be placed in the same class only if their interests are substantially similar in legal character. This tends to produce more classes than is the case in Canada. However, its effect is ameliorated by the existence of a "cram down" power

---

65 *Ibid* at 580, Lord Escher.

66 *Ibid* at 583, Lord Bowen.

67 *Norcen Energy Resources Ltd v Oakwood Petroleums Ltd*, above note 63; *Re Woodward's Ltd* (1993), 20 CBR (3d) 74 (BCSC).

that permits a court to force a plan on a dissenting class if certain conditions are satisfied.[68]

The Canadian approach is often referred to as the non-fragmentation approach. It is premised on the idea that excessive fragmentation of classes will defeat the underlying purpose of restructuring law, and that some degree of difference in the legal rights held by members of the class can be tolerated. Claimants with different legal claims therefore may be placed in the same class so long as their legal rights are not so dissimilar that it is not possible for them to consult with one another with a common interest.[69]

In applying the non-fragmentation approach, the first step in the analysis is to determine whether the legal rights held by the various claimants within the class are the same or different. If they are the same, then there is no basis for giving the applicant the right to vote in a separate class. If the legal rights are different, the second stage of the analysis is engaged and it becomes necessary to determine whether the difference in legal rights is such that the parties do not have a sufficient commonality of interest.

b) Determination of Legal Rights

In deciding whether the legal rights of claimants within a class are the same or different, the court must look to the nature and character of the legal rights held by the claimant and must not consider external matters that might influence a claimant in voting on the plan. In other words, the focus is on the legal character of the rights of the claimant and not on the nature, identity, or motivation of different claimants.[70]

Trade creditors, tort victims, and banks with unsecured loans all have identical legal rights. Each has an unsecured claim against the debtor. It may well be that the motivation of the different creditors in voting on the plan differs. Trade creditors may be influenced by the desire to preserve a future customer, while tort victims may be primarily concerned with obtaining a settlement of their claims as soon as possible. However, these factors are not relevant, and a claimant cannot use them to argue that the claimant should occupy a separate class for voting on a plan.

Legal rights are different if their priority ranking differs. The most obvious example of this is the difference between secured claims and unsecured claims. However, even unsecured creditors may have dif-

---

68 See Tabb, *The Law of Bankruptcy*, above note 25 at 854–56.

69 *Re Woodward's Ltd*, above note 67; *SemCanada Crude Company (Re)*, 2009 ABQB 490.

70 *Re Woodward's Ltd*, above note 67.

ferent legal rights. This may occur where one of the claimants has the status of preferred creditor in bankruptcy proceedings, since this gives the creditor the right to have the preferred claim satisfied before the general creditors receive anything. They also differ if some of the claimants have different remedies for enforcement than those available to other members in the same class.[71] However, creditors will not be considered to have different legal rights if their rights against the debtor are the same but the difference arises out of a subordination agreement under which one creditor has agreed to postpone its claim to another.[72]

In determining whether the legal rights are different, it is necessary to establish how the legal rights of the claimants are being affected by the plan. Equipment lessors who hold true leases and secured financers have different legal rights and remedies. However, if the plan affects only the lessor's claim for damages for breach of the lease and the secured financer's deficiency claim, they can be treated as having identical legal rights. The plan affects only their unsecured claims against the debtor.[73] Although their proprietary rights differ, their unsecured claims share the same legal characteristics.

c) Commonality of Interest

If the members of the class do not possess identical legal rights, the next step is to decide whether the difference in legal rights prevents the creditors from sharing a sufficient commonality in interest. Secured creditors will usually have different rights from other secured creditors either because they will have security on different assets of the debtor or because the ranking of their claims will differ. Their rights will be identical only if they have taken a security interest in the same asset and they enjoy the same priority ranking in respect of their claims.[74] Despite the differences in their legal rights, courts have upheld classification schemes in which secured creditors are placed in the same class. The fact that they have security in different assets and that some may be oversecured while others may be undersecured is not by itself a sufficient justification for requiring the division of secured creditors into separate classes.[75]

---

71 *Re San Francisco Gifts Ltd*, above note 36.

72 *Re Stelco Inc*, above note 48.

73 *Re Woodward's Ltd*, above note 67; *Re Armbro Enterprises Inc* (1993), 22 CBR (3d) 80 (Ont Ct Gen Div).

74 *Citibank Canada v Chase Manhattan Bank of Canada* (1991), 5 CBR (3d) 165 (Ont Ct Gen Div).

75 *Norcen Energy Resources Ltd v Oakwood Petroleums Ltd*, above note 63.

The commonality of interest test cannot be assessed in isolation but must be considered in the context of the restructuring plan. Suppose that a plan provides that all secured creditors will be limited to their right to repossess and sell their collateral, and that they will lose any right to claim a deficiency from the debtor. This creates a substantial rift between secured creditors who are oversecured and those who are undersecured. The oversecured creditors are not detrimentally affected in the same manner as the undersecured creditors, and it would be inappropriate to place them in the same class. However, if the plan provides for equal treatment of secured creditors up to the value of their collateral and permits the secured creditors to participate in the plan as unsecured creditors to the extent of any deficiency claims, the differences in their legal rights should not prevent them from acting with a common interest.[76]

It may be difficult to justify a classification scheme in which a secured creditor entitled to priority is placed in the same class as a secured creditor who has a subordinate security interest in the same collateral.[77] The senior secured creditor has the right to full satisfaction of its claims before the junior creditor receives anything. However, the classification scheme may be acceptable if the value of the collateral is such that both secured creditors are fully secured.

d) Identical Treatment of Different Legal Rights

Although it is permissible to place all the unsecured creditors in the same class, it is inappropriate to do so if the plan denies some of the creditors a valuable right to which they would otherwise be entitled. In *Re Woodward's Ltd*,[78] a plan provided for payment to unsecured creditors of 37 percent of the value of their claims. The problem was that the same payment was offered to creditors who had claims solely against the debtor company and to creditors who were holders of an unsecured guarantee given by an affiliated company. In a liquidation of the two companies, the unsecured creditors who held claims against both companies would obtain a greater recovery than creditors who held a claim only against one of the companies. The court held that the holders of guarantees should have the right to vote on the plan as a separate class. The fact that the holders of guarantees would receive more than they would in a bankruptcy does not alter the fact that the creditors who held guarantees were liable to have a valuable right confiscated by a

76 *Ibid.*

77 *Re Wellington Building Corp*, above note 23; *Re Fairview Industries Ltd* (1991), 11 CBR (3d) 71 (NSSCTD); *Contech Enterprises Ltd v Vegherb, LLC*, 2015 BCCA 99.

78 *Re Woodward's Ltd*, above note 67.

vote of a majority that would force them to accept the same proportionate payment.

This does not mean that the appropriate response always is to place the objecting creditors in a different class for the purposes of voting on the plan. To do so may give that class of creditor an unwarranted power to threaten to veto the plan. As an alternative, the court may decide to make some other kind of order that is designed to safeguard the unique interest of the creditor. It may do so by ordering that the plan be amended to compensate the creditor for the loss of their unique legal right or directing that it be amended to provide for the survival of the unique right.[79]

Under certain circumstances, it may be legitimate to afford identical treatment to claimants who have different legal rights. It may even be appropriate to place a secured creditor in a class of unsecured creditors rather than in a class of secured creditors. Suppose that a creditor has a subordinate security interest, and the obligation secured by the security interest of the higher-ranking secured creditor exceeds the value of the collateral. Although the subordinate creditor has different legal rights from the unsecured creditors, the reality is that these additional rights are valueless.[80]

e) Different Treatment of Identical Legal Rights

The controversy in many of the cases arises when creditors with different legal rights are placed in the same class for the purposes of voting on the plan. However, problems may also arise when the plan affords different treatment to creditors who have identical legal rights. For example, a plan may create separate classes for trade creditors and landlords and propose to pay 40 percent to landlords in respect of their claims for damages for breach of leases that have been disclaimed and 35 percent to trade creditors. These two kinds of claims are identical in respect of the legal rights that pertain to them since they both constitute simple unsecured claims, but the plan affords more favourable treatment to one type of creditor over another. Courts are reluctant to interfere in such cases. Restructuring law does not require that creditors with the same rights receive equal treatment.[81] The debtor develops

---

79 *Re San Francisco Gifts Ltd*, above note 36.

80 See *Minds Eye Entertainment Ltd v Royal Bank of Canada* (2004), 1 CBR (5th) 89 (Sask CA). See also *Re Doman Industries Ltd* (2003), 41 CBR (4th) 29 (BCSC), in which holders of common shares and holders of preferred shares were placed in the same class despite the higher ranking of the preferred shares on the basis that the rights of both types of shareholders had no economic value.

81 *Re Keddy Motor Inns Ltd* (1992), 13 CBR (3d) 245 (NSCA).

a plan that is put before the creditors, and it is up to the creditors to decide whether or not to approve it. Creditors who object to the second-rate treatment that their class of claims is being offered can negotiate for a better deal, backed up with the threat that they will vote against the unamended plan.

A plan will sometimes subdivide a class of claims in order to furnish different treatment to different members of the class but nevertheless provide for a single class vote. For example, a plan might provide for a single class of unsecured creditors and provide for payment of 80 percent of the claims for creditors with claims of $1,000 or less, payment of 60 percent of the amount of claims that exceed $1,000 but are less than $10,000, and issuance of shares in the restructured corporate debtor in respect of claims in excess of $10,000. Courts have upheld such schemes despite the fact that the creditors receive different treatment under the plan depending upon the amount of their claims.[82] In doing so, the courts have rejected a principle that creditors who are afforded different treatment under a plan should vote in separate classes. Even so, these sorts of plans are vulnerable if they are designed to force unfavourable treatment upon a subclass of creditors. For the sake of illustration, consider an extreme example where the following payout is proposed:

Subclass A: Creditors with claims of $1,000 or less	100%
Subclass B: Creditors with claims greater than $1,000 but less than $10,000	40%
Subclass C: Creditors with claims in excess of $10,000	80%

The favourable treatment of subclass A claimants may ensure that the plan is approved by a majority in number of creditors in the class, while the favourable treatment of subclass C creditors may be such that the plan will be approved by creditors having two-thirds of value of the claims. Subclass B claimants should not be forced to accept unfavourable treatment by virtue of a majority vote, since it amounts to a confiscation of their rights by the other creditors.

2) The Statutory Rules

The *BIA* sets out a set of rules that are to be applied in deciding whether secured creditors should be placed in the same class.[83] The *CCAA* was

82 *Re Sammi Atlas Inc* (1998), 3 CBR (4th) 171 (Ont Ct Gen Div); *Re Steinberg Inc* (1993), 23 CBR (3d) 243 (Que Sup Ct).

83 *BIA*, s 50(1.4).

originally silent on this question. The 2009 amendments have added a new provision that is substantially similar to the *BIA* provisions, except that it applies to both secured and unsecured creditors.[84] The statutory provisions permit the classification of creditors if their interests are sufficiently similar to give them a commonality of interest, taking into account the following factors:

- the nature of the debts giving rise to the claims;
- the nature and rank of any security in respect of the claims;
- the remedies available to the creditors in the absence of the plan, and the extent to which the creditors would recover their claims by exercising those remedies;
- the treatment of the claims under the plan, and the extent to which the claims would be paid under the plan; and
- such further criteria consistent with those set out above.

These rules are consistent with the judicial approach to classification in which the priority of the secured claim, the value of the collateral, and the treatment of the secured creditors under the plan are considered in determining whether the secured creditors share a commonality of interest. The statutory formulation also provides that a relevant consideration is the nature of the debts giving rise to the claims. It is unlikely that this was intended to alter the principle that it is the legal character of the rights of the claimant that is relevant, rather than the nature, identity, or motivation of the claimant who holds those rights.

3) Objecting to the Classification Scheme

In the first instance, the person who develops the plan — almost always the debtor — devises the classification scheme.[85] A claimant who is dissatisfied with the fairness of this scheme may seek an order requiring the use of a different scheme. A creditor who objects to the classification scheme for voting on a plan should not wait until the fairness hearing when the court decides whether or not to approve the plan. Courts have held that it is too late to bring an objection at this stage in the proceedings unless it involves a substantial injustice.[86]

The *BIA* provides that a court, on application made at any time after a notice of intention or proposal is filed, may determine the classes of secured claims appropriate to a proposal.[87] Although the legislation

84 *CCAA*, s 22(2).

85 See *Northland v Excelsior Life*, above note 39 at para 15.

86 *Re Armbro Enterprises Inc*, above note 73.

87 *BIA*, s 50(1.5).

does not provide a similar procedure in respect of unsecured creditors who object to the classification scheme in a proposal, it is likely that a court will permit a similar procedure in respect of unsecured creditors who object to the classification of their claims.

Under the *CCAA*, the onus was on a creditor to bring its objection to the proposed classification of claims before the court. However, in many restructurings the company would apply to court for an order approving the classification scheme. The 2009 amendments have codified this practice. The *CCAA* now provides that the debtor must apply to court for approval of a classification scheme for voting at a meeting.[88]

E. THE TREATMENT OF SHAREHOLDER CLAIMS

1) Shareholder Approval of Fundamental Changes

The *BIA* and the *CCAA* deal only with voting on a plan by creditors, and do not make any provision in respect of shareholders. The *CCAA* provides that the provisions of the Act may be applied together with the provisions of any federal or provincial legislation that authorizes or makes provisions for the sanction of compromises or arrangements between a company and its shareholders.[89] The *BIA* does not contain a comparable provision. Both the *CCAA* and the *BIA* provide that a court may order that the constating instrument be amended to reflect any change that can be lawfully made under federal or provincial law.[90]

The restructuring plan may involve a sale of substantially all the assets to a purchaser. The corporate law that governs the debtor corporation may provide that shareholder approval is required before the transaction can be completed. Alternatively, the restructuring plan may involve a change to the articles of incorporation, an amalgamation, or some other fundamental change that requires the approval of the shareholders. The question that arises is whether shareholder approval is needed to implement the restructuring plan.

If shareholder approval is needed, the shareholders will generally be able to receive some consideration or maintain some participation in the restructured corporation as the price for obtaining their consent to the transaction. If shareholder approval is not needed, the restructuring may

---

88 *CCAA*, s 22(1).

89 *Ibid*, s 42.

90 *Ibid*, s 6(2); *BIA*, s 59(4).

eliminate their claims on the basis that they are of no economic value. The latter approach is the one that has been embraced by the courts.

Many of the Canadian corporation statutes, such as the *Canada Business Corporations Act*,[91] provide that a court may make an order amending a corporation's articles of incorporation in connection with a restructuring under the *CCAA* or the *BIA*. The legislation further provides that shareholders do not have a right of dissent. This permits a court to cancel the existing shares in respect of the restructured company.[92]

Other corporation statutes do not contain similar provisions, and courts have been called upon to decide whether the provisions of the corporation legislation that require shareholder approval of fundamental changes must be satisfied. In *Re Loewen Group Inc*,[93] the court held that the provisions of the corporations statute requiring shareholder approval are inapplicable in cases where the disposition is pursuant to a vesting order issued pursuant to the *CCAA*.

A further issue is whether the same approach can be applied in respect of restructuring proceedings under the *BIA*. This issue was addressed in *Fiber Connections Inc v SVCM Capital Ltd*.[94] The court came to the conclusion that shareholder approval was not required for two reasons. First, a court could resort to the oppression remedy to override the veto power that could otherwise be exercised by a shareholder whose shares have no economic value. Second, a court may draw upon its inherent jurisdiction to make such orders. Although it was acknowledged that there is much less scope for the use of the concept in connection with the more detailed rule-based approach of the *BIA*, the court held that it may be invoked to permit a court to make an order setting aside a unanimous shareholder agreement and amending the share structure of the debtor corporation.

Although courts have not hesitated to eliminate shareholder equity in restructuring proceedings where it is obvious that the interest of shareholders is clearly of no economic value, the same approach should not be applied where there is legitimate uncertainty or disagreement over the going-concern value of the firm. If there is a reasonable possibility that the interests of the shareholders retain some value, the shareholders may legitimately expect to participate in the restructuring.

---

91 RSC 1985, c C-44, s 191. See also Alberta *Business Corporations Act*, RSA 2000, c B-9, s 192; Ontario *Business Corporations Act*, RSO 1990, c B.16, s 186.

92 *Re Stelco Inc* (2006), 17 CBR (5th) 78 (Ont SCJ); *Re Beatrice Foods Inc* (1996), 43 CBR (4th) 10 (Ont Ct Gen Div).

93 (2001), 32 CBR (4th) 54 (Ont SCJ).

94 (2005), 10 CBR (5th) 192 (Ont SCJ).

2) The Treatment of Equity Claims

Shareholders are on the very bottom rung in the scheme of priorities. They are not entitled to anything until the claims of creditors are fully satisfied. Shareholders have attempted to enhance their low status by asserting claims for damages against the corporation for fraud or misrepresentation in connection with the issuance of the shares. Alternatively, they may seek to rescind the contract and recover the money that they paid for the shares in an action for restitution. If successful, the claimant will be able to participate in the restructuring as an unsecured creditor who has an unliquidated claim for damages or for the recovery of money. Shareholders may also seek to cast their claims as unsecured creditor claims if the rights associated with their shares include a right to be paid money in respect of a corporate distribution, such as a right to be paid a dividend, a right of redemption, or a retraction right.

Courts have refused to allow the use of such claims to elevate the priority ranking of shareholders. They have used the doctrine of equitable subordination to prevent the shareholders from participating with the unsecured creditors.[95] The subordination was justified on the basis that this reflects the reasonable expectations of both the shareholders and the creditors. The shareholders assume the risk of loss of such activities and therefore should be denied recovery until the creditors are paid in full. Courts also subordinated shareholder claims for some corporate distributions on the basis that they did not fall within the definition of a claim.[96] The subordination of shareholder claims was not a complete solution. Although subordinated, claims for damages or for the recovery of money were nevertheless regarded as claims under the *BIA* or the *CCAA*. If shareholders were placed in their own class and given the right to vote on the plan, they would obtain the ability to veto it.

The 2009 amendments to the *BIA* and the *CCAA* specifically address this situation. The statutes now contain a definition of an "equity claim."[97] An equity claim covers claims for dividends and other corporate distributions as well as claims for monetary loss connected with the ownership, purchase, or sale of an equity interest or with the rescission of a contract for the purchase or sale of an equity interest. The *BIA*

---

95 *Re Blue Range Resource Corp* (2000), 15 CBR (4th) 169 (Alta QB). And see Chapter 9, Section B(3)(c).

96 *Re Central Capital Corp* (1996), 38 CBR (3d) 1 (Ont CA). However, a claim for a declared dividend was recoverable as a debt. See *Re I Waxman & Sons Ltd*, 2008 CarswellOnt 1245 (SCJ).

97 *BIA*, s 2 "equity claim"; *CCAA*, s 2(1) "equity claim."

and the *CCAA* provide that creditors holding equity claims must be placed in the same class and that the class does not have a right to vote on the plan unless the court orders otherwise.[98] Both the *BIA* and the *CCAA* also provide that a court may not sanction a plan that provides for payment of an equity claim unless it provides that all claims that are not equity claims are to be paid in full before equity claims are paid.[99] The characterization of a claim as an equity claim is not altered by the fact that the claimant obtains a judgment before the commencement of insolvency proceedings.[100] The definition of an equity claim focuses on the nature of the claim rather than the identity of the claimant.[101] Claims by auditors or underwriters against a debtor for contribution and indemnity fall within the definition of equity claims.[102]

F. THIRD-PARTY RELEASES

A plan will afford affected creditors with the rights specified in the plan and the affected creditors will in turn provide a release of their former claims against the debtor. In many instances the creditors will also release their claims against the directors and officers of a debtor corporation. In some cases there is a release of claims against the monitor, chief restructuring officer, and financial advisors.[103] In others, the plan contains even broader releases under which the affected creditors release claims against other third parties that are not directly connected with the debtor or the restructuring. Third-party releases will bind dissenting creditors and therefore the requirements of dual majority voting and court approval provide one degree of protection.[104] A further protective requirement is that courts have held that the release of the claim in question must be justified as part of the compromise or arrangement between the debtor and its creditors in that there must be a reasonable connection between the third-party claim being released and the restructuring achieved by the plan so as to warrant the inclusion

98 *BIA*, s 54.1; *CCAA*, s 22.1.
99 *BIA*, s 60 (1.7); *CCAA*, s 6(8).
100 *Bul River Mineral Corporation (Re)*, 2014 BCSC 1732.
101 *Sino-Forest Corporation (Re)*, 2012 ONCA 816.
102 *Ibid.*
103 *Aveos Fleet Performance Inc/Aveos Fleet Performance aéronautique inc (Arrangement relatif à)*, 2013 QCCS 5924. The release of the monitor was regarded as excessive and not approved.
104 *Metcalfe & Mansfield Alternative Investments II Corp (Re)*, 2008 ONCA 587 [*Metcalfe*].

of the third-party release in the plan.[105] The same criteria has been applied to third-party releases in *BIA* commercial proposals.[106]

Although a court has the power to approve plans that provide releases in respect of fraud, these types of releases will be carefully scrutinized so as not to condone serious civil wrongdoing.[107] The provision may nevertheless be justified when the release is critical to a successful restructuring. In some instances, courts have authorized a limited carve out under which claims based on common law fraud are not released whereas claims based on constructive or equitable fraud are released.[108]

G. APPROVAL BY THE COURT

In order to be binding on the creditors, the court must also approve the plan. The court may not approve a plan if the creditors have rejected it. Under both the *BIA* and *CCAA*, one of the central issues is the plan's fairness and reasonableness. However, the approach under the two statutes is not the same in all respects, so it is necessary to give separate consideration to the formulations that are employed. The fairness requirement under both statutes will be considered under the same heading.

1) Court Approval under the *CCAA*

Before approving or rejecting the plan, the court will consider the report of the trustee or monitor.[109] The *CCAA* provides that a court may sanction a plan that has been approved by the creditors. The *CCAA* does not provide any criteria to assist a court in deciding whether to approve the plan. The relevant considerations have been developed by the courts in a series of decisions dealing with court approval of a plan. The courts have set out the following principles for approving a plan:[110]

- there must be strict compliance with the statutory criteria;
- there must be no unauthorized conduct; and
- the plan must be fair and reasonable.

---

105 *Ibid*; *Sino-Forest Corporation (Re)*, 2012 ONSC 7050; *Bul River Mineral Corporation (Re)*, 2015 BCSC 113.

106 *Kitchener Frame Limited (Re)*, 2012 ONSC 234.

107 *Metcalfe*, above note 104.

108 *Ibid*; *Holley v The Northern Trust Company, Canada*, 2014 ONSC 889.

109 *BIA*, s 59(1); *CCAA*, s 23(1)(i).

110 *Northland v Excelsior Life*, above note 39; *Olympia & York*, above note 22.

The requirement of strict compliance with statutory criteria covers matters such as the insolvency requirement and the requirement that the total claims exceed $5 million. It also means that the correct procedure for the calling of meetings must have been followed and the votes correctly counted.[111] Disputes over whether particular parties had the right to vote or whether they were entitled to vote in a different class are sometimes delayed until the court hearing, and these issues sometimes are rendered moot if the resolution of the dispute does not affect the outcome. The court makes a series of orders under the *CCAA* in respect of a wide variety of matters. Compliance with these orders is of significance, since unauthorized conduct is one of the grounds for refusing to approve a plan.

2) Court Approval under the *BIA*

The *BIA* provides a different set of criteria that are to be applied by a court in deciding whether to approve a proposal. A court is directed to refuse a proposal if:[112]

- the terms of the proposal are unreasonable; or
- the terms of the proposal are not calculated to benefit the general body of creditors.

In addition to these two factors, courts have added the requirement that the proposal must be made in good faith.[113]

The court is also directed to refuse approval of the proposal if one of the facts that would justify a refusal to grant an absolute discharge is established, unless the debtor provides reasonable security for the payment of not less than fifty cents on the dollar. A court may refuse to approve a proposal if it is established that the debtor has committed an offence under the *BIA*. Courts have indicated that, in deciding whether to approve a proposal, the court should consider the interests of the debtor, the interests of the creditors, and the interests of the public in maintaining the integrity of the insolvency system.[114]

---

111 *Re Canadian Airlines Corp*, above note 36 at para 62.

112 *BIA*, s 59(2). See also *Kitchener Frame Limited (Re)*, above note 106.

113 *Magnus One Energy Corp (Re)*, 2009 ABQB 200; *Contech Enterprises Ltd v Vegherb, LLC*, above note 77.

114 *Re Stone* (1976), 22 CBR (NS) 152 (Ont HCJ); *Re WRT Equipment Ltd* (2003), 41 CBR (4th) 288 (Sask QB).

3) Assessing Fairness and Reasonableness

Although the formulation of the tests for court approval under the *CCAA* and the *BIA* differs somewhat, the central question is the same. The court reviews the plan to determine if it is fair and reasonable. A court is not required to approve a plan that has been approved by each class of creditor. However, courts recognize that it is the creditors who bear the economic consequences of the success or failure of the restructuring proceedings, and their evaluation of the situation should not be dispensed with lightly. They also recognize that it is not their role to descend into the negotiating arena and substitute their own business judgment in place of that of the participants.[115] The parties know best what is in their interests, and the court should not second-guess their judgment on the business aspects of the plan. Courts have also indicated that it is appropriate to consider the public interest in deciding whether to approve or reject a plan.[116] Where the plan contemplates the continued operation of the debtor, this factor will generally weigh in favour of court approval of the plan in order to protect the interests of employees, suppliers, customers, and the larger community.

These factors work in favour of court approval of the plan, but they can be outweighed by other factors that justify rejection. The court must be satisfied that the plan is fair and reasonable. Unfairness may arise from the conduct of the debtor. This may occur if the debtor makes misrepresentations to the creditors to induce them to vote in favour of the plan. Unfairness may also arise from the conduct of other creditors. The fairness hearing ensures that dissident creditors who are unwillingly bound to a plan are not abused or unfairly treated by the majority.[117] The fact that a creditor may have voted in favour of a plan does not prevent the creditor from raising an objection to it at the fairness hearing.[118]

a) Procedural Unfairness

Majority approval of a plan by the creditors is undermined if that approval was obtained through unfair means. Here, the focus is on the fairness of the process that was used in developing and voting on the plan rather than on the plan's substantive features. The creditors will not have given a genuine consent to the plan if it is obtained through

---

115 *Olympia & York*, above note 22.

116 *Re Canadian Airlines Corp*, above note 36. And see *Re San Francisco Gifts Ltd*, above note 36 at para 31.

117 *Re Keddy Motor Inns Ltd*, above note 81 at para 49.

118 *Re Eagle Mining Ltd* (1999), 42 OR (3d) 571 (Gen Div).

misrepresentations on significant matters or material non-disclosure of relevant information.[119] The assent can also be vitiated if it has been obtained by secret side deals that benefit some of the creditors.[120] Although the misclassification of creditors is also a species of procedural unfairness, there is an expectation that a creditor who is dissatisfied with the classification scheme will object to it before the fairness hearing.[121]

b) Lesser Recovery than in Liquidation

A plan will not be considered fair or reasonable if a creditor obtains an amount that is less than the creditor would receive on a bankruptcy or other liquidation of the debtor.[122] The participants in restructuring proceedings bargain over the surplus value that is created when bankruptcy is avoided. Although a minority creditor may be forced to accept a plan, that creditor is not required to sacrifice its interest for the benefit of other creditors or stakeholders.

c) Changes in Priority Ranking

Under Chapter 11 of the United States Bankruptcy Code, a court may exercise its power to "cram down" a plan on a dissenting class of creditors. In order to do so, the plan must comply with the "absolute priority rule." This rule is satisfied if the dissenting class is paid in full or if no class of lower-ranking claimants receives anything under the plan.[123]

Neither the power to "cram down" a plan nor the absolute priority rule is a feature of Canadian restructuring law. An affected class of creditors that rejects a plan cannot be bound by it. However, Canadian restructuring law does not demand as high a degree of homogeneity in respect of the rights or interests of creditors within a class. So it is conceivable that some of the creditors within a class may hold different rights or be afforded different treatment under the plan. This creates a greater potential for unfairness within a class of creditors. It is therefore possible that some of the creditors who would normally be entitled to priority in bankruptcy proceedings will be afforded treatment only equal or inferior to that of creditors who have a lower priority.

---

119 *Re Mayer* (1994), 25 CBR (3d) 113 (Ont Ct Gen Div); *Re Mister C's Ltd* (1995), 32 CBR (3d) 242 (Ont Ct Gen Div).

120 See Section C(5), above in this chapter.

121 *Re Global Light Telecommunications Inc* (2004), 2 CBR (5th) 210 (BCSC); *Re Armbro Enterprises Inc*, above note 73.

122 *Re Sumner Co (1984) Ltd* (1987), 64 CBR (NS) 218 (NBQB); *Re Canadian Airlines Corp*, above note 36.

123 See Tabb, *The Law of Bankruptcy*, above note 25 at 854–56.

Courts in Canada have indicated that a plan that unfairly deprives a subclass of creditors of the priority to which they would otherwise have been entitled may result in its rejection.[124] This is not to say that a plan cannot alter the priority ranking that would otherwise apply. The creditors may, for example, vote in favour of a plan that provides that the unsecured creditors are paid in full and the secured creditors receive only partial payment.[125] So long as the secured creditors receive more than they would in a bankruptcy and there is a sufficient commonality of interest among the secured creditors, a dissenting secured creditor will be bound by the vote of the majority. The unfairness arises when the interests of the members of the class or the treatment that they are afforded is not the same, since it is in these situations that the spectre of confiscation or abuse of the minority can arise.

d) Composition of the Vote

Courts often take into consideration the size of the majority vote that approved a plan. Often they identify the fact that the vast majority of creditors voted in favour of the plan as a reason favouring court approval of it. Of course, this will be of little relevance if the favourable vote has been obtained through fraud, misrepresentation, or material non-disclosure. Although a sizeable majority vote in favour of a plan is often influential, the fact that a plan has been passed by a thin majority will not cause a court to reject it on this ground alone. The thinness of a majority vote may, however, be used to buttress some other ground for rejection.

e) Unlikely to Resolve Financial Crisis

In reviewing a plan, the court is not limited to considering the interests of existing creditors. A plan that is unlikely to succeed places future creditors at risk and undermines the integrity of the insolvency system. A court may refuse to approve a plan if it is of the opinion that the plan will not resolve the insolvency crisis faced by the debtor.[126] The report of the trustee or monitor will usually assist the court in making this determination.

---

124 *Re Woodward's Ltd*, above note 67; *Canadian Bed & Breakfast Registry Ltd* (1986), 65 CBR (NS) 115 (BCSC).

125 *Citibank Canada v Chase Manhattan Bank of Canada*, above note 74.

126 *Re McNamara* (1984), 53 CBR (NS) 240 (Ont HCJ); *Re Booth* (1998), 4 CBR (4th) 45 (Ont Ct Gen Div).

H. THE LEGAL EFFECT OF APPROVAL OR REJECTION

When a plan has been approved by the creditors and by a court, it binds every creditor in each class of creditor that voted in favour of it and also binds the debtor. It does not bind creditors who are not covered by the plan (unaffected creditors) or classes or creditors that voted against it. Upon court approval, the obligations owed by the debtor to affected creditors are discharged and replaced with the obligations that are provided for in the plan.

Under the *BIA*, a refusal of a proposal by the unsecured creditors results in an automatic bankruptcy of the debtor.[127] If the unsecured creditors are divided into classes, each class must approve the proposal. If they do not, the proposal is rejected and an automatic bankruptcy ensues. Rejection of a proposal by a class of secured creditors does not have the same effect. If one or more classes of secured creditors vote against approval of the proposal, the members of the dissenting class of secured creditors are treated as unaffected creditors.[128] A refusal of a proposal by a court also results in an automatic bankruptcy of the debtor.[129]

The *CCAA* does not provide for an automatic bankruptcy on refusal of the plan by the creditors. Nor does the *CCAA* contain a provision for the automatic termination of the stay of proceedings upon a refusal of the plan by the creditors. The creditors will therefore need to bring an application before the court to terminate the stay of proceedings or else wait until the designated period for the stay of proceedings expires. Thereafter, the creditors may apply for a bankruptcy order or otherwise enforce their claims against the debtor or the debtor's assets.

I. POST-APPROVAL DEFAULT

A plan that has been approved by the creditors and by the court may nevertheless fail to rescue the debtor from insolvency. The treatment of post-approval default under the *CCAA* is relatively straightforward. Upon approval of the plan, the previous obligations are replaced by new obligations. A default under these new obligations will give the creditors the normal enforcement remedies associated with those rights. If

127 *BIA*, s 57.
128 *Ibid*, s 62(2).
129 *Ibid*, s 61(2).

the financial crisis is not alleviated, the debtor may attempt to initiate a second round of restructuring proceedings.

The position under the *BIA* is more complicated. Proposals that are made in respect of smaller firms or individuals are more likely to involve terms that require future performance. The performance terms may involve putting a lease into good standing or making future payments in accordance with a schedule of payments set out in the proposal. The *BIA* provides a system for the judicial annulment of a proposal. The annulment of a proposal is significant since it results in the automatic bankruptcy of the debtor.[130]

A court may annul a proposal if there has been a default under the provisions of a proposal, if it appears to the court that the proposal cannot continue without injustice[131] or undue delay, if the approval of the court was obtained by fraud, or if the debtor has been convicted of a bankruptcy offence.[132] The trustee must inform the creditors and the official receiver of a default in the performance of any provision in a proposal unless the default is waived or it is remedied within thirty days.[133] The power to annul a proposal is discretionary and a court is not required to order an annulment on a default in performance. It is not necessary for creditors to demonstrate that they would receive any benefit on a bankruptcy of the debtor.[134]

An annulment of a proposal does not affect the validity of any sale, disposition of property, or payment duly made or anything duly done under or in pursuance of the proposal.[135] Creditors affected by the proposal as well as post-filing creditors rank equally in the subsequent bankruptcy, and the affected creditors may prove for the original value of their claims less any amounts received under the proposal.[136] If the proposal provides that post-filing creditors will be given priority in respect of their claims, this provision is effective even if the proposal is annulled.[137] If the proposal provides for the granting of a security interest in favour of pre-proposal creditors and does not subordinate it to creditors whose claims arise thereafter, the security remains valid

130 *Ibid*, s 63(4).

131 See *Re Garritty* (2006), 21 CBR (5th) 237 (Alta QB).

132 *BIA*, ss 63(1) and (3).

133 *Ibid*, s 62.1; *Bankruptcy and Insolvency General Rules*, above note 7, s 93.

134 *Re Northlands Cafe Inc* (1996), 44 CBR (3d) 164 (Alta QB); *544553 BC Ltd v Sunshine Coast Mechanical Contractors Inc* (2000), 18 CBR (4th) 153 (BCCA).

135 *BIA*, s 63(2).

136 *In Re Lipson* (1924), 4 CBR 432 (Ont CA); *Re J LeBar Seafoods Inc* (1981), 38 CBR (NS) 64 (Ont HCJ).

137 *Re Thoun* (1925), 7 CBR 251 (Ont HCJ); *Re Eco Superwood BC Ltd* (1996), 43 CBR (3d) 242 (BCSC).

following an annulment of a proposal and is effective in giving the pre-filing creditors priority over the subsequent creditors on annulment of the proposal.[138]

FURTHER READINGS

BAIRD, D, & D BERNSTEIN. "Absolute Priority, Valuation Uncertainty, and the Reorganization Bargain" (2006) 115 *Yale Law Journal* 1930

CHARLES, SK. "Trading Claims in Chapter 11 Cases: Legal Issues Confronting the Postpetition Investor" (1991) *Annual Survey of American Law* 261

LIEB, R. "Vultures Beware: Risks of Purchasing Claims against a Chapter 11 Debtor" (1993) 48 *Business Lawyer* 915

LOPUCKI, L, & G TRIANTIS. "A Systems Approach to Comparing US and Canadian Reorganization of Financially Distressed Companies" in J Ziegel, ed, *Current Developments in International and Comparative Corporate Insolvency Law* (Oxford: Clarendon Press, 1994) 109

MACPARLAND, N. "How Close Is Too Close? The Treatment of Related Party Claims in Canadian Restructurings" in Janis P Sarra, ed, *Annual Review of Insolvency Law, 2004* (Toronto: Thomson Carswell, 2005) 355

QUINN, JJ. "Corporate Reorganization and Strategic Behaviour: An Economic Analysis of Canadian Insolvency Law and Recent Proposals for Reform" (1985) 23 *Osgoode Hall Law Journal* 1

SARRA, J. "From Subordination to Parity: An International Comparison of Equity Securities Claims in Insolvency Proceedings" (2007) 16 *International Insolvency Review* 181

138 *Re Model Craft Hobbies Ltd* (1981), 39 CBR (NS) 97 (Ont HCJ).

PART THREE

RECEIVERSHIP LAW

CHAPTER 17

THE FOUNDATIONS OF RECEIVERSHIP LAW

A. A SHORT HISTORY OF RECEIVERSHIP LAW

Receivership law emerged from two different sources. One body of substantive principle governed court-appointed receivers, while a different body of law governed privately appointed receivers. More recently, federal and provincial governments have passed statutes that regulate receiverships. These statutes do not codify receivership law, and so it remains necessary to delve into the two original bodies of law. However, the statutes have significantly altered the legal landscape. They set out a common set of rules that applies to both types of receiverships. Furthermore, the impact of these new statutory rules has been one-sided. The rules governing privately appointed receivers have been modified to a much greater degree than the rules governing court-appointed receivers. As a consequence, there is a now greater similarity in the legal rules and principles that govern these two types of receiverships.

There have been two recent fundamental shifts in the law and practice relating to receiverships in Canada. The first has been the dwindling use of the privately appointed receiver. The other has been the emergence of the national receiver appointed under the *BIA*. When receiverships first began to be widely used in Canada in the 1980s, the privately appointed receiver was very much the norm and the court appointed receiver was exceptional.[1] This no longer holds true. The 2009 *BIA* amendments permit the court appointment of a receiver who has the authority to act throughout Canada (a practice that had started through the appointment of interim receivers under the *BIA*), and it is now the case that most receivers are appointed under this provision.

1) The Historical Bifurcation of Receivership Law

The courts of equity provided a remedy in the form of the appointment of a receiver to protect the interests of a secured creditor. The court-appointed receiver would take possession of the property, collect the rents and profits, and apply them against the secured obligation. The courts of equity provided the remedy in other contexts as well, such as disputes over partnership property or in cases where ordinary judgment remedies were inadequate.[2] Under this regime, the receiver is appointed by the court and is accountable to it. The receiver does not act as agent for either the secured party or the debtor and does not obey their directions.[3]

In order to produce a quicker and less expensive procedure, debtors would appoint a receiver at the request of a secured creditor. Later, it became common for the parties to stipulate that the secured creditor would appoint the receiver and that the receiver would act as the debtor's agent. The secured creditor was viewed as acting as agent for the debtor in making the appointment of the receiver.[4] This led to the creation of the privately appointed receiver, also referred to as an instrument-appointed receiver, a document-appointed receiver, or an out-of-court-appointed receiver. Whereas the substantive law governing court-appointed receivers was largely derived from principles of equity, the substantive law governing privately appointed receivers was largely derived from principles of agency and contract law.

As industrialization progressed, it became common for lenders to take security on the entire undertaking of an operating business. In these circumstances, it was not enough simply to appoint a receiver to collect income and rents generated from land. Increasingly, commercial

---

1 P Farkas, "Why Are There So Many Court-Appointed Receiverships?" (2003) 20 *National Insolvency Review* 37.

2 Since these do not involve insolvency proceedings, nothing further will be said about these other types of court-appointed receivers.

3 *Bacup Corporation v Smith* (1890), 44 Ch D 395; *Parsons v Sovereign Bank of Canada*, [1913] AC 130 (PC).

4 The historical development of the privately appointed receiver is described in *Gaskell v Gosling*, [1896] 1 QB 669 at 691–92, Rigby LJ.

documents provided for the appointment of a person who had the power of management over the business in addition to the powers of a receiver. In making receivership orders, courts would similarly provide for the appointment of a receiver-manager. This practice has become so dominant that it is rare that a receiver is not also given a power of management, so much so that the term "receiver" usually denotes persons who have the power of a receiver and manager alike.[5] This usage will be adopted here, but it should be kept in mind that the document or court order must specifically confer on the receiver the power to manage the business in order for the receiver to exercise the powers of a receiver-manager.

The division between privately appointed receivers and court-appointed receivers remains highly relevant. Although both types of receiverships have the same objectives, there are many important differences in the substantive law that governs these two types of receiverships.

2) Overlapping Legislative Regimes

For many years, the basic division between the court-appointed receiver and the privately appointed receiver prevailed in Canada, and there was very little in the way of legislation that modified this position. Historically, a strong case could be made that receivership law was primarily a remedy of a secured creditor and did not provide a collective insolvency proceeding. This view is no longer tenable in Canada. The legislative regulation of receiverships has given a number of important rights to the debtor and to other interested parties. Although receivership law continues to be heavily geared to the enforcement of a secured creditor's security interest, it contains a number of elements that one would expect to find in collective insolvency proceedings.

During the 1970s and 1980s, the use of receiverships to protect and enforce the rights of secured creditors became increasingly common. However, the greater reliance on the remedy was accompanied by concerns over its effect on other interested parties. The debtors as well as the other creditors of the debtor were largely left in the dark concerning the activities of the receiver.[6] They had little ability to obtain any information or an accounting from the privately appointed receiver.

---

5 Provincial PPSA defines "receiver" as including a receiver-manager. See, for example, *Personal Property Security Act*, RSA 2000, c P-7, s 1(1)(nn) "receiver."

6 See Canada, Advisory Committee on Bankruptcy and Insolvency, *Proposed* Bankruptcy Act *Amendments: Report of the Advisory Committee on Bankruptcy and Insolvency* (Ottawa: Advisory Committee on Bankruptcy and Insolvency, 1986) at 37 [Colter Report].

There was also a concern that the privately appointed receiver had the interests only of the secured creditor at heart, and that the legitimate interests of all other interested persons were liable to be sacrificed. During this period, legislation was passed that gave creditors greater access to information and that made receivers more accountable to other interested parties for their actions.

Unfortunately, the legislative response has been highly fractured. Instead of a single legislative solution, there are several different layers of statutes that enact similar but not identical rules. The first legislative intervention was taken in federal business corporation legislation[7] and was followed by a similar approach adopted in many provincial business corporation statutes.[8] Although the majority of receiverships involved corporate debtors, the legislation did not apply if the debtor was not a corporation governed by the federal or provincial business corporation statutes. In order to remedy this deficiency, personal property security legislation provided for statutory regulation of receiverships.[9] These provisions applied to all kinds of entities, including sole proprietorships and partnerships.[10]

In the 1992 amendments to the *BIA*, federal provisions regulating receiverships were added to the *BIA* for the first time. The provisions do not apply to all receiverships, as they are restricted to receiverships in which the debtor is a bankrupt or insolvent person.[11] This limitation was presumably included in order to ensure that the provision would not exceed Parliament's power to enact laws respecting bankruptcy and insolvency.

Although the statutes were passed in order to redress serious problems associated with the appointment by secured creditors of privately appointed receivers, it has given rise to two problems. The first is that it is often difficult to navigate through the fractured and overlapping legislative provisions, since a receivership may attract the operation of several different legislative regimes. The second difficulty is that no Canadian

---

7 *Canada Business Corporations Act*, RSC 1985, c C-44, ss 94–101.

8 See, for example, *Business Corporations Act*, RSA 2000, c B-9, ss 93–100. The Ontario business corporations statute does not contain equivalent provisions regulating receiverships.

9 See, for example, *Personal Property Security Act*, RSA 2000, c P-7, s 65. The Ontario Act has a less extensive set of provisions regulating receivers. See *Personal Property Security Act*, RSO 1990, c P.10, s 60.

10 In Saskatchewan, the receivership provisions in the business corporations statute were removed so that the only provincial regime governing receiverships is that set out in the *Personal Property Security Act, 1993*, SS 1993, c P-6.2, s 64.

11 *BIA*, ss 243(1) & (2).

court to date has provided a detailed discussion of the effect of the legislative provisions on the status, rights, and obligations of receivers.

3) The Expansion of the Interim Receivership

The 1992 amendments to the *BIA* provided for the appointment of an interim receiver under the *BIA*. The functions of an interim receiver were likely intended to be of limited scope and duration and were included in order to prevent the prejudice that might otherwise be caused by the imposition of a new statutory notice period that was also added in 1992. These amendments require a secured creditor who intends to enforce a security interest against substantially all the assets to give to the debtor a notice of intention. The secured creditor cannot enforce the security until a ten-day period has elapsed.[12] This gives the debtor the opportunity to commence restructuring proceedings, which would have the effect of staying the enforcement remedies of the secured creditor. A secured creditor may be concerned that the debtor may dissipate the assets during this period. In order to protect the interests of the secured creditor, the court is given the power to appoint an interim receiver.[13]

Although the drafters of these provisions likely intended them to have a limited role, the courts took a different tack. The legislation provided that, in addition to taking possession and control over the debtor's assets, the court could take such other action as it considered advisable.[14] This was given a very wide interpretation by the courts. Courts took the view that they could "enlist the services of an interim receiver to do not only what 'justice dictates' but also what 'practicality demands.'"[15] Orders were granted that provided for a wide stay of proceedings against third parties, borrowing powers secured by a priority charge, protection from environmental liability and successor liability, the power to assign the debtor into bankruptcy, and the power to terminate contracts.[16] Interim receivers were appointed by courts and given broad powers to manage the business as well as selling the business as a going concern and distributing the proceeds to the creditors according to their priority

---

12 *Ibid*, s 244.

13 *Ibid*, s 47(1).

14 This language was originally contained in *BIA*, s 47(2) but was deleted when the 2009 amendments were proclaimed into force.

15 *Canada (Minister of Indian Affairs & Northern Development) v Curragh Inc* (1994), 27 CBR (3d) 148 at para 16 (Ont Ct Gen Div).

16 See P Macdonald & B Harrison, "Receivership Orders — Where Do We Go From Here?" (2004) 21 *National Insolvency Review* 65.

ranking.[17] In other words, interim receivers were given the same types of powers that were ordinarily granted to court-appointed receivers.

One of the reasons for conferring such wide powers on interim receivers was that it effectively gave rise to a national receivership. Prior to this, receivers were appointed pursuant to provincial law and it was necessary to seek the assistance of courts of other provinces to give effect to the order there. The availability of a national receivership meant that an order had full force and effect in every Canadian province and territory.

The growth of the interim receivership had anomalous effects. Suppliers who provided goods to the debtor were ordinarily able to exercise their right to repossess thirty-day goods as against the debtor's trustee in bankruptcy or a receiver. However, the definition of receiver used in this provision did not include a court that was exercising its jurisdiction in bankruptcy.[18] This meant that a supplier could not repossess thirty-day goods if an interim receiver were appointed but could do so if a receiver were appointed pursuant to the court's ordinary jurisdiction.[19] It also meant that none of the statutory provisions in the *BIA* that governed the conduct of receivers applied to interim receivers. For example, the provision that required receivers to act in a commercially reasonable manner[20] would not apply to an interim receiver. An interim receiver was also exempt from the notification and reporting obligations that were imposed on other court-appointed receivers.

4) Judicial Scrutiny of Overreaching Powers

The growing use of the interim receivership was accompanied by another phenomenon. The interim receivership orders that were granted by courts conferred extensive powers on the receiver and also purported to exempt the receiver from liability pursuant to employment

17 *Ibid*. But see *Re Big Sky Living Inc* (2002), 37 CBR (4th) 42 (Alta QB), in which the court at para 8 indicated that the "section does not appear to contemplate that the interim receiver will actually carry on the business of the debtor." The point was not pursued on account of the lack of opposition on this issue.

18 *BIA*, s 243(1). The section defined "court" as a court that was not exercising its bankruptcy jurisdiction. The provision was changed in the 2009 amendments so that the receivership provisions now govern receivers who are appointed under the *BIA* as well as receivers who are appointed by courts not exercising their bankruptcy jurisdiction.

19 *Bruce Agra Foods Inc v Everfresh Beverages Inc (Interim Receiver of)* (1996), 45 CBR (3d) 169 (Ont Ct Gen Div); *Harris Trust & Savings Bank v Anicom Multimedia Wiring Systems Inc* (2001), 24 CBR (4th) 203 (Ont SCJ).

20 *BIA*, s 247.

legislation and environmental legislation. This practice was given an abrupt jolt following the decision of Justice Slatter in *Re Big Sky Living Inc*.[21] The secured creditor had given the debtor a notice of intention to enforce its security and also applied *ex parte* for the appointment of an interim receiver. Justice Slatter agreed that an appointment of an interim receiver was necessary for the protection of the creditors, but he was of the opinion that many of the powers that were requested went far beyond what was necessary to protect the creditors, and in some instances went beyond the power of the court to grant. He was concerned that the proposed order detrimentally affected the rights of persons who had not been given notice of the proceedings. He was also concerned that the order was "legislative" in nature, since it purported to immunize the receiver from liabilities well beyond the protections provided in the *BIA*.

Although some Ontario insolvency lawyers expressed the opinion that the *Big Sky* decision might be limited to Alberta, this view was simply untenable. Interim receiverships are national in scope and therefore any future Ontario decision would need to consider the matters discussed in the case. Subsequent cases from Ontario endorsed the view that "a draft order that gives the receiver extensive powers, while at the same time cloaking it with immunity from responsibilities to parties who are not before the court, can no longer be sanctioned."[22]

5) The Development of Template Receivership Orders

Uncertainty over the legitimate scope of receivership orders provided the impetus for the creation of template receivership orders. This initiative was designed to make it easier for insolvency practitioners to choose the types of provisions to include in draft receivership orders. The template receivership orders also made it easier for judges to determine whether the often-lengthy draft orders contained unusual provisions that required special scrutiny. In Ontario, a subcommittee of the Commercial List User's Committee developed a standard-form receivership order together with an explanatory note.[23] The template order provides a starting point, and it remains possible to add or delete provisions in order to meet the special circumstances of the case at hand. However, proposed changes are to be brought to the attention of

---

21 Above note 17.

22 *GMAC Commercial Credit Corp - Canada v TCT Logistics Inc* (2004), 48 CBR (4th) 256 at para 62 (Ont CA), Feldman J, rev'd on other grounds, [2006] 2 SCR 123.

23 See online: www.ontariocourts.ca/scj/practice/practice-directions/toronto/#Commercial_List_Forms_including_Model_Orders.

the court by blacklining the additions or striking through the deletions. Committees in Alberta, British Columbia, and Saskatchewan have developed similar template receivership orders.

The template receivership orders involved the appointment of an interim receiver pursuant to the *BIA* as well as the appointment of a court-appointed receiver pursuant to provincial or federal statute. The latter appointment ensured that the various statutory regimes that regulated receivers were brought into operation. This meant that the receiver had to observe the statutory reporting and notification requirements. In addition, suppliers who had a right to repossess thirty-day goods were able to exercise this right in respect of receivers who were appointed pursuant to a template receivership order. This eliminated the anomaly of operating under different substantive rules where an interim receiver was appointed.

6) Liability Concerns and the Substitutability of Insolvency Regimes

Despite the wide-reaching powers that were given to court-appointed receivers, insolvency professionals who acted as receivers became concerned about the potential liability under successor employer legislation.[24] Some courts handled this by making a declaration in the order appointing an interim receiver that the receiver shall not be deemed or considered to be a successor employer. However, the Ontario Court of Appeal in *GMAC Commercial Credit Corp - Canada v TCT Logistics Inc*[25] held that only the labour relations board had jurisdiction to determine who was a successor employer. The declaration in the court order was therefore of no effect. Under the *BIA* it is necessary to obtain leave of the court before bringing action against an interim receiver.[26] The caselaw had established the principle that the threshold for obtaining leave was relatively light since it was designed to screen out claims that were frivolous or vexatious or that did not disclose a cause of action.[27] The Ontario Court of Appeal held that the court may legitimately go beyond this role in respect of claims arising out of successor employer legislation and may consider factors such as any detrimental effect on the maximization of stakeholder value.

---

24 See R Davis, "From *St. Mary's Paper* to *TCT Logistics*: The Fate of Receivers in a Constitutional Law Battlefield" (2005) 42 *Canadian Business Law Journal* 1.

25 Above note 22 (Ont CA).

26 *BIA*, s 215.

27 *Mancini (Trustee of) v Falconi* (1989), 76 CBR (NS) 90 (Ont HCJ), aff'd (1993), 61 OAC 332 (CA).

On appeal to the Supreme Court of Canada, the Court agreed with the Ontario Court of Appeal that a bankruptcy court does not have jurisdiction to decide whether an interim receiver is a successor employer.[28] A majority of the Court disagreed with the Ontario Court of Appeal and held that the leave provisions were designed to protect the interim receiver from well-founded litigation, and that it was not legitimate for a court to use these provisions to pursue broader bankruptcy objectives in exercising the power to withhold leave.

During the period in which this litigation was ongoing, the concern over potential liability of the receiver under successor employee legislation resulted in a decrease in the use of the receivership. In many instances, liquidation proceedings that would ordinarily be conducted through receivership proceedings were instead carried out through restructuring proceedings.[29] The 2009 amendments have attempted to eliminate these concerns over potential liability by expressly providing that a trustee or receiver is not personally liable for any liability, including that as a successor employer, that exists before the appointment of the trustee or receiver or that is calculated by reference to a time period prior to the appointment.[30]

7) The National Receiver and Other Legislative Reform

The 2009 amendments to the *BIA* have produced a further evolution in Canadian receivership law. The interim receiver provisions were changed in order to make it clear that an interim receiver may be appointed for only a relatively short period of time. The appointment cannot extend beyond thirty days after the order is made, unless the court specifies a longer period.[31] The appointment will also come to an end if a court-appointed receiver, privately appointed receiver, or trustee in bankruptcy takes possession of the debtor's property. The powers that can be exercised by an interim receiver have been more precisely defined to include the power to take conservatory measures and the power to dispose summarily of assets that are perishable or likely to

---

28 Above note 22 (SCC). On the implications of the decision see R Davis, "The Way Forward: Policy Implications of the Supreme Court Decision in *TCT Logistics*" (2007) 44 *Canadian Business Law Journal* 357; JC Carhart, "The Decision of the Supreme Court of Canada in *TCT Logistics* and the Future of Receiverships in Canada" (2007) 44 *Canadian Business Law Journal* 376.

29 P Macdonald & B Harrison, "Receivership Orders — Where Do We Go from Here?" (2004) 21 *National Insolvency Review* 65 at 73.

30 *BIA*, s 14.06(1.2).

31 *Ibid*, s 47(1).

depreciate rapidly in value.[32] The discretion to make such orders as the court considered advisable has been eliminated. As a result, an interim receiver can no longer be used to dispose of the business as a going concern, and the appointment of an interim receiver is available only as a temporary measure to protect the assets until a trustee or receiver can take over possession of the assets.

Instead of using an interim receiver as a means of appointing a receiver who can operate nationally, the amendments give the bankruptcy courts the power to appoint a national receiver. The court may give the receiver the power to take possession of the debtor's property, exercise control over the debtor's business, and take any other action that the court thinks advisable.[33] This gives the court the ability to make the same wide-ranging orders that it formerly made in respect of interim receivers, including the power to sell the debtor's property out of the ordinary course of business by way of a going-concern sale or a break-up sale of the assets. A court is directed not to appoint a receiver in respect of a debtor who has been given a notice of intention to enforce until the ten-day notice period has expired, unless the debtor consents to an earlier appointment or the court considers it appropriate to do so.[34] If the secured creditor is concerned that the debtor may dissipate the assets, the secured creditor may seek the appointment of an interim receiver.[35] A receiver who is appointed under the *BIA* may also be given the benefit of a priority charge on the assets of the business in respect of the receiver's claim for fees or disbursement.[36]

The *BIA* now provides that the application is to be made in a court having jurisdiction in the judicial district of the locality of the debtor.[37] There was no similar restriction in the former *BIA* provision governing the appointment of an interim receiver. As a result, applications for the appointment of interim receivers were sometimes brought in jurisdictions other than the location where the debtor had its principal place of business. Although the ability to do so was convenient for the creditor (usually a large financial institution) who brought the application, it was potentially prejudicial to other smaller claimants who were unable to participate in the proceedings because of the higher cost. The legislation also imposes a new qualification requirement on both court-

32 *Ibid*, s 47(2).
33 *Ibid*, s 243(1).
34 *Ibid*, s 243(1.1).
35 *Ibid*, s 47.
36 *Ibid*, ss 243(6)–(7). The court is permitted to do so only if secured parties who would be materially affected by the order have been notified.
37 *Ibid*, s 243(5).

appointed and privately appointed receivers by providing that only a trustee may be appointed to act as a receiver.[38]

The legislative reforms may result in a re-evaluation of the template receivership orders that are currently in use. These orders adopted the practice of concurrent appointments under the *BIA* and under provincial law. This was done in order to bring into operation the *BIA* provisions that regulate receiverships. It is no longer necessary to resort to concurrent appointments to achieve this result, and it is possible that the practice will disappear in favour of a single national appointment under the *BIA*.[39]

8) The National Receiver and Federal Paramountcy

The creation of a national receiver has given rise to a constitutional issue. Now that receivers are appointed pursuant to a federal statute, it can be argued that provincial legislation that is inconsistent with the receiver's powers are rendered inoperative through the constitutional principle of federal paramountcy. This matter was considered by the Saskatchewan Court of Appeal in *Lemare Lake Logging Ltd v 3L Cattle Company Ltd*,[40] and has been appealed to the Supreme Court of Canada.[41] Provincial legislation in Saskatchewan provides that a secured creditor who wishes to enforce against land must give notice, participate in a mediation and review process, and may apply to court for permission to commence foreclosure proceedings only after the expiry of 150 days following the completion of the mediation process. Provincial law is inconsistent with federal law in two situations: (1) if dual compliance is impossible; and (2) if provincial law frustrates the purpose of the federal law. The Saskatchewan Court of Appeal held that although dual compliance was possible, the provincial law frustrated the purpose of the federal receivership provisions by dramatically increasing the ten-day notice period provided by the *BIA*, and by layering new criteria for the granting of a receivership order.

The federal receivership provisions have no counterpart to section 11 of the *CCAA* that permits a court to override provincial or federal legislation. The court therefore does not have the power to override

38 *Ibid*, s 243(4). As well, a court can appoint a trustee only as an interim receiver. See *BIA*, s 47(1).

39 See Chapter 18, Section C(2).

40 2014 SKCA 35.

41 Appeal to SCC heard and reserved 21 May 2015.

provincial legislation that requires the consent of encumbrancers in order to register property as a condominium.[42]

9) The Dwindling Use of the Privately Appointed Receiver

There are several reasons for the dwindling use of the privately appointed receiver in Canada. The privately appointed receiver was initially favoured over a court appointment because of the reduced cost, the speediness of the process, and the fact that receivers owed a duty primarily to the secured creditor who was responsible for the appointment. Although greater costs are associated with a court appointment, several of the other advantages have been diminished. Federal legislation has imposed a ten-day notice period before a receiver can be appointed. Provincial legislation has imposed significantly greater duties on the privately appointed receiver. Moreover, court appointment has a number of advantages. Court supervision provides the receiver a greater degree of comfort that the receiver's decisions will not be challenged after the fact, and also provides a convenient venue for the resolution of disputes or the seeking of directions. As well, a court appointment may be the best option when disposing of land or when dealing with businesses that operate in different provinces or different countries. A vesting order also provides prospective purchasers with a stronger assurance that they obtained good title to the assets.

B. THE OBJECTIVES OF RECEIVERSHIP LAW

1) Replacing Inefficient Management

Secured creditors take security on the debtor's assets for a number of reasons. They do so in order to ensure that their claims will have priority over those of other creditors once the debtor's assets are disposed of and the proceeds are available for distribution among the creditors. However, this is not the only advantage of obtaining a security interest in the debtor's assets. A security interest prevents the debtor from selling or disposing of the collateral outside the ordinary course of business without the authorization of the secured creditor. A security interest also gives the secured creditor the right to enforce the security interest in the event of a default by the debtor. This permits a secured

---

42 *Railside Developments Ltd (Re)*, 2010 NSSC 13.

creditor to enforce the security interest through seizure and sale of the collateral, and this right is not affected by a bankruptcy of the debtor.

In addition to these rights, a secured creditor who takes a security interest in all of the debtor's present and after-acquired assets may be able to exercise a special kind of control right through the appointment of a receiver. The appointment of a receiver terminates the managerial powers of the current managers of the business, and the receiver will take over the operation of the business. Receivership proceedings therefore provide a means by which a secured creditor can quickly move to replace the managers of a financially distressed business with more competent management. This is particularly important if the managers are acting fraudulently or if they are engaging in more risky ventures in the hope that their gamble will pay off and lift the firm out of the financial crisis that it faces.

A secured creditor does not obtain a direct right to take control or manage the business through the appointment of a receiver. Rather, the control right merely gives the secured creditor the right to remove the existing managers and substitute a receiver in their place. If the secured creditor attempts to go further and to give directions to the receiver, the secured creditor risks becoming liable for any negligent acts or omissions of the receiver.[43]

2) Enforcement of the Secured Party's Security Interest

A secured creditor who has taken a security interest in the entire undertaking of the debtor can employ the receivership as a means of enforcing its security interest in the collateral. The invocation of receivership proceedings gives the secured party the ability to utilize the services of an experienced insolvency professional. The persons who act as receivers are qualified to act as trustees in bankruptcy, and the individuals who serve in these roles have an expertise in conducting liquidations of financially distressed businesses. Because the receiver takes control over management, the receiver will gain access to the debtor's inside information concerning its assets and its customers. This will make it easier for the receiver to enforce the security interest against the collateral.

---

43 *American Express International Banking Corp v Hurley*, [1985] 3 All ER 564 (QBD).

3) Facilitating Going-Concern Sales of the Business

The use of a receivership permits the secured creditor to maximize its recovery in the event of a debtor's default under the security agreement. An ordinary seizure of assets by a secured creditor will generally disrupt the continuity of the business operations. The assets will be sold piecemeal to buyers, with the result that the secured creditor will recover the break-up or liquidation value of the assets rather than their value as part of a going concern. The use of receivership proceedings is a method by which enforcement of the secured creditor's security interest does not result in a discontinuity in the business operations, thereby allowing a sale of the business as a going concern. It is not always feasible for the assets to be sold to a buyer as a going concern. In such cases, receivership proceedings may provide a convenient method for holding closing-out sales.

C. THE FUNDAMENTAL PRINCIPLES OF RECEIVERSHIP LAW

1) Title to the Debtor's Assets Does Not Vest in the Receiver

The appointment of a receiver does not have any effect on the debtor's ownership of its assets. Unlike a bankruptcy, there is no automatic vesting of the debtor's assets in the receiver. The receiver therefore has no right to bring an action in his or her own name in respect of a debt owed to the debtor. The action is properly brought by the receiver in the name of the debtor, since the cause of action does not vest in the receiver.[44]

2) Control over Management Is Transferred to the Receiver

Upon the appointment of a receiver, the former managers of the business cease to have powers of management over the business. The receiver obtains control over the business and exercises the power of management in respect of the activities of the business. This conferral of managerial power occurs by virtue of the court order in the case of a court-appointed receiver and by virtue of a contractual provision in

---

44 *Franco Belgium Investment Co v Dubuc*, [1918] 2 WWR 684 (Alta SC).

the security agreement in the case of a privately appointed receiver. The appointment of a receiver does not terminate the appointment of the corporate directors. The directors remain in office, but they cannot exercise their powers until such time as the receiver is discharged.[45]

It is not uncommon to have concurrent receivership proceedings and bankruptcy proceedings. This is usually arranged in order for the secured creditor to obtain a more favourable priority status as against other competing interests.[46] This practice may have unintended consequences. The invocation of bankruptcy results in the vesting of the assets in the trustee. A contractual provision in a security agreement that deems a privately appointed receiver to be the agent of the debtor loses its effect upon this event.[47] This means that a receiver no longer acts as agent of the debtor in carrying on business. Instead, the receiver becomes personally liable on new contracts. Although court-appointed receivers ordinarily incur liability in a personal capacity, this results in a significant change in status in relation to privately appointed receivers.

3) Power to Dispose of the Assets

A receiver has two different types of powers. The first is the receiver's power of management and control over the business, which is discussed above. The second is the receiver's right to enforce the security interest through sale of the assets. These two powers can overlap. In carrying out the management of the business, a receiver may sell or transfer some of the assets to third parties. This often will take the form of sales of inventory to customers and payments to creditors, both as part of the ordinary course of business of the debtor. In carrying out these types of transactions, the receiver has no greater ability to transfer good title to the transferee than that possessed by the debtor.

A receiver may also sell the debtor's assets outside of the ordinary course of business. In a court-appointed receivership, the sale process is supervised by the court and the transfer is completed through a vesting order. In a private appointment, the receiver enforces the secured creditor's security interest, and this will confer a good title in the assets to the buyer free of junior security interests and lower ranking encumbrances. The receiver's right to dispose of the assets is unaffected by a bankruptcy of the debtor.

---

45 *Canada Business Corporations Act*, above note 7, s 96.

46 See Chapter 5, Section B(6).

47 *Gosling v Gaskell*, [1897] AC 575 (HL).

4) Distribution of the Proceeds

Unlike a trustee in bankruptcy or a liquidator, the receiver does not act as a representative of the creditors. The primary duty of the receiver is to dispose of the assets and pay the proceeds to the secured creditor after paying out higher-ranking claims that are secured against the assets. For the most part, the priorities are determined according to ordinary non-insolvency law principles. However, in recent years there has been a growing practice of making the bankruptcy priority rules applicable to receiverships. A supplier's right to recover thirty-day goods,[48] the security in favour of suppliers of agricultural products,[49] the charge on land that secures environmental damage,[50] and the charges that secure unpaid wages[51] and pension contributions[52] apply to bankruptcy proceedings and receivership proceedings.

In the event that there is a surplus after disposition, the receiver is not responsible for the proof and valuation of claims or the distribution to the creditors. The usual practice would be to initiate a bankruptcy in order to dispose of any surplus. The insolvency professional who has acted as receiver will often perform the role of trustee, since he or she will be familiar with the circumstances of the insolvent debtor.

5) The Court's Supervisory Role

The privately appointed receiver, unlike the court-appointed receiver, was not originally subject to the supervision of the court. This position no longer holds true. The court now exercises general supervisory power that permits it to exercise the same jurisdiction available to it in respect of court-appointed receivers. The court may remove or replace a receiver or give directions to a privately appointed receiver. A privately appointed receiver is not an officer of the court, and the privately appointed receiver's power to manage the business and to sell the assets is not derived from a court order. However, a court has the ability to intervene on the application of an interested party and supervise the activities of a privately appointed receiver.

48 *BIA*, s 81.1.
49 *Ibid*, s 81.2.
50 *Ibid*, s 14.06(7).
51 *Ibid*, s 81.4.
52 *Ibid*, s 81.6.

6) The Creditors' Right to Information

The receiver is under an obligation to report and provide information to other interested parties. This obligation existed under the common law in respect of court-appointed receivers, but it has been widened by legislation in order to impose the obligation to provide information on privately appointed receivers as well.

FURTHER READINGS

ARMOUR, J, & S FRISBY. "Rethinking Receivership" (2001) 21 *Oxford Journal of Legal Studies* 73

BAIRD, DE. "The Section 47 Interim Receiver: A Modern Trojan Horse Designed by Secured Creditors or the Right Approach for Our Times?" in Janis P Sarra, ed, *Annual Review of Insolvency Law, 2005* (Toronto: Thomson Carswell, 2006) 37

BUCKLEY, FH. "The Canadian Private Receivership" in J Ziegel, ed, *Current Developments in International and Comparative Corporate Insolvency Law* (Oxford: Clarendon Press, 1994) 473

BUCKWOLD, T. "The Treatment of Receivers in the Personal Property Security Acts: Conceptual and Practical Implications" (1997) 29 *Canadian Business Law Journal* 277

CARHART, JC. "The Decision of the Supreme Court of Canada in *TCT Logistics* and the Future of Receiverships in Canada" (2007) 44 *Canadian Business Law Journal* 376

COHEN, D, & D KOLESAR. "Interim Receivership: Decline of the Private Receiver in Ontario?" (2002) 19 *National Insolvency Review* 37

DAVIS, R. "The Way Forward: Policy Implications of the Supreme Court Decision in *TCT Logistics*" (2007) 44 *Canadian Business Law Journal* 357

FARKAS, P. "Why Are There So Many Court-Appointed Receiverships?" (2003) 20 *National Insolvency Review* 37

MACDONALD, P, & B HARRISON. "Receivership Orders — Where Do We Go from Here?" (2004) 21 *National Insolvency Review* 65

WOOD, R. "The Regulation of Receiverships" in Janis P Sarra, ed, *Annual Review of Insolvency Law, 2009* (Toronto, Carswell, 2010) 243

ZIEGEL, JS. "The Privately Appointed Receiver and the Enforcement of Security Interests: Anomaly or Superior Solution?" in J Ziegel, ed, *Current Developments in International and Comparative Corporate Insolvency Law* (Oxford: Clarendon Press, 1994) 450

CHAPTER 18

COMMENCEMENT, ADMINISTRATION, AND SUPERVISION OF THE RECEIVERSHIP

There are two different methods of commencing receivership proceedings. The first is through the appointment of a privately appointed receiver. This form of receivership is not possible unless the parties have contractually agreed to the exercise of this power by the secured creditor. The second is through the appointment of a court-appointed receiver. A secured creditor may also convert a private receivership into a court-appointed receivership through a court application made after a receiver is privately appointed. The rules and principles that govern the commencement, administration, and supervision of receivership proceedings differ depending upon whether a privately appointed receiver or a court-appointed receiver is involved. In addition, there are certain preliminary steps that must be satisfied before either type of receivership proceeding can be invoked.

A. PRELIMINARY REQUIREMENTS

1) The Requirement of a Valid Security Interest

The validity and priority of the secured creditor's security interest is of critical importance to receivership proceedings. There are two reasons why this is the case. First, the ability of the receiver to give clear title to a buyer depends upon the priority of the secured creditor. If the secured creditor does not have priority to the asset, the enforcement sale will not give the buyer clear title. An enforcement sale by a secured creditor cuts off only security interests of subordinate secured creditors.[1] The buyer will therefore take the property subject to the interest of those parties that are entitled to priority over the secured creditor. Although a court can make a vesting order that conveys the property to a purchaser free and clear of any encumbrances against the property, the prior and subsequent encumbrancers must be given notice.[2] A court will not grant the vesting order unless the claims of higher-ranking claimants are fully protected.

Second, the receiver's ability to manage the business and to enforce the security interest will be seriously compromised if third parties are able to claim priority to some or all of the assets. Because a receiver's possession and control of the debtor's assets can be displaced by the superior right of a higher-ranking secured creditor, the appointment of a receiver by a junior-ranking creditor is generally a risky undertaking.[3]

Receivership proceedings will not generally be feasible where the security interest covers only some of the business assets. The receiver will lack the enforcement remedies available to secured creditors in respect of the assets that are not given as collateral under the security interest. For this reason, courts have refused to make an order appointing a receiver unless the secured creditor's security interest covers all the business assets.[4]

2) The Requirement of Notice

a) The Reasonable Notice Doctrine

Prior to 1992, a secured creditor's right to appoint a receiver to take possession and control of the debtor's assets upon default under a security agreement was not restricted by legislation. Secured creditors would demand payment and within a matter of hours appoint a receiver to take over control of the business. Canadian courts began to develop the reasonable notice doctrine in order to curtail potential abuses of this power. The security interest given to the secured creditor often secured a demand loan. The courts held that a secured creditor was not entitled to make a demand for payment and then immediately appoint a receiver. The secured creditor was required to give the debtor

1 See, for example, *Personal Property Security Act*, RSA 2000, c P-7, s 60(12) [Alta *PPSA*].

2 *Roynat Ltd v Canawa Holdings Ltd* (1978), 28 CBR (NS) 285 (Sask CA).

3 See R Cuming, C Walsh, & R Wood, *Personal Property Security Law*, 2d ed (Toronto: Irwin Law, 2012) at 675–76.

4 *First Investors Corp v 237208 Alberta Ltd* (1982), 20 Sask R 335 (QB).

a reasonable period of time to pay before a receiver could take control of the business or institute other measures to enforce the security. The Supreme Court of Canada ultimately endorsed the reasonable notice doctrine in *Ronald Elwyn Lister Ltd v Dunlop Canada Ltd.*[5]

There were two difficulties with the reasonable notice doctrine. The first was that it was difficult to predict how much notice was sufficient in any given case, and this uncertainty produced much litigation. The amount of notice that was required to be given depended on a number of factors including the amount of the loan, the risk to the creditor of losing its money or security, the length of the relationship between the debtor and the creditor, the character and reputation of the debtor, the potential ability to raise the money required in a short time, and the circumstances surrounding the demand for payment.[6] In this respect, the Canadian doctrine represents a major departure from the position in England and other Commonwealth countries that adopt a mechanics of payment test. Under this test, the debtor is given only sufficient time to withdraw the funds from an existing bank account or other source.[7]

The second difficulty concerned the juridical foundation of the doctrine. The doctrine was not limited to demand loans but applied to term loans where the debtor had defaulted in making one or more of the scheduled payments[8] and also to any instance in which the lender was asserting some other event of default.[9] Furthermore, the reasonable notice doctrine was regarded as a substantive legal rule that could not be waived or varied by the security agreement. This suggests that the doctrine was based on an underlying principle of unconscionability, but this was never clearly articulated in the cases. The reasonable notice doctrine also appeared to be in conflict with the personal property security legislation of many jurisdictions, which provided that a

---

5 [1982] 1 SCR 726.

6 *Mister Broadloom Corp (1968) v Bank of Montreal* (1979), 25 OR (2d) 198 (HCJ), rev'd on other grounds (1983), 44 OR (2d) 368 (CA).

7 *Bank of Baroda v Panessar*, [1987] 2 WLR 208; *ANZ Banking Group (N.Z.) Ltd v Gibson*, [1986] 1 NZLR 556 (CA).

8 *Roynat Ltd v Northern Meat Packers Ltd; Roynat Ltd v Bourgoin* (1986), 29 DLR (4th) 139 (NBCA), leave to appeal to SCC refused (1987), 78 NBR (2d) 90n.

9 *Jim Landry Pontiac Buick Ltd v Canadian Imperial Bank of Commerce* (1987), 40 DLR (4th) 343 (NSSC); *Kavcar Investments Ltd v Aetna Financial Services Ltd* (1989), 70 OR (2d) 225 (CA); *Waldron v Royal Bank of Canada* (1991), 78 DLR (4th) 1 (BCCA).

secured creditor was entitled to immediately enforce a security interest on default.[10]

b) The Statutory Notice Period

The uncertainty associated with the application of the reasonable notice doctrine has been largely eliminated by the introduction in 1992 of a statutory notice period. A secured creditor who intends to enforce a security on all or substantially all of the inventory, accounts, or other property of a business debtor must give the debtor a notice of intention to enforce the security.[11] The secured creditor is not permitted to enforce the security until the expiry of ten days after the notice is sent.[12] A debtor is permitted to consent to an earlier enforcement of the security, but this consent can be given only after the notice of intention is given to the debtor.[13] After receiving the notice, a debtor may decide to respond by initiating restructuring proceedings under the *BIA* or the *CCAA*. If this is done, the stay of proceedings associated with the restructuring proceedings will prevent the secured creditor from enforcing the security interest through the appointment of a receiver or otherwise.[14]

Although the statutory notice period required under the *BIA* does not replace the reasonable notice doctrine, it will be very rare that the reasonable notice period extends beyond the ten-day statutory notice period.[15] The courts have held that the ten-day period is not an add-on that is tacked on to the end of the reasonable notice period, and that a statutory notice can be combined with the common law demand for payment within a reasonable time.[16]

---

10 See Cuming, Walsh, & Wood, *Personal Property Security Law*, above note 3 at 627–28.

11 *BIA*, s 244(1). Enforcement against a single aircraft did not constitute a enforcement against substantially all of the debtor's assets. See *London Life Insurance Co v Air Atlantic Ltd* (1994), 27 CBR (3d) 66 (NSSC).

12 *BIA*, s 244(2).

13 *Ibid*, s 244(2.1). This provision prevents the debtor from contracting out of the statutory notice requirement by signing a security agreement that contains a waiver clause.

14 See Chapter 13, Section C.

15 See *Whonnock Industries Ltd v National Bank of Canada* (1987), 42 DLR (4th) 1 (BCCA), in which Seaton JA stated: "The Canadian law demonstrated in the decisions does not contemplate more than a few days and cannot encompass anything approaching thirty days. In the decisions noted nothing approaching the seven days permitted here has been classed as unreasonable."

16 *Prudential Assurance Co (Trustee of) v 90 Eglinton Ltd Partnership* (1994), 18 OR (3d) 201 (Gen Div); *Delron Computers Inc v ITT Industries of Canada Ltd*

3) Qualification Requirements

There were originally no statutory qualification requirements on persons who could be appointed as receiver. The 2009 amendments to the *BIA* provide that only a licensed trustee may be appointed as a receiver.[17] This requirement extends to court-appointed receivers as well as to privately appointed receivers. As a consequence, the same rules governing the licensing and qualification of a trustee in bankruptcy now also apply to a receiver.[18]

4) The Definition of Receiver

Part XI of the *BIA* defines a receiver so as to include (1) a national receiver appointed under the *BIA*; (2) a person appointed to take possession or control — of all or substantially all of the inventory, accounts receivable, or other property of an insolvent person or bankrupt that was acquired for or used in relation to a business carried on by that person — under a security agreement; and (3) a receiver appointed by a court under federal or provincial statute. The second enumeration covers a privately appointed receiver, but there is some question on whether it covers other persons as well. In *Colour Box Ltd (Re)*,[19] the court held that the wording is broad enough to cover a secured creditor who takes possession of the property pursuant to a security agreement. As a consequence, the secured creditor was obliged to comply with the notification and reporting requirements of the *BIA*. The decision should be reconsidered in light of the 2009 amendment that added a qualification requirement that the receiver be a licensed trustee. If *Colour Box* is correct, a secured party would be unable to enforce a security agreement against all or substantially all the inventory or accounts because the secured creditor is not a licensed trustee. This would be a highly surprising result, and there is absolutely no evidence that Parliament intended to restrict the enforcement remedies of secured creditors in this way. Moreover, *Colour Box* appears to have misconstrued the Saskatchewan decision of *Farm Credit Corp v Corriveau*.[20] *Corriveau* held that the *BIA* draws a distinction between a secured creditor and a receiver, and that the definition of receiver in Part XI was intended to

---

(Receiver of) (1995), 31 CBR (3d) 75 (Sask QB); *Beresford Building Supplies (1984) Ltd v Caisse Populaire de Petit-Rocher Ltée* (1996), 38 CBR (3d) 274 (NBQB).

17 *BIA*, s 243(4).

18 See Chapter 8, Section B(1).

19 (1995), 21 OR (3d) 746 (Gen Div) [*Colour Box*].

20 (1993), 20 CBR (3d) 124 (Sask QB).

cover the traditional concept of a receiver and was not intended to regulate a secured creditor who enforces its security against the property otherwise than through the appointment of a receiver.

The definition does not encompass an interim receiver. The duties and obligations that are imposed on a receiver under Part XI of the *BIA* therefore do not apply to an interim receiver.

B. APPOINTMENT OF AN INTERIM RECEIVER

Since 1992, the *BIA* has given the bankruptcy court the power to appoint an interim receiver when a secured creditor had sent or was about to send a notice of intention to enforce its security.[21] Because the secured creditor was required to wait ten days following the notice before it could enforce its security, there was a danger that the debtor might dissipate the assets or otherwise engage in conduct that would harm the interests of the secured creditor. The ability to appoint an interim receiver provided a means through which the interests of the secured creditor could be protected. Some courts began to use the power to appoint an interim receiver as an alternative to the usual court appointment of a receiver.[22] The orders appointing the interim receiver conferred wide powers that permitted the interim receiver to operate in the same manner as a court-appointed receiver.

The 2009 amendments have curtailed the use of an interim receiver for this purpose. The appointment is effective for only thirty days unless a court renews it,[23] and the appointment also comes to an end if a court-appointed receiver, privately appointed receiver, or trustee takes possession of the property. The powers that may be given to an interim receiver have been limited too. The interim receiver may take possession of and exercise control over the property, take conservatory measures, and sell perishable property.[24] The court no longer has the power to make any other order that it thinks advisable. A court is therefore unable to confer the same wide powers on an interim receiver that formerly permitted the interim receiver to dispose of the property and distribute the proceeds. The application must be brought in the judicial

---

21 *BIA*, s 47(1).

22 *Canada (Minister of Indian Affairs & Northern Development) v Curragh Inc* (1994), 27 CBR (3d) 148 (Ont Ct Gen Div). And see Chapter 17, Section A(3).

23 *BIA*, s 47(1).

24 *Ibid*, s 47(2).

district of the locality of the debtor.[25] Only a licensed trustee may be appointed as an interim receiver.[26]

An interim receiver may be appointed only if it is shown that it is necessary for the protection of the debtor's estate or the interests of the secured creditor that sent the notice of intention.[27] Prior to 2009, courts differed on what was needed to satisfy this requirement. Some courts held that the applicant must demonstrate an actual and immediate danger of dissipation of assets rather than a concern based on suspicion and speculation.[28] Other courts held that it is enough to show that the interim receiver would be able to carry out his or her duties more effectively and efficiently than a privately appointed receiver.[29] These cases were decided before the changes in the law that restricted the powers of an interim receiver. Currently, the interim receiver is appointed on a temporary basis in order to protect and preserve the property. The test should therefore correspond to the test that is used to protect the assets after a bankruptcy application is brought but before a bankruptcy order is granted.[30] The applicant should be required to demonstrate on a balance of probabilities that the secured creditor has the right to enforce the security and that there is some imminent threat to the property.

In making the order, a court should give the interim receiver only the powers that are needed to alleviate the threat or potential prejudice to the secured creditor and should not be any more intrusive than is necessary.[31] In some circumstances it may not be necessary to give the interim receiver possession or control of the assets. For example, it may be sufficient to give the interim receiver access to the debtor's premises and records.[32]

---

25 *Ibid*, s 47(4).

26 *Ibid*, ss 47(1) and 2 "trustee."

27 *Ibid*, s 47(3).

28 *Royal Bank of Canada v Zutphen Brothers Construction Ltd* (1993), 17 CBR (3d) 314 (NSSC). And see *Maxium Financial Services Inc v Corporate Cars Ltd Partnership* (2006), 29 CBR (5th) 110 (Ont SCJ).

29 *Bank of Nova Scotia v DG Jewelery Inc* (2002), 38 CBR (4th) 7 (Ont SCJ); *Re Pension Positive Inc* (2006), 19 CBR (5th) 277 (Ont SCJ).

30 *BIA*, s 46. And see Chapter 3, Section C(8).

31 See *2 NJ Finance Corp v Raghunan Development Group Inc*, 2013 ONSC 1033.

32 *Great Atlantic & Pacific Co of Canada v 1167970 Ontario Inc* (2002), 37 CBR (4th) 277 (Ont SCJ).

C. METHOD OF APPOINTMENT

1) Private Appointment

The security agreement under which a debtor grants a security interest in all of the debtor's assets to a secured party will typically provide that the secured creditor has the power to appoint and remove a receiver upon the debtor's default. The security agreement will usually set out the powers of the receiver. In most cases, the receiver is given the power to carry on the business of the debtor. If the security agreement merely provides for the appointment of a receiver and does not give the receiver the power to manage the business, the receiver will have only the power to receive the income from the property, to pay the liabilities connected with the property, and to realize the security interest.[33] In order to operate the business, the receiver must be given the power to manage the business.

In the event of a default by the debtor, the secured creditor may choose to initiate the receivership by appointing a receiver. This is typically done through a letter of appointment. The receiver will then notify the debtor of the appointment and take possession and control of the business. However, the secured creditor is not compelled to enforce its security through the appointment of a receiver. It may choose instead to enforce its security through the seizure or sale of the collateral or through some other enforcement remedy available to it.

2) Court Appointment

Instead of appointing a receiver pursuant to a power conferred in a security agreement, a secured creditor may apply to a court for the appointment of a receiver. A secured creditor may also apply to court to have a receiver who has been privately appointed converted into a court-appointed receiver. One of the complicating features in the present state of the law is that there are several different statutes that provide for the court appointment of a receiver, and the secured creditor must decide to bring the application pursuant to one or more of these statutes. For example, the Alberta template receivership order[34]

---

33 *Standard Trust Co (Liquidator of) v Turner Crossing Inc* (1992), 15 CBR (3d) 79 (Sask QB). And see *Canada Business Corporations Act*, RSC 1985, c C-44, s 94 [*CBCA*].

34 See Template Receivership Order Committee, "Alberta Template Receivership Order Explanatory Notes," online: https://albertacourts.ca/court-of-queens-bench/commercial-practice.

provides for the court appointment of a receiver under potentially four different statutes: namely, the *Judicature Act*,[35] the *Business Corporations Act*,[36] the *Personal Property Security Act*,[37] and the *BIA*.

Prior to the 2009 amendments to the *BIA*, the practice was to seek a concurrent appointment of an interim receiver under the *BIA* and under one or more of the relevant provincial statutes. By doing so, the rights of suppliers to repossess thirty-day goods were preserved and the receiver was rendered subject to the reporting and other obligations imposed on receivers under the *BIA*. This is no longer a factor. This device was needed because the appointment of an interim receiver under the *BIA* did not activate these rules, but an appointment of a receiver under provincial law did. The use of the interim receiver is now sharply limited. In its place, appointment of a national receiver under the *BIA* is possible. A national receiver appointed under the *BIA* is considered to be a receiver for the purposes of the thirty-day goods provision[38] and the *BIA* provisions that regulate reporting and other obligations.[39]

The use of concurrent appointments may decline or disappear in the future. A court appointment of a receiver under the *BIA* is desirable, since this will produce an order that is national in scope and readily enforceable. It is less clear whether there will be any need for a concurrent application under the provincial regimes. This will depend on whether the applicant is convinced that the *BIA* provisions are sufficient and that there is no need to draw upon the provincial receivership statutes for any additional rights or powers. If this is not the case, concurrent appointments can be expected to continue. One of the difficulties with such appointments is that the rules concerning appeal periods and other procedural matters differ depending upon whether the court is exercising its bankruptcy jurisdiction or its jurisdiction as a superior court.

Although it is possible to obtain the appointment of a receiver on an *ex parte* application, courts will make such orders only on an emergency basis where a failure to act would cause irreparable harm.[40] The applicant must act in good faith and make full, fair, and candid disclosure of the facts, including those that are adverse to the applicant's position.[41]

---

35 RSA 2000, c J-2, s 13(2).

36 RSA 2000, c B-9, s 99.

37 Above note 1, s 65(7).

38 *BIA*, s 81.1(12) "receiver."

39 *Ibid*, s 243(2).

40 *Royal Bank of Canada v W Got & Associates Electric Ltd* (1997), 47 CBR (3d) 1 at para 21 (Alta CA).

41 *Hover v Metropolitan Life Insurance Co* (1999), 91 Alta LR (3d) 226 (CA).

D. GROUNDS FOR APPOINTMENT

In order for the private appointment of a receiver to be valid, there must be a default, the notification requirements must have been satisfied, and the security agreement must give the secured creditor the power to appoint a receiver. Beyond this, a secured creditor does not need to demonstrate any additional grounds for the private appointment of a receiver.

A court may appoint a receiver where it appears to the judge that it is just or convenient to do so. This traditional test has not been substantially altered by any of the statutory regimes governing receiverships. Courts have been prepared to make such orders where it is necessary for the protection or preservation of the secured creditor's security interest in the debtor's property. Courts will also appoint a receiver to preserve the property pending realization where ordinary legal remedies are defective, or to preserve property from some danger that threatens it.[42] In deciding whether or not to appoint a receiver, the court may consider such matters as the nature of the property, the likelihood of maximizing return to the parties, and the costs associated with the appointment.[43]

A number of courts have endorsed a more extensive set of factors that a court can consider in determining whether to appoint a receiver, namely:

- whether irreparable harm might be caused if no order were made, although it is not essential for a creditor to establish irreparable harm if a receiver is not appointed, particularly where the appointment of a receiver is authorized by the security documentation;
- the risk to the security holder taking into consideration the size of the debtor's equity in the assets and the need for protection or safeguarding of the assets while litigation takes place;
- the nature of the property;
- the apprehended or actual waste of the debtor's assets;
- the preservation and protection of the property pending judicial resolution;
- the balance of convenience to the parties;
- the fact that the creditor has the right to appoint a receiver under the documentation provided for the loan;

---

42 *Tim v Lai* (1984), 53 CBR (NS) 80 (BCSC).

43 *Paragon Capital Corp v Merchants & Traders Assurance Co*, 2002 ABQB 430 [*Paragon*]; *Business Development Bank of Canada v Pine Tree Resorts Inc*, 2013 ONSC 1911.

- the enforcement of rights under a security instrument where the security-holder encounters or expects to encounter difficulty with the debtor and others;
- the principle that the appointment of a receiver is extraordinary relief which should be granted cautiously and sparingly;
- the consideration of whether a court appointment is necessary to enable the receiver to carry out its duties more efficiently;
- the effect of the order upon the parties;
- the conduct of the parties;
- the length of time that a receiver may be in place;
- the cost to the parties;
- the likelihood of maximizing return to the parties;
- the goal of facilitating the duties of the receiver.[44]

Courts have also considered the fact that a secured creditor had the ability of appoint a privately appointed receiver under its security agreement, although the significance of this factor has cut both ways. Some courts have refused to make an order appointing a receiver if the secured creditor has the power to appoint a receiver under the security agreement.[45] The order will be granted only if the secured creditor can demonstrate that the powers of the privately appointed receiver are inadequate in some respect. Other courts have been more willing to grant an order appointing a receiver despite the fact that the secured creditor has the power to appoint a privately appointed receiver. It is not necessary to show that a private appointment is inadequate; it is sufficient to demonstrate that a court appointment would enable the receiver to carry out his or her duties more effectively and efficiently.[46]

The weight of authority has now firmly shifted to this latter view. Most courts have adopted the view that the "just or convenient" test is more easily satisfied where the security agreement provides that the secured creditor may appoint a receiver. The remedy is not viewed as extraordinary, and the inquiry is whether or not it is in the interests of

---

44 *Paragon*, above note 43; *Enterprise Cape Breton Corporation v Crown Jewel Resort Ranch, Inc*, 2014 NSSC 128 [*Enterprise Cape Breton*]; *Maple Trade Finance Inc v CY Oriental Holdings Ltd*, 2009 BCSC 1527.

45 *Royal Bank of Canada v White Cross Properties Ltd* (1984), 53 CBR (NS) 96 (Sask QB); *Macotta Co of Canada v Condor Metal Fabricators Ltd* (1979), 35 CBR (NS) 144 (Alta QB); *Royal Bank of Canada v Cal Glass Ltd* (1978), 29 CBR (NS) 302 (BCSC).

46 *Bank of Nova Scotia v DG Jewelery Inc* (2002), 38 CBR (4th) 7 (Ont SCJ); *Re Pension Positive Inc* (2006), 19 CBR (5th) 277 (Ont SCJ).

all concerned to have the receiver appointed by the court.[47] In British Columbia, some courts have proceeded even further down this path and have held that the order should follow as a matter of course if the security agreement provides for the appointment of a receiver.[48]

E. STAY OF PROCEEDINGS

The appointment of a privately appointed receiver does not result in a stay of proceedings in respect of the actions or remedies of creditors who have claims against the debtor, or in respect of actions brought against the receiver. Despite the absence of a stay of proceedings, the unsecured creditors of the debtor are unlikely to pursue their remedies against the debtor or debtor's assets. The secured creditor ranks in priority to the claims of the unsecured creditors. The unsecured creditors therefore have no incentive to expend further funds in futile litigation or collection efforts. A claimant who has priority over the secured creditor has a superior right of enforcement and may demand that the receiver give up possession of the asset.[49]

A court order appointing a receiver usually contains a provision that stays any proceedings against the debtor or the property of the debtor.[50] The drafting of the stay provisions in the template receivership order was heavily influenced by the drafting of the stay provisions in the template *CCAA* initial orders. Alberta, British Columbia, and Saskatchewan have also produced similar template receivership orders.

The first component of the stay provisions is an order that prevents parties from bringing proceedings against the receiver without leave of the court. This is substantially similar in effect to the provision of the *BIA* that prevents parties from bringing actions against a trustee without leave of the court.[51] The threshold for obtaining leave is not high, since the provision was designed to protect the trustee against frivo-

---

47 *Bank of Montreal v Carnival National Leasing Limited*, 2011 ONSC 1007; *Enterprise Cape Breton*, above note 44; *Textron Financial Canada Limited v Chetwynd Motels Ltd*, 2010 BCSC 477.

48 *United Savings Credit Union v F & R Brokers Inc*, 2003 BCSC 640; *Canadian Imperial Bank of Commerce v Can-Pacific Farms Inc*, 2012 BCSC 437.

49 See Cuming, Walsh, & Wood, *Personal Property Security Law*, above note 3 at 675–76.

50 The order will generally permit actions to be commenced if it is necessary to do so to prevent the action from being barred by a statutory limitation period.

51 *BIA*, s 215.

lous or vexatious actions.[52] However, if the receiver has received court approval of the activities or if the receiver has been discharged and considerable time has passed, the applicant must demonstrate a strong *prima facie* case.[53] The court may grant leave *nunc pro tunc* in the event that the applicant failed to seek leave before commencing the action.[54]

The second component prevents commencement or continuation of any proceedings against the debtor or the debtor's property without the written consent of the receiver or the leave of the court. The third component provides that all rights and remedies against the debtor or the receiver or affecting the property are stayed except with the consent of the receiver or the leave of the court. The stay does not empower the receiver to carry on business that the debtor is not lawfully entitled to carry on; exempt the debtor or receiver from compliance with statutory or regulatory provisions relating to health, safety, or the environment; or prevent a creditor from registering a security interest or lien. The template orders contain language that replicates the provisions of the *CCAA* that ensure that the stay of proceedings does not affect eligible financial contracts.[55]

The fourth component prevents any person from terminating, repudiating, or failing to perform any right, renewal right, contract, or licence without the written consent of the receiver or the leave of the court. The fifth component prevents a person from discontinuing the supply of goods or services pursuant to an agreement or a statutory or regulatory mandate. This prevents a utility from threatening to discontinue water, electricity, or other services until the arrears in payment are paid.

Although the template orders have brought a greater degree of predictability to the law, they have not eliminated all problems. Some of the orders continue to contain wide provisions that led to legislative intervention when similar provisions were used in the context of the *CCAA*. For example, the template receivership orders of Alberta, British Columbia, and Saskatchewan provide that the stay of proceedings prevents a third party from exercising a right of set-off. A third party who is unable to exercise a right of set-off may be forced to pay an obligation that it owes to the debtor without the benefit of set-off. This effectively destroys the right and does not merely stay its effect. The *CCAA* was

---

52 *GMAC Commercial Credit Corp - Canada v TCT Logistics Inc* (2006), 22 CBR (5th) 163 (SCC).

53 *Bank of America Canada v Willann Investments Ltd* (1993), 23 CBR (3d) 98 (Ont Ct Gen Div); *Gallo v Beber* (1998), 7 CBR (4th) 170 (Ont CA).

54 *RoyNat Inc v Allan* (1988), 69 CBR (NS) 245 (Alta QB); *80 Aberdeen Street Ltd v Surgeson Carson Associates Inc* (2008), 40 CBR (5th) 109 (Ont SCJ).

55 See Chapter 13, Section F.

modified in order to ensure that the right of set-off could be exercised despite the stay of proceedings.[56]

There are also some significant variations in the template orders across jurisdictions. For example, the template order in Alberta permits the commencement of a proceeding in order to prevent the claim from being barred by a statute or an existing agreement.[57] The other template orders require the claimant to apply to court to lift the stay. The Alberta and BC template orders do not apply to regulatory bodies except when they are enforcing a payment order,[58] whereas the Ontario template order only exempts compliance with statutory or regulatory provisions relating to health, safety or the environment.[59]

The stay of proceedings is effective to prevent the exercise of enforcement remedies by a higher-ranking secured creditor or other claimant who is entitled to priority over the secured creditor who has applied to court for the appointment of a receiver.[60] A party who is entitled to priority over a specific asset may bring the matter before the court by invoking the comeback provision that is found in the court order to request that the stay of proceedings be lifted in respect of the asset. The court may decide to lift the stay and permit enforcement by the creditor, but it is not required to do so. A court-appointed receiver acts in the interests of all persons who have an interest in the assets and does not act as agent of the secured creditor who applied for the court appointment.[61] The court may conclude that the asset should be sold as part of a going-concern sale in order to benefit all the interested parties if doing so does not prejudice the interests of the party entitled to priority.

F. COURT SUPERVISION OF THE RECEIVERSHIP

Courts had very little ability at common law to supervise the conduct of a privately appointed receiver. There was no convenient mechanism

56 *CCAA*, s 21.

57 Above note 34 at para 8.

58 *Ibid*.

59 Online: www.ontariocourts.ca/scj/practice/practice-directions/toronto/#Commercial_List_Forms_including_Model_Orders at para 10.

60 *Merchants Consolidated Ltd (Receiver of) v Canstar Sports Group Inc* (1994), 25 CBR (3d) 203 (Man CA).

61 *Alberta Treasury Branches v Tetz* (1998), 2 CBR (4th) 119 (Alta QB).

by which interested parties could seek the intervention of the court.[62] Although other parties with an interest in the property under receivership might seek to obtain an injunction to prevent anticipated harmful conduct, they usually were left in the dark concerning the activities of the receiver. The reality was that they had little opportunity to intervene. The courts therefore did not play an active role in the supervision of the receivership. Instead, they became involved after the fact when litigation was commenced alleging wrongful conduct on the part of the secured creditor or the receiver. The position was entirely different where a court-appointed receiver was involved. The receiver was an officer of the court, and the court had the power to control the conduct of the receivership. This provided interested parties with the means to obtain information concerning the receivership and to have issues brought before the court.

Provincial and federal legislation has significantly altered the common law position and given courts a general supervisory power over both court-appointed and privately appointed receivers. The personal property security statutes and the business corporations statutes give courts the power to make the following orders:[63]

- an order removing, replacing, or discharging a receiver;
- an order giving directions on any matter relating to the duties of the receiver;
- an order approving the accounts or fixing the remuneration of a receiver;
- an order requiring the receiver or the secured creditor to make good any default in connection with the receiver's custody or management of the property and business;
- an order relieving a receiver or secured creditor from any default on such terms as the court thinks fit; and
- an order confirming any act of the receiver.

The personal property security statutes also provide that a court has the same power to make orders in respect of privately appointed receivers as it has in respect of court-appointed receivers.[64]

---

62 See Canada, Advisory Committee on Bankruptcy and Insolvency, *Proposed* Bankruptcy Act *Amendments: Report of the Advisory Committee on Bankruptcy and Insolvency* (Ottawa: Advisory Committee on Bankruptcy and Insolvency, 1986) at 36 [*The Colter Report*].

63 See, for example, *CBCA*, above note 33, s 100; *Personal Property Security Act*, RSO 1990, c P.10, s 60(2) [Ont *PPSA*].

64 See, for example, Alta *PPSA*, above note 1, s 65(7)(e). The Ontario *PPSA* is less clear on this point. See Ont *PPSA*, above note 63, s 60(2)(d).

These statutory provisions have their greatest effect on privately appointed receivers, since courts were already able to exercise most of these powers in respect of court-appointed receivers. In some cases, the statutory powers given to the court are wider than those that were formerly available in respect of court-appointed receivers. For example, a court is permitted to order that a secured creditor make good any default in connection with a receiver's custody or management of the property or business.[65] A court-appointed receiver is an officer of the court who acts in his or her own right and not as an agent of the secured creditor.[66] A court therefore should not normally make an order that renders a secured creditor liable for the acts of the receiver unless it is shown that the receiver was acting on the instructions of the secured creditor.[67]

G. FINANCING THE RECEIVERSHIP

A receiver may think it expedient to borrow funds in order to pay employees, landlords, and suppliers and to meet other periodic expenses. Many security agreements contain a provision that permits the receiver, with the consent of the secured creditor, to borrow money in order to carry on the business of the debtor or to maintain the collateral. As this is merely a contractual provision between the secured creditor and the debtor, it cannot give these borrowings any priority over senior ranking interests in the collateral. In many instances, the secured creditor who appoints the privately appointed receiver will provide the financing, and these amounts become part of the obligation secured by the collateral.

A court-appointed receiver does not have the power to borrow unless authorized to do so by the court. The template receivership orders contain a standard provision that allows the receiver to borrow up to a stated maximum amount. A receiver who borrows funds pursuant to this power will issue a receiver's certificate that evidences the amounts that are borrowed. The amounts borrowed pursuant to receiver's certificates rank *pari passu*.

The template receivership orders provide for the creation of a receiver's charge that secures the fees and disbursements of the receiver as

65 See, for example, Alta *PPSA*, above note 1, s 65(7)(f); *CBCA*, above note 33, s 100(d). The Ontario *PPSA* does not contain a similar provision.

66 *Alberta Treasury Branches v Tetz*, above note 61.

67 See T Buckwold, "The Treatment of Receivers in the Personal Property Security Acts: Conceptual and Practical Implications" (1997) 29 *Canadian Business Law Journal* 277.

well as a receiver's borrowing charge that secures amounts borrowed by the receiver. Both are charges on all of the assets of the debtor that rank in priority to all security interests, trusts, liens, charges, and encumbrances, statutory or otherwise. The receiver's charge ranks ahead of the receiver's borrowing charge. Courts have held that a receiver can claim this priority only if notice has been given to the secured creditor.[68] Priority can be asserted over secured creditors in the absence of notice if the secured creditors gave their approval to the appointment of the receiver, or if the receiver expended money for the necessary preservation or improvement of the property.

The 2009 amendments to the *BIA* have added a specific statutory rule that codifies the recovery of the fees and disbursements of a receiver appointed under the *BIA*.[69] A court is permitted to make any order that it considers appropriate, including one that gives a receiver a charge ranking ahead of that of a secured creditor. A court is not permitted to grant a priority charge unless it is satisfied that the secured creditors who are materially affected by the order have been notified and given an opportunity to make representations. The charge secures fees and disbursements of the receiver but does not encompass payments made in the operation of the business of the debtor.

The priority that is afforded to the receiver's charge and the receiver's borrowing charge gives rise to the same issue concerning the allocation of expenses amongst the subordinate secured creditors that is encountered in respect of the allocation of administrative expenses in restructuring proceedings.[70]

H. PRIORITIES

As a general principle, the occurrence of a receivership does not affect the priority status of a secured creditor in relation to other parties who have competing interests in the debtor's assets. Unlike bankruptcy, the statutes that govern receiverships do not provide a scheme of distribution and they do not contain priority rules that override the ordinary priority rules that apply in circumstances in which the debtor is not insolvent. If a secured creditor is subordinate to a landlord who has

---

68 *Robert F Kowal Investments Ltd v Deeder Electric Ltd* (1975), 21 CBR (NS) 201 (Ont CA) [*Kowal Investments*]; *Lochson Holdings Ltd v Eaton Mechanical Inc* (1984), 52 CBR (NS) 271 (BCCA) [*Lochson Holdings*].

69 *BIA*, s 243(6).

70 See *Hickman Equipment (1985) Ltd (Re)*, 2004 NLSCTD 164. And see Chapter 15, Section B(11).

exercised a right of distress under provincial law, this priority is not altered by the fact that a receiver has been appointed. The same holds true for Crown claims that are secured by deemed statutory trusts or by statutory liens, charges, or security interests. The secured creditor's priority vis-à-vis the competing third party is unaffected by the receivership.

There are a number of special provisions contained in the *BIA* that create special priority rules that operate if the debtor is bankrupt or a receiver has been appointed. A special right of repossession is given to a supplier in respect of thirty-day goods.[71] A farmer, fisherman, or aquaculturalist who has sold products to a purchaser within fifteen days of a receivership of the purchaser has a security on all the inventory of the purchaser to secure the unpaid price.[72] Statutory charges secure claims of unpaid wage earners[73] and unpaid pension contributions.[74] A first-ranking charge is also created in respect of environmental remediation claims.[75] These provisions give the claimants priority over secured creditors, thereby affording them a different priority from what they would have received if the ordinary priority rules of provincial law were applied.

There are two further qualifications on the general principle that the priorities are unaltered on receivership. The first qualification is that there is currently some uncertainty whether provincial statutory devices that confer priority on wage earners will be held to be inoperative by virtue of the enactment of the *BIA*'s statutory charge in favour of wage earners. Although the matter is not beyond debate, it is likely that the provincial provisions do not conflict with the federal *BIA* provisions, since they simply afford an additional right to employees.[76]

The second qualification is that a secured creditor may attempt to invoke a bankruptcy in order to obtain a more favourable priority ranking over competing creditors. The occurrence of bankruptcy causes the bankruptcy priority rules to come into operation.[77] These are often dif-

---

71 *BIA*, s 81.1(1). See Chapter 5, Section C(1).

72 *BIA*,s 81.2(1). See Chapter 5, Section C(2).

73 *BIA*, s 81.4. See Chapter 5, Section D(1).

74 *BIA*, s 81.6. See Chapter 5, Section D(2).

75 *BIA*, s 14.06(7). See Chapter 5, Section F.

76 See T Buckwold & R Wood, "Priorities" in S Ben-Ishai & A Duggan, eds, *Canadian Bankruptcy and Insolvency Law: Bill C-55, Statute c. 47 and Beyond* (Markham, ON: LexisNexis Canada, 2007) 101 at 126–27.

77 Although secured creditors will often invoke a bankruptcy in order to obtain a more favourable priority status, this fundamentally alters the status of a privately appointed receiver and can lead to unanticipated consequences. See Chapter 19, Section B(3).

ferent from the ordinary priority rules of provincial law. Non-consensual security interests in favour of the Crown[78] and deemed statutory trusts[79] are generally afforded a lower priority ranking in bankruptcy. A creditor who ranks as a preferred creditor in bankruptcy is also precluded from asserting any provincial law that would give the creditor a higher priority.[80]

The commencement of bankruptcy proceedings does not bring an end to the receivership proceedings, and the two proceedings will therefore operate concurrently. Since the receivership will usually be invoked by a secured creditor who has a security interest in all of the assets of the debtor, the bankruptcy proceedings will play a subordinate role. The only assets that will be available for distribution among the unsecured creditors will be any surplus value remaining once the secured creditors and other priority claimants are paid in full. In many cases there is no surplus value, so that the primary effect of the bankruptcy proceedings is to alter priorities, usually to the detriment of the unsecured creditors.

I. SALE OF THE ASSETS

At common law, the privately appointed receiver was viewed as acting in a fundamentally different capacity than the court-appointed receiver in selling the assets. A privately appointed receiver acted as an agent of the secured creditor in enforcing the security interest. The receiver therefore had the same rights and was subject to the same obligations as a secured creditor, and in selling the collateral was required to observe the same enforcement procedures as required of a secured creditor.

A court-appointed receiver acted not as an agent of the secured creditor but on behalf of all persons who had an interest in the assets. The power to sell the assets was derived from the order of the court rather than from the provisions of the security agreement. Consequently, the court-appointed receiver was not required to follow the procedures imposed by provincial law on the enforcement of security interests by secured creditors. Instead, the receiver was required to follow the sale process mandated by the court. The court typically gives the receiver the power to sell assets in the ordinary course of business, but requires court approval in respect of substantial sales of assets outside the ordinary

---

78 *BIA*, ss 86–87. And see Chapter 5, Section E.

79 *BIA*, ss 67(2)–(3). And see Chapter 4, Section C(1)(d).

80 *BIA*, s 136(1). See Chapter 5, Section B(6).

course of business. The court-appointed receiver will often seek directions from the court in respect of his or her plan for marketing and selling the property, and frequently appraisals are obtained and filed with the court.

The common law position has been modified by provincial personal property security legislation. The statutes provide that a reference to a secured party includes a receiver for the purposes of most of the enforcement provisions of the Acts. A privately appointed receiver is clearly subject to the enforcement provisions of the Acts. This means that, in the conduct of the sale, the receiver must give the pre-sale notice and comply with the other requirements of provincial personal property security legislation. A pre-sale notice is not required in respect of sales that are conducted by the receiver in the ordinary course of the debtor's business.[81] If the personal property is sold together with real property, the secured creditor may proceed against both in a single action, and the procedure for enforcement against land rather than the enforcement provisions of the PPSA will govern.[82]

Personal property security statutes contemplate the appointment of both privately appointed receivers and court-appointed receivers but do not otherwise distinguish between them.[83] This means that the enforcement provisions of the PPSA apply to both privately appointed receivers and court-appointed receivers. This is subject to an important exception. The PPSAs give the court the power to relieve the parties from compliance with the Act's enforcement provisions.[84] This power is exercised by courts in the template receivership orders, which dispense with the PPSA notice requirements.

In a court-appointed receivership, the court order will typically authorize the receiver to sell assets in the ordinary course of business and will as well authorize sales out of the ordinary course of business not exceeding a specified monetary value. Sales exceeding this value must be authorized by court order. A court will consider the following factors in determining if the sale should be approved:[85]

---

81 See, for example, Ont *PPSA*, above note 63, s 63(7); Alta *PPSA*, above note 1, s 65(9).

82 See, for example, Ont *PPSA*, above note 63, s 59(6); Alta *PPSA*, above note 1, s 55(4).

83 See, for example, Ont *PPSA*, above note 63, s 60(1); Alta *PPSA*, above note 1, ss 65(1) and 65(7).

84 See, for example, Ont *PPSA*, above note 63, s 67(1(d); Alta *PPSA*, above note 1, s 64(c).

85 *Royal Bank of Canada v Soundair Corp* (1991), 7 CBR (3d) 1 (Ont CA); *Royal Bank of Canada v Fracmaster Ltd* (1999), 11 CBR. (4th) 217 (Alta CA).

- whether the receiver has made a sufficient effort to get the best price and has not acted improvidently;
- whether the interests of all parties have been served;
- whether the process by which offers were obtained has been marked by efficacy and integrity; and
- whether there has been unfairness in the working out of the process.

In many instances, the receiver will also seek prior court approval of the marketing and sales process in order to avoid subsequent questioning of the process. Courts have authorized stalking horse bid sales processes similar to those that have been used under the *CCAA*.[86]

Following the sale, a court will often grant a vesting order in respect of the assets which operates as a conveyance of title of the property.[87] The template receivership orders authorize a receiver to apply to a court in another jurisdiction for an order granting recognition to the order or assistance in carrying out its terms. It is unlikely that a receiver who is appointed under the *BIA* will need to obtain such recognition or assistance in other provinces, since the vesting order is an order issued under a federal statute that has national effect.[88]

J. DISTRIBUTION OF THE PROCEEDS

The distribution rules in respect of receiverships are relatively simple. Unlike bankruptcy, no statutory scheme of distribution is provided. Instead, the entitlement to the proceeds of sale will largely be determined by the priority ranking of the secured creditor's security interest. In some instances, the receiver will have sold the assets despite the fact that they are subject to a senior-ranking claim. This most often occurs when the assets are subject to a deemed statutory trust that secures Crown claims, such as unremitted source deductions of income tax, CPP, and EI contributions. Because the Crown lacks an effective sale mechanism, it usually relies upon the receiver to dispose of the assets and then claims priority in respect of the proceeds of sale.

---

86 See *Crate Marine Sales Ltd (Re)*, 2015 ONSC 1062. And see Chapter 13, Section G(2).

87 *Re Regal Constellation Hotel Ltd* (2004), 50 CBR (4th) 258 (Ont CA).

88 *BIA*, s 188. But see *Enterprise Cape Breton*, above note 44, in which the court questioned whether Part XI of the *BIA* gives the court the authority to make a vesting order. The contrary view is that it is authorized by s 243 which provides that a court may "take any other action that the court considers available."

The costs of the receivership are generally paid out first. In the case of a privately appointed receiver, there is usually a contractual provision in the security agreement to this effect, and the PPSA provides that the proceeds of disposition of the collateral are to be directed first to the reasonable expenses of enforcing the security interest and then to the satisfaction of the obligations secured by the security interests.[89] Difficulties may arise if the receiver has sold property that is subject to a higher-ranking claim of another party. The receiver or secured creditor should ensure that the third party has consented to the sale and has agreed that the costs of the receivership should be paid first out of the proceeds of sale. In the absence of such an agreement, the lower-ranking secured creditor may nevertheless be able to recover the costs of enforcement if the efforts lead to an enhanced recovery and benefits the higher-ranking creditor.[90]

In the case of a court-appointed receivership, the court will approve the distribution of the proceeds to those who are entitled to them according to the priority ranking of their claims. The court order usually provides that the fees and costs of the receiver are a first charge on the assets and have priority over all security interests, trusts, liens, or encumbrances. However, a court should not make an order giving the charge priority over higher-ranking interests unless notice has been given to the party that such an order is being sought. The requirement of notice is unnecessary if the party has consented to or approved of the appointment of the receiver or if the expenses are absolutely necessary for the preservation of the property.[91]

Where different secured creditors have security interests in different assets, it may become necessary to allocate a portion of the receiver's fees against each set of assets. In making this allocation, it is not always the case that each secured creditor must be allocated the same proportion of the costs. In making an unequal allocation, the court may consider the differences in type of security held by the creditors and the degree of potential benefit that could be derived from the receivership.[92] Thus, a smaller proportion might be allocated to the costs associated with the disposal of real property if a greater portion of the

89 See, for example, Ont *PPSA*, above note 63, s 63(1); Alta *PPSA*, above note 1, s 60(1).

90 *Father & Son Investments Inc v Maverick Brewing Corp* (2007), 37 CBR (5th) 74 (Alta QB).

91 *Kowal Investments*, above note 68; *Lochson Holdings*, above note 68.

92 *Re Hunters Trailer & Marine Ltd* (2001), 30 CBR (4th) 206 (Alta QB); *JP Morgan Chase Bank NA v UTTC United Tri-Tech Corp* (2006), 25 CBR (5th) 156 (Ont SCJ).

receiver's work was directed towards the enhancement of the value of the personal property.

K. TERMINATION OF THE RECEIVERSHIP

A receivership ordinarily comes to an end when all the realizable assets have been disposed of and the proceeds have been distributed to parties according to their priority ranking. In the case of a court-appointed receiver, the receiver will pass its final accounts and seek a discharge. Although there is not a formal discharge of the receiver in the case of a private receivership, the receiver is under an obligation to render a final account of the administration[93] and interested parties may apply to court to have the receiver's fees reviewed.[94]

The appointment of a receiver can also come to an end before the duties of the receiver have been completed. This may occur through death, resignation of the receiver, or removal. The secured creditor who appointed a privately appointed receiver has the power to dismiss the receiver. Legislation has given courts the power to remove and replace a privately appointed receiver.[95] Only the court that appointed a court-appointed receiver may remove the receiver from office. Creditors will typically apply to have a court-appointed receiver removed and replaced when they think that the receiver is in a conflict of interest or has failed to consider impartially the interests of all of the claimants.[96]

FURTHER READINGS

BENNETT, F. *Bennett on Creditors' and Debtors' Rights and Remedies*, 5th ed (Toronto: Carswell, 2006) ch 14

———. *Bennett on Receiverships*, 2d ed (Toronto: Carswell, 1998) ch 2

---

93 *BIA*, s 246(3).

94 *Ibid*, s 248(2); *CBCA*, above note 33, s 100; Ont *PPSA*, above note 63, s 60(2).

95 See, for example, Ont *PPSA*, *ibid*, s 60(2)(a); Alta *PPSA*, above note 1, s 65(7)(b); *CBCA*, above note 33, s 100.

96 *Canada Trustco Mortgage Co v York-Trillium Development Group Ltd* (1992), 12 CBR (3d) 220 (Ont Ct Gen Div); *Royal Bank of Canada v Vista Homes Ltd* (1985), 57 CBR (NS) 80 (BCSC).

BUCKWOLD, T, & R WOOD. "Priorities" in S Ben-Ishai & A Duggan, eds, *Canadian Bankruptcy and Insolvency Law: Bill C-55, Statute c. 47 and Beyond* (Markham, ON: LexisNexis Canada, 2007) 101

CARHART, J. "Appointing a Receiver and Seizing Equipment" (2005) 22 *National Insolvency Review* 53

CUMING, R, C WALSH, & R WOOD. *Personal Property Security Law* (Toronto: Irwin Law, 2005) ch 12

MCELCHERAN, K. *Commercial Insolvency in Canada* (Markham, ON: LexisNexis Butterworths, 2005) ch 3

CHAPTER 19

THE STATUS, POWERS, DUTIES, AND LIABILITIES OF THE RECEIVER

A. THE STATUS OF THE RECEIVER

1) The Traditional View

Historically, there was a significant difference in the status of a court-appointed receiver and the status of a privately appointed receiver. A court appointed receiver has an independent status and does not act as agent of either the secured creditor or the debtor.[1] A privately appointed receiver acts as an agent of either the secured creditor or the debtor depending on the function undertaken by the receiver.[2] In managing the business, the receiver acts as agent for the debtor; in realizing the security, the receiver acts as agent of the secured creditor. This difference was significant in its legal effect. A court appointed receiver enters into new contracts with third parties as a principal. The court-appointed receiver therefore becomes personally liable on the contracts[3] but has a right of indemnity from the assets under receivership.[4] A privately appointed receiver enters into new contracts as agent of the debtor and therefore does not become personally liable on them. As well, a

1 *Parsons v Sovereign Bank of Canada*, [1913] AC 160 (PC).

2 *Peat Marwick Ltd v Consumers' Gas Co* (1980), 35 CBR (NS) 1 (Ont CA) [*Peat Marwick*].

3 *Re Ashk Development Corp* (1988), 70 CBR (NS) 72 (Alta QB).

4 *Burt, Boulton & Hayward v Bull*, [1895] 1 QB 276; *Re Smith & Son* (1929), 10 CBR 393 (Ont HCJ).

court-appointed receiver is an officer of the court, whereas a privately appointed receiver does not have this status.

This status of a privately appointed receiver has not been directly changed by statute. However, it is possible that provincial personal property security legislation has modified the powers and duties owed by the privately appointed receiver to such an extent that it is better to view the privately appointed receiver as having the same independent status as a court-appointed receiver.

2) The Effect of the Personal Property Security Acts

Personal property security legislation has been adopted in every Canadian common law jurisdiction. These statutes contain provisions that govern receiverships. The legislative provisions in most of these jurisdictions regulate receiverships in the following manner.[5] First, they provide that the receiver may take possession and control of the assets and may manage the business if appointed as a receiver and manager. Second, they give a court the power to appoint, replace, and discharge receivers and give directions to them. These powers are not restricted to court-appointed receivers. It is thus possible for an interested party to seek a court order replacing a privately appointed receiver, or for a privately appointed receiver to apply to court for directions. Third, they impose a number of accounting and reporting duties on receivers. Fourth, provisions that relate to the enforcement remedies of secured creditors are made applicable to receivers. A receiver who is realizing the collateral is therefore required to fulfil the same obligations that are imposed on a secured creditor in the exercise of these remedies.[6]

The traditional view was that a privately appointed receiver acted as agent of the debtor in managing the business but as an agent of the secured creditor in enforcing the security interest.[7] It is likely that personal property security legislation has altered this position. The legislation directly imposes statutory obligations on a privately appointed receiver, and this suggests that the receiver's duties and liabilities are no longer to be viewed as being derived from the receiver's status as agent of the secured creditor. Instead, the privately appointed receiver

---

5 The Ontario *PPSA* contains less extensive receivership provisions than those contained in the *PPSA*s of other Canadian jurisdictions.

6 See R Cuming, C Walsh, & R Wood, *Personal Property Security Law*, 2d ed (Toronto: Irwin Law, 2012) at 669–71.

7 *Peat Marwick*, above note 2.

may be regarded as acting in an independent capacity in much the same way as a court-appointed receiver when enforcing the security interest.[8]

More problematic is whether the legislation has changed the effect of a deemed agency clause on the status of the privately appointed receiver in relation to the management of the business. The deemed agency clause provided that a privately appointed receiver acted as agent of the debtor. This provided continuity in the contractual relations following the invocation of receivership proceedings. The privately appointed receiver was thereby able to perform the debtor's contracts because the receiver acted as the debtor's agent in doing so. Many of the personal property security statutes and business corporations statutes provide that a person who is appointed receiver and manager has the right to carry on the business of the debtor.[9] It may be that a deemed agency clause is no longer needed to provide contractual continuity in light of the statutory grant of authority to manage the business.

It might also be argued that these provisions go further and give the receiver an independent status to operate the business.[10] This would mean that a privately appointed receiver would be treated in much the same way as a court-appointed receiver in entering into new contracts. The receiver would contract in the receiver's personal capacity and the debtor would not be liable on the contract. The treatment of set-off would also change. The legislative provisions merely empower a receiver to carry on the business and do not provide any guidance on whether the receiver does so as agent of the debtor or in an independent capacity. It therefore can be argued that clearer language would be expected if the intent was to change the status of the privately appointed receiver to such a major extent. Courts have, to date, shown no inclination to take this step. For this reason, the discussion will proceed on the basis that the traditional view concerning a privately appointed receiver's power to manage the debtor's business is not altered by personal property security legislation.

---

8 See T Buckwold, "The Treatment of Receivers in the Personal Property Security Acts: Conceptual and Practical Implications" (1997) 29 *Canadian Business Law Journal* 277 at 296–99. See also J Ziegel, "The Privately Appointed Receiver and the Enforcement of Security Interests: Anomaly or Superior Solution?" in J Ziegel, ed, *Current Developments in International and Comparative Corporate Insolvency Law* (Oxford: Clarendon Press, 1994) 450 at 463–66.

9 See, for example, *Personal Property Security Act*, RSA 2000, c P-7, s 65(2)(a) [Alta *PPSA*]; *Canada Business Corporations Act*, RSC 1985, c C-44, s 95 [*CBCA*].

10 See Buckwold, above note 8 at 307–10.

B. THE SOURCE OF THE RECEIVER'S POWERS

1) The Powers of the Court-Appointed Receiver

The powers of a court-appointed receiver are those enumerated in the court order. A court-appointed receiver must be careful not to act in excess of the powers conferred in the court order, since this may result in a loss of the right to receive an indemnity for fees and expenses.[11] The receiver who has been privately appointed and who is subsequently appointed pursuant to a court order is limited to the powers conferred by the court order and may not exercise any of the powers previously obtained pursuant to the private appointment.[12]

The template receivership order that has been developed in several provinces sets out the powers of the court-appointed receiver. These include the following powers:[13]

- to take possession and control of the property and to protect and preserve it;
- to manage, operate, and carry on the business;
- to cease to carry on all or part of the business and to cease to perform any contract;
- to engage consultants and experts;
- to commence, continue, or defend a legal action and settle or compromise legal proceedings;
- to market the property for sale; and
- to report to and meet interested stakeholders and to discuss with them matters concerning the property.

The order will not give the receiver an unrestricted power to sell the assets outside the ordinary course of business, since the expectation is that the court will be required to grant its approval to any proposed sale. However, the template receivership order gives the receiver the power to sell property outside the ordinary course of business without the need for approval if it falls below a certain value specified in the order. The order also gives the receiver the power to borrow money up to a specified amount and provides that such borrowings are secured by a first charge on the assets and have priority over all other interests including security interests.

---

11 *Re Ursel Investments Ltd* (1992), 10 CBR (3d) 61 (Sask CA).

12 *Price Waterhouse Ltd v Creighton Holdings Ltd* (1984), 54 CBR (NS) 116 (Sask QB).

13 See online: www.ontariocourts.ca/scj/practice/practice-directions/toronto/#Commercial_List_Forms_including_Model_Orders.

The template order does not give the receiver the power to make an assignment in bankruptcy or consent to a bankruptcy order. Although this provision was included in some orders in the past, it was thought that the court should decide whether this course of action is appropriate since bankruptcy may have the effect of reversing the priority ranking of some of the creditors.[14]

2) The Powers of the Privately Appointed Receiver

The traditional view is that the privately appointed receiver's powers are derived from both the secured creditor and the debtor. From the secured creditor, the receiver acquires the power to enforce the security interest against the collateral. This includes the right to take possession of the collateral, the right to sell it, and the right to apply the proceeds of sale against the secured obligation. These rights are proprietary rights that can be asserted not only against the debtor but also against a third party who has possession and control of the collateral, unless the third party holds a competing proprietary right that is entitled to priority over the secured party. It is no longer necessary to adopt an agency analysis in respect of a receiver's power to enforce a security interest that is governed by personal property security legislation. The statutes give a receiver the right to enforce the security interest and impose liability on the receiver for the failure to comply with the enforcement regime.[15]

From the debtor, the receiver acquires the power to manage the business. The security agreement that creates the right to appoint a receiver contains a clause that provides that the receiver is deemed to act as agent for the debtor. Deemed agency clauses have been upheld and given effect by courts in England and Canada. The powers that are conferred upon the receiver are derived from the debtor, even though it is the secured creditor who makes the appointment. The unusual feature of this power is that the debtor is unable to terminate or limit the exercise of this power by its agent (the receiver) without the consent of the secured creditor.

The leading Canadian decision that recognizes the dual agency of the privately appointed receiver is that of the Ontario Court of Appeal in *Peat Marwick Ltd v Consumers' Gas Co.*[16] The court held that, by virtue of the deemed agency clause, the receiver acts as the agent of the debtor in

14 See online: https://albertacourts.ca/docs/default-source/Court-of-Queen's-Bench/receivership-order-explanatory-notes-(pdf).pdf.

15 See Section A(2), above in this chapter.

16 Above note 2.

occupying the premises of the debtor and in carrying on the business. In realizing the collateral, the receiver acts as the agent of the secured creditor.

The source of the receiver's powers is significant for a number of reasons. One of the functions of a deemed agency clause is to protect the secured creditor from liability for the acts of the receiver. Since the receiver acts as agent of the debtor in managing the business, the secured creditor will not be liable for the acts of the receiver. This insulation from liability does not operate when the receiver exercises his or her powers to realize the property or on bankruptcy of the debtor, since the receiver does not act as agent of the debtor in these circumstances.

A number of other issues also turn on whether the receiver is acting as agent of the secured creditor or agent of the debtor. Because the receiver manages the business as agent of the debtor, existing contracts are unaffected by the appointment of the receiver. In the absence of a deemed agency provision in the security agreement, the receiver would not act as agent of the debtor and therefore would have no right to perform existing contracts on behalf of the debtor. The clause also gives the receiver the power to enter into new contracts and to repudiate existing contracts on behalf of the debtor. If the appointment of the receiver is invalid, the deemed agency clause will not come into operation and the secured creditor will be liable for the acts and omissions of the receiver.

Neither the secured creditor nor the receiver is liable in respect of new contracts that are entered into by the receiver following the appointment. The receiver acts as agent of the debtor and so does not incur liability to a party with whom he or she contracts, unless the receiver additionally agrees to be personally liable on the contract. However, if a privately appointed receiver makes representations to the effect that parties who enter into new contracts will be paid, this likely indicates that the receiver has undertaken personal liability on the new contracts.[17]

3) The Effect of Bankruptcy on the Powers of a Receiver

A bankruptcy of the debtor brings to an end the operation of the deemed agency provision.[18] Upon bankruptcy, the debtor's property vests in the trustee in bankruptcy, and the debtor loses the capacity to deal such property. The receiver can no longer be regarded as acting as the agent of the debtor, since the debtor no longer has title to the assets or the

---

17 See Review Committee of Insolvency Law and Practice, *Report of the Review Committee of Insolvency Law and Practice*, Cmnd 8558 (London: HMSO, 1982) at 108–9 [*Cork Report*].

18 *Gaskell v Gosling*, [1897] AC 575 (HL); *Thomas v Todd*, [1926] 2 KB 511.

capacity to deal with them. A bankruptcy of the debtor does not affect the receiver's right to enforce the security.[19]

It is not uncommon for a secured creditor to initiate a bankruptcy in order to obtain a more favourable priority ranking in bankruptcy.[20] This advantage should be weighed against a number of potential problems that it creates. The bankruptcy prevents the receiver from acting as agent of the debtor, which in turn prevents the receiver from entering into new contracts on behalf of the debtor. If new contracts are concluded, the receiver does so only in his or her personal capacity or as agent of the secured creditor. A receiver also has no right to perform existing contracts that were entered into by the debtor without the consent of the other contracting party. A receiver is therefore exposed to greater potential liability.

A bankruptcy of the debtor has no effect on the powers of a court-appointed receiver. The court-appointed receiver does not act as agent of the debtor and therefore is unaffected by the bankruptcy.

4) The Effect of a Receivership on the Powers of Directors

The appointment of a receiver causes the directors of a corporate debtor to lose their power of management over the assets of the corporation. The appointment of a receiver does not cause a removal of the directors,[21] who are therefore entitled to exercise powers that do not involve dealings with the assets. Some courts have taken the view that there remains a residual role for directors following the appointment of a receiver in that the directors may bring legal actions in the name of the corporation so long as these actions do not prejudice the secured creditor's interest in the assets.[22] Canadian decisions have since departed from this position.[23] These courts have held that the common law position has been altered by the provisions in business corporations statutes that expressly provide that the directors may not exercise any powers that are authorized to be exercised by the receiver.[24]

---

19 See Chapter 5, Section B(2).

20 See Chapter 5, Section B(6).

21 *Toronto Dominion Bank v Fortin* (1978), 26 CBR (NS) 168 (BCSC).

22 *Newhart Developments Ltd v Co-operative Commercial Bank Ltd*, [1978] QB 814; *First Investors Corp v Prince Royal Inn Ltd* (1988), 69 CBR (NS) 50 (Alta QB). And see M Wylie, "Legal Proceedings by a Board in Corporate Receiverships" (1990) 5 *Banking and Finance Law Review* 137.

23 *Maple Leaf Foods Inc v Markland Seafoods Ltd* (2007), 29 CBR (5th) 270 (NLCA) [*Maple Leaf Foods*]; *Lang Michener v American Bullion Minerals Ltd* (2006), 21 CBR (5th) 118 (BCSC) [*Lang Michener*].

24 See, for example, *CBCA*, above note 9, s 96.

The directors of a corporation may allege that a secured creditor acted wrongfully in appointing a privately appointed receiver. Although a receiver is generally given the power to prosecute and defend actions, a receiver is not entitled to exercise this power in relation to litigation between the debtor corporation and the secured creditor in respect of the appointment of the receiver, since this would constitute a conflict of interest.[25] The directors therefore retain the power to bring actions on behalf of the corporation against the secured creditor or the receiver. This principle applies equally in respect of a court-appointed receiver.[26]

A related controversy arises over whether the directors are permitted to look to the debtor's assets, which are in the control of the receiver, to fund the litigation against the secured creditor or against the receiver. Courts have made orders permitting directors to do so. In making such orders, the court will attempt to weigh the interests of the various parties and may consider:[27]

- the nature of the proceeding the directors wish to bring;
- the merits of the proceeding;
- the impact on the secured creditor if the application for funds is allowed;
- the impact on other creditors of allowing or not allowing the application; and
- the impact on the proposed proceedings if the application is denied.

C. CONTRACTUAL DEALINGS

1) New Contracts

A privately appointed receiver will typically enter into new contracts as agent of the debtor and therefore will not incur personal liability on the contract unless the receiver has expressly or impliedly assumed this liability.[28] The receiver does not act as agent of the debtor in the absence of a deemed agency provision in the security agreement, in the case of an invalid appointment of a receiver, upon the bankruptcy

25 *Maple Leaf Foods*, above note 23; *Lang Michener*, above note 23.

26 *Toronto Dominion Bank v Fortin*, above note 21; *Royal Bank of Canada v Tower Aircraft Hardware Inc* (1991), 3 CBR (3d) 60 (Alta QB).

27 *Standard Trust Co (Liquidator of) v 2448956 Manitoba Ltd* (1993), 18 CBR (3d) 251 (Man QB) and *Amcan Industries Corp v Toronto-Dominion Bank*, [1998] OJ No 3014 (Gen Div), both quoting from M Wylie, Case Comment, *Royal Bank of Canada v West-Can Resource Finance Corp* (1990) 3 CBR (3d) 70 at 72.

28 *Peat Marwick*, above note 2.

of the debtor, or if the receiver acts on the instructions of the secured creditor. In these situations, the receiver will be personally liable on any new contracts.[29]

A court-appointed receiver contracts in his or her own right and therefore is personally liable for post-receivership obligations.[30] However, a court-appointed receiver who incurs such liabilities is entitled to be indemnified out of the assets of receivership in priority to other creditors.[31] This position has been modified by statute in British Columbia. A receiver is not personally liable on a contract if the receiver discloses in the contract that he or she is acting as a receiver.[32]

2) Executory Contracts

a) Affirmation

Upon being appointed, a receiver must decide either to perform or to repudiate existing contracts. A privately appointed receiver acts as agent of the debtor and therefore is not liable for any default in performance for pre-appointment or post-appointment breaches, since the liability is that of the debtor and not of the agent. A decision to affirm an existing contract does not render a court-appointed receiver liable for the debtor's breaches that occurred before the receiver was appointed,[33] but a court-appointed receiver is liable for any contractual breaches that occur after affirmation of the contract.[34]

The position is more complicated if the debtor was in breach of the agreement. If the breach merely gives the counterparty a right to recover damages for breach of contract, a privately appointed receiver may elect to perform the contract, and the counterparty has a claim as an unsecured creditor in respect of the contractual damages. If the breach allows the counterparty to treat any future obligations as terminated (thereby relieving both parties of any future performance), the receiver is in no different position than the debtor and cannot compel performance by the counterparty.[35] An *ipso facto* clause that terminates

---

29 *Gaskell v Gosling*, above note 18; *American Express International Banking Corp v Hurley*, [1985] 3 All ER 564 (QBD).

30 *Re Smith & Son* (1929), 10 CBR 393 (Ont HCJ); *Re Ashk Development Corp*, above note 3.

31 *Crédit foncier franco-canadien v Edmonton Airport Hotel Co* (1966), 55 WWR 734 (Alta SCTD).

32 *Personal Property Security Act*, RSBC 1996, c 359, s 64(5). And see *Bank of Montreal v Pioneer Meat Packers Ltd* (1981), 38 CBR (NS) 40 (BCCA).

33 *Bank of Montreal v Scaffold Connection Corp* (2002), 36 CBR (4th) 13 (Alta QB).

34 *Bayhold Financial Corp v Clarkson Co* (1991), 10 CBR (3d) 159 (NSCA).

35 *Peat Marwick*, above note 2.

or amends an agreement or calls for accelerated payment or forfeiture of the term is fully effective. Unlike the *BIA* and the *CCAA*, no legislative provisions have been enacted that limit the use of such clauses in respect of a receivership.[36]

The analysis proceeds along a different path in the case of a court-appointed receiver. The court-appointed receiver is not an agent for the debtor, and so the rights of the receiver vis-à-vis the counterparty do not depend upon whether the counterparty has a right to terminate the contract.[37] Instead, the matter is controlled through the stay of proceedings that is granted by the court when the receiver is appointed. The template receivership orders prohibit any person from terminating, repudiating, or ceasing to perform any agreement without the consent of the receiver or leave of the court. Suppliers are similarly prevented from terminating contracts for the supply of goods and services but are entitled to recover from the receiver the price of any post-receivership supply at the normal contract rate. A counterparty can invoke the comeback clause in the receivership order and apply to court for an order lifting the stay in respect of the contract so as to permit the party to terminate the agreement.

b) Disclaimer

A receiver may wish to disclaim an existing contract. If this is done, the counterparty will have a claim for damages against the debtor for breach of contract.[38] However, the counterparty will not have a claim against a receiver for disclaiming the contract.[39]

Historically, the courts exercised greater control over a receiver's ability to repudiate contracts in respect of a court-appointed receivership than they did in respect of a privately appointed receivership.[40] The court-appointed receiver is under an obligation to consider the interests of all interested parties, and courts can control the receiver's exercise of this power. A court-appointed receiver must act in a fair and equitable manner and consider the interests of all parties. If the court concludes that a disclaimer of a contract would cause unfair prejudice to a counterparty, the court may refuse the receiver permis-

---

36 See Chapter 6, Section B(2) and Chapter 13, Section D(1).

37 *Canadian Commercial Bank v Universal Tank Ltd* (1983), 49 CBR (NS) 226 (Alta QB).

38 *Parsons v Sovereign Bank of Canada*, above note 1.

39 Above note 34.

40 *Re Newdigate Colliery Ltd*, [1912] 1 Ch 468 (CA).

sion to disclaim a contract.[41] Although template receivership orders give court-appointed receivers the power to cease to perform any contract, counterparties may invoke the comeback provision in order to bring the receiver's decision to disclaim the contract before the court for review.

Courts did not have the same latitude to control the disclaimer of a contract by a privately appointed receiver. However, it is possible that the changes resulting from the legislative regulation of receiverships have altered this position in relation to the privately appointed receiver. Courts have been given the power to exercise the same supervisory power over privately appointed receivers that they have in respect of court-appointed receivers.[42] This suggests that the courts may now have the power to exercise control over the disclaiming of contracts by privately appointed receivers. The matter would not be brought before the court pursuant to a comeback clause, since no court order is required to initiate the receivership proceedings. Instead, the matter would be brought before the court using the procedure provided by the personal property security legislation or business corporations legislation that gives an interested party the right to ask the court for directions or to seek relief.[43]

c) Assignment

The contract between the debtor and the counterparty may prohibit the debtor from assigning the benefit of the contract to another party without the consent of the counterparty. In the case of a privately appointed receiver, the receiver is bound by the provision to the same extent that the provision binds the debtor. Although the 2009 amendments to the *BIA* and the *CCAA* permit such transfers in bankruptcy proceedings and restructuring proceedings,[44] no similar provision was enacted in respect of receivership proceedings.

Prior to these amendments, courts in *CCAA* proceedings made orders permitting the transfer of rights to third parties in spite of anti-assignment clauses. These orders were made through the exercise of their inherent jurisdiction.[45] The *BIA* receivership provisions provide that the court may appoint a receiver to take any other action that the

---

41 *Bank of Montreal v Probe Exploration Inc* (2000), 33 CBR (4th) 173 (Alta QB), aff'd (2000), 33 CBR (4th) 182 (Alta CA).

42 See, for example, Alta *PPSA*, above note 9, s 65(7)(e). The Ontario *PPSA*, below note 43, is less clear on this point. And see Chapter 18, Section F.

43 See, for example, *Personal Property Security Act*, RSO 1990, c P.10, s 60(2) [Ont *PPSA*]; *CBCA*, above note 9, s 100.

44 *BIA*, s 84.1; *CCAA*, s 11.3.

45 *Re Playdium Entertainment Corp* (2001), 31 CBR (4th) 302 (Ont SCJ).

court considers advisable. It is possible that a court may use this provision to justify a similar order in respect of court-appointed receiver.

3) Employment Contracts

Although there is some authority that suggests that a court-appointed receivership automatically terminates contracts of employment between the debtor and its employees,[46] the template receivership orders provide that the employees remain the employees of the debtor until the receiver, on behalf of the debtor, terminates the employment relationship.[47] A private receivership does not automatically terminate employees, since the deemed agency provision is given effect and the receiver is treated as agent of the debtor. However, if the debtor goes bankrupt, the appointment of a trustee will automatically terminate any contracts of employment.[48] As well, if the business is sold as a going concern, the contracts of employment will come to an end because the debtor has made further employment impossible.[49] If the privately appointed receiver decides to terminate some or all of the employees, the terminated employees can pursue their common law and statutory claims for wrongful dismissal against any funds that remain after the secured claims are paid.

4) Set-Off

Before modern personal property security legislation was introduced into Canada, the appointment of a receiver had the effect of crystallizing a floating charge. When this occurred, the courts held that the accounts owed to the debtor were assigned in equity to the secured creditor.[50] The appointment of a privately appointed receiver therefore resulted in a loss of mutuality so that debts that arose after the appointment of a receiver could not be set-off against a debt that arose before the appointment of a receiver.[51] This no longer holds true. The enactment of modern personal property security legislation in the provinces

46 *Parsons v Sovereign Bank of Canada*, above note 1.

47 Above note 13 at para 14.

48 *Re Rizzo & Rizzo Shoes Ltd*, [1998] 1 SCR 27.

49 *Addison v M Loeb Ltd* (1986), 25 DLR (4th) 151 (Ont CA); *White v Stenson Holdings Ltd* (1983), 22 BLR 25 (BCSC).

50 *Biggerstaff v Rowatt's Wharf Ltd*, [1896] 2 Ch 93 (CA); *Simpson Shatula Redi-Mix & Building Ltd v Keir Tire Ltd* (1982), 45 CBR (NS) 26 (Sask QB).

51 *Canadian Imperial Bank of Commerce v Tucker Industries Inc* (1983), 48 CBR (NS) 1 (BCCA).

has changed the legal analysis that is to be applied, although the end result is much the same as before.[52] The concept of a floating charge has no meaningful role within the context of the new legislation. A security interest that is taken in all present and after-acquired property attaches immediately when the security agreement is executed and value is given, and the debtor has rights in the collateral.[53]

The assignment of the account by way of security in favour of the secured creditor occurs immediately once the conditions for attachment have been satisfied and is not delayed until the appointment of a receiver. The account debtor is permitted to set-off debts accrued before the debtor has knowledge of the assignment.[54] Knowledge of the appointment of a receiver will almost certainly be regarded as knowledge of the assignment. The account debtor will therefore be unable to set-off debts that arise after knowledge of the appointment of a receiver. However, if the secured creditor notifies the account debtor of the assignment at some earlier date, the account debtor will lose the ability to set-off any debt that subsequently arises. Notice of the assignment will have no effect on the ability of the account debtor to claim equitable set-off in respect of closely connected contracts or events.[55] There is an exception to the rule that legal set-off cannot be claimed against debts that arise after knowledge of the assignment. If a receiver elects to continue an existing executory contract, the counterparty may assert a legal set-off in respect of pre-receivership obligations owed to it by the debtor.[56]

An application of the set-off principle in the context of a receivership is illustrated in the following scenario. A debtor corporation (D) is indebted to C. D defaults on a secured loan, and the secured creditor appoints a receiver who takes control and management of D's business. The receiver subsequently sells goods to C on credit and, when payment of the price is due, C seeks to set-off the debt owed by D. Legal set-off is not permitted in this case, since C knows of the assignment of the account. However, if the contract for the sale of goods was a pre-existing contract that the receiver elected to perform, C could set-off the two debts. Set-off would also be permitted if the goods had been

---

52 See *Re Associated Investors of Canada Ltd* (1989), 76 CBR (NS) 185 (Alta QB) for the pre-*PPSA* position.

53 Cuming, Walsh, & Wood, *Personal Property Security Law*, above note 6 at 246–48 and 260–63.

54 See, for example, Alta *PPSA*, above note 9, s 41(2); Ont *PPSA*, above note 43, s 40(1.1).

55 *Ibid*. And see *Parsons v Sovereign Bank of Canada*, above note 1.

56 *Rother Irons Works Ltd v Canterbury Precision Engineers Ltd*, [1974] 1 QB 1.

sold to C before C knew of the assignment, even if the price was not payable until sometime after the appointment of the receiver.[57]

D. DUTIES OF THE RECEIVER

1) The Nature of the Duties

A court-appointed receiver is an officer of the court and acts in a fiduciary capacity in relation to all parties who have an interest in the assets under receivership.[58] The court-appointed receiver is not subject to the control or direction of the secured creditor and is under an obligation to make the same information available to all the parties.[59] The standard of care expected of a court-appointed receiver at common law is that which a reasonable person would exercise in respect of his or her own property or business.[60]

Under the common law, a much less extensive duty was imposed on a privately appointed receiver. The privately appointed receiver's duties were owed primarily to the secured creditor who appointed the receiver, although the receiver also owed a more limited duty to the debtor and to persons holding lower-ranking interests in the assets to act in good faith and to obtain the best price reasonably obtainable.[61]

A major difference between the duties owed by the court-appointed receiver and those exercised by the privately appointed receiver at common law was that a court-appointed receiver must consider the interests of all persons who have an interest in the assets, while the privately appointed receiver need consider only the interests of the secured creditor. Third parties had no right to complain about the timing of the sale despite the fact that a temporary delay might greatly benefit other interested parties without any detriment to the interests of the secured creditor.[62]

The common law position likely has been altered by statute. The *BIA* as well as provincial personal property security legislation and

---

57 *Christie v Taunton, Delmard, Lane & Co*, [1893] 2 Ch 175 (Ch D).

58 *Re Newdigate Colliery Ltd*, [1912] 1 Ch 468 (CA); *Ostrander v Niagara Helicopters Ltd* (1973), 19 CBR (NS) 5 (Ont HCJ) [*Ostrander*].

59 *Royal Bank of Canada v Vista Homes Ltd* (1984), 54 CBR (NS) 124 (BCSC) [*Vista Homes*]; *Re Ravelston Corp* (2007), 29 CBR (5th) 34 (Ont SCJ).

60 *Re Ursel Investments Ltd*, above note 11.

61 *Ostrander*, above note 58; *Downsview Nominees Ltd v First City Corp Ltd*, [1993] AC 295.

62 *Cuckmore Brick Co Ltd v Mutual Finance Ltd*, [1971] Ch 949; *South Sea Bank Ltd v Tan Soon Gin*, [1990] 1 AC 536.

business corporations legislation impose an obligation on a receiver to act in good faith and in a commercially reasonable manner.[63] This statutory duty of care is expected both of court-appointed and of privately appointed receivers. Furthermore, a privately appointed receiver may seek directions from a court, and this procedure may be used if the receiver is uncertain about the appropriate course of conduct where the interests of the stakeholders are in conflict. It is therefore reasonable to think that courts will assimilate the duties owed by both types of receivers and hold that the privately appointed receiver now owes the same duty to other interested parties as that owed by a court-appointed receiver.[64]

2) Accounting and Reporting Obligations of the Receiver

Provincial personal property security legislation, the federal business corporations statute, and several of the provincial business corporations statutes contain provisions that regulate receiverships. There is a high degree of duplication in the statutory provisions, but the duties imposed on receivers are not identical. Therefore, it is necessary for a receiver to ensure that all of the duties imposed by the applicable statutory regimes have been satisfied. The statutes apply to both court-appointed receivers and privately appointed receivers.

The statutes impose the following duties on a receiver:[65]

- to take the collateral into the receiver's custody and control;
- to notify immediately the corporate registrar of the receiver's appointment or discharge if the debtor is a corporation;
- to open and maintain a bank account in the receiver's name and to deposit all money coming under the receiver's control as a receiver;
- to keep detailed records, in accordance with accepted accounting practices, of all receipts, expenditures, and transactions relating to the assets;
- to prepare, at least once in every six-month period after the date of the receiver's appointment, financial statements of the receiver's administration; and
- to render a final account of the receiver's administration on completion of the receiver's duties, and to provide the corporate registrar with a copy if the debtor is a corporation.

---

63 *BIA*, s 247; *CBCA*, above note 9, s 99; Alta *PPSA*, above note 9, s 66(1).

64 See Buckwold, above note 8 at 296–99.

65 See, for example, *CBCA*, above note 9, s 101; Alta *PPSA*, above note 9, s 65(2).

The *BIA* provides additional reporting duties. A receiver must, forthwith upon taking control of the assets, prepare a statement that sets out the name of each creditor and the amount of their claim, a list of the property and its book value, and the receiver's intended plan of action to the extent that it has been established.[66] A receiver is also required to prepare interim reports at least every six months and a final report that contains a statement of receipts and disbursements.[67] The receiver must provide a copy of the reports to the Superintendent of Bankruptcy, the debtor, and any creditor who requests a copy.

E. LIABILITY OF THE RECEIVER

1) Sources of Liability

A receiver may be liable in respect of new contracts concluded by him or her after the commencement of the receivership. This will always be the case in respect of a court-appointed receiver but will usually not be the case in respect of a privately appointed receiver.[68] A receiver may also be liable for loss caused by a failure to act in a commercially reasonable manner.[69] This might occur if the receiver sells the property at an unreasonably low price that is sufficient to pay out the secured creditor but that results in a lesser recovery by the lower-ranking claimants. A guarantor may also seek to recover loss caused by an improvident realization of the assets by the receiver.[70] The mere fact that a receiver is appointed by a court is not a bar to an action against the receiver.[71]

In addition to these two sources of liability, a receiver is potentially subject to liability that is not based upon contract or tort but rather is imposed by statute. Environmental protection statutes impose liability for the costs of remediation on persons who exercise control of the property. In 1997 the *BIA* was amended in order to extend to receivers the same protection afforded to trustees in connection with environmental liability. A receiver is not personally liable for any environmental damage that occurred before his or her appointment, but only

66 *BIA*, s 246(1); *Bankruptcy and Insolvency General Rules*, SOR/98-240, s 125.

67 *BIA*, ss 246(2)–(3); *Bankruptcy and Insolvency General Rules*, above note 66, ss 126–27.

68 See Section C(1), above in this chapter.

69 See Section D(1), above in this chapter. See also Cuming, Walsh, & Wood, *Personal Property Security Law*, above note 6 at 647–50.

70 *Standard Chartered Bank Ltd v Walker*, [1982] 3 All ER 938 (CA).

71 *Vista Homes*, above note 59.

for post-appointment damage caused by the receiver's gross negligence or wilful misconduct.[72]

Employment statutes are another potential source of statutory liability. The issue is whether a receiver who continues to operate a business is liable as a successor employer. The Supreme Court of Canada in *GMAC Commercial Credit Corp - Canada v TCT Logistics Inc*[73] held that the bankruptcy courts do not have the jurisdiction to decide this question, but that it is properly a matter to be decided by the labour relations tribunal. The question that remains is whether these tribunals will decide that receivers are liable as successor employers. The 2009 amendments to the *BIA* have expanded the statutory liability shield for trustees and receivers. A receiver who continues to operate a business or continues the employment of the debtor's employees is not personally liable for any liability, including that of a successor employer, in respect of claims arising before or upon the receiver's appointment or that are calculated by reference to a period before the receiver's appointment.[74]

2) Protective Devices

Courts have attempted to create a liability shield in favour of receivers through the use of a stay of proceedings in the order appointing the receiver or through provisions limiting the liability of a receiver. These attempts have subsequently been rendered ineffective for the most part. The Supreme Court of Canada in *TCT Logistics* has held that these can be used only to screen out frivolous and vexatious claims, and not to pursue broader bankruptcy objectives.[75] In *Re Big Sky Living Inc*,[76] the court indicated that a court should not make orders that expand or extend the statutory liability shield provided in the *BIA*.

FURTHER READINGS

BAIRD, D, & R DAVIS. "Labour Issues," in S Ben-Ishai & A Duggan, eds, *Canadian Bankruptcy and Insolvency Law: Bill C-55, Statute c. 47 and Beyond* (Markham, ON: LexisNexis Canada, 2007) ch 4

72 *BIA*, s 14.06(2).
73 [2006] 2 SCR 123.
74 *BIA*, s 14.06(1.2).
75 Above note 73.
76 (2002), 37 CBR (4th) 42 (Alta QB).

BENNETT, F. *Bennett on Receiverships*, 2d ed (Toronto: Carswell, 1998) ch 5 and 7

BLANCHARD, P, & M GEDYE. *Private Receivers of Companies in New Zealand* (Wellington: LexisNexis, 2008) ch 10 & 11

BUCKWOLD, T. "The Treatment of Receivers in the Personal Property Security Acts: Conceptual and Practical Implications" (1997) 29 *Canadian Business Law Journal* 277

WYLIE, M. "Legal Proceedings by a Board in Corporate Receiverships" (1990) 5 *Banking and Finance Law Review* 137

ZIEGEL, J. "The Privately Appointed Receiver and the Enforcement of Security Interests: Anomaly or Superior Solution?" in J Siegel, ed, *Current Developments in International and Comparative Corporate Insolvency Law* (Oxford: Clarendon Press, 1994) 450

PART FOUR

OTHER INSOLVENCY REGIMES

CHAPTER 20

ALTERNATIVES TO CONSUMER AND FARM BANKRUPTCY

This chapter covers three different insolvency regimes. The consumer proposal provisions and the orderly payment of debts provisions of the *BIA* both deal with consumer debtors. The *Farm Debt Mediation Act*[1] covers farmers. All of them operate as alternatives to bankruptcy. By invoking these regimes, the consumer or farm debtor will avoid a bankruptcy and will be entitled to keep his or her assets.

The consumer proposal provisions permit consumers to make a proposal to their creditors. The provisions differ from the commercial proposal under the *BIA* in that the process is quicker and simpler and the voting rules make it easier for the debtor to obtain the approval of the creditors. The orderly payment of debts provisions, which operate in only four of the provinces, do not require the approval of creditors. They merely create a process through which the various debts of the consumer debtor may be consolidated into a single sum. The farm debt mediation statute provides a process through which a voluntary arrangement can be concluded between a farmer and his or her creditors. Unlike commercial restructuring proceedings, there is no mechanism to bind a dissenting creditor.

1 SC 1997, c 21 [*FDMA*].

A. CONSUMER PROPOSALS

A consumer proposal differs from a consumer bankruptcy in several respects. First, the property of the debtor does not vest in an insolvency administrator. A consumer debtor may consider a consumer proposal to be a better option since the debtor is able to keep his or her house, vehicle, and other property. Payments to the creditors are generally made from the future income or other earnings of the debtor over the course of the consumer proposal. A consumer may also choose a consumer proposal to avoid the stigma of bankruptcy or in the hope of procuring a more favourable credit history. Second, the insolvency process does not involve a liquidation of the debtor's assets. Instead, the process involves the preparation of a proposal and its acceptance or rejection through a vote of the creditors. The proposal binds creditors even if they have voted against it, so long as a majority of the creditors have approved of it. The voting rules are heavily skewed towards obtaining approval of a consumer proposal, since silence is taken as consent to the proposal.[2]

The choice between making a consumer proposal and making an assignment in bankruptcy is generally done in consultation with a trustee, since both bankruptcies and consumer proposals require the services of a licensed trustee. However, the *BIA* attempts to dissuade debtors from choosing bankruptcy if a consumer proposal is a viable option. A court is not permitted to grant an absolute discharge if the bankrupt could have made a viable proposal but chose to proceed to bankruptcy as the means to resolve the indebtedness.[3]

1) Eligibility

A consumer proposal is a voluntary process that can be initiated only by a debtor.[4] In order to be eligible to make a consumer proposal, the debtor must fall within the Division II definition of a "consumer debtor."[5] To qualify as a consumer debtor, the debtor must:

---

2 Registrar Nettie in *Re Sztojka*, 2005 CarswellOnt 7449 at para 2 (SCJ) observed that the consumer proposals provisions are "drafted in such a manner as to favour creditor apathy, and result in deemed creditor acceptance and deemed Court approval in the vast majority of proposals filed under Division II."

3 *BIA*, ss 172(2) and 173(1)(n). A mediation process is used to resolve this question if it is the only grounds for objection to the discharge. See *BIA*, ss 170.1(1)–(2).

4 *Ibid*, s 66.12(1).

5 *Ibid*, s 66.11(1) "consumer debtor."

- be an individual;
- be bankrupt or insolvent; and
- have aggregate debts, excluding any debts secured by the person's principal residence, that are not more than $250,000.[6]

All secured obligations, other than the debt secured against the debtor's principal residence, must be included in the calculation of the $250,000 monetary limit. Two or more consumer proposals may be dealt with as one consumer proposal where the debts of the individuals making the joint proposal are substantially the same.[7] However, the $250,000 monetary limit also applies to a joint proposal. A consumer cannot make a consumer proposal if an earlier one has been annulled or is deemed to be annulled, unless a court orders otherwise.[8] A bankrupt must obtain the approval of the inspectors, if any, before making a consumer proposal.[9]

The ineligibility of the debtor does not result in the invalidity of a consumer proposal. If it is later discovered that the debtor is ineligible, the creditors and the official receiver must be notified.[10] This gives them the ability to object to the proposal or seek to have it annulled.[11]

2) The Administrator

In order to make a consumer proposal, the consumer debtor must obtain the assistance of an administrator.[12] Licensed trustees are qualified to act as administrators.[13] The administrator conducts an investigation of the financial affairs of the debtor, provides the debtor with financial counselling, prepares the consumer proposal and statement of affairs, and files it with the official receiver.[14] The administrator must prepare a report that sets out the result of the investigation and the administrator's opinion as to whether the consumer proposal is reasonable and fair to the consumer debtor and the creditors, and whether the consumer

6 The monetary limit was raised from $75,000 to $250,000 by the 2009 amendments.

7 *BIA*, s 66.12(1.1) and Superintendent's Directive No 2R (19 December 1997).

8 *BIA*, s 66.32(1).

9 *Ibid*, s 66.4(2). Approval or deemed approval of the consumer proposal by a court annuls the bankruptcy and revests the property in the consumer debtor.

10 *Ibid*, s 66.13(4).

11 *Re Jalal* (2003), 42 CBR (4th) 260 (Ont SCJ).

12 *BIA*, s 66.13(1).

13 *Ibid*, s 66.11(1) "administrator." The definition also covers a person appointed or designated by the superintendent to administer consumer proposals.

14 *Ibid*, s 66.13(2).

debtor will be able to perform it.[15] The administrator is required to send the report together with the consumer proposal, statement of affairs, and a proof of claim form to every known creditor.[16]

3) Effect of Making a Consumer Proposal

An automatic stay of proceedings comes into effect upon the filing of a consumer proposal with the official receiver and continues until the consumer proposal is withdrawn, refused, annulled, or deemed annulled or the administrator has been discharged.[17] A stay of proceedings does not come into effect if a consumer proposal has been made within six months of the filing of a previous consumer proposal.[18]

The stay of proceedings is very similar in effect to that which arises upon a bankruptcy of the debtor.[19] It prevents a creditor from commencing or continuing any action against the debtor or exercising any remedy. Like the automatic bankruptcy stay, it does not apply to a secured creditor.[20] The filing of a consumer proposal renders a wage assignment ineffective in respect of any wages earned after the filing of the consumer proposal.[21] An employer is prohibited from dismissing an employee by reason only that a consumer proposal has been filed in respect of the employee.[22]

The filing of a consumer proposal has the same effect on a writ or judgment as the commencement of bankruptcy proceedings.[23] The judgment enforcement is not afforded any special priority but must share with the other unsecured creditors pursuant to the terms of the consumer proposal.[24] Upon the filing of a consumer proposal, parties who have entered contracts with the debtor are not permitted to invoke clauses

---

15 *Ibid*, s 66.14(a). The report also sets out a list of the creditors whose claims exceed $250.

16 *Ibid*, s 66.14(b). The materials that are sent to the creditors must also contain a statement that a meeting of creditors will be held only if required and court review of the consumer proposal will occur only if requested.

17 *Ibid*, s 69.2(1).

18 *Ibid*, s 69.2(2).

19 See Chapter 6, Section A.

20 *BIA*, s 69.2(4). Although the automatic stay does operate against secured creditors, the debtor may apply to court for a temporary stay of proceedings against a secured creditor.

21 *Ibid*, s 66.35. Note that several jurisdictions prohibit or restrict the use of wage assignments. See, for example, *Employment Standards Act*, RSBC 1996, c 113, ss 22–24.

22 *BIA*, *ibid*, s 66.36.

23 *Ibid*, s 70(1). And see Chapter 6, Section A(4).

24 *Toronto-Dominion Bank v Phillips*, 2014 ONCA 613.

that permit the other contracting party to exercise *ipso facto* clauses. These are contractual provisions that permit the other contracting party to terminate or amend the contract or to claim an accelerated payment or forfeiture of the term by reason of the insolvency of the debtor or the filing of a consumer proposal.[25] However, contractual provisions that permit termination, amendment, or acceleration may be invoked if some other event of default is triggered. For example, a secured consumer-loan agreement may provide that a term loan is accelerated and immediately payable if the debtor fails to repay an instalment when it is due. Although a secured creditor cannot accelerate the loan because of the debtor's insolvency, it may do so because of the debtor's failure to repay. However, the applicable provincial law may provide the consumer debtor with a right to reinstate a security agreement and thereby deactivate the effect of an acceleration clause.[26]

If the consumer debtor has leased property, the lessor is not permitted to terminate the agreement for default so long as post-filing lease payments are made when they are due.[27] Similarly, a public utility is not permitted to discontinue service so long as post-filing payments amounts are paid as they become due.[28] A court may declare the provision inapplicable if the contracting party applies to the court and convinces it that the operation of the provision would likely cause significant financial hardship.[29]

4) Terms of the Consumer Proposal

A consumer proposal must be made to the creditors generally and must provide that its performance is to be completed within five years.[30] The consumer proposal must provide for payment of preferred claims in priority to the payment of other claims and must provide for payment of the costs of administration and counselling.[31] It must also specify the manner of distributing dividends. All amounts payable under the consumer proposal must be paid to the administrator, who in turn must distribute these funds to the creditors in accordance with the

---

25 *BIA*, s 66.34(1). This cannot be evaded by a waiver clause or other contractual exemption in the agreement. See *BIA*, s 66.34(5).

26 See, for example, *Personal Property Security Act*, RSA 2000, c P-7, s 63(1); *Personal Property Security Act*, RSO 1990, c P.10, s 66(2).

27 *BIA*, ss 66.34(2) and (4).

28 *Ibid*, ss 66.34(3) & (4).

29 *Ibid*, s 66.34(6).

30 *Ibid*, ss 66.12(3) and (5).

31 *Ibid*, s 66.12(6).

terms of the consumer proposal after payment of the relevant fees and expenses.[32] The consumer proposal will typically specify the frequency of payments and the time period over which they are to occur. A consumer proposal may include provisions or terms that provide for the supervision of the affairs of the consumer debtor.[33] The British Columbia Court of Appeal held that a consumer proposal may validly include a term that the administrator has the power to extend the time for making a payment pursuant to the proposal.[34]

5) Meeting of Creditors

There is no requirement for a meeting of creditors, and in most consumer proposals a meeting is not convened. The administrator must call a meeting of creditors if, within the forty-five-day period following the filing of the consumer proposal, the administrator is directed to do so by the official receiver or requested to do so by creditors together holding at least 25 percent of the value of the proven claims.[35] The creditors may appoint up to three inspectors of the estate of the consumer debtor. The inspectors have the same powers as inspectors in a bankruptcy, unless these powers are extended or restricted by the consumer proposal.[36] The reality in most consumer proposals is that a meeting of creditors is not called, no inspectors are appointed, and hence the administrator is the only conduit between the consumer debtor and the creditors.[37]

6) Voting on the Consumer Proposal

If a meeting is requested, the administrator must send a voting form and a proxy form to the creditors.[38] The proxy form is used to permit another person to attend the meeting and vote on behalf of the creditor. The voting letter is used to direct the administrator to vote for or against the proposal. The creditors are notified of the meeting and creditors who have proven their claims may indicate their assent

---

32 *Ibid*, s 66.26(1).

33 *Ibid*, s 66.2.

34 *Dondale (Re)*, 2009 BCCA 10. The court declined to follow *Re Sztojka*, above note 2, which indicated that this type of provision was not permissible.

35 *BIA*, s 66.15(2).

36 *Ibid*, s 66.21.

37 *Re Dondale* (2007), 34 CBR (5th) 113 at para 5 (BCSC).

38 *BIA*, s 66.15(3).

to or dissent from the consumer proposal.[39] Unless it is rescinded, any assent or dissent that is received by an administrator has the same effect as if the creditor had been present and voted at the meeting.[40] The creditors are deemed to accept a consumer proposal if a meeting of creditors has not been requested or if a meeting is requested but there is no quorum.[41]

Only creditors who have proven their claims prior to the meeting are permitted to vote. The creditors vote for or against the consumer proposal as a single class.[42] Each creditor is entitled to one vote for each dollar of proven claim.[43] A creditor who is related to the consumer debtor may vote against but not for the acceptance of the consumer proposal.[44] The administrator, as a creditor, is not entitled to vote.[45] A consumer proposal is accepted by a simple majority of votes.

Courts have divided over the question as to how votes cast by secured creditors should be counted in respect of a consumer proposal. The voting rules indicate that the creditors are to vote as a single class.[46] Some courts have held that this permits a secured creditor to vote the full value of its claim.[47] Others have held that this must be read in light of other bankruptcy provisions that require a secured creditor to either value its collateral and vote only in respect of the difference or surrender its security and vote the full value of the claim.[48] The latter view accords better with the underlying objectives of the legislation as the former view gives disproportionate power to secured creditors despite the fact that their rights as secured creditors cannot be affected by the consumer proposal.[49]

---

39 *Ibid*, s 66.17(1). The dissent or assent must be given at or prior to a meeting of creditors or prior to the forty-five-day period following the filing of the consumer proposal.

40 *Ibid*, s 66.17(2).

41 *Ibid*, ss 66.18(1) & (2).

42 *Ibid*, s 66.19(1).

43 *Ibid*, s 115.

44 *Ibid*, s 66.19(2). The definition of a related person is found in *BIA*, s 4.

45 *Ibid*, s 66.19(3).

46 *Ibid*, s 66.19(1).

47 *Laforge (Proposition de)*, 2007 QCCS 1074.

48 *Schryburt (Re)*, 2011 ONSC 880.

49 *BIA*, s 66.19(1) indicates that the voting rules are subject to the rights of a secured creditor. Secured creditors are therefore only affected to the extent that they seek to recover the difference between the obligation secured and the value of the collateral. See also s 66.28 which holds that a secured creditor is bound only to the extent that they have filed a proof of claim.

An administrator may file an amendment to a consumer proposal.[50] The same rules for voting and approval apply to the amended consumer proposal.

7) Approval of a Consumer Proposal

If the creditors approve the consumer proposal or are deemed to have done so, it does not become binding until a completion of a process that permits court review of it. The official receiver and any other interested party may request the administrator to apply for a court review of the proposal within fifteen days of its acceptance or deemed acceptance by the creditors.[51] If the administrator receives no request within this period, the consumer proposal is deemed to be approved by the court.[52] If the administrator receives a request, the administrator must apply to court for a review and give notice of the hearing to the consumer debtor, the creditors with proven claims, and the official receiver.[53] A consumer debtor may withdraw the consumer proposal after it has been accepted but before the process for court review has been completed.[54]

The court has the power to approve or to refuse approval of the consumer proposal[55] but not to amend it.[56] The court shall refuse to approve a consumer proposal if it is of the opinion that the terms of the consumer proposal are not reasonable or are not fair to the consumer debtor and the creditors.[57] A court must also refuse approval of a consumer proposal if it does not comply with the statutory requirements for a consumer proposal.[58] The court has the discretion to refuse approval of a consumer proposal if the debtor has committed a bankruptcy offence or if the debtor was not eligible to make the consumer proposal when it was filed.[59]

There is little caselaw on what factors will be considered in determining whether a consumer proposal is fair and reasonable to the debtor and the creditors.[60] One standard against which it may be tested is the distribution that would be available to the creditors on a bank-

---

50 *Ibid*, s 66.37.
51 *Ibid*, s 66.22(1).
52 *Ibid*, s 66.22(2).
53 *Ibid*, s 66.23.
54 *Ibid*, s 66.25.
55 *Ibid*, s 66.24(4).
56 *Re Sztojka*, above note 2.
57 *BIA*, s 66.24(2).
58 *Ibid*, s 66.24(3). See Section A(4), above in this chapter.
59 *BIA*, s 66.24(2). And see *Re Ter Mors* (1998), 5 CBR (4th) 109 (Man QB).
60 *Re McLaughlin*, 2005 CarswellNS 535 (SC).

ruptcy of the consumer debtor. A creditor should not in principle be forced to accept an outcome that is less favourable than that obtained on a bankruptcy. In the case of a consumer proposal that is made by a bankrupt, a court may consider whether the terms of the consumer proposal are ones that the court would grant in connection with an order for a conditional discharge.[61]

8) Binding Effect of a Consumer Proposal

Once a consumer proposal is approved or is deemed to be approved by a court, it is binding on all the unsecured creditors of the consumer debtor, as well as on secured creditors who have filed proof of claims in respect of the difference between the amount owing and the value of their collateral.[62] Creditors with claims that arose after the filing of the consumer proposal do not participate in the consumer proposal and are not affected by it.[63] Non-dischargeable claims are not released unless the consumer proposal explicitly provides for the compromise of the debt or liability and the creditors holding such claims have voted for the acceptance of the consumer proposal.[64] The acceptance and approval of a consumer proposal does not affect claims of the creditors against third parties who have guaranteed a debt of a consumer debtor or who co-signed the obligation.[65]

9) Effect of Rejection or Withdrawal of a Consumer Proposal

Unlike a commercial proposal under Division I of the *BIA*, rejection of a consumer proposal by the creditors, refusal by a court to approve it, or withdrawal of it by the debtor does not result in an automatic bankruptcy of the debtor. The stay of proceedings ceases to operate and the

---

61 *Re Dunn* (2002), 31 CBR (4th) 237 (Alta QB).

62 *BIA*, s 66.28(2).

63 *Ibid*, s 66.28(1).

64 *Ibid*, s 66.28(2.1). This provision was added in the 2009 amendments to the *BIA*. The previous version provided that non-dischargeable debts were not released unless the creditors assented. In *Re Cardwell* (2006), 20 CBR (5th) 175 (Sask QB) and *Re Slaney* (2004), 4 CBR (5th) 95 (BCSC), the courts held that there must be an express term in the consumer proposal for the release of the non-dischargeable debt. However, this left open the possibility that creditors who did not vote against it would be deemed to assent to it. The new provision therefore requires both an express term in the consumer proposal and a positive vote in favour of it by the creditor holding the non-dischargeable claim.

65 *BIA*, s 66.28(3).

creditors are free to exercise their collection and enforcement remedies against the consumer debtor. The consumer debtor may make an assignment in bankruptcy, or may attempt another consumer proposal. The administrator is required to notify the consumer debtor, the creditors, and the official receiver of a refusal of a consumer proposal by the creditors or by a court or a withdrawal of it by the consumer debtor.[66]

10) Annulment by a Court

Two types of annulment of a consumer proposal are provided for in Division II: annulment ordered by a court and deemed annulment. A court may annul a consumer proposal in any of the following situations:[67]

- there is a default in the consumer proposal;
- the debtor was not eligible to make the proposal;
- the consumer proposal cannot continue without injustice or undue delay;
- the approval of the court was obtained by fraud; or
- the consumer debtor is afterwards convicted of a bankruptcy offence.

In determining whether it will exercise its discretion and annul a consumer proposal, a court will consider the conduct of the parties and the need to maintain the integrity of the consumer proposal provisions.[68] Upon the annulment of a consumer proposal by a court, the debtor is deemed to have made an assignment in bankruptcy on the date of the annulment.[69]

11) Deemed Annulment

If payments under a consumer proposal are to be made monthly or more frequently, a deemed annulment occurs when the consumer debtor is three months in default for an amount greater or equal to three payments. If payments are to be made less frequently than monthly under the consumer proposal, a deemed annulment occurs three months after a default in respect of any payment.[70] The deemed annulment will not operate if a court has previously ordered otherwise or if an amendment

---

66 *Ibid*, s 66.27. The notice must be given within five days of the refusal or withdrawal.

67 *Ibid*, ss 66.3(1) and (3).

68 See *Re Newsham* (2003), 48 CBR (4th) 121 (Alta QB); *Automotive Finance Corp v Davies* (2002), 33 CBR (4th) 22 (BCSC).

69 *BIA*, s 66.3(5)(a).

70 *Ibid*, s 66.31(1)

to the consumer proposal has been filed. A deemed annulment does not operate as a deemed assignment in bankruptcy.

Originally, neither a court nor an administrator had any power to suspend or relieve the operation of the deemed annulment.[71] This was changed by the 2009 amendments to the *BIA*. The administrator now has the discretion to attempt to revive a consumer proposal that is deemed to be annulled. A revival of a consumer proposal is possible only if the consumer debtor is not a bankrupt. The administrator must send a notice to the creditors informing them that the consumer proposal will be automatically revived sixty days after the date of the deemed annulment.[72] If no objection is sent in, the proposal is automatically revived.[73] If an objection is filed, the administrator must notify the creditors that the consumer proposal is not going to be automatically revived.[74] The administrator may apply to court for an order reviving the consumer proposal, and the court may make the order on any terms and conditions that it considers appropriate.[75] In determining whether an order for revival is appropriate, a court will consider the likelihood of success of the proposal, the conduct of the debtor, the interests of creditors, and the position of the Superintendent of Bankruptcy.[76] If a consumer proposal is revived, the administrator must notify the creditors and the official receiver.[77] The revival of a consumer proposal does not affect the validity of any act done by a creditor in exercise of its revived rights during the period after the deemed annulment of the consumer proposal and its revival.[78]

12) Effect of Annulment or Deemed Annulment

Upon an annulment or deemed annulment of a consumer proposal, the stay of proceedings comes to an end and, unless permitted to do so by

---

71 *Re Schrader* (1999), 13 CBR (4th) 256 (NSSC); *Re Dziewiacien* (2002), 37 CBR (4th) 250 (Ont SCJ).

72 *BIA*, s 66.31(6). The notice must be given not later than thirty days after the day of the deemed annulment unless some other time period is prescribed. The sixty-day period for automatic revival can also be varied if a different time period is prescribed in the General Rules. The official receiver must also be notified.

73 *Ibid*, s 66.31(7).

74 *Ibid*, s 66.31(8).

75 *Ibid*, s 66.31(9). Courts have taken the view that this allows them to amend the terms of the consumer proposal. See *Tavita (Re)*, 2012 SKQB 42. Notice of the application must be given to the creditors and to the official receiver.

76 *Birns v Kinequon*, 2013 SKQB 164.

77 *BIA*, s 66.31(10).

78 *BIA*, s 66.31(11).

the court, the debtor cannot make another consumer proposal until all proven claims are paid in full or extinguished by virtue of his or her bankruptcy.[79] The rights of the creditors are revived less any dividends they received under the consumer proposal.[80] The annulment or deemed annulment does not affect the validity of any acts done under the consumer proposal, and any guarantee that was given pursuant to the consumer proposal remains in full force.[81] If payments are thereafter made to the administrator, they will be distributed to the creditors, but this will not affect the revival of their claims in full.[82] If a consumer debtor who is bankrupt makes a consumer proposal that is subsequently deemed to be annulled, the consumer bankrupt is deemed to have made an assignment on the date of the deemed annulment.[83]

B. ORDERLY PAYMENT OF DEBTS

The orderly payment of debts provisions are set out in Part X of the *BIA*. These were introduced in 1966 after similar provisions contained in provincial legislation in Alberta were held to be unconstitutional.[84] Part X of the *BIA* (the "OPD") does not apply throughout Canada, since jurisdictions must proclaim it into force in order to bring it into operation.[85] The OPD is currently available only in Alberta, Saskatchewan, Nova Scotia, and Prince Edward Island.

A consolidation order under the OPD provisions differs from a consumer proposal in several important respects. A consolidation order is not voted upon by the creditors or approved by a court. It is a mechanism under which the various debts are consolidated into a single amount that is paid to the clerk of a court and then distributed to the creditors by way of dividend. A consolidation order does not permit a compromise of the claims. The debtor must pay the debts in full, except

---

79 *BIA*, s 66.32(1). In order to satisfy a court that it is appropriate to order otherwise, the debtor must show that there was a reasonable explanation for the default and that the second proposal contemplated has a reasonable prospect of being accepted by the creditors. See *Re Bartlett* (2001), 25 CBR (4th) 207 (NSSC).

80 *BIA*, s 66.32(2).

81 *Ibid*, ss 66.3(2) and 66.31(5).

82 *Re White* (2001), 31 CBR (4th) 128 (NSSC).

83 *BIA*, s 66.31(4).

84 See Chapter 1, Section B.

85 *BIA*, s 242.

that the interest on the debts that accrues after the consolidation order is fixed at 5 percent.[86]

1) Eligibility

The OPD originally was restricted to claims that did not exceed $1,000, but the monetary restriction has been eliminated by regulation.[87] The debtor must reside in a province in which the OPD provisions are in force.[88] The debtor must be an insolvent person but cannot be a corporation.[89] A debt that is incurred by a debtor in connection with a trade or calling or a debt associated with a mortgage or agreement for sale of land cannot be included in a consolidation order.[90]

2) Application for a Consolidation Order

A debtor may apply to a clerk of the court by filing an affidavit that sets out details of the debtor's financial situation.[91] The clerk of the court reviews the information and settles the amount and frequency of payments into court.[92] In doing so, the clerk of the court is not empowered to adjudicate upon the reasonableness of the debtor's estimate of what can be paid to the creditors, but must accept the amount proposed by the debtor.[93] The creditors are notified and given an opportunity to object to the amount entered as owing to the creditor or to the amounts and times for payment by the debtor under the consolidation order.[94] The consolidation order must provide for payment in full of all debts covered by it within a period of three years unless all creditors agree or a court approves the order.[95] The dividends are paid rateably to the creditors at least once every three months.[96]

---

86 *Ibid*, s 225(2); *Orderly Payment of Debts Regulations*, CRC, c 369, s 31 [*OPD*].

87 *BIA*, ss 218(1) and 240; *OPD*, above note 86, s 28. The regulations also extend the *OPD* to debts owing to public authorities which were originally excepted from the application of the *OPD*.

88 *BIA*, s 219(1).

89 *Ibid*, s 217 "debtor."

90 *Ibid*, s 218(2).

91 *Ibid*, s 219(2).

92 *Ibid*, s 220(1).

93 *Re Prince* (2004), 3 CBR (5th) 87 (Alta QB).

94 *BIA*, s 221.

95 *Ibid*, s 226. A creditor is deemed to consent if no objection is made within thirty days after the receipt of a request.

96 *Ibid*, s 235.

3) Effect of a Consolidation Order

The making of a consolidation order stays any process issued by a court in respect of a debt that is covered by the consolidation order.[97] A secured creditor is not subject to the stay of proceedings and can elect to enforce its security interest.[98] The consolidation order operates as a judgment in favour of each creditor.[99] A public utility is not permitted to discontinue service to the debtor by reason of the non-payment for services rendered prior to the consolidation order.[100] An employer is prohibited from firing an employee by reason only that the debtor has applied for a consolidation order.[101]

4) Termination of a Consolidation Order

A consolidation order can be terminated automatically through a default by the debtor in making payments or by a court order obtained by application of a creditor named in the consolidation order.[102] A consolidation order is terminated if the debtor defaults in making payments and the default continues for a period of three months. A court is given the power to forgive the default if the debtor satisfies it that the circumstances giving rise to the default were beyond his or her control. On application of a creditor, a court may terminate a consolidation order if the debtor has failed to comply with its terms, any other proceeding for recovery of money is brought against the debtor, or if the debtor has incurred further debts in excess of $500.

C. FARM DEBT MEDIATION

The purpose of the *Farm Debt Mediation Act*[103] is to provide for mediation between an insolvent farmer and the creditors of the farmer in an attempt to permit them to reach a mutually acceptable arrangement. If requested by the farmer, a stay of proceedings can be imposed on the creditors. In the period from 2007 to 2011, there were 1,525 applica-

97 *Ibid*, s 229.
98 *Ibid*, s 232(1).
99 *Ibid*, s 225(2).
100 *Ibid*, s 239.2.
101 *Ibid*, s 239.1.
102 *Ibid*, s 233; *OPD*, above note 86, s 16.
103 Above note 1.

tions, of which 1,278 (75 percent) resulted in an arrangement.[104] A farmer is not prevented from attempting to reach an arrangement with creditors by using the commercial proposal provisions of the *BIA*. One of the advantages of the *FDMA* is that financial review and mediation services are provided free of charge by the federal government. One potential disadvantage to the *FDMA* provisions is that a dissenting creditor cannot be bound by an arrangement even if the majority of creditors consent to it.

1) Eligibility

In order to make an application for a financial review and mediation, the debtor must fall within the definition of a farmer and must be insolvent. The *FDMA* uses a definition of insolvency that is substantially the same as that contained in the *BIA*.[105] A farmer is defined as any individual, corporation, cooperative, partnership, or other association of persons that is engaged in farming for commercial purposes.[106] The "commercial purposes" requirement means that that the enterprise must be intended to make a profit.[107] This was intended to exclude hobby farmers or others who own or reside on rural land that they use for purposes other than farming.[108] The *FDMA* definition of "farming" covers the production of field-grown crops, cultivated and uncultivated, and horticultural crops, the raising of livestock, poultry, and fur-bearing animals, and the production of eggs, milk, honey, maple syrup, tobacco, fibre, wood from woodlots, and fodder crops.[109] Farmers who apply under the *FMDA* are not required to demonstrate that they are insolvent, but if there is evidence that shows that they are not insolvent they will not be eligible.[110]

---

104 Canada, Agriculture and Agri-Food Canada, *Report to Parliament on the* Farm Debt Mediation Act, *Farm Debt Mediation Service and Farm Consultation Service* (Ottawa: Agriculture and Agri-food Canada, 2011) [*Report to Parliament*].

105 *FDMA*, above note 1, s 6. And see Chapter 1, Section E(2).

106 *FDMA*, above note 1, s 2 "farmer."

107 *Community Futures Development Corp of South Fraser v Litzenberger* (2006), 23 CBR (5th) 182 (BCSC).

108 *Graybriar Land Co v Kovacs* (2006), 25 CBR (5th) 291 (Alta QB). And see *Harding v 0780194 BC Ltd*, 2010 BCSC 5.

109 *FDMA*, above note 1, s 2 "farming."

110 *Ibid*, s 6. And see *Chrysler Financial Canada v Morris*, 2009 SKQB 510.

2) Application for Financial Review and Mediation

The *FDMA* provides two different ways of proceeding. A farmer may apply simply for a financial review and mediation. Alternatively, a farmer may apply for a financial review and mediation together with a stay of proceedings.[111] The farmer may amend the application and choose the other alternative at any time before termination of the mediation.[112] The application must contain the names and addresses of all the farmer's creditors.

Administrators are federal civil servants.[113] They will review the application and determine if the applicant is eligible to apply under the *FDMA*.[114] The administrator must issue a thirty-day stay of proceedings and notify all the creditors of the application if the farmer requested a stay. If the farmer did not request a stay, only the secured creditors are notified of the application.[115] The administrator will then engage private-sector financial consultants and mediators to conduct the financial review and mediation. The federal government, through Agriculture and Agri-Food Canada, pays the consultants, and neither the farmer nor the creditors are charged for these services.[116]

The financial review must include the preparation of an inventory of all the assets of the farmer and financial statements, and may include a financial recovery plan. Once a report is prepared, a mediator is appointed and the relevant creditors are notified. The role of the mediator is to assist the farmer and the creditors to arrive at a mutually acceptable arrangement, not to provide advice to the farmer.[117]

3) Stay of Proceedings

The issuance of a stay of proceedings by an administrator prevents any creditor from enforcing any remedy against a farmer or commencing or continuing any judicial or extra-judicial action or proceeding for the recovery of the debt, the realization of security, or the taking of any property of the farmer.[118] The purpose of the stay is to provide "a short standstill period within which the farmer has an opportunity to dem-

---

111 *FDMA*, above note 1, s 5(1).
112 *Ibid*, s 8.
113 *Ibid*, s 4.
114 *Ibid*, s 7(1)(c).
115 *Ibid*, s 7(1)(a).
116 See *Report to Parliament*, above note 104.
117 *FDMA*, above note 1, s 10(2).
118 *Ibid*, s 12.

onstrate long-term viability to creditors."[119] The initial stay of proceedings is for a thirty-day period, and it may be extended for a maximum of three further periods of thirty days each if the administrator considers it essential to the formulation of an arrangement.[120]

The administrator must also appoint a person as guardian of the farmer's assets when a stay of proceedings is issued.[121] The farmer or any other qualified person can be appointed guardian. The guardian must prepare an inventory of all the assets of the farmer, verify periodically the presence and condition of those assets, and advise the administrator of any act or omission that would jeopardize those assets.[122]

The *FDMA* provides for the termination of a stay of proceedings if the administrator later makes a determination that the applicant is not eligible to make an application under the *FDMA*.[123] The administrator is given the discretion to terminate the stay if the administrator is of the opinion that the mediation will not result in an arrangement between the farmer and the majority of the creditors, or if the farmer has jeopardized his or her assets or obstructed the performance of duties of a guardian of these assets.[124] The stay of proceedings automatically terminates when an arrangement is signed or the farmer makes an assignment in bankruptcy.[125]

4) Appeal Boards

The *FDMA* sets up a number of appeal boards for various regions.[126] A farmer or creditor may appeal a decision of an administrator concerning the eligibility of a farmer to make an application or the termination of a stay.[127] The termination of the stay of proceedings comes into effect on the expiration of the appeal period or upon dismissal of the appeal.[128]

---

119 *M & D Farm Ltd v Manitoba Agricultural Credit Corp*, [1999] 2 SCR 961 at para 19.

120 *FDMA*, above note 1, s 13.

121 *Ibid*, s 16.

122 *Ibid*, s 17(2).

123 *Ibid*, s 14(1).

124 *Ibid*, s 14(2).

125 *Ibid*, s 14(5).

126 *Ibid*, s 15(1); *Farm Debt Mediation Regulations*, SOR/98-168, s 5.

127 *FDMA*, above note 1, s 15(2). A decision of an Appeal Board is final and is not subject to appeal. See *FDMA*, *ibid*, s 15(5).

128 *Ibid*, s 14(4); *Farm Debt Mediation Regulations*, above note 126, s 11.

5) Notice by Secured Creditors

A secured creditor who intends to enforce any judicial or extra-judicial remedy or proceeding against the property of a farmer must give a written notice of intention to do so and inform the farmer of the right to make an application under the *FDMA*.[129] The farmer is not required to show that he or she is insolvent in order to take the benefit of this provision.[130] The definition of secured creditor in the *FDMA* covers creditors who have security interests in land or personal property.[131] The security interest can arise by agreement or by operation of law as in the case of a builder's lien.[132] Courts have held that a lessee who holds under a lease of real property combined with an option to purchase is not a secured creditor.[133] The definition does not extend to a person who is given a personal guarantee by a farmer.[134]

A farmer cannot validly waive the notice requirement even if the terms of an arrangement between the farmer and creditor waive any non-compliance.[135] The notice must be given at least fifteen business days before the remedy or proceeding is taken. A failure to give the notice renders any act of the creditor null and void, except that a person who acquires title to property of a person who purchased the property in good faith from the creditor is protected unless related to the creditor.[136] The guardian prepares an inventory of all the farmer's assets, periodically verifies their presence and condition, and advises the administrator of any act or omission that would jeopardize them.

---

129 *FDMA*, *ibid*, s 21(1). The *Farm Debt Mediation Regulations*, above note 126, s 17 and the *Farm Debt Secured Creditors Notice Regulations*, SOR/86-814 provide rules concerning proper service of the notice.

130 *McKenna v Marshall* (2004), 1 CBR (5th) 251 (Ont CA).

131 *FDMA*, above note 1, s 2 "secured creditor."

132 *Cash and Carry Lumber Ltd v Jacques*, 2001 SKQB 444.

133 *Rai v Can-Pacific Farms and Packers Ltd*, 2013 BCSC 545. It is uncertain whether courts will draw a distinction between true leases and security leases of personal property as they have done in restructuring law. See Chapter 13, Section A(5).

134 *Canadian Imperial Bank of Commerce v Verbrugghe* (2006), 24 CBR (5th) 33 (Ont SCJ).

135 *Intec Holdings Ltd v Grisnich* (2003), 49 CBR (4th) 240 (Alta QB).

136 *FDMA*, above note 1, s 22. The *Farm Debt Mediation Regulations*, above note 126, s 1(2) provide that a person who is an officer, director, partner, or employee of the creditor or a person who directly owns or indirectly owns, controls, or holds 25 percent or more of the shares of the creditor is considered to be a related person.

6) Arrangements

The *FDMA* does not contain any provisions concerning an arrangement that is concluded between the farmer and the creditors except for a requirement that the administrator shall ensure that it is in writing and signed by the parties.[137] The law of contracts will therefore supply the rules and principles that govern the operation of the arrangement. This means that there is no ability to bind a dissenting creditor to an arrangement by virtue of the consent of a majority of the creditors. Each creditor must consent to the arrangement in order for it to bind the creditor. Nor are there any provisions in the *FDMA* for the termination or annulment of an arrangement for non-disclosure or non-compliance with its terms. In the absence of a contractual provision in the arrangement, a court must determine whether the breach is so serious as to terminate the agreement. If so, the creditors will be able to enforce their claims against the farmer and the farmer's property.

FURTHER READINGS

BEN-ISHAI, S, & V TORRIE. "Farm Insolvency in Canada" (2013) 2 *Journal of the Insolvency Institute of Canada* 33

CANADA, OFFICE OF THE SUPERINTENDENT OF BANKRUPTCY, PERSONAL INSOLVENCY TASK FORCE. *Final Report of the Personal Insolvency Task Force* (Ottawa: Office of the Superintendent of Bankruptcy, 2002)

ZIEGEL, J. "Philosophy and Design of Contemporary Consumer Bankruptcy Systems: A Canada-United States Comparison" (1999) 37 *Osgoode Hall Law Journal* 205

137 *FDMA*, above note 1, s 19.

CHAPTER 21

SPECIALIZED INSOLVENCY REGIMES

There are two specialized insolvency regimes that apply to particular types of debtors or economic sectors. The *Winding-up and Restructuring Act* is used primarily in respect of insolvencies of banks, insurance companies, trust companies, and loan companies. It is sometimes used to wind-up federal corporations, such as the liquidation of the assets of the Christian Brothers of Ireland in Canada as a result of the claims of boys who suffered abuse at the Mount Cashel Orphanage in Newfoundland. There is also a special insolvency regime that governs railway companies.

Unfortunately, the use of specialized insolvency regimes in these sectors has produced a creeping statutory obsolescence.[1] While the general insolvency regimes are frequently amended in order to create an efficient and modernized insolvency system, these amendments are usually not introduced into the specialized insolvency regimes.[2] The

1 One need only examine the definition of "trading company" in the *Winding-up and Restructuring Act*, RSC 1985, c W-11, s 2(1) [*WURA*], to be nostalgically transported back to an earlier era of "apothecaries, auctioneers, bankers, brokers, brickmakers, builders, carpenters, carriers, cattle or sheep salesmen, coach proprietors, dyers, fullers, keepers of inns, taverns, hotels, saloons or coffee houses, lime burners, livery stable keepers, market gardeners, millers, miners, packers, printers, quarrymen, sharebrokers, ship-owners, shipwrights, stockbrokers, stock-jobbers, victuallers, warehousemen, wharfingers . . . ."

2 There have been two exceptions to this tendency. Provisions found in other insolvency statutes that limit the application of the legislation to aircraft objects and to eligible financial contracts have also been added to the *WURA*.

differences between the general insolvency regimes and the specialized regimes grow progressively greater, and the specialized regimes fall into mounting disrepair. Indeed, the provisions relating to railway insolvencies seem more appropriately included in a museum of railway antiquities than in the statute books.

In addition to these two specialized insolvency regimes, the arrangement provisions of the *Canada Business Corporations Act*[3] are increasingly used to restructure insolvent corporations in cases where an arrangement alters the rights of holders of corporate securities and does not involve a compromise of the claims of the trade creditors.

A. THE *WINDING-UP AND RESTRUCTURING ACT*

1) Historical Origins

The repeal of the Canadian insolvency statutes[4] in 1880 meant that there was no longer an expedient method available to liquidate insolvent companies. In 1882, at the behest of boards of trade of the larger cities, a new winding-up statute was enacted.[5] The new statutory regime that governed the liquidation of a company was modelled on the English system of company liquidation. It was vastly different from the federal bankruptcy regime that was subsequently enacted in 1919. Whereas the property of a bankrupt vests in the trustee in bankruptcy, the ownership of the assets of the insolvent company does not vest in the liquidator under the winding-up statute. Instead, the control and management of the company is taken from the directors and given to the liquidator.

Despite the enactment of this legislation, a bifurcated insolvency system — in which a bankruptcy statute governs personal insolvency of individuals and a separate liquidation statute governs corporate insolvencies — did not evolve in Canada. From its inception, the bankruptcy regime was available to both individuals and corporations. This meant that a choice had to be made as to which of the insolvency regimes would be employed in respect of the liquidation of an insolvent company. This was changed in 1966, when the bankruptcy legislation was amended to provide that bankruptcy proceedings took precedence

3 RSC 1985, c C-44, s 192 [*CBCA*].

4 See Chapter 2, Section A(2).

5 *Insolvent Banks, Insurance Companies and Trading Corporations Act*, 45 Vict, c 23.

over winding-up proceedings.[6] Thereafter, the winding-up statute was primarily used for the liquidation of insolvent financial institutions, including banks, trust companies, and insurance companies, since these cannot be liquidated under the *BIA* and cannot be restructured under the *CCAA*.[7]

2) Application of the Act

The *Winding-up and Restructuring Act* (*WURA*) applies to the following entities:[8]

- federal corporations;
- banks, trust companies, insurance companies, and loan companies; and
- trading companies, wherever incorporated, doing business in Canada.

The Act does not apply to railway companies,[9] since railway insolvencies are governed by their own insolvency regime. The Act also does not apply to a federal corporation incorporated under the *Canada Business Corporations Act* (*CBCA*), since that statute specifically provides for the non-application of the *WURA*.[10] The Act is not limited to insolvency proceedings but may be employed for the voluntary liquidation of solvent federal companies that cannot be liquidated under the *CBCA*.[11] In respect of an authorized foreign bank, the winding-up proceedings apply only to the winding-up of its business in Canada and to the liquidation of its assets.[12]

3) Commencing Proceedings

Proceedings are commenced through an application to a court by way of a petition for a winding-up order. The proceedings must be brought before the superior court of the province where the company's head

---

6 SC 1966, c 32, s 169A; now *BIA*, s 213.

7 *BIA*, *ibid*, s 2 "corporation" and *CCAA*, s 2(1) "company."

8 *WURA*, above note 1, s 6.

9 *Ibid*, s 7.

10 See *DX Ashe Holdings Ltd v Money's Mushrooms Ltd*, 2003 CarswellBC 1822 (SC).

11 Although the *CBCA*, above note 3, contains provisions in ss 207–28 governing the voluntary liquidation of corporations, these do not apply to companies that are enacted under their own special statutes. The *WURA* therefore provides a procedure for their voluntary liquidation. Corporations that are incorporated under the *CBCA* can be voluntarily liquidated only under that statute and not under the *WURA*.

12 *WURA*, above note 1, s 6(2).

office is situated or where its chief place or one of its chief places of business in Canada is situated.[13] A court may make a winding-up order where a company is insolvent.[14] If a winding-up order is sought on the grounds of insolvency, the application may be brought by the company, a creditor, or a shareholder.[15] A company is deemed to be insolvent upon the occurrence of certain specified events.[16] These are similar but not identical to the acts of bankruptcy, and include an inability to pay debts as they become due, an acknowledgment of insolvency, a disposition of property made with intent to defraud, defeat, or delay its creditors, and a seizure of its property under execution that is permitted to remain unsatisfied until within four days of the sale or for fifteen days after the seizure. A company is also deemed to be insolvent if a creditor to whom more than $200 is owed has served the company with a written demand for payment and the company neglects to pay it for sixty days after the service of the demand.[17]

4) Stay of Proceedings

An automatic stay of proceedings comes into operation as soon as a court makes a winding-up order.[18] No suit, action, or other proceeding may be proceeded with or commenced against the company without leave of the court. A court, on application, may also order a stay of proceedings after the proceedings are commenced but before a winding-up order is granted on such terms as the court thinks fit.[19] As the purpose of the stay of proceedings in winding-up proceedings is the same as that in bankruptcy proceedings, a similar approach is to be taken in determining the scope of the stay and the reasons that might convince a court to lift it.[20] Unlike bankruptcy proceedings, winding-up proceedings do

---

13 *Ibid*, s 12. And see s 2(1) "court."

14 *Ibid*, s 10(c). There are a number of other grounds on which a court can make a winding-up order, such as for just and equitable grounds.

15 *Ibid*, s 11(b). The claim of the creditor must be for the sum of at least $200. Except in the case of banks and insurance companies, a shareholder may bring the application if holding shares of at least $500 par value or five shares not having par value.

16 *Ibid*, s 3.

17 *Ibid*, s 4.

18 *Ibid*, s 21.

19 *Ibid*, s 17.

20 *Canada (Attorney General) v Reliance Insurance Co* (2007), 36 CBR (5th) 273 (Ont SCJ). The stay of proceedings covers extra-judicial proceedings such as arbitration.

not bind the Crown.[21] The stay of proceedings in winding-up proceedings therefore does not bind the Crown.

5) Effect of a Winding-Up Order

A winding-up order does not cause the assets of the insolvent company to vest in the liquidator.[22] Instead, the Act provides that the company shall cease to carry on business except as required for the beneficial winding-up of the company.[23] The winding-up is deemed to commence at the time of the service of the notice of presentation of the petition for winding up.[24] The effect of this deeming provision is uncertain. It resembles the relation-back doctrine that was at one time employed in bankruptcy law. Under this doctrine, a bankruptcy was deemed to have occurred at the date of the application for a bankruptcy order. The doctrine produced difficulties in that it had the effect of invalidating transactions that were entered into by the debtor after the application was brought but before the order was granted. It is not clear if the doctrine has a similar effect in winding-up proceedings. A court might conclude that the company lacks the capacity to enter into post-petition transactions, since it is permitted to carry on business only under the control of the liquidator. However, the *WURA* goes on to provide that all the powers of the directors of the company cease upon the appointment of a liquidator.[25] This supports the view that it is the actual appointment of the liquidator and not the winding-up order or its deemed retrospective effect that results in the loss of the directors' managerial power. On this view, transactions entered into by the company before the appointment of a liquidator are valid and effective.

The Act provides that every attachment, sequestration, distress, or execution put in force against the estate or effects of a company after the making of a winding-up order is void.[26] The wording is different from that contained in the bankruptcy statute, and its meaning is ambiguous. The provision refers to an execution or other process that is "put in force" after the winding-up order. It might be argued that a process that is put into place prior to the winding-up order is preserved. However, this interpretation would undermine a fundamental objective of

21 The *WURA* has no counterpart equivalent to *BIA*, s 4.1.

22 *Coopérants, Mutual Life Insurance Society (Liquidator of) v Dubois* (1996), 39 CBR (3d) 253 (SCC).

23 *WURA*, above note 1, s 19.

24 *Ibid*, s 5.

25 *Ibid*, s 31.

26 *Ibid*, s 22.

insolvency law in that it would not result in a single insolvency proceeding in which the assets of the debtor are liquidated on behalf of all the creditors. It is therefore likely that the provision was intended to invalidate all enforcement proceedings following the winding-up order unless they have been fully executed by payment of the money to the creditor.[27]

6) Powers and Duties of the Liquidator

On making a winding-up order, the court may appoint one or more liquidators.[28] The liquidator must be a licensed trustee.[29] Unless a court orders otherwise, the creditors and shareholders of a corporation must be notified of the proposed appointment.[30] A court may appoint a provisional liquidator after the bringing of a petition for a winding-up order but before it is granted.[31] The court also has the power to remove a liquidator if due cause is shown.[32]

A liquidator is required to take custody and control of the company's assets and perform all duties imposed by the court.[33] Within 120 days of the appointment, the liquidator must prepare a statement of the assets, debts, and liabilities of the company.[34] The liquidator carries out the liquidation under the supervision of the court, and the court may authorize the liquidator to bring or defend legal actions, carry on business to the extent that it is necessary to the beneficial winding-up of the company, sell the assets of the company, and borrow money on the security on the company's assets.[35] The Act allows a court to appoint one or more inspectors[36] and permits the court to call a meeting of creditors,[37] but it is silent as to the role that these parties are expected to perform in the insolvency proceedings.

---

27 See also *ibid*, s 86, which lends further support in favour of this interpretation.

28 *Ibid*, s 23(1).

29 *Ibid*, s 23(2). An exception is made for the appointment of the Canada Deposit Insurance Corporation as liquidator.

30 *Ibid*, s 26.

31 *Ibid*, s 28.

32 *Ibid*, s 32.

33 *Ibid*, s 33.

34 *Ibid*, s 34.

35 *Ibid*, s 35. The court may authorize the liquidator to carry on these activities without the need for a court order approving the particular acts or transactions. See *Kendall v Webster* (1910), 15 BCR 268 (CA).

36 *WURA*, above note 1, s 41.

37 *Ibid*, s 63.

A liquidator acts as agent of the company in respect of transactions and dealings that occur following the making of the winding-up order.[38] The *WURA* does not contain a counterpart to the provisions contained in the *BIA* that limit the liability of a trustee or receiver in respect of matters that arose prior to the commencement of insolvency proceedings.[39]

7) Set-Off

The *WURA* takes the same approach to set-off as that employed in bankruptcy proceedings. The law of set-off applies in the same manner and to the same extent as if the business of the company was not being wound up.[40] Despite the fact that the assets do not vest in the liquidator, courts have held that the commencement of winding-up proceedings results in a loss of mutuality. As a result, post-petition debts cannot be set-off against pre-petition debts.[41]

8) Avoidable Transactions

The *WURA* contains its own set of provisions for the avoidance of preferences and fraudulent transfers. These provisions use different terminology and different approaches from those used in the bankruptcy statute. For example, the *WURA* refers to a "company unable to meet its engagements." It is uncertain whether this test is materially different from the *BIA* requirement that the debtor be insolvent at the time of the transaction.

Transfers without consideration made within three months immediately preceding the commencement of winding-up proceedings are presumed to be made with fraudulent intent.[42] If the transfer is made for consideration, it is void if the company was unable to meet its engagements and if both the company and the recipient intended to defeat or delay the creditors.[43] Intent to defraud on the part of the

---

38 *Coopérants, Mutual Life Insurance Society (Liquidator of) v Dubois*, above note 22.

39 See *BIA*, s 14.06.

40 *WURA*, above note 1, s 73(1). See the discussion in Chapter 4, Section B(8).

41 See *Maritime Bank of the Dominion of Canada v J Morris Robinson* (1887), 26 NBR 297 (SC). And see K Palmer, *The Law of Set-Off in Canada* (Aurora, ON: Canada Law Book, 1993) at 209–10.

42 *WURA*, above note 1, s 96.

43 *Ibid*, s 99. A court may avoid the transaction if it occurred within a thirty-day period prior to the commencement of the winding-up even if the recipient did not have the fraudulent intent, but it must do so on terms that protect the

recipient is presumed if the recipient knew of the company's inability to meet its engagements.[44]

The *WURA* also contains a provision that allows recovery against a creditor who has received a preference. A transfer of property to a creditor made "in contemplation of insolvency" and that gives that creditor an unjust preference is recoverable.[45] This has been interpreted to mean that both the company and the recipient must be aware of the financial position of the company.[46] If the transfer or payment occurs within a thirty-day period prior to the commencement of winding-up proceedings, it is presumed to be made in contemplation of insolvency whether or not it was made voluntarily or under pressure, and evidence of pressure shall not be admissible to support the transaction.[47] Courts have held that the statutory presumption is not conclusive, but is rebuttable.[48] A different rule is applied in the case of a payment to a creditor. The payment must have occurred within a thirty-day period prior to the commencement of winding-up proceedings, both the company and the recipient must know of the inability of the company to meet its engagements, and a statutory presumption of knowledge does not operate.[49]

9) The Claims Procedure

Any claim, including an unliquidated or contingent claim, that is in existence at the time of commencement of the winding-up proceedings may be proven.[50] The valuation of unliquidated or contingent claims is to be determined by the court.[51] The court is given the power to establish the claims procedure by fixing the time periods for submission of the claims by the creditors and by determining the manner of notice that is to be given to the creditors by the liquidator.[52] The liquidator

recipient from actual loss or liability. See *WURA*, *ibid*, s 98. See also *Royal Bank of Canada v Pioneer Trust Co* (1988), 68 CBR (NS) 124 (Sask QB).

44 *WURA*, above note 1, s 97.

45 *Ibid*, s 100(1).

46 *Dominion Trust Co v Royal Bank of Canada*, [1921] 1 WWR 90 (BCSC).

47 *WURA*, above note 1, s 100(2).

48 *Hammond v Bank of Ottawa* (1910), 22 OLR 73 (CA).

49 *WURA*, above note 1, s 101.

50 *Ibid*, s 71(1).

51 *Ibid*, s 71(2).

52 *Ibid*, s 74. For a discussion of the claims procedure created in respect of multiple tort claims, see R Wood, "Assessing Institutional Abuse Claims in Liquidation Proceedings: *Re Christian Brothers of Ireland in Canada*" (2005) 20 *Banking and Finance Law Review* 449.

may accept the claim or may require the creditor to prove it to the satisfaction of the court. The court on hearing the matter may allow or disallow the claim, and a failure to attend the hearing results in a disallowance of the claim.[53] A creditor or other interested party may object to any claim filed with the liquidator.[54] Secured creditors and claimants who assert a proprietary right in assets that are in the hands of a liquidator must pursue their remedies through an order of the court by way of a summary petition.[55]

10) Treatment of Secured Creditors

The rules governing the treatment of secured creditors are roughly parallel to those that apply in the case of a bankruptcy. The secured creditor must specify the nature and amount of the security and must value it.[56] The liquidator may consent to the retention of the collateral by the secured creditor, or may redeem it by paying the amount specified by the secured creditor as its value.[57] If the right to redeem is not exercised, the secured creditor may claim as an unsecured creditor any deficiency between the obligation secured and the value of the collateral in the winding-up proceedings.[58]

11) Scheme of Distribution and Priorities

The *WURA* contains only two provisions that relate to priorities. The costs, charges, and expenses of the liquidation are payable out of the assets of the company, in priority to all other claims.[59] Wage claims of employees for unpaid wages accrued during the three-month period preceding the winding-up order are given a preference over the other unsecured creditors.[60] The priority rules are therefore drawn from applicable federal and provincial law. There is no counterpart in the *WURA* to the priority provisions governing Crown claims or thirty-day goods. As well, the *Wage Earner Protection Program Act* does not

---

53 *WURA*, above note 1, s 75.

54 *Ibid*, ss 87–92.

55 *Ibid*, s 135. And see *Stewart v LePage* (1916), 53 SCR 337. This applies only in respect of claims to assets in the hands of a liquidator. Claims by the liquidator against third parties must be brought in the ordinary way in civil courts. See *Ross Brothers & Co v Vermette* (1952), 32 CBR 229 (Que QB).

56 *WURA*, above note 1, s 78.

57 *Ibid*, s 79.

58 *Ibid*, s 80.

59 *Ibid*, s 94.

60 *Ibid*, s 72.

apply to wage claims in respect of winding-up proceedings. Several of the federal statutes that govern financial institutions set out a scheme of distribution. For example, the *Bank Act*[61] and the *Trust and Loan Companies Act*[62] provide a scheme of distribution under which Crown claims are given first priority.

12) Sector-Specific Rules

The *WURA* contains two additional parts that create two sets of sector-specific rules. The first deals with authorized foreign banks.[63] These provisions are designed to restrict the winding-up proceedings to the bank's assets, liabilities, and business in Canada. The second provides additional provisions that govern the winding-up of insurance companies.[64] A special scheme of distribution is provided that gives priority first to the costs of liquidation, second to the satisfaction of the preferred claims, and third to the claims of policyholders.[65] The creditors are paid only after these priority claims are satisfied. A liquidator with the consent of a court is permitted to arrange for the transfer or reinsurance of policies,[66] and the court may modify the terms of the policies so long as the modifications do not have an adverse material impact on the policyholders.[67] Both parts also contain provisions that authorize a liquidator to transfer the assets of a foreign company to a liquidator in the country of its head office.[68]

13) Restructuring Proceedings

The *WURA* contains incomplete and skeletal provisions governing restructurings. A court is authorized to call a meeting of creditors to consider a proposed compromise or arrangement,[69] and may sanction it if it is approved by a majority in number, representing three-fourths of the value of proven claims, of each class of creditor.[70] Upon court sanction, the compromise or arrangement binds all the creditors.

---

61 SC 1991, c 46, s 369.
62 SC 1991, c 45, s 374.
63 *WURA*, above note 1, Part II, ss 150–58.3.
64 *Ibid.*, Part III, ss 159–72.
65 *Ibid*, s 161(1).
66 *Ibid*, s 162.
67 *Ibid*, s 162.2.
68 *Ibid*, ss 158.2 and 165.
69 *Ibid*, s 65.
70 *Ibid*, s 66.

B. RAILWAY COMPANIES

The *Canada Transportation Act*[71] (*CTA*) contains a brief set of provisions that establishes the only insolvency regime that can be employed in respect of insolvent railway companies. (The *BIA*, the *CCAA*, and the *WURA* exclude railway companies from their application.[72]) The *CTA* provisions provide a skeletal set of rules for the restructuring of a railway company but provide no mechanism for its liquidation. This may reflect the fact that restructuring rather than liquidation is the only feasible manner of dealing with insolvent railway companies on account of the very specific types of assets they hold and the difficulty in reallocating them to any other use.

The proceedings are commenced when the directors of an insolvent railway company prepare and file a scheme of arrangement between the company and its creditors in the Federal Court.[73] Once it is filed, the court may restrain any action against the company.[74] The stay of proceedings cannot prevent a secured creditor from taking possession of the rolling stock unless, within sixty days from the filing of the scheme of arrangement, the railway company agrees to perform all its obligations under the security agreement and cures any default.[75]

The scheme must be assented to by the shareholders and by claimants holding three-quarters of the value of (a) mortgages, hypothecs, bonds, and debenture stock of the company; (b) any rent charge, or other payment, charged on the receipts of or payable by the company in consideration of the purchase of the railway of another company; and (c) each class of preferred share.[76] The assent of a class is not needed if the class is not prejudicially affected by the scheme.[77] The Federal Court may confirm the scheme if it has been properly assented to and if no sufficient objection to the scheme has been established.[78] Once confirmed and registered in the Federal Court, it becomes binding on the company and all persons.[79]

---

71 SC 1996, c 10, ss 106–10 [*CTA*].

72 See B Jolin & S Gaudet, "When a Railway Company Is Not Really a Railway Company" (2002) 19 *National Insolvency Review* 57, for a discussion of what entities are considered to be railway companies.

73 *CTA*, above note 71, s 106(1).

74 *Ibid*, s 106(4).

75 *Ibid*, s 106(5).

76 *Ibid*, s 107(1).

77 *Ibid*, s 107(3).

78 *Ibid*, s 108(3).

79 *Ibid*, s 108(4).

These provisions are wholly inadequate for proceedings that involve trade creditors or tort victims. This was recognized in the aftermath of the Lac-Mégantic rail disaster that killed forty-seven people and destroyed a large part of the town. The court in *Montréal, Maine & Atlantique Canada Co (Arrangement relatif à)*[80] held that a railway company that was incorporated pursuant to the general corporations statute was permitted to commence proceedings under the *CCAA*. It held that the reference to "railway company" in the statutes was limited to those companies that were incorporated pursuant to a special Act of Parliament or a provincial legislature..

C. *CANADA BUSINESS CORPORATIONS ACT* ARRANGEMENTS

The arrangement provisions of the *Canada Business Corporations Act* (*CBCA*)[81] can be used in conjunction with a restructuring under the *CCAA* or the commercial proposal provisions of the *BIA* in order to reorganize the capital structure of the corporation. Where this is done, it operates in a supplementary role. However, section 192 of the *CBCA* has also been employed essentially as an independent insolvency regime. This may seem surprising given that the statute expressly provides that it applies only to a corporation that is not insolvent, but courts have interpreted this requirement in a manner that allows it easily to be satisfied. It is primarily used in instances where an arrangement is sought with a specific holder of securities rather than the ordinary business creditors of the debtor. The process is often speedier, less costly, and less dependent on court supervision than restructuring proceedings under the *CCAA* due to its more limited scope.[82] Arrangements are also possible under provincial business corporation statutes, but as the requirements vary according to the jurisdiction, the discussion will limit itself to *CBCA* arrangements.

---

80 2015 QCCS 3236. And see P Rubin & H Sevenoaks, "Keeping on the Right Track: An Examination of Recent Railway Cases to Explore Judicial Authority and the Impact on Exclusionary Clauses" in Janis P Sarra, ed, *Annual Review of Insolvency Law, 2013* (Toronto: Thomson Carswell, 2014) 473.

81 Above note 3.

82 M McGregor & P Casey, "*CBCA* Section 192 Restructurings: A Streamlined Restructuring Tool or a Statutory Loophole?" in Janis P Sarra, ed, *Annual Review of Insolvency Law, 2013* (Toronto: Thomson Carswell, 2014) 683.

1) Scope and Application

There are four requirements that must be satisfied before the arrangement provisions in section 192 of the *CBCA* are available.[83] First, the corporation must be one that is incorporated under the *CBCA*. Second, the proposed plan must be in the nature of an arrangement.[84] The *CBCA* sets out a non-exhaustive list of arrangements that can be effected under the provision. It encompasses share cancellations, amalgamations, debt-equity swaps, and asset sales. Third, it must be impracticable to effect a fundamental change under any other provision of the *CBCA*. Fourth, the corporation must not be insolvent.

2) The Insolvency Requirement

Courts have held that the insolvency requirement can be satisfied through two different methods. First, it is sufficient if the corporation is no longer insolvent at the completion of the restructuring even though it may have been insolvent at the commencement of the proceedings.[85] Second, it is sufficient if one of the corporations involved in the restructuring is insolvent, even if the primary beneficiary of the proceedings is insolvent.[86] Courts have permitted an insolvent corporation to incorporate a solvent wholly owned subsidiary to serve as applicant and satisfy the solvency requirement.[87]

The definition of insolvency that is used differs from that used in the federal insolvency statutes.[88] A corporation is insolvent if (1) it is unable to pay its liabilities as they become due; or (2) the realizable value of the assets of the corporation are less than the aggregate of its liabilities and stated capital of all classes.[89] The first test is substantially the same as the cash flow test. However, the second test differs from the balance sheet test in that the stated capital must be added to the liabilities for the purposes of the test.

83 *CBCA*, above note 3, s 192(3).
84 *Ibid*, s 192(1).
85 *Re GT Canada Medical Properties Inc*, 2010 ONSC 6760.
86 *Trizec Corp (Re)*, [1994] 10 WWR 127 (Alta QB).
87 H Clarke & W Gray, "Arrangements and Reorganizations of Insolvent Companies under the *CBCA* and Provincial/Territorial Corporate Law" (2013) 29 *Banking and Finance Law Review* 1 at 19.
88 See Chapter 1, Section E.
89 *CBCA*, above note 3, s 192(2).

3) Commencement of Proceedings and the Stay

Proceedings are commenced through application by the corporation for an initial order. The *CBCA* provides that the court may make any order that it sees fit, including an order concerning notice of the proceedings or dispensing with notice, an order appointing counsel to represent shareholders, an order concerning meetings, and an order approving an arrangement.[90] Although the Act does not expressly provide for the granting of a stay of proceedings, a court has the power to make such orders under their general power. The wide stay of proceedings that is found in *CCAA* initial orders is usually not appropriate since the general creditors are unaffected by the arrangement, and the order when granted is usually more selective.[91] Nonetheless, courts have in appropriate cases made orders that restrain the termination of agreements or the discontinuance of the supply of goods or services as well as orders that declare that the proceedings do not constitute an event of a default under other agreements.[92] The typical order does not provide for the appointment of a monitor. The Director of Corporations must be notified, and the Director's function is to ensure that the proceedings are consistent with the policy of the statute.[93] The Director has published a policy statement that outlines the factors that the Director takes into consideration.[94] The Director does not have the power to block an arrangement, but the Director has the right to appear before the court and make known any concerns about the use of the process.

4) Voting on the Arrangement

The arrangement contemplated by the *CBCA* is one that is concluded between the debtor corporation and the holders of securities, which are defined so as to include a bond, debenture, note or other evidence of indebtedness or guarantee of a corporation, whether secured or

---

90 *Ibid*, s 192(4). The list also mentions an order for a dissent and appraisal right, but this will not generally be appropriate if the corporation is insolvent. The court cannot dispense with notice to the Director of Corporations.

91 W Kaplan, "Stays of Proceedings under the *Canada Business Corporations Act*: A Question of Balance" in Janis P Sarra, ed, *Annual Review of Insolvency Law, 2011* (Toronto: Carswell, 2012) 135.

92 See *45133541 Canada inc (Arrangement relatif à)*, 2009 QCCS 6444; *8440522 Canada Inc (Re)*, 2013 ONSC 2509.

93 *CBCA*, above note 3, s 192(5).

94 Industry Canada, "Policy Concerning Arrangements under Section 192 of the CBCA," Policy Statement 15.1 (4 January 2010), online: hwww.ic.gc.ca/eic/site/cd-dgc.nsf/eng/cs01073.html#opinions.

unsecured.[95] Arrangements that are intended to affect the claims of ordinary trade creditors are to be undertaken under the insolvency law restructuring statutes. Claimants whose legal rights are not affected by the arrangement are generally not permitted to vote even though the arrangement may affect the economic value of their investment.[96]

The interim order will typically set out the process rules for the meeting, the voting rules, and the fairness hearing for court approval. Unlike the *CCAA*, the *CBCA* arrangement provisions do not establish any voting approval thresholds, but leave this entirely to the discretion of the court. Courts have consistently denied voting rights to classes of claimants who are "underwater" in the sense that they no longer hold a valuable economic stake in the entity.[97] Unlike the *CCAA*, the court has the power to cram down the arrangement against a class that votes against the arrangement if the court is of the view that they have been fairly treated.[98] Where the claims of holders of corporate debt are affected, it is usual for the corporation to obtain a fairness opinion from an independent financial advisor indicating that the arrangement gives the affected party more than what they would receive in liquidation proceedings.[99]

5) Court Approval

If the plan of arrangement is approved by the necessary threshold, the corporations must obtain court approval. The onus is on the corporation to establish that (1) the statutory procedures have been met; (2) the application has been put forth in good faith; and (3) the arrangement is "fair and reasonable in the sense that: (a) the arrangement has a valid business purpose; and (b) the objections of those whose rights are being arranged are resolved in a fair and balanced way.[100]

95 *CBCA*, above note 3, s 2(1) "security," "debt obligation" and ss 192(2)(f) and 192(4)(c).
96 *BCE Inc v 1976 Debentureholders*, 2008 SCC 69 at para 133 [*BCE*].
97 *Savage v Amoco Acquisition Co* (1988), 59 Alta LR (2d) 260 (QB).
98 *BCE*, above note 96 at para 150.
99 Industry Canada, above note 94 at paras 4.03 to 4.05.
100 *BCE*, above note 96 at para 156.

FURTHER READINGS

CARFAGNINI, JA. "Proceedings under the *Winding-Up Act* (Canada)" (1988) 66 CBR (NS) 77

CLARKE, HE, & WD GRAY. "Arrangements and Reorganizations of Insolvent Companies under the *CBCA* and Provincial/Territorial Corporate Law" (2013) 29 *Banking and Finance Law Review* 1

INSOLVENCY INSTITUTE OF CANADA. "The *Winding-up and Restructuring Act*: Recommendations for Reform" (14 June 2000)

JOLIN, B, & S GAUDET. "When a Railway Company Is Not Really a Railway Company" (2002) 19 *National Insolvency Review* 57

KAPLAN, W. "Stays of Proceedings under the *Canada Business Corporations Act*: A Question of Balance" in Janis P Sarra, ed, *Annual Review of Insolvency Law, 2011* (Toronto: Carswell, 2012) 135.

RUBIN P, & H SEVENOAKS. "Keeping on the Right Track: An Examination of Recent Railway Cases to Explore Judicial Authority and the Impact on Exclusionary Clauses" in Janis P Sarra, ed, *Annual Review of Insolvency Law, 2013* (Toronto: Thomson Carswell, 2014) 473

TELFER, T, & B WELLING. "The *Winding-up and Restructuring Act*: Realigning Insolvency's Orphan to the Modern Law Reform Process" (2008) 24 *Banking and Finance Law Review* 233

WOOD, RJ. "Assessing Institutional Abuse Claims in Liquidation Proceedings: *Re Christian Brothers of Ireland in Canada*" (2005) 20 *Banking and Finance Law Review* 449

CHAPTER 22

CROSS-BORDER INSOLVENCIES

Cross-border insolvencies, also known as transnational or international insolvencies, involve a foreign element. The debtor may be located in another country, some or all of the assets may be located in another country, or some or all of the creditors may be foreigners. This book has been structured around the various insolvency regimes that have been legislatively created. This structure, together with the fact that the *BIA* contains a separate Part on cross-border insolvencies, may lead the reader to think that this chapter is about an international insolvency regime that governs such insolvencies. Such is not the case. Although many believe that the best solution to the problem of cross-border insolvencies is the creation of an international convention that would create a single, universal body of substantive insolvency law principles for transnational businesses, this is currently a hope rather than a reality.[1]

The 2009 amendments to Canadian insolvency statutes have implemented many features of the UNCITRAL Model Law on Cross-Border Insolvency. Several other countries, including the United States, the United Kingdom, and New Zealand, have done so as well. The Model Law does not create a separate insolvency regime for international insolvencies. It does not purport to create substantive insolvency law at all. Instead, it provides a mechanism to facilitate cooperation and coordination of international insolvencies by providing for the recognition of

1 See JL Westbrook, "A Global Solution to Multinational Default" (2000) 98 *Michigan Law Review* 2276.

foreign insolvency proceedings. Although these provisions can by no stretch of the imagination be regarded as a transnational insolvency regime, it is possible that they may be the first stage in a process that will eventually realize the universalist ideal. Only time will tell.

A. FUNDAMENTAL PRINCIPLES

1) The Rival Principles of Universalism and Territorialism

There are differing views on the most appropriate way to deal with cross-border insolvencies. At its most basic level, the debate is about the relative merits of the principle of universalism over its rival, the principle of territorialism. Universalism contemplates an insolvency proceeding that deals with all of the debtor's assets regardless of where in the world they may be located. Territorialism envisages insolvency proceedings that are limited to the assets located in a particular country. This dichotomy gives rise to two further opposing principles: unity and pluralism. The principle of unity gives carriage of the proceedings to a single court in the location of the debtor's home jurisdiction. The principle of pluralism accepts that there will be concurrent insolvency proceedings in different jurisdictions.

A territorialist approach to international insolvencies must by necessity also adopt a pluralist approach. Because the proceedings are territorially limited, an international insolvency must involve concurrent proceedings in each jurisdiction where assets are located.[2] For the territorialist, the solution to cross-border insolvencies is to foster greater cooperation and coordination among the courts and administrators in the parallel insolvency proceedings. This has been referred to as cooperative territoriality.

In its pure form, a universalist approach would involve a single court administering the debtor's assets on a worldwide basis. This would most likely be achieved by the adoption of an international insolvency law regime. As this requires the negotiation of an international multilateral convention, it is not regarded as a realistic possibility in the short term. The interim solution for the universalist is a system of modified universalism in which ancillary or parallel proceedings in different jurisdictions are accepted as necessary, but in which the insolvency courts and administrators in the various jurisdictions cooperate

---

2 See *Orient Leasing Co v "Kosei Maru"* (1978), 94 DLR (3d) 658 (FCTD).

with the mutual goal of achieving a worldwide collection and distribution of assets.

Although these approaches, modified versions of the pure forms of universalism and territorialism, clearly converge towards one another, they do not meet and therefore cannot be regarded as merely two different ways of expressing the desirability of international cooperation in insolvency matters. Cooperative territorialism requires that parallel insolvency proceedings be brought in each jurisdiction. There is no hierarchy among these proceedings. Each is supreme within its own territory. Modified universalism is not premised on this view. It is inclined to regard the insolvency proceeding in the home jurisdiction as the main proceeding, with other insolvency proceedings in other jurisdictions playing an ancillary role.

2) The Principle of Pragmatism

Canadian insolvency legislation is universalist in that it purports to cover all of the debtor's assets wherever located and permits foreign creditors to participate in the insolvency proceedings. This is fine in theory, but the reality is that this goal cannot be realized unless the insolvency proceedings are recognized and given effect by other states. The other state may embrace a universalist approach to insolvency, or it may adopt a more territorial approach. There is an infinite variation in the circumstances and the kinds of problems that can arise in international insolvencies.[3] The principle of pragmatism accepts that concurrent insolvency proceedings will often be necessary, and that the best means of attaining a fair and efficient outcome is for the courts and administrators to cooperate and coordinate their efforts. This may result in a variety of different approaches being considered, since flexibility is required in this kind of environment.[4]

The pragmatic approach is often manifested by the use of protocols that are negotiated between the insolvency administrators of the different jurisdictions and approved by each of their courts. These protocols provide for an agreed-upon set of rules and procedures to govern the parallel insolvency proceedings. The protocols will typically confirm the independent jurisdiction of the courts over their own proceedings but will also involve an undertaking of the courts to use their best efforts to coordinate their activities and to defer to the judgment of the

---

3 See *Holt Cargo Systems Inc v ABC Containerline NV*, [2001] 3 SCR 907 at para 85.

4 See I Fletcher, *Insolvency in Private International Law*, 2d ed (Oxford: Oxford University Press, 2005) at paras 1.16 to 1.19. Fletcher refers to the pragmatic approach as the "internationlist principle."

other court where feasible. The protocols often provide for mutual recognition of stays of proceedings, confer a right of interested parties to be heard, establish methods of communication by telephone or video link, and enshrine the principle of non-discrimination among creditors.[5]

3) The Principle of International Comity

The Supreme Court of Canada has described the principle of international comity as "the deference and respect due by other states to the actions of a state legitimately taken within its territory."[6] The classic statement of the principle is found in the decision of the United States Supreme Court in *Hilton v Guyot*:[7]

> "Comity" in the legal sense, is neither a matter of absolute obligation, on the one hand, nor of mere courtesy and goodwill, upon the other. But it is the recognition which one nation allows within its territory to the legislative, executive, or judicial acts of another nation, having due regard both to international duty and convenience, and to the rights of its own citizens or of other persons [who] are under the protection of its laws.

The principle of international comity is increasingly being used to support the idea that courts should make efforts to assist and coordinate their efforts with foreign courts on cross-border insolvency proceedings, and in appropriate cases to recognize that the proceedings in another jurisdiction ought to be regarded as the primary proceedings.[8] Because of its emphasis on cooperation and flexibility, it is often associated with the principle of pragmatism.

Adherence to the principal of international comity does not mean that Canadian courts must cede their authority and jurisdiction over their own process or over the application of the substantive laws of their own jurisdiction whenever any difference between the two jurisdictions may arise.[9] Canadian courts will be reluctant to stay Canadian insolvency proceedings, to authorize the transfer of assets out of the jurisdiction, or to force Canadian creditors to participate in foreign

---

5 An example of a protocol between Canada and the United States is reproduced in J Sarra, *Rescue! The Companies' Creditors Arrangement Act* (Toronto: Thomson-Carswell, 2007) at 487.

6 *Morguard Investments Ltd v De Savoye*, [1990] 3 SCR 1077.

7 159 US 113 at 163–64 (1895).

8 See, for example, *Roberts v Picture Butte Municipal Hospital*, [1999] 4 WWR 443 (Alta QB); *Re Babcock & Wilcox Canada Ltd* (2000), 18 CBR (4th) 157 (Ont SCJ).

9 *Menegon v Philip Services Corp* (1999), 11 CBR (4th) 262 at para 48 (Ont SCJ).

insolvency proceedings where to do so would undermine important matters of public policy or cause undue prejudice to the creditors.[10]

4) The Principle of Non-discrimination

States that adhere to a universalist approach to the application of their own insolvency laws will almost invariably adopt a principle that there should be no discrimination against foreign creditors. Foreign creditors are permitted to prove their claims and participate in the insolvency proceedings as fully as domestic creditors. The principle of non-discrimination is a corollary of the universalist principle. If there is to be a single, worldwide insolvency proceeding covering all the assets, it would be grossly unfair to exclude or discriminate against foreign creditors.

The flip side of the non-discrimination principle is that Canadian creditors must be afforded equal treatment in foreign insolvency proceedings. The willingness of Canadian courts to cooperate in respect of foreign insolvency proceedings will generally be conditioned on the other jurisdiction's willingness and ability to afford equal and non-discriminatory treatment to Canadian creditors. The equality principle can also be seen in the hotchpot rule. Under this rule, a creditor who has obtained some of the debtor's assets from enforcement activities or insolvency proceedings in another country must account for the amount recovered elsewhere and is entitled to a dividend only once the other creditors have received a dividend equal in value to the amount received.[11]

The non-discrimination principle is also illustrated in *Re Sefel Geophysical Ltd*,[12] in which a United States court made an order authorizing the transfer into Canada of the US assets. This order was made on the understanding that the United States creditors would be afforded equal treatment with the Canadian creditors. The difficulty was that many of the claims constituted foreign revenue claims. This gave rise to two problems. The first involved the application of the long-standing rule that courts will not entertain an action for the enforcement either directly or indirectly of a penal law or the revenue laws of a foreign state.[13] The second problem was that, although claims of municipalities were given a preferred status under Canadian bankruptcy law, this preferred

---

10 See *Re SemCanada Crude Company (Companies' Creditors Arrangement Act)*, 2009 ABQB 90.

11 *Banco de Portugal v Waddell* (1880), 5 App Cas 161.

12 (1988), 70 CBR (NS) 97 (Alta QB).

13 *United States v Harden*, [1963] SCR 366.

status did not extend to claims of US municipalities. Justice Forsyth held that the rule against the enforcement of foreign revenue laws was not applicable to the Canadian insolvency proceedings and that the US creditors must be afforded an equivalent status. The application of these principles would lead to an injustice since the US assets had been turned over on the understanding that the US creditors and the Canadian creditors would be treated the same.[14]

5) The Problem of Corporate Groups

The difficulties associated with international insolvencies are further compounded when corporate groups are involved. Consider the case of a US parent company and a Canadian subsidiary. Each corporate entity is a separate juridical person. Each corporation owns its own assets and owes obligations to its own creditors. One of the corporations may be financially healthy, while the other may be financially distressed. One approach to the problem of corporate groups is to give full effect to the separate identities of their members and to require separate insolvency proceedings in the home jurisdiction of each insolvent member of the group. This is not an application of the principle of territorialism. Rather, it proceeds from the premise that the corporations are different legal persons.

This solution becomes less attractive when the activities of the related corporations are closely integrated.[15] The corporations may have given intercorporate guarantees, so that it is not particularly helpful to segregate the creditors of one corporation from those of the other. The affairs of the businesses may be such that it is factually difficult to separate their business activities. A restructuring attempt might work best by the formulation of a plan that encompasses all the members of the group. In such instances, it might be more efficient to have a single insolvency proceeding that encompasses all the corporate entities that comprise the group.

It is important to distinguish procedural consolidation of cross-border insolvency proceedings from substantive consolidation.[16] Procedural consolidation simply provides that the carriage of the proceedings

---

14 The court relied on the principle of unjust enrichment and the rule in *Ex parte James; Re Condon* (1874), LR 9 Ch App 609 in holding that it would be unjust under the circumstances to permit the Canadian creditors to claim priority over the US creditors.

15 See J Opolsky, "COMI's Fifth Year in Canada: Centre of Main Interest and the Inescapable Corporate Group" in Janis P Sarra, ed, *Annual Review of Insolvency Law, 2013* (Toronto: Carswell, 2014) 233.

16 See Chapter 12, Section B.

will be given to a single administrator under the supervision of a single court. Substantive consolidation involves a pooling of the assets and the claims so that the joint assets of the related companies are used to satisfy the claims of all of the creditors. Substantive consolidation has a major impact on the amount recoverable by creditors and therefore is limited to cases where it becomes impractical to attempt to determine the separate assets and liabilities of each corporation.

B. CANADIAN INSOLVENCY PROCEEDINGS INVOLVING A FOREIGN ELEMENT

1) Jurisdiction under Canadian Bankruptcy and Insolvency Legislation

Canadian bankruptcy and insolvency legislation is universalist in its application. Bankruptcy proceedings that are commenced in Canada are not limited to the property that is located in Canada but extend to property located in other jurisdictions as well.[17] Of course, it often will be necessary to seek recognition of the Canadian bankruptcy order in a court outside Canada in order to enforce it. In respect of an involuntary bankruptcy, it is not necessary that the debtor be located in Canada. It is sufficient that the debtor carry on business in Canada, even if Canada is not the chief place of business. In respect of a voluntary bankruptcy, the debtor does not need to be located in Canada at all. It is sufficient that the bankrupt merely has property located in Canada.[18] There is no restriction placed on the ability of foreign creditors to apply for a bankruptcy order or to prove their claims in the Canadian bankruptcy proceedings, even if the debts or other claims were entered into outside Canada and governed by foreign law.[19] Furthermore, many of the acts of bankruptcy expressly extend to conduct that occurs outside Canada. The most commonly used act of bankruptcy is the failure to meet obligations when they become due. This has been interpreted to apply where there is a failure to pay foreign creditors, even though the claims of creditors in Canada are kept in good standing.[20]

---

17 *BIA*, s 2 "property." The definition covers "property, whether situated in Canada or elsewhere."

18 *Ibid*, s 2 "insolvent person."

19 *Re Kaussen Estate* (1988), 67 CBR (NS) 81 (Que CA).

20 *Ibid*.

The jurisdiction of Canadian courts in respect of restructuring proceedings is also very wide. The *CCAA* applies to any company that is incorporated in Canada and to any company that is incorporated outside Canada if it carries on business in Canada.[21] Restructuring proceedings under the *BIA* have an even greater potential application, since the proceedings can be commenced by a debtor who does not reside or carry on business in Canada but who has property located there.[22] There is no limitation in the Canadian insolvency statutes that prevents foreign creditors from participating in the Canadian restructuring proceedings or that otherwise discriminates against such creditors.

2) Discretion to Abstain from Exercise of Jurisdiction

A court that hears an application for a bankruptcy order in respect of an involuntary bankruptcy is given the discretion to refuse the order if it is of the view that there is sufficient cause to do so.[23] A court that hears an application under the *CCAA* may also refuse to make an order if it thinks that it is appropriate to do so.[24] A voluntary bankruptcy is commenced without the need for a court order, but a court may subsequently annul the bankruptcy proceedings.[25] It is possible that a Canadian court may exercise its discretion and refuse an order where there is little connection to Canada and foreign insolvency proceedings have been brought in another country.[26] In doing so, it would very likely apply a *forum non conveniens* analysis.[27] This does not mean that a Canadian court will decline jurisdiction whenever foreign insolvency proceedings have been commenced. There is long-standing authority that Canadian insolvency proceedings may be brought concurrently.[28] Rather, the principle is that a Canadian court may choose to decline

---

21 *CCAA*, s 2(1) "company." The *Winding-up and Restructuring Act*, RSC 1985, c W-11 [*WURA*], uses a similar approach to jurisdiction. See *WURA*, s 6(1).

22 *BIA*, ss 2 "insolvent person" and 50(1).

23 *Ibid*, s 43(7).

24 *CCAA*, s 11.02(3).

25 *BIA*, s 181(1).

26 It may be more difficult to do so in respect of restructuring proceedings under the *BIA*, since a court order is not needed to commence the proceedings and the grounds upon which a court may terminate the proceedings or refuse their extension are not as open-ended. See *BIA*, ss 50.4(8) and (11).

27 See I Fletcher, *Insolvency in Private International Law*, 2d ed (Oxford: Oxford University Press, 2005) at paras 2.45–2.54. And see *Spiliada Maritime Corp v Cansulex Ltd*, [1987] AC 460 (HL) and *Amchem Products Incorporated v British Columbia (Workers' Compensation Board)*, [1993] 1 SCR 897.

28 See *Allen v Hanson* (1890), 18 SCR 667.

jurisdiction where the concurrent proceedings would not lead to the more efficient administration of the insolvency but would instead create conflict.[29]

3) Choice of Law Issues

Where Canadian insolvency proceedings are commenced, Canadian courts will apply Canadian insolvency law on matters concerning the administration of the insolvency. This is generally uncontroversial in relation to matters of procedure. The matter becomes more complicated when dealing with substantive issues. It may be necessary to apply the law of some other jurisdiction to resolve an issue that arises in the Canadian insolvency proceedings. For example, an issue may arise in connection with the validity of the claim of a foreign creditor. In respect of contractual claims, the outcome will be determined by application of the proper law of the contract. In respect of tort claims, it will be determined by the place where the wrong occurred.[30] A court may also need to determine the validity or priority of a security interest. In these types of cases there is no real controversy. Canadian insolvency legislation is silent on these issues, and therefore it is entirely appropriate to apply the choice of law rules of private international law.

The analysis becomes more difficult where the Canadian insolvency statute sets out a substantive rule, and the court must decide if it should be applied where a foreign element is implicated in the Canadian insolvency proceedings. In some cases, the Canadian insolvency legislation may not clearly indicate the extent to which it is territorially limited, and a court may need to determine this issue as an exercise in statutory interpretation. If a court concludes that the legislation is not territorially limited, it may need to consider directly the appropriateness of applying the substantive law rule. Questions relating to the application of the impeachment powers in respect of pre-bankruptcy transactions can give rise to particularly difficult problems.[31]

The statutory provisions that give an insolvency administrator the power to impugn a pre-bankruptcy transaction are not expressly limited by any territorial constraint as to the location of the property or the location of its recipient. The application of these provisions to a transfer that has little connection to Canada can create harsh results for the

---

29 See *Holt Cargo Systems Inc v ABC Containerline NV*, [2001] 3 SCR 907 at paras 79–80.

30 *Jensen v Tolofson*, [1994] 3 SCR 1022.

31 See J Westbrook, "Choice of Avoidance Law in Global Insolvencies" (1991) 17 *Brooklyn Journal of International Law* 499.

recipient of the property. For example, a foreign creditor who obtains property located in another country may discover that the transaction is being impugned in Canada even though it was perfectly valid in the country in which the transaction took place. The problem is compounded by the fact that there is great diversity across jurisdictions in the approach taken to the avoidance powers. A transaction that is legitimate under the insolvency laws of one jurisdiction may be subject to impeachment under the laws of another jurisdiction.

If the statutory provision gives the court a discretion to make the order, one approach is for the court to refuse to exercise its discretion if the recipient does not have a sufficient connection to Canada. In making this determination, the court has regard to the nature and purpose of the transaction impugned, the nature and locality of the property involved, and whether under foreign law the recipient would have unimpeachable title in foreign insolvency proceedings.[32] This approach can be applied in respect of the impeachment powers that confer a discretion on the court, but this is only a partial solution since many of the statutory powers do not involve a discretionary element.[33]

If the impeachment provision is not subject to a territorial limitation on its application and if there is no scope for the exercise of discretion, the courts may be called upon to consider whether a choice of law analysis should be applied in respect of the impugned transaction. This issue was considered in the United States in connection with the insolvency of Robert Maxwell's media empire.[34] The court looked to a number of factors, such as the primary location of the debtor's business, assets, and creditors, in order to determine which jurisdiction's laws and policies were implicated to the greatest extent. The court concluded that the closest connection was with England, and therefore declined to apply United States avoidance law. It remains to be seen whether Canadian courts would be prepared to apply a similar approach.

C. RECOGNITION OF FOREIGN PROCEEDINGS

The traditional common law approach gave recognition to foreign insolvency proceedings that were made in the jurisdiction of the debtor's domicile. For individuals, this was the place where they had their most permanent connection. For corporations, this was the place of their

---

32 *Re Paramount Airways Ltd (No 2)*, [1993] Ch 223 (CA).

33 See Chapter 7, Section D(6).

34 *In re Maxwell Communication Corporation plc*, 93 F3d 1036 (2d Cir 1996).

incorporation. There was one qualification to this recognition. A foreign order for the discharge of a bankrupt did not have the effect of releasing debts governed by the proper law of some other country.[35] More recently, Canadian courts have departed from this approach in favour of a broader basis for recognition. They have given recognition to foreign insolvency proceedings if the debtor has a substantial connection with the foreign jurisdiction.[36] In doing so, they have applied the decision of the Supreme Court of Canada in *Morguard Investments Ltd v De Savoye*.[37]

1) The 1997 Amendments

In 1997 the *BIA* and the *CCAA* were amended by the addition of provisions dealing with international insolvencies. These provisions were modest in their scope. The *BIA* amendments allowed a court to limit a Canadian bankruptcy to the property located in Canada if foreign bankruptcy proceedings were instituted,[38] and permitted a foreign representative to commence concurrent Canadian proceedings.[39] A foreign representative could also apply for the appointment of an interim receiver for the protection of the debtor's estate or the interests of creditors.[40] The hotchpot rule was also codified.[41] The amendments empowered a court to make such orders and grant such relief as it considered appropriate to facilitate, approve, or implement arrangements to coordinate the Canadian and the foreign insolvency proceedings.[42] The provisions made it clear that they did not compel a court to make any order that was not in compliance with the laws of Canada,[43] and that they did not prevent a court from applying any legal or equitable rules governing the recognition of foreign insolvency orders and assistance to foreign representatives that were not inconsistent with the statutory provisions.[44]

The 1997 amendments were based on the view that the best approach to international insolvencies is through the use of concurrent

---

35 *Gibbs v La Societe Industrielle et Commerciale des Metaux* (1890), 25 QBD 399 (CA); *International Harvester Co v Zarbok*, [1918] 3 WWR 38 (Sask KB).

36 *Microbiz Corp v Classic Software Systems Inc* (1996), 45 CBR (3d) 40 (Ont Ct Gen Div); *Roberts v Picture Butte Municipal Hospital*, [1999] 4 WWR 443 (Alta QB).

37 Above note 6.

38 *BIA*, s 268(2) [now repealed].

39 *Ibid*, s 270 [now repealed].

40 *Ibid*, s 271(3) [now repealed].

41 *Ibid*, s 274 [now repealed].

42 *CCAA*, s 18.6(2) [now repealed]; *BIA*, s 268(3) [now repealed].

43 *CCAA*, s 18.6(5) [now repealed]; *BIA*, s 268(6) [now repealed].

44 *CCAA*, s 18.6(4) [now repealed]; *BIA*, s 268(5) [now repealed].

insolvency proceedings in both Canada and the foreign jurisdiction, and the promotion of cooperation between the courts and administrators of the respective jurisdictions. They did not contemplate the recognition of a foreign insolvency as the main proceeding in respect of which the role of the Canadian court was to assist and grant relief in respect of the foreign main proceeding. Courts have nevertheless taken the view that the 1997 amendments did not prevent them from doing so in appropriate cases. In *Re Babcock & Wilcox Canada Ltd*,[45] Justice Farley held that the amendments expressly permitted a court to apply legal or equitable rules governing the recognition of foreign bankruptcy proceedings and assistance to foreign representatives, and that this empowered the court to stay proceedings in Canada.

The controversial aspect of the *Babcock* decision was that the stay of proceedings was made in respect of a Canadian subsidiary that was not insolvent and that was not a party to the US insolvency proceedings.[46] A similar request for recognition of a US order that covered a Canadian subsidiary was refused in *Re Singer Sewing Machine Co of Canada Ltd*[47] on the basis that recognition should not be afforded to a foreign insolvency order in respect of a Canadian company carrying on business only in Canada and owning property only in Canada.

2) The 2007 Cross-Border Insolvency Provisions

The 2007 amendments to the *BIA* and the *CCAA* introduce a shift in favour of a modified universalist approach to cross-border insolvencies. The amendments are based on the UNCITRAL Model Law on Cross-Border Insolvency, but the provisions of the Model Law are not fully replicated. Some of the provisions of the Model Law are omitted and others contain substantive variations.[48] The *BIA* and the *CCAA* are amended by the addition of a Part concerning cross-border insolvencies.[49] These replace the 1997 provisions on international insolvencies.

45 (2000), 18 CBR (4th) 157 (Ont SCJ).

46 The case is extensively analyzed in J Ziegel, "Corporate Groups and Canada-US Crossborder Insolvencies: Contrasting Judicial Visions" (2001) 25 CBR (4th) 161.

47 (2000), 18 CBR (4th) 127 (Alta QB).

48 The difference are identified and discussed in J Ziegel, "Cross-Border Insolvencies" in S Ben-Ishai & A Duggan, eds, *Canadian Bankruptcy and Insolvency Law: Bill C-55, Statute c. 47 and Beyond* (Markham, ON: LexisNexis Canada, 2007) at 296–306.

49 *BIA*, Part XIII, ss 267–84; *CCAA*, Part IV, ss 44–61.

a) Scope of Application

The cross-border insolvency provisions come into play when a foreign representative applies to a Canadian court for an order recognizing a foreign proceeding.[50] The terms "foreign proceeding" and "foreign representative" are defined by the legislation, and these definitions control the scope of application of the cross-border insolvency provisions.

A "foreign proceeding" is defined as "a judicial or an administrative proceeding, including interim proceedings, in a jurisdiction outside of Canada dealing with the creditors' collective interests generally under any law relating to bankruptcy or insolvency in which a debtor's property and affairs are subject to control or supervision by a foreign court for the purpose of reorganization or liquidation."[51] The definition requires that the foreign proceedings deal with the creditors' collective interests. This will likely exclude privately appointed receivers, since these are not proceedings that deal with the collective interests of creditors.

A foreign representative is defined differently in the *BIA* and *CCAA* provisions. The former defines a foreign representative as a person or body who is authorized in a foreign proceeding to administer the debtor's property or affairs for the purpose of reorganization or liquidation or to act as a representative in respect of the foreign proceeding.[52] The latter limits the definition to a person or body authorized to monitor the debtor company's business and financial affairs for the purpose of reorganization or to act as a representative in respect of the foreign proceeding.[53] The United States uses a debtor-in-possession concept in respect of its restructuring law. A debtor company that has this status should qualify as a foreign representative because it is viewed as a separate legal entity that is authorized to administer the assets in the reorganization and to act as a representative in the insolvency proceedings.

b) Types of Foreign Proceedings

There are two types of foreign proceedings: a foreign main proceeding and foreign non-main proceeding. A foreign main proceeding is defined as a foreign proceeding in a jurisdiction that is the centre of the main interest of the debtor (COMI).[54] Any other kind of foreign proceeding

---

50 *BIA*, s 269(1); *CCAA*, s 46(1).

51 *BIA*, s 268(1) "foreign proceeding." The *CCAA* definition is the same except that the foreign proceedings must be for the purpose of reorganization. See *CCAA*, s 45(1) "foreign proceeding."

52 *BIA*, s 268(1) "foreign representative."

53 *CCAA*, s 45(1) "foreign representative."

54 *BIA*, s 268(1) "foreign main proceeding"; *CCAA*, s 45(1) "foreign main proceeding."

falls within the definition of a foreign non-main proceeding.[55] This difference is important because the effects of recognition differ depending upon which of the two types of foreign proceeding is involved.

c) Determining the Centre of Main Interest

The ascertainment of the debtor's centre of main interest is of great importance, since it will determine whether the foreign proceedings will qualify as foreign main proceedings. The centre of main interest is not defined, but a rebuttable presumption is provided.[56] In the case of an individual, the centre of main interest is, in the absence of proof to the contrary, the debtor's ordinary place of residence. In the case of non-individuals, it is the debtor's registered office.

The legislation does not enumerate the relevant factors or considerations that might cause a court to conclude that the COMI is in a location other than the registered office. Some courts have developed an extensive list of the following factors in determining the COMI:

- the location where corporate decisions are made;
- the location of employee administrations, including human resource functions;
- the location of the company's marketing and communication functions;
- whether the enterprise is managed on a consolidated basis;
- the extent of integration of an enterprise's international operations;
- the centre of an enterprise's corporate, banking, strategic, and management functions;
- the existence of shared management within entities and in an organization;
- the location where cash management and accounting functions are overseen;
- the location where pricing decisions and new business development initiatives are created; and
- the seat of an enterprise's treasury management functions, including management of accounts receivable and accounts payable.[57]

---

55 *BIA*, s 268(1) "foreign non-main proceeding"; *CCAA*, s 45(1) "foreign non-main proceeding." In this respect, the Canadian version differs from the Model Law. The Model Law adds a further requirement that the debtor have an establishment in the jurisdiction of the foreign non-main proceedings.

56 *BIA*, s 268(2); *CCAA*, s 45(2).

57 *Angiotech Pharmaceuticals Ltd (Re)*, 2011 BCSC 115. See also *Probe Resources Ltd (Re)*, 2011 BCSC 552.

Other courts have identified the following three considerations as of primary importance:

- the location is readily ascertainable by creditors;
- the location is one in which the debtor's principal assets or operations are found; and
- the location is where the management of the debtor takes place.[58]

Neither the UNCITRAL Model Law nor the Canadian cross-border insolvency provisions sets out any special rules for the determination of the centre of main interest in respect of members of a corporate group.

d) Recognition of Foreign Proceedings

A foreign representative may apply to a Canadian court for the recognition of the foreign proceeding.[59] In the case of an application under the *BIA*, it is to the superior court exercising bankruptcy jurisdiction; in respect of the *CCAA*, it is to the superior court of the province or territory. The application must be accompanied by a certified copy of the instrument that commenced the foreign proceedings, a certified copy of the instrument that conferred authority on the foreign representative to act in that capacity or an order of the foreign court affirming the foreign representative's authority to act, and a statement identifying all foreign proceedings in respect of the debtor that are known to the foreign representative.[60] The documents may be accepted without further proof of the foreign proceedings and the foreign representative's authority to act.[61] The court may require the documents to be translated.[62]

If the court is satisfied that the application for the recognition of a foreign proceeding relates to a foreign proceeding and that the applicant is a foreign representative, it is required to make an order recognizing the foreign proceeding and must specify in the order whether the foreign proceeding is a foreign main proceeding or a foreign non-main proceeding.[63]

---

58 *Lightsquared LP, Re*, 2012 ONSC 2994; *Massachusetts Elephant & Castle Group, Inc (Re)*, 2011 ONSC 4201.

59 *BIA*, s 269(1); *CCAA*, s 46(1).

60 *BIA*, s 269(2); *CCAA*, s 46(2). If these documents are not provided, the court may nevertheless hear the application and accept any other evidence of the existence of the foreign proceeding and of the foreign representative's authority. See *BIA*, s 269(4); *CCAA*, s 46(4).

61 *BIA*, s 269(3); *CCAA*, s 46(3).

62 *BIA*, s 269(5); *CCAA*, s 46(5).

63 *BIA*, ss 270(1) & (2); *CCAA*, ss 47(1) & (2).

e) Legal Effect of Recognition

The making of a recognition order has the following legal effects:

- Recognition of a foreign proceeding as a foreign main proceeding results in mandatory relief in the form of a stay of proceedings and a suspension of the debtor's right to sell or otherwise dispose of assets outside the ordinary course of business.
- Recognition of a foreign proceeding (main or non-main) gives the foreign representative the right to seek discretionary relief from a court in Canada.
- Recognition of a foreign proceeding (main or non-main) gives the foreign representative the standing to commence or continue Canadian insolvency proceedings.
- Recognition of a foreign proceeding (main or non-main) imposes an obligation on Canadian courts and insolvency officials to cooperate with the foreign representative and the foreign court.
- Recognition of a foreign proceeding (main or non-main) imposes an obligation on the foreign representative to inform the court of substantial changes in respect of the foreign proceedings.
- Recognition of a foreign proceeding (main or non-main) imposes an obligation on Canadian courts to review their orders to ensure consistency when multiple proceedings are brought.

f) Mandatory Relief

Recognition of a foreign main proceeding will result in mandatory relief being granted. The nature of this mandatory relief is different depending on whether the application for foreign recognition is brought under the *BIA* or the *CCAA*. The basic concept is that recognition of a foreign main proceeding will give rise to a stay of proceedings and will also suspend the debtor's right to sell, dispose, or encumber the property, but that the Canadian rules governing the scope, modification, and termination of the stay and suspension should apply to the stay and suspension.[64] Because the nature of the stay of proceedings under the *BIA* differs from that under the *CCAA*, the cross-border insolvency provisions in each Act have been drafted to reflect the different characteristics of the stay. A recognition order under either the *BIA* or the *CCAA* does not preclude the commencement or continuation of Canadian insolvency proceedings.[65]

Under the *BIA*, the effect of a recognition order is automatic and non-discretionary in respect of a foreign main proceeding, and it arises

64 See UNCITRAL, *Model Law on Cross-Border Insolvency*, art 20.

65 *BIA*, s 271(4); *CCAA*, s 48(4).

immediately upon making the recognition order.[66] There are two legal effects of the order. First, it operates as a stay of proceedings. No person is permitted to commence or continue any action, execution, or other proceedings concerning the debtor's property, debts, liabilities, or obligations. Second, it prohibits the debtor from selling or disposing of the debtor's property in Canada, other than transactions that occur in the ordinary course of the debtor's business. This is subject to two important qualifications. First, the recognition order will not have these legal effects if proceedings under the *BIA* have been commenced in respect of the debtor at the time the order recognizing the foreign proceeding is made.[67] In such a case, the Canadian property will be subject to an automatic stay of proceedings by virtue of the *BIA* proceedings. However, in the case of involuntary bankruptcy proceedings, the stay will not commence until a bankruptcy order is made.[68] Second, the legal effects of the recognition order are subject to the exceptions, specified by the court in the recognition order, that would apply in Canada had the foreign proceeding taken place there under the *BIA*.[69] This means that the stay will not affect secured creditors in respect of foreign liquidation proceedings, but that it will affect secured creditors in respect of foreign restructuring proceedings.

If the application for recognition is made under the *CCAA*, the court, on making an order recognizing a foreign main proceeding, must also make an order providing for a stay of proceedings.[70] The order shall also prohibit the sale or other disposition of the debtor's property in Canada outside the ordinary course of business. Although the stay and the prohibition of non-ordinary course sales arise by virtue of the court order, the court does not retain a discretion to grant the order. The *CCAA* requires the court to make the order on making the recognition order in respect of the foreign main proceeding. The order may be made on such terms and conditions as the court thinks appropriate and must be consistent with an order that may be made under the *CCAA*.[71] The recognition order will not have these legal effects if proceedings

66 *BIA*, s 271(1).

67 *Ibid*, s 271(2).

68 The creditors may bring an application for the appointment of an interim receiver if they have grounds to believe that the property may be jeopardized. See Chapter 3, Section C(8).

69 *BIA*, s 271(3).

70 *CCAA*, s 48(1). The provision adopts language that is parallel to the *CCAA* provision that empowers a court to make an order staying proceedings.

71 *Ibid*, s 48(2).

under the *CCAA* have been commenced in respect of the debtor at the time the order recognizing the foreign proceeding is made.[72]

g) Discretionary Relief

On application of the foreign representative, a court may grant discretionary relief if it is satisfied that it is necessary for the protection of the debtor's property or the interests of a creditor or creditors.[73] The discretionary relief may be granted in respect of both a foreign main proceeding and a foreign non-main proceeding. Under both the *BIA* and the *CCAA*, the court may give to a foreign non-main proceeding the relief that is conferred on a foreign main proceeding. Both Acts also permit a court to make orders respecting the examination of witnesses, the taking of evidence, or the delivery of information concerning the debtor's property, affairs, debts, liabilities, and obligations.

The *CCAA* cross-border provisions permit the making of an order authorizing the foreign representative to monitor the debtor company's business and financial affairs in Canada for the purpose of reorganization.[74] The *BIA* cross-border provisions permit the court to entrust the administration or realization of all or part of the debtor's property located in Canada to the foreign representative, and also permit the court to make an order appointing a trustee as receiver to take possession of the property and exercise control over the business.[75] The discretionary relief must be consistent with any order obtained pursuant to Canadian insolvency proceedings.[76] The granting of the relief does not preclude the commencement or continuation of such Canadian insolvency proceedings.[77]

On several occasions Canadian courts have exercised this power to grant discretionary relief through the appointment of an information officer.[78] An information officer is an officer of the court, and the rights and duties of the information officer are set out in the court order. The order will typically provide that the information officer will provide assistance to the foreign representative, report to the court, respond to reasonable requests for information from stakeholders, and have access

72 *Ibid*, s 48(3).

73 *BIA*, s 272(1); *CCAA*, s 49(1).

74 *CCAA*, s 49(1)(c).

75 *BIA*, ss 272(1)(c) & (d).

76 *Ibid*, s 272(2); *CCAA*, s 49(2).

77 *BIA*, s 272(3); *CCAA*, s 49(3).

78 *See Lightsquared LP (Re)*, above note 58. And see P Boparai, K Jackson, & V Tickle, "The Appointment and Role of the Information Officer" (2013) 2 *Journal of the Insolvency Institute of Canada* 201.

to the debtor's books and records.[79] The role of an information officer has been described as one of a watchdog.[80]

h) Standing of Foreign Representatives

Upon the making of a recognition order, a foreign representative is given the same right as that afforded to a creditor or a debtor to commence or continue Canadian insolvency proceedings.[81] In the absence of this provision, the foreign representative might encounter difficulties commencing Canadian insolvency proceedings. For example, in involuntary bankruptcy proceedings, only a creditor has standing to bring an application for a bankruptcy order.

i) The Duty to Cooperate and Coordinate

On making a recognition order, Canadian courts are charged with a duty to cooperate, to the maximum extent possible, with the foreign representative and the foreign court involved in the foreign proceeding.[82] A similar duty is imposed on any person who exercises any powers or performs duties and functions in connection with Canadian insolvency proceedings.[83] The provisions state that cooperation may be provided by any appropriate means, including:[84]

- the appointment of a person to act at the direction of the court;
- the communication of information by any means considered appropriate by the court;
- the coordination of the administration and supervision of the debtor's assets and affairs;
- the approval or implementation by courts of agreements concerning the coordination of proceedings; and
- the coordination of concurrent proceedings regarding the same debtor.

This clearly contemplates the use of direct court-to-court communication through protocols and other methods currently employed in fostering communication and coordination.

---

79 *Tucker v Aero Inventory (UK) Limited*, 2009 CanLII 63138 (Ont SCJ). And see Foreign Main Proceeding – Supplemental Order, online: www.ontariocourts.ca/scj/practice/practice-directions/toronto/#Commercial_List_Forms_including_Model_Orders.

80 *Lear Canada (Re)* (2009), 55 CBR (5th) 57 (Ont SCJ).

81 *BIA*, s 274; *CCAA*, s 51.

82 *BIA*, s 275(1); *CCAA*, s 52(1).

83 *BIA*, s 275(2); *CCAA*, s 52(2).

84 *BIA*, s 275(3); *CCAA*, s 52(3).

j) The Duty to Inform

Once a court makes a recognition order, the foreign representative is obliged, without delay, to inform the court of any substantial change in the status of the recognized foreign proceeding, any substantial change in the status of the foreign representative's authority to act in that capacity, and any other foreign proceeding in respect of the same debtor that becomes known to the foreign representative.[85] The foreign representative must also publish a notice in one or more newspapers in Canada after a recognition order is granted.

k) Concurrent and Multiple Proceedings

The Canadian cross-border insolvency provisions contemplate the existence of concurrent insolvency proceedings. Recognition of foreign insolvency proceedings does not prevent the commencement or continuation of Canadian insolvency proceedings. Equally, the commencement of Canadian insolvency proceedings does not terminate the recognition that was given to the foreign proceeding. The legal effects in Canada of recognition of the foreign proceedings coexist with the Canadian insolvency proceedings. It is therefore necessary to coordinate the proceedings to ensure that they are not inconsistent. The same kind of problem can arise when there are multiple foreign proceedings, i.e., when more than one foreign proceeding is recognized in Canada in respect of the same debtor.

The Canadian provisions contain three different rules that cover concurrent insolvency proceedings. The first rule applies when an order recognizing foreign proceedings is made and is followed by the commencement of Canadian insolvency proceedings.[86] In this case, the court must review any discretionary order that was made and amend it or revoke it to ensure that there are no inconsistencies with the Canadian insolvency proceedings. The same must be done in respect of any mandatory relief that was afforded in respect of a foreign main proceeding. The operative principle is that the Canadian insolvency proceeding takes pre-eminence over the recognition order.

Both the second and the third rule deal with multiple orders for recognition of foreign proceedings. The second rule covers the situation where an order recognizing a foreign non-main proceeding is made and a court thereafter makes an order recognizing a foreign main proceeding. Here the court is obliged to review the order in respect of the foreign non-main proceeding and amend it or revoke it to ensure that

85 *BIA*, s 276; *CCAA*, s 53.
86 *BIA*, s 277; *CCAA*, s 54.

there are no inconsistencies. The operative principle is that the foreign main proceeding order takes pre-eminence over the foreign non-main proceeding order.

The third rule covers the situation where an order recognizing a foreign non-main proceeding is made and a court thereafter makes an order recognizing another foreign non-main proceeding. Here the court is obliged to review the first order and amend it or revoke it to ensure that there are no inconsistencies with the later order. The operative principle is that the later foreign non-main proceeding order takes pre-eminence over the earlier foreign non-main proceeding order.

l) The Hotchpot Rule

The cross-border insolvency provisions of the *BIA* and the *CCAA* provide a statutory codification of the hotchpot rule.[87] The rule applies where there are concurrent insolvency proceedings in both Canada and another country. A dividend or distribution of property that is received by the creditor in a foreign insolvency proceeding is taken into account in the Canadian insolvency proceeding by treating it as if it had been received by the creditor in the Canadian proceeding.

The provision does not require that the creditor give up the payment received in the foreign proceeding. Rather, the creditor cannot claim a dividend in the Canadian proceeding until the other creditors receive the same percentage as the creditor received in the foreign proceeding. Thus, if a creditor received ten cents on the dollar in the foreign proceeding, that creditor cannot receive anything in the Canadian insolvency proceeding until all the other creditors have first received ten cents on the dollar in respect of the Canadian insolvency proceedings.

The Canadian version of the hotchpot rule is not limited to amounts that are received as a result of a dividend or distribution in the foreign insolvency proceedings. They apply as well to any property that is obtained by a creditor outside Canada by way of a transfer that could be impeached as a preference or transfer at undervalue if it were subject to Canadian insolvency legislation. Through this method, *BIA* provisions respecting preferences and transfers at an undervalue can be effectively imposed on transfers that occur outside Canada, even though the transactions could not be impugned by the application of foreign avoidance law in the foreign insolvency proceeding.

87 *BIA*, s 283; *CCAA*, s 60.

m) The Presumption of Insolvency

The Canadian cross-border insolvency provisions provide that a certified copy of an insolvency or reorganization order in a foreign proceeding is proof, in the absence of evidence to the contrary, that the debtor is insolvent.[88] Some countries, such as the United States, do not require proof of insolvency as a precondition for the commencement of insolvency proceedings. The provision creates a rebuttable presumption, and therefore a party may adduce evidence to show that the debtor was not insolvent. Thus, if concurrent restructuring proceedings are brought in the United States and in Canada, the proof of the US proceedings can be used as proof of insolvency in the absence of evidence to the contrary. However, proof that the debtor is not insolvent will have a significant effect on the relief that can be granted to the foreign representative. Because the scope of the relief that can be granted in Canada is limited to orders that could be made in Canadian insolvency proceedings,[89] a stay of proceedings is not available in respect of a solvent debtor.[90]

n) Miscellaneous Provisions

The Canadian cross-border insolvency provisions do not prevent a court from applying any legal or equitable rules governing the recognition of foreign insolvency orders and assistance to foreign representatives that are not inconsistent with the statutory provisions.[91] A court may refuse to do something required by the provisions if to do so would be contrary to public policy.[92]

FURTHER READINGS

AMERICAN LAW INSTITUTE. *Transnational Insolvency Project — International Statement of Canadian Bankruptcy Law* (Philadelphia: American Law Institute, 2003)

BERENDS, A. "The UNCITRAL Model Law on Cross-Border Insolvency: A Comprehensive Overview" (1998) 6 *Tulane Journal of International & Comparative Law* 309

---

88 *BIA*, s 282; *CCAA*, s 59.
89 *BIA*, s 271(3); *CCAA*, s 48(2).
90 See Chapter 1, Section E(5).
91 *BIA*, s 284(1); *CCAA*, s 61(1).
92 *BIA*, s284(2); *CCAA*, s 61(2). And see *Stanford International Bank Ltd (Dans l'affaire de la liquidation de)*, 2009 QCCA 2475.

BOPARAI, P, K JACKSON, & V TICKLE. "The Appointment and Role of the Information Officer" (2013) 2 *Journal of the Insolvency Institute of Canada* 201

FLETCHER, I. *Insolvency in Private International Law*, 2d ed (Oxford: Oxford University Press, 2005)

GOODE, R. Principles of Corporate Insolvency Law, 3d ed (London: Sweet & Maxwell, 2005) ch 14

HONSBERGER, J. "Reaching Canadian Assets of Foreign Debtors through Local or Foreign Bankruptcy Proceedings" (1993) 18 CBR (3d) 301

KENT, A, S DONAHER, & A MAEROV. "UNCITRAL, Eh?: The Model Law and Its Implications for Canadian Stakeholders" in Janis P Sarra, ed, *Annual Review of Insolvency Law, 2005* (Toronto: Carswell, 2006) 187

LOPUCKI, LM. "Cooperation in Internationalist Bankruptcy: A Post-Universalist Approach" (1999) 84 *Cornell Law Review* 696

SARRA, J. "Northern Lights, Canada's Version of the UNCITRAL Model Law on Cross-Border Insolvency (2007) 16 *International Insolvency Review* 19

UNCITRAL. *Model Law on Cross-Border Insolvency with Guide to Enactment* (30 May 1997)

WESTBROOK, JL. "A Global Solution to Multinational Default" (2000) 98 *Michigan Law Review* 2276

ZIEGEL, JS. "Corporate Groups and Canada-US Crossborder Insolvencies: Contrasting Judicial Visions" (2001) 25 CBR (4th) 161

———. "Cross-Border Insolvencies" in S Ben-Ishai & A Duggan, eds, *Canadian Bankruptcy and Insolvency Law: Bill C-55, Statute c. 47 and Beyond* (Markham, ON: Lexis Nexis Canada, 2007) ch 12

TABLE OF CASES

INDEX

ABOUT THE AUTHOR

Roderick J Wood is the FR (Dick) Matthews QC Professor of Business Law at the Faculty of Law, University of Alberta, Edmonton. He teaches and publishes in the areas of bankruptcy and insolvency law, personal property security law, and commercial law. He has co-authored books on secured transactions law in Canada and in New Zealand, and has written extensively in various law journals. He is the 2004 recipient of the Tevie H Miller Teaching Excellence Award for the Faculty of Law, a 2005 recipient of the AC Rutherford Award for Excellence in Undergraduate Teaching at the University of Alberta, and a 2006 recipient of a McCalla Professorship for his contribution to research in law at the University of Alberta. Professor Wood was appointed as the inaugural Estey Chair in Business Law at the College of Law, University of Saskatchewan, during the 2014–15 academic year.

Professor Wood has served as associate dean (1997 to 1999) at the Faculty of Law, as a board member of the Alberta Law Reform Institute (1997 to 2001), and as commissioner of the Law Commission of Canada (2001 to 2006). Professor Wood was a member of the Canadian delegation at diplomatic conferences in Luxembourg in 2007 and Berlin in 2012 that produced international instruments governing the secured financing of rail assets and space assets, and was a member of the drafting committee that produced the text of the *Luxembourg Protocol to the Unidroit Convention on International Interests in Mobile Equipment.*